Supernatural

'The modern world was not alive to the tremendous Reality that encompassed it. We were surrounded by an immeasurable abyss of darkness and splendour. We built our empires on a pellet of dust revolving round a ball of fire in unfathomable space. Life, that Sphinx, with the human face and the body of a brute, asked us new riddles every hour. Matter itself was dissolving under the scrutiny of Science; and yet, in our daily lives, we were becoming a race of somnambulists, whose very breathing, in train and bus and car, was timed to the movement of the wheels; and the more perfectly, and even alertly, we clicked through our automatic affairs on the surface of things, the more complete was our insensibility to the utterly inscrutable mystery that anything should be in existence at all.'

Alfred Noyes, *The Unknown God*, Sheed and Ward, London, 1934, pp.176-177

For my father, Donald M. Hancock, 7 December 1924 –
16 September 2003.
Ride in green pastures.

Supernatural

*Meetings with the
Ancient Teachers
of Mankind*

Graham Hancock

DOUBLEDAY CANADA

Doubleday Canada and colophon are trademarks.

Library and Archives Canada Cataloguing in Publication applied for.

Printed and bound in the USA

Published in Canada by
Doubleday Canada, a division of
Random House of Canada Limited

Visit Random House of Canada Limited's website: www.randomhouse.ca

BVG 10   9   8   7   6   5   4   3   2   1

CONTENTS

Acknowledgements   vii

Part I: The Visions

1   The Plant that Enables Men to See the Dead   3
2   The Greatest Riddle of Archaeology   13
3   Vine of Souls   33

Part II: The Caves

4   Therianthropy   69
5   Riddles of the Caves   94
6   The Shabby Academy   133
7   Searching for a Rosetta Stone   159
8   The Code in the Mind   194
9   Serpents of the Drakensberg   230
10 The Wounded Healer   262

Part III: The Beings

11 Voyage into the Supernatural   289
12 Shamans in the Sky   308
13 Spirit Love   338
14 The Secret Commonwealth   357
15 Here is a Thing that Will Carry Me Away   370
16 Dancers between Worlds   392

Part IV: The Codes

17 Tuning in to Channel DMT   415

18 Amongst the Machine Elves   428

19 Ancient Teachers in Our DNA?   457

20 The Hurricane in the Junkyard   474

Part V: The Religions

21 The Hidden Shamans   495

22 Flesh of the Gods   531

Part VI: The Mysteries

23 Doors Leading to Another World   563

Appendices

Critics and Criticisms of David Lewis-Williams'
    'Neuropsychological Theory' of Rock and Cave Art   591

Psilocybe semilanceata – a hallucinogenic mushroom native to
    Europe. By Professor Roy Watling, OBE.   614

Interview with Rick Strassman MD   618

Notes and References   631

Index   703

ACKNOWLEDGEMENTS

My father Donald Hancock died when research on this book was in its early stages. He influenced me, and the work I have done, more than I think he ever realised. I miss his warmth, his wise advice, his enduring love, and his celebration of the mysteries and spiritual truths that lie at the heart of this life of ours. I retain the hope, and the expectation, that our dialogue is not over and that death is not the end of all things but simply a transition to another level of consciousness. As ever my wife and partner Santha was with me, stood by me, gave me love, gave me support, gave me understanding – every step of the way. I can't thank her enough. I am also grateful for the encouragement of our six children, Sean, Shanti, Ravi, Leila, Luke and Gabrielle. Each one of them contributed an insight into what was needed to get this book done. Thanks to my mother and to my uncle James Macaulay for reading and commenting on the manuscript,

In South Africa special thanks go to Bokka du Toit for bringing his unique skills and understanding to our research adventures in that ancient land that he loves so much, and to Ann Steyn for her friendship and help during our stay in Jeffries Bay. I am extremely grateful to all the excellent staff at the superb Bushman's Kloof in the Cedarberg for their hospitality and knowledge of the local rock art, and to Judy Soul of the Monkey Valley Resort in Cape Town for her kindness shown to us during our stay there. Thanks to Chris Henshilwood and his team at Blombos cave for their hospitality and for a most instructive day spent with them in the midst of an active, newsbreaking excavation. And thanks to David Lewis-Williams for revolutionising scientific understanding of the factors at work in the birth of modern human behaviour.

My research in the Amazon would not have been possible without the fantastic back-up, local knowledge and organisational skills of

Francesco Sammarco and Ignazia Posadinu of El Mundo Magico (www.ayahuasca-shamanism.co.uk) who again and again put me on the right track in the jungle and in contact with absolutely the right people. Additional thanks go to the shamans who introduced me to ayahuasca during my stay – notably Don Francisco Montes Shuna of Sachamama, Don Leoncio García Sampaya, Don Alberto Torres Davilla (in the Aucayacu), Dona Otilia Pashmino and Don Alberto Alvarez Vela. I'm also grateful to Ruber del Castillo Ramirez and his wonderful family for the hospitality and kindness that they extended to us when we stayed with them on their homestead in the Aucayacu. Additional thanks go to Clever Hoyos who worked with us as an insightful and resourceful translator during our stay in the Peruvian Amazon. Finally, thanks and deep appreciation to Pablo Amaringo (www.pabloamaringo.com) for kind permission to reproduce some of his luminous and inspiring paintings of his ayahuasca visions. In every case, with these remarkable images, a picture says far more than a thousand words. Thanks also to the anthropologist Luis Eduardo Luna (www.wasiwaska.org) who worked with Pablo on their wonderful book *Ayahuasca Visions: The Religious Iconography of a Peruvian Shaman*.

In Brazil special thanks go to the *Uniao de Vegetal* and in particular to *Mestre* Antonio Francisco Fleury. In France I would like to thank the administration of *la Grotte du Pech-Merle* and in particular M. Zimmermann who took the time to show me around on my private visit to the cave and to share his insights with me.

I am most grateful to Dr Rick Strassman for discussing with me at such length his breakthrough research with DMT and human volunteers at the University of New Mexico. Thanks, too, to Professor Benny Shanon of the Hebrew University in Jerusalem for our discussions and for his remarkable work which has advanced the scientific understanding of the phenomenology of ayahuasca experiences to a level not hitherto reached by any other researcher. I am also most grateful to the anthropologist Jeremy Narby for his hospitality in Switzerland and for his remarkable book *The Cosmic Serpent: DNA and the Origins of Knowledge* which opened my eyes to many possibilities that I simply had not seen before. Thanks to Professor Roy Watling for contributing Appendix II of this book documenting the ancient Old World provenance of the hallucinogenic mushroom *Psilocybe semilanceata*. Thanks to the late Professor John Mack for his pioneering work at the borders of consensual reality and for his tremendous intellectual courage. Thanks to Hattie Wells for seeing me safely through my first ibogaine session. One of the great untold stories of this book is the remarkable success that Hattie and other healers all around the world have achieved administering ibogaine to drug addicts as a cure for heroin, cocaine and alcohol addiction. In many cases two to three ibogaine sessions have been sufficient to produce virtually symptom-free withdrawal, a strong determination not to relapse, and a transformed outlook on life on the part of the individuals concerned.

Thanks and appreciation to Simon Macara for his kind and sincere help on several occasions in making difficult things easy, to Helen Vinckier for looking after us in Belgium, to Zoe Kenway for her excellent work under intense time-pressure on so many of the black-and-white illustrations in this book, and to Steve Nixon for the cover design. Thanks to Shanti Faiia for her specialised research into the human-rights implications of current drug laws, and to Damian Walter for his excellent and professional bibliographic research. Thanks to my literary agents Bill Hamilton and Sara Fisher for wise advice and good practical encouragement at all times. Thanks to Tim Andrews at Century in London for working so professionally with me on the final stages of the editing and production of *Supernatural*. Last but not least particular thanks and appreciation to Mark Booth, my editor at Century. As well as having had the guts to take on such a controversial subject in the first place he was a real friend who read the chapters and give me his reactions over the course of a year as the writing progressed.

Graham Hancock
Bath, England, October 2005
www.grahamhancock.com

PART I
The Visions

CHAPTER ONE

The Plant that Enables Men
to See the Dead

I lay on a couch in the darkened drawing room of a 200-year-old townhouse in the English city of Bath. The streets outside were deserted and offered few clues to remind me of the familiar world. It was reassuring to find that I could still read the luminous dial of my wristwatch if I held it in front of my eyes. Ten minutes passed, then 20, then 35. I began to feel bored, restless, even a little blasé. After 45 minutes I closed my eyes and directed my thoughts inwards towards contemplation, still noticing nothing unusual. But at the end of the first hour of my vigil, when I tried to stand up and walk around, I was amazed to discover that my legs would not work. Out of nowhere, an enervating feebleness had ambushed my limbs, the slightest physical effort set off uncontrollable tremors and stumbling, and I had completely lost my sense of balance.

A wave of giddiness and nausea washed over me and I fell back exhausted on the couch, drenched in cold sweat. I remembered with a shudder of finality that I could not change my mind because there was no antidote. Once it was underway, the process I was going through could not be stopped and would simply have to be endured.

My hearing was the next faculty affected. At intervals, there would be a tremendous ringing and buzzing in my ears, blotting out all other sounds. My eyesight also rapidly deteriorated, soon becoming so obstructed at the edges with strange black lines, like fence-posts or gratings, that I could no longer see my watch and had to abandon all control of time. For what felt like a very long while the poison remorselessly

3

tightened its grip and I fell prey to indescribable sensations of physical and psychic unease. There was a great deal of pain, weakness and discomfort. It was as if my body were being slowly and systematically smashed and dismembered and I began to fear that I might never be able to put it back together again.

In a moment of stillness when my eyes were closed a vision popped up – a vivid moving tapestry of intertwining branches and leaves, elaborate arabesques and Celtic knotwork. I blinked my eyes open. Instantly the writhing patterns vanished and the darkened drawing room returned. But as soon as I closed my eyes the patterns came back.

More unmeasured time passed while the patterns continued to expand and multiply. Then another great gust of dizziness hit me and I winced at the terrifying new sensation it brought of balancing on a swaying tightrope over a bottomless abyss. I found that if I lay on my back, looked straight up at the ceiling and stayed absolutely still I could minimise these uncomfortable effects. But all it took was the slightest movement of my head to left or right to bring on another spectacular surge of vertigo.

When at last I closed my eyes again the sinuous intertwined patterns reappeared with renewed intensity and then were abruptly overwritten by a profile view of a heavily built blond young man with his eyes turned towards me in a glare of reproach. He appeared right at my side, startlingly close. His skin was pallid and his brow blotched with patches of green mould.

Shamanic portals

In the Central African countries of Gabon, Cameroon and Zaire certain age-old ancestor cults still flourish in the twenty-first century. Their members share a common belief, based they say on direct experience, in the existence of a supernatural realm where the spirits of the dead may be contacted. Like some hypothetical dimension of quantum physics, this otherworld interpenetrates our own and yet cannot ordinarily be seen or verified by empirical tests. It is therefore a matter of great interest, with highly suggestive research implications, that tribal shamans claim to have mastered a means, through the consumption of a poisonous shrub known locally as eboka or iboga, by which humans may reach the otherworld and return alive. How they mastered this skill is told in the origin myth of the indigenous secret society known as the Bwiti:

> Zame ye Mebege [the last of the creator gods] gave us *Eboka*. One day . . . he saw . . . the Pygmy Bitamu, high in an Atanga tree, gathering its fruit. He made him fall. He died, and Zame brought his spirit to him. Zame cut off the little fingers and little toes of the cadaver of the Pygmy and planted them in various parts of the forest. They grew into the *Eboka* bush.[1]

The pygmy's wife was named Atanga. When she heard of the death of her husband she went in search of his body. Eventually, after many adventures, she came to a cave in the heart of the forest in which she saw a pile of human bones:

> As she entered the cave she suddenly heard a voice – as of the voice of her husband – asking who she was, where she came from, and whom she wished to speak with. The voice told her to look to the left at the mouth of the cave. There was the *Eboka* plant. The voice told her to eat its roots . . . She ate and felt very tired . . . Then she was told to turn around in the cave. The bones were gone and in their place stood her husband and other dead relatives. They talked to her and gave her a [new] name, *Disoumba*, and told her that she had found the plant that would enable men to see the dead. This was the first baptism into Bwiti and that was how men got the power to know the dead and have their counsel.[2]

Today several million people distributed across Gabon, Cameroon and Zaire have no difficulty resisting well-financed efforts at conversion aimed at them by Christian and Islamic missionaries. Their allegiance instead is to the Bwiti, into which they have been initiated by consuming huge amounts of eboka root-bark shavings and experiencing a journey into supernatural realms.

Eboka, also known as iboga (the spelling that I will use from now on), is classified scientifically as *Tabernanthe iboga* and is a member of the *Apocynacae* (Dogbane) family. Its root bark turns out to be very special, as the myth of the pygmy asserts, and contains more than a dozen unusual chemicals belonging to a class known as the indole alkaloids. One of them, ibogaine, is the potent hallucinogen responsible for the convincing and life-changing visions experienced by Bwiti initiates, notably 'encounters with supernatural beings' and 'encounters with the spirits of the dead'. Many report meeting their deceased fathers or grandfathers, who act as guides for them in the spirit world. However, the bark must be eaten in toxic quantities if the visionary state is to be attained, and initiates confront an ever-present risk of fatal overdose as they seek out their ancestors.[3]

Tabernanthe iboga. Its root bark is the source of the powerful hallucinogen ibogaine.

Iboga root bark and ibogaine hydrochloride (the pure extract of the psychoactive alkaloid) are both illegal drugs in the United States; they are classed under Schedule I alongside other major hallucinogens, such as LSD, and addictive narcotics and stimulants like heroin and crack cocaine. By contrast, in Britain and several other European countries, where there is growing scientific recognition of a number of startling therapeutic effects claimed for ibogaine, the drug has not been banned. It may be purchased legally and openly from specialised botanical suppliers and consumed freely in any private place.

Research

Even without the barbaric threat of a jail sentence, ibogaine is a very serious business, so I had not gone lightly into the decisions that had led me to this couch, this night, and this state of helpless prostration to whatever was coming next.

My primary motive, unabashedly, was research. I had deliberately submitted myself to this ordeal as part of a wider, longer-term investigation into a mysterious 'before and after moment' that took place in human prehistory, perhaps as recently as 40,000 years ago. Before it, other than a very few widely scattered and isolated examples, there is nothing in the archaeological record left by our ancestors that we would instantly recognise as modern human behaviour. After it, the signs that creatures exactly like us have arrived are everywhere, most notably in the first definite evidence for beliefs in supernatural realms and beings – evidence, in other words, for the birth of religion.

The clearest possible illustration of this is in south-west Europe where sophisticated religious art – the oldest so far discovered in the world – appears suddenly, with no apparent antecedents, between 40,000 and 30,000 years ago and then endures until approximately 12,000 years ago. This is the art of the great painted caves such as Chauvet, Lascaux, Pech Merle and Altamira – surely amongst the most beautiful and enigmatic of all human creations. The cave paintings are rightly famous for their realistic images of Ice Age mammals. Much less well known is the fact that numerous supernatural and chimerical beings, often half human, half animal, are also depicted.

An ingenious explanation for the bizarre appearance of these beings, as well as for other intriguing features of the caves which we'll explore in later chapters, has been put forward by a prestigious international group of anthropologists and archaeologists. The essence of their argument is that the cave art expresses mankind's first and oldest notions of the supernatural, of the 'soul', and of realms of existence beyond death – notions that took shape in 'altered states of consciousness' most likely brought on by the consumption of psychoactive plants. Although not to the liking of some scholars, this has been the most widely accepted theory of cave art since the mid-1990s. It is therefore an embarrassment that none of the experts currently advocating it have ever actually consumed any psychoactive plants themselves; nor do they have any first-hand idea of what an 'altered state of consciousness' is, or any desire to experience one. To give fair consideration to their arguments, and to the views of their critics, I felt I needed to be able to judge on the basis of personal experience whether plant-induced visions could be made of strong enough stuff to have convinced early humans of the existence of supernatural realms and of the survival after death of some essence of deceased ancestors.

This, in a nutshell, was why I had taken ibogaine – for sound, solid, common-sense research reasons. But I have to acknowledge that there was another, much more personal motive as well. It had to do with my own father's painful death from bone cancer the previous autumn and my inexcusable failure to be at his bedside during the last few days of his life. Part of the appeal of this slightly risky experiment with ibogaine was undoubtedly its promise of 'encounters with the ancestors' and – however tenuous – the possibility of closure and quietus that it seemed to offer.

Long night of iboga

I've probably given the impression up till now that I was alone during my vigil in Bath, but this wasn't the case. The psychoactive dose of ibogaine that I consumed[4] was administered by an experienced and reputable healer who remained on hand the whole night, my wife Santha was also in the room, and we had a medical doctor present as well. At first I'd been acutely aware of all three, but as the malaise and paralysis deepened they faded into insignificance and I seemed to see them – if at all – through panels of thick glass. The same odd disconnection applied to the bowl I'd been given to vomit in. I was able to hold on to it and retch over it, but I was in one place, it was in another.

As the night wore on I could feel my couch undergoing an insidious process of transformation until eventually it had become a stone sarcophagus within which I was laid out. I experienced a strong sense of constriction and immobility, as though a great weight were pressing down on my chest, and wondered: Is this death? At the same instant the room became very full of people – not the healer, my wife and the doctor, who might as well have been locked away in a soundproof capsule, but a large and somehow threatening crowd of uninvited guests. They did not vanish when I opened my eyes, as my earlier visions had done, but stayed firmly in view, for the most part anonymous and shadowy, shoulders hunched, heads down. A few showed their faces, but like the young blond man I'd seen earlier, with his mildewed skin, they had the look of the grave.

I grew conscious that someone was watching me from far back in the jostling crowd. Lean and middle-aged, with a solemn manner, he was dark-skinned and his features were unmistakably African. His eyes were huge and black as obsidian. He was not old and grey as was usually the case in the visions of the Bwiti, but the thought came to me that this might be the legendary 'Spirit of Iboga', here to abduct my soul:

> Iboga is intimately associated with death; the plant is frequently anthropomorphised as a supernatural being, a 'generic ancestor' who can so highly value or despise an individual that it can carry him away to the land of the dead.[5]

I fell into a dream state for what seemed like a very long time, and as with most dreams I now find it hard to remember the details. All I can confirm is my absolute certain conviction that *something* happened – something of lasting importance to me. Did I hallucinate an encounter with my father? I don't remember clearly enough to be absolutely sure, but I get flashbacks of that night in which I see him amongst the crowd of phantoms gathered round me. Sometimes the flashbacks are so poignant and intense that I can almost believe he must really have been out there, walking by with dignity and pain as he did when he was fighting his cancer.

As well as these tantalising recollections of my father, I've managed to dredge up a few other broken images from those hours of fevered dreams which add to my sense that something momentous occurred. At one point I felt very strongly that I had awakened. I opened my eyes expecting to see the familiar outlines of the darkened drawing room. Instead I found myself in a very strange place that I had never seen before, with billowing draperies hanging from the walls, trees growing within, and a ceiling transparent to the stars. It seemed like some exotic temple, part sanctuary, part palace, part desert tent. To one side, absorbed in the motions of a dance, I could see a giant figure dressed in flowing white robes with black vertical markings.

Was I dreaming, or awake? Was what I was seeing *real* in some way – as it very convincingly seemed to be – or was it all just a grand illusion? And did the spirit of my father still survive in some other dimension or reality? These were weighty questions, not easily settled. But for now, at least, my interest was narrower. Plants like *Tabernanthe iboga* were available to our ancestors and would have had the same effects on them as they do on us. I remembered the overwhelmingly eerie sense I had experienced for much of the night of crowds of the dead gathered round me – crowds of ghosts, crowds of my forebears. Of course it was reasonable and potentially productive to ask whether it was not precisely experiences of this general sort that gave rise – in remote antiquity – to mankind's first notions of the spirit world. Since scholarship as yet has no complete or satisfactory explanation for the origins of religion, this is an area that remains ripe for investigation.

Towards morning, with light beginning to filter through gaps in the curtains, I was not surprised to go through a mild out-of-body experience. These are common amongst Bwiti initiates under the influence of iboga, and I wasn't completely new to the phenomenon myself. The last time it had happened to me was when I was 16 years old and nearly killed by a massive electric shock. Now, as then, my consciousness seemed to float near the ceiling of the room for a few moments, looking down on my own body. Now, as then, I felt detachment and curiosity, certainly not fear, and revelled in the lightness of being and freedom of flight I seemed to be able to enjoy in the disembodied state. Now, as then, the hallucination – or whatever it was – rapidly faded and the out-of-body view was quickly lost.

I was left with a philosophical reflection in the form of a cartoon image of a large sausage tightly knotted at one end. This is what we are, the image seemed to be saying. The message was obvious, almost a cliché – that it is pointless to dwell on the physical and material aspects of life because ultimately our bodies are just overstuffed sausage skins.

Healing with spirits

For more than 12 hours after the visions ended I remained violently ill and was unable to walk. It was not until the second night that my strength began to return, the muscle tremors stopped and I recovered my sense of balance. By the following morning I felt completely better and ravenously hungry and went through a long active day without any sense of fatigue.

Iboga is a shamanic drug. In the Bwiti scheme of things it brings healing in this world by reconnecting us to the world of spirits. My visions, I knew, had been relatively subdued and unspectacular by comparison with those of the Bwiti initiates, but I too, in my own limited way, had experienced contact with some sort of otherworld through consumption of their sacred plant. Was it really a supernatural realm that the ibogaine took me into, or just a crazy hallucination? As I've emphasised, this was not something I was yet in a position to judge; nor was it easy to disentangle cause from effect. But what was miraculous nonetheless was the dramatic turnaround in my mood that I benefited from after my ibogaine session. For months beforehand I had been intensely depressed and irritable, filled with morbid thoughts and gloomy anxiety. My guilt at what I perceived as my dismal failure of my father, and my grief at his loss, had been compounded by feelings of worthlessness and anguish so deep that I frequently saw no point in taking any further initiatives in life. Better by far, I had persuaded myself, to withdraw from the world, abandon research and avoid all new intellectual challenges – which, anyway, I would certainly fail.

I hadn't expected ibogaine to make a difference, but it did. From the moment I woke up with my strength recovered I knew that it had flipped some sort of switch in me because I was no longer able to see anything in the world in the same negative and nihilistic way as I had done before. From time to time a morbid thought would still stray across my mind and try to drag my mood down; previously I would have dwelt on it obsessively until it made me miserable; now I found it easy to dismiss it and move on. I didn't feel so bad about my dad either. I'd not been at his bedside, and I couldn't change that. But somehow, now, I no longer ached so much.

Whether this healing was achieved through contact with the spirit world, or whether it was just a beneficial side-effect of shaking up my brain chemistry, I felt grateful to ibogaine. Regardless of the explanation, or the mechanism, it had put me through something I would never forget – something very much like a religious experience. It had swept away the cobwebs of ingrained bad habits and moods. And it had most persuasively demonstrated the worth of a hitherto neglected line of research into the spiritual life of the ancients.

CHAPTER TWO

The Greatest Riddle of Archaeology

Pech Merle cave in south-western France is a sacred sanctuary at least five times older than the Great Pyramid of Egypt. Like the pyramid it has a labyrinthine system of internal corridors, passageways, chambers and galleries. But unlike the pyramid, which is entirely man-made – for the most part with quarried blocks – the innards of Pech Merle were reamed out of a limestone massif by an underground river millions of years ago.

When the river changed its course the cave system it left behind was four kilometres long. It remained untouched and unvisited – except occasionally by hibernating bears – until human beings took possession of it around 25,000 years ago in the epoch now known as the Upper Palaeolithic. They do not seem ever to have lived in it – hardly surprising since its entrance was cramped and inaccessible and it was impenetrably dark and dripping with damp within. But they began a programme of subtle modification and embellishment that went on continuously, though at widely spaced intervals, between 25,000 years ago and about 15,000 years ago, after which it appears that all knowledge that there had ever been a holy place here was lost. Around 10,000 years ago, at the end of the Ice Age, a landslide completely sealed off the cave's entrance from the outside world. From then until its rediscovery in 1922 no one visited or even had the faintest idea that wonders and clues to the secrets of our origins lay entombed within, encoded in sacred images, shrouded in millennial darkness.

Shapes and shadows

Chaperoned by M. Zimmermann, an official of the Pech Merle Museum, I descend the stairway that leads to the modern entrance of the cave, a few metres to one side of the original entrance. The first sensations I register are of a change in the air, chill humidity, rivulets of running water underfoot. We already seem to be deep inside the mountain when we reach a massive security door. M. Zimmermann ceremoniously unlocks it and ushers me through to the halls of mystery that lie beyond.

My eyes are still adjusting to the contrast with the sunny early spring afternoon outside, and the lighting is dim, so for the first few moments I can see almost nothing. But the people of the Upper Palaeolithic would have seen even less 25,000 years ago when they began to make use of Pech Merle. My imagination is already at work on the shapes and shadows around me. How much more dramatic, possibly even fearsome, the cave system must have appeared in the low, guttering light cast by the simple torches and stone lamps that we know were used here by the ancients.

Besides, in several parts of Pech Merle's four kilometres of corridors and galleries the access has been artificially enlarged, improved and made safe in modern times. In antiquity the people who held the cave sacred would have been obliged to negotiate perilous deadfalls, and crawl on their bellies through narrow and constricting slits and gullies, before reaching the main rooms. Each visit must have been a terrifying experience, calling for courage and a determined effort of will – by no means the sort of venture that anyone would undertake lightly. Archaeological evidence points conclusively to a history of relatively few visits by relatively small numbers of people spread out over a period of more than 10,000 years, *but all coming to do the same thing* – namely to paint (and perhaps to venerate) beautiful and enigmatic images on certain carefully selected rock surfaces. From this and other important clues, which we'll return to in later chapters, scholars reasonably conclude that a religion was being practised here, one of the earliest true religions of mankind, and that the practitioners must have been ritual specialists, who worked largely

14

alone or with a few acolytes to create their mysterious art. It seems clear also, as is obvious in many other painted caves, that some special qualities were recognised in the place itself that led the artists to select it as their canvas.

Anteroom to the underworld

Pech Merle is first and foremost a marvel of nature – shaped, as though with cunning artifice, in such a way that it could hardly fail to make a powerful and numinous impact upon any human who encounters it. Even in modern times, with permanent electric lighting, it remains a spectacularly eerie and otherworldly subterranean realm.

After M. Zimmermann closes the security door behind us we find ourselves in a long, sinuous descending corridor, three metres high and wide, carved out of the bedrock by the ancient river. Gnarled and glistening stalactites and stalagmites the colour of old ivory are stacked up in niches like ranks of organ pipes or folded into weird curtains and drapes that seem to caress the rock walls. There are no cave paintings yet, but the further we penetrate, the stranger and more wildly chimerical and dreamlike the atmosphere becomes. I find it easy to imagine that I am descending into some parallel universe, some kingdom of the dwarves and elves – frozen and preserved like a time capsule come down to us from a legendary age or a snapshot glimpse across the borders of another dimension.

Now we arrive at the first piece of Upper Palaeolithic art on the route that all modern visitors take around Pech Merle – although it is by no means the first in terms of its age relative to other paintings here. About seven metres wide by two and a half metres high, it's a horizontal composition, imposed on a slightly concave expanse of cave wall to our left, where the rock face, sheltered beneath an overhang, is unusually pale, dry, and smoothly polished. Archaeologists refer to it as the Frise Noire because its principal figures of cold-adapted woolly mammoths, bison, aurochs (wild ancestors of modern cattle) and a horse with a disproportionately small head are dreamlike free-hand drawings done in black manganese. The figures all date from about 16,000 years ago and are thought to be the work of a single artist. On

Animals and polka dots of the Frise Noire

casual inspection they seem to form the entire subject matter of the panel, but a closer look shows them to be superimposed upon copious quantities of red iron oxide ochre. It was daubed and smeared about 4,000 years earlier across the lower part of the wall, here and there marshalled into distinct groups of polka dots, and at a couple of points attenuated into the faint outlines of animals.

Floating over the red foreground of the panel, the Ice Age mammals of the Frise Noire conspire in the convincing illusion of a three-dimensional array. Through the clever use of tricks of perspective the impression is somehow conveyed that the closest figures have emerged from the rock face itself while the ranks of other creatures beyond them seem almost to fade and disappear into its distant depths.

Emergence

The bestiary of the Frise Noire stands near the entrance of the so-called Salle Préhistorique, the large primary chamber that contains the vast majority of the Upper Palaeolithic art at Pech Merle. It is a mystery why other areas of the cave system – such as the spectacular and sepulchral Salle Rouge – were left untouched by the prehistoric artists, but there is no doubt that the Salle Préhistorique provides a uniquely atmospheric and awe-inspiring setting. As much as 40 metres wide in places, it supports a labyrinth of side passages and tunnels,

Plan of Pech Merle.

and is further complicated by rock falls and scree deposits that create a series of different floor levels. At some points the cave roof is low overhead, at others it soars away to disappear in the lofty darkness above, out of which, drawn down by the force of gravity, a frozen deluge of stalactites descends. Some are metres in length, jagged, multi-pointed, dripping like giant icicles in a thaw. Others join with stalagmites rising out of the floor below to form huge, irregular multi-fluted columns like fossilised leg bones or stacked vertebrae in a mausoleum of primordial giants.

Turning away from the the Frise Noir, M. Zimmermann leads me to our right up a flight of stairs installed in modern times within what must originally have been a steeply sloping natural tunnel. At the top we emerge on to a ledge, also natural, running along the cave wall at a height of about 10 metres above the floor and providing a fantastic vantage point over important areas of the Salle Préhistorique. Outlined in black manganese on the ceiling above the ledge, the spectral figures of two bison and a mammoth float into view. Then beneath us in the dark depths of the main chamber a spotlight snaps on to show me a distant glimpse of Pech Merle's masterpiece, the world-famous panel of the spotted horses. Tantalisingly, M. Zimmermann switches off the spot again almost immediately but reassures me that we will eventually come to the panel when he brings me to the lower level of the chamber.

We seem to have reached the end of the ledge now and descend 10 modern steps over what must have been a difficult scramble in prehistoric times. This brings us to a shallow natural cleft in the cave wall. To the right of the cleft M. Zimmermann points out the painted figure of a bison, the head of a second bison with a distinct mane of bushy hair, and the back, head and trunk of a mammoth – all in black manganese. To the left, at a slightly higher elevation, the ancient artist somehow 'found' the form of another mammoth immanent in the natural bulges, indentations and fissures of the rock, then teased out the apparition with suggestive black lines. 'The Cro-Magnon man used the natural shape of the rock,' explains M. Zimmermann, help-fully tracing the figure with a laser-pointer. 'You can see the head here, with the trunk. You see the front legs and the back legs. And you have two lines, one for the back and the tail and one for the stomach – here.'

Again, as at the Frise Noire, the essential quality of these painted animals seems to be that of dwelling in and emerging from the rock face. This feels true to me not only of the wonderful three-dimensional 'emergence' of the mammoth but also of the whole composition, which somehow contrives to suggest that the creatures depicted have emerged, from hidden depths beneath, through the junction of the cleft around which they cluster.

Engravings

We descend another flight of 10 steps to a lower level of the chamber where the floor is littered with huge piles of giant boulders through which we follow a winding path. Above us – I would estimate three metres above my head at this point – M. Zimmermann shows me an expanse of ceiling decorated with what looks at first like a mean-ingless scrawl of crudely inscribed lines but resolves on careful study into pattern and form. 'The ceiling is very soft,' M. Zimmermann explains, 'and they made the drawings with their fingers. You have maybe two periods – one with only lines, and in the second period you have figures.' His laser lights up the outline of a huge faintly incised mammoth: 'Here we have the back, here the head; this is the trunk; the front legs; the stomach.' A second mammoth looms nearby, and to its right hovers an exaggerated, cartoon-like figure of a naked woman with immense buttocks and breasts and a very tiny head – a classic Upper Palaeolithic 'Venus', one amongst many such voluptuous representations of the female form that have been found in the painted caves of old Europe. 'We have thirteen human representations in Pech Merle,' comments M. Zimmermann, 'two men and eleven women.'

'And the women are all Venus-type, very big, like this one?'

'Yes. Like this. You see another here, without head. You see the breast. You see the stomach here. You see the legs. You see the bottom. And the back.'

It was up the piles of tumbled boulders – almost blocking the floor at this point – that the ancients climbed to compose art on the ceiling with their fingers. Somewhere around 20,000 years ago they also painted the figures of two animals in black manganese on the boulders themselves: a mammoth at shoulder height and a large bison above head height.

We walk on for some tens of metres on a path that seems – in Pech Merle's characteristic labyrinth-like way – to wind first up a little, then steeply down. We find ourselves in the Hall of Discs, so called after its beautiful concentric formations of crystallised calcite. At the far side, to the right of our path, there is a sheer wall scored high up with four parallel scars. 'The claw marks of a cave bear,' explains M. Zimmermann. 'This bear was three metres tall.'

The mystery of the children

At the corner of the wall where the claw marks are impressed we come to the foot of a modern staircase. It rises 20 steps in two right-angled flights, where the ancients would have had a steep climb up treacherous scree. At the top we reach a natural alcove a few metres above and behind the claw marks, and on the floor of the alcove M. Zimmermann shows me the footprints of a child aged about 12. They were made almost 20,000 years ago, in what was originally soft mud, and have survived in fossilised form. Some of the prints are extremely clear, as though they were left this morning, and I find it impossible to look at them without forming some mental image of the intrepid young person – we know it was a single individual but we don't know if it was a girl or boy – who made them. With their neatly rounded heels and toes, the prints powerfully reinforce the common bond of shared humanity that ties us remotely but firmly to the cave artists despite the passage of millennia. It is this same bond that allows us to respond emotively to the art itself, to be affected by it – perhaps in many of the same ways that it affected the ancients – and to recognise its subtle qualities of abstraction and symbolism even while the meaning of its symbolic lexicon continues to elude us.

Pech Merle is not the only painted prehistoric cave in which there is evidence that children were in some way associated with the artists. Why should this have been so?

Gallery of the Bear

Beyond the little area of preserved footprints, deep in the mountain and about 50 metres underground, we enter the Galerie de l'Ours, or Gallery of the Bear, a very ancient part of the Pech Merle system. It contains no paintings but a riot of stalactites and stalagmites, deeply fluted and withered pillars, and improbably immense calcite phalluses lewdly erect. To our right, protecting a dark sanctuary, a rank of polished columns, so symmetrical as to appear man-made, forms a distinct architectural feature, like a scaled-down version of an ancient Egyptian temple. We climb a modern flight of eight steps then follow a low narrow corridor to our left where the roof clearance is just a few centimetres above my head. But in prehistoric times it was even lower, explains M. Zimmermann – crawl space only.

Twenty thousand years before the access was expanded for the benefit of modern visitors, what possible motive could the ancients have had to crawl in here? The answer soon presents itself in the form of more art incised high up on the corridor walls – most distinctively the beautifully shaped head and eye of a brown bear etched in profile. Beside it are patterns of vertical and horizontal lines. Cut into the opposite wall of the corridor four triangles lie partially superimposed upon one another, and alongside them a curious and as yet unidentified symbol somewhat resembling the horn of a bull.

Wounded man

The corridor reconnects us to the main painted gallery of Pech Merle by way of a zig-zag path recently cut into the side of a scree slope from which breathtaking views unfold. The effect is of being in the heart of an immense gothic edifice, consecrated to the worship of the mineral gods and furnished in the dark depths of the earth with great halls and vaults, soaring archways, flying buttresses, and pillars of calcite and alabaster. Surely in his famous opium trance it must have been some vision of sunless otherworldliness like this that inspired Coleridge when he described the measureless caverns of Xanadu and the stately pleasure dome of Kubla Khan? The place seems surreal and enchanted, as though a spell of death-like sleep was cast over it by the magicians of the Ice Age and has never since been lifted.

Halfway down, M. Zimmermann draws me aside into an alcove to show me a strange representation of a human, or human-like, figure, the so-called 'wounded man', painted in red ochre on the low ceiling. I have to stoop to see it properly but, again, this is an area that has been dug out for modern convenience and it would have been much harder to access in prehistoric times. In fact in the Upper Palaeolithic the ceiling here was little more than a metre above the floor. The artist would therefore have had extremely limited room for manoeuvre and could only have worked lying on his back. Those who came after to view the painting – assuming that was what happened – would have been obliged to adopt the same posture.

The wounded man is so named because of a series of lines, drawn as harsh slashes (and often interpreted as spears), that pass directly through his chest, torso and buttocks. Against the background of the ceiling he seems to be rising slowly into the air. His head is a most peculiar shape. Some archaeologists say it is birdlike. But with its prominently domed skull, narrow pointed chin and oblique slit eyes, the

The wounded man
of Pech Merle

forceful first impression it makes on me is not of any kind of bird but of the traditional image of an elf or goblin from the realm of fairytale.

Directly above the wounded man's head, the back of which it touches, is a large sign also daubed in red ochre. Variations of the same symbol, and indeed of the wounded man himself, have been found in other caves, though none quite identical to this one. Archaeologists describe the symbol as 'tectiform' (somewhat like a building) or 'aviform' (somewhat like a bird). It has the shape of an inverted outlined letter T with thinner single lines extending down at angles from either end of its crossbar.

Possibly – or possibly not – part of the same composition is the figure of a powerful aurochs (an extinct species of wild bull) with lyre-shaped horns. It too is done in red ochre and floats on the ceiling of the alcove very close to the wounded man. A little further off there is a stylised ibex (mountain goat) also painted in red ochre. Between the two there are several associated symbols, including one that is distinctively branched or Y-shaped.

The whole complicated multi-media display of signs and pictures seems to pulse and vibrate with ineffable meaning.

Reaching out

We continue our descent to the floor of the main gallery and come in a moment to a pattern of red ochre polka dots painted on the cave wall. To their left is the ghostly negative image, also outlined in red, of a graceful female hand.

It is an intimate encounter.

When a woman stood here 20,000 years ago, spreading her fingers against the wall, what thoughts were going through her head? Was she young, or old, or in the prime of life? What was her relationship to the artist, who had chewed up a solution of ochre in his mouth, mixing it with his saliva, so that he could use his breath to spray it over her hand? Or was she herself the artist as well as the model?

Negative handprint
and dots

Either way, what was her purpose in leaving her spectral handprint here?

An alcove extends back into the rock face beneath and behind the hand. On the right wall of the alcove M. Zimmermann points out a representation, again in ochre, of eight female figures, all highly stylised in the familiar 'Venus' form with disproportionately large breasts and buttocks. There is, however, an ambiguity about them that leads some experts to class them as composite beings, part animal, part human. The French prehistorian A. Leroi-Gourhan called them 'bison-women'.[1] One of them is superimposed on the head of a horse. The same composition also includes two roughly circular groups of polka dots (one consisting of 7 and the other of 14 dots) and the outline of a mammoth. A few metres away, on the opposite wall of the passage, the head of a stag looms over us outlined in red ochre.

A palimpsest of spotted horses

A walk of only a few seconds brings us to the acknowledged master-piece of Pech Merle's gallery of prehistoric art, the spectacular panel of the spotted horses that M. Zimmermann had first pointed out to me from above. Now, close up, I see that the panel is framed by more negative handprints – this time men's hands, silhouetted in black, one apparently with six digits instead of the usual five. Whether intended by the ancients or not, the impression created is that these hands have merged with the rock beneath – as though, by the process of painting, the former was drawn into and incorporated with the latter. It seems to me that this is the exact corollary of the other gift of the cave artists, the gift of finding and drawing out the forms of animals already dwelling in the rocks they chose to paint. Yet that gift, too, is expressed in this panel, which culminates, to the right, in a naturally formed spur of bedrock shaped unmistakably like the head of a horse. There is little reasonable doubt that this is why two beautiful dappled horses, each about two metres in length, were painted here (rather than elsewhere in the cave or not at all) and why the horse at the right of the composition is oriented so that its head overlaps the suggestive spur.

The spur is of the correct size and in the correct place to serve with only minimal decoration as the horse's head. Nevertheless it is an illusion.

The panel of the spotted horses

A closer look at the panel reveals that this otherwise realistic animal, as is the case with its counterpart to the left, already possesses a painted head of its own – one that is preposterously out of scale with the rest of the body and seems at first glance to be a mere continuation of the mane. These tiny heads, perched on the end of robust necks and bodies, give the spotted horses of Pech Merle a phantasmagoric quality, as though they have been drawn forth through the rock wall from a dimension that is similar to ours and yet also strikingly and bizarrely different.

Like other works of art in the cave, the frieze is a palimpsest in which compositions from different eras have been superimposed on one another. The horses, for example, were entirely created with an organic paint based on wood-charcoal mixed with saliva and sprayed orally on to the rock wall. Wood charcoal is eminently datable and fragments of paint from the horse on the right are now known to be more than 24,000 years old.[2] But there are other ingredients in the panel, executed in red ochre, that are younger, dating to approximately 20,000 years ago. Particularly notable amongst these is an impressive two-metre-long lake fish, a pike, superimposed over the back and part of the mane of the horse on the right. There are also red ochre polka dots, about the same size as – and mingled with – the black dapples of the horse's body. Lastly there are seven indecipherable signs shaped like bent thumbs, and a range of other more abstract symbols including lines, triangles, dots and a circle.

The symbolic revolution

The spotted horses with their tiny heads are not the only weirdly distorted and phantasmagoric images at Pech Merle. In the narrow Combell gallery, which is presently off-limits to the public, there are three more 'imaginary animals'. These are loosely based on antelopes and once again have disproportionately small heads. Dating back an estimated 25,000 years, they are the oldest paintings in the cave. The composition of which they form part also includes several dots and signs, more horses, and a large cave lion portrayed as though about to leap on its prey.

Not for the first time the limitations of present knowledge are such that we may only shrug our shoulders and ask: What does it all mean?

Twenty thousand years, more or less, separate us from the inspired religious artists of Pech Merle, and almost 35,000 years from the oldest cave art so far found in Europe.[3] No traditions or accounts of any kind have come down to us about these long-forgotten Stone Age visionaries, and despite their frequent use of signs and symbols they had no written language and so have left us no inscriptions that we might one day hope to decipher. It is therefore hardly surprising that we do not know the meaning of any of their paintings, that almost everything they did, and their reasons for doing it, is completely mysterious to us, and that many scholars in this field have given up theorising about prehistoric art and prefer to spend their time simply accumulating and sorting data. The consequence is that we are ignorant of the mechanisms and driving forces behind by far the greatest evolutionary transformation ever to have overtaken the human race – the so-called symbolic revolution, of which the cave paintings that first began to appear in Europe more than 30,000 years ago are a rich and already fully evolved expression.

Despite a very few deeply puzzling anomalies,[4] it is the expert consensus that our hominid predecessors did not behave symbolically *at all* during approximately the first five to seven million years of evolution that separate us from our last common ancestor with the chimpanzee.[5] What we see throughout this period is a dull and stultifying copying and recopying of essentially the same patterns of behaviour and essentially the same 'kits' of crude stone tools, without change or innovation, for periods of hundreds of thousands, even millions of years. When a change is introduced (in tool shape, for example), it then sets a new standard to be copied and recopied without innovation for a further immense period until the next change is finally adopted. In the process, glacially slow, we also see the gradual development of human anatomy in the direction of the modern form.

By 196,000 years ago,[6] and on some accounts considerably earlier,[7] humans had achieved 'full anatomical modernity'. This means that they were in every way physically indistinguishable from the people of today and, crucially, that they possessed the same large, complex brains as we do. One mystery is that their behaviour at first lagged behind their acquisition of modern neurology and appearance – because it was not until around 100,000 years ago that they began to show the first unmistakable signs of symbolic ability that we associate with almost every aspect of modern human life. Another mystery is that these developments seem to have taken place only in Africa.

Outside the African continent much more primitive hominids still prevailed. From mainland Asia there is evidence that a species known as *Homo erectus* (whose brain was two thirds the size of ours and whose forebears had left Africa more than a million years previously) may have survived virtually unchanged until first contact with modern humans 50,000 years ago or less.[8] During 2004, archaeologists working on the remote Indonesian island of Flores unearthed the remains of another 'primitive' hominid that also survived into recent times – in this case until less than 20,000 years ago, when it too came into contact with modern humans. Nicknamed 'the hobbit' because of its very small stature, it is now scientifically classified as *Homo floresiensis*. Initial investigations suggested that this newly discovered species might be a descendant of a *Homo erectus* population that had become marooned on Flores hundreds of thousands of years previously and thereafter pursued its own distinctive evolutionary course. Like other animals living on the island (where there were also pygmy elephants the size of ponies), this meant dwarfism.[9] Later researchers suggested that the creature was not just a dwarf *Homo erectus* but a previously unknown species 'on a different branch of humanity's family tree'.[10] The matter remains in dispute, but whatever the final outcome, the remains of *Homo floresiensis* indicate that full-grown adults reached a height of only about one metre and had a brain capacity of around 380 cubic centimetres, which, to put it in perspective, is about the same size as the brain of a chimpanzee, one third the size of a *Homo erectus* brain, and just over one quarter the size of a modern human brain. What is striking, despite his ape-sized brain, is that *Homo floresiensis* made and used stone tools; but neither he, nor his larger-brained ancestor, *Homo erectus*, appears to have made any use of symbols.[11]

Meanwhile in Europe, *Homo neanderthalensis*, the thickset, beetle-browed species better known as Neanderthal Man, had been the sole master of all he surveyed from perhaps as early as 250,000 years ago until he too began his fatal encounter with modern humans less than 50,000 years ago.[12] Neanderthal Man was far ahead of *Homo erectus* and *Homo floresiensis* on the evolutionary scale, but he also – and greatly to his disadvantage – seems to have had no knowledge of symbols.[13]

The multiple survival advantage that the ability to use symbols bestowed on our anatomically modern ancestors – from improved hunting strategies to improved transmission of vital lore from generation to generation – are too obvious to require enumeration here. It is by no means necessarily the case, however, that all groups of humans everywhere became adept manipulators of symbols at exactly the same moment. Common sense suggests that some probably caught on much earlier than others and that there may have been lags of many thousands of years in isolated examples.

This is broadly what the archaeological record shows, with the earliest evidence of symbolism (though not all scholars are willing to accept it as such) turning up in southern Africa between approximately 110,000 and 90,000 years ago. At a number of sites exquisitely made and often impractically fragile bone tools have been found, dating to this period, that seem to have been hoarded and exchanged rather than used. The obvious implication is that these objects must have had important symbolic value to their owners.[14]

The next big landmark in symbolic thinking that archaeologists have identified again occurs in southern Africa. Chris Henshilwood's excavations at Blombos Cave on the Cape have produced the earliest uncontested example of purely symbolic art so far found anywhere in the world – an abstract geometrical composition inscribed on a small block of red ochre. It is nothing very much to look at, yet for reasons that will become clear to the reader in Chapter Eight, the fact that these specific patterns appear on the world's earliest artwork may be

Red ochre block with geometrical patterns (left), and drilled shell beads (right), from Blombos Cave, South Africa, estimated to be around 77,000 years old.

highly significant. In 2004 Henshilwood also excavated the earliest uncontested example of personal adornment so far found anywhere in the world: a set of minute drilled shell beads. Both the ochre and the beads were found in a stratum dated to 77,000 years ago.[15]

It is worth remembering that in archaeology a turn of the spade can change everything. Still, on today's evidence, it looks very much as though the human symbolic revolution remained 'stuck' more or less at the Blombos phase (of shell jewellery and geometric patterns) for rather a long while – from 77,000 years ago until the great cave art began to appear in Europe more than 40,000 years later. For most of this immense period the evidence points to Africa, and neighbouring parts of the Levant, as *the only region in the world* where ancestral modern humans were present – and for most of it their surviving symbolism is confined to the relatively low level of abstract patterns and personal adornments found at Blombos.

There is, however, a single intriguing exception. Australia, never populated by any other hominid species, was colonised by anatomically modern humans at an astonishingly early date – as early as 60,000 years ago on some estimates, and possibly (though such 'extreme' dates are hotly contested) as far back as 75,000 years ago.[16] As well as making the immense overland journey from their home in Africa, apparently over a very few generations, and perhaps even within one generation, these pioneering humans were finally obliged to mount a feat of open-ocean sailing (to reach Australia from south-east Asia) that would surely have been impossible without advanced symbolic abilities.

The mystery deepens when we realise that the earliest evidence for the presence of modern humans in south-east Asia (which straddles the overland route that migrants from Africa would have had to follow) dates back less than 40,000 years – i.e. at least 20,000 years *after* the arrival of modern humans in Australia.[17] There are also controversial claims of extremely ancient works of rock art in Australia, featuring simple engraved geometrical patterns, some possibly more than 40,000 years old, and some, again, with an 'extreme' suggested antiquity of 75,000 years that is close to the age of the engraved patterns at Blombos.[18]

Whether we find its traces in Australia, Asia, Africa or Europe it is impossible to overstate the uniqueness and peculiarity of the evolutionary event by which we were drawn into fully modern consciousness and the fully modern capacity for symbolism and culture, religion and art. No ancestor in the human lineage had ever made use of any form of symbolism before, and needless to say no other animal species had ever done so either. But the switching-on of humanity's symbol-making capacity between approximately 100,000 and 40,000 years ago was the change that changed everything. Before it, other than scattering their stone tools for us to find, the generations of our ancestors appear to have come and gone leaving no more impression upon the earth than any other animals; after it our behaviour and achievements began to diverge very rapidly from those of the rest of the animal kingdom. While it is undoubtedly the case that there was a lengthy build-up to this, it is also obvious that some sort of 'critical mass' was reached, at least in south-west Europe, when the great caves began to be painted between 40,000 and 30,000 years ago. Subsequently, notes Richard Klein, Professor of Anthropology at Stanford University, 'ever more closely packed cultural revolutions have taken humanity from the status of a relatively large mammal to something more like a geologic force'.[19]

What adds to the mystery of this amazing stepping-up of our effectiveness and competitiveness is that it was not accompanied or immediately preceded by any obvious anatomical change. There was, for example, no increase in human brain size between 100,000 and 40,000 years ago. On the contrary, the fossil record shows that today's average of around 1,350 cubic centimetres had already been attained by our ancestors in Africa as early as half a million years ago – even before full anatomical modernity was reached – and has since remained relatively stable. We are therefore obliged to ask why it was that humans with identical brains, looks and genes to ours nevertheless behaved so very differently from us for the first 100,000 years of their existence (i.e. from roughly 200,000 to roughly 100,000 years ago) – so differently, in fact, that they seem almost like another species.[20] And why did they then embark on an immense behavioural metamorphosis – that would not hit critical mass until around 40,000 years ago – to become innovative and artistic, symbolic and cultured, religious and self-aware? What caused the momentous change of direction and destiny, hitherto unparalleled in the history of life on earth, that gave birth to modern human culture?

Dr Frank Brown, whose discovery of 196,000-year-old anatomically modern human skeletons in Ethiopia was published in *Nature* on 17 February 2005, points out that they are 35,000 years older than the previous 'oldest' modern human remains known to archaeologists:

> This is significant because the cultural aspects of humanity in most cases appear much later in the record, which would mean 150,000 years of *Homo sapiens* without cultural stuff . . .[21]

Brown's colleague, John Fleagle, of Stony Brook University in New York State, also comments on the same problem:

> There is a huge debate regarding the first appearance of modern aspects of behaviour . . . As modern human anatomy is documented at earlier and earlier sites, it becomes evident that there was a great time gap between the appearance of the modern skeleton and 'modern behaviour'.[22]

For Ian Tattershall of the American Museum of Natural History the problem posed by this gap – and what happened to our ancestors during it – is 'the question of questions in palaeoanthropology'.[23] His colleague Professor David Lewis-Williams of the Rock Art Research Institute at South Africa's Witwatersrand University describes the same problem as 'the greatest riddle of archaeology – how we became human and in the process began to make art and to practise what we call religion'.[24]

Clues to follow

The admission by scholars that we simply do not understand the artistic and religious revolution of the Stone Age, or the part it played in putting us on the fast track forward to the Space Age, highlights an obvious direction for new research. The libraries are already full of weighty books and learned papers generated by more than a century of mainstream academic study of prehistoric art. The data mountain is huge; yet ironically, concludes Professor Lewis-Williams, all the efforts that went into building it have brought us no closer to finding out the one thing we really need to know about the Upper Palaeolithic: 'why the people of that period penetrated the deep limestone caves of France and Spain to make images in total darkness'.[25]

Why indeed? What motives led them to pick out such extreme and difficult places? What did they themselves believe they were doing all this for?

Such were the questions that had brought me to Pech Merle – off-season, when the whole cave was closed to the public, so that I might have the opportunity to experience its great works of art in something like the conditions of solitude and silence that would have prevailed when they were created. Whatever the true nature of the process that transformed the lives of our ancestors, it is clear that it involved symbolic expression above all else. Whether at Pech Merle or at dozens of other Upper Palaeolithic sites, the images they left behind may therefore be the best clues we have if we want to uncover the secret of our own humanity.

CHAPTER THREE

Vine of Souls

Most human characteristics that are genuinely universal are easily accounted for in evolutionary terms, and the arguments are widely known. For example, we all live in families and societies because to do so aids our survival and the propagation of our genes. We all have the capacity for love because it is an emotion that promotes family and social life. We all have laws of one kind or another because these, too, reinforce family and social ties and thus make us stronger and more competitive. We all eat food and drink water because we will soon die if we don't. We all use the unique human gift of language to communicate more effectively than other species on the planet, to preserve knowledge handed down from previous generations, and to create culture – thus further sharpening our competitive edge.

But there's one very odd thing that all of us at all periods of history seem to have done that defies an obvious evolutionary explanation. Against logic and reason, lacking irrefutable proof that we are right, and sometimes contrary to our own objective interests, every society that we know about since the appearance of modern humans on the planet has maintained a steadfast belief in the existence of supernatural realms and beings. Even in this rational and scientific century (the twenty-first since the crucifixion of a supernatural being called Jesus), more than a billion Christians still believe in Heaven and Hell, God and the Devil, angels and demons. Muslims, Hindus, Buddhists, the ancient Egyptians, the Maya, the Druids and the practitioners of all other known religions living and dead have all also entertained similar ideas. The exact nature and multiplicity of the beings may change, the number and character of the realms may change, but in all cases, at root, what unites us are our unproven irrational beliefs of one kind or another in non-material dimensions of reality, inhabited by incorporeal beings that interact with us and frame our destiny in mysterious ways.[1]

Many evolutionary scientists claim that beliefs of this sort are 'hard wired' into our brains. This 'neurological adaptation' is said to have been selected because, despite some obvious aberrations and exceptions, religious beliefs generally strengthen society and therefore aid the survival of our species – just like our propensity to love, or our universal inclination to live by laws. But even if religion does exactly what the evolutionists say it does, the central problem remains. We may have learnt something more about the workings of society and its institutions, but we are no nearer to understanding why the common ground of all religions everywhere should consist of remarkable, unproven and deeply illogical beliefs in spiritual and supernatural levels of reality and their alleged influences upon our daily lives.

I want to re-emphasise that there is no dispute here about the social usefulness of religious beliefs. I take that for granted. The problem is better phrased if we ask why human societies have so consistently opted for *these particular beliefs* – in supernatural realms and beings – rather than others that might have served the same function without requiring such a radical disconnection from observed reality. To put the issue in some kind of perspective, one can hardly imagine that lions would be more efficient predators if they lavished large amounts of their time and energy on placating nonexistent beings from other worlds. And what about the gazelles? Would they have any chance of escaping the cheetahs if they kept being diverted by parades of spirits, elves or angels? Because it is hard to see the evolutionary advantage of such impractical distractions for animals, it is all the more difficult to understand how they could provide any possible advantage to humans. Yet if they provide no advantage, then how are we to explain the fact that every human society throughout recorded history in which religion has played an important role – which is as good as saying *every* society, ever, without exception – has been so thoroughly dominated and entranced by precisely such beliefs?[2]

Shared neurology

The anthropological theory that I had set out to test, outlined briefly in Chapter One, offers a partial answer to this question. While it does not explain the long-term survival and massive historical influence of any religion in particular, it does offer a very reasonable, logical and simple explanation for the strange notions of supernatural realms and supernatural beings that form the foundation of all religions. According to Professor David Lewis-Williams, the leading proponent of the theory, such ideas are not part of the normal, predictable currency of everyday life but arise from the universal human neurological capacity to enter 'altered states of consciousness' (ASCs) – i.e. states of deep trance in which extremely realistic hallucinations are seen. Many anthropologists are convinced that as far back as the Upper Palae-olithic our ancestors placed a high value on hallucinations and made extensive use of psychoactive plants to induce them.[3] In addition it is well known that rhythmic drumming and dancing, hyperventilation, self-mutilation, starvation and a variety of other more or less unpleasant techniques can also bring on hallucinations.[4] In hunter-gatherer soci-eties such work is typically not the responsibility of all people but only of the shamans – those ritual specialists who are able to make the perilous journey to the hallucinatory otherworld and return with healing knowledge.[5]

Supported by David Whitley, one of the leading North American rock art specialists, Jean Clottes, the world-renowned expert on the French prehistoric painted caves, and a growing number of other scholars from many different countries, Lewis-Williams takes the view that the first notions of the existence of supernatural realms and beings, the first 'religious' ideas about them, the first art representing them, and the first mythologies concerning them were all derived from the experiences of hallucinating shamans.[6] By this theory, the art of Pech Merle and of the 300 or so other painted caves of south-west Europe

35

is an art of visions – in other words, the extraordinary images that confront us there depict hallucinations seen by shamans in altered states of consciousness. Since both we and the shaman-artists of the Upper Palaeolithic share the same modern human neurology, and since ASCs are a universal phenomenon of that neurology, it follows that there may after all be some possibility of a bridge between us and them – some possibility for us to see what they saw and, despite the passage of tens of thousands of years, to gain direct experiential insight into the roots of their beliefs.

The limits of objective research

David Lewis-Williams began to develop his 'neuropsychological model' of cave art and the origins of religion in the early 1980s and has been testing and defending it virtually non-stop since 1988, when he and his co-researcher Thomas Dowson officially put it before their peers in the scholarly journal *Current Anthropology*.[7] Despite widespread acceptance of the model, criticisms have recently begun to mount which Lewis-Williams remains active in rebutting. As he admitted when I met him at Witwatersrand University in 2004, however, there is one thing he has not done and is not prepared to do in the name of science, and that is to experiment directly and personally with the altered states of consciousness he has made a career out of researching and writing about. Like many Westerners, he told me, he was too much of a 'control freak' to put himself into trance by dancing or drumming, he had no intention of starving himself for 40 days, and he certainly wasn't going to take any psychoactive drugs – by far the easiest, the most certain and, throughout history, the most common method used by shamans to attain the visionary state.

'Why not?' I asked.

Lewis-Williams shrugged: 'I don't want to fry my brains and frankly I'm not in the least bit interested in the experience.'

I protested that as the leading exponent of the visionary theory of Upper Palaeolithic art I would have thought that he of all people should be extremely interested in such experiences, but Lewis-Williams maintained steadfastly that he was not. He pointed out that

36

the scientific literature already contains a huge number of studies of trance states and hallucinations, and that for him to add a few hallucinations of his own would change nothing. Better to stand back, stay objective, and focus on the search for common patterns in the cave art on the one hand and in what the psychiatric and psychological experts have reported about hallucinations on the other. That was the way to flesh out the neuropsychological theory – with an overwhelming deluge of evidence and common sense. There was nothing to be gained from seeking a personal tour of the shamanic 'otherworld', which – we now know as our ancestors did not – is just a silly illusion.

Though I understood perfectly where Lewis-Williams was coming from, I could not agree with him and objected that we do not know any such thing. We might feel very sure that there is no more to reality than the material world in which we live, but we cannot prove that this is the case. Theoretically there could be other realms, other dimensions, as all religious traditions and quantum physics alike maintain. Theoretically the brain could be as much a receiver as a generator of consciousness and thus might be fine-tuned in altered states to pick up wavelengths that are normally not accessible to us. Depending on our point of view and our experiences, we might find the proposition that such 'otherworlds' are real more or less improbable, but it is important to register that no empirical evidence exists that rules them out entirely.

At this point Lewis-Williams politely expressed impatience at the speculative direction in which he felt I was taking the conversation and we moved on to discuss weightier matters. At the back of my mind, however, I couldn't help feeling there was a problem with the way that academic researchers who studied the religious impact of visions were so sure they were just 'silly illusions'. Lewis-Williams was probably 100 per cent right that they were 'mere' hallucinations and figments which had tricked our foolish ancestors into believing in nonexistent otherworlds for thousands of years. Still, I thought he was 100 per cent wrong to express that view with such force and authority without ever having experienced visions himself.

I had reason to believe that such experiences might have influenced his take on the matter; they had certainly influenced mine . . .

South American shamans, on drugs, painting their hallucinations

Six months before the ibogaine session that I described in Chapter One, and three months before I met Professor Lewis-Williams in Johannesburg, I spent five weeks in the Peruvian Amazon with indigenous Indian shamans drinking the sacred plant hallucinogen known in the Quechua language of the Incas as ayahuasca. This is a composite word that means, literally, the 'Vine of the Dead' or, in some translations, the 'Vine of Souls'. It reflects the alleged capacity of the South American brew, very much like iboga in Africa, to propel those who ingest it into realms that seem convincingly spiritual and supernatural where, very often, they encounter their deceased ancestors. Since I sought to test the hypothesis that the first religious ideas of mankind, and the cave art that expressed them, were inspired by visions induced by psychoactive plants, I was intrigued to learn of the existence of Indian tribal shamans in the Amazon who routinely paint scenes from their ayahuasca visions.[8] Certain shamans, such as the renowed Pablo Amaringo and his cousin Francisco Montes Shuna, had even gained international renown for their ayahuasca-inspired art – the latter contributing a mural to the Eden Project in Cornwall, England, the former having collections of his paintings exhibited in New York and published in a prestigious art book.[9]

Scientists know why ayahuasca produces visions. It does so because one of its two principal plant ingredients is rich in N,N-dimethyl-tryptamine (DMT), an extremely potent and fast-acting hallucinogen that is also secreted naturally in minute, usually sub-psychedelic quantities by the human brain. Despite being present in our bodies, both DMT in its pure form and DMT in solution in the ayahuasca brew are classified as Schedule 1/Class A illegal drugs in the United States and Britain and you can go to jail for a long time for possessing them. In countries bordering the Amazon Basin, however, where ayahuasca has been an integral part of indigenous Indian culture for thousands of years, it is not illegal; on the contrary, in Peru, Brazil, Colombia and Ecuador its consumption is protected under laws of individual religious freedom. Those good and decent laws, and the relative accessibility of indigenous shamans working as *curanderos* – healers – in their local communities were reason enough for me to do most of my ayahuasca sessions in the Peruvian Amazon. But I also participated in one session in Brazil with a modern syncretic cult known as the Uniao de Vegetal (UdV). It uses ayahuasca as its sacrament and has brought the archaic shamanic experience of visionary revelation alive for a rapidly expanding community of otherwise very 'normal', middle-class, well-educated Brazilians.

A number of plants growing in different parts of the Amazon contain the DMT that gives ayahuasca its extraordinary visionary powers, and all of these have long been known to indigenous shamans. One of the most widely used is *Psychotria viridis*. It is a bush of the

Psychotria viridis. Its leaves contain dimethyltryptamine (DMT), the active ingredient of ayahuasca.

Rubiaceae family and its leaves release psychotropic quantities of DMT if cooked together with water. Whether the DMT is extracted from this plant, however, or from one of the half-dozen or so other known sources, there is a problem to overcome. Monoamine oxidase, an enzyme that occurs naturally in our stomachs, so efficiently destroys DMT on contact as to render it entirely orally inactive. It is at this point that the other principal ingredient of the brew – the ayahuasca vine itself – comes into play. Classified scientifically as *Banisteriopsis caapi*, and a member of the *Malpigia* family of giant forest lianas, it contains chemicals known as monoamine oxidase inhibitors which

Banisteriopsis caapi, the ayahuasca
'vine of souls'

cleverly switch off the stomach enzyme and allow the DMT from the *Psychotria viridis* leaves (or from any of the other sources) to go to work.[10]

Anthropologist Jeremy Narby comments:

> So here are people without electron microscopes who choose, among some 80,000 Amazonian plant species, the leaves of a bush containing a hallucinogenic brain hormone, which they combine with a vine containing substances that inactivate an enzyme of the digestive tract which would otherwise block the hallucinogenic effect. And they do this to modify their consciousness. It's as if they knew about the molecular properties of plants *and* the art of combining them, and when one asks them how they know these things, they say their knowledge comes directly from hallucinogenic plants.[11]

The renowned ethnobotanist Richard Evans Schultes was struck by the same problem:

> One wonders how peoples in primitive societies, with no knowledge of chemistry or physiology, ever hit upon a solution to the activation of an alkaloid by a monoamine oxidase inhibitor. Pure experimentation? Perhaps not. The examples are too numerous.[12]

So the substance I had gone to South America to drink had a mysterious history. It was intimately connected to religious ideas and to the religious art of the region. Its very existence was biochemically unlikely and contrary to the laws of probability, and the shamans who used it claimed it transported them to supernatural worlds where they encountered spiritual beings of great power.

In the pages that follow, I set out the highlights of my own visions, woven into a sequential narrative. I participated in ayahuasca sessions ten times in Peru and Brazil and once in Europe. But no matter where I drank the brew, its extraordinary effects always brought me, pretty soon, to the same complex, internally consistent and deeply strange universe.

The vine and the leaf

I accompany the great shaman Francisco Montes Shuna to the place in the jungle where ayahuasca is prepared. Gathered there on the ground there is already a pile of cut sections of ayahuasca vine, which is a tough, liana-like creeper that hangs from the tall trees. Francisco selects several large pieces, each approximately as thick as my arm, consisting of three or four vines coiled around one another in long, tight knots like mating serpents. These large pieces are chopped into 22 segments each about a foot long. Then we pick approximately 300 fresh green leaves of *Psychotria viridis* from bushes nearby. Finally the 22 sections of vine are smashed with a heavy wooden club – methodically smashed, mainly by Francisco, although I inexpertly assist him with three of them.

Once macerated in this way the inner part of the vine is exposed. It is very fibrous but also damp and turning a red colour. Francisco places a thick layer of the smashed vine into the bottom of a large iron cooking pot, on top of this a layer of all the *P. viridis* leaves, then another layer of the rest of the vine. Next the whole mass is wedged down beneath two sticks jammed transversely into place and several litres of cold water from the creek are added until all the contents are covered. This is left to marinate overnight.

The following morning, around 8 a.m., I go to see the brew being cooked. It has already been on the fire for two hours and is bubbling steadily at a slow boil. This first water is eventually decanted into a second large iron pot and fresh water is added to cover the mass of vine and leaves once again. This will happen three more times. Then all the substance-rich water collected in the second pot, many litres, will be boiled slowly down to less than a litre of pure, concentrated ayahuasca. The vines and leaves from the first pot, having now served their function, are thrown away.

The ceremony begins

It is always night when the ceremony begins, around nine or ten in the evening. The rich velvet darkness of the rain forest envelops everything. The setting may be a small, simple hut out on the far edge of Iquitos, or the temple at Sachamama established by Francisco Montes Shuna, or a homestead beside a stagnant creek on a remote tributary

Jungle ayahuasca session

of the Amazon, or just a clearing in the jungle. Sometimes I'm alone with the shaman; usually my wife Santha is there as well; frequently people from the local community who also want to drink join in.

The shaman is almost always a man, dressed in the nondescript Westernised clothes of the villages. You wouldn't notice anything particularly special about him if you passed him in the street, but he knows a great deal about the plant medicines of the jungle and how they may best be harnessed for the benefit of human beings. As a practising *ayahuasquero* he is likely to have been drinking the sacred brew since childhood and to have travelled so frequently in the super-natural realms, to which ayahuasca affords a portal, that he is truly the master of all the strange experiences to be encountered there. He will long ago have acquired his own 'spirit animals' who meet him in the hallucinatory otherworld, act as his guides and protectors throughout the trance, and assist him in his vocation as a seer and healer. Sometimes also he has in his possession a number of 'power objects' – for instance pebbles of quartz crystal, a piece of magnetised iron, a bundle of feathers, and certain small statuettes of wood, bone or terracotta – which provide additional assistance to him in his struggles in the spirit world.

Wherever we hold the ritual, and whichever shaman is leading it, an essentially similar routine is followed. The shaman puffs on huge

Painting of an ayahuasca session in a jungle *maloca*, by
Peruvian shaman Pablo Amaringo

hand-rolled cigarettes of sacred tobacco and blows clouds of smoke over himself and the drinkers and into the neck of the bottle containing the ayahuasca. There is much muttering of invocations, brushing of the air with rustling leafy branches, and sprinkling of

Agua Florida, a cheap cologne. The shaman clears his throat several times and spits. Then he begins to sing the *icaros*, ancient chants and whistles, handed down since time immemorial, to draw in the spirits around our circle.

Usually by the time the ayahuasca is poured more than half an hour has passed. Modes of preparation vary. In some cases – for example the UdV in Brazil – large glasses of a very diluted brew are served. More commonly the ayahuasca is concentrated by repeated boiling into a thick, dark, viscous liquid – of the kind I saw Francisco Montes Shuna prepare – and is presented in a small cup.

First in line at the very first session I attend is a middle-aged woman who wants to contact the spirit of her dead husband. She sips. Pauses. Looks down into the cup. Then drains the rest at a gulp. The same grubby china cup is used by all participants, with the shaman seeming to assess each individual carefully (body weight? aura?) before pouring out a dose. In each case he whispers incomprehensible words into the cup before handing it over to the participant. In each case the measure he has poured looks much the same as the last – roughly equivalent in volume to a double shot of spirits.

My turn. I'm sitting on my heels on the grass mat that is spread out in front of the shaman. His lined features are folded like leather into a beatific expression. He weighs me up, pours from the bottle into the cup the standard double shot of ayahuasca, whispers the incomprehensible words, passes the cup over to me.

I take a tentative sip of the vile-tasting liquid – so strong and bitter-sweet and salty, so dark, so concentrated and so textured as to be repellent. There are jangling discordant notes of cocoa, medicine and jungle rot. And there is the definite sense that I am partaking here of something formidable and elusive – a 'living spirit' as the old myths say – that announces its presence in the sheer mass and energised heaviness of the brew.

I raise the cup to my lips again. About two thirds of the measure that the shaman poured for me still remains, and now I drain it in one draught. The concentrated bittersweet foretaste, followed instantly by the aftertaste of rot and medicine, hits me like a punch in the stomach. I shudder. Will I throw up? Will I shit myself? I have heard that such inconveniences are always a risk with ayahuasca, which, as well as its unsurpassed qualities as a hallucinogen, is also an extremely strong and efficient purgative (indeed, one of the many names and nicknames by which ayahuasca is known throughout the Amazon is La Purga – the purge). Vomiting and diarrhoea are common amongst participants in ayahuasca sessions and one must simply deal with these effects if they strike. Feeling slightly apprehensive, I thank the shaman and wander back to my place on the floor.

Geometry and nets

Time passes but I don't keep track of it. I've improvised a pillow from a rolled-up sleeping bag and I now find I'm swamped by a powerful feeling of weariness. My muscles involuntarily relax, I close my eyes, and without fanfare a parade of visions suddenly begins, visions that are at once geometrical and alive, visions of lights unlike any light I've ever seen – *dark* lights, a pulsing, swirling field of the deepest luminescent violets, of reds emerging out of night, of unearthly textures and colours, of solar systems revolving, of spiral galaxies on the move ... Visions of nets and strange ladder-like structures. Visions in which I seem to see multiple square screens stacked side by side and on top of each other to form immense patterns of windows arranged in great banks. Though they manifest without sound in what seems to be a pristine and limitless vacuum, the images possess a most peculiar and particular quality. They *feel* like a drum-roll – as though their real function is to announce the arrival of something else.

I begin to pay attention to one image in particular, or rather to one area of my inner visual field where complex interlaced patterns of geometry prove on more careful inspection to be part of the skin of a snake – a gigantic snake, apparently alive not dead, with its head and its tail away from me. I zoom in for a closer view. I can make out the individual scales and the way that they overlap each other. They're rectangular, outlined in black, like windows. There's a circle in the centre of each rectangle. Zoom in again. The circles are purple, spinning like fireworks, glowing with the otherworldly dark light that I'm already getting used to here.

45

Here? Where is here? Why is it a place where I see colours that do not exist in everyday life?

Closer still. Focus on a single one of the spinning circles.

Detail from a painting of an ayahuasaca vision by Peruvian shaman Pablo Amaringo

What is it? A sense of familiarity dawns before all becomes clear. It's the iridescent eye from the display feathers of a peacock . . . It's a spiral galaxy, swirling and turning in the darkness of space . . .

Then the shaman begins to chant the *icaros* again. His performance is very quiet at first but it builds up . . . builds up. For what feels like half an hour, maybe more, the whole atmosphere rustles with melodious chanting and whistling, as though great wings are stirring, and I find myself relaxing into this sound-realm.

Something interesting begins to happen. Quite smoothly, like an automatic gear-change, the parade of patterns and unearthly colours that have assailed me until now, the geometrical pulse, the swirling lights, all begin to beat in time to the underlying rhythm of the chant. I have the sense of rising up through ethereal levels – as though the Gnostics of old were right that reality consists of a series of layers extending upwards from grossest matter to purest spirit.

My whole visual field gets less static and crystalline, more fluid and organic. Suddenly it feels like a night dive. I'm looking up from the bottom of a clear ocean at a mass of purple jellyfish bobbing at the surface. There are so many of them that they all seem joined into a single voluptuous fabric, each one – I now observe – with a ring of luminous pearls, like the landing lights of a miniature space ship, arranged amongst its undulating skirts. As the chants and whistles rise and fall, this vast repetitive pattern glides slowly and majestically overhead – strobing bright and dark, bright and dark, like a well-synchronised *son et lumière*.

Other than these amazing visuals, I feel completely down to earth. I've experienced some intense moments of nausea, but the worst seems to have passed and I haven't thrown up yet. There's no particular sign that I'm going to shit myself. And if I open my eyes the visions instantly disappear – *whoomph!* – like vampires at dawn.

It's an unsettling sensation to see with my eyes closed a decidedly non-ordinary universe and with my eyes open an absolutely mundane world, and to be able, to a limited degree, to switch back and forth between the two – blink, ordinary, blink, non-ordinary, etc., etc. But I can also feel reason and measure reasserting themselves and already the quality of supernatural immanence that has characterised my experience so far is beginning to dull and fade.

I look at my watch. It is around one in the morning. Now even with my eyes closed the visions are weak and intermittent. I'm 100 per cent back on planet earth, sober, rational, not about to visit any parallel dimension.

I reached the anteroom and saw the wallpaper there. That's the realistic assessment. I fastened my seatbelt and trundled down the runway but couldn't build up enough speed to take off. I stood at the doors of perception but didn't pass through.

Although the prospect is still daunting and horrible, although the mere thought of the taste makes me gag and retch as if I've inhaled mustard gas, I resolve to drink another cup of the brew.

I go outside, pee, look at the stars, come back in again, take off my shoes, have a few swigs of water. Drinking ayahuasca is an ordeal – everything about it is difficult, nothing is easy. Yet I have no choice but to persevere if I want to understand this mysterious substance. I know of several examples of people who have taken ayahuasca and experienced nothing very remarkable during their first two or three sessions, only to get the full return ticket to a parallel world on their third or fourth attempt.

I shuffle up to the shaman again, tell him I think I'm ready for a second dose. He pours out the usual double-shot measure into the cup and whispers the usual incomprehensible words into it before handing it to me to drink.

I intend to drain it in one gulp, because it's only a small amount after all. But once again it seems formidable – the way a toad might seem formidable if blended as a beverage and served in a cup. My flesh recoils from it and I hesitate, then take a preliminary sip exactly as before. There's something unique and indescribable about the taste: ayahuasca from the Amazon. The Vine of Souls. The rancid medicine of the gods . . . I tip my head back, tilt the cup upright and swig down the remainder of its contents.

As I wander back to reoccupy my place on the floor I'm thinking that with the first dose still presumably in my system, and certainly not vomited out, is it reasonable to hope that this second dose will do the trick? I already know that the answer is 'maybe' and that it really does depend – because the effects of ayahuasca differ so much from person to person and from day to day, even from hour to hour.

After about 40 minutes the parade of images reappears – the geometry, the nets, ladders and banks of windows, the spirals, the swastikas spinning in the void, the furious zig-zags, the kaleidoscope of unearthly colours – and I find myself back in the anteroom to the ayahuasca realm. As before, sound and vision have effortlessly synchronised and the whole scene pulses and vibrates hypnotically. As before, I have the ability to zoom in on small areas of the scene. As before, I see what looks like the flank of a gigantic serpent and, when I come closer, the patterned rectangles of individual scales – each one of which proves to enclose a swirling, iridescent eye.

For a while not much else happens. Then suddenly, without preamble, I get a display of zig-zags, pyramids, tribal masks. One after the other, as though briefly illuminated by the brightest spotlight, they seem to jump out of the darkness, then disappear. It's the grand finale of another visit to the ayahuasca anteroom. As the display fades, ordinary reality replaces it and my consciousness engages itself completely with the material world again.

Vision serpents, light-elves, a celestial temple and an angry supernatural

During my second session I know things are going to be different when the opening parade of patterns and geometry gets overlaid with a lot of snakes, like a game of snakes and ladders. The snakes are very large and their whole bodies from head to tail are clearly visible to me. The main colours are browns and yellows.

Painting of an ayahuasca vision by Peruvian shaman Pablo Amaringo

I've been expecting them to show up. Reading round the subject before coming to the Amazon I've learnt that people from all parts of the world and many different cultures routinely meet snakes on the ayahuasca journey. The shamans say this is because the spirit of ayahuasca, like the vine itself, takes snake form. In my vision the snakes arrange themselves into patterns of interlaced wheels and spirals. Then they merge into one large mass and finally break apart into pairs of individuals that wind around each other like the DNA double helix.

The nausea comes on strong and I'm out in the dark, puking. The vomiting racks me to the core until I'm drenched from head to foot in sweat and have only dry heaves left. I sink to the ground on hands and knees, slump against one of the support poles of the hut and then change my mind when I find myself face to face with a large poisonous spider.

My head has cleared. I go back inside, take my place in the circle, close my eyes. More snakes, a recurrence of the geometrical patterns. Then suddenly two beings made all of white light pop up in my face, one behind and to the side of the other. They are quite small – three or four feet tall – but I'm only aware of their upper bodies from the waist up. I don't see their feet. Their white light faces glow like neon and are approximately heart-shaped with big domed foreheads and

Sketch of an ayahuasca vision from the author's field research notebook

narrow pointed chins. Nostrils and mouths, if they have them at all, are just slits in their otherwise smooth features. Their eyes are completely black and apparently without pupils.

They seem to have business with me. They want to communicate. The communication, or communication attempt, feels telepathic, but somehow it is not getting through. I sense eagerness and . . . frustration on their part.

Then the nausea comes on again, really strong, and I'm outside for another protracted bout of vomiting and retching. Seated on a tree stump, looking up at the stars, I have a strange sense of being possessed by the spirit of my father, as though he's inside me somehow, merged with me and my consciousness.

On another night the visions begin very differently. After an initial

Painting of an ayahuasca vision by Peruvian shaman Pablo Amaringo

bout of geometry and ladders I find myself inside a building – a huge structure a bit like the ancient Egyptian temple of Edfu at its entrance but opening out into something quite other. Fantastic architecture on an extraordinary scale. I have a computercam point of view and can fly around, zoom in or zoom out anywhere. I fly up into a vast dome, examine the patterns of nested curves that decorate its ceiling. Then the vomiting takes me again and the visions are gone.

Around the fifth night of my stay in the Amazon I drink ayahuasca in a natural clearing in the jungle. The name given by the Indians to clearings like this is *supay chakra*, which means 'the devil's farm'. Two makeshift benches have been set up by a huge ancient fig tree, and we hang hammocks and mosquito nets at the edge of the clearing. Dark falls, surrounding us with the sounds of the jungle night. We wait until around 8 p.m. to start the ceremony.

I begin to vision very mildly after about 45 minutes – a dreamlike state enhanced by the weird luminous glow given off by thousands of dead leaves carpeting the forest floor. When my eyes are open I see this real jungle with its glowing floor. When I close them another jungle appears – a jungle of trees, stems, shoots, each traced with a line of fire and overcast with strangeness.

I also see snakes again, not very large this time, but with wide-open mouths. Then a tiny mannequin appears amongst the high jungle plants. It has the outline and size of a gingerbread man, but is glowing all neon-white. It behaves like a puppet operated on strings by a puppeteer who is so far above us as to be out of sight. The mannequin dances through the tall trees.

In the morning Don Alberto, the shaman, says that the spirit of the *chakra* was with us, watching us the whole time, hiding behind the big fig tree. Apparently he was not happy that we vomited – and worse! – in his *chakra*. But Don Alberto reassures us that he intervened on our behalf to make everything OK with this angry supernatural being.

Transformations

22 January: This night I go through what I've come to think of as the scrying mirror into the otherworld. I tolerate the ayahuasca well and about 90 minutes pass before I vomit.

In my hour of strong visions I'm surrounded by intelligent plants, which seem almost like animals, waving, weaving leaves – in dark

Detail from painting of an ayahuasca vision by
Peruvian shaman Pablo Amaringo

colours but with their own fire. Then I meet a big boa constrictor. Its head alone is about two feet long and a foot high. It allows me to stroke it and I hear myself saying in my vision, 'It's a beauty' or 'You're a beauty.' Something like that.

I see a yellow and black spotted butterfly, the size of a dinner plate, flitting from plant to plant in the hallucinatory jungle. I follow it until we reach a clearing where a second huge serpent awaits. There is no butterfly now, only this immense yellow and black serpent radiating sentience and magical force. Before my eyes it spectacularly and mysteriously transforms into a powerful jaguar with yellow and black spots and confronts me face to face. There is a sort of telepathy. Then the creature abruptly turns away and vanishes. For what feels like a long

Detail from painting of an ayahuasca vision by Peruvian shaman Pablo Amaringo

while afterwards I continue to sense its presence still out there, camouflaged amongst the otherworldly jungle plants. At no point do I feel afraid of it or threatened by it.

Both it and the beautiful boa, the butterfly, even the plants, seem filled with vibrant energy and life and communicative intelligence. They also seem utterly and convincingly real – not stuff my brain is just perversely cooking up out of some hitherto unknown jungle-scenes image bank in my temporal lobes, but real perceptions of real beings that ordinarily exist outside the range of my senses.

The visions left me thinking and the following morning I wrote in my notebook:

Matter and spirit. As above so below. Science teaches us to believe that the material world is the primary and only reality. But from the ayahuasca perspective this is absolutely not the case. What we call the material world, our 'consensual reality', is only part of the pattern – probably not even the primary part. Viewed through the lens of ayahuasca, another 'world' becomes visible, another reality, perhaps many of them. And because these worlds interpenetrate our own, *effects* in this world may turn out to have *causes* in the other worlds. Perhaps the material world is indeed the creation of spirits but if so then presumably they made it because they need it (for their own experience/evolution/development?). The material world, if cut off from the spirit world, becomes meaningless and empty. So the material world *needs* the spirit world too. Ayahuasca, and similar 'master plants', appear to provide a direct means of communication with the spirit realm for sentient beings of the material world. The plants educate us by allowing us to experience in visions the reality of the supernatural – something normally impossible or very difficult for us to do as material-bound creatures.

Purple prose? A bit New Age and over the top? Even lunatic fringe? I don't deny it and in a way that's exactly my point. If I, with all the knowledge and rationalism of the twenty-first century at my disposal, could be so persuaded by the apparently supernatural realms and spirit beings that ayahuasca introduced me to, then what would our ancestors have thought if they had chanced upon similar hallucinogenic plants 30,000 years ago and seen similar wonders? What about the two elf-sized 'light-beings' I'd met? What would they have been taken to be in the Upper Palaeolithic? What about the serpent transforming into a jaguar? What about the geometry and the architecture? Wouldn't it have all come together as a seamless otherworld? Not the way we tend to see such scenes now – as some sort of derangement of perception devalued by the modern idea of 'hallucinations' – but as a veridical experience of another level of reality?

Introspection

24 January: Don Francisco pours me a generous cupful of dense and rancid ayahuasca which I almost throw up on the last swallow. The taste and smell are extremely strong and for some reason I feel nervous and out of sorts this evening. There are waves of nausea but I control them, breathe into them.

I suppose that half an hour passes before the visions become strong. Tonight I see predominantly snakes, most of them about three or four feet in length. Again the sense I get is that these are intelligent beings who mean us well, not harm. I experience none of the archetypal fear that snakes supposedly evoke. As usual my eyes are closed, but I can 'see' my legs and feet below me as though bathed in light. One of the serpents coils around my left calf and then rears its head up from knee

Detail from painting of an ayahuasca vision by
Peruvian shaman Pablo Amaringo

level towards my face. Its body and head are coloured a deep and brilliant gold. It seems to be inspecting or examining me but I feel no fear.

I meet a lot of these snakes, coiling round the vegetation and around each other. They are everywhere, in the foreground, and often the background, of all my visions.

There are patterns and lights. I see something that looks like a very large inverted bowl rising up into a purple sky, glowing with light.

I witness a complex series of transformations of snakes into felines.

I have a sense of flying, as though I am a bird (or riding on a bird?) accompanied by two other birds.

Detail from painting of an ayahuasca vision by Peruvian shaman Pablo Amaringo

I go through what feel like long periods of intense introspection. Something in the ayahuasca leads me to examine my own moral failings and weaknesses in an utterly unsympathetic light – holds them up to my view and shows me how much, in how many ways, I am inadequate, venal, not good. In particular I flagellate myself mercilessly about my father. Why wasn't I with him those last five days of his life? Why did I feel so driven to go back and finish my work? There are no excuses. Plain and simple, I should have been there and I wasn't. Several times I ask to see Dad's spirit, to meet him again and to talk to him.

But this grace the Vine of Souls does not grant me.

Aliens and dragons

27 January: The visions begin with 20 minutes of geometry; then suddenly I find myself looking, at very close range, into a shockingly 'alien' face, grey in colour, with a wide domed forehead and a narrow pointed chin – heart-shaped like the faces of the 'light-beings' I'd encountered a few days earlier. But this creature doesn't look friendly. Its eyes are multi-segmented like those of a fly. Frankly, it's the sort of image you'd expect to see adorning some far-fetched *X-Files* exposé,

Sketch of an ayahuasca vision from the author's field research notebook

and since aliens and ETs have never been interests of mine, I'm really puzzled to experience such a hallucination. In the part of my mind that is still dealing with reasoning I can already see the way that sceptics who have never taken ayahuasca are bound to read it. They must argue that there is no mystery in the appearance of entities like this in my hallucinations because, regardless of my lack of enthusiasm for aliens, my brain has had the opportunity to borrow such imagery from popular culture. Still, I feel unaccountably shaken and perplexed by what I've just seen.

A short while later, out of a background of shifting geometrical patterns, a beautiful Egyptian goddess appears. I see only her head and headdress clearly. She's in full regalia. Then she vanishes as abruptly and mysteriously as she arrived.

29 January: Strange and terrifying (briefly), although it didn't start that way. I drink at 8.05 p.m. For the first half-hour, as usual, nothing much happens, just queasy and formless luminescences. Then I begin to see snakes, not a lot and not spectacular. By 9.05 I'm feeling more intoxicated, giddy and nauseous. But still just snakes. Not many. Mid-size. They're coiling and writhing around a bit more. I begin to wonder (foolish bravado) if this is all I'm going to get.

The nausea increases and the whole visionary experience ratchets up a notch and becomes more sinister. My eyes are closed throughout but when I 'look' up, the visions are 'up' and when I 'look' down they're 'down'. I have the sense of gazing through a tunnel – a tunnel of vision with serpents coiled at the side of it, close to my eyes, threatening to fall on me.

I throw up over the back of the bench I'm sitting on. As I shift position the serpents shift with me. The visions stay strong while I'm vomiting. As I stop and return to the seated position everything ratchets up another notch. The serpents morph into Chinese dragons with beards and long serpentine bodies. Serpents and serpentine dragons with beards and rows of teeth. It's as though a Chinese painting has come to life. And again – where did the ancient Chinese originally mine this imagery from, if not from the visionary world? I'm convinced it's not a matter of my vision being inspired by Chinese paintings – which I hardly ever think of. I'm getting a glimpse into the same visionary realm that inspired the Chinese artists – and count-less other mythologies in which dragons feature.

Then another upwards crank of the ratchet. The overall atmosphere – I can't explain why – is now distinctly terrifying and sinister. I see the grey heart-shaped face of an alien again, but with an even stranger,

Sketch of an ayahuasca vision from the author's field research notebook

58

harsher expression than before. And I see what could be space ships – flying saucers – associated with this commanding, unpleasant alien presence. What's frightening is something that would be easy to

Detail from painting of an ayahuasca vision by
Peruvian shaman Pablo Amaringo

interpret as an abduction experience – the feeling that if I allow the vision to continue I'm going to be taken up into those metal ships. They rotate and pulse with light from beneath, seeming to rise through a tube or funnel in the universe. I distinctly don't want to be taken and open my eyes to stop what I'm seeing. But the strangeness persists. I'm back in the real world but just out of sight I can feel serpents, dragons, demonic aliens and space ships whirling all around.

Detail from painting of an ayahuasca vision by
Peruvian shaman Pablo Amaringo

There's a sense in which the serpents/dragons morph into the alien who dominates this vision, and a sense in which the alien is different – not so much a serpent/dragon as some sort of huge insect with humanoid features. I also see four or five other insect-like creatures associated with him. They seem more like 'workers' – less intelligent,

Sketch of an ayahuasca vision from the author's field research notebook

Drawing by a Barsana Indian shaman of an ayahuasca vision
(source Reichel-Dolmatoff, *The Shaman and the Jaguar*, fig 56)

or not intelligent. Like giant ants in a way. These worker beings – and they do seem to be working as a team on something – are about three feet high I would guess.

Two other images, both of planets, stand out in my memory of this complex vision. In the first the planet is immense and surrounded by rings or discs in the plane of its equator. In the second I see a transparent earth sphere with the fragility, texture and glittering iridescent colours of a soap bubble. Etched on its surface are the outlines of the familiar continents, and I can see through them from one side to the other. The sphere is rotating and seems to float in space between two cupped hands.

Half animal, half human

My final ayahuasca session in Peru is with a 74-year-old Shipibo Indian shaman named Don Leonceo in his tambo in the jungle beyond Iquitos. As well as the usual ingredients of *Psychotria viridis* leaves and the *Banisteriopsis caapi* vine, his ayahuasca includes datura, another well-known visionary plant, and tastes unspeakably awful.

I have a series of generally small and certainly not terrifying visions. There are a few snakes. Several times I see multiple rows of green pyramids laid out in long tapering strips. I seem to be flying over these strips. I also see a sphere, a cube and a triangle, and rows of serpent or alligator mouths full of teeth.

But the single most memorable aspect of my visions this night unfolds over what feels like just a few seconds. I seem to be inside a large, quite dark room with an opened doorway to one side. Light floods into the doorway and through it I can see a beautiful, spacious balcony overlooking what is perhaps a vast river, or a lake, or even the sea.

On the left side of the balcony, at the rear just outside the open doorway through which I'm looking, I suddenly become aware of the presence of a figure. It is an imposing statue, about six feet high and apparently carved in one piece from some green stone – perhaps jade.

Detail from painting of an ayahuasca vision by
Peruvian shaman Pablo Amaringo

The sculptor provided excellent detailing of fine robes, and a belt, and something – possibly a sword? – suspended from the belt.

At first this stunning piece of sculpture seems just that – a harmless, inanimate statue. I'm curious to see more of it and move my point of view a little closer to get a look at its face. To my surprise the statue is half animal, half human. It has the body of a powerful and well-muscled man but the head of a crocodile, like Sobek, the ancient Egyptian crocodile god. And now I suddenly realise it is alive – a living being, a supernatural guardian. At this moment its eyes swivel sideways and it is looking at me, taking note of me.

The look is intelligent, appraising, somehow sly, but yet not threatening. What is this living statue, this being of jade? The vision fades . . .

Shamanism comes to suburbia

After leaving Peru, Santha and I flew to Brazil so that I could attend a session with the Uniao de Vegetal (UdV) in the beautiful district of Ilha de Guarantiba, about one hour's drive west of the centre of Rio de Janeiro.

The *mestre* – Master of the ceremony – is Antonio Francisco Fleury. He's a distinguished, intellectual-looking gentleman in his sixties with a grey moustache. Altogether about 100 people attend. It is a family affair with age ranges present from babes in arms, young kids, teenagers, through to grandparents in their seventies. The UdV allows kids to drink ayahuasca (they call it their *cha* – tea) once a month from the age of 14, twice a month from age 18.

This is demonstrably a prosperous, middle-class group including many professionals such as doctors, lawyers and architects. The temple is in a specially dedicated villa overlooking magnificent countryside. It has a kitchen, a dining area, a patio, a large area to one side for cooking the ayahuasca (strictly *Banisteriopsis caapi*, *Psychotria viridis* and water), and the temple itself, a large rectangular hall with space for congregations of 100 or more, all comfortably seated.

What is striking is the extremely positive atmosphere of friendliness, support, rationality and love among the congregation. For any

Westerner, used to strict drug prohibition, it is quite surprising to discover that these responsible, courteous people and families, all upright citizens, are gathered to take a powerful hallucinogen – and to do so as the basic sacrament of their own intensely philosophical religion. All wear a uniform for the session, representing their place in the hierarchy. The men wear white slacks and white shoes. The women wear orange slacks. All wear green, short-sleeved, button-up shirts. Entry rank is signalled by the white letters UdV on the left breast pocket. Councillors – the next rank – have the letters UdV and CDC in yellow on the breast pocket. Higher rank is indicated by gold stars. The top rank is the *mestre*, signalled by a blue shirt and a star. Visitors are allowed to wear civilian clothes.

The *cha* is dispensed from a large glass urn placed at the head of a central table. The *mestre* decides how much each person gets, partly on body weight, partly on other factors (past experience?). The dispensing of the *cha* is done for the top ranks first – the *mestre*, then the councillors, then down through beginners, and finally visitors like me. We all line up to have our glasses filled, and wait till everyone is ready, then on a word from the *mestre* we all drink. The *cha* is watery and about the colour of an overbrewed milky tea. The taste as usual is hideous and at least four people exit to vomit straight away.

The rest of us sit down. One of the councillors reads from several documents about the philosophy and founding of the UdV. Another councillor stands and clarifies certain points. A third councillor intones a hymn.

The first hour is mainly passed in silence, reviewing our visions and thoughts, although occasionally a member of the congregation will raise a hand to ask a question which one of the councillors answers. Sometimes others elaborate.

Later in the session many members of the congregation (one by one) come to the table to stand and address the assembly. Some talk about their visions and thoughts during this session, others about some recent event or idea that has affected them deeply. It is all very earnest, genuine, spiritual and philosophical.

Sometimes CDs of haunting melodies are played. Sometimes the leading councillor intones hymns.

The session runs from 9 p.m. until about 1.20 a.m. I drink my brew at 9.20 p.m. and am having good visions by 9.45. The first hour after drinking – until 10.20 – passes in what feels, subjectively, like an instant. My visions are familiar and positive – perhaps more brightly lit (less 'darkness visible') than before. What I remember clearly are large snakes (again!), light-coloured boas, huge, coiling around each other and around branches. I also get pyramid shapes built around a lattice or framework of some kind.

But the best part of the evening is when the same Egyptian goddess whom I last saw in Peru reappears – this time on the left side of my visual field. At first she is concealed, in shadow. I look closely and see a slender female figure holding a dark blue mask in front of her face – one of those masks on a stick. Then she removes the mask and I see her face clearly in the instant before she vanishes once more. She glows the colour of molten gold.

Where the impossible becomes real

If I were to nominate the single defining quality of the visions I experienced under the influence of ayahuasca it would have to be their remarkable sense – no matter how 'otherworldly' they were – of being real. It is surprising enough to encounter something so improbable as a 'light-being', or an intelligent giant snake that transforms into a jaguar, or a hybrid crocodile-man, or an insect-man like my 'aliens' – especially when any thought of such entities is normally very far from one's mind. But to encounter them in all their strangeness, yet bolstered by an unassailable aura of certainty and solidity, is doubly disturbing and disorienting.

So some months before I met David Lewis-Williams, what I had learnt from personal experience in the Amazon had already begun to convince me of the force of his argument. If our ancestors in the Upper Palaeolithic had consumed psychoactive plants – and we'll see that there was an excellent candidate available in Europe in the Ice Age that could have produced ayahuasca-like effects[13] – then because we share the same neurology it is safe to say that they would have had experiences rather like mine (not in every minute detail, of course, but broadly and with something like the same general atmosphere).[14] It had begun to seem highly plausible to me, as Lewis-Williams suggests, that hallucinations could have given rise to early religious notions about supernatural realms and beings, and the survival of death by the 'soul'. Indeed, where else could our ancestors ever have acquainted themselves with such ideas in the first place if not in the visionary realms where the shamans of all cultures in all periods have always made their 'spirit journeys'?

There, as I'd already found out for myself, hybrid man-beasts, light-beings, transformations, and encounters with the deceased all become possible. Is the hard evidence for such encounters documenting the birth of religion really painted inside the deep caves of Upper Palae-olithic Europe, as Lewis-Williams claims?

Author's note: I had not seen any of Pablo Amaringo's paintings before experiencing my own ayahuasca visions. That I was later able to find similarities to my visions in several works by the Peruvian shaman reproduced in this chapter is an illustration of the astonishing common imagery and identical 'parallel worlds' that are reported by people from many different cultures who have experienced ayahuasca. We will look further into this mystery in Chapter Twenty-Three.

PART II
The Caves

CHAPTER FOUR

Therianthropy

There is an extreme and unprecedented concentration of cave art dating from the Upper Palaeolithic in a small area of Europe, but our ancestors who lived in many other parts of the world at the same time also painted and engraved rock, and carved delicate, beautiful objects out of bone and ivory.

Such art is astonishingly widely distributed,[1] and although Asia and the Middle East remain poorly represented in what has survived from the more ancient periods,[2] Australia, the Americas and Africa join Europe in being particularly well endowed with prehistoric rock art which dates back in some cases more than 20,000 years. Predictably, given the self-evident diversity and idiosyncrasies of human cultures, not all of the art in all these places shares the same concerns or can be accounted for with a single overarching explanation.[3] Indeed, one feels intuitively that there ought to be almost as many different motivations behind it as there are different societies or even different individuals. Nevertheless, it is the bold claim of David Lewis-Williams that his 'neuropsychological' theory can provide a single parsimonious explanation, not for all but for certain large bodies of this ancient art as far afield as the California Great Basin, southern Africa and Europe.[4]

No texts or scrolls have come down to us from the Upper Palaeolithic, thousands of years before the first written languages began to evolve, and very little thought has been given to the possibility that the world's vast heritage of prehistoric rock images could (like well-known bodies of art in the historic period)[5] be encoded with messages concealed in rich non-alphabetic symbolism. Besides, even if there *are* hidden messages in the art, which is hypothetically possible, we still can't go back in time and communicate directly with the artists – so how can we possibly hope to deduce what they had in mind?

It is to precisely this problem of access to the lost mental world of the cave artists that Lewis-Williams claims to have found a solution. If he's right then his neuropsychological approach offers us the means to decode the contents of some of those ancient halls of records. This is a very exciting idea if feasible – almost like opening a door in space-time between our world and the Upper Palaeolithic and stepping through to share the experience of the people on the other side.

Lots of questions, not many answers

If Lewis-Williams' theory is really as big a breakthrough as its supporters claim, then it must, first and foremost, be able to answer questions and solve mysteries where previous theories have failed. It so happens, after more than 100 years of academic study of prehistoric art, that a great many unanswered questions and unsolved mysteries remain.

During much of the twentieth century scholarly research was disproportionately weighted towards Europe, so it is there we might reasonably expect the most progress to have been made. The European art is dominated by thousands of naturalistic images of Ice Age animals, painted on the walls of 300 or so caves. We know that the animals were present in the general area of the caves at the time the paintings and engravings were made, and we have enough knowledge of their anatomy from fossils to confirm that they have been represented accurately. Other than their beauty and technical accomplishment, however, the first instinct of most researchers is to suppose that there is nothing particularly unusual about such images *in themselves*. The animals were part of the natural environment, they were seen and they were painted, end of story. All we have to do is work out why.

Surprisingly, even this has proved impossible for the scholars. During the past 100 years many theories have been proposed, but we'll see in Chapter Six that not a single one of them has been accepted by the general academic community. The main reason is lack of progress with a far bigger underlying puzzle presented by other more obscure and difficult images that are also found in the caves, side by side with the naturalistic depictions – images of creatures that do not exist, and have never existed. The presence of these fantastic beasts, hybrids, chimeras and monsters, which have no concrete reference points in the material realm, of course casts doubt on the naturalism of all the other figures with which they share the rock walls. Indeed, if Lewis-Williams is right then it is possible that *none* of the art is 100 per cent naturalistic and that what the whole corpus really reveals is imagery from the inner mental universe of the ancients.

One of the most mysterious of these images occurs repeatedly in numerous variations not only in Upper Palaeolithic Europe but in rock and cave art all around the world from many different periods. The figure is part human and part animal, and scholars refer to it by the technical term therianthrope (from the Greek *therion* = 'wild beast' and *anthropos* = 'man'). It seems to have been with us from the beginning.

The oldest art

On 20 October 2000, *Science* magazine reported a momentous archaeological discovery:

> Traces of what could be the world's oldest-known cave paintings have been found in northern Italy. Stone slabs bearing images of an animal and a half-human, half-beast figure were uncovered during excavations by an Italian team at the Fumane Cave northwest of Verona. The slabs, painted with red ochre, had apparently fallen from the cave roof and become embedded in floor sediments previously dated to between 32,000 and 36,500 years ago.[6]

How old does that make the paintings themselves? Securely situated within well-dated sediments, good archaeological procedure says that they have to be *at least* 32,000 years old, the minimum age of the layer in which they were found. On the other hand, they might easily be older than that. This is not just a matter of the age differences within the layer (spanning 32,000 to 36,500 years ago). A much bigger problem, since there is no test that can date red ochre directly, is the impossibility of knowing how long the paintings remained intact on the ceiling before they fell to the floor and began to be covered by datable sediments. Millennia could have passed, in which case they might, theoretically, be considerably older than the maximum age of the layer – i.e. more than 36,500 years old.

The other contenders for the title of the world's most ancient cave paintings are the spectacular images of the Grotte Chauvet in the Ardèche region of southern France. Unlike the red ochre used in Fumane, which is of mineral origin, many of the Chauvet paintings were done with a charcoal emulsion containing organic residues that are relatively easy to date by the tried-and-tested Carbon 14 method. More than 30 charcoal samples have been taken in Chauvet and the dates produced directly from the paintings vary between roughly 30,000 and 32,500 years ago with margins of error of up to 700 years in either direction.[7] So although an overlap is possible at the younger end of Fumane's range, it does look likely that the Italian paintings are a few thousand years older than the paintings in Chauvet and thus may rightly be claimed as the oldest in the world – at least until some new discovery is made that pushes the boundary back even further.

The therianthropes of Fumane and Chauvet

Fumane became important for my research because of the mysterious subject matter of the painted stone slabs excavated there by the archaeologists. Despite close study the red ochre images on two of the slabs are so faint that they cannot be made out. Two others depict 'unrealistic' animals, one with a weirdly elongated neck and the other with five legs.[8] Another slab carries the image of the bizarre creature rightly described by *Science* magazine in the extract cited above as 'half-human, half-beast'. This figure, which is about 18 centimetres high, has the head of a horned bovid, such as a bison or an aurochs (the wild ancestor of modern cattle), a man's arms and torso, and upright hind legs that

'Half-man, half-beast':
the Fumane therianthrope

seem to be a mixture of both human and animal characteristics. The reader will recognise such blending and fusion of species as the attributes of a fully fledged therianthrope – a composite mythical being of the same general category as the 'crocodile-man' whom I encountered during my final ayahuasca vision in the Peruvian Amazon.[9]

As well as their great age, Fumane and Chauvet have something else in common. The aurochs/bison-man of the oldest Italian cave finds a close counterpart in the oldest French cave – for Chauvet turns out to have a mysterious and eye-catching bison-man of its own.[10] This eerie charcoal figure is painted on a spur of smooth rock that juts down from the ceiling of the last and deepest of Chauvet's great galleries, the appropriately named End Chamber. Bent sharply forward at the abdomen, as though in pain, the figure combines the horned head, chest and characteristic hump of a bison, with human legs in a slightly flexed standing position, and an unmistakably human arm and hand with long fingers that hang downward.[11] Moreover, although he is already quite strange enough, the Chauvet bison-man becomes stranger still when our eyes adjust to the gloom and we realise that he seems to straddle the left side of the lower body and prominent pubic triangle of a gigantic human female. She is portrayed headless, but her foreshortened right arm – as though to compensate

Chauvet bison-man straddling
lion-woman

– seems to have transformed into the head of a large felid,[12] perhaps a cave lion.

What weird and distorted universe do such images come from – images of blended humans and animals, images of astonishing transformations?

The German lion-men

If we look further afield, the mystery deepens.

The oldest art of Germany dates from the same period as the therianthropes of Chauvet and Fumane – roughly 30,000 to 35,000 years ago. The principal sites are the caves of Vogelherd, Hohlenstein-Stadel, Geissenklosterle, and Hohle-Fels in the Swabian Jura mountains in the south-west of the country. Although there are some hints of what could once have been extensive wall-paintings,[13] the key discoveries in the caves are 19 identifiable pieces of sculpture carved from mammoth ivory.[14] Most are exquisitely crafted miniatures that rarely exceed five centimetres in length. Some are drilled so that they could be hung as neck pendants. All have a minimum age – set by the age of the sediments from which they were excavated – of around 32,000 years, but some of the pieces could be significantly older than that, and one was found in a layer with an upper age-limit of 36,800 years.[15]

The subjects of these ancient sculptures include horses, bears, a bird, several mammoths, four felids, two bovids, two vaguely humanoid 'anthropomorphs', and one quadruped that so far has not been identified.[16] Most were excavated from floor sediments in the living areas of the caves. However, there is one piece, from Hohlenstein-Stadel, that seems to have been singled out as special. Measuring 29.6 centimetres tall and weighing almost three-quarters of a kilogram, it is more than five times the size of any of the other statuettes and was found within a recess deep inside the cave where archaeologists believe the ancients ventured only rarely.[17]

Like the oldest art of Italy and the oldest art of France, this strange ivory figure of Hohlenstein-Stadel was made at least 32,000 years ago and depicts . . . a therianthrope. In this case it is not 'Bison-Man' but 'Lion-Man'. The arms and legs are human but the extremities are much more like the paws of a felid than human hands and feet. The body and general posture are human but the head is that of a large

The lion-man of Hohlenstein-Stadel

felid.[18] The obvious notion that the figure must represent a man in some sort of ritual lion mask has been specifically rejected by scholars who have studied it closely.[19] Through and through it seems to depict a being in transformation, neither all lion nor all man but both welded together into a single supernatural entity. A second such sculpture was also recently discovered in Hohle-Fels Cave in the same district. It too is a lion-man, but it is tiny – only four centimetres tall – and weighs just a few grams.[20]

A widespread belief system?

So, to take stock, we now know that the world's three oldest collections of figurative art all prominently feature those fabulous creatures, part beast, part human, that scholars of myth and religion label as therianthropes.

We are familiar with therianthropes in popular culture today – werewolf and Dracula, for instance, are both therianthropes. And a moment's thought reveals that such creatures have kept humanity company since the beginning of recorded history. From ancient Egypt 5,000 years ago the god Anubis, part hound, part man, is a therianthrope, the god Sobek is part man, part crocodile, the avenging goddess Sekhmet is part lioness, part woman, and the Great Sphinx of Giza is part lion, part man. Bellowing in the dark subterranean labyrinth of Crete, the Minotaur has a man's body and a bull's head – a classic bovid therianthrope. And what is the centaur of Greek legend but an improbable and phantasmagoric combination of horse and man? As we confront the therianthropes of Chauvet, Fumane and the German caves, however, it becomes obvious that such ideas and images originated much earlier than the beginning of recorded history a mere 5,000 years ago. The fully formed appearance of lion-men and bison-men in the art of 30,000 to 35,000 years ago pushes the birth of the peculiar concept of human-animal transformation back to an almost impossibly remote epoch.

It is a puzzle why such a concept should ever have arisen at all, let alone why it should have been expressed independently in the oldest surviving cave art from three different regions of Europe. As Randall White, Professor of Anthropology at New York University, commented when the discovery of the strange horned therianthrope of Fumane was announced:

We now have this image at three different places during this early time period. It is one thing to represent a horse, but another thing to

76

represent something that doesn't exist in reality. People had ideas about the world that were abstractions, which we can only describe as religious. We are looking at a widespread belief system that is very ancient.[21]

The beast-man of Apollo-11 Cave

About as far away from Europe as you can get, southern Africa is thought by scientists to be the cradle of anatomically modern humans. Is it just an amazing coincidence, or a hint of some hidden long-distance connection, that the oldest rock paintings so far discovered in southern Africa also turn out, like those of France, Germany and Italy, to include a prominent depiction of a therianthrope?

It is one of a series of monochrome and polychrome images that were painted by unknown prehistoric artists on flat rock plaquettes, brought to a cave in Namibia,[22] and eventually abandoned on its floor. Thereafter natural processes that we have seen at work elsewhere set in and the plaquettes were gradually buried beneath accumulating layers of sediment. Much more time passed and more layers of sediment piled up. Finally, in 1969, a team of archaeologists from the University of Cologne led by Dr Wolfgang Erich Wendt explored and began to excavate the cave – to which, in honour of that July's lunar landing, they gave the name Apollo-11.[23] Amongst many other objects of great interest, they found seven of the painted plaquettes buried in floor sediments dated between 25,500 and 27,500 years ago – thus establishing a minimum age of 25,500 years for the paintings themselves.[24] Once again, as at Fumane, it is perfectly possible that the paintings could have been completed hundreds or perhaps even thousands of years before ending up on the floor of the cave.

Experts have recognised five animals depicted on the Apollo-11 plaquettes, including a black rhinoceros and two zebras.[25] But my interest was focused on the therianthrope, a creature from the realm of nightmare combining the feet, legs, hindquarters and prominent phallus of a human being with the body, forelegs, head and massive jaws of a powerful felid[26] – perhaps a lion or a leopard.[27] That such a distinctive 'beast-man' image should prove to be part of the oldest

77

Human-like hind legs and feet blend with an animal body:
the beast-man of Apollo-11 Cave

hoard of rock art in its region felt almost inevitable in the light of what I knew about the very similar discoveries at Fumane, Chauvet and Hohlenstein-Stadel.

The same strange figure after 17,000 years . . .

Long after therianthropes had made their first appearance in the cave art of Europe and southern Africa between 35,000 and 25,000 years ago they continued to feature prominently in the artistic traditions of both regions.

For example, the 32,000-year-old bison-man hanging suspended on his spur of rock from the ceiling of Chauvet Cave in France is matched quite closely in general outline by a bison-man from the cave of El Castillo in northern Spain that the ancient artists created by enhancing the natural form of a stalagmite jutting up from the cave floor.[28] But unlike the Chauvet therianthrope, which marks the beginning of cave art in Europe, the El Castillo example is thought to date from around 15,000 years ago, the time of a last creative flourish – archaeologists refer to it as the 'Magdalenian culture complex' – that occurred just before the end of the cave art epoch.[29] The difference between 32,000 years ago and 15,000 years ago is

Chauvet bison-man (left), El Castillo bison-man (right)

17,000 years, a period of time so long in human terms that it is difficult to comprehend – more than five times longer than the entire
span of ancient Egyptian civilisation and more than eight times longer
than the whole story of the Christian religion. Yet throughout this
immense interval the evidence before our eyes if we visit the painted
caves is that the outlandish image of a man transforming into a bison
was maintained and repeatedly recreated.

Thus essentially the same figure appears twice in the cave of Trois
Frères, again dating from the Magdalenian, in France's Ariège region,[30]
and yet again in the nearby cave of Gabillou on a rock wall at the

Left and centre, bison-men of Trois Frères (Breuil, 1952);
right, bison-man of Gabillou

end of a long tunnel.[31] Here he is captured at the precise moment of transformation, with a bison's rump and human legs merged. Another prominent man-bison – although this time only the face of the creature is human – dominates the great polychrome ceiling of the cave of Altamira in Spain.[32] And let us not forget the figures that the prehistorian André Leroi-Gourhan identified as 'bison-women' on the walls of Pech Merle.[33]

Proteus

Not all the therianthropes in the caves of Upper Palaeolithic Europe are human-bison blends. The lion-men of Hohlenstein-Stadel and Hohle Fels are the oldest exceptions, but there are several others.

In Trois Frères, for example, there are also two large engraved owls which scholars recognise as possessing distinctly humanoid characteristics.[34] Much more spectacular, however, presiding over the small round chamber known as the Sanctuary – with its engraved panels displaying hundreds of animal figures from a total of 13 different species[35] – is the so-called 'Sorcerer' or 'Beast-Master' of Trois Frères. Perched in a niche in the eroded rocky ceiling more than three metres above the floor, this amazing protean figure, which is deeply engraved

The 'Sorcerer' of Trois Frères – part owl, part wolf, part stag, part horse, part lion and part human. (Breuil, 1952)

and outlined in black charcoal, combines owl-like eyes and a beak-shaped nose with the ears of a wolf, the antlers of a stag, the tail of a horse, the claws of a lion, and the feet, legs, body and penis of a human being.[36]

The Unicorn and the bird-man of Lascaux

One of the very first paintings that the visitor confronts on entering the Hall of Bulls in the famous French cave of Lascaux is the misleadingly-named 'Unicorn' – misleading because if the lines jutting from the front of its head are to be taken as horns then there are certainly two of them rather than one as the name suggests. The figure is a clumsy looking quadruped about the size and approximate shape of a horse. It has a swollen belly and six circular markings along its body like the spotted coat of a large felid.[37] Some researchers argue

The so-called 'Unicorn' of Lascaux. Its hind legs are thought to represent those of a human

that it has a bearded human face[38] but most identify it as a therianthrope on account of its thick hind legs with pronounced thigh and calf muscles which are said to resemble those of a man.[39]

The Unicorn is painted on the left (north) wall of the Hall of Bulls, soon after the entrance. Straight ahead at the eastern end of the hall is the vulva-like opening into the Axial Gallery, a fabulously decorated dead-end passageway. Another passage exits the hall through its right (south) wall and runs more or less due south. After less than 30 metres it brings the visitor to an area of the cave called the Apse, which contains the remains of large numbers of paintings and engravings on its walls and ceiling, amongst them a claviform (club-like) sign and a geometrical grid.[40] Here the main passageway continues south while a side-branch turns west to the Shaft of the Dead Man – surely the most engimatic and otherworldly of all Lascaux's wonders. Reached through a narrow cleft followed by a sheer drop of around five metres, the sides of the shaft are worn smooth and shiny, suggesting that large numbers of people made their way here during prehistoric times, probably with the help of some sort of rope.[41] Yet the shaft is just a deep natural pit in the rock, so why did they go to all that trouble?

The answer seems to lie on a ledge at the very bottom, where a most unusual scene is painted. To the left, seemingly walking away, we see a black rhinoceros with its tail in the air.[42] Behind it there is a pattern of six black dots. The centre ground is taken up by a humanoid stick-figure with an erect penis. The figure is positioned at an odd

The enigmatic shaft scene at Lascaux

angle to the vertical, as though it is falling over backwards. Beside or just below it is a short pole or rod surmounted by a bird. Lastly, to the right, directly confronting the falling stick-figure, there is a large bison, apparently badly wounded, with its entrails spilling out. Its head is lowered in a threatening manner as though it is about to attack.

The stick-figure at the centre of all this action – the 'dead man' after whom archaeologists named the shaft – is a therianthrope. His body, arms, legs and penis are fully human but his head has a beak rather than a mouth and is, in fact, identical to the head of the bird on the pole depicted near him. In an article published in *Antiquity*,

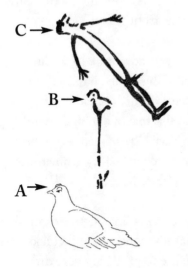

(A) The characteristic supra-ocular comb of the capercaillie grouse; (B) The grouse on the staff; (C) supra-ocular comb on the humanoid stick figure. The presence of this distinguishing feature, together with the four digits on each of the stick-figure's hands, suggest that what is depicted here is a man at the moment of transformation into a bird (after Davenport and Jochim, 1988).

researchers Demorest Davenport and Michael A. Jochim have identified the bird as a male capercaillie grouse. They demonstrate that the characteristic supra-ocular comb of this species is shown on the beak of the bird itself and on the beak of the stick figure.[43] They also point out that the figure's hands, though they look human at a superficial glance, only have four digits each:

> Four is the precise number of digits that a bird has. The replacement of each human hand with a four-fingered bird's foot was a deliberate and indeed sophisticated ploy of the artist to make the image more bird-like . . . The humanoid is not a man and not a bird but a man/bird, if downed by the bison, apparently struck at the moment of transformation into a grouse.[44]

Beauty and the Beast

In the little cave of El Juyo in northern Spain dated to around 14,000 years ago, less than two millennia before the end of the immense cave art epoch, yet another therianthropic transformation is depicted. Here the ancients gave pride of place to a large natural boulder which was sculpted and reshaped by hand. With its 'eye', 'nose', 'mouth', and even the suggestion of a 'moustache', the right side of the boulder bears an unmistakable resemblance to a human face. According to the cave's excavators, L.G. Freeman and J. Gonzalez Echegaray:

> To represent the mouth, the artist had taken advantage of a natural curved fissure in the rock; the central part of this fissure has been regularized by engraving to strengthen the shape of the lips and to suggest teeth. The general impression thus produced is that of a smiling mouth. The lower edge of the stone is naturally wavy – 'festooned' is the best description – and the festoons have been retouched by (sometimes deep) engraving to suggest a beard of moderate length.[45]

So far so good, but all these human features are on the right side of the face. Again taking advantage of natural contours and cracks, the ancient artist reshaped the left side of the face to produce a very different sort of likeness. Here, 'the eye is a deep, more or less triangular hole, a concavity suggesting a tear duct extends some distance below, and

Beauty and the Beast at El Juyo
(after J.L. Casado in Freeman
and Echegaray, 1981)

the inner corner of the eye meets a deep natural fissure in the rock which produces a clean-cut division of the face into two halves'.[46] Once again it is the story of Beauty and the Beast – for just as the right side depicts a visage that is wholly human, this left side shows us:

> a large carnivore, with oblique eye, large lachrymal, and a moderately long nose ending in a good depiction of a naked *rhinarium*. The chin

is triangular and a sharply pointed tooth projects above the mouth. On the muzzle there are three subparallel lines of black spots suggesting the bases of whiskers or vibrissae, a characteristic feature of felids. Taken as a whole, these features represent a large cat, probably a lion or a leopard.[47]

Now you see them, now you don't: mysteries of the San

All in all it appears irrefutable from the evidence that ideas about human-animal transformations, as well as paintings and sculptures depicting such transformed beings, were present at the very beginning, and survived to the end, of the cave art epoch in Europe. We've seen that precisely the same unlikely notion that a human can transform into an animal was also expressed in the very earliest rock art of southern Africa – the painted plaquettes from Apollo-11 Cave in Namibia, thought to be around 27,000 years old, which feature a therianthropic image of a man-lion or a man-leopard. Here, too, as in Europe, the concept was to prove a long-lived one; as we'll see, the rock art of the San bushmen of southern Africa continued to feature large numbers of therianthropes right through until the end of the nineteenth century when their age-old hunter-gatherer culture was forced into extinction.

I don't use the phrase 'age-old' lightly. The truth is nobody knows exactly how long the San had been in southern Africa before they were ethnically cleansed by land-hungry white settlers, but scholars are confident that it was a very long time. The paintings themselves are mostly done with mineral pigments and so cannot be directly dated in the same way, for example, as the charcoal emulsion paintings of Chauvet. Still, there are clues, particularly certain artefacts and remains associated with the San and with their painted rock shelters, that start turning up in the southern African archaeological record around 10,000 years ago.[48] 'We've got tortoise carapace bowls with ochre staining that are certainly 8,000, 9,000, 10,000 years old,' commented John Parkington, Professor of Archaeology at the University of Cape Town, when I interviewed him in April 2004:

There are bits of exfoliated paintings in Namibia which were certainly on the walls of caves and I think that goes back to 7,000, 8,000, 9,000 . . . I would say we're on pretty good grounds going through the Holocene to 10,000 years ago . . . I would be very surprised if people weren't painting on the caves at 10,000 years ago. Apollo-11 sticks out like a bit of a sore thumb at the moment, and it would be very nice to have other examples of what people were painting at that time.[49]

The reason Apollo-11 sticks out 'like a bit of a sore thumb' is simply that there are *no other examples* from the entire southern African region of 'what people were painting at that time'. The approximate age of 27,000 years normally suggested for the painted plaquettes is *17,000 years older* than the earliest acceptable evidence, cited by Parkington, for the appearance of the San rock-art tradition in southern Africa 10,000 years ago. Yet by style and subject matter the Apollo-11 paintings look very much like the work of the San. Could the archaeologists who excavated the cave somehow have got the chronology wrong and overestimated the age of the art? 'No,' says Parkington, 'it's very hard to dispute the date. There are about 30 radiocarbon dates so it's really hard to dispute.'[50]

Here's the executive summary: rock art very much like that of the later San, with identical themes, is created in southern Africa 27,000 years ago; then, after a mysterious absence from the region lasting 17,000 years, it reappears 10,000 years ago and thereafter continues to be created and renewed, in an unbroken tradition, until the final destruction of San culture in the nineteenth century.

The insect-men of Kondoa

One speculative scenario that would account for all the evidence is that the ancestors of the historical San were indeed in southern Africa 27,000 years ago and were responsible for the art from Apollo-11 Cave. At that time the entire population of the region would have been extremely small, probably a few hundred or a thousand individuals at most, and it would have been natural and relatively simple for them – in the face of some hypothetical environmental disaster or catastrophic

86

climate change in southern Africa – to migrate elsewhere. The San were always hunter-gatherers – a way of life that they preserved from the Stone Age and that their last relatives, the bushmen of Namibia and the Kalahari, still adhere to today. Such people do not hesitate to move great distances if it is necessary for survival and there are huge areas of the African continent, never excavated or even visited by archaeologists, where the ancestral San might theoretically have gone and stayed for 17,000 years – or even longer – without our knowing anything about it. To complete the scenario, we need only suppose further climate changes around 12,000 or 10,000 years ago that allowed the migrant San to return at last to their ancestral homelands in the south – thus accounting for the firm traces of their presence and artistic activities that begin to appear in the archaeological record at precisely this time.

The notion of prehistoric San migrations into and out of southern Africa helps to explain some anomalous rock-art sites elsewhere in the continent that archaeologists have studied but find very hard to categorise. Far to the north, for example, there is an isolated concentration of a few hundred painted rock shelters in the Kondoa district of Tanzania.[51] To the untrained eye it is immediately obvious that these Tanzanian paintings have many similarities to the rock art of the San, known from more than 20,000 sites in southern Africa. The experts agree, admitting that the paintings 'invite comparison with the southern tradition, even though separated from the nearest southern site by 1,500 kilometres'.[52]

Like the art of the southern San, the Tanzanian art is largely executed in mineral pigments that cannot be directly dated; nevertheless there are hints that it may be extremely ancient. At a number of the decorated sites, excavations have produced 'ochre fragments, ochre pencils, and stained "palettes"' – all items that are strongly indicative of painting – in strata dated to around 29,000 years ago.[53] The Italian prehistorian Emmanuel Anati supports this date and specifically links the Tanzanian paintings to those from Apollo-11 Cave in far-off Namibia.[54] The palaeoanthropologist Mary Leakey also maintains there is a family resemblance between the Apollo-11 plaquettes and the Tanzanian rock art – for which she has suggested the even more ancient date of 40,000 years ago.[55]

87

Few other scholars would be prepared to accept that the Kondoa paintings are so old, and since attempts to derive dates from associated archaeological deposits have not met with anything like universal agreement, there is still no consensus either about the provenance or about the age of these mysterious images. The only thing that everyone seems to agree on is that they are in some way connected to the southern San rock-art tradition.

But whether they're the work of a far-flung outpost of southern San culture sometime during the past 10,000 years, or whether they're part of an as yet largely undiscovered reservoir of much more ancient San art hidden away in other parts of Africa, it is surely of interest that the Tanzanian paintings prominently feature therianthropes. These include animal-headed figures of the general type with which the reader is already familiar.[56] There are also some most unusual variations on the therianthropic theme – notably a group of thin, elongated anthropomorphs at Kondoa's Kolo I rock shelter which were painted using multiple fine parallel lines of red ochre. Frequently misidentified as men with elaborate hairstyles or headdresses,[57] these otherworldly figures prove on close inspection to have the heads

The insect-men of Kondoa

neither of humans nor of animals. Their bodies, arms and legs are human enough, but their hands and feet, and particularly their heads, which have 'feelers' – and in one case even eyes on stalks – are decidedly insect-like.[58]

Southern Africa: therianthropes everywhere

The extraordinary idea of humanoid insects evoked by the Tanzanian paintings is found in southern San rock art and mythology, where the praying mantis is particularly favoured. At Brandhoek rock shelter in the Cedarberg wilderness of the Western Cape, a tall and muscular human female figure seems to turn a mantis-like head to look back over her shoulder.[59] The name of the San creator god, Kaggen, means,

San images of a woman (left, from the Cedarberg, after Slingsby, 1997) and man (right, from the Karoo) transforming into a mantis

literally, 'the Mantis'.[60] He principally manifests in human form – usually as a San hunter and shaman – but can transform at will into his insect avatar.[61] I have seen painted images in San rock shelters in South Africa's rugged Karoo region in which the deity is depicted as a man in precisely this process of metamorphosis into a large mantis.[62]

Kaggen – who can also appear as an eland, a snake or an eagle[63] – is a protean shape-shifter, like the sorcerer of Trois Frères, and dances to the same tune of human-animal transformation that was played in Namibia more than 27,000 years ago by the therianthrope of Apollo-11 Cave. In the vast archive of San rock art dating between 10,000 and just 100 years ago that is scattered across the length and breadth of southern Africa it is a tune that is played again and again – for depictions of therianthropes of all kinds are frequent and ubiquitous.[64]

In Wide Valley in the Maclear district of South Africa's North-Eastern Cape, San artists used white paint to portray a tall therianthrope with the legs and hoofs of a buck, hands resembling paws, and a human face.[65]

At an isolated rock shelter called Syfer, 30 kilometres from Clanwilliam in the Cedarberg, there is an arresting image painted in red ochre. The subject is a group of freakish-looking human figures with

Humans transforming into antelopes

greatly extended arms and legs standing on all fours on a thick zig-zag line in the posture of a herd of antelope. I step forward for a closer inspection. Now I can see that one of the figures has grown horns and all the others are at various stages in the process of metamorphosis into antelopes.[66]

Another San image from South Africa's Western Cape Province shows a group of a dozen or so anthropomorphic figures depicted ambiguously as though in flight or swimming. They have human heads,

Bird-men or mermen?

90

arms and upper bodies, but in place of human legs they have the tails either of fish or perhaps of birds – swallows have been suggested.[67]

Amidst the spectacular scenery of the Giant's Castle Nature Reserve in the Drakensberg Mountains there is an extensive rock-art site, now known as Main Caves, where the two central figures are both therianthropes with human legs, buttocks and arms, and the heads of mountain reedbuck.[68] One of the figures seems lumpy and malformed and a closer look shows why. It is wrapped up in the coils of gigantic serpents, suggesting the possibility of further levels of metamorphosis.

Throughout South Africa by far the most frequently represented therianthrope is a man transforming into an eland, the largest of the

Human-eland transformations in the Drakensberg

antelopes. In one of many such scenes from the Drakensberg – at Game Pass in the Kamberg Nature Reserve – we see an eland with its hind legs crossed in a posture of collapse, suggesting it is about to die. Behind it, holding on to its tail, is the figure of a tall man with his legs crossed in exactly the same manner. Instead of a human head and feet he has the head and hoofs of an eland.[69] To the right is the

San therianthropes.

91

figure of a dancer, also partially transformed, and two further theri-anthropes, one with the body of a man and the head of an unidentified animal with pointed ears, the second again with the body of a man but with the hoofs and horns of an eland.[70]

Other transformed figures favoured by the San artists include elephant-men,[71] jackal-men,[72] some spectacular bird-men,[73] an archer with the head and tail of a baboon but the legs and arms of a human,[74] 'upside-down' therianthropes with animal heads emerging from the buttocks of headless human bodies,[75] and, inevitably, lion-men.[76]

A man transforms into a lion

The one common theme

It would be possible to say much more about the bewildering variety of therianthropes depicted by the San, but the point has been made. Over a period of at least 27,000 years, the rock art of southern Africa consistently and repeatedly represented the mystery of human beings transforming into animals – just as we now know the cave art of prehistoric Europe did also, from its earliest beginnings.

Why should this be so even in one let alone both of these far-flung regions?

Dr Paul Tacon, Senior Scientist at the Australian Museum in Sydney, and Dr Christopher Chippendale of Cambridge University's Museum of Archaeology and Anthropology recently undertook a detailed survey of prehistoric rock art in locations as widely separated as Australia, France, South Africa and Spain. The purpose of the survey was to identify any obvious common themes, but in the end the researchers found only one that could be said to be truly universal:

> We looked at art that goes back to the dawn of humanity and found it had one common feature: animal-human hybrids . . . Werewolves and vampires are as old as art, in other words. These composite beings, from a world between humans and animals, are a common theme from the beginning of painting.[77]

The French prehistorian Jean Clottes agrees that the 'belief in therianthropic beings' is not only conclusively demonstrated in the oldest cave art, but is 'attested in the whole world in all periods'.[78] In his view, therefore, it must form 'part of the universals of the human mind'.[79]

This sounds like an impressive explanation of the amazing resilience and ubiquity of therianthropic images, but a moment's thought reveals that it simply begs the question. If a belief in therianthropes is one of the universals of the human mind, then what we really should be asking is *why* is it universal? Since our minds are supposedly the products of Darwinian evolution, it is axiomatic that any forms of behaviour that endure in human culture for thousands of years must have proved themselves useful for the long-term survival of our species. We therefore need to figure out why it was useful for our ancestors to be so passionately interested in nonexistent man/animal hybrids that they made them the subjects of their very first artistic endeavours – at Chauvet, Fumane, Hohlenstein-Stadel and Apollo-11 Cave – and continued to represent them, in one form or another, for tens of thousands of years.

No theory that claims to tell us what cave art is or means can hope to succeed if it is unable to provide a complete and persuasive explanation for this puzzling state of affairs.

CHAPTER FIVE

Riddles of the Caves

In the summer of 1991 Henri Cosquer, a scuba diver from Marseilles, found a hidden wonderland while exploring underwater caves off the south-west coast of France. At a depth of almost 40 metres he entered a terrifying upwards-sloping tunnel more than 150 metres long, eventually surfacing within the dome of the huge cave that is now named after him. Its entrance had been submerged by rising sea levels at the end of the Ice Age and Cosquer was the first person for more than 18,000 years to come here.[1] In the period between 27,000 years ago and 18,000 years ago, however, it had been extensively decorated.[2] Thanks to its special topography (with its main galleries at a much higher level than its entrance), most of its wonderful Upper Palaeolithic paintings and engravings were still not only intact and above water, but in pristine condition.

There are so many fantastic images in the Cosquer Cave that prehistorians can hardly be blamed for initially paying relatively little attention to what looks like one of the least impressive. It is an engraving 28 centimetres long, not an eye-catching painting, and it is positioned obscurely on a ceiling overhang. During the preliminary archaeological study in 1992 it was given a cursory examination and identified as the figure of a diving seal impaled by harpoons.[3] Since the Cosquer galleries feature depictions of a number of different sea animals, including at least eight other impaled seals in various parts of the cave, this was regarded as nothing unusual.[4]

94

It was not until much later that members of the archaeological team began to have doubts about the image because:

The body has a roughly rectangular shape, with a clearly indicated curve in the back. A pronounced curve shapes the rump . . . We became intrigued by the strange shape of the hindquarters. If this were a seal, they should have been tapered rather than curved. Comparing the slides and highly enlarged black-and-white photographs at our disposal, we then noticed that what we had at first taken to be an animal's fore-flipper was in fact a very elongated arm ending in an obvious hand, with the fingers depicted by several deeply engraved parallel lines . . . We had to accept the evidence: this was not one more pinniped [the order of aquatic mammals to which seals belong] but a human.[5]

Close examination led to a further revision of the identification to allow that the creature is partly a pinniped after all. To be specific, the experts now agree that its hand and arm, and the general shape of its head, body and rump, are those of a human, but its lower limbs have been shortened and tapered to make them more like a seal's hindflippers and 'the three light but clear marks on top of the head are reminiscent of a seal's moustache'.[6]

The seal-man of Cosquer Cave. The figure's hindquarters are oriented up, to the left, while its head is oriented down, to the right, as though it is falling backwards with its legs in the air. The figure's mid-back, shoulders, neck and face area are shown impaled by three deeply scored lines.

So finally we know what we're dealing with in the Cosquer Cave – yet another therianthrope captured in the process of transformation from man to wild beast. This time, however, there's something new. The most notable characteristic of the figure (presumed to be male, although no sexual organs are shown) is that he is *impaled* by three deeply scored lines. One of these, thought to represent a harpoon, is almost twice as long as the figure itself. It extends far behind him, enters his mid-back, passes diagonally though his chest, and exits the front of his body at throat level before striking and completely obliterating most of his face. The second line is shorter and may represent the barbed head of the first massive harpoon rather than a separate projectile. It does not extend behind the body of the figure, but it too exits at throat level and is involved in the disfigurement of the face. The third line again extends behind the figure, though not so far as the first, and penetrates his back at the level of the shoulder blades. Like the other two it exits at the throat and culminates in the face.[7]

This ravaged form, says Jean Clottes, 'represents a human killed, or rather the *idea* of a human killed'.[8] For this reason, despite its therianthropic characteristics, he calls it 'the killed man'[9] and points out its many obvious similarities to figures, usually referred to as 'wounded men', that have been found in a small number of other caves.[10]

Images of the wounded man

I first encountered one of these mysterious images during my visit to the cave of Pech Merle, and have already described it in Chapter Two. The reader will recall that the features of the Pech Merle wounded man have been compared by some authorities to a muzzle or a beak.[11] Its legs are human, but disproportionately stocky and short, and it has only vestigial arms with no obvious hands. Its body – again human – is pierced by three long lines, usually interpreted as spears, which pass completely through it and extend for some distance on either side, one at the level of the buttocks, one through the sternum, and one through the upper part of the back and chest. Another line, perhaps indicating a penis rather than a piercing of the body, hangs down from

The wounded man
of Pech Merle

the groin. Two more spear-like lines penetrate the figure higher up, near neck level, one from the front, the other from the back.

In the cave of Cougnac, 40 kilometres from Pech Merle, I had the opportunity to study two more wounded men. They feature in a stunning series of interlinked panels covering perhaps a third of the available wall-space in a spectacular, almost circular underground grotto. Roughly in the centre of this beautiful fairyland there is a large 'island' of stalagmitic columns, two of which were daubed with red ochre by the cave artists more than 20,000 years ago while a third, which had formerly stood between them, was cut down. The two columns provide a perfect frame through which to view one of the central and most prominent images on the main panel – a large male ibex painted in red ochre with delicately beautiful, steeply curved horns.

A few metres to the left of the ibex, also outlined in red, is the figure of a megaceros, a species of giant deer that became extinct at the end of the Ice Age. The forelegs, neck and head of this animal face to the left, hugging the natural relief of the rock face. Painted in black on its shoulder, and oriented to the right, is the first of the two wounded men.

What should seem immediately odd is the way that the figure seems to lack head, neck, shoulders and arms. But the image, though simple, has been skilfully outlined in such a way as to create the illusion that the missing parts are still attached to its upper body and simply thrust out of our sight behind a change of tone in the rock surface – as it might look, for example, if it were seen hauling itself, upper body first, through a narrow opening into a concealed chamber above. There is much the same feeling about the feet – still attached but not visible, as though obscured by fog. Like other wounded men, the legs are stocky and foreshortened. The buttocks are clearly shown, so the figure is naked. Three lines, presumed to be spears, strike it from behind, one in the rump, one in the lower back and the third in mid-back.

The wounded men of Cougnac Cave

Cougnac's second wounded man is positioned almost exactly as far to the right of the ibex at the centre of the panel as the first wounded man is positioned to its left. This second figure is again painted in black and superimposed on the outline of a large animal in red ochre facing towards the left – here a mammoth – which, again, conforms closely to the natural contours of the rock face. Some other points of comparison may be noted. The vestigial upper limbs of the second wounded man are very like those of the Pech Merle figure, while the body follows the same general plan as the 'killed man' of Cosquer, including the human torso and buttocks and the shortened and tapered lower limbs without feet. The head of the second wounded man, frequently described as 'bird-like',[12] faces left and, provocatively, is painted to fit exactly inside the much larger skull of the underlying red ochre mammoth in the position of its brain. To complete the

Cougnac wounded man in context. The figure is superimposed over the head and forequarters of a large mammoth.

picture this second wounded man of Cougnac is pierced by no fewer than eight spears that seem to skewer him from all directions. One strikes him high in the rump, a second lower down in the thigh, a third in the middle of his back, the fourth and fifth penetrate his belly, the sixth his side, the seventh his shoulder and the eighth his neck.

What could possibly be the meaning of such symbolism? For it is symbolism. Most of the wounded men, including the killed man of Cosquer, seem to 'float' in random orientations, without reference to any local horizon, as though weightless. And although all the figures are different, there is in every case a distinct lack of naturalism, typified by the predicament of the Cosquer figure, struck from behind by a 'harpoon' almost twice its own length yet depicted as though lying on its back with its legs in the air. Very simply, as Jean Clottes points out, 'a person hit in the back by such a weapon would fall forward'.[13]

Other than the one Cosquer figure, Pech Merle (also just one figure) and Cougnac (two figures),[14] images of the wounded man that have come down to us from the European Upper Palaeolithic are exceptionally rare.

One is in a little-known cave in the Dordogne called Sous-Grand-Lac. As is usually the case, he is mildly therianthropic, but this time, instead of a bird's head or a seal's flippers, he has a tail-like appendage

99

combined with an otherwise normal human body, arms, legs and head. He has an erect penis and seems to have been struck in the upper back by three barbed spears descending almost vertically from above.[15]

The final wounded man is a figure we've met before. On the one hand he's the bison-human therianthrope of Gabillou (see Chapter Four); on the other, with a 'spear' line through his thigh and two shorter slashes penetrating the front of his face, he very definitely

Gabillou: therianthrope and wounded man combined

qualifies as a wounded man too.[16] Like the Cosquer figure, he seems to merge both identities in complex ways, suggesting that whatever it was that led a person to believe he could become a therianthrope might also, under different circumstances, lead him to identify with the agonised figure of the wounded man.

What does it all mean?

'Without some extraordinary discovery,' say the experts, 'it is an illusion to think that we will one day arrive at certainty in this area or in so many others.'[17]

The wounded men of southern Africa

Despite predictable differences in style, a figure that is essentially identical to the rare wounded men of Upper Palaeolithic Europe appears – equally rarely – in the Stone Age art of southern Africa. The most striking example, painted in a rock shelter in Eastern Free State, is a wounded man who would not be out of place in Cougnac or Pech Merle – right down to the hint of therianthropy that many of the French subjects share.[18] The figure is shown prone, seemingly floating,

The wounded man was also painted by the San.
This figure is from Eastern Free State, South Africa. (RARI)

and multiply penetrated in the legs and torso by close to 50 harsh, stabbing lines, presumed to represent spears or arrows.[19]

In the Mutoko district of Zimbabwe, east of the capital Harare, another of these San wounded men appears, pierced by what look like

San wounded man, Mutoko, Zimbabwe (after Garlake, 1995)

eight or nine arrows. Again he is shown prone in a manner that suggests floating.[20]

Two further examples also come from Zimbabwe and are both part of the same large painted rock face in Makoni district, south of Mutoko. One shows a running figure with a grotesquely distended head, a long body and foreshortened legs, pierced in the rump, lower back, stomach and face by four spear lines.[21] The second figure, with

Wounded men, Makoni, Zimbabwe (after Garlake, 1995)

two spear lines in its back and one in its abdomen, has a man's legs and body combined therianthropically with the tail of an elephant.[22]

The problem of the signs

Therianthropes and wounded men, and the strange equivalences between them, are amongst the major unsolved mysteries of cave art. In later chapters we'll look closely at the way David Lewis-Williams' neuropsychological model responds not only to these mysteries but also to a number of others that have come to be considered as hopelessly obscure and beyond solution.

Very high on the list is the problem of the 'signs' that appear with greater or lesser frequency, scattered throughout the majestic bestiaries of Ice Age animals, in almost all the Upper Palaeolithic painted caves of Europe. These include zig-zag and wavy lines, lattice, chequerboard, grid and ladder patterns, figures that resemble spiders' webs, striped and cross-hatched quadrilaterals and triangles, honeycombs, occasional nested catenary curves known as festoons (formed out of multiple parallel arcs), fields of polka dots (sometimes cohering into almost recognisable shapes, sometimes attenuated into lines) and a number of other, often geometrical devices.[23]

No generally accepted explanation of such figures, and their precise relationship with the supposedly naturalistic images of animals for which the caves are famous, has ever been proposed.[24] In many cases the signs are inextricably intertwined and superimposed upon the naturalistic representations, yet it is an unproven dogma, frequently repeated by cave-art specialists, that these are two distinct and unrelated 'systems of depictions': 'One of them is figurative, extremely realistic, revealing the artist's skill in observing nature; the second system, which comprises not forms but signs, is symbolic and its meaning is still unknown.'[25]

These two systems appear to have been running in parallel from the very beginning of Upper Palaeolithic art. Chauvet Cave in France contains some of the most ancient paintings and engravings of animal and therianthropic figures anywhere in the world, and also some of the earliest-surviving examples of the system of patterns, named 'signs'

Chauvet: left, the form of an animal emerges from a cloud of dots; right, parallel arcs and a cross

by the archaeologists – though the matter is far from settled – that would continue in use until the end of the cave-art epoch. Located soon after the narrow entrance passage, the lofty and extensive Bunuel Chamber is particularly richly equipped with such signs, including three panels of large red-ochre polka dots and a bizarre sheaf of nested curved lines surmounted by a cross.[26]

Further into Chauvet's labyrinth of passageways and chambers the visitor comes to the so-called Gallery of the Red Panels. Between two

Chauvet: feline and dots

human handprints and the head of a large feline there extends a semi-circle of about a dozen small red dots.[27]

Nearby is the 'Panel of the Signs' on which is painted a most intriguing geometrical figure. At its centre, placed vertically, is a narrow, approximately rectangular outline, a little wider at the top than at the bottom, crossed by a rack of six slightly curved horizontal lines

Chauvet: geometry?
or an insect?

that extend noticeably to either side.[28] It is almost – *but not quite* – as though the upright rectangle is the body of some large insect and the curved lines are its legs, However, the presence of 'very similar but more geometrical shapes' elsewhere in the cave led the excavators of Chauvet to be 'circumspect about any zoological or figurative inter-pretation' and to classify this puzzling image with the abstract motifs.[29] As such it is, of course, considered to be beyond any further investigation – part of that broad class of signs that cave-art authority Anne Sieveking describes as 'a language for which we have no vocabulary'.[30]

We saw in Chapter Four that the mammoth-ivory statuettes from the German caves of Vogelherd, Geissenklosterle, Hohle Fels and Hohlenstein-Stadel are about the same age as the paintings in Chauvet, i.e. around 32,000 years old or perhaps a little more. Quite a number of these beautiful figurines are deeply marked with geometrical patterns greatly resembling the mysterious signs of the painted caves. For example, a lion statuette from Vogelherd is decorated with

Vogelherd: lion figure with dots and criss-crossed incisions

dots and engraved with criss-crossed incisions that form a grid of diamond shapes.[31] The top of the head of a second statuette is patterned with dots.[32] A third figure is engraved with nested curved lines and multiple series of dots and dashes.[33]

Vogelherd figures: grids, dots and arcs (after Dowson and Porr, 2001)

Moving forward in time a few thousand years, Pech Merle has particularly rich and intriguing patterns of polka dots at several different points, some painted in black charcoal emulsion, some in black manganese, some in red ochre. In the cave's Combel Gallery, dated to about 25,000 years ago, the reader will recall that there are several depictions of 'imaginary animals' – a problem that we will return to – but the same gallery also contains a small side-chamber decorated with a series of quadrangular signs formed by dots.[34] Surrounding the handprint of the young woman that so arrested my attention in Pech Merle there is another curious geometrical pattern of red-ochre dots. Nearby, beside the therianthropic bison-women, there are two further dot patterns, both roughly circular. On the panel of the spotted horses the dapples on the animals' coats are formed by black polka dots, but red

Overlapping dots and figures on the panel of the
spotted horses at Pech Merle

dots have also been added and these patterns of dots – both black and red – extend beyond the main figures on to the surrounding rock face. The mane, head and throat of the right-hand horse, dated to 24,640 years ago,[35] are shadowed by lines of black dots.

Moving forward in time again we find a painting of a large aurochs in the Tête du Lion Cave in the Ardèche dated to around 22,000 years ago; above it a quadrangular grid sign is picked out in red-ochre polka dots.[36] In Cosquer Cave from the same period there is a striking engraved pattern of eight nested curved festoons with four sets of arcs

Left, aurochs with pattern of dots at Tete du Lion Cave. Centre and right, nested arcs and figure composed of lines and arcs, Cosquer Cave.

oriented one way and four sets oriented the other.[37] Of note elsewhere in the cave is a curious, almost anthropomorphic composition featuring a ladder-like rack of short parallel straight lines, four parallel catenary curves (nested arcs), and a roughly quadrangular grid overlaid with a diamond shape.[38] There are also numerous zig-zag patterns, either standing alone or incorporated into other geometric shapes or into the figures of animals.

Zig-zags standing alone and incorporated into geometrical and animal figures at Cosquer Cave

The frequency with which such signs appear in cave art increased as the millennia passed. By the Magdalenian epoch, between approximately 17,000 and 12,000 years ago – and thus at the other end of the Upper Palaeolithic from Chauvet and Vogelherd – they were everywhere abundant.[39]

107

The cave of Niaux dates from this period. On the main panel of its Black Room, more than half a kilometre from the entrance, the sweeping curved horns of a mountain ibex are elegantly combined with a curving zig-zag line. From Trois Frères, in the same period, an extraordinary composition in the Sanctuary includes an image of a large bear covered in patterns of open dots. Above it floats the figure of a bison overlaid with wavy and zig-zag lines.

Left, ibex with zig-zag horn, Niaux. Right, bear with dots, and bison with wavy and zig-zag lines, Trois Frères (Breuil, 1952)

In Lascaux, the best known of the Magdalenian caves, the Axial Gallery running east out of the Hall of Bulls contains many examples of signs combined with animal figures. On the ceiling as you enter there is a rectangular yellow-ochre grid amongst the fantasia of aurochs cows and magnificent Chinese horses dancing above you. Deeper in, on the south wall of the narrow gallery, 13 polka dots have been painted beneath the figure of a stag with elaborate filigree antlers. The line of dots terminates at an open quadrilateral sign beneath the stag's head, then seems to restart again, after a short distance, in front of an odd-looking pot-bellied horse with an improbably small head. At the level of the horse's forelegs, the line of dots becomes sinuous and forms an oxbow meander.

A few metres further and you see two more horses advancing towards you on the ceiling. Above the mane of the closest one is a pattern of four vertical parallel lines crossed at the top by two

Dots and a quadrangular sign combined with animal figures at Lascaux

horizontal lines. Ahead again another five metres and you come to a large cow jumping with its forelegs extended so that it almost seems to be flying. Immediately in front of it is a grid of five parallel vertical lines flowing with the relief of the wall crossed by three parallel

Lascaux: jumping aurochs cow and grid

horizontal lines. Another three metres brings you close to the eastern end of the gallery. There a pair of ibexes have confronted one another for the past 17,000 years separated by a prominent rectangular grid resembling a window with six panes.[40]

Elsewhere in Lascaux there are further quadrangular signs. The Apse has more than 40 of them and there are four in the Nave.[41] One of

Two ibexes separated by a 'window-pane' grid at Lascaux

the latter, stunningly beautiful in its simplicity, has the form of a large square window with nine polychrome panes.[42] There are also numerous sequences and patterns of polka dots. In the Hall of Bulls there are six dots on the shoulder of the fourth aurochs and four dots on the breast of the third. In the Axial Gallery, as well as the line of dots already described between the stag and the horse, there are also two further groups of dots where the gallery ends. In the remotest parts of the cave, at the bottom of the shaft and at the end of the Chamber of the Felines, there are groups of six dots, each arranged in parallel lines of three to form rectangular signs.[43]

In northern Spain, the works of art in the world-renowned cave of Altamira, dating from between 16,500 and 14,500 years ago,[44] again

Nets, starbursts and web patterns from the ceiling of Altamira

show a dazzling and perplexing mixture of geometric signs and naturalistic images of Ice Age animals. On the great polychrome ceiling of the main chamber there are nets and grids, zig-zags, 'starbursts', spider-web patterns of nested lines, and another quadrilateral figure with panes like a window.[45] In a small side gallery off Room II, five narrow 'ladder' signs (each consisting of two parallel vertical lines of red ochre crossed by dozens of horizontal steps) spill down the left wall, becoming sinuous and intertwined towards the floor. At the very

Ladder-like patterns at the rear of a small side gallery in Altamira

back of the gallery, again in red ochre, are four slightly distorted upright rectangles with horizontal divisions.[46]

Deeper into the cave, in the narrow, winding terminal passage called the Horse's Tail, eerie 'masks' of therianthropic bison-human faces have been crafted by adding just a few lines of black charcoal emulsion to invitingly shaped outcrops of the natural rock face. Amongst these spectres, scattered here and there, are painted groups of black navicular figures and a quadrilateral. The latter is an upright rectangle with slight curving at the outer edges. It is divided into five vertical registers, three with ladder-like horizontal steps, two filled with diamond cross-hatching, and, at the centre, an empty horizontal band. The naviculars are approximately boat-shaped, with flat 'decks' crossed by horizontal lines, curved 'keels' again crossed by horizontal lines,

Altamira: some of the curious patterns in the 'Horse's Tail'

and sometimes a second nested horizontal line parallel to the keel. In one case the whole figure is further subdivided into more than 50 small quadrilateral panels.[47]

A few kilometres south of Altamira, the caves of El Castillo and La Pasiega, deep inside a mountain above the town of Puente Viesgo, both contain paintings and engravings spanning an immense period from almost 30,000 years ago down to the end of the Magdalenian around 13,000 years ago. In La Pasiega you walk through a gallery lined with several dozen animal figures, mainly deer, horses, bison and aurochs, then, suddenly – disposed inside and around the entrance of a narrow fissure at the end of the gallery – you are confronted by a

La Pasiega

mystifying array of more than 20 red quadrangular signs and ladder-like patterns.[48] El Castillo similarly has a small side gallery dominated by a spectacular display of signs.[49] Here flowing meanders of red dots are organised into formalised geometrical patterns, including a cross, and into thick vertical parallel lines like tassles or dangling strings of beads.[50] Side by side with these there are also ten conspicuous quadrangular signs with multiple panels. Some incorporate tall, narrow 'ladders'. One, a slightly curved and distorted rectangle with six panes, weirdly prefigures the famous Microsoft 'flying windows' logo by about

Left, overview of geometrical patterns at El Castillo; right, detail of the same composition

14,000 years. In another part of El Castillo the wall of a narrow passageway is decorated at chest height with huge quantities of large red polka dots arranged into a continuous wavy line, doubled in some sections, that runs for more than 50 metres.[51] A little further on, a small human handprint is seen, outlined in negative by spray-painting. A metre to its left and slightly lower, there is a pattern of crossed zigzag lines, almost like a section of the double helix.[52]

At the beginning of the second century of academic research into the painted caves, what is to be made of all this? 'It is very probable that we shall never know the meaning of Palaeolithic art,' says Anne Sieveking, voicing the opinion of large numbers of scholars in this field, 'for, although the naturalistic element is potentially comprehensible, the idiomatic and schematic are not.'[53]

The bottom line of such defeatist thinking, as David Lewis-Williams points out, is that 'The so-called signs of European Upper Palaeolithic art have been a persistently intractable challenge to archaeologists [and] no explanation . . . has won general acceptance.'[54]

Signs of the San

Having seen that the prehistoric rock art of the San of southern Africa has so much else in common with the cave art of Upper Palaeolithic Europe, it hardly comes as a surprise to discover that ladders and ladder-like patterns, some strongly reminiscent of similar figures described above in the caves of Altamira and El Castillo in Spain, are also present in the rock shelters of South Africa.[55] Indeed, it is not too difficult to find virtually identical examples of the whole range of signs seen in the European caves.

Ladder patterns in southern African rock art

Zig-zags are common. In one remarkable case in the Drakensberg Mountains of KwaZulu-Natal, the legs and neck of a (six-fingered!)

Drakensberg figure with six fingers
and zig-zag legs

human figure are painted as elaborate zig-zags.[56] At Shaman Cave near the town of Uniondale there is a remarkable zig-zag pattern with the hint of a human form.[57] Near Bushman's Kloof in the Cedarberg, at a shelter called Charlie Brown, a group of dancing women are prominently marked with parallel zig-zag lines. Grid and net patterns

The Cedarberg: left, dancing women with zig-zags; right, White Net

are also common in the Cedarberg – at the eponymous White Net, for example, positioned deep beneath an overhang so low one can only reach it by lying on one's back.[58] Numerous grids enclosed in squares, ovals and circles, some closely resembling the quadrangular window-pane patterns of Lascaux and El Castillo, are also seen amongst many

Geometrical engravings,
Riet River, Northern Cape

other geometrical engravings near the Riet River in the Northern Cape.[59] In the Guruve district of northern Zimbabwe, geometric grids are frequently enclosed within oval designs.[60] In Murewa, in the north-east, we see streams of dots painted between pairs of wavy parallel lines, and a large chequerboard pattern in which squares of solid colour alternate with squares of dots.[61]

A few kilometres north of the Brandewyn River in South Africa's Western Cape is a site called Salmanslaagte set amongst scrub country filled with ravines, dried-up river beds and outcrops of boulders. Here an extensive rock face 60 metres in length is densely painted with the same sort of curious mixture of naturalistic figures of animals and

Left and centre, 'magic carpet' and zig-zag patterns of the Western Cape. Right, a net of fine lines painted in a San rock shelter in the Karoo.

humans, combined with idiomatic and schematic geometrical signs, that is normal in Europe. My eye was drawn to the so-called 'magic carpet' – a rectangle filled with finger-sized dots that overspill its edges, several cross-hatched grids or nets, zig-zag patterns, and a composition of nested curved lines with a superimposed animal figure.[62]

Particularly noteworthy at Salmanslaagte is a pattern of opposed nested curves[63] directly comparable in general structure and outline to

Western Cape: left, parallel arcs and a superimposed animal figure; right festoons and a complex 'navicular' (boat-shaped) figure

116

the pattern of festoons from Cosquer Cave described earlier. The same site also features a prominent navicular – boat-shaped – figure, painted in red ochre, with a similar curved 'keel' to the naviculars of Altamira, and enclosing multiple nested curved lines.[64]

This sign of nested catenary curves (parallel arcs) arranged in the shape of boats recurs often in many different contexts in rock shelters across southern Africa and is sometimes incorporated into more complex designs. For example, in the Harriesmith District in North-

North-eastern Free State: sky-boat of the therianthropes (RARI).

Eastern Free State, one such navicular sign has evolved into a fully fledged boat, with a high prow and stern, the base of its keel marked with five zig-zag parallel lines. It gives the appearance of floating in the sky (since birds are present). The figures of two antelope-headed therianthropes with human arms and bodies peer curiously down at the ground from the curved upper deck.[65] A third therianthrope is positioned below.

As is the case in the caves of Upper Palaeolithic Europe, patterns of dots are common features of southern African San art, and one interesting painting, from Eastern Cape Province, bears close comparison to the panel of the spotted horses in Pech Merle.[66] Both compositions feature clouds of dots in two different colours, and in both cases the dots are taken into the design of animal figures with which they overlap – horses in Pech Merle, an eland in the Eastern Cape.[67]

Additional geometric elements in the Eastern Cape painting – a horizontal zig-zag line at the base and a grid imposed over the body of the eland – are not found at Pech Merle, but, as we know, are found at numerous other European Upper Palaeolithic caves.

Above, panel of the spotted horses, Pech Merle. Below, San rock painting from the Eastern Cape (RARI)

The final element of the South African composition is a gigantic horned serpent that seems to emerge out of a natural crack in the rock face. Although there are no such figures in the European caves, the way that the serpent uses the rock face like this – darting out of it and creating the illusion that half of its body is still hidden from view behind it – is highly reminiscent of one of the most consistent and effective techniques of the Upper Palaeolithic painters and sculptors.

The dynamic rock face

I have visited 17 of the European decorated caves – 13 of them in France and four in Spain.[68] What they all have in common is an almost magical level of imagination and creativity in the use of the natural contours of the rock, a characteristic highlighted, by specialists and non-specialists alike, in virtually every study of every cave ever published.

In Chapter Two I recount my own first experiences of this phenomenon in the cave of Pech Merle – where the inspired treatment of natural bulges, indentations and fissures, sometimes with just a few lines of paint, repeatedly generates the illusion of groups of Ice Age animals flowing into and out of the rock face. Clearly the positioning of these animal figures could not have been determined by any preconceived plan or grand design on the part of the artists but had much more to do with the attractions of suitably formed natural surfaces. Indeed, it has been sensibly suggested that certain wholly natural features in Pech Merle may have been critical in the selection of this cave for decoration in the first place, and particularly in the choice of mammoths – 27 of them in total – as the most frequently represented animal.[69] The Italian prehistorian Paolo Graziosi points to certain stalagmitic formations found throughout the cave which are indeed evocative of mammoths with long trailing coats and round domed skulls of exactly the kind painted so frequently at Pech Merle.[70]

In Cougnac the remarkable panel I described earlier – featuring a large red ibex and two figures of wounded men – repeatedly integrates ancient calcite 'draperies' into the paintings. Thus the legs of the ibex are each formed from vertical flows of calcite enhanced with a

Cougnac: ibex (left) and megaceros (right) with superimposed wounded man

surrounding line of red ochre; further calcite formations conjure up the shagginess of the animal's coat. The neckline, front legs and hind legs of the megaceros over which the first wounded man is superimposed are all also defined by calcite flows touched up with red ochre.

The same is true for much of the body of the mammoth over which the second wounded man is superimposed. (See p. 99).

Hundreds of miles north-west of Cougnac, in the cave of Arcy-sur-Cure in central France the same technique is used with, for example, the painted legs, body and head of a mammoth completed by a calcite trunk. Deeper into the cave, near the back of the so-called Sea Waves Room, another mammoth is painted around bulges in the wall in such a way that it appears in almost full relief. Close by there is the figure of a megaceros, outlined in black with some red ochre, where both antlers are formed by natural cracks and ridges in the wall. On my way out I notice a complex stalagmitic concretion high up on the wall of the so-called Chaos Room. It is entirely natural but bears an astonishing resemblance to the well-endowed female 'Venus' figures that have been found painted and sculpted in many Upper Palaeolithic caves.[71] The artists of Arcy-sur-Cure also recognised the likeness because although they did not alter the shape of the concretion, they did daub red ochre on it in the position of its stomach and breasts. Directly opposite, as though to re-emphasise the significance of the formation, a human handprint appears – not in negative, like the woman's handprint at Pech Merle, but a positive print achieved by applying paint directly to the inside of the hand and pressing it against the wall. Further on still I pass a second such natural Venus, 'growing' out of the cave wall as concretions do, again purposely daubed with red ochre.[72]

The great majority of the amazing polychrome images of Lascaux are integrated in a variety of ways with the folds and ridges of the rock wall.[73] In the Hall of Bulls, for example, a natural ridge forms the back, head and ears of a small image of a bear; nearby the hindquarters of an aurochs have been described by the French scholar Annette Laming-Emperaire as 'outlined by a horizontal protuberance of the rock . . . When viewed in slanting light the flank and bony rump stand out in remarkable relief.'[74]

In Lascaux's Axial Gallery it is worth taking a second look at the scene of the stag and the small horse described earlier. As well as the open quadrilateral sign that separates them, the reader will recall that there is a line of black dots that begins under the head of the stag. It seems to stop at the open sign, is interrupted by a light-coloured bulge in the wall and then reappears again as an intact line of dots on the

The dots seem to form a continuous line woven in and out of the rock face

other side where it curves down in front of the horse. The effect is almost as though a rope, strung along the rock face, has been threaded through a hole in the side of the bulge, passed beneath it out of sight, and then brought out again into the open through another hole.[75]

The same sort of illusion is deployed at the ancient cave of Chauvet in France, where we see the forequarters of an aurochs emerging out of a hollow in the rock as though it is about to draw the rest of its

Chauvet: the hint of an aurochs emerging from the shadows

body forth from the darkness beneath.[76] And at Rouffignac we find a horse's head painted on a flint nodule sticking out of the cave wall.

The effect, which can only be intentional, is that the body of the horse is somehow present on the other side of the wall.[77]

A few kilometres away, in the cave of Bara Bahau, another embedded nodule has been co-opted to a different purpose. It is integrated into the painted forms of two animals superimposed over it – serving both as the hoof of a horse and as the eye of an aurochs.[78] In Font de Gaume the figure of a bison is similarly oriented around a natural pattern in the cave wall that forms its eye. A red-ochre dot is painted in the centre of the eye. Further on in the same beautiful cave 12 more of these animals (in the eponymous 'Chapel of the Bison') are all painted to take maximum advantage of natural relief and seem at the point of bursting out of the cave wall.[79] Famously the same is also true of the great polychrome ceiling of Altamira in Spain from which hang down about a dozen very large nodules, some more than a metre in diameter, creating a distinctly knobbly effect. On every one of these natural embossments the figure of a bison has been painted; most are curled up but each has a different posture suggested by the under-lying relief.[80]

In Le Portel in France the outlines of two men in red ochre have been painted around calcite deposits used to represent their genitals.[81] A kilometre inside the cave of Niaux, in a place of total darkness, an irregularly shaped hole in the rock is coincidentally suggestive of the head of a deer viewed from the front. Around 15,000 years ago someone with a lamp came here, saw the potential of the similarity, and painted

Niaux

a set of black antlers to complete the head.[82] Exactly the same prin-ciple – of drawing out the potential of a natural feature – is seen in the way that the bison-man therianthrope of El Castillo (Chapter Four) is integrated into the form of a stalagmite. Here again, contours, ridges and folds naturally present in the calcite are used to provide relief characteristics for the outlined figure and to define its overall upright stance.[83] If the electric lights of the cave are turned off, and a flickering lamp is held in front of the stalagmite, an additional bonus is the shadow of a giant bison projected on to the rear wall where it fuses with a set of painted bison legs.[84]

It would be possible to extend this list almost endlessly, through virtually every one of the nearly 300 decorated caves that are now known in Europe, but sufficient examples have been given here to make the point. There is much that is difficult to fathom about the ancient artists but there is one thing we can be certain of: they did not treat the rock face as a blank canvas but rather as a dynamic part of their paintings and perhaps even the factor that determined whether a painting was to be made at all. Any theory that seeks to explain the art of the caves must therefore be able to explain why such a special emphasis was put on this relationship with the rock.

Before moving on, one last understated image comes to mind. From a site called La Chaire à Calvin in France's Charente region, it is a rare scene of two horses copulating.[85] The graceful contours of the animals break through the rough surface of the rock in low relief as the forms of dolphins at play momentarily break the surface of a choppy ocean before disappearing from view again into the depths below.

The strong sense that is conveyed is of an independent world and its inhabitants – animals, humans, hybrids, even monsters as we shall see – existing on the other side of the rock face and sometimes, through a strange sorcery, becoming visible to us.

Walls have ears

In this matter, as in so much else, it is striking how the prehistoric art of southern Africa – though disconnected geographically and even (to some extent) chronologically from the painted caves of Europe – nevertheless exhibits precisely the same sort of dynamic relationship with the rock face. And as with Europe, where it is found in virtually every cave, it is a relationship that expresses itself, in one way or another, in almost all of the 20,000 or so painted and engraved rock shelters so far discovered in southern Africa. A few examples will have to stand for many:

- Just like images in the caves of Upper Palaeolithic Europe, numerous paintings throughout southern Africa imply that we are seeing only part of a figure and that the rest of it is hidden. In Lesotho there is a well-preserved scene showing the head, neck, front legs and body of an antelope, but not its hind legs. Often when this happens it is simply because the missing part has faded away, but that is not the case here and the depiction is obviously deliberate: 'The painting seems to imply that the rest of the animal is behind the rock face and out of sight,' comments David Lewis-Williams.[86]
- At a site in the North-Eastern Cape, a red-ochre zig-zag line has been painted down the front of the calcite flow. At the top, two white ears have been added to give the impression of an animal's head viewed from the front.[87]
- At Elephant Hunt shelter in the Western Cape a small human

Figures merge with natural features of the rock face

figure is depicted wrapped around a natural ovoid hole in the rock wall.[88] Likewise at Gxalingenwa in KwaZulu-Natal Drakensberg a naturally formed hole in the rock face has been incorporated into a painting of a human figure, serving as its chest and distended abdomen.[89] We saw above how the same technique was used at Niaux to transform another such hole into a deer's head and antlers.

- A deep natural pocket in the rock at a site in the North-Eastern Cape has been smeared black, creating a patch of shadow. Protruding

A mysterious underwater scene composed around a
natural pocket in the rock face (RARI)

out of it the ancient artist painted the upper body of a large antelope-headed therianthrope and a number of other extraordinary creatures. Several swimming fish are present, indicating that this is an underwater scene. We will learn the significance of this 'underwater' or 'river' imagery in later chapters.

A huge serpent, bleeding from the nose, winds through the rock face

- At Barkly East on the Eastern Cape border an astonishing serpent, with two short horns and an antelope-like head that bleeds from the nose, slithers across the rock face.[90] The serpent is quarter of a

metre wide and very long. After almost four metres its body 'disappears' for 40 centimetres behind a natural ridge, then its neck and head reappear on the other side.[91] In the Axial Gallery at Lascaux, the dots between the stag and the horse form a line, described earlier, that enters and leaves the rock face in exactly the same way.

Chimeras

The serpent with horns or tusks and the head of an antelope mentioned above brings to mind another of the mysteries shared by the prehistoric rock art of southern Africa and the art of the European painted caves. Alongside the naturalistic animal figures found in both regions are a number of profoundly *non*-naturalistic depictions of fantastic or chimerical animals that combine parts of several different species, or that are equipped with extra heads, legs or tails, or that are just plain monstrous. Obviously any theory seeking to explain either the European or the southern African art cannot afford to pass such figures by but must be able to account for them. A few examples will be sufficient to give the reader a sense of the problem:

- France, Bara Bahau Cave: a half-horse, half-lion hybrid – with the body of the former and the head of the latter.[92]
- France, Trois Frères: two bears, one with the head of a wolf, one with a bison's tail.[93] Cosquer: an animal with an elongated horse's head and two horns similar to a bison's.[94] Chauvet: a bear/feline/bison.[95] Combarelles: horse with three front legs.

Horse with three front legs from the cave of Les Combarelles (Breuil, 1952)

- South Africa, Heaven Cave, the Karoo: a composite animal, part lion, part antelope.[96]

Heaven Cave, the Karoo: antelope-feline chimera

- France, Pair-non-Pair: the so-called Agnus Dei (Lamb of God), an engraving of an animal with the body of a deer and the heads of both an ibex and a horse.[97] France, Trois Frères: a lion with two heads and two tails.[98]

Trois Frères: lion with two heads and two tails

- South Africa, the Eastern Cape, Chamisso shelter: a lion with two tails.[99] South Africa, Drakensberg: an eland with three hind legs.[100]
- France, Chauvet: a bison with seven legs;[101] a mammoth with three tusks.[102] Italy, Fumane Cave: an unidentified animal with five legs.[103]

Left: two-tailed Chamisso lion; right, mammoth with
three tusks from Chauvet

- South Africa, the Cedarberg, Site 2 on the Sevilla Trail: 'The
  Monsters', paintings in red ochre of three gruesome creatures, two
  with long necks and gaping dinosaur jaws, the third nicknamed 'the
  devil' for its cloven hoofs, spiny back and apparent horns.[104]

'Monsters' of the
Cedarberg

- France, Pergouset Cave: 'The Monsters', an entire room full of
  engravings of bizarre, distorted, 'impossible' animals.[105]

Detail of the 'monsters'
of Pergouset

- South Africa, the Cedarberg, Fallen Rock shelter: an antelope with a monstrous head and gaping jaws; on close examination the head and jaws prove to be formed by an abstract pattern of nested curves and zig-zag lines similar to one of the group of abstract and geometrical signs discussed earlier.[106]

Fallen Rock 'monster'
(after Slingsby, 1997).

- Zimbabwe, near Harare, southern Africa: three monstrous composite creatures with wings, horns and human faces.[107]
- France, Le Portel: a monstrous animal bearing no relationship to any known species.[108] Chauvet: indeterminate mammal with the beak of a large bird.[109] We also saw in Chapter Two that the Combel Gallery of Pech Merle cave contains images of outlandish unclassifiable animals.
- France, Lascaux, the Hall of Bulls: dwarfed by giant aurochs it is easy to miss the fantastic intricacy and elaboration of the antlers of a small group of red deer stags.[110] Also, why does the only image of a reindeer in the cave have webbed feet like a water bird?[111]

Similarities

We may conclude that the cultures that created the ancient cave and rock shelter art of Upper Palaeolithic Europe and of southern Africa held certain rather complex, peculiar and seemingly inexplicable ideas, and expressed these in their paintings, engravings and sculptures:

- People can be part animal, part human and can transform fully into animals.

- Certain people are sometimes impaled by spears, arrows or harpoons when they are transforming into animals.
- Animals can transform into other animals or appear as hybrids of two or more species.
- Distorted-looking animals and utterly unfamiliar monsters exist.
- There are geometric patterns everywhere.
- The rock face is dynamic and permeable, not a blank canvas to be decorated.

Further striking similarities between the prehistoric arts of southern Africa and Europe include a passion for superimposition, with sometimes as many as half a dozen different images overlapping and obscuring each other – apparently scrawled without consideration of the earlier work. Both systems also feature an almost total absence of ground or horizon lines, so that figures seem to float in limitless and directionless space, and both disregard relative scale (so that a creature that is small in reality, like a deer or an antelope, may be shown much bigger than a mammoth or an elephant placed near it). The decorated caves of Upper Palaeolithic Europe and the prehistoric rock

Handprints: southern Africa (left); southwest Europe (right)

shelters of southern Africa both feature large numbers of human handprints.[112] In both cases the same basic palette turns up – red and yellow ochre, black manganese and charcoal – coupled with the same basic suite of painting and engraving techniques. In both southern Africa and Europe, the ancient artists selected for depiction certain very specific animals appropriate to their very different environments while completely ignoring other animal species also present in those environments. In both cases excavations have shown that the animals portrayed were not the animals they hunted.[113] Last but not least, it was unusual in both areas for decorated caves or rock shelters to be lived in. They appear, predominantly, to have been sacred sanctuaries that were rarely visited except for specific ritual purposes.[114]

Explanation

It would be wrong to take any of this to imply that there are *no* differences at all between the Stone Age art of southern Africa and its counterpart in Upper Palaeolithic Europe. On the contrary, there are very important differences. For example, the European art stopped for ever around 12,000 years ago, whereas in southern Africa it continued to be made until just 100 years ago. Another big difference concerns the locations of the art – dark subterranean caves in Europe, well-lit open rock shelters in southern Africa. A third example is that the ancient artists in southern Africa painted huge numbers of human figures – amounting to tens of thousands of individual images, and almost equal to the number of animals depicted. By contrast there are barely more than 100 human figures in all the 300 painted and engraved caves of Europe, and animals are the dominant subject-matter.[115]

But none of this should surprise us, argues Lewis-Williams:

> The differences between southern African San rock art and the temporally and spatially remote west European Upper Palaeolithic art are, after all, to be expected; it is the ways in which the arts resemble one another that are striking and that require explanation.[116]

As my research progressed, I was amazed to discover that dismally little has been achieved to explain anything by more than a century of formal academic study of Upper Palaeolithic art in Europe, and by the parallel study – for almost as long – of the rock art of the San in southern Africa. To be frank, for the first 80 years of the twentieth century, until David Lewis-Williams' radical ideas first began to shake things up, nothing was achieved at all.

That is how it seems to me, anyway. I'll give my reasons in the next chapter.

CHAPTER SIX

The Shabby Academy

In the whole world there are only a few hundred academic specialists who study prehistoric art. The members of this small and tight-knit intellectual community bear a heavy responsibility. In Europe, where their efforts have been sustained for several generations, where they enjoy the full backing of governments, and where funding has always been relatively plentiful, they have seen to it that more than 90 per cent of all the known painted and engraved caves of the Upper Palaeolithic are permanently closed to the public. Of course this is necessary, even unavoidable, if we wish to preserve these special places for the future, but it has practical consequences. It means that the accredited experts, who continue to be able to enter and leave pretty much at will, enjoy a monopoly over basic research. This in turn allows them to control much of the production of knowledge on the subject and ensures that the story our society is told about the caves meets with their approval.

It is not a conspiracy, or anything like one, because we routinely hand control over vital areas of knowledge to limited elites. Take the case of nuclear physicists – to pick one example amongst many. No one is surprised or offended that they should control knowledge about nuclear physics or that they should enjoy privileged access to relevant research facilities from which the public are barred. By the same token, why shouldn't archaeologists keep the keys to the painted caves?

Besides 'the Academy' in this case is far from a monolithic archaeological establishment. Anthropologists are also present in force amongst the leading researchers, plus a smattering of scholars from other disciplines who bring an eclectic breadth and depth to the subject that is missing in most forms of scientific enquiry. In addition, as we'll see later, cave-art specialists are prone to quarrel with one another in the pages of highly regarded academic journals. From the pungent phrases used and the personal tone of some of the attacks, one senses that these are much more than 'friendly disagreements' amongst colleagues, and that, in this field, there is really no such thing as a united front. On the contrary, these unruly prehistorians seethe and boil with territorial rivalries and deeply felt intellectual divisions.

84 years in the wrong direction, 20 more of dithering and inaction

Though no doubt painful for the protagonists, the state of competition amongst prehistorians must be healthy for the search for truth about the caves and for the quality of public information available on the subject. But it is also a very recent phenomenon. There was no significant dissent or disagreement at all during most of the first nine decades of the twentieth century, just two massive intellectual orthodoxies of French-dominated scholarship that smoothly succeeded one another. The first gave way to the second on the death of the Abbé Henri Breuil in 1961; his ideas and immense personality had towered over the study of cave art from its formal inception in 1902. The second fell apart in 1986 immediately after the death of its main proponent, the structuralist prehistorian André Leroi-Gourhan, who had been Breuil's student and who replaced his mentor's ruling theory with one of his own.

When Leroi-Gourhan died, no new ruling personality emerged to take his place and the discipline rapidly collapsed into the state of schism and utter mutual contempt amongst the main camps that defines its behaviour today. The only thing that all of them seem to agree on – looking back on the twentieth century from the vantage point of the twenty-first – is that the intellectual duopoly of Breuil followed by Leroi-Gourhan was more or less a complete waste of time. Certainly these 'great authorities' have a number of technical and clerical achievements to their credit – working out what sorts of pigments were used, counting the number of figures in each cave, etc., etc. But when it comes to furthering our understanding of the *meaning* of the art there is agreement today that Breuil and Leroi-Gourhan's best efforts have proved utterly fruitless and spurious and that in the 84 years that cave art was under their stewardship nothing of real value was achieved at all.

While awarding the modern prehistorians ten out of ten for honesty about their predecessors, I wonder why there haven't been louder public and media yells of impatience and annoyance over this admission. After all, if our governments had given a monopoly position to any other group of scientists to allow them to investigate important matters and they had failed so badly, over nearly a century, to get any worthwhile results, it is almost certain that someone would have objected. Despite the dismal record of the first 84 years, therefore, how are we to explain the fact that the successors of Breuil and Leroi-Gourhan continue to monopolise the caves without facing any objections or having to account for themselves at all? Worse, because their predecessors promoted grand theories that were wrong, the new generation of prehistorians have been permitted to declare a tacit 'moratorium on explanation'[1] that has lasted – with the notable exception of David Lewis-Williams and the growing support that now exists for his theory – from 1986 until the present.

What the moratorium has meant in practice has been a growing emphasis on empirical work, data collection and quantification decoupled from any form of theory – justified on the grounds that when enough data has been amassed the right theory will emerge.[2] To date, however, a theory on which all can agree has not emerged and the only promising contender – David Lewis-Williams' neuropsychological approach – has provoked particularly bitter confrontations.

Seeing Altamira

To understand the promise that Lewis-Williams' work holds for unravelling the mystery of modern human origins, and to make sense of the furore that he has stirred up amongst contemporary prehistorians, we need to look back briefly over what has happened in this field in the past hundred years.

The official 'beginning', it is generally agreed, was 1902, when the Abbé Henri Breuil visited the cave of Altamira in Spain on an expedition led by the eminent French prehistorian Emile de Cartailhac. The two scholars spent a month working inside the cave and emerged to declare that the magnificent art painted on its walls and ceilings was absolutely genuine and belonged to the Palaeolithic period. Only once their patrician seal of approval had been granted did the formal academic study of cave art begin across Europe – with Breuil and Cartailhac naturally amongst its leading lights from the start.

The story has a prequel. Altamira had been investigated, and quickly recognised for what it was, as early as 1879. But thereafter, for reasons that are still difficult to understand, it was denied the proper study that it deserved for 23 years by a cabal of 'sceptical' scholars who used every technique of black propaganda to convince the world that the paintings in the cave were recent and probably forged. The prime movers in this campaign to vilify and discredit Altamira were the imperious Gabriel de Mortillet, a man of a dry, scientific frame of mind – at the time the undisputed doyen of French prehistorians – and, ironically, Emile de Cartailhac, who so much later would be forced to eat his words and vouch for the authenticity of the paintings.

The actual discovery of Altamira took place sometime between 1868 and 1872. The find was made by a tenant farmer, Modesto Cubillas, paid to look out for caves on the estates of local landowner and dedicated amateur archaeologist Marcelino Sanz de Sautuola.[3] Initially Sautuola did not follow up the tip but in 1875 he made a first visit to the cave, explored it and conducted minor excavations within. It was not until 1879, however, on his second visit – fortuitously accompanied by his eight-year-old daughter Maria – that he noticed the extraordinary array of paintings on the Great Polychrome Ceiling for which the cave is today famous. Indeed, as Sautuola himself reported the incident, it was not he but Maria who first spotted the spectacular images of bison and other animals that we now know had been painted there about 14,000 years previously.[4]

Sautuola can hardly be blamed for not seeing the paintings on his first visit. He was a person of his times, as we all are, and came to the cave with the preconceptions of those times. By the 1870s many pieces of portable art (engraved bones, antlers, mammoth ivory, etc.) had been found in a number of different Upper Palaeolithic caves in France and correctly identified as belonging to the prehistoric period.[5] The problem was that nobody imagined for a moment that the same people who had made the small portable pieces could also have been capable of wall and ceiling art on such a grandiose scale as Altamira. So Sautuola was not prepared psychologically to see paintings in the cave and did not see them until his daughter pointed them out.

Principal figures on the Great Polychrome Ceiling at Altamira (Breuil, 1952).

To his lasting credit, however, once the paintings had been brought to his attention he very quickly recognised them for what they were. Through his own research and travels Sautuola was quite familiar with the portable art that had previously been collected from the French caves and knew that many of the pieces were engraved with the figures of Ice Age animals.[6] Now he realised that the animals on the walls and ceilings of Altamira belonged to the same bestiary and shared the same stylistic conventions. From this it followed, if the prehistoric date of the portable art was accepted – which it was – that the Altamira paintings must also belong to the same period.

The logic was impeccable, but when the Spanish amateur archaeologist made his discoveries in Altamira public it got him into deep trouble with the Academy of his day and ultimately ruined his life.

Stupid, petty and shabby

In retrospect, looking back on the whole case, we can see that although Sautuola was absolutely right about the antiquity of the art, he nevertheless made three very big mistakes when he sought to convince the academics of this. The first was being Spanish, the second was finding the cave in Spain, and the third was being an amateur archaeologist.

Stupid and petty as it may seem, the downside of his being Spanish and finding the cave in Spain was that all the pieces of portable Upper Palaeolithic art hitherto recognised had come from France and all the leading authorities on the subject were also French. They had a very definite tendency, perhaps inspired by patriotism or habit – or a bit of both – to respond positively to claims of great antiquity for new sites discovered in France but negatively to rival claims from sites in other countries. When it turned out, in addition, that Sautuola was not a member of the Academy, but an outsider with no qualifications, he was more or less doomed to be crushingly snubbed and ridiculed. What made this fate certain for him, however, was that Altamira began to attract a great deal of attention, and became hugely popular, after he first announced his discoveries there. For a couple of years it was widely hailed in the media as the site of the oldest-known art in the world (as indeed it was then) and was even visited by King Alfonso XII of Spain.[7] This level of exposure and interest infuriated the academics, who resented Sautuola's new-found fame, believing that they alone had the right to introduce prehistoric art to the public and to bathe in whatever kudos might be attached.

So perhaps Altamira's art wasn't prehistoric after all? That was one of many lines of insinuation that were deployed to bring down the intruder. Perhaps it was graffiti left behind by Roman soldiers 2,000 years ago and Sautuola was simply too inexperienced and naïve to tell the difference? Or perhaps the paintings were ingenious modern fakes? If so they had no doubt been intended to make fools of the academic authorities but had ended up only duping poor obsessed Sautuola. Finally, perhaps Sautuola himself was involved in the scam? After all, it was hinted darkly, there could be many motives for manufacturing an archaeological forgery of this magnitude.

The hatchet-job begins

In September 1880 Sautuola published an important, modest, understated paper on his discoveries at Altamira, and his conclusions about the antiquity of the art: *Breves Apuntes Sobre Alguno Objectos Prehistoricos de la Provincia de Santander.*[8] It has gone down in the annals of scholarship as a breakthrough that added something fundamental to human knowledge – the first ever written account of prehistoric cave paintings and, moreover, one that future research would vindicate conclusively. But the truth about the cave – which today would have won a Nobel Prize for Sautuola – was not appreciated by the experts at the time and the wide public circulation of his paper only served to intensify the academic hate campaign that was by then already underway against him.

A further development, also in 1880, came when one of Sautuola's very few and utterly consistent academic supporters, Professor Vilanova y Piera of the University of Madrid, took the case for Altamira's antiquity to the IXth International Congress of Anthropology and Prehistoric Archaeology held in the Portuguese capital of Lisbon. Amongst the many other distinguished participants were Emile de Cartailhac and Gabriel de Mortillet, then the two biggest names in the field.

Vilanova, for his part, was Spain's foremost palaeontologist[9] but because he had chosen to support the work of a despised amateur his presentation at the Congress was shunned and not one of the delegates took up his invitation to go and see Altamira for themselves.[10] Indeed, throughout the whole 'Altamira affair', which lasted 23 years, from 1879 until Breuil and Cartailhac finally bestowed official recognition on the cave in 1902, the vast majority of the academics who were quick to vilify Sautuola's discovery as a worthless hoax never visited the site themselves and based their damning judgements on poor-quality reproductions of the paintings.

Gabriel de Mortillet was typical in this regard and all the more dangerous because his views were so influential. When asked to comment on reproductions of the paintings in May 1881 he rapidly concluded as follows:

Simply by looking at the drawings you sent me in your letters I can see that it is a farce, nothing more than a hoax. They have been done and shown to the whole world so that everyone can have a laugh at the expense of palaeontologists and prehistorians who would believe anything.[11]

It was part of a co-ordinated attack by a man who had opposed the authenticity and significance of the paintings from the outset. That same month in 1881 a devastating report was circulated by the engineer and palaeontologist Edouard Harle who Mortillet and Cartailhac had commissioned to go to Altamira on their behalf. Scholars now think that Harle was so influenced and overawed by the negative views of these two very powerful authorities that he was 'already prejudiced against Altamira before he arrived, and his paper thus concluded to the same effect'.[12] As Miguel Angel García Guinea, Professor of Archaeology at the University of Santander, points out:

The reasons he [Harle] gave against the authenticity of the paintings seem today – seen with our present-day knowledge – lacking in foundation. For example that there would have been traces of smoke on the walls of the cave if they had been painted by prehistoric man, or the supposition that the paint was recent because of its slight fluidity. He also stated that the paintings could in some cases not have been made with anything other than a modern paintbrush.[13]

Many years later, Harle was to admit that his 1881 report on Altamira had been a 'stain' on his scientific reputation.[14] However, despite the glaring weaknesses and absurdities that are obvious in it now, it was enthusiastically endorsed and accepted at the time by the nineteenth-century academic community led by Mortillet whose prejudices it endorsed. The supposed credibility of the report was further reinforced when it appeared in full in the pages of what was then the most influential journal of prehistory in the world, *Matériaux pour l'Histoire Primitive et Naturelle de l'Homme*. Securing publication for Harle's egregious nonsense in a journal of such high standing was not difficult, since the editor was Emile de Cartailhac.[15]

Smear campaign

One of the nastiest, most insidious suggestions in Harle's report is that the paintings of Altamira were modern forgeries of very recent date, most probably completed in the interval between Sautuola's first and second visits to the cave, i.e. between 1875 and 1879.[16] Harle did not bluntly accuse Sautuola of complicity with the supposed forger, but either complicity or extreme naïvety on Sautuola's part was nevertheless clearly implied.

The Spanish press, which previously had fêted Sautuola, now turned against him and a vile public campaign (which today would have ended in a costly libel suit) was mounted to smear his name. It was noted that that Sautuola had a French painter in his employ, a certain Paul Ratier, who never spoke to anyone but was constantly in and out of the cave of Altamira. This was all true. Ratier never spoke because he was mute, and he was constantly in and out of Altamira because Sautuola had employed him to make good copies – for the benefit of other researchers – of the paintings on the Great Polychrome Ceiling.[17] It should have been obvious to everyone that there was nothing untoward about this arrangement. Nonetheless an unscrupulous commentator appeared under the pseudonym of El Parlante who loudly and enthusiastically put two and two together to make five. In sensational tabloid fashion he accused Sautuola of hiring Ratier not just to copy but to forge all the original paintings in the cave.[18] Sautuola challenged El Parlante to 'remove his mask or the pseudonym he hides behind and face the consequences of his statements',[19] but the unprincipled attacks in the newspapers continued.

In 1883 Gabriel de Mortillet published his grand survey of the prehistoric world – *Le Préhistorique*. Since he considered the paintings of Altamira to be a modern hoax – 'a laughing stock, a joke, a disgrace',[20] he naturally made no mention of them.[21]

In 1886, an art expert, Don Alberto Lemus y Olmo, head of Spain's national copper-printing industry, renewed the charges of forgery. After visiting Altamira he wrote: 'I felt an overwhelming disillusion upon seeing the paintings which I had always thought were prehistoric. I felt the coldness of he who has been deceived and hoaxed.' Lemus concluded loftily that the transcendent artworks of Altamira were 'not in the least characteristic of the Stone Age . . . They are merely the expression of a mediocre follower of the Modern School.'[22]

Also in 1886, Emile de Cartailhac published what was then supposedly the definitive book about the 'prehistoric age'. In it he accepted Altamira as a prehistoric site and included reproductions of flints, harpoons, a needle, etc., that had been excavated there, but pointedly made no mention whatsoever of the paintings.[23] It was as though they simply did not exist.

In 1888 Sanz de Sautuola died, broken-hearted and broken-spirited. Following the publication of his monograph on the cave in 1880, as his grandson was much later to recall, the life of the enterprising amateur archaeologist had 'become one of bitterness, reproach and continuous attack'.

> All the great European scientists of the epoch, headed by the Frenchman Mortillet, and with only very few exceptions in Spain . . . fiercely and viciously attacked my grandfather's thesis and accused him of being an imposter.[24]

Sautuola was not the type to shrug such insults off. Understandably he took them to heart. Finally, in his grandson's assessment, it was this sustained, cancerous hostility of the academic elite that 'provoked his premature death in sadness and discouragement'.[25]

The frightening power of preconceived ideas

It is difficult to comprehend how and why highly intelligent scholars like Mortillet and Cartailhac were unable to do what Sautuola did instantly – i.e. make a simple comparison of the images painted on the walls and ceiling of Altamira with the images of Ice Age animals they already knew from prehistoric portable art. What their own testimony suggests is that they were deeply immersed in a world view, derived from the then recently adopted Darwinian theory of evolution, that required Stone Age people to be 'primitive', 'savage', 'ignorant' and 'barbaric'. Since the Altamira paintings were sophisticated and 'modern' (and since, moreover, they were in Spain, where no prehistoric art had hitherto been found), we shouldn't be surprised at the initial negative and sceptical reaction of the experts.

Much more surprising, however, is the way that these same experts, almost to a man, resolutely refused to visit Altamira themselves – while the few who did go were pumped up with so much preconceived opposition to the authenticity of the paintings that nothing they saw was going to change their minds. Looking back on this phenomenon now, modern scholars have concluded that it had much to do with the misuse of evolutionary thinking. According to Professor García Guinea of the University of Santander:

> If the works of art that had been discovered had been primitive, deformed and badly executed, nobody would have put them at odds with the theory of evolution . . . However, it happened to be a refined and perfected art, an art which could easily be compared to contemporary art, to that of Manet and Monet . . . Could it then be believed that these techniques had been conceived and mastered by troglodytes, primitive cavemen, who had not yet discovered the plow?[26]

The idea was an affront to everything that scientists like Mortillet and Cartailhac stood for. 'The discovery of Altamira disturbed the current prehistorical theories,' concludes Professor García Guinea:

> and opened unsuspected perspectives in the understanding of the soul of our remotest forebear. One might even say that Sautuola's mark on the scientific thought of the time was so trenchant that it produced first a commotion of amazement and denial, and then a rapid bound forward, a revolution . . .[27]

That revolution was not brought about by any willing change of heart on the part of the group of scholars who had defamed the great discovery and achievement of Sautuola's life and surrounded him for so long in 'a storm of opposition and inflexible negation'.[28] What happened, instead, was that they were gradually overwhelmed by a remorseless flood of new evidence – in the form of more painted caves – which confirmed Altamira's authenticity.

Volte-face

Nor was the new evidence admitted into court easily. Throughout the 1890s prehistoric caves continued to be discovered or re-explored – now that people knew what to look for – and several turned out to have painted or engraved walls and ceilings. Such caves included Figuier, 1890, La Mouthe, 1895, Marsoulas, 1897,[29] and Les Combarelles and Font de Gaume, 1901.[30] Since they all had the capacity to vindicate Altamira, Cartailhac worked hard to discredit them. As late as 1897, for example, he joined other scholars in mocking suggestions that there were authentic prehistoric paintings in the cave of Marsoulas in the Pyrenees, supporting the argument instead that they were modern and the work of children. He also used his influence as editor of the journal of the Société Archéologique de Midi to suppress evidence on the antiquity of the paintings submitted for publication by local scholar Felix Regnault.[31]

But the tide was turning. At another French cave, Pair-non-Pair (Heads-or-Tails), wall engravings were discovered in 1896 partially buried under Upper Palaeolithic occupation layers – making them at least Upper Palaeolithic in age. By 1898 the elderly Mortillet, in his last published paper before his death, admitted that this was decisive and that Pair-non-Pair obliged him to abandon his long-held opposition to the authenticity of wall art.[32]

Cartailhac doggedly clung on to the old view for a few more years. This must have required some mental gymnastics, or frank dishonesty, since he himself, while excavating at La Mouthe, had scraped away Palaeolithic deposits and exposed part of the painting of an animal securely sealed beneath them on the wall.[33] He kept quiet about that initially. What finally tipped the balance for him, however, was the barrage of new finds of undeniably Upper Palaeolithic wall art at Les Combarelles and Font de Gaume in 1901. 'These discoveries,' comments British archaeologist Paul Bahn, 'together with all that had gone before, finally penetrated Cartailhac's stubbornness.'[34]

The next step, in 1902, was the historic research visit to Altamira with the Abbé Henri Breuil (who, emerging from obscurity, had also assisted Cartailhac with a visit to Marsoulas earlier that same year).[35] At the end of their one-month hands-on study of Altamira we have already seen how the two men declared its previously disgraced paintings to be authentic and of Palaeolithic age.

Such a volte-face as this represented could not go unnoticed and it was obviously necessary for Cartailhac to make some sort of statement about his former position on Altamira. The ugly fact was that he had 'changed his mind only at the last minute when the evidence became overwhelming',[36] and his problem now was to spin this to his advantage. Against all the odds, he did so masterfully before the end of 1902 by publishing an article titled 'Mea Culpa d'un sceptique' in the journal *L'Anthropologie*.[37] In it he admitted disarmingly that he had participated in 'an error, committed for twenty years, an injustice that must be acknowledged and made reparation for publicly . . . For my part I must bow to reality, and render justice to M. de Sautuola.'[38]

It is one of the weird things about the cave-art Academy that to this day it still frequently lauds Cartailhac for his supposed 'honesty', 'courage' and 'integrity' in publishing his *mea culpa* but has lavished little praise or recognition on Sanz de Sautuola, who first saw the truth about Altamira, and brought it to the world's attention, and whom Cartailhac destroyed.[39]

The takeover

Something else remarkable happened after Cartailhac issued his *mea culpa*. He was able to transform himself, literally overnight, from the most bitter opponent of cave art into the revered and respected father figure of the new discipline of cave-art studies. *And nobody thought this was odd.* He even purchased the cave of Marsoulas out of concern for its preservation.[40] Meanwhile, Breuil, who would soon assume absolute control of the discipline, slid quietly into place as his anointed second-in-command.

Keeping in mind the diligence with which Cartailhac had ruined

Sautuola's life and spent nearly quarter of a century mocking and belittling the paintings of Altamira, I was particularly repulsed to discover the content of an interview that this arrogant French academic had given on 6 October 1902. Altamira, he told the newspaper *El Cantabrico*, was 'beautiful and impressive . . . Spain should take pride in protecting it, so that scholars from all over the world will always be able to study it.'[41]

Three days later, on 9 October, Cartailhac wrote to a friend: 'The Abbé Breuil and I wish you were here with us in the cave of Altamira. It is the most beautiful, the strangest, and the most interesting of all the painted caves . . .'[42]

The confident, slightly patronising tone of the first quote, and the almost loving, proprietorial mood of the second speak for themselves. Smoothly and effortlessly, like an easy conquest, the cave that had been delivered to the world by a free-thinking, intuitive amateur had now been possessed, body and soul, by men of a very different temper.

Genuinely bad ideas

Emile de Cartailhac died in 1921 but faded from prominence long before that, allowing his protégé Breuil to take on his mantle. Thus from being dominated by a bigoted, deeply conservative and unimaginative stick-in-the mud, the new discipline passed into the hands of a *maître* (as Breuil's fawning underlings insisted on addressing him)[43] who would prove in many ways to be even more rigid and authoritarian, even more arrogant and self-confident, and thus, if anything, even more inclined to impose his preconceptions on the evidence and distort the truth.

Thereafter generations of French archaeologists slavishly devoted themselves to Breuil's ideas as though they were the word of God.[44] However, every major contribution that he made to the discipline between 1902 and his death 59 years later in 1961 has subsequently been thrown out by modern scholars as utterly worthless, irrelevant and wrong. Nor is this simply a matter of the usual professional bitchiness applied retrospectively to one of the founders of cave-art studies. Breuil's ideas, as well as those of others that he co-opted or supported, were genuinely bad and have long since been refuted by the empirical evidence.

There are not many fields where one can say this about almost the entire output of a scientific discipline for nearly 60 years, but cave-art research is one of them. Still, a brief summary of what people were thinking about in those lost decades will be helpful.

Ideas before Breuil

First, let's not forget that there were ideas before Breuil.

One popular but short-lived theory was that ancient tribes had selected particular animals as their totems and painted them in the caves. Then it was realised that if these were really totemic images, 'one would expect to find homogeneous art centred around a particular animal in each cave (for example the ibex cave, the lion cave, the reindeer cave, etc.), instead of the mixture of species we see at each site'.[45]

The execrable Gabriel de Mortillet, when not furiously assaulting poor Sautuola, advocated another early theory – that the portable art of the caves (and later the wall art when he finally accepted its authenticity) had been made purely for the fun of it, because people liked it, and with no deeper motive.[46] As an arch-Darwinist (and also as the strident anti-clericalist that he is known to have been) it is easy to see why Mortillet promoted this notion of 'art for art's sake'. It meant he need not confront the possibility – which seems to have been inconceivable to him – that our 'primitive' Stone Age ancestors might have had spiritual aspirations or perhaps even possessed something as advanced and sophisticated as a religion.[47]

Unusually, Emile de Cartailhac had disagreed with Mortillet on this, but as the twentieth century got underway, it was Cartailhac's successor Breuil who was to demonstrate conclusively that 'art for art's sake' could not possibly be the correct explanation. Together with other scholars such as Capitan and Salomon Reinach, he pointed out a number of simple but fatal flaws in the theory.[48] For example, how could this be art for the sheer aesthetic pleasure of the thing when so many cave paintings and engravings were made directly on top of

Compositions such as this one at Trois Frères, where huge numbers of figures are superimposed directly over other figures in a confused tangle of images, convinced experts that whatever else the cave artists were doing it was not 'art for art's sake' (Breuil, 1952).

earlier paintings and engravings? In many sites one could find places where dozens of different figures were superimposed on one another so densely that the final effect was almost a meaningless scrawl – even when clean panels of rock face were available nearby that had never been decorated. Another uncomfortable fact – capable on its own of falsifying the theory – was the presence of paintings and engravings in the deepest, darkest and most remote parts of the caves. If this was art for art's sake, then what was the point of putting so many spectacular images where hardly anyone would ever have the chance even to see them, let alone enjoy them?

Hunting magic

Obviously some other motive must have been at work, and Breuil was the most senior and influential of those who proposed 'hunting magic' as the solution to the mystery, and through whose influence it rapidly became dogma.[49] According to this theory, the paintings and engravings had not after all been made for frivolous aesthetic reasons but to aid the serious economic quest for the 'cave man's' daily needs. Writing in 1929, Breuil's colleague Count Begouen (the owner of Trois Frères) simply expressed what was by then the well-established conventional wisdom when he explained that 'he [the cave man] hoped through pictorial representation to augment his power over the beasts he hunted, just as many primitive peoples do to this day'.[50]

In this new orthodoxy of hunting magic, now safely under the aegis of 'the Pope of Prehistory' (as Breuil was sometimes affectionately, but tellingly nicknamed),[51] the same narrow ideas were recirculated, without significant development, innovation or challenge, for several decades. To give an example of the theory in action, hunting-magic proponents explained the well-known use of the relief of the cave wall by the ancient artists as a device to ensure that the animals depicted were not simply two-dimensional but were so far as possible 'doubles' of the animals to be hunted – because 'the man who possesses the image actually has some power over the creature'.[52] Another favourite argument was that the quadrangular window and grid signs which are so common in the caves – often intermingled with the animal figures, as we have seen – must be depictions of prehistoric snares or traps, while 'the round dots in black or red, arranged along the walls in lines, circles, or scattered irregularly . . . represent numbers of stones to be used as projectiles'.[53] Last but not least, Breuil pointed to the paintings and engravings, which he claimed were numerous, showing animals pierced by arrows and spears. Self-evidently these were hunting scenes and therefore further proof that hunting magic was the true purpose of cave art.[54]

It took Breuil's death in 1961, and the succession of Leroi-Gourhan, before the hunting-magic theory was dropped definitively, for reasons that we will consider below. Meanwhile, Breuil's other big idea – which was co-opted and superseded, but not outright abandoned after his death – had to do with the supposed evolution and development of cave art over long periods. After much painstaking work he felt able to identify two successive cycles, the 'Aurignaco-Périgordian' and the 'Solutreo-Magdalenian', each of which, at different stages in the Upper Palaeolithic:

had progressed from simple to complex forms, starting with 'primitive' or archaic figures, and leading on to more complex and detailed images.

149

There was an overall progression from schematic to naturalistic and finally degenerate forms.[55]

Breuil is dead; long live Leroi-Gourhan

In retrospect, it is difficult to understand how anyone as intelligent and as deeply acquainted with prehistoric art as Breuil could have held on to such an easily refuted idea as hunting magic for so long.

For example, if this is really what it was all about, one would expect to see a correspondence, even a close correlation, between species depicted in the caves and the species that archaeological excavations have proved people were eating in the vicinity. But Leroi-Gourhan's statistical studies following Breuil's death showed that the correlation was extremely poor and that 'species percentages in depictions rarely correspond to those in animal bones'.[56] Lascaux provides a typical case in point: reindeer were the main item on the menu, contributing by far the largest number of bones found, but there is only one reindeer image in the cave (and, as we've seen, it has webbed feet like a duck!).[57] Reindeer were also the main food item around the cave of Villars, but none at all were depicted there. And at Pair-non-Pair, although the ibex is the most frequently painted animal, its bones are not present in the archaeological layers.[58]

Another fatal issue for the theory was Breuil's claim that spears or other projectiles could be seen sticking into many of the images.[59] Leroi-Gourhan's analysis showed this to be spurious. While some caves like Niaux do have quite a number of images that could be interpreted that way,[60] a broader survey reveals that just 3 to 4 per cent of Palaeolithic animal figures have 'missiles' anywhere on or near them.[61] Bison are the most 'pierced' species, but even in their case the figure is less than 15 per cent.[62] Moreover, there are many caves in which no pierced species are shown at all.[63] None of this supports the hunting-magic thesis – which would predict a majority of animals 'marked with "arrows" or wounds';[64] on the contrary, it suggests strongly that some other explanation must be sought for the relatively few images of piercing or wounding that do exist (which we know are not confined to animals, but include human and therianthropic figures as well).

So, after 50 years' service as the only explanation that serious people could accept, the hunting-magic theory was suddenly worthless and discredited. Quite rightly, Leroi-Gourhan retained nothing of it from Breuil. What he did hold on to, however, was the essence of his mentor's other theory, according to which a suitably trained expert could classify the art of the caves into a series of stylistic phases arranged along a continuum from simple to ever more complex and ultimately decadent forms.

In addition Leroi-Gourhan is remembered for his structuralist theory of cave art – the new dominant orthodoxy from the mid-1960s until his death in 1986 – according to which every cave was laid out to a secret grand design that researchers might hope to unravel by intense statistical study of every known painting and engraving. In this he was closely supported by and identified with another high-ranking researcher of the period, Annette Laming-Emperaire (1917–78). Amongst other things, she was responsible for the completely useless idea (because impossible to prove or disprove, and basically just her opinion) that depictions of horses in the caves represented the abstract concept of 'femaleness' while bison represented 'maleness'.[65] Later she abandoned this herself and proposed instead that tribes, and the structure of society, together with creation myths were at the root of the art.[66] But since we can know nothing about tribes, the structure of society, or creation myths in the Upper Palaeolithic this was yet another untestable academic whimsy based on nothing at all.

Leroi-Gourhan's obsessional fantasies

Laming-Emperaire also argued that engravings and paintings in the caves should be studied as planned compositions that were part of an overall design and had not been painted 'one at a time, according to the needs of the hunt'.[67] She advocated rigorous data-collection using distribution maps that would show 'position of the works in a cave, associated archaeological remains, signs of use, and content or form of representation'.[68] It was this scheme, broadly speaking, that Leroi-Gourhan adopted as the basis of his own elaborate programme of research,[69] and what it revealed, he argued, was indeed the planned and structured grouping of images, 'with a place for everything and everything in its place',[70] that Laming-Emperaire suspected.[71]

Geometrical forms were no longer to be seen as weapons and traps, but as meaningful signs that were a counterpart to the animal images. The images were to be viewed as mythograms, and their structure could be revealed in the same way as that of myths recounted by living ethnographic informants.[72]

All of it, of course, was unmitigated nonsense. For example, Leroi-Gourhan counted the number of figures of each species of animal in 66 caves and divided them arbitrarily into four different groups (horses, reindeer and hinds in the first group; bison and aurochs in the second; deer, ibex, mammoths and some other animals in the third; bears, felids and rhinos in the fourth).[73] Rather after the fashion of Laming-Emperaire, he assigned gendered symbolism to the first two groups – horses, reindeer and hinds represented 'maleness', he insisted; bison and aurochs represented 'femaleness'.[74] As a final piece of obsessional madness, he divided each cave into four zones – entrance, central area, side chambers and dark ends – and then established what proportion of which groups of animals was found in each zone. From all this the *maître* (Breuil's old title that Leroi-Gourhan had now acquired)[75] sublimated a grand theory, set to become the new prehistoric dogma of its times, that there existed 'an ideal or standard layout to which the topography of each cave was adapted as far as possible'.[76]

In other words, these caves (like modern churches in which there is also an ideal or standard layout for the sacred art) were 'organised sanctuaries' conforming to the blueprint of the religion that lay behind them.[77]

The problems with this superficially attractive scheme are too many to recount here, but two are fundamental. First, the decision to lump particular animals together in groups (e.g. the deer/ibex/mammoth group) was taken by Leroi-Gourhan on the basis of purely subjective criteria; there is no evidence that the cave artists saw any such 'groupishness' connecting these different species. Equally, the zoning of the caves was also arbitrary and it is most unlikely that the ancients shared Leroi-Gourhan's sense of space and how it should be divided up. So what we have here amounts to little more than speculation piled upon fantasy and then treated for a couple of decades as though it were a serious academic theory. Little wonder, as Paul Bahn wryly observes in a recent review of the whole débâcle, that 'Leroi-Gourhan sometimes had to adopt bizarre itineraries within caves in order for his scheme to fit – even going to the wall furthest from the entrance to find the "first series" of big signs, and then coming back again.'[78]

The second fundamental problem with Leroi-Gourhan's notion that the layout of the art in the caves reflects an underlying blueprint has to do with the character of the art itself. As we have seen in previous chapters, these amazing paintings and engravings are nothing if not spontaneous and opportunistic. In very many cases their location is determined by the presence of suitable natural features in the cave wall – a small flint nodule becomes a bison's eye, a flow of calcite becomes a mammoth's trunk, etc., etc. – that could not possibly have been accommodated in such intricate detail if a pre-existing scheme were involved.

An additional major weakness that undermines the theory is the extent to which it relies on the relative frequency of appearance of different animal species in cave art as a whole. As well as being based from the start on a sample of 66 caves (rather than on all caves), this made it susceptible to major new discoveries featuring animals in different frequencies – e.g. a cave such as Chauvet, discovered in 1994, that turned out to contain more depictions of rhinos than all other known Upper Palaeolithic caves put together.[79]

Refuting everything

As noted earlier, Leroi-Gourhan's other main contribution to this field was his developmental chronology – an elaboration and refinement of Breuil's 'evolutionary' scheme according to which suitably trained investigators could classify the paintings and engravings into a series of stylistic phases or stages. Style I was supposed to be the oldest, between 40,000 and roughly 25,000 years ago, characterised by crude, stiff figures placed only in daylight settings of caves and shelters. Style II, between 25,000 and 20,000 years ago, featured much more pleasing representations of animals – clearly an improvement although still a little crude – that were again restricted to daylight areas. Style III, 20,000–15,000 years ago, ventured into the darker parts of caves and introduced some of the strange-looking animals like the horses with disproportionately small heads at Pech Merle. Only in Style IV, after 15,000 years ago and near the end of its very long story, did cave art reach its full fruition with penetration of the deepest, darkest sanctuaries and elaboration of the fullest, most mature paintings and engravings.[80]

'The basis of this endeavour,' points out the Australian rock-art expert Robert Bednarik:

> was the assumption that researchers possessed the ability to readily identify those variables of the art that determined the stylistic conventions of particular cultures. It was never satisfactorily explained why the researchers should have these abilities, how they had acquired them, and how one would define and test them.[81]

An even bigger problem for Leroi-Gourhan's chronology was its basis in evolutionary ideas which presumed a progression from early, crude and primitive daubings to ever more advanced and sophisticated works of art.[82] Subsequent direct dating was to prove him far wrong on some of his specific stylistic attributions – e.g. the small-headed horses at Pech Merle date from more than 24,000 years ago, not from less than 20,000 years ago as he thought.[83] But the discovery that would finally bring the entire edifice tumbling down was – once again – Chauvet Cave.

Quite simply, everything about it refutes the *maître*'s theory. For instance, lions and rhinos occupy positions of great importance on Chauvet's main, centrally located panels, yet if Leroi-Gourhan was right these species should only have been found elsewhere – the lions should have been either in the entrance or in an obscure position at the end of the cave.[84] Even more damaging, however – indeed, conclusively so – was the simple fact that Chauvet's art was 32,000 years old and yet was clearly every bit as advanced and sophisticated as the much later masterpieces like Lascaux dating from less than 20,000 years ago.[85] Clearly an evolutionary scheme that required only crude daubings 32,000 years ago could not stand in the face of such evidence, and as Jean Clottes puts it today: 'Leroi-Gourhan's theories are no longer tenable after Chauvet.'[86] Likewise, Robert Bednarik concludes that as a consequence of Chauvet and other evidence, 'all evolutionary stylistic schemas of Palaeolithic rock art formulated in the course of the entire 20th century must now be regarded as squarely refuted'.[87]

Southern Africa didn't escape

The setback to human knowledge caused by the theories of Breuil and Leroi-Gourhan also had ramifications outside Europe. Well into the 1980s, it is noteworthy how much of the research into the Stone Age rock art of southern Africa continued to be deeply influenced by Leroi-Gourhan's elaborate but useless and irrelevant structuralist ideas. This led to the pursuit of a great many red herrings and had a tendency – as it did in France – to suppress original and innovative thinking by scholars who were too much in awe of the *maître*'s reputation.

Perhaps one of the reasons Leroi-Gourhan's scheme was so eagerly taken up by researchers in southern Africa was that the intellectual ground had already been prepared by that earlier *maître*, the Abbé Breuil, who had spent several years there during World War II as an exile from Nazi-occupied France. On his say-so, a prehistoric San bushman painting in Namibia was attributed to Phoenician explorers – since the ancestors of the bushmen were considered to be too primitive to have produced such a transcendent work of art (supposedly being capable only of 'hideous little figures').[88] To add insult to injury, Breuil also insisted that the figure – which he dubbed the 'White Lady of the Brandenberg' – had a Mediterranean profile and was white-skinned.[89]

The racist and pseudoscientific underpinning of this approach should be obvious, but what is remarkable is how long other scholars were prepared to accommodate it. Close examination at any time would have shown them what we know now – namely that the White Lady is in fact a man, complete with a penis, is certainly *not* a Phoenician in profile but resembles tens of thousands of other bushman images, and carries a bow and arrow that are distinctively those of a bushman. As to the white colour of the figure's legs, David Lewis-Williams and his colleague Thomas Dowson point out that the bushmen rock artists often used colour unrealistically and that white figures – most of them clearly bushmen – abound in their art. Moreover, the realism of this painting was already called into question by another detail of the composition that Breuil ignored (because his theory had no way of explaining it). Just above the so-called White Lady there is an antelope with human hind legs.[90]

The void

By the start of the 1990s, with Breuil's mad ideas long gone, Leroi-Gourhan's structuralist 'grand schemes' abandoned, and a voluntary 'moratorium on explanation' already in place since 1986, cave and rock-art scholarship in both Europe and southern Africa entered what Lewis-Williams describes as 'an interpretive void'.[91]

Most researchers, recognising the climate of the times, simply concentrated their energies on empirical work and data-gathering. As noted earlier, the hope was that eventually, from a sufficient mass of data, a good new theory would emerge. Meanwhile others like Lewis-Williams argued that there was already quite enough data. What was needed was a new way of looking at it – and in various shapes and forms, despite the moratorium, a number of investigators have continued to propose theories that attempt to do just that.

Unfortunately, however, the character of explanation offered is in every case unappealing, bloodless and, worse still, brings us no nearer to understanding what the art means. I have in mind here the so-called theory of Cambridge archaeologist Anne Sieveking, who sought an explanation for the art in terms of territorial and social divisions that she felt arose in south-west Europe during the Ice Age as a consequence of seasonally shifting settlement.[92] Clive Gamble, Professor of Archaeology at the University of Southampton, likewise proposes a social basis for the art and suggests that the stimulus for its appearance in the late Upper Palaeolithic was provided by certain 'changes in the amount and kind of information needed by Palaeolithic societies'.[93]

No doubt the social and economic matrix surrounding the art is of interest and worthy of investigation, but is it really likely that we're going to get inside the mental world of the artists this way or grasp the meaning of their work? Certainly some scholars think so, but many others do not, and the end result, as anthropologists Olga Soffer and Margaret Conkey admit, is that: 'A century of study . . . has not produced a definitive theory about this "art", but rather has brought forth a number of conflicting claims.'[94]

Paul Bahn agrees: 'Since the death of André Leroi-Gourhan in 1986, no new all-embracing theory has been put forward for Palae-olithic art, or at least none by anyone who is well-acquainted with the data and which, therefore, can be taken seriously.'[95]

The deep problems of Humanity . . .

Bahn himself clearly shares the opinion of the growing number of specialists – for he cites them approvingly – who 'abandon any serious attempt at interpretation as a waste of effort'.[96] But if this is so, and if many of the big names studying cave art today just want to concentrate on what are basically counting and filing tasks, then I'm not sure that any further extension of their monopoly over the caves is justified. Whatever these amazing and numinous places meant to the people of the Upper Palaeolithic – and we definitely don't know yet – we can all agree that they are a precious heritage and legacy for humanity. Those academics presently enjoying privileged access to this legacy do indeed bear a heavy responsibility when they keep the rest of us out so that they can study in peace. It is thus absolutely infuriating, and an insult, to discover that they and their predecessors, who achieved nothing in the twentieth century, now make a virtue of giving up 'any serious attempt at interpretation' and plan to spend the twenty-first century counting every dot and squiggle in the caves.

True, we don't know yet what the art meant to the people of the Upper Palaeolithic, but this is not something we should just give up on. Moreover, if the task really is impossible – which I don't believe for a moment – and since it seems to be amply demonstrated that the academics can't use the caves well, then perhaps these wonderful and transformative spaces should be reclaimed for some sacred purpose? The questions raised by the art of Upper Palaeolithic Europe touch directly on the mysterious origin of our humanity – which we sense very strongly is at least as much our own business as it is the business of specialists and experts. I think that many of us would agree with Professor Miguel García Guinea of the University of Santander that:

> The images are of hieratic profundity, full of religious force, and thus can clearly be classified as Sacred Art, the first in the history of humanity. Works such as Altamira or Niaux surpass the label of a simple work of art and must be seen and valued from the point of view of philosophy and the deep problems of Humanity.[97]

Perhaps it is because David Lewis-Williams succeeds in valuing the ancient images from precisely this point of view, touching on the enigmas of our consciousness and the essence of what it is to be human, that his neuropsychological theory stands out head and shoulders above all other attempts to explain cave art. It was to respect that theory, and test it as far as I could, that I undertook my experiments with ibogaine and ayahuasca and my journeys to the caves of France and Spain and the rock-art sites of southern Africa. In particular I would say that I was intrigued and challenged by the questions that David Lewis-Williams posed: Could the prehistoric artists have been hallucinating and painting their visions? And was it possible that such practices could lie at the foundation of art and religion, the most exalted achievements of mankind?

CHAPTER SEVEN

Searching for a Rosetta Stone

The evolution of anatomically modern humans – *Homo sapiens sapiens* – was a late event in the 4.5 billion-year story of the Earth. We will recall that the oldest modern human skeletons so far known to archaeologists are from Ethiopia and date to just 196,000 years ago.[1] These direct ancestors of ours were at first found exclusively in Africa. For a very long time their behaviour was indistinguishable from other earlier (and smaller brained) hominid species. We find it hard to recognise anything they did as being definitively 'us'.

Between about 100,000 and 50,000 years ago, the evidence occasionally lights up with precocious hints of the revolution in behaviour that is to come. In Chapter Two I cited the example of Chris Henshilwood's excavations at Blombos Cave in South Africa. From deposits dated to around 77,000 years ago, Blombos has yielded the earliest piece of abstract art in the world – a small ochre slab engraved with a cross-hatched grid – and the oldest example of personal ornamentation in the world in the form of a necklace of seashells. Around the same time anatomically modern humans, looking just like us, were beginning to leave traces of their presence outside Africa, apparently even mastering the open-ocean sailing skills needed to get them to Australia.

Somewhere between 50,000 and 40,000 years ago, personal ornaments and items of portable art, previously known only from rare examples in Africa, began to turn up in Europe where they had never been seen before, along with the first signs of the presence of anatomically modern humans. The archaeological record testifies to the subsequent rapid multiplication of *Homo sapiens sapiens*, as well as proof of our characteristic penchant for personal adornment, from as far east as Bulgaria to as far west as El Castillo Cave in Spain – where modern human occupation layers have been dated to 42,000 years ago.[2] Many other lifestyle changes are also witnessed in the record, but it is this sudden, widespread and sustained appearance of complex symbolic objects and images that warns us of a momentous shift now underway in the character and condition of humanity.

It is a shift that concerns anatomically modern humans *exclusively*. The archaeological record shows our cousins the Neanderthals, with whom we do not ever seem to have interbred,[3] going into a long and catastrophic decline after our arrival in Europe, culminating in their total extinction by around 27,000 years ago.[4] Despite some evidence of imitation very late in the day,[5] not a single uncontested and original Neanderthal carving, sculpture, art object, painting or intentional engraving has come down to us from the entire period, 200,000 years long, when *Homo neanderthalensis* was the only kind of human being in Europe.[6] The possibility that firm evidence of Neanderthal symbolism might eventually be turned up by excavators cannot be entirely ruled out, but if it ever existed, the absolute paucity of its traces in the European archaeological record tells us already that it was never a big part of the Neanderthal way of life. By contrast, having been entirely absent from the European stage in all previous periods, *Homo sapiens sapiens* seems to have arrived out of Africa less than 50,000 years ago and has left for us not only a treasure trove of beautiful and effective stone, bone and ivory tools, but also – as we know – thousands of art objects and the crowning glory of the painted caves.

The oldest items of personal adornment so far discovered in Europe are from Bulgaria and are dated to between 46,000 and 42,000 years old. They include a bear incisor tooth, and a fox canine tooth, both drilled to be worn as pendants, and a facsimile of a red-deer tooth sculpted from deer antler.[7] By approximately 35,000 years ago the earliest figurative art to have survived anywhere in the world was painted at Fumane Cave in northern Italy, and by 32,000 years ago the magnificent underground cathedral of Chauvet had been decorated. We've seen that the earliest surviving examples of figurative art from Africa – the paintings from Apollo-11 Cave in Namibia – date from 27,000 years ago. Other equally ancient paintings and engravings have been found as far afield as Australia.[8] Clearly we have no choice but to conclude, notwithstanding the undeniable evidence of a slow, piecemeal build-up of human abilities from 100,000 years ago or earlier, that some sort of 'critical mass' was reached after 50,000 years ago leading to the birth of the phenomenon that we call modern culture.

Rosetta Stone

For reasons that are by no means clear, this critical-mass event seems to have begun a little earlier in Europe than in some other regions and must already have been well launched by the time of those Bulgarian drilled pendants around 42,000 years ago. Its greatest and most enduring expressions, however, spanning the immense period from 35,000 years ago down to about 12,000 years ago, were the painted and engraved caves of Italy and Franco-Cantabria. These are surely the ultimate proof of the unprecedented change mankind was then passing through all over the world. Yet the huge and complex body of work that the cave artists left behind in Europe – with its amazing geometrical and animal figures, its sinuous interaction with the rock face, its curious affinities to the generally much later bushman art of southern Africa, and its astonishing 23,000-year lifespan stretching back into deepest prehistory – can often seem so alien and remote as to be incomprehensible to us. When in addition we take into account the more mysterious apparitions in the cave art – its wounded men, its therianthropes, its monsters – it seems even less likely that we can ever hope to extract its meaning. We turn in desperation to the experts, the great scholars who have monopolised the production of knowledge in this field for a century, in the sure and certain expectation that they at least must have got to the heart of the matter. As we saw in Chapter Six, however, everything they thought they knew has turned out to be wrong and now large numbers of their successors make a virtue of either ridiculing or evading all attempts to enquire into the meaning of the art they are charged with studying.

This is a most unfortunate waste of time and a distraction from the investigation of the enigmatic change that overtook our species less than 50,000 years ago and made us what we are today. In particular, no thought whatsoever seems to have been given to the possibility that cave art itself, habitually viewed as part of the mystery, might also contain the clues to its solution.

Even to begin to explore so radical an idea we would need some kind of Rosetta Stone or cryptographic key that could unlock the meaning of the art. Since the grand schemes of Breuil and Leroi-Gourhan collapsed, large numbers of scholars have regarded it as anathema to suppose that any such key exists or could ever be found. We saw in the last chapter how the definition of the research task has been reduced and narrowed until – for perhaps as many as half of all cave-art specialists – it has become a stark matter of neutral data-collection devoid of theory.

David Lewis-Williams has taken a refreshingly different and independent line on this matter – as first became evident during the period following Leroi-Gourhan's death in 1986. Everyone else had declared a moratorium on explanation, but the South African scholar was busy elaborating the new theory that he and Thomas Dowson would soon jointly present to a sceptical academic community in a controversial article, 'The Signs of All Times', published in 1988 in the prestigious academic journal *Current Anthropology*.[9] Stated bluntly, the fundamental claim of that article is that a Rosetta Stone to decode European Upper Palaeolithic cave art does in fact exist, but lies concealed in a place where we would least expect to find it – deep inside our own minds.

Bringing the right pieces of information together

Great ideas rarely shoot up out of nowhere with no softening of the ground first. The 'neuropsychological theory' of cave art is not an exception. It is most unlikely that David Lewis-Williams would have formulated it at all if he had not prepared himself for a long time in advance through the chance acquisition of exactly the sorts of information he would need to put it together. What he brought to the subject was an open and innovative approach, but what impelled him towards the theory was his extensive first-hand knowledge of Upper Palaeolithic European cave art and of the prehistoric rock art of the San in southern Africa, his recognition of the many puzzling similarities between the two, his deep dissatisfaction with the state of research on both continents – particularly its collapse into 'neutral' data-collection – and his rejection of the defeatist view that no explanations of the art are possible.

All of this on its own, however, would have counted for nothing if Lewis-Williams had not also possessed three other vital pieces of information.

First, in the 1970s, in pursuit of greater understanding of San rock art, he began an in-depth study of ethnographic records compiled by nineteenth-century scholars in South Africa. Based on extensive interviews with bushmen elders in the decades immediately before their culture became extinct, these records of a lost mythology shed a wholly unexpected light on the art of the San and completely transformed Lewis-Williams' perspective on the scale of the mystery.

Secondly, because his personal research interests had taken him that way, it so happened that he knew about some interesting and unusual work done in the 1970s with indigenous Indian tribes in the Amazon rain forest. Undertaken by the Colombian anthropologist Gerardo Reichel-Dolmatoff, this was a landmark investigation into shamanism and the use of hallucinogenic plants. It too would contribute several vital building blocks to the evolution of Lewis-Williams' theory, and it put him, quite naturally as we will see, on the trail of the third bit of information he would need. Accumulated by scientists in many different countries over a large part of the twentieth century, this was a body of data focused on what neuropsychologists call 'altered states of consciousness' (ASCs) and anthropologists generally refer to as 'trance states'.[10]

ASCs and how to get into them

I will be using the terms 'altered states of consciousness', 'altered consciousness', 'ASCs', 'trances' and 'trance states' interchangeably in the pages that follow, as I have done in earlier chapters, and will take this opportunity to emphasise that I mean the same thing by them. The reader should also keep in mind that alterations of consciousness can be and routinely are achieved through the use of a wide range of very different techniques.

Amongst the dwindling numbers of traditional peoples still adhering to that ancient form of spirituality known as shamanism – in which practitioners deliberately cultivate trance states – the ritual consumption of psychoactive plants is by far the most common means used to alter consciousness. According to anthropologist Michael Ripinsky-Naxon:

> The majority of shamans throughout the world . . . depend on some kind of psychoactive substance in their repertoire. This ethnographic fact represents a genuine aspect of shamanism. Hallucinogenic experiences during shamanistic seances constitute the key religious expression for such a society.[11]

As we recall, that's the way it is done across the Amazon basin; there the hallucinations seen in trances induced by ayahuasca and other psychoactive brews, snuffs and smokes are of fundamental importance in the shamanistic religions still surviving both in the cities and in the remotest tribal reservations. In the rain forests of Africa, that's the way it is done amongst the Bwiti with their consumption of iboga, 'the plant that enables men to see the dead'. That's the way it was done amongst the Aztecs and Maya of Central America – with mushrooms and psychoactive water lilies and Morning Glory seeds – before the Spanish conquest imposed Christianity upon them.[12] That's the way it is still done by members of the Native American Church in the United States who have won a legal exemption to consume peyote, a powerful hallucinogenic cactus, in order to induce the visions that are central to their religious life.[13]

Although the use of hallucinogens is ancient and widespread, a number of shamanic cultures have explored and developed effective alternative means to enter altered states of consciousness – often in areas where psychotropic plants do not exist or have not been identified. As Arnold M. Ludwig, one of the most respected scientists in this field, points out: 'ASCs may be produced in any setting by a wide variety of agents or manoeuvres.' Amongst these, as well as 'the administration of numerous pharmacological agents', he lists: 'the absolute reduction of sensory input, the change in patterning of sensory data, or constant exposure to repetitive monotonous stimulation'; 'excitatory mental states resulting primarily from sensory overload or bombardment, which may or may not be accompanied by strenuous physical activity or exertion'; 'mental states which appear to result primarily from focused or selective hyperalertness'; and 'mental states which appear to occur mainly as a result of what might be described as a "passive state of mind" . . . [i.e.] mystical, transcendental, or revelatory states'.[14]

From this list of techniques, which also includes dehydration, sleep deprivation and hyperventilation,[15] it is possible to recognise a number of the well-established routes other than plant drugs that shamans in different parts of the world use to induce trance.

To give just a few examples here, the Sun Dance of the Native American Lakota tribe involves agonising body piercing – Ludwig would no doubt call it 'sensory overload' – by means of which participants plunge themselves into deeply altered states of consciousness and attain visions.[16] Amongst the Saora of Orissa in north-west India it is music built around a pentatonic scale that does the trick[17] – the out-of-body journeys to the 'underworld' made by Saora shamans provide a classic example of the mental effects of 'repetitive monotonous stimulation'.[18] Similarly, Magar shamans in Nepal use drums and bells to induce the altered states of consciousness in which they believe that their souls travel to the spirit world,[19] and in some parts of tribal south-east Asia anthropologists have observed that 'shamans may enter trance by rhythmically swishing a handful of rice in a winnowing fan'.[20]

Last but not least, in the extinct culture of the San bushmen of southern Africa – a primary focus of our attention here – an arduous form of dance leading to dehydration and hyperventilation was the preferred trance vehicle. In all cases, just as though the participants had consumed a powerful hallucinogen, the altered states of consciousness induced by these non-drug techniques were and are sought out because of the visionary experiences that they afford – in other words because they unleash floods of extraordinary hallucinations.

The mystery of the universal patterns

It is here that what is known about shamans' visions – whether induced by drugs or other techniques – begins to dovetail neatly, and to the advantage of David Lewis-Williams' evolving theory, into what neuropsychologists have learnt by deliberately inducing altered states of consciousness in human volunteers under modern laboratory conditions. Some trials use entirely new, non-shamanic, methods such as direct electrical and electromagnetic stimulation of the brain. Sensory deprivation, strobing lights and other techniques have also been tried out with varying success. But most often, for obvious reasons of efficiency, the neuropsychologists devising these studies have resorted to the rapid and certain route to trance offered by the extracted active ingredients of plant hallucinogens – notably mescaline, derived from the peyote cactus, psilocybin, derived from widely distributed psilocybin mushroom species, and LSD – a hallucinogen synthesised from the psychoactive fungus ergot.[21]

Over the course of many such experiments a very curious fact has become apparent. At some stages of the visionary experience subjects in laboratory tests report seeing displays of specific kinds of abstract geometrical patterns. What is interesting is the evidence that such patterns are universal and culture-free. Once we have entered a state of consciousness that has been altered deeply enough – itself a universal neurological capacity of the human race – it seems that everyone, everywhere, experiences visions containing very much the same combinations of patterns and shapes. Since these 'form constants', 'phosphenes' or 'entoptics', as they are variously known, will be seen in altered states of consciousness by German bankers and Amazonian hunter-gatherers alike, the very strong implication is that they are not the products of our cultural backgrounds but must in some way be hard-wired into the human nervous system as part of the evolutionary package of being who and what we are.

Scientists are close to certain that neither the average size of our brains nor their basic wiring (to stick with that rather restrictive metaphor) has changed at all in the last 50,000 years (or even within the longer span of 196,000 years that have passed since the earliest anatomically modern humans identified by archaeologists lived in Africa). David Lewis-Williams was the first to realise that this tells us something important we might not previously have considered about the anatomically modern *Homo sapiens sapiens* cave artists of Upper Palaeolithic Europe. Though separated from us by tens of thousands of years, they would have had the capacity to enter altered states of consciousness just as we do. Once in such states, again just as we do, they would have seen those universal, culture-free, hard-wired visionary shapes and patterns that the neuropsychologists call entoptic phenomena, phosphenes or form constants.

For reasons that will become clear in the next chapter, all this was to have the greatest importance for the development of David Lewis-Williams' ideas.

Walking the walk

At first sight the differences between European Upper Palaeolithic cave art and the rock art of the San in southern Africa seem overwhelming; but we saw in Chapters Four and Five that there are in fact many striking similarities. The presence in both arts of the same kinds of abstract geometrical patterns – nets, ladders, quadrilaterals, zig-zag lines, nested curves, spider's webs, honeycombs, etc., etc. – is particularly noteworthy and unexplained. So, too, is the combination of these patterns with apparently naturalistic figures of humans and animals – again a distinctive feature of both arts. Then, as we've seen, there are other mysterious commonalities. For example, both treat the rock face as a dynamic part of the art; both make frequent use of multiple superimpositions; both lack horizon or ground lines so that figures often seem to float; both disregard scale; both contain images of weird monsters and hybrid animals; both depict clearly non-naturalistic wounded men; and both feature therianthropes.

Thanks to special arrangements made for him by André Leroi-Gourhan, David Lewis-Williams first visited a number of the Upper

Palaeolithic painted caves in south-west Europe in 1972. By this point he had already devoted five years of his academic life to the exploration of San rock-art sites across southern Africa, with a particular focus on the Drakensberg region.[22] He admits that the principal influence on him and other South African researchers at that time was the structuralist school of Leroi-Gourhan and Annette Laming-Emperaire. In line with the outlook and methods of this school, Lewis-Williams' approach, and that of his colleagues, involved massive amounts of data-collection built around a framework of categories that – fatally – were those of the researchers, not of the artists. And while the general framework was structuralist and French, the apparatus for their specific investigation had been developed by another South African researcher, Patricia Vinnicombe, who had sorted data on punch-cards recording 20 different characteristics for each of 8,478 individual images.[23]

After some while, Lewis-Williams says it began to dawn on him that these pre-defined characteristics or categories jeopardised the whole unwieldy exercise. For example, Vinnicombe's system included a category of 'Scene Description' which required the recorder to decide what the group of images in question depicted. The options listed were strictly limited: hunting, fighting, domestic activities, dancing, acrobatics, and a category of 'ceremonial, ritual or mythical scenes'. But making this choice was not nearly as easy as it looked in the absence of any knowledge about what the paintings had actually meant to the artists:

> Every time a scene was recorded, the recorder had to interpret it. Is this a 'dance'? If so could it be said to be 'mythical' or 'ritual'? The system of recording thus depended on *a priori* interpretations and the notion that one could determine what a scene depicted by simply looking at it. Interpretation was molding the statistics, not deriving from them.[24]

In 1972, the year that he made his first field-trip to the French painted caves, Lewis-Williams published an article in the *South African Archaeological Bulletin* about the state of research on San rock art. In it he argued that the quantitative method wasn't working, and that 'The only possibility of clarifying the themes which most deeply moved the mind of the prehistoric Bushmen lies in the, albeit fragmentary, mythology.'[25]

The problem was that the culture of the southern San bushmen responsible for the rock art had been extinct for nearly 100 years – so their oral traditions, and hence their myths, seemed lost beyond recovery. As late as 1972, few researchers were aware that extensive ethnographic records of the bushmen – their 'myths, accounts of rituals, personal histories, and much about daily life'[26] – had been set down in writing in the late nineteenth and early twentieth centuries, shortly before the last San died out. Once interest in these records spread amongst scholars, and proper study of them began, everything changed. But in 1972, Lewis-Williams did not yet appreciate the value of this material, and so 'persevered with quantitative analysis' until 1975 – this time in the Barkly East district of South Africa's Eastern Cape Province, where he and his colleagues recorded 2,361 images in detail in 38 rock shelters.[27] 'But no matter how long we stayed in a rock shelter – hours, days, or weeks – we were no closer to understanding the meaning of the images or why the San had placed them there.'[28]

Looking back on that whole period, those years of literally 'walking the walk' in South Africa's rugged mountains and wildernesses, Lewis-Williams is clearly angered by what he now regards as 'an enormous waste of time and energy' – not only his, but everyone else's as well.[29] Today, he insists:

> I would not advocate quantitative techniques in rock art research unless important questions can be formulated in such a way that they can be answered numerically . . . [Harald] Pager's 1971 book *Ndedema* contains an 80-page inventory that gives numerical descriptions of 3,909 individual rock paintings. As far as I am aware, no one has used this compilation to answer any questions that Pager himself did not pose. This is a cautionary tale for those who gather 'objective' numerical data in the hope that others will be able to use them.[30]

Based directly on his own extensive personal experiences studying San rock art, his growing knowledge of European Upper Palaeolithic cave art, and the comparisons between the two that were beginning to intrigue him, it was this edge of anger and frustration over failed and fruitless policies that set Lewis-Williams searching for some new theoretical approach that might yield results in a way that previous ones had not.[31]

Numinous notebooks

The first breakthrough was the mythology. The key nineteenth-century records of San traditions are set down in around 100 handwritten notebooks, running to more than 12,000 pages in total. These are records of interviews undertaken in the 1870s in the Cape Town area with San informants from central parts of the British Cape of Good Hope Colony.[32] The interviews were conducted by the German philologist Wilhelm Bleek and his sister-in-law Lucy Lloyd, two scholars, very far ahead of their time, who anticipated with absolute clarity the annihilation then looming over San culture. They did what they could to preserve its essence for the larger benefit of humanity by arranging for San elders – who had been imprisoned for cattle theft or other 'crimes' against the whites – to live with them in their home over the period of several years that the interviews took to complete.

After Bleek's premature death in 1875, Lloyd continued with the work on her own, but lacked the contacts or expertise to attract scholarly attention to it. Nothing was published until a short selection appeared in 1911, three years before Lloyd herself died. Thereafter the contents of the notebooks remained undisturbed and undisclosed until the 1930s, when a South African journal that was virtually unknown in Europe published further selections.[33] Another long period of disuse and neglect followed, but interest began to well up again in the late 1960s and early 1970s,[34] finally drawing David Lewis-Williams away from his fruitless quantification efforts and into the detailed study of bushman mythology that he had previously believed would never be possible.[35] He describes his awakening in the mid-1970s by 'the uncanny experience of paging through the numinous notebooks' that

Bleek and Lloyd had compiled a century earlier. They were, he says, to become 'indispensable' to his work on San rock art and had a determining effect on the future path his research would take.[36]

Usually referred to as the Bleek and Lloyd documents, the notebooks today reside in a protected vault at the Jagger Library in the University of Cape Town, where I had the opportunity to glance through them in 2004. Making use of a special phonetic script devised by Bleek, their orderly, neatly ruled pages give us verbatim handwritten transcripts, in the San language, of well in excess of a million words of testimony from the informants. Each page is confronted by a facing page providing the literal translation in English of the words actually spoken at the time. Although the San language still had a few hundred speakers at the end of the nineteenth century (and Bleek was fluent in it), it is now officially classified as extinct.[37]

I think David Lewis-Williams is right to use the strong word 'numinous' to describe the notebooks, suggesting something awe-inspiring about them – something capable of arousing spiritual or religious emotions. They are numinous because their pages are stalked by the ghosts of a murdered culture and because it appears, against all the odds, that they do miraculously preserve something of that culture's essence. Even more miraculously, as Lewis-Williams was to discover, the mythology rescued in those 12,000 pages is a natural counterpart to the hitherto mute and entirely mysterious rock art. Properly used, each has the capacity to illuminate the other in hitherto unimagined ways.

The Bleek and Lloyd documents are not the only source of ethnographic information to have come down to us from the nineteenth century, when the declining remnant of the San still struggled to preserve their Stone Age culture and when the very last rock paintings at the end of a 27,000-year tradition were still being made.[38] Other records and accounts are also extremely valuable. In the 1830s, for example, the French missionaries Thomas Arbousset and Francis Daumas left important eyewitness descriptions of San rituals.[39] And in the 1870s the English magistrate Joseph Millard Orpen travelled for several months in the Drakensberg mountains with a San elder named Qing whom he interviewed extensively. Qing and Orpen frequently camped in abandoned decorated rock shelters, and as Orpen wrote: 'When happy and at ease, I got from him . . . stories and explanations of paintings, some of which he showed and I copied on our route.'[40]

Also in the 1870s, the geologist George William Stow, a gifted artist, completed copies of a large number of San rock paintings. These were sent to Wilhelm Bleek in Cape Town in 1875. He was delighted with the fine-quality reproductions and showed them to his San informants who, in most cases, were immediately able to recount their meaning. 'An inspection of these pictures, and their explanation by the Bushmen, has only commenced,' wrote Bleek at the time, 'but it promises some valuable results, and throws light upon many things hitherto unintelligible.'[41]

Unfortunately 1875 was the year of Bleek's death and he was not able to take this insight further.

Shamanism

About a hundred years later, during the second half of the 1970s, Lewis-Williams' in-depth study of the Bleek and Lloyd documents, as well as Orpen's material, and many other sources, began to pay off. Despite the use of colourful allusions and metaphors, which sometimes make for ambiguity, it turned out that the nineteenth-century San informants had been on the whole remarkably clear about the beautiful and mysterious rock art of their ancestors – which in their day was still being made in rare instances. They indicated that the paintings and engravings were the work of functionaries in their society known as *!gi:ten*, singular *!gi:xa*. The exclamation marks and other signs used by linguists to transcribe spoken San represent 'clicks' and other sounds not found in Western languages. In the word *!gi:xa* the first syllable *!gi* (preceded by a click) means 'supernatural power' and the second syllable, *xa*, means 'full of'. So these were people who the San thought of as literally 'full of supernatural power' or 'possessors of supernatural power'.[42]

The ethnographic sources further make it clear that the vast archive of rock art for which the *!gi:ten* had been responsible since prehistoric times across huge areas of southern Africa played a vital part in expressing, symbolising and facilitating interactions between this world and a supposed spirit world which the San believed human beings must have dealings with. Control of the weather, particularly rain-making, control over the movements of animals to aid hunters in times of scarcity, the ability to do battle with spiritual enemies on the psychic plane, the ability to discover the whereabouts of far-off friends and relatives, knowledge of the pharmacological properties of plants, and, crucially, the ability to heal the physical and psychological ailments of the tribe were all regarded as vitally dependent upon regular access to the spirit world and contacts with its supernatural inhabitants. In San society it was the *!gi:ten* who were responsible for nurturing, main-taining and extending these all-important spirit-world contacts. Their supernatural power (*!gi*) was thus, explicitly, the power to leave the earthly plane and to travel out-of-body in the realm of the spirits.

Such responsibilities, concerns and supposed powers are character-istic of all those ancient systems of religion, usually but not exclusively associated with hunter-gatherers, that modern anthropologists loosely categorise as 'shamanistic'.[43] The word 'shaman' itself has very specific origins, being derived from the Tungus-Mongol noun *saman*, meaning, broadly speaking, 'one who knows'.[44] It is used generally not because the Tungus mysteriously contacted and influenced other cultures but because Tungus shamanism was the first example of the phenomenon to be studied by European travellers. The Tungus word entered Western languages through their enthusiastic written reports and has subsequently continued to be applied in all parts of the world where systems very similar to Tungus shamanism have been found.

It is the shaman – usually a man but sometimes a woman – who stands at the heart of these systems. And what all shamans have in common, regardless of which culture they come from, is an ability to enter and control altered states of consciousness. Shamanism, there-fore, is not a set of beliefs, nor the result of purposive study. It is first and foremost the set of techniques needed to achieve trance and thus to occasion particular kinds of experiences – hallucinations – which are then in turn used to interpret events and guide behaviour:

The true shaman must attain his knowledge and position through trance, vision and soul-journey to the Otherworld. All these states of enlightenment are reached . . . during a shamanic state of consciousness, and not by purposive study and application of a corpus of systematic knowledge.[45]

Underlying the notion of soul-journeys to the otherworld is a model of reality which is diametrically opposite in every way to the model presently favoured by Western science. This remotely ancient shamanistic model holds our material world to be much more complicated than it seems to be. Behind it, beneath it, above it, interpenetrating it, all around it – sometimes symbolised as being 'underground' or sometimes 'in the sky' – is an otherworld, perhaps multiple otherworlds (spirit worlds, underworlds, netherworlds, etc., etc.), inhabited by supernatural beings. Whether we like it or not, we must interact with these non-physical beings, which, though generally invisible and intangible, have the power both to harm us and to help us. Most people are passive in the matter. Once born into the physical world, their spirits become so attached to it that they are only able to leave it again when they die. But it is the special burden and responsibility of the shaman that he is able to leave his body here on earth, send his spirit to the otherworld to contact and negotiate with the beings there, and then return again to his body and resume normal life.

Since the Tungus provide something of an archetype for the concept of shamanism worldwide, what are the purposes of their trance journeys? 'Divination of the causes of various troubles,' answers the American anthropologist Weston La Barre:

discovery of the future, curing the sick, transporting souls back and forth from the underworld and managing them there, sacrifice to spirits, including those of 'animal masters', and initiating new shamans . . . Some shamans eat narcotic mushrooms and in their hallucinations visit the world of spirits, where they get the answers to questions posed to them . . .[46]

Though hallucinogenic plants were little used by the nineteenth-century San,[47] we'll recall that their shamans, the *!lig:ten*, those men and women who were full of supernatural power, had developed a different specialised technique to enter the spirit world, negotiate with its supernatural inhabitants, and return with the help needed by the tribe. The technique was a very distinctive, long drawn-out and arduous form of dance. Once this was understood, many other elements in the nineteenth-century ethnographic reports not only made sense themselves but began to shed light on the meaning of some of the hitherto most obscure and perplexing features of the rock art.

Solving the mysteries

Of particular significance was the fact that the reports offered a solution to the long-standing mystery of the therianthropes. According to the San informants, these figures depicted shamans in the act of

Mysterious hybrid figures such as these are common in southern African rock art. It is now known that they represent San shamans, in deep trance, shape-shifting into the animal forms in which they travel in the spirit world.

transformation into the animal forms – elephants, elands, lions, birds, jackals, serpents – that they adopted for their journeys in the spirit world.[48] In order to achieve such transformations, the informants explained, a circular dance, frequently also shown in the rock art, had been performed. During these dances, which could last for 24 hours at a time, the *!gi:ten* entered trance – described sometimes as descending through a waterhole into the bowels of a subterranean realm, or sometimes as flying up into the sky, or sometimes as dying.[49]

San rock art contains numerous images of the circular 'trance dance' used by shamans to enter altered states of consciousness and make contact with the spirit world

Once in this deep altered state of consciousness, comparable in some mysterious way to death, they transformed into their animal avatars and undertook terrifying and enlightening psychic voyages in what

San shamans depicted transforming into animal spirits in the trance dance. The sticks on which they support their weight as they lean steeply forward were part of the ritual paraphernalia of the dance.

they experienced as a spirit world.[50] When they returned to normal consciousness they informed the community about what they had learnt during their out-of-body journeys, and painted on the walls of the rock shelters some of the strange beings and scenes they had encountered amongst the spirits.[51]

In San art another figure is repeated almost as regularly as the therianthropes. This figure is often fully human – usually dancing, almost always a man – with a bleeding nose. But very frequently theri-

Figures in the rock art that are shown bleeding from the nose – whether human, animal or therianthrope – are to be understood as references to shamans undergoing the rigours and transformations of the trance dance

anthropes are also shown bleeding from the nose. Sometimes even elands, and other animals, are shown bleeding from the nose. For decades, until the ethnographic evidence was consulted, none of this made any sense. Once that evidence was taken into account, however, the meaning of the images became perfectly clear: these figures also depict shamans in various stages of transformation from human beings into spirit animals.[52] The nineteenth-century San reported that during extended dances it was quite normal for the *!gi:ten* to bleed conspicuously from the nose at the point of entering deep trance (we now know that the physical cause of this phenomenon was dehydration and haemorrhage of fragile nasal blood vessels). The description given by Qing, one of the more important informants, couldn't be clearer: 'It is a circular dance of men and women, following each other, and it is danced all night. Some fall down; some become as if mad and sick; blood runs from the noses of others . . .'[53] Figures in the rock art that are shown bleeding from the nose – whether human, animal or therianthrope – are therefore to be understood as references to shamans or the shamanic state.[54]

Qing's testimony also sheds light on another mystery of the art. During their travels in the 1870s, he and Joseph Orpen visited a rock shelter that still exists named Melikane in a remote part of the Moloti mountains (just inland from the Drakensberg). In the shelter an ancient painted rock panel features a group of three therianthropic figures with human bodies and the heads of antelopes. Qing had this to say about them: 'They are men who had died and now lived in rivers, and were spoilt at the same time as the elands and by the dances of which you have seen paintings.'[55]

Decoding this, on the face of things rather odd, remark is reasonably straightforward, as David Lewis-Williams has shown. Death, the state of being 'spoilt' and the state of being underwater – including the specific notion of living in rivers (or sometimes of descending underground through a waterhole) – are all well established from the ethnography as San metaphors for the shamanic trance state.[56] The majestic eland, largest of the antelopes, was also another common metaphor for the shaman. Moreover, many of the rock paintings exploit an observed similarity between the behaviour of a shaman in trance and the behaviour of a dying eland.[57] This analogy is especially appropriate, Lewis-Williams adds, when we consider

an eland that is succumbing to the effect of a poisoned arrow. Both shaman and animal tremble violently, sweat profusely, stagger, lower their heads, bleed from the nose, froth at the mouth, and finally crash to the ground. In addition, a dying eland's hair stands on end and San people told Bleek and Lloyd that lion's hair sometimes grows on a shaman's back.[58]

Last but not least, it cannot be an accident that the surviving *Ju/'hoansi (!Kung)* bushmen in the Kalahari, whose culture shares so much with the lost culture of the southern San, use the single word *kxwia* to mean both 'spoil' and 'to enter deep trance'.[59] Citing the work of American anthropologist Megan Biesele, Lewis-Williams notes that when a *Ju/'hoansi* shaman

> lies completely unconscious and possibly cataleptic, people say that he has been 'spoilt'. That Qing meant this and not 'spoil' in the daily sense is confirmed by his statement that the men with rhebuck [antelope] heads were 'spoilt . . . by the dances of which you have seen paintings'.[60]

It is not such a strange idea. In England today we say someone is 'smashed' when we mean he is in a drunken stupor. By the same token, San or *!Kung* shamans who fell into a deep hallucinatory state after dancing for hours were said to be 'spoilt'. So when Qing used the word for the figures in the rock paintings it was his idiom to tell us that they depicted trancing shamans.

Another big puzzle to researchers had been scenes which show

Rain animal of the spirit world, wallowing in water. (RARI)

179

strange hybrid animals, possibly part buffalo, part hippo, being led by ropes – often by groups of men and therianthropes bleeding from the nose.[61] We know already that the latter features mean shamans were at work. The informants further explained that these fantasy beasts were 'rain animals' and that they lived in immense pools of water in the realm of the spirits. The paintings show what was done when the San were afflicted by drought. Then groups of shamans would enter trance together, cross over into the spiritual domain, capture a rain animal and bring it back to our world, where it would be 'cut' or

San shamans capturing a rain animal in the spirit world and leading it back through the rock face into this world. (RARI)

'milked', producing the much-needed downpour. The paintings often show rain animals as though they are being pulled through the rock wall itself[62] – perhaps because the realm of the spirits was believed to lie on the other side of it.

In this way, enigma by enigma, Lewis-Williams discovered that many of the problems of interpretation surrounding the rock art of southern Africa had already been cleared up by nineteenth-century bushmen. Not only were they direct descendants of the prehistoric artists, but also, even more valuable, they still participated in their age-old traditions, sharing in thousands of years of accumulated experience of the trance dances and of shamans' out-of-body journeys, and continuing to paint depictions of what they had seen in the otherworld on the walls of their rock shelters.

A rose by any other name is still a rose

In all his published work David Lewis-Williams refers to the San *!gi:ten* quite explicitly as 'shamans'. To my mind he is absolutely right to do so. Nevertheless he has been criticised by a small but vociferous group of fellow academics who have filled many boring pages in the scholarly journals arguing that the *!gi:ten* were not shamans. The principal technique used in these attacks, which seems almost to be derived from a standardised debunkers' manual, is for the critic to apply some personal, deeply idiosyncratic, highly restrictive definition of shamanism (without informing readers of exactly what the definition is) and then to declare on the basis of this private yardstick that – for example – the trance healing by *!gi:ten* was not shamanistic trance healing but some other sort of healing and therefore that the San did not have or practise shamanism.

As Lewis-Williams points out, those who use this line of attack often commit the elementary error of confusing a word with a thing. Frequently it is not clear if they are objecting to what they see as a misuse of the word 'shamanism' in certain specified contexts or to the efforts to interpret some rock arts that have been labelled 'shamanistic'.

> Perhaps, if amicable discussion were possible, we could agree to find some other word (though I do not see the need; better definition is what is required), but the nature of San beliefs and practices and my understanding of their images would remain the same.[63]

And this is really the crucial point. *There is a phenomenon here*, and whether we call it 'shamanism' or something else, it is in fact a universal phenomenon with very distinctive, recognisable and eerily consistent characteristics amongst the San, the Tungus, and scores of other peoples and cultures throughout history and on all inhabited continents. These prominent universal characteristics are based upon the neurological capacity of all humans (by means of a range of techniques varying from rhythmic dancing to the ingestion of hallucinogenic drugs) to enter altered states of consciousness, to experience hallucinations in those altered states that are interpreted as supernatural contacts with a spirit world or otherworld (usually said to be located above us in the sky or beneath us underground), and to use these contacts to bring back to this world what are believed to be healing powers, control over the weather, control over the movements of animals and other useful benefits.[64]

This is the phenomenon that we are interested in and that the ethnographic records demonstrate was found amongst the southern San and provided the inspiration for their rock paintings. It is the same phenomenon that Lewis-Williams suggests may have inspired the cave paintings of Upper Palaeolithic Europe. And it is a phenomenon – I repeat with some emphasis – that rests on the neurological capacity of all humans to enter altered states of consciousness.

Although the precise ways in which this capacity is used in different societies and cultures may vary from place to place and epoch to epoch, it is the capacity itself that is fundamental. Many people never in their whole lives exercise it. Some only do so rarely in private and individual settings – whether through the use of drugs, deep meditation or other techniques. What marks shamans out is simply that they exercise this capacity to alter consciousness more frequently than others, that they do so on behalf of their community, and that they build up high levels of skill, familiarity and confidence in navigating the hallucinatory spirit world and negotiating with the supernatural beings who they are convinced inhabit it. In many societies such individuals may acquire some sort of formal position or rank; in others they may not. But if they go into trance, travel out of body amongst the spirits, can see far-off places and people, and claim to be able through these powers to cure sickness, control the movements of animals and make rain, then they rightly deserve to be called shamans.

Because all humans can experience altered states of consciousness and hallucinations, say Lewis-Williams' critics, and precisely because these are fundamental to shamanism, there is a danger that we will end up calling 'everyone who experiences an altered state of consciousness a shaman, in which case we are all shamans, and the word loses all meaning, becoming synonymous with human being!'[65] But perhaps this is the point – not that the word is synonymous with human being but that all human beings have the capacity to be shamans and that in some societies the proportion of men and women in the population who exercise this capacity may be quite large without the word in any sense becoming meaningless.

We'll see below that amongst the *Jul'hoansi (!Kung)* around half of all the adult men in any band and almost a third of all the women are shamans. Similarly there are probably 100,000 shamans in Peru. There they are called *curanderos* ('healers') or *brujos* ('sorcerers') but their tasks and personal experiences are virtually identical to those of their southern African and Siberian Tungus counterparts – i.e. entering a trance state (in Peru always through the ingestion of hallucinogens), travelling out of body to the otherworld, negotiating with spirits there, and returning to this world to heal the sick, control the weather and the movements of game animals, etc., etc. Interestingly, both in Peru and amongst the San there is also the notion that out-of-body battles are constantly going on unseen all around us in which 'good' shamans struggle to defend their people against the psychic attacks of 'bad' shamans. In neither case does the concept of the shaman become meaningless or irrelevant to the understanding of the society concerned simply because many people are or can be shamans.

In the semantic debate over the meaning and application of the words 'shaman' and 'shamanism' we therefore appear to be confronted by a line of attack on Lewis-Williams that proves baseless on close examination. The fact is that his work focuses on an extraordinary universal capacity of the human race which many scholars refer to as shamanism, but which would not be one whit diminished as a phenomenon if we were to agree to call it 'grglism' or 'qwrzlzat'. It is unfortunate that some scholars have succeeded in distracting attention from the great interest of the phenomenon itself with tedious and irrelevant wrangling about its name.

I have found that the same goes for almost all other attacks on Lewis-Williams' work. It has been my burden, as a responsible author, to have to study these attacks in depth. I have found very little of merit in them and very much that smacks of sour grapes and petty cavilling rather than proper scholarly criticism. For readers who wish to know more, full details will be found in Appendix I.

The living trance dance

If the rediscovery of the nineteenth-century ethnographic records was a breakthrough for researchers of San rock art, so too was the parallel recognition that surviving bushman communities in the Kalahari Desert, spanning Botswana and Namibia, still preserve ancient lore, customs and traditions that shed light on the art. This had not at first been expected. The *Ju/'hoansi* bushmen of Botswana (also known as the *!Kung*) speak a language that is unrelated to the extinct tongue of the southern San rock artists and have no rock-art tradition of their own. Nevertheless, with the help of Megan Biesele, an anthropologist working with the *Ju/'hoansi*, and drawing also on research into the beliefs of the bushmen done by Lorna and Elizabeth Marshall, Richard Katz, and others, Lewis-Williams had established by the late 1970s that these superficial differences mask fundamental similarities from which certain legitimate inferences follow concerning the rock art.

The most important similarity is the survival amongst the *Ju/'hoansi* of the trance dance shown in the ancient rock art, and spoken of in the nineteenth-century ethnographic records, as the means by which shamans took on the forms of spirit animals in order to gain access to the otherworld. In the same way, the *Ju/'hoansi* shamans dance themselves into a deeply altered state of consciousness in which they experience hallucinatory transformations into animal spirits – very frequently lions – and undertake out-of-body journeys.[66] Because their language is not the same as the southern San's, the shamans of the *Ju/'hoansi* are not called *!gi:ten* but *n/om k"xausi*. The concept is identical, however, for *k"xausi* means 'possessor of' and *n/om* means 'supernatural power'.[67] So these *Ju/'hoansi* shamans are possessors of supernatural power, just as the *!gi:ten* were, and to this day the dance is their portal to the otherworld, as it has perhaps been for tens of thousands of years.

Anthropologists have noted that in any *Ju/'hoansi* camp it is normal to find that about half of all the adult men are shamans as well as about a third of the women.[68] Whenever a trance dance is necessary to resolve problems originating in the otherworld, the entire camp will gather at night around a fire. Women sit closest to the fire, in a circle, shoulders touching. They sing and clap time to certain potent songs that open the way to supernatural experiences. Around them, the men, including established shamans, and novices who hope to make their first spirit journey, form a wider circle and begin to dance, rhythmically and energetically, edging out into the enveloping darkness. Most of them hold ceremonial fly-whisks, used only for this ritual, which they swish from side to side. Rattles, worn around their calves, are activated by repeated stamping of the feet. During the dance female shamans sometimes leave their position at the fire to join in. Even at the most intense moments, however, it is notable that all members of the community, including young children, are present. As David Lewis-Williams observes:

> While the dance proceeds, children play around, sometimes hilariously mimicking the shamans in trance. No one seems to find this mixing of what we may see as 'sacred' with 'secular' activities in any way disruptive or disrespectful.[69]

As hours pass and the dancers become more and more exhausted and overheated, pouring with sweat, the experienced shamans are the first to enter trance (a state referred to in the *Ju/'hoansi* language as *!kia*).[70] Because the dehydration and physical stress that pitch them into an altered state of consciousness also cause blood vessels in the delicate lining of their nasal passages to rupture, this process is routinely accompanied – as the rock art indicates – by copious nose bleeds. There is also what has been described as a terrifying feeling of rising inner heat. According to a *Ju/'hoansi* shaman interviewed by the anthropologist Richard Lee:

> Trance medicine really hurts! As you begin to trance the *n/om* slowly heats inside you and pulls at you. It rises up and grabs your insides and takes your thoughts away. Your mind and your senses leave and you

don't think clearly. Things become strange and start to change. You can't listen to people or understand what they say. You look at them and they suddenly become very tiny. You think, what's happening? Is God doing this? All that is inside you is the *n/om*; that is all you can feel.[71]

Staggering around the dance circle, shamans in this first stage of trance catch splatters of their own nasal blood in their hands and mix it with sweat from their armpits to create a medicine filled with *n/om* which they then smear over the bodies of the sick in the community. Another method of transferring *n/om*, frequently depicted in the prehistoric rock paintings and still practised today in the Kalahari, is for the shaman to lie directly on top of the sick person, pressing him down with the weight of his body.[72]

A puzzling body posture

On other major issues and problems of the rock art to which the nine-teenth century ethnography offers no obvious answers, David Lewis-Williams reports several further examples of illumination

The puzzling arms-back body posture frequently depicted in San rock art

provided by the *Ju/'hoansi* trance dance. For instance, a feature of many of the paintings and engravings in the Drakensberg is the presence of human or therianthropic figures bent forwards at the waist with their arms held out behind their backs:

Because this curious posture is widely depicted, researchers realised that it must have some specific meaning, but what it meant could not be ascertained. No ethnographer of the nineteenth or twentieth century seems to have recorded the posture.[73]

But then a fortunate encounter occurred during a research trip:

In 1975 I was in the Kalahari Desert with Megan Biesele, the American anthropologist. She speaks the !Kung [*Ju/'hoansi*] language fluently and was translating what a group of shamans was telling us. Without prompting from me, one of the men stood up and, bending slightly forward, adopted the arms-back posture. At once I realised that a long-standing puzzle was about to be solved. This, the man said, was the way some shamans danced when they were asking god to put more potency in their bodies. One of the most important mysteries of the Drakensberg art was explained. It was one of those rare, rewarding moments when the past seems to brush against the present.[74]

All in all, then, the nineteenth-century ethnography was paying dividends, and the study of contemporary communities of bushmen in the Kalahari was providing further hints of the meaning of the prehistoric rock art of southern Africa and its connection to altered states of consciousness. But David Lewis-Williams still needed input from other areas of scholarship before he would be ready for his own attempt at a grand theory that would explain the meaning not only of the southern African art but also of the art of the painted caves of Upper Palaeolithic Europe.

Painted visions of the Tukano

He found the first essential pointers to the information he needed in the work of the Colombian anthropologist Gerardo Reichel-Dolmatoff. In 1975, at exactly the time that Lewis-Williams was beginning to gain real insights into the San rock art, Reichel-Dolmatoff published his important monograph, *The Shaman and the Jaguar: A Study of Narcotic Drugs amongst the Tukano Indians of Colombia*.[75] The use of the term 'narcotic' in the title is unfortunate, since the drug in question is not strictly speaking a narcotic but a hallucinogenic. It is in fact my old friend ayahuasca, the vile and bitter brew of the Amazon in which the principal active ingredient is the potent psychotropic alkaloid dimethyltryptamine.[76] Scattered across the Amazon basin, more than 70 different tribal cultures use ayahuasca and many of them have their own names for it (*natema, caapi, cipo, shori*, etc.).[77] The Tukano of Colombia call it *yaje* (pronounced ya-hé) but it is identical to the ayahuasca that I drank in Peru and Brazil.

I will have more to say about Reichel-Dolmatoff's discoveries in later chapters. What is interesting here is a curious fact to which his 1975 study drew attention: the Tukano paint geometrical patterns and abstract designs on fabrics and musical instruments, on their houses and on the communal *malocas* where they consume *yaje*.[78] The Colombian anthropologist also reported the results of an intriguing experiment he carried out in which he asked members of a Tukano community to make crayon drawings of what they saw when they were drinking *yaje*. (The drawings were of course made from memory, after the drinkers had returned to normal consciousness.) The results, broadly identical to the designs on the houses and fabrics, included a triangle flanked by vertical lines ending in spirals, a rhomboid, a rectangular design filled with parallel lines, patterns of parallel undulating lines drawn horizontally, a number of different oval and U-shaped elements, rows of dots or small circles, a vertical pattern of little dots, grid patterns, zigzag lines, nested rectangles, nested parallel arcs (catenary curves), etc., etc.[79] Significantly, the Tukano also paint identical shapes and patterns on rock faces in the hills of the north-west Amazon, where they combine them with red-painted animal figures.[80]

For a man of Lewis-Williams' broad experience, all this was, of course, a colossal clue as to the possible source of exactly the same sort of abstract and geometrical shapes and patterns in the rock art of the San and in the painted caves of Upper Palaeolithic Europe.[81]

Stages of visions

A second idea that Lewis-Williams would develop in his later work, though it has never been indispensable to his arguments, also had its precursor in Reichel-Dolmatoff's 1975 study. This is the idea that hallucinatory experiences tend to proceed in stages.

The Tukano report three such stages after drinking *yajé*/ayahuasca, and it is in the first stage that they claim to see the majority of the abstract and geometrical figures that they prefer to paint, in which 'grid patterns, zigzag lines and undulating lines alternate with eye-shaped motifs, many-coloured concentric circles or endless chains of brilliant dots'.[82] Interestingly, when speaking of visions of this sort, they use the generic term *nomeri*, a word that designates any patterned luminous sensations, but which could be translated as 'to paint with coloured dots'.[83]

Reichel-Dolmatoff's informants added that the *nomeri* patterns eventually faded and disappeared as the second stage of their visions began. These featured 'larger shapes, looking like people, or animals, or unknown creatures'.[84] During this second stage it was said that experienced shamans were able to enter the spirit realm, frequently depicted as being 'under the waters', and to encounter there – in his deeply hidden abode – the powerful supernatural being known as the Master of Game Animals. Less experienced *yajé*-drinkers might see terrifying monsters, huge snakes or jaguars in this second stage of the trance.[85]

Finally, in the third stage, the informants reported a calming down and a mood of reflection accompanied by 'soft music and wandering clouds, seemingly carried by a gentle breeze'.[86]

Entoptic phenomena

Another big theme developed in Lewis-Williams' later work is the realisation that modern neuropsychological research focusing on the problem of 'phosphenes' (also called 'entoptic phenomena' and 'form constants' as we recall) might hold the key to at least part of the code of prehistoric rock art.[87] This theme too is prefigured by Reichel-Dolmatoff, who reports that phosphene-like patterns dominate contemporary Tukano rock paintings, and reminds us:

Phosphenes are subjective images, independent of an external light source, and are the results of self-illumination of the visual sense. As they originate within the eye and the brain, they are common to all men. Occasionally phosphenes can appear quite spontaneously, especially when the person has been deprived for a certain time of visual stimuli . . . They can also be produced by external stimuli: pressure on the eyeballs, a sudden shock, or the act of looking into the darkness when one wakes up at night . . . Moreover phosphenes can be induced by a number of chemical agents. Hallucinogenic drugs such as LSD, psilocybin, mescaline, bufotein and harmaline are known to produce phosphenes of abstract design motifs, and frequently the after-images can be observed for several months after the experience.[88]

Phosphene patterns of Western volunteers (after Reichel-Dolmatoff, 1975)

In this connection, Reichel-Dolmatoff's 1975 study brings into evidence the laboratory experiments of scientist Max Knoll. He used electrical stimulation of the brain to induce phosphenes in more than 1,000 Western volunteers, who were then asked to draw what they

Hallucinatory design motifs of the Tukano Indians.
(After Reichel-Dolmatoff, 1975)

had seen. The parallels with the Tukano informants drawing their *yaje* visions were striking since the Amazonian Indians and the Western laboratory test subjects both produced almost exactly the same range of abstract patterns and geometry.[89] 'These correspondences are too close to be mere coincidences,' comments Reichel-Dolmatoff. 'They seem to demonstrate that the motifs seen by the Indians under the influence of *yaje*, especially those of the first stage of intoxication, are phosphenes which are then interpreted in cultural terms as having a specific significance.'[90]

A single explanation?

Once again, what is exciting about this, and what Lewis-Williams immediately realised, is the obvious possibility of a single explanation. Could it be that the geometrical and abstract motifs found inside the painted caves of Europe, in the rock shelters of the San, amongst the Tukano Indians in the Amazon, and amongst Western laboratory subjects all derive from the same essential source? Could they all be representations of entoptic phenomena generated universally by the particular neurology of anatomically modern humans once they enter into altered states of consciousness?

If that does turn out to be what they are, then we could be on the way to learning a great deal about the hitherto elusive prehistoric cultures that have left their legacy in rock art all around the world but for which no ethnographic record has survived. The point remains valid even though it is certain that different cultures at different times would construe and interpret the mysterious shapes and patterns seen in altered states of consciousness in very many entirely different ways. We should not expect the construal put on entoptic patterns by a Tukano *yaje* drinker to be the same as the construal of a San trance dancer – or of an Upper Palaeolithic cave artist for that matter. Nor should we expect that all people who experience entoptic phenomena will attempt to make paintings of them. One may safely assume that most will not.

Nevertheless, the very fact that exactly the same shapes and forms keep on turning up in the rock art of different times and places suggests that some powerful common factor must be at work and invites the formulation of a tentative hypothesis: if recognisable phosphene-like patterns are prominent in a prehistoric art, as they are in the art of the San, and of the Tukano, and of Upper Palaeolithic Europe, then it may be a clue to the use of altered states of consciousness in the cultures that produced the art. With the San and the Tukano we already know that altered states of consciousness *are* involved, in both cases expressed through shamanism. There really does appear to be a significant and widespread pattern here and Reichel-Dolmatoff has already given us the reason for it. As phosphenes originate within the eye and the brain, 'they are common to all men'.[91]

Mysteries of the brain

Even if it is agreed that phosphenes are depicted, these are rarely the only features of rock art. We've seen that amongst the Tukano the entoptic grids and other patterns are painted alongside and sometimes directly over the top of animal figures, and we know that animals – again mixed up with the familiar patterns and signs – are likewise of immense importance in the rock art of the San and of the painted caves of Upper Palaeolithic Europe. Clearly all these very different figures of animals and humans – and, even more complicated, of therianthropes – cannot be produced entoptically (simply and mechanistically 'in the optical system') in the same way as the universal shapes and patterns. But it is also obvious that there are many extraordinary underlying similarities from culture to culture – in the ways that figures are superimposed on one another, seem to float without ground or horizon, make use of features in the rock face, etc., etc. – that are again suggestive of a common source.

David Lewis-Williams knew that the answer to the conundrum was probably not as simple as some sort of improbable and unprecedented diffusion of ideas across vast tracts of space and time. Like the entoptic phenomena, with which they are intimately involved, these strange and even eerie similarities must also have to do with altered states of consciousness and the mysteries of the human brain. Though it was unexpected ground for an archaeologist to enter, David Lewis-Williams was about to learn much more than he had ever thought he would need to know about the findings of neuropsychologists.

CHAPTER EIGHT

The Code in the Mind

It takes courage to throw off unproductive methods and approaches that the majority of scholars in your field have unquestioningly yoked themselves to for decades. Most people find it simpler just to stay with the herd, so David Lewis-Williams showed strength of character when he broke with the legacy of Breuil and Leroi-Gourhan in the mid-1970s and began to mark out a path of his own. Like a detective tracking down a master-criminal he slowly and patiently followed the clues where they led him. Along the way he stirred up controversy and the fierce opposition of other scholars with vested interests in established ideas, but he was confident of his sense of direction and willing to take the flak. The result, over the next 30 years, was that he would come closer than anyone before him to breaking the code of the world's most ancient and enigmatic religious art.

With a local tradition extending back at least as far as the painted stone slabs of Apollo-11 Cave in Namibia 27,000 years ago, southern Africa is one of the great repositories of the mysterious globally distributed art of our remote forefathers. By the early 1980s, thanks to Lewis-Williams' efforts, it was clear from the ethnographic evidence that many of the puzzling and apparently impenetrable scenes painted and engraved within thousands of rock shelters were 'essentially shamanistic over a huge area from the semiarid Kalahari Desert to the much better watered Drakensberg over 1,000 km to the south-east'.[1]

More than this, there were aspects of the art, for example its use of very specific abstract and geometrical patterns, which were matched point-for-point even further away in the rock paintings of the Tukano Indians of the Colombian Amazon. This was intriguing and suggested a common cause. However, to eliminate coincidence and lay the foundations for a more general theory it would be necessary to know if other rock-art traditions around the world featured such motifs, and whether there were cases with surviving ethnography linking the patterns to altered states of consciousness.

Meanwhile the most immediate hope of a way forward lay in another direction. Western volunteers, asked to paint what they had seen during laboratory experiments in which their brains had been stimulated electrically to produce an altered state of consciousness, depicted sequences of abstract and geometrical patterns that were essentially identical to those painted by the San and the Tukano. The reader will recall from the last chapter that such patterns are instantly familiar to neuropsychologists, who refer to them variously as 'phosphenes', 'form constants' and 'entoptic phenomena', and can be elicited by hallucinogenic drugs such as ayahuasca and LSD as reliably and consistently as by electrical stimulation. Lewis-Williams had abandoned the old-style quantitative methods of rock-art research – widely favoured because they were felt to be scientific – that simply counted different characteristics of prehistoric images. But he had certainly not abandoned science and now found himself enormously attracted to the possibility that rigorous empirical data produced under properly controlled laboratory conditions might shed light on the origin of the curious patterns that kept turning up in rock-art traditions from different parts of the world. He recognised fully that how they were interpreted would have varied from epoch to epoch and from place to place. But his decision to concentrate his initial research more or less exclusively on these patterns was strengthened by the fact that their form at least appeared to be uninfluenced by local cultural considerations, suggesting them to be 'a feature of altered states completely controlled by the nervous system'.[2]

In this way, by focusing on elements of the art least likely to have been shaped by cultural considerations, he hoped to avoid being accused of making crude ethnographic analogies between peoples and cultures widely separated in time and space. His aim, so far as possible, was to see if these strange patterns were truly universal, as his initial research had suggested, and to establish more clearly their exact link to altered states of consciousness. In the back of his mind was the hope that a 'neurological bridge' could be found that would offer us a way over the vast gulf of culture and years and allow us genuine access to the minds and motives of the Upper Palaeolithic cave artists.

Entoptic phenomena

With terms like 'phosphenes', 'form constants' and 'entoptic phenomena' all being used at once to mean the same or very similar things, it is easy to become confused. David Lewis-Williams prefers to stick to 'entoptic phenomena' (defined as 'visual sensations derived from the structure of the optic system anywhere from the eyeball to the cortex).'[3] This is also the term that I will generally use here for these largely geometric visual percepts.

Lewis-Williams makes a further point of insisting that entoptic phenomena be clearly distinguished from true hallucinations, which 'have no foundation in the actual structure of the optic system [and] include iconic visions of culturally controlled items such as animals, as well as somatic [body] and aural [sound] experiences'.[4] In the laboratory work that has been done in several different countries, subjects routinely reported a tendency for the visions seen in altered states of consciousness to proceed through a series of stages with entoptic patterns at one end of the continuum and full-scale 'iconic' visions of animals, humans, hybrid beings, etc., at the other. Regardless of cultural differences amongst the subjects, the shift into this last stage was often said to have been accompanied by powerful fast-moving imagery of a spiral or a vortex, sometimes in the form of tunnels, funnels, alleys and cones.[5] The very universality of these spiral/vortex images suggests an origin within the structure of the optic system, but Lewis-Williams regards them as sufficiently distinct from other entoptics to deserve separate treatment[6] – to which we will return in the next two chapters.

The universal ability of the human nervous system to generate entoptic phenomena was not systematically studied until the 1920s. The German-born neurologist and experimental psychologist Heinrich Kluver, a professor in the Division of Biological Sciences at the University of Chicago, did the first serious work. Published in 1926, 1928 and 1942, his findings closely linked such visions to altered states of consciousness brought on by the use of psychotropic drugs.[7] Kluver's investigations, which were later confirmed and elaborated by many other neuropsychologists and psychiatrists (such as Mardi Horowitz and Ronald K. Siegel in the 1970s, for example),[8] also established a definite catalogue of recognisable entoptic phenomena.[9] From these, as a guideline for his own research, Lewis-Williams drew up the following list of six of the commonest types, which in all cases are experienced as 'incandescent, shimmering, moving, rotating, and sometimes enlarging patterns':[10]

I A basic grid and its development in a lattice and expanding hexagonal pattern
II Sets of parallel lines
III Dots and short flecks

ENTOPTIC PHENOMENA		
	A	B
I		
II		
III		
IV		
V		
VI		

Entoptic phenomena (after Lewis-Williams and Dowson, 1988)

IV Zig-zag lines crossing the field of vision (reported by some subjects as angular, by others as undulating)
V Nested catenary curves (in a developed form the outer arc comprises flickering zig-zags)
VI Filigrees or thin meandering lines[11]

Kluver had also remarked on a tendency for entoptic forms to be 'frequently repeated, combined, or elaborated into ornamental designs and mosaics of various kinds'.[12] Drawing on this initial observation, and on the work of other later researchers in the field, Lewis-Williams eventually isolated and codified seven general principles that always seem to underlie the ways in which entoptic phenomena are perceived. These are: *replication* (the simple reproduction of one of the six basic entoptic forms); *fragmentation* ('research has shown that an entoptic phenomenon may be broken down into minimal components'); *integration* ('for instance a grid may blend with a series of zigzags'); *superpositioning* ('one entoptic form may be projected against another'); *juxtapositioning* (the placing of one entoptic form beside another); *reduplication* ('what may start as a single image becomes a series of duplicated images, such as festoons of catenary curves'); and finally *rotation* ('entoptic phenomena rotate in the field of vision').[13]

Three stages of trance and some drugs that will get you to all of them

A further important matter to settle, as noted above, concerned the progression – or stages – of 'non-real' experiences in altered states of consciousness.[14] Reviewing neuropsychological research undertaken over several decades (prior to the effective global ban on the use of hallucinogens in clinical trials since the mid-1970s), Lewis-Williams concluded that there appeared to be 'three broadly conceived stages in the progression of mental imagery during altered states of consciousness'.[15]

In Stage 1, subjects experience entoptic phenomena alone . . . In Stage 2 subjects try to make sense of entoptics by elaborating them into iconic forms [e.g. a zigzag entoptic might be construed as a snake] . . . As subjects move from this stage into Stage 3, marked changes in imagery occur. Many laboratory subjects report experiencing a vortex or rotating tunnel that seems to surround them . . . The sides of the vortex are marked by a lattice of squares like television screens. The images on these 'screens' are the first spontaneously produced iconic hallucinations; they eventually overlie the vortex as entoptics give way to iconic images [i.e. full-scale hallucinations].[16]

These stages, Lewis-Williams warned, did not necessarily follow one another sequentially, nor were they necessarily discrete from one another. On the contrary, it was clear from the reports of the test subjects that the stages were often hopelessly mixed up – for example entoptic patterns from Stage 1 were frequently superimposed on iconic figures from Stage 3.[17] A rigid structure of three stages is thus *not* an essential or indispensable part of the neuropsychological model but can be considered as a useful analytical tool to accommodate different kinds and degrees of imagery seen in trances.

Another reservation concerned how the entoptic and hallucinatory phenomena studied by the neuropsychologists had been generated in the first place. Although there had been some work with electro-magnetic fields and direct electrical stimulation of the brain (for example Max Knoll's studies cited in Chapter Seven), almost all the laboratory research since Kluver had been done either with mescalin, psilocybin or LSD.[18] Unfortunately, however, this promising research had to be discontinued in the mid-1970s when the so-called 'War on Drugs' began to make further investigations in this field impossible. It was thus not clear, Lewis-Williams admitted, 'if the trajectory of mental imagery is the same for all drugs and for non-drug-induced states'.[19] Nonetheless, when he published the first detailed results of his neuropsychological investigation into rock and cave art (jointly with Thomas Dowson in the pages of *Current Anthropology* in April 1988), he argued that 'a broad similarity can be accepted'.[20] As one example of a different drug having broadly similar effects, he cited the experiences of the Tukano Indians under the influence of ayahuasaca[21] – in which the active hallucinogen is dimethyltryptamine. The reader will recall from Chapter Seven that the Tukano also experience three stages of trance, in the first of which their visions consist entirely of what we now recognise as classic entoptic phenomena.

Help from the San and the Coso

In summary, though suitably hedged around with scholarly qualifications and restrictions, the 1988 *Current Anthropology* paper that launched Lewis-Williams' neuropsychological theory proposed a model comprising 'six entoptic forms, seven principles governing the perception of entoptic phenomena and iconic hallucinations, and three stages in the progression of altered states of consciousness'.[22] With that analytical apparatus in place, the next step was to give the model a 'trial run' on two bodies of rock art from different continents that were already known from ethnographic records to have been linked to shamanism and altered states of consciousness. If the model proved 'appropriate to these arts', the reasoning was that it could then be used to assess other arts – such as the cave art of Upper Palaeolithic Europe – where no ethnographic evidence has survived to tell us whether or not altered states of consciousness played a role.[23] Should such arts also respond to the model then the involvement of altered states at some stage in their production would, at the very least, be strongly implicated.

The two cultures Lewis-Williams selected because their rock art was known to have been shamanistic were the San of southern Africa and the Native American Shoshonean Coso culture of the California Great Basin. We saw in the last chapter that nineteenth-century ethnographic records were crucial in confirming the shamanistic character of the San paintings and engravings and their basis in altered states of consciousness. In the same way ethnographic information collected from elders amongst the fast-disappearing Indian tribes of the US in the nineteenth and early twentieth centuries rescued the evidence that confirms the shamanistic foundations of Coso and much other Native American rock art.[24]

To give just a couple of brief examples here, there was a tradition in the California Great Basin that tribal shamans (*po 'hage*, literally 'doctors') had 'painted their spirits [*anit*] on rocks, to show themselves, to let people see what they have done'.[25] Other informants believed that the rock art was not the work of the shamans themselves but of supernatural beings, referred to as 'water babies', said to serve the shamans as spirit-helpers.[26] Also spoken of as 'rock babies' and 'mountain dwarfs',[27] these mysterious entities were not normally visible but could be seen 'in jimsonweed trances'.[28] Since jimsonweed is *Datura stramonium*, a potent hallucinogen,[29] the connection with altered states of consciousness is unambiguous.

An important traditional use of datura amongst Native Americans was in the shamanic practise of 'vision-questing',[30] which we'll hear more of in later chapters. Today it is also sometimes added to the ayahuasca brew in the Amazon where shamans similarly believe that it enhances the clarity and power of the resulting visions. I would not quarrel with that: on the night I drank ayahuasca with an admixture of datura my visions included an eerily convincing part-man, part-crocodile therianthrope.[31]

Testing the model

Beginning with the six most common categories of entoptic phenomena listed earlier, detailed comparisons with the shamanic rock art of the San and the Coso reveal a sequence of blatant and completely unmistakable similarities. That such parallels should exist at all is striking in itself; but it becomes all the more significant and curious when we remember the wide geographical separation between southern Africa and California and the certainty that at no period of history or prehistory did the San and the Coso ever have any contact with one another. The results are best appreciated visually. As the following figure shows, all six categories of entoptic phenomena – grids or lattices, sets of parallel lines, dots and short flecks, zig-zag lines, nested catenary curves, and filigrees – are present, often in abundance, in the rock art both of the Coso and of the San.[32]

The correspondences with the other main analytical categories of the model – the seven principles of perception (e.g. the tendencies of entoptic phenomena towards 'replication', 'fragmentation', 'integration',

ENTOPTIC PHENOMENA		SAN ROCK ART		COSO
		ENGRAVINGS	PAINTINGS	
A	B	C	D	E
I				
II				
III				
IV				
V				
VI				

Comparison of entoptic phenomena with elements of the rock art of the San and the Coso (after Lewis-Williams and Dowson, 1988)

'reduplication', etc.) and the three stages of trance (in which entoptic phenomena merge gradually into full-blown hallucinations) – are equally intricate and close. In their 1988 paper, by way of example, Lewis-Williams and Dowson focus on the transformations of two of the six basic entoptics – zig-zag lines and nested catenary curves (which themselves sometimes incorporate zig-zag lines or flickering zig-zags at the outer edges of the arcs). These are followed through the complex series of permutations that the different stages and principles of perception generate in the art of the San and the Coso.[33]

Again the model's effectiveness and relevance is best appreciated visually. In the figure below, line I shows *replication* – i.e. simple reproduction – of boatlike nested catenary curves from the first stage of trance in the rock art of the San and the Coso. Line II, again arising from entoptic phenomena in the first stage of trance, shows the *fragmentation* of zig-zags into chevrons in both arts. Still within the first, exclusively entoptic stage of trance, line III shows the *integration* of two entoptic phenomena – zig-zags and grids in this case – again in both arts.[34]

Mental imagery of different stages of trance illustrated in the rock art of the San and the Coso (after Lewis-Williams and Dowson, 1988).

The images from San and Coso rock art in line IV of the illustration are typical of those that laboratory subjects draw of their visions in the second stage of trance. This is the stage identified in the neuropsychological studies in which subjects try to make sense of, or impose meaning on, the entoptic phenomena dancing across their visual fields – typically construing them as iconic images of animals and natural objects. In the San example, nested catenary curves are construed as a honeycomb with accompanying bees. In the Coso example the construal is of a bighorn sheep with the curved horns recalling the classic form of the entoptic while 'the body is an entoptic boat shape to which head, legs and tail have been added'.[35]

Lines V and VI illustrate animal and human figures in the rock art of the San and the Coso which closely match full-blown hallucinatory images seen in the third and final stage of trance. As both these examples show, such images frequently co-exist – in states of *superimposition* and *juxtaposition* – with zig-zags and other entoptic elements encountered in the first stage of trance.[36]

All in all, therefore, it seems Lewis-Williams is right to claim that his model, based on neuropsychological research into mental imagery in altered states of consciousness, does have broad explanatory power with regard to the rock art of the San and the Coso. That explanatory power is best understood by imagining the predicament of an archaeologist with no access to the relevant nineteenth- and twentieth-century ethnography who is required to interpret the two traditions and discover where they fitted into the life of the cultures that produced them. We know that the old methods of rock-art research offer no help in the face of such a challenge. But it cannot be denied that if our archaeologist were armed with the neuropsychological model, applied it properly, and observed the presence, development and elaboration of entoptic and visionary motifs in both arts, he or she would be more or less compelled to conclude – correctly – that both must have had a strong basis in shamanistic altered states of consciousness.

The ability of the model to make correct predictions about arts like those of the San and the Coso that are known to be shamanistic increases confidence that its predictions will also be correct with arts where no such knowledge is available. In the final part of their 1988 paper, therefore, Lewis-Williams and Dowson set out to apply the neuropsychological model to the enigmatic cave art of Upper Palaeolithic Europe.

Applying the model to Upper Palaeolithic art

The reader is already well aware from previous chapters that the European painted caves contain huge numbers of abstract and geometrical patterns such as zig-zags, grids, arrangements of dots, etc., which archaeologists have habitually referred to as 'signs'. We also know that these so-called signs are matched point-for-point in San (and now Coso) rock art by virtually identical abstract and geometrical patterns – which the neuropsychological model associates clearly with entoptics seen in altered states of consciousness. Indeed, as the next figure shows, the six formal categories of entoptic phenomena identified by the model were all used as widely by the artists of Upper Palaeolithic Europe as they were by the artists of the San and the Coso. This is true both of the paintings and engravings on the cave walls (for which the technical term is 'parietal art') and of the many small portable pieces ('mobile art').[37] Confronted by such a tight interlock between their model and the European evidence, it is difficult to disagree with

ENTOPTIC PHENOMENA		SAN ROCK ART		COSO	PALEOLITHIC ART			
		ENGRAVINGS	PAINTINGS		MOBILE ART		PARIETAL ART	
A	B	C	D	E	F	G	H	I
I								
II								
III								
IV								
V								
VI								

Comparison of entoptic phenomena with elements of the rock art
of the San, the Coso and of Upper Palaeolithic Europe
(after Lewis-Williams and Dowson, 1988)

Lewis-Williams and Downson's cautious conclusion: 'The presence of all six [entoptic categories] suggests that at least some of the art originated in certain altered states.'[38]

Turning to the seven principles of perception built into the neuropsychological model, Fig. 8.4 repeats the San and Coso information from Fig. 8.2 and compares this with examples from the Upper Palaeolithic. Thus the final column of line I provides an example from the Upper Palaeolithic of *replication* of the basic entoptic category of nested catenary curves – here in a very simple, unadorned form.[39] Lewis-Williams and Dowson point out that the European caves also contain more elaborate versions where this entoptic is further developed by *reduplication*

		SAN	COSO	PALAEOLITHIC
STAGE 1 ENTOPTICS	I			
	II			
	III			
STAGE 2 CONSTRUAL	IV			
STAGE 3 ENTOPTICS AND ICONICS	V			
	VI			(i) (ii)

Mental imagery of different stages of trance illustrated in the rock art of the San, of the Coso, and of Upper Palaeolithic Europe (after Lewis-Williams and Dowson, 1988) into a festoon, or where it is symmetrically inverted.[40] Line II illustrates *fragmentation*, in this case 'a zigzag line, a set of overlapping chevrons which form, in effect, a zigzag, and a number of discrete chevrons. The derivation of the chevrons from the continuous zigzag line seems clear.'[41] In line III, *juxtapositioning* of two different entoptic forms is seen – a grid placed next to a series of zigzags.[42]

As with the San and Coso examples, all the images in lines I, II and III are characteristic of the first stage of trance. But in line IV, the figure of an ibex from the Cave of Niaux in France is characteristic of the second stage in which subjects attempt to make sense of entoptic phenomena by construing them as iconic figures. Lewis-Williams and Dowson argue that this ibex with its exaggerated curved horns is a construal from an entoptic of two nested catenary curves with a zig-zag on the outer arc.[43]

Arrival of the therianthropes: the origins of religion

Finally coming to the full-blown hallucinatory imagery seen in Stage 3 of trance, the last column in lines V and VI of the figure on page 206 gives examples of corresponding animal and human depictions found in the art of the European Upper Palaeolithic. The bison in line V is one of many such images from the caves which additionally feature some degree of *superimposition* of entoptic patterns on the iconic figures – in this case zig-zag lines.[44] Similarly in line VI a zig-zag entoptic is superimposed over the non-realistic humanoid figure on the left. The creature on the right is the 'Sorcerer' from the cave of Gabillou in France whom we met in Chapter Four. The adjacent quadrilateral grid provides an excellent example of the *juxtapositioning* of entoptic and iconic forms predicted by the neuropsychological model.[45] The 'Sorcerer' himself is, of course, a thoroughly non-realistic integration of both human and animal characteristics in a single, visionary therianthropic figure – a classic Upper Palaeolithic bison-man. But such hybrids are also quite characteristic of the range of outlandish entities routinely encountered by modern people in Stage 3 of trance, 'when images are fantastically combined, and the subject inhabits . . . a bizarre hallucinatory world'.[46]

For example, Kluver, the founding father of this field of neuropsychological research, frequently self-experimented with mescalin, a powerful psychotropic alkaloid derived from the buttons of the peyote cactus. He reports that in one typical vision he observed a human head becoming overgrown with the hair of a cat and then transforming fully into a cat's head.[47] Likewise, experiences of therianthropy in which 'subjects begin to feel dissociated from their bodies and frequently become part of their own imagery' are common under the influence of a wide range of psychoactive drugs and can even be induced by substances as minimally hallucinogenic as hashish: 'I thought of a fox,' reports one subject, 'and instantly I was transformed into that animal. I could distinctively feel myself a fox, could see my long ears and bushy tail, and by a sort of introversion felt that my complete anatomy was that of a fox.'[48]

In the case of southern Africa, we already know from the ethnographic sources that the depiction of therianthropes in the rock art was inextricably linked to visions seen by trancing San shamans.[49] This evidence on its own invalidates the counter-claim made by some commentators that the images depict hunters wearing masks.[50] Besides, as Lewis-Williams and Dowson point out, the southern African therianthropes include 'numerous non-realistic painted features such as hoofs, long streamers emanating from the shoulders, and flywhisks protruding from the shoulders or head'.[51] Often overlooked on a casual inspection, such details, further 'suggest that therianthropes are hallucinatory rather than realistic paintings'.[52]

The same is also very likely to be true of the European therianthropes. Lewis-Williams and Dowson are prepared to allow 'that in certain rituals, Upper Palaeolithic people may have attached antlers or horns to their heads'.[53] Nevertheless:

> The Palaeolithic therianthropes are also better explained by hallucination than ritual costume because they, like the southern African ones, clearly have non-realistic features . . . [We] suggest that the rather unlikely concept of a half-man/half-animal was initially presented to early people by the nervous system as, in altered states, it integrated different iconic images.[54]

Thus, in a reticent and understated manner, one of the most significant and far-reaching themes of Lewis-Williams' work was first put before the public. It is, bluntly, the very hypothesis that I had consumed ibogaine and ayahuasca to test – namely that mankind's first representations of supernatural beings, and with them our earliest religious ideas, were derived from hallucinatory experiences. This is a matter to which I'll return in much greater detail in later chapters. Meanwhile, it is of course perfectly obvious that the half-man/half-animal concept is fundamental to the imagery of huge numbers of gods and spirits from virtually all the world's religions and suggests some kind of continuity with therianthropic imagery going back at least 27,000 years in the rock art of southern Africa and as much as 35,000 years in the painted caves of Europe.

Midwives of art

Another big new claim advanced quietly in Lewis-Williams' and Dowson's mould-breaking 1988 paper is that our ancestors' hallucinations in altered states of consciousness were not simply *depicted* in the earliest rock and cave art, but also played a far more fundamental role as the catalysts that led to its creation. In other words, as with religion, if we seek out the origin of art we will sooner or later come to the otherworlds of altered states of consciousness, and to the strange beings, experiences and perceptions that are to be encountered there.

Perhaps the most basic artistic skill is the ability to represent three-dimensional objects with two-dimensional marks. But how did people ever get the idea to do this in the first place? The old view in cave-art studies was that an evolutionary process had been involved and that full-scale representational painting and engraving had developed from earlier, initially accidental, non-representaional marks and signs – i.e. the abundant abstract and geometrical patterns in the caves. This argument has been challenged by modern dating evidence which shows that full-scale representational art with extremely sophisticated animal figures was being painted in Chauvet Cave 32,000 years ago at the same time that the earliest abstract and geometrical patterns were being made there – so, logically, the former could not have evolved from the latter. Then, too, there is the now well-established fact that although the patterns and marks are present at all epochs of cave art, they become much more numerous in the later phases of the Upper Palaeolithic, roughly from the time of Lascaux onwards – i.e. at least 15,000 years after the main phase of decoration at Chauvet. Again this is not what we would expect of an evolutionary process in which 'primitive', abstract, non-representational forms 'develop' over thousands of years into sophisticated representational art.

Another argument, almost equally unsatisfactory, has been that the patterns/marks/signs on the one hand, and the iconic images on the other, form two parallel and distinct graphic systems.[55] But even if this is taken to be an accurate description of the evidence that confronts us, it still brings us no nearer to knowing *why* precisely the same two graphic systems that we see in European Upper Palaeolithic cave art keep on turning up again and again in very distant parts of the world and in different periods in other prehistoric rock arts like those of the San and the Coso.

The solution that Lewis-Williams and Dowson propose returns us once again to the operation of the human nervous system. Laboratory subjects of modern neuropsychological research into altered states of consciousness consistently report that their visions of entoptic phenomena, as well as their full-blown iconic hallucinations of animals and other entities, are seen as though localised on nearby walls and ceilings.[56] Some of the descriptions given convey this sense clearly, comparing the experience to 'pictures painted before your imagination' or to watching a projected 'motion picture or slide show'.[57] Follow-up studies further confirm that many subjects experienced vivid recurrences over periods of several months of entoptic phenomena seen in altered states of consciousness. Known technically as 'after-images', these were also perceived as though projected on to nearby surfaces such as walls and ceilings.[58] Interestingly, outside the laboratory framework, Reichel-Dolmatoff's Tukano informants in the Colombian Amazon reported the same experiences arising from ayahuasca trances. Their visions began with large quantities of entoptic phenomena (which, as we saw in Chapter Seven, also turn out to form the core motifs of traditional Tukano art). As with Western subjects, the entoptic patterns, and subsequent full-blown hallucinations, were perceived by the Tukano trancers as though projected on to nearby plane surfaces in their immediate vicinity. And as with Western subjects the Tukano reported the recurrence of projected afterimages over periods of several months.[59]

Lewis-Williams and Dowson reasonably conclude from such reports that prehistoric humans with the same neurology as ours experiencing altered states of consciousness would also have experienced similar projection of mental imagery and afterimages on to nearby surfaces. 'Their surroundings were thus already invested with "pictures".'[60] It follows, should the ancients have found a way to put themselves into altered states within the confines of the deep caves of Upper Palae-olithic Europe, that the surfaces thus 'invested' would have been the walls and ceilings of the caves themselves.

Once all this is considered, argue Lewis-Williams and Dowson, it is even less likely to be an accident that so many of the established characteristics of mental imagery seen in altered states of conscious-ness turn out to match so closely the well-known and oft-repeated characteristics of Upper Palaeolithic cave art. These include, in both cases, 'distorted and geometric percepts', iconic figures that are 'completely disengaged from any kind of natural surroundings', located 'without regard to size or position relative to one another' and projected on to nearby surfaces where they attain their 'own free-floating exist-ence, independent of scene or surface'.[61]

In other words:

Early people were neurologically provided with the salient features of Upper Palaeolithic art. They did not have to 'invent drawing'... Tracing projected mental images with a finger in the sand or on the soft wall of a cave to experience them more fully would have 'fixed' them and would have been an initial step in the history of art.[62]

As a bonus, this radical new theory of art origins also solves the problem, with which the reader is already thoroughly familiar, of the co-occurrence of abstract and geometric patterns with fully iconic representations within single 'compositions'. Long admitted by the experts as one of the central puzzles of Upper Palaeolithic art, the answer, explain Lewis-Williams and Dowson

> is not that man invented and purposefully maintained two parallel or complementary systems . . . In Upper Palaeolithic Western Europe, southern Africa, the Great Basin, and elsewhere, entoptic phenomena were intentionally associated with iconic images, simply because this is the way the human visual system works; the association is intrinsic to altered states of consciousness . . .[63] Moreover, because the action of 'fixing' the images would have been the same for entoptic phenomena and iconic hallucinations, there is no need to postulate different origins or a genetic [evolutionary] relationship between Upper Palaeolithic signs and representational art. Both signs and iconic representations are 'realistic' in that they both depict what people 'really' experienced . . .[64]

What is at stake

Arguably art and religion are our two most prized cultural institutions, the saving human graces from which have arisen many of the most noble virtues and glorious achievements of our species. But if Lewis-Williams is right, we need to be brutally honest about where the first incarnations of these institutions came from. Their birth was not assisted by the operation of any of the faculties that we admire in the twenty-first century – such as reason, intelligence, the scientific application of logic, sensitivity to nature, or even consciously driven creativity. Instead it seems that art and religion were bestowed upon us like secret and invisible powers, by inner mental realms that our societies now despise and legislate against – the realms of altered states of consciousness, most commonly entered (by us as by our predecessors) through the consumption of potent hallucinogenic drugs.

If Lewis-Williams is right, in other words, then sooner or later we must ask ourselves whether we are wise today to censor and ferociously repress the very kinds of shamanistic explorations of consciousness that brought art and religion into being at the dawn of the modern human story. Above all else, we who say that we are 'free' in the economically advanced and democratic nations of the world, and who arrogantly set up our societies as models for others to follow, need to pause and reflect. What do we have to preach about where freedom is concerned, when we as individuals are not even free to exercise that basic sovereignty over our own consciousness that our ancestors claimed as their birthright? And on what authority do we portray our kind of 'freedom' as a universal example, or claim to possess great and useful knowledge about the human condition, when we ourselves are denied the freedom that is still granted today to any peasant-farmer or hunter-gatherer drinking ayahuasca in jungle clearings in the Amazon – namely the freedom to investigate the mysterious depths of our own minds?

How not to be the victim of an academic mugging

Lewis-Williams and Dowson describe their 1988 paper as only 'a conservative beginning to an investigation of possible Upper Palaeolithic mental imagery'.[65] Having gone through it closely now, I have no doubt, and nor do any of the growing number of top-rank scholars who have publicly endorsed the neuropsychological theory since 1988, that the authors make their case well, and that there is indeed

> a strong suggestion that at least a significant component of Upper Palaeolithic art . . . derives from altered states of consciousness and that many of the 'signs' depict entoptic phenomena in the various transformations we have described.[66]

This in itself is quite a breakthrough. For the first time in more than a century, thanks to David Lewis-Williams' bloody-mindedness, originality and initiative, we have before us an inviting, intelligent, well thought out and persuasive theory, backed by hard evidence, that explains the overall phenomenon of European cave art extremely well. Unlike some previous, failed theories this fresh approach has managed to avoid simplistic ethnographic analogies in dealing with the art (despite some tempting lifestyle similarities shared by, say, San and Upper Palaeolithic hunter-gatherers). Instead, the focus has been kept rigorously on areas of perception belonging to the neurological common ground of all humanity. Lewis-Williams has also rejected interpretations based on spurious quantitative analyses or on 'expert' 'feelings' about the style, meaning, etc. of specific images. By substituting hard evidence from the empirical discipline of neuropsychology for the habitual waffle and favoured hobbyhorses of archaeologists, he has created the first ever theory of cave art that is in principle testable – i.e. subject to potential validation or refutation by further research. It is also a theory that has already proved its worth as an explanatory tool in the analysis of several different and culturally unrelated systems of rock art.

Good new ideas are often very annoying to people who have built their careers around old bad ones. I was therefore not startled to learn that Lewis-Williams' work has been violently attacked by a faction of his fellow scholars. In this respect he is like every innovator in this field of study since the Spanish amateur archaeologist Marcelino Sanz de Sautuola first tried to tell the world the truth about the cave of Altamira. As we saw in Chapter Six, de Sautuola's good name was destroyed, and his life shortened, by the vile assaults and insults of a cabal of leading nineteenth-century prehistorians. The fact that Sautuola was right and the prehistorians were wrong didn't make any difference at the time because his opponents so heavily outweighed him in the academic pecking order and because really only one mainstream scholar – the redoubtable Vilanova y Piera of the University of Madrid – was prepared to offer him open support.[67]

Despite the hostility that he too has aroused, I think I can predict with confidence that David Lewis-Williams is never going to end up in the same sort of tight spot as poor Sautuola.

First there is the matter of credentials. Sanz de Sautuola was not a qualified archaeologist. This meant that the snobbish academic establishment of his day didn't take him seriously. By contrast, Lewis-Williams, founder of the highly respected Rock Art Research Institute at the University of Witwatersrand, is a full Professor of Archaeology with 40 years' experience in the field and has been internationally acclaimed for his lifetime work on ancient rock art.[68] With a long list of important publications to his credit, he is, by any standards, one of the major figures worldwide in this area of study and his thinking commands and deserves special attention for that reason.

Secondly there is the 'common-sense' factor – the downright basic good sense of the majority of people. Until the academic hatchet-job began, most of the visitors who flocked to Altamira in droves in the nineteenth century agreed with Sautuola that the sophisticated paintings before their eyes really were extremely ancient. Eventually they were persuaded otherwise by authorities like Cartailhac and Mortillet, who had not even seen the art for themselves, and thereafter shunned Altamira until 1902, when those same authorities finally admitted that Sautuola had been right all along. Today a common-sense factor also underlines public support for Lewis-Williams and what he has to say about ancient shamanism, the caves, neuropsychology, the amazing art and its astonishing cross-cultural similarities with other systems of rock art around the world. It should be added that it accords particularly with the common sense of those large numbers of members of the public who at one stage or another in their lives have tried a hallucinogenic drug and explored the strange realms of geometry, visions and experience to which these substances give access. Nowadays when an academic diktat not only confounds our common sense but also contradicts our direct personal experience, we tend to reject the diktat, not just accept it blindly.

Thirdly there is the matter of the political lobby. Sanz de Sautuola didn't have one, and apart from his friend Vilanova y Piera, no other experts took his side. By contrast one of the many reasons Lewis-Williams' theory has prospered despite its enemies is that the South African archaeologist has lobbied extensively and effectively for his own work and has the considered backing of dozens of top researchers.

Jean Clottes, France's leading living authority on European cave art, is one of them, and this is no small thing since today (as in the nineteenth century) French academics are the dominant players in this field. In 1996, following joint expeditions with Lewis-Williams to dozens of caves, Clottes became so convinced that the South African's theories were indeed applicable to French cave art that he co-authored a book with him, *The Shamans of Prehistory*, which has subsequently been highly influential.[69]

Such strategic alliances have worked well and, according to the prestigious *Cambridge Archaeological Journal* (*CAJ*), Lewis-Williams' theories have in recent years 'come to dominate the field, marginalising interest in other cultural themes such as totemism and records of everyday foraging'.[70] Leading US rock-art expert David Whitley, who makes active use of the neuropsychological model in deciphering Native American shamanic art, goes so far as to state that Lewis-Williams' contributions represent 'a landmark in the development of Western archaeology'.[71]

The fight with Bahn and Helvenston

But still there is a fight. The leading protagonists in the anti-Lewis-Williams camp are British archaeologist Paul Bahn and his colleague Patricia Helvenston, a retired American clinical psychologist. I refer the reader to Appendix I for a point-by-point investigation of all the main charges that these scholars have levelled against Lewis-Williams. I find little or no merit in any of them. However, there is one accusation of sufficient importance to justify the reader's attention here. This is Bahn and Helvenston's claim, made in a privately published paper in 2002 (*Desperately Seeking Trance Plants*) and again in the influential *Cambridge Archaeological Journal* in 2003 ('Testing the Three Stages of Trance Model'), that no altered states of consciousness 'except those elicited by mescaline, LSD or psilocybin'[72] are consistent with the types of hallucinations and experiences described in the neuropsychological model. Both in *Desperately Seeking Trance Plants* and in their *CAJ* article they then set a test whereby Lewis-Williams' theory is to be regarded as refuted unless the remains of plants containing one of these substances can be found in the archaeological sediments of the painted caves themselves.[73] Finally they proceed to argue that no such plant remains have been found either in the caves or anywhere else in Europe for the whole period of the Upper Palaeolithic:[74]

> Mescaline ... is found only in plants of the New World. This inescapable fact certainly discredits the 'three-stage' model with respect to Palaeolithic cave art being inspired by mescaline-induced trance.[75]

LSD was found in Europe [but] evidence for its deliberate ingestion is non-existent.[76]

Unfortunately for the 'three stage model', the only psilocybin-containing mushrooms that have ever been used for hallucinatory purposes are New World species, so they have to be ruled out as inspiring Upper Palaeolithic cave art in Europe.[77]

In conclusion, mescaline, LSD and psilocybin are the only substances that produce a form of trance with which the 'three stage' model bears correspondence. Yet plants containing two of these substances, mescaline and psilocybin, were unavailable in Europe and the third, LSD, is highly unlikely to have ever been deliberately ingested . . .[78]

To refute the point that the two critics are making here, as we will see at the end of this chapter, it is not even necessary to demonstrate that they are wrong when they state so confidently that mescaline, psilocybin and LSD are the only substances compatible with Lewis-Williams' model. I will therefore simply mention in passing that they *are* wrong. We've already established (and further evidence will be presented in Chapter Nine) that the trances of the San, which are *not* induced by any of the above-named drugs but by strenuous rhythmic dancing, *do* result in combinations of entoptic and iconic hallucinatory images exactly as predicted by the neuropsychological theory. Nor, if we look at drug-induced trances, are Bahn and Helvenston right to claim that mescaline, psilocybin and LSD are the only suitable agents, since I know from my own experience that at least one other well-known psychoactive substance, dimethyltryptamine (DMT – the active ingredient of ayahuasca), is also available from plants and also very frequently produces a progression of hallucinations from abstract and geometrical patterns to full-scale iconic figures as the model requires.[79]

I cannot blame Bahn and Helvenston for being unaware of my personal experiences with ayahuasca/DMT! But these researchers, who castigate others for not using the latest references, should have known that the only large body of research done since the 1970s into the effects on consciousness of any major hallucinogen has focused on ayahuasca/DMT. One part of this is the experimental lab work done during the 1990s by Dr Rick Strassman at the University of New Mexico with DMT and human volunteers, and published in 2001. The other part is the immense phenomenological investigation of ayahuasca-induced hallucinatory experiences published in 2002 by Dr Benny Shanon, Professor of Psychology at the Hebrew University in Jerusalem. Both studies, as we will see in later chapters, chart precisely the kinds of hallucinations moving between geometric and iconic figures that Lewis-Williams and Dowson envisage in the neuropsychological model.[80]

Nor, to refute Bahn and Helvenston, is it necessary to deal with their constant misnaming of the neuropsychological model as the 'three stages of trance' (TST) model. This is a straw man, because Lewis-Williams and Dowson nowhere call their model by any such name or focus any kind of special attention on its three-stagedness. What is correct is that a notion of trances that fall into three broadly defined stages is one of the parameters of the model, but the focus throughout is on the changing and overlapping nature of the hallucinations experienced during these stages rather than the stages themselves. Lewis-Williams and Dowson have also been at pains to make clear, even in their earliest work on the subject, that not everybody goes through all three stages and that the boundaries between stages as well as the order in which they occur are flexible.[81] Moreover, contrary to the impression that Bahn and Helvenston most strongly seek to convey, the truth is that three-stagedness has never been an essential 'stand-or-fall' quality of the model, but rather one of its more peripheral characteristics.[82] What *is* essential, whether three, or five, or no stages are involved, is that the model implicates a distinctive type of hallucinatory process involving abstract and geometrical patterns and full-scale iconic figures in a presentation of an alternative reality so powerful that the natural tendency of humans experiencing it is to think they are confronting a spirit world. By trying to focus our attention on the stages, rather than the imagery and the experiences of these hallucinations, Bahn and Helvenston misrepresent the neuropsychological model.

Last but not least, to refute the two critics on their main line of attack it is not even necessary to expose the absurd nature of their proposed 'empirical test' – namely that the model should be regarded as invalid unless traces of plants containing LSD, psilocybin or mescaline are found in the archaeological sediments of the painted caves themselves. As archaeologist Christopher Chippendale points out in a response to Bahn and Helvenston's *CAJ* article, this test is incapable of invalidating the model (and is thus irrelevant) because:

> One can envisage many plausible scenarios for Palaeolithic Europe in which plant-induced visionary experience *does* explain the art but does *not* leave that kind of trace. Suppose, for instance, the central metaphor of the visionary experience was of drowning in noisy darkness; so the hallucinogens were taken on the rocks just by large river channels, adjacent to waterfalls or rapids where the flow is swirling and loud and dangerous, and during moonless nights. Suppose any unused hallucinogenic agents were invariably committed to the waters as the act of ceremony closed. Suppose, in some complementary ritual business, the same or other specialists recorded their journeys to the spirit world by engraving and painting in varied places, especially deep in the caves whose isolating disorienting darkness was recognised as repeating what was experienced by the river. Outcome: cave-art deriving from visionary experience, with no trace of the inducing plant agents either in the cave sediments or in any surviving outside deposits.[83]

Liberty Cap

Bahn and Helvenston repeatedly emphasise the extremely clear and simple point that they regard as fundamental to their case, namely that a suitable hallucinogenic agent was not available in Europe during the Upper Palaeolithic. At the end of their presentation in the *Cambridge Archaeological Journal* in 2003 they summarise their argument. It won't hurt to remind ourselves once more here of the issues that they regard as the most important:

> Lewis-Williams and Dowson indicated their evidence for trance-induced Palaeolithic rock art was that geometric figures and complex

animal or therianthropic images were depicted in such art. They argued that such a combination of images only occurred in trance states. But since only mescaline, psilocybin, and LSD-induced trances produce that particular pattern of images, and those substances weren't used in Europe, let alone found in cave-art sites or at camp sites, then that entire rationale for trance-inspired Palaeolithic cave art in Europe collapses ... The TST model ... has now been refuted ... One can only conclude that anyone who continues henceforth to cite or apply the TST model is either ignorant of the facts or has little respect for truth in scholarship.[84]

Such shrill claims of refutation, such easy dismissals of the life work of other scholars, are characteristic of Bahn and Helvenston. Their certitude seems ironclad and they never for a moment consider the possibility that their own central propositions could be wrong. If by chance they are wrong, however, then the model stands and they themselves are refuted. On their own terms that would require the following demonstrations:

(a) that any one of the plant-based psychedelics they list – psilocybin, mescalin, or LSD – was in fact available in Europe in the Upper Palaeolithic, and

(b) that expert testimony exists, of the kind and level Bahn and Helvenston have shown they trust, confirming the possibility that the substance in question could have been used as a hallucinogen by the people of Europe at that time.

I don't propose to take up the concession about LSD being found in Europe. In fact LSD-25, the famous hallucinogen of the 1960s, is a synthetic substance that does not appear spontaneously in nature. It was, however, synthesised from ergot, a fungus that grows on various species of wild grasses found in Europe, and it is true that other psychoactive lysergic acid amides, ergine and lysergic acid-hydroxethylamide are found in ergot. These were responsible, as Bahn and Helvenston rightly observe, for the convulsive form of ergotism ('St Anthony's Fire'), a deadly disease that killed thousands during the Middle Ages, and are 'unlikely candidates for hallucinogen use at any time'.[85]

There is one exception to this rule – the possibility, which we will explore in Chapter Twenty-One, that the Eleusinian Mysteries of Ancient Greece made use of an ergot-based LSD-like potion to induce powerful visionary experiences amongst initiates. For present purposes, however, I am content to accept with Bahn and Helvenston that even if substances similar to LSD were theoretically available on wild grasses in Upper Palaeolithic Europe they are 'highly unlikely to have ever been deliberately ingested' at that time.[86] Who knows, perhaps they were. But I'm not going to insist on it.

I'm also with Bahn and Helvenston on mescaline. I agree that it is only found in New World plants – principally in the San Pedro cactus of South America, and the peyote cactus of Mexico and neighbouring parts of the US. No point, then, in trying to argue that mescaline had anything to do with the cave paintings of Upper Palaeolithic Europe.

But on the third substance – psilocybin – Bahn and Helvenston are just plain wrong.

This is their claim:

Unfortunately for the 'three stage model', the only psilocybin-containing mushrooms that have ever been used for hallucinatory purposes are New World species, so they have to be ruled out as inspiring Upper Palaeolithic cave art in Europe. There may have been a species of psilocybin-containing mushroom, *Stropharia cubensis*, that was found in both the New World and North Vietnam. There is no evidence that this species was ever used outside the New World for hallucinogenic purposes.[87]

A brief footnote on the same page adds the following nugget of information:

A closely related species, *Psilocybe semilanceata*, was reported to be found in Europe by Pollock, but nothing was cited as to whether it had ever actually been used as a hallucinogen.[88]

The reference is to an article in the 1975 volume of the *Journal of Psychedelic Drugs* by Steven Hayden Pollock.[89]

Let us dispense with *Stropharia cubensis* at once as a possible source of hallucinogenic experiences for the cave artists of Upper Palaeolithic Europe. This mushroom, which grows in subtropical areas on the dung of cattle and elephants,[90] could not have survived in the brisk Ice Age climate of Franco-Cantabria, and its mention by Bahn and Helvenston on page 37 of *Desperately Seeking Trance Plants* is simply a diversion. The real interest lies with *Psilocybe semilanceata*, the mushroom they consign to a footnote. What is interesting about it is that it is *a native European species* which today grows very comfortably in cold northern latitudes – indeed as far north as Norway[91] – and would have thrived in the Franco-Cantabrian pastures and valleys during the Ice Age. Best known as the Liberty Cap, this very popular little brown 'magic mushroom' is now used for hallucinatory purposes all around the world, but mycologists are unanimous as to its ancient European provenance.[92] Bahn and Helvenston themselves furtively acknowledge this in their little footnote, where they attribute the information to Pollock who – they nevertheless hasten to reassure us – says nothing 'as to whether it had ever actually been used as a hallucinogen'.[93]

In their usual argumentative style they then deploy this *absence* of comment by Pollock as though it is *positive evidence* to prove that even though the Liberty Cap may grudgingly be admitted to have been available in Upper Palaeolithic Europe, it was in fact never used there for hallucinatory purposes. Astonishingly this is the *only* reason they have to reject this 'extremely potent'[94] European psilocybin mushroom as the possible source of the geometric and iconic hallucinations amongst the cave artists that Lewis-Williams' theory calls for.

The problem is the very test constructed by Bahn and Helvenston to bring Lewis-Williams down. Setting aside the ridiculous demand that the remains of the hallucinogenic agent should actually be found in archaeological sediments on site, and focusing instead on the bigger question of whether or nor psilocybin could have been available in any mushroom species in Upper Palaeolithic Europe, the answer – in the form of the Liberty Caps – has to be a resounding YES.

One of the principal sources that Bahn and Helvenston draw on is the classic reference book *Plants of the Gods* (a global compendium of the ritual use of psychoactive plants) by Richard Evans Schultes, former Director of the Botanical Museum at Harvard University, and Albert Hoffman, the Swiss scientist who first synthesised LSD.[95] Indeed, Bahn and Helvenston cite *Plants of the Gods* frequently (for instance at the beginning of their footnote on *Psilocybe semilanceata*[96]) and thus cannot deny knowledge of the work. First published in 1992 and revised in 1998, it is also a much more recent and up-to-date source on psilocybin mushrooms than Pollock's 1975 article. How then are we to account for the fact that Bahn and Helvenston cite only Pollock on this matter and not *Plants of the Gods*?

It's not that *Plants of the Gods* has nothing relevant to say about Liberty Caps, or even that what it has to say is obscurely hidden away where Bahn and Helvenston might reasonably have missed it. On the contrary, half a minute's work in the index looking up either 'Liberty Caps' or '*Psilocybe semilanceata*' will lead the reader like a guided missile to page 72, where the following clear, strong and to-the-point statement appears:

> **Liberty Cap:** *Psilocybe semilanceata*. It is possible that this fungus has been used for psychoactive purposes in Central Europe for about 12,000 years. Earlier it was used as a hallucinogen by the Alpen nomads and it has also been used in European witchcraft.[97]

So the latest edition of *Plants of the Gods* actually confirms (in much more detail than Pollock) the presence of an entirely suitable hallucinogenic agent in Europe in the Upper Palaeolithic – the Liberty Cap mushroom.

Expert opinion

Astonished that Bahn and Helvenston could have got things so wrong, I wondered if there was some reason to doubt *Plants of the Gods* on this matter and sought a second opinion from the British Mycological Society at Kew Gardens. Their former president, Professor Roy Watling OBE, winner of the Royal Society of Edinburgh's Patrick

Neill Medal for research in mycology, wrote to me on 23 November 2004 to confirm that *Psilocybe semilanceata* is indeed native to the Old World and is

> well-distributed from the northernmost Scandinavian countries thru' to the Mediterranean countries . . . Judging from the DNA analysis of other widespread agarics there is little doubt that *Psilocybe semilanceata* would be around in the Palaeolithic in much the form as it is today occurring in nitrophilous enriched areas (but not directly on dung) in woodland clearings and in marginal grassy spots much the same as now . . . No doubt tribal peoples, if not before, soon tested fungi for food and so found that some were 'feel goods' . . .[98]

How could Bahn and Helvenston get out of this? I pressed them on the matter through Chris Scarre, the editor of the *Cambridge Archaeological Journal*, who emailed me their reply on 16 December 2004. To cut a long story short (the reader will find fuller details in Appendix II), they claimed that *Plants of the Gods* and Roy Watling were wrong and that *P. semilanceata* was not in fact an Old World mushroom. Since it is found today in the New World too, they proposed that it originated there and was only introduced to Europe after contact in 1492.[99]

I asked Roy Watling to comment on this latest manoeuvre of the Bahn and Helvenston argument. He replied that *P. semilanceata* occurs widely in Europe:

> from lowlands to subarctic localities and I would think a newly intro-duced species [i.e. post-1492] would not have been able to travel so far . . . I do not know of any European mycologist who thinks that this is nothing other than a good European species . . . It was probably already around during the Palaeolithic and as man started to migrate following animals and later burning small areas of woodland then this fungus would happily have been taken along and may have spread from its normal habitats associated with deer, etc.[100]

Besides, he added, 'why pick on poor old *P. semilanceata*' when there are other native European species that are also rich in psilocybin and could in theory have been used in the Upper Palaeolithic for hallucinogenic purposes:

There are several common *Panaeolus* species which are undoubtedly European growing on dung which contain hallucinogens of the psilocin group . . . *Panaeolus sphinctrinus, P. campanulatus* and *P. papilonaceus* are all widespread in Europe on dung of domesticated and wild herbivores and can supply such compounds. *P. subbalteatus* is found in disturbed ground and *Panaeoina foenisecii* is called the Haymaker being associated with grassland during the hay period. Both contain suitable compounds.[101]

Internationally renowned ethnobotanist and ethnomycologist Giorgio Samorini strongly reinforced this line of argument. In an email to me on 17 December 2004 he wrote:

In Europe more than 30 species of psilocybin mushrooms have been identified; therefore it is not only a matter of *P. semilanceata*, which is surely a very old European mushroom, and for which, clearly, as a mycologist, I have all the demonstrable documentation. Indeed I don't have time to lose with anthropologists and neuropsychologists who pretentiously believe to have in their hands all the knowledge of science other than anthropology and neuropsychology. It is their problem to have difficulties to accept the worldwide historical use of psychoactive drugs and their poor scientific debate doesn't deserve my attention.[102]

US mushroom expert Paul Stamets (author of the highly respected reference book *Psilocybin Mushrooms of the World*[103] wrote to me on 1 January 2005 to say that he found the whole argument ridiculous:

Currently the genus *Psilocybe* has more than 220 species, with about half of them being psilocybin-producing. Are these so-called anthropologist mushroom experts prepared to argue that all of them come from the New World? I think if they knew these numbers, and their distribution, they would temper their enthusiasm for this ill-grounded hypothesis.[104]

Settling the matter with DNA

Having come to know Bahn and Helvenston's style of debate, I somehow doubted that their enthusiasm would be tempered. They were more or less obliged to fight this one out because if it stopped being a matter of expert opinion and could in some way be proved that *P semilanceata* was an ancient Old World species then the entire basis of their attack on Lewis-Williams would fall apart. That other psilocybin-containing mushrooms – such as the *Panaeolus* species – were now also confirmed to have been present in Europe in the Upper Palaeolithic already effectively invalidated their case. And besides, as the example of the San clearly shows, hallucinogenic plants are not the only way to enter the shamanic state of consciousness called for by the neuropsychological model. The artists of the Upper Palaeolithic might just as easily have entered trance, and seen the appropriate visions, through rhythmic dancing. Nevertheless I decided to push for hard, indisputable scientific evidence – something decisive like DNA – on the true provenance of *P semilanceata*.

Again I enlisted the help of Professor Roy Watling, and on 6 January 2005 he kindly agreed to compare the DNA of *P semilanceata* collections from the Old World and *P semilanceata* collections from the New World. A total of 12 such collections are referenced in the international Genbank archive. Five of them are from Europe and were isolated and analysed by Watling himself together with his colleague Maria Martin of Spain's Royal Botanical Gardens in Madrid.[105] The other seven collections are all from North America, one being from the US (North Carolina) and the other six from Canada.[106]

It turned out that the North Carolina data was irrelevant since the US researchers had not looked at the same sections of *P semilanceata* DNA as those studied by Watling and Martin. The closest matches were with the Canadian studies, which, Watling said do not look at all the bits we did. However, there is some common ground and interestingly even in the bits we have the Canadian material varies in itself, but what is significant is that there are important differences with the European material in some cases by as many as eight base pairs, which is significant.[107]

But exactly how significant is this difference between the DNA of European *P semilanceata* and that of North American *P semilianceata*? Well, as it turns out, very significant indeed. Far smaller differences have settled court cases. As Watling explained in an email to me on 16 January 2005, what an eight-base-pair difference indicates beyond any serious dispute is that

> there has been geographical isolation within this species and that it is in both US and Europe which would fit in with what I have said before and that any evolution in Europe to explain the differences could not have happened in historic times.[108]

I cannot predict whether Bahn and Helvenston will ultimately be prepared to accept the DNA evidence that destroys their case against Lewis-Williams, but it is certainly good enough for me. As well as around 30 other species of psilocybin-containing mushrooms, we can now be sure that *P semilanceata* was present in prehistoric Europe and cannot have been introduced recently after first historical contact with the New World in 1492 as Bahn and Helvenston would like to argue. This is what the DNA evidence says, and since Bahn and Helvenston have already admitted that people who have ingested psilocybin do see visions of geometric and therianthropic figures of precisely the kind that are painted on the cave walls, it seems they are obliged to concede that those figures might indeed depict visions seen in psilocybin-induced trances.

Two celibates arguing about sex

There's a funny side to David Lewis-Williams and Paul Bahn arguing about the subjective experience of hallucinations and citing screeds of scholarly references and research studies to support their differing points of view. Lewis-Williams cheerfully admits that he has never taken a hallucinogen in his life, while it is evident from Bahn's writing that he dislikes the whole idea of using such 'artifical means' to alter consciousness. Listening to the two of them on this subject, therefore, is a bit like tuning in to two curmudgeonly lifetime celibates arguing earnestly about the ten best positions for sex. One notes quite soon that both of them have read all the 'how-to' manuals but that they are embarrassingly naïve and misinformed at the level of direct personal experience.

My guess is that a few hefty doses of LSD, mescaline or psilocybin would change them both in fundamental ways – although I have to admit there's a danger that Bahn wouldn't respond well. I suspect the very real and sometimes terrifying sense of loss of control at the edge of a deeply altered state of consciousness might cause him to reject the experience. Still, if he could work through that fear, then I think that an intense hallucinatory journey might persuade him – as such journeys have persuaded me – that the neuropsychological model is very far from being 'Piffle-Lite' (as he insultingly described it in one of his papers).[109]

For this fundamentally is a matter that will *not* be resolved one way or another by clever scholarly arguments and debating tricks. It has nothing to do with whether there are 'stages' or not, or how many of them there are. We won't ever get to the truth by finagling about what shamanism is or by enumerating the 1,001 different kinds of trance (another irritating aspect of Bahn and Helvenston's critique – see Appendix I). It is of no significance whether our sources date from 1953 or 2005. It is simply a fact, and not even a controversial one, that all human beings everywhere, at all periods of history and prehistory, have had the ability – through the use of psychoactive plants and other means – to enter states of consciousness so deeply altered that they believe themselves transported to an otherworld where they can interact with its supernatural inhabitants. As I've said before, not all human beings *use* this ability, but all of us have it, and this is not in dispute. Moreover, its central place in a universal phenomenon of human culture – which some call shamanism – is supported by tens of thousands of examples that could be extracted from anthropological reports and ethnographic records, as well as from the world's religious traditions. Lewis-Williams is right to alert us to the possibility that this phenomenon could be responsible for the extraordinary and haunting art of the deep caves of Upper Palaeolithic Europe.

Once I had some hard-won direct experience of the otherworld through my ayahuasca and ibogaine trances, I knew – at a personal level – how utterly convincing its supernatural inhabitants could be. Whether *in fact* they are supernatural, or in any sense 'real' – rather than just tricks of the mind – are questions that I will not drop simply because science finds such ideas abhorrent. Meanwhile I believe it is entirely reasonable to suppose that such encounters – including, in my case, a half-man/half-crocodile therianthrope – could have convinced our pre-scientific ancestors of the sometimes visible existence of an alternative reality or parallel world of the spirits. It also makes perfect sense to me that the shamans of some prehistoric cultures might have wished to paint images of the strange and powerful beings they encountered on their supernatural journeys. And since they would have seen geometric patterns as well, it is obvious that they would have painted them too. Exactly where and on what surfaces the images would be painted would vary from culture to culture, and some would not bother to paint them at all. But if there was a culture that had wanted to paint these images in southern Africa, then the rock shelters would have provided the ideal canvas. And if there was a culture that had wanted to paint these images in south-west Europe, then how could they possibly have failed to notice the attractions of the walls and ceilings of the deep dark caves – especially if those caves reminded them, more than any other locations on earth of the appearance and atmosphere of the otherworld?

CHAPTER NINE

Serpents of the Drakensberg

Until 1927, the year in which the last official permit was issued for hunting bushmen, it was legal for whites in South Africa to murder the San – whose body parts were kept and boastfully displayed as trophies by the killers. This was around the time that the Abbé Breuil, the 'Pope of Prehistory', who dominated European cave-art studies for much of the twentieth century, made the first of his many visits to southern Africa.[1] The reader will recall the case of the White Lady of the Brandenberg, reported in Chapter Six, in which Breuil wrongly identified a large polychrome rock painting of a bushman as a depiction of a white-skinned woman with a 'Mediterranean profile'. Most other prehistoric San art Breuil wrote off as nothing more than 'hideous little Bushman figures';[2] but certain polychrome images like this one, which made liberal use of the colour white, really took his fancy. He regarded them as the highest art and therefore attributed them to supposed Minoan or Phoenician migrants.[3]

Against the background of this climate of automatic racism and state-sanctioned genocide, it is little wonder that southern San culture was to all extents and purposes extinct by the middle of the twentieth century, represented only by a tiny diminishing remnant of elders scattered as refugees amongst Xhosa, Zulu, Pondomise, Sotho and other Bantu-speaking African tribes who had been prepared to give them sanctuary. As this last generation died out, the San language and the oral mythology that had been transmitted faithfully for thousands of years died out too, a slow falling of silence leaving behind the majestic panorama of the rock art, seemingly mute.

Yet we have seen that the silence was not quite total. The Bleek and Lloyd documents and other nineteenth- and early twentieth-century ethnography saved something of the essence of bushman religious, spiritual and mythological thought, keeping the window open on the lost otherworld of the southern San for anyone with the initiative to look.

Nor is the written ethnography the only such resource. A second important refuge for San culture, which scholars are beginning to explore, has been the series of syncretistic unions it managed to form with the cultures of the surrounding Bantu-speaking tribes. These were the very cultures that gave the last surviving bushmen their protection. They did so because they and their ancestors had lived alongside the San since the first migrations of Bantu peoples from further north began to arrive in southern Africa many hundreds of years previously. For the most part the relationship they struck up with the indigenous inhabitants was a harmonious one, with a great deal of mutual interchange and, frequently, intermarriage.[4] Indeed, so close did the connection become in the case of Bantu tribes such as the Xhosa, the Pondomise, the Thembo and others (known collectively as the Nguni) that their languages acquired and permanently incorporated the characteristic 'click' sounds of spoken San. One sixth of the Xhosa language, for example, contains these click sounds, hinting at just how strong the bushman legacy in this culture really may be.[5]

San influence was also powerful amongst the Sotho (not part of the Nguni group), who revered the bushmen as the original and wise inhabitants of the land and sought out their participation in ritual affairs.[6] There are reports of Sotho healers chipping pigment from San rock paintings to incorporate in their medicines since the pigment itself was believed to possess curative powers.[7]

Likewise, even today, the Nguni in remote rural areas still 'speak about the San of long ago, and a few people are known to be of San descent'.[8] There are also suggestions of a close, teacher–pupil relationship involving a transfer of 'medicines', quite possibly hallucinogens, between San !gi:ten on the one hand and Nguni apprentices on the other. As David Lewis-Williams puts it:

According to Nguni tradition, San shamans give Nguni acolytes certain medicines that enable them to understand the San language . . . After the 'language medicine' the shamans give the novices other medicines that enable them to 'see more clearly in their dreams'. During dreams and trance experiences a shaman and a novice go on extended journeys to the spirit world where, together, they see wild animals . . . According to the Nguni, some of these creatures are monsters that cannot be seen by ordinary people.[9]

Both the Nguni and the San use altered states of consciousness to enter into contact with what they believe is the spirit world. Amongst the Xhosa this often traumatic and difficult work (frequently involving spirit possession during trance) is done by ritual specialists known as *igqirha*, a title that derives directly from the San *!gi:xa*, meaning shaman.[10] Another area of overlap, which again suggests the possibility that much of value from San culture may have survived amongst the Nguni, is that San shamans also joined Nguni tribes permanently as professional rainmakers[11] – a skill, as we know, that they believed they exercised by entering trance, passing over to the spirit world, capturing a 'rain animal' and bringing it back to 'cut' or 'milk' it in this world over the area suffering drought.[12] The association of rain with certain kinds of spirit animals is a concept shared in both cultures. Amongst the Nguni, however, the rain animals most typically envisaged were not the hybrid creatures of the bushmen – part buffalo, part hippo – but much more often gigantic serpents whose dwelling place was said to be deep within rivers. Gigantic serpents in their turn are also a feature of San rock art, particularly in the mountainous wilderness of the Drakensberg.[13]

Centuries of living together, in short, meant that the indigenous San tribes picked up some aspects of Bantu culture and influenced the culture of the Bantu immigrants equally strongly in return. There were important differences and San shamanism was not the same as the shamanism of the Sotho and Nguni. Nevertheless, the similarities were sufficiently close to enable San shamans to participate frequently in Sotho and Nguni initiation rites.[14] It probably would be impossible to disentangle this complex web completely, but enough common points have emerged from it for scholars to feel justified in drawing certain limited inferences about the spiritual world of the San from what is known about the spiritual world of the Sotho and Nguni peoples.[15]

It was for this reason, during my research visit to South Africa in April 2004, that I was glad to take up the offer of a local ethnographic filmmaker, Bokka du Toit, to introduce me to a leading Nguni shaman living in the area of Jeffrey's Bay on the Southern Cape. Named Mama Magaba, she turned out to be an enormous, powerful woman of mixed Xhosa and San descent. I had been told before meeting her that she would soon be conducting an initiation ceremony for two spiritual healers – twins, a man and a woman in their forties, both apparently well advanced on the shamanic path. The ceremony would take place on the banks of the Gamtoos River, near the town of Hankey, and would last three days. I asked if I might attend it and, after some discussion mediated by Bokka, Mama Magaba agreed that I could witness the closing rituals that would take place on the final morning at sunrise.

As I made these arrangements I had no idea that the spirit world – or perhaps I should say, cautiously, the power of belief in the spirit world – would make its presence felt so graphically, or with such tangible force, in that cold dawn by the river.

The claiming of a soul

I reported the wars in Ethiopia and Somalia in the 1970s and 1980s. I have seen people killed by machine-gun bullets and mortar bombs. But I've never seen anyone killed directly by *belief* before, or for that matter by anything as intangible as 'spirits'. So what happened that morning on the banks of the Gamtoos, when I witnessed a man in his forties lose his life suddenly – at the whim of what he certainly believed were spirits – was something that I was absolutely unprepared for by anything in my previous experience.

When we arrived, the sun was not yet above the local horizon but a pearl-grey first light was seeping across the sky. Walking through thick undergrowth soaking with dew, we passed a large grass hut with an open fire burning in front of it. From there we followed a narrow path towards the river and I began to hear the sound of chanting. We walked on and soon I could make out a second hut in the distance with a large group of people standing beside it, many of them wrapped in shawls and blankets against the penetrating cold and the faint damp mist that hugged the ground.

Coming closer, I saw that the hut overlooked the river and that the people were observing, with rapt attention, the activity that was taking place in the river itself, where Mama Magaba, in all her massive solemnity, stood waist deep in the slow-moving icy current wearing voluminous white robes. Beside her, naked, was a smaller, leaner, grey-haired woman, already up to her chest in the water, who Mama Magaba now proceeded to duck beneath the surface repeatedly – perhaps as many as a dozen times – while the observers continued their chanting. I couldn't help thinking how shocking and uncomfortable it must have felt, being plunged under the freezing water like that, and not just plunged quickly in and out but held under for some time before coming back up for air and then going down again. Though a different approach to the San trance-dance, this is precisely the sort of physical stress that has the capacity to bring on altered states of consciousness.

When the woman initiate came out of the river, others rushed to wrap her warmly in a thick blanket. She was shivering at first but quite soon stopped. All in all she seemed in surprisingly good shape, considering the ordeal she had just been through, and joined in happily with the rest of the crowd to witness her brother's ceremony.

He stripped down to his underwear, revealing a scrawny body, and entered the water with Mama Magaba. There was more chanting and singing, hands clapping to the rhythm. Once again the repeated immersions began, ten times, maybe twenty; I lost count. Then the two of them came out again and the initiate, like his sister, was wrapped in a blanket.

For a moment he seemed fine. He was smiling, talking quietly, but then little by little his demeanour changed, slackness came over his features, a far-off, unfocused look settled in on his eyes. We all walked back now to the first hut we had passed on the way in and the initiate's condition worsened. As he came near to the fire his legs and body suddenly lost all strength and he dropped heavily to the ground. Others picked him up and tried to help him to stand but it was as though he had no bones or muscles. It didn't occur to me that he was dying, because he was certainly still alive at that time, but his eyes were wide and wild and he looked very frightened, as though he had seen something that terrified him. He fell again, and lost consciousness. Bokka rushed him to hospital in the back of his pick-up truck, but it was too late.

Probably it was a heart attack brought on by stress and cold, but when we questioned Mama Magaba about what had happened, she told us that everyone, including the initiate himself, had been expecting this and that it was a good death for a man to pass over to the world of the spirits at the time of such a ceremony. When I asked why the death was expected, she explained that the night before, when they had all been gathered in the hut on the river bank, they had been visited by powerful supernatural beings who she called the 'river people'. She described them as very tall and black-skinned with golden hair, and said, in a most matter-of-fact way, that they lived in the depths of great rivers but could emerge from the waters and move amongst ordinary mortals on the land – sometimes to do good, sometimes to do harm. Last night, in the company of a procession of serpents and river animals, they had surfaced from the deep, entered the hut with water still dripping from their glistening bodies, and claimed the soul of the initiate.

Mystery of the river people

Later I was able to research the matter a little further. In Nguni languages the traditional name given to the mysterious river people is the *abantubomlambo*. Spoken of in hushed tones as both malevolent and benevolent in nature – and always unpredictably so – they take the form not only of strange-looking human beings, but also of snakes.[16] Perhaps this therianthropic ambiguity is why they are always closely associated with gigantic aquatic serpents called *ichanti*, said to live alongside them in the underwater otherworld,[17] and to which several scholars have turned for a possible explanation of San rock paintings of serpents in the Drakensberg mountains.[18] Particularly noteworthy in light of the San's age-old shamanic theme is that these mysterious *ichanti* are 'masters of transformation' capable of shape-shifting with hypnotic rapidity: '*Ichanti* can assume the appearance of almost anything from a snake to a goat and transform itself from an iron chain to a feather to a honeycomb.'[19]

Interviewed in the 1920s, Xhosa healers talked about the way they perceived these apparently random transformations:

> They likened the rapidly changing patterns they observed in a kaleido-scope to *ichanti*. Perhaps because of these rapid transformations it is believed that *ichanti* have the power to mesmerise people.[20]

In 1931 the anthropologist J.H. Soga was the earliest to note that accounts of the *ichanti* – which he called 'water-sprites' – sound a lot like hallucinations.[21] Indeed, with the benefit of what we know today, we can be more specific than that. The Xhosa elders' descriptions of rapidly changing geometric patterns merging with iconic images are reminiscent of the hallucinatory process that stands at the heart of the neuropsychological model of rock and cave art. Anthropological reports add weight to this suspicion of a hallucinatory origin for the *ichanti* and for the river people (who are sometimes also snakes) with whom they are invariably linked:

> During the period of their initiation, diviners from many Nguni groups travel in dreams and trance to underwater realms in rivers, where they encounter a large underwater serpent, the *ixanti* [*ichanti*], surrounded by snakes which are directly associated with the ancestral spirits. Initi-ates are required to capture one or more of these snakes . . . Other ancestral beings known as the River People, *abantubomlambo*, are also encountered in this realm . . .[22]

A final level of the puzzle noted by anthropologists is that Nguni shamans are themselves commonly associated with snakes: 'They are believed to be able to control snakes, and in some cases to turn into these creatures.'[23]

All in all, therefore, we are in familiar visionary territory with this complex of beliefs involving spirit beings, the otherworld and therianthropic transformations. Even the underwater theme, as we have seen in previous chapters, is quite standard global shamanic fare built around the imagery of waterholes, funnels, vortices and whirlpools.[24] It is for this reason that David Lewis-Williams is unwilling to include suggestive spiral and vortex patterns sometimes seen in rock and cave art in the general category of entoptic phenomena, but prefers to regard them – together with accounts of being underground, underwater, etc. – as part of the flow of hallucinations at the edge of the deepest levels of trance.[25] He also points out that Westerners tend to use words like 'funnels', 'cones', and 'vessels' to describe the vortex.[26] In other cultures the same neurological phenomenon is frequently experienced as entering an underground tunnel filled up with rushing water:

> probably because of the rushing and roaring heard in certain altered states of consciousness . . . When the Inuit are living on the ice, the route to the underworld is through the sea: 'He almost glides as if falling through a tube' (Ramussen, 1929, 124). The hole down which a Tavgi Samoyed shaman moves leads to a river with streams flowing in opposite directions. Reports of culture-specific apprehensions of this universal, neurologically determined hallucination of subterranean and subaqueous travel could easily be multiplied.[27]

Perhaps not surprisingly, one place in which such reports could be multiplied is southern Africa. Modern anthropological studies amongst the *Ju/'hoansi* (*!Kung*) bushmen of the Kalahari have produced statements from several shamans who speak of travelling underwater and down through the depths of the earth as their trances deepen.[28] Likewise from the Bleek and Lloyd documents we know that San informants in Cape Province in the nineteenth century:

> spoke of shamans going into a 'waterpit' where the water was 'alive'; there they captured the hallucinatory *!khwa-ka xoro*, the rain animal, which they killed so that its blood and milk would fall as rain. /Kaggen,

the San trickster deity, who was himself a shaman, dived into water-holes during trance episodes.[29]

And at the bottom of the waterholes lived gigantic serpents, in their turn sometimes seen as rain animals, which the Nguni tribes called *ichanti* and which shared their subaqueous otherworld with the race of spirits called the *abantubomlambo* – the river people. They were hallucinations and yet they could emerge from the depths, their long hair dripping, stride along the river banks accompanied by a retinue of water serpents, and steal away with the souls of men.

Eight major anomalies

After leaving the Gamtoos river, the final leg of my research trip in South Africa in April 2004 took me through the rugged Drakensberg mountains where there are many thousands of San rock paintings – amongst them quite a number showing gigantic serpents that scholars connect with the *ichanti*.[30] One very good reason that they do this is again derived from the ethnography. In the nineteenth century the artist George William Stow several times showed his excellent reproductions of San rock paintings to surviving bushmen. One of these reproductions features a huge horned serpent slithering through the rock face. An elderly San woman named Kou'ke immediately recognised it and claimed that in the days of her forefathers such enormous and powerful serpents had 'lived in rivers'.[31] Since we know that 'living in rivers' is one of the common underwater metaphors for trance, this was as good as saying that the horned serpents were creatures of trance – as are the river-dwelling *ichanti*.

However, this wasn't the only reason that I was curious to see these images. My own visionary encounters with gigantic serpents when I was under the influence of the Amazonian hallucinogen ayahuasca had left me with the weird conviction that such apparitions were somehow much more than mere hallucinations – that I might even, as the shamans claim, have confronted intelligent spiritual entities of some kind who were communicating with me. Now such ideas, I am fully aware, sound really crazy from a twenty-first-century scientific perspective that knows (or thinks it knows) a great deal about brain chemistry. But to our prehistoric ancestors, who had no such perspective, the sense of absolute, seamless, impermeable reality that surrounds the strong hallucinations of deep trance would, I think, have been utterly convincing – and utterly persuasive of the existence of a supernatural dimension inhabited by non-physical, shape-shifting beings.

Human nature being what it is, it seems to me virtually inevitable that those who had entered trance (by whatever means), and who had undergone such powerful, deeply felt and poorly understood experiences, would have wanted to talk about them. Our ancestors had the same sense of wonder and curiosity as we do. They would have felt compelled to describe the amazing things they had seen, discuss them with others who had cultivated similar experiences, and try to make sense of it all – thus, over a few generations, transforming their visions of the otherworld into an evolved and agreed mythology.[32]

By the same logic I find it reasonable that some people in some cultures might have wanted to paint or engrave their visions on to enduring surfaces – perhaps even on the walls and ceilings of rock shelters and caves. Accordingly, I once again cannot agree with Lewis-Williams' critics Paul Bahn and Patricia Helvenston (writing in the *Cambridge Archaeological Journal*) when they describe the notion that 'rock art is produced by visionary experience' as a 'startling assumption'.[33] Humankind has a very old, very deep and very complex relationship with plant hallucinogens (see Chapters Twenty-One and Twenty-Two). Given this long history, it is not 'startling', but wholly predictable, that trance-inspired rock and cave art should exist at a number of locations in the wide world – and that some of it should be extremely ancient. Such a possibility, comments archaeologist David Pearce in reaction to Bahn and Helvenston's critique

is startling only in a twenty-first century view that apportions low value to the less rational aspects of consciousness and condemns outright the use of mind-altering drugs. A brief survey of world ethnography would reveal a long list of cultures that do value and cultivate these very states. It is doubtful that they would find the proposition that some rock art was related to altered states of consciousness 'startling'.[34]

The more closely I examined all the competing theories and arguments, therefore, and the more carefully I considered the alternative points of view generated and abandoned by a century of scholarship, the more sure I felt that Lewis-Williams was right that the rock art of the San in southern Africa and the cave art of Upper Palaeolithic Europe had been inspired by the experiences of shamans in deeply altered states of consciousness. Indeed, in the case of the San, thanks to the surviving ethnography, many scholars already regard this as the most plausible explanation of the art. In the case of the Upper Palaeolithic cave artists, we can never be so sure while we lack any form of ethnography from their times. Nonetheless it is a fact that the art they left behind raises many of the same questions as the art of the bushmen and that any theory purporting to explain the strong and superficially very different imagery in both places also has to be able to account for the most glaring and anomalous similarities as well. As we saw in Chapter Five, these include:

1. The therianthropes.
2. The chimeras – hybrid animals blending the characteristics of two or more different species.
3. The monsters – bizarre, fantastic and often wildly distorted creatures.
4. The frequent appearance of abstract and geometrical patterns and their recurrent combination with fully iconic figures.
5. The way that both systems treat the rock face as though it were a permeable veil or membrane beyond which lie hidden worlds.
6. The multiple superimpositions of images on top of earlier images.
7. The absence of ground and horizon lines and the disregard of relative scale.
8. The strange figures of 'wounded Men' penetrated by many arrows or spears.

Explanations with the neuropsychological model

We have seen in previous chapters that figures from categories 1, 2 and 3 listed above feature prominently in the oldest rock art of Europe and Africa.[35] This has to be significant, because in normal waking consciousness we humans never routinely encounter therianthropes, chimeras or monsters, nor have we ever done so in the past. Daily experience, therefore, is most unlikely to have inspired the emotionally charged depictions of such entities that have come down to us from prehistory.

Could the unaided creative imagination of individual artists be the simple answer? Perhaps, but we would still need to explain why idiosyncratic talent keeps on coming up with the same weird formulae of man-beasts, hybrid animals and freakish monsters, and why it has been doing so since human beings first began to make art. Jungian concepts like the collective unconscious could be brought to bear on such shared imagery, of course, but then those very concepts would in turn call for further explanation. What, after all, is the collective unconscious? Has its existence ever been satisfactorily demonstrated? How does it work? Whence and how does it derive its store of common imagery? And isn't it in essence a description of a mystery that needs to be solved rather the solution to that mystery?

I don't rule out the notion of a collective unconscious at all, but I don't need to use a phenomenon that is itself problematic and unexplained in order to understand the distinctive presence of therianthropes, chimeras and monsters in the cave art of Upper Palaeolithic Europe and the rock art of southern Africa.

Regarding the latter, it is worth repeating what we already know from the ethnography – that many of the extraordinary paintings and engravings were inspired by the hallucinations of San shamans (who were also the artists) and depict their visionary encounters and transformations in the spirit world where they believed they were able to travel in the form of animals.[36]

But such elaborate hallucinatory encounters are not unique to shamans or to the San. We know now that they are a global phenomenon of altered states of consciousness. And while we cannot actually interview people from the Upper Palaeolithic, we can be almost as certain that some of them hallucinated as we can be that they ate and drank. In Part III we will see just how universal such encounters have been throughout human history and how frequently they feature therianthropes, chimeras and monsters. It is no surprise, therefore, that therianthropes, chimeras and monsters should play the role they do in the art of the caves.

Albeit on a small scale, my own experiences bear this out. I have seen therianthropes, chimeras and monsters depicted in the rock art of the San – art that I know reproduces the visions of hallucinating shamans. And under the influence of ayahuasca, as I reported in Chapter Three, I found myself in the presence of an extremely compelling and surprising therianthrope, saw a butterfly transform into a serpent and a serpent into a jaguar, and was obliged to confront monstrous dragons and a huge insect with humanoid features. I therefore have no hesitation in agreeing with David Lewis-Williams that the inspiration for the therianthropes, chimeras and monsters in the cave art of Upper Palaeolithic Europe is very likely to have been similar trance experiences.

What makes this all the more probable are the recurrent combinations of abstract and geometric 'signs' with iconic figures that we've documented throughout the rock art of the San and from the very beginning to the very end of the cave art story in Europe – category 4 in the list above. As with the first three categories, David Lewis-Williams' neuropsychological model really does offer the only logical, coherent and internally consistent single solution to the 'persistently intractable' mystery of these signs.[37] They are depictions of entoptic phenomena seen in trance states. The case that they are universal because they are controlled by the structure of the human nervous system has been extremely well made.

It is the same story with categories 5, 6 and 7, and again, all the evidence has already been put before the reader in the previous chapters. Why is the rock face dynamically incorporated into the paintings in such a way that it seems a permeable veil between this and other worlds? Why are images again and again superimposed upon one another? Why didn't the artists care about scale or give us ground and horizon lines – so that their figures often seem to 'float' abstractly? Where other attempts at explanation flounder, the neuropsychological model suggests a simple scenario that offers sensible answers to all three questions:

- first the artists entered altered states of consciousness in the caves and rock shelters (by trance-dancing in southern Africa; probably by the ingestion of *Psilocybe semilanceata* or other psilocybin-containing mushrooms in Upper Palaeolithic Europe – although a form of trance-dance, or other physical techniques of altering consciousness, cannot be ruled out there also);
- secondly they experienced hallucinations which were seen to emerge from behind the walls and ceilings of the caves and rock shelters – as though they were literally breaking through a veil or membrane of rock into this world – very frequently one crowding in on top of the other or 'floating' here and there with no relative scale or positioning;
- thirdly, after the trance state had passed, the artists devoted themselves to reproducing the highlights of their visions in the places that they had seen them on the walls of the caves/rock shelters, thus 'fixing' or memorialising these places as portals to the spirit world.

It doesn't need to have happened exactly like that, but a scenario of this general sort does provide a plausible explanation for what are otherwise extremely puzzling and indeed inexplicable features of the rock and cave art of southern Africa and Upper Palaeolithic Europe. When we remember that this explanatory power derives from the same model that has already successfully solved other 'intractable' mysteries of these arts – the therianthropes, the chimeras, the monsters, the geometry – it becomes more and more obvious how valuable a key to our own past David Lewis-Williams has presented us with.

Indeed, out of the list of eight major anomalies that link the rock art of southern Africa and the cave art of Upper Palaeolithic Europe, his neuropsychological key has so far proved its capacity to unlock the first seven. The eighth is the figure of the 'wounded man' – which any theory that claims to be broadly correct must of course be able to explain. There is also a ninth anomaly that we need to consider, but it is limited to the European art: why were so many of the wonderful paintings and engravings placed inside very deep, very dark caves where they could only be approached with great difficulty and only be seen with artificial light?

One of the most 'user-friendly' features of the neuropsychological model is its ability to suggest answers to unanswered questions and, as we'll see in Chapter Ten, it does have answers to these last two anomalies. But an almost equally significant test of its truth is the way that it is capable of proving its usefulness and explanatory power again and again, in front of almost any panel of rock or cave art belonging to the southern African and European prehistoric traditions. In the case of South Africa, thanks to the ethnography, we often have the added satisfaction of being sure that the explanation is right.

This was brought home to me as I continued my journey in the Drakensberg mountains after witnessing the strange events on the banks of the Gamtoos river.

Solving the mysteries of the Long Panel and Snake Rock

At Main Caves (not true caves but a series of large rock shelters) in what is today the Giant's Castle Nature Reserve in the heart of the Drakensberg, I was able to spend some hours studying an extraordinary composition more than five metres in length known unimaginatively as the Long Panel. The two central figures that dominate the entire composition have already been described briefly in Chapter Four. They are therianthropes with human legs, buttocks and

The Giant's Castle therianthropes. Note the serpents with reedbuck heads coiled around the upper body of the figure on the right

arms, and the heads of mountain reedbuck. The figure on the right is additionally entwined within the coils of two gigantic serpents which, on close examination, both also prove to be hybrid figures – chimeras with the bodies of snakes and the heads, again, of reedbuck (one of them complete with horns). The figure on the left is not thus encumbered but has two long feather-like appendages protruding out of its mid-back. Meanwhile, positioned about a metre or so further to the left and a little higher on the rock face is another impressive chimera, this time an eland/feline with the tail and spotted coat of a

Eland-feline

leopard but with the hind legs of a large antelope. An additional curiosity are small dots, each extending some distance beyond the body, that are painted in a row along the spine of the animal and down part of its tail.

Lying on the ground a few metres to the right of the Long Panel is a large, thick, jagged slab of rock – Snake Rock – probably weighing a couple of tons, that fell in antiquity after detaching itself from the ceiling. Sometime after it fell, perhaps when the Long Panel was painted, San shamans came here and covered it with a complex series of images in red ochre including depictions of two serpents. The first, which has the head and ears of an antelope and is bleeding copiously from the nose, seems to emerge from a crack in the rock face. It hangs suspended, spattering nasal blood over a crowded, difficult composition directly beneath it in which the second serpent forms the centrepiece. This one isn't a hybrid, being 100 per cent snake from

'Snake Rock',
the complete scene

head to tail, but it too bleeds from the nose. It is coiled in four large, thick loops around a strangely abstract human figure with unnaturally elongated body and legs. Several more of these attenuated, stretched-out humans seem to 'float' nearby.

'Snake Rock', detail

Without the neuropsychological theory and the boost given to it by the San ethnography, how could we ever hope to explain any of these puzzling images? With these tools, however, the paintings begin to speak eloquently to us of trance experiences.

The two therianthropes in the Long Panel are shamans, transforming into reedbuck, travelling in the spirit world. The feathers protruding from the back of one may signal a further level of transformation into a bird or into one of a species of winged therianthropes frequently portrayed in San rock art which combine avian and antelope anatomy.

universally as subjects enter the profoundest levels of trance. As we saw in Chapter Eight:

> Many laboratory subjects report experiencing a vortex or rotating tunnel that seems to surround them . . . The sides of the vortex are marked by a lattice of squares like television screens. The images on these 'screens' are the first spontaneously produced iconic hallucinations; they eventually overlie the vortex as entoptics give way to iconic images.[53]

Of course Upper Palaeolithic people did not have the concept of television screens. But if they were looking for locations in the everyday world where they could best reproduce their impressions

Image from El Castillo Cave, approximately 15,000 years old. 'The sides of the vortex are marked by a lattice of squares like television screens'.

of the vortex as they entered the spirit world, then the walls and ceilings of the deep dark caves would have cried out for attention. Indeed, like shamans of all times and places, it seems almost inevitable that these early psychic voyagers would have seen the caves – to repeat Eliade's insight – as 'concrete symbols of passage into another world, or a descent to the underworld'. Here was darkness, here were tunnels, here were calcite formations in the form of monsters or mammoths seeming to grow like living things out of the rock face, here were vast echoing chambers, forests of glittering stalagmites, steep deadfalls, narrow fissures and diverticules, underground rivers. For those who had already been ushered by psilo-cybin or by trance-dancing into chthonic hallucinatory realms it is easy to see how the deep caves of Franco-Cantabria could have been perceived as gateways to the land of the spirits, perhaps even as its border territories. And there is no doubt, with the low flickering lighting provided by simple Upper Palaeolithic lamps, that shamans in suitably altered states of consciousness inside the caves would have seen utterly convincing visions of the denizens of the spirit world 'floating' through the thin membrane of the rock walls and begin-ning to materialise before their eyes surrounded by scintillating geometrical patterns.

Since that, more or less, is exactly what we see painted on the walls of the caves, since paintings and engravings were frequently made in extremely remote locations that would have been difficult and dangerous to access, and since we have such figures as the wounded men, it makes perfect sense to conclude that a profound and mysterious shamanic quest lay at the heart of Upper Palaeolithic religion. Moreover, this was no slight or primitive effort but an immense project, sustained over more than 25,000 years, that used altered states of consciousness systematically, in carefully controlled settings, to explore and chart the antipodes of the mind. It was, in a sense, the longest-running neuropsychological experiment in history – one that has the potential to unlock the deepest mysteries of human consciousness – and its origins are inextricably interlinked in the archaeological record with the still poorly understood process by which fully modern human behaviour first emerged. Indeed the hypothesis cannot be dismissed that it may well have been shamanic explorations of hallucinatory realms during the Upper Palaeolithic that played the catalytic role in extracting our ancestors from the five-million-year torpor of the hominid line, galvanised their intu-ition and creativity, helped them to build a stable and nurturing, non-violent society that lasted for 25,000 years – in itself a stag-gering accomplishment – and set them on a dramatically new course of evolution.

Scientific sacrilege

Could it be, as shamans in the Amazon repeatedly assert, that the plants really do open a channel of communication to supernatural realms and teachers? Could it be, as the *!Kung* bushmen of the Kalahari tell us with equal vehemence, that their ability to enter deeply altered states of consciousness through their trance dances really does give them access to powerful non-physical entities capable of influencing events in this world? And isn't it logical to conclude, since evolution has bestowed these peculiar and distinctive abilities on the human race, that contact with the supernatural must have offered some profound adaptive advantage to our ancestors and could, conceivably, continue to do so today?

Even to whisper such questions amounts to scientific sacrilege of the worst order – for the assumption on which science is built is that there is no such thing as the 'supernatural', no such thing as 'spirits', and that all unexplained phenomena, no matter how mysterious they may at first appear to be, will prove on proper examination to have natural causes that are fully explicable in terms of established physical, chemical and biological laws.

In the case of shamanism, everything is quite the opposite. Here the bedrock of the entire edifice is the conviction that the supernatural *does* exist. More than merely existing, it is believed to be the senior and pre-eminent dimension and to have a profound influence on all

'Fallen Rock' Shelter, Western Cape. Central figure: the spirit of a trance-dancing shaman separating from the body to explore the supernatural realm.

other levels of reality. From the perspective of shamanic cultures, no one disputes that we need to take proper account of the supernatural, and make every effort to learn what we can about it, if we wish to lead full and balanced lives as material creatures on the physical earth.

The common response of scientists who do not believe in the supernatural is to dismiss all such ideas as hallucinations. But we will see in later chapters that this is disingenuous – to say the least! – since science does not yet really have the faintest idea what hallucinations are, or how they are caused, or why our brains should have evolved in such a way that certain plants can induce them. It is a more or less automatic assumption for I would guess close to 99 out of 100 educated people in the technologically advanced countries today that hallucinations are simply 'wanderings of the mind', foolish tricks of brain chemistry to which it would be mad to attribute any objective reality. Yet the truth is that science has never proved this to be the case, and indeed has not yet even progressed very far in understanding the neurological basis of normal day-to-day perception,[54] let alone what is involved in occasioning the fantastic mental imagery that is characteristic of hallucinations.

There is an unspoken assumption that the brain is some sort of factory that simply manufactures hallucinations, whereas, with the images of 'normal' perception, we tend to think of the brain more as a receiver picking up and processing relevant data from the outside world. But there is another possibility which science, with its materialist mindset, has never seriously pursued and this is that the brain may be operating as a receiver with hallucinations too. By this reckoning, hallucinogens and other means of inducing altered states of consciousness work by temporarily 'retuning' the brain to pick up frequencies, dimensions and entities that are completely real in their own way but that are normally inaccessible to us.

This, in a nutshell, is the anti-scientific idea at the heart of shamanism – which does not doubt that the mind can be retuned to experience other levels of reality but rather seeks to harness that capacity to explore those other realms and to channel and maximise the benefits derived there for the good of society as a whole. It is ironic that we today, who have criminalised the use of hallucinogens, and can offer our young people no wise advice when they pursue the natural human yearning for altered states of consciousness, have the temerity to imagine that we know better about these remarkable substances than other cultures that have lived with them and made controlled use of them for thousands of years. It is equally absurd to suppose, in the 50 or so years in which Western neuropsychologists were able to conduct systematic research with hallucinogens – before being stopped by the 'War on Drugs' – that they could have learnt even a fraction as much as is already known through long accumulated experience by any shaman in the Amazon jungle today.

Nevertheless, by the early 1970s, just before the War on Drugs really began to take prisoners, a few neuropsychologists were beginning to give serious consideration to what look in retrospect like profoundly shamanistic ideas – including 'discussions of hallucinogenic drug use as a threshold to paranormal phenomena'.[55] Another mystery, which we'll explore in later chapters, is that a broad range of volunteers from very different backgrounds and cultures, who had not met and had no opportunity to compare notes, repeatedly gave lab researchers descriptions of what appear to have been *the same* intelligent, communicative, non-physical 'entities' encountered on their trance journeys.

Who are we to say that such entities are just figments of consciousness that have no real existence? What do we really understand about the place that shamans call the 'spirit world', or of the states of trance that they must enter in order to explore it? What confidence can we possibly have in anything we've been told, when the very scientists who pronounce so loftily on the non-existence of spirits and the impossibility of the supernatural turn out never to have experienced a deeply altered state of consciousness in their lives and profess to hate and despise the plants that could offer them such an experience in an instant? Their assessments of hallucinatory realms and beings are therefore based exclusively on their preconceptions about the nature of reality rather than on direct personal knowledge; as such they should rightly be disregarded.

By contrast, it is precisely because of their own repeated personal experiences, and deep explorations of hallucinatory phenomena, that shamans of all lands and times are unanimous in the opinion that only a thin veil separates the world of everyday reality from supernatural otherworlds where powerful spirits dwell. David Lewis-Williams' genius has been to demonstrate how this shamanic perception of reality, and the specific kinds of hallucinations seen and experienced in the altered states of consciousness entered by shamans, provide by far the most plausible explanation for the most ancient art of mankind, for the dawn of religion, and, intriguingly, perhaps even for the mysterious 'x-factor' in our evolution that jolted our ancestors not only into the practice of religion and the creation of great art but also into the complete suite of fully modern behaviour that begins to be widely documented in the archaeological record after about 40,000 years ago.

It is, however, at this point that Lewis-Williams' work, having pursued a wildly unorthodox trajectory by giving such importance to altered states of consciousness, merges back smoothly and without protest into the mainstream. As I've indicated several times in previous chapters, he is of absolutely one mind with the mass of scientists on the subject of the 'spirit world' and 'spirit beings'. Whatever the cave artists saw in their trances, and no matter how devoutly they may have believed that what they were seeing was real, Lewis-Williams is adamant that the entire inspiration for 25,000 years of Upper Palaeolithic cave paintings reduces to nothing more than the fevered illusions of disturbed brain chemistry – i.e. to hallucinations. In his scientific universe there is simply no room, or need, for the supernatural, no space for any kind of otherworld, and no possibility that intelligent non-physical entities could exist.

Quest for the ancient teachers of mankind

I found I couldn't leave the matter there, with the inspiration for cave art and the birth of religion neatly accounted for by disturbed brain chemistry, with the earliest spiritual insights of mankind rendered down to mere epiphenomena of strictly biological processes, with the sublime thus efficiently reduced to the ridiculous. At risk of repetition, I need to stress again that to have established the role of hallucinations as the inspiration for cave art is one thing – and David Lewis-Williams, in my opinion, has successfully done that. But to understand what hallucinations really are, and what part they play in the overall spectrum of human perceptions, is another thing altogether, and neither Lewis-Williams nor any other scientist can yet claim to possess such knowledge, or to be anywhere near acquiring it. Gifted and experienced shamans the world over really do know more – much more – than they do. So if we were smart we would listen to what the shamans have to say about the true character and complexity of reality instead of basking mindlessly in the overweening one-dimensional arrogance of the Western technological mindset.

Because I had been shaken to the core by my experiences with ayahuasca and ibogaine, I decided to take my investigation further and to explore the extraordinary possibility that science is unwilling even to consider and that David Lewis-Williams dismisses out of hand. This is the possibility that the Amazonian and African hallucinogens had obliged me to confront face to face and that shamans contend with on a daily basis – the possibility that the spirit world and its inhabitants are real, that supernatural powers and non-physical beings do exist, and that human consciousness may, under certain special circumstances, be liberated from the body and enabled to interact with and perhaps even learn from these 'spirits'. In short, did our ancestors experience their great evolutionary leap forward of the last 50,000 years not just because of the beneficial social and organisational by-products of shamanism but because they were literally helped, taught, prompted and inspired by supernatural agents?

The very idea, I know, sounds preposterous at first to anyone educated in the Western logical positivist tradition. The more closely I pursued it, however, the more convinced I became that it is a matter of extraordinary substance and that science has done us an immense disfavour by its policy of ridiculing and discouraging all rational enquiry in this area.

PART III
The Beings

CHAPTER ELEVEN

Voyage into the Supernatural

The ocean of the supernatural is vast and treacherous. It cannot be navigated without charts. Wherever possible, landmarks must be sought from which to take one's bearings.

My first landmark, and the mystery that originally drew me to this enquiry, was the realisation that encounters with supernatural beings are documented in the oldest representational art that has so far been found anywhere in the world – art depicting therianthropes and dating back more than 30,000 years. The discovery that shamans in surviving hunter-gatherer cultures routinely experience encounters with virtually identical beings when they enter trance, and that I could and did encounter such beings myself under the influence of the same hallucinogens that the shamans use, convinced me that there was a real mystery to explore here.

Yes, by all means, the 'beings' that ayahuasca and ibogaine brought me literally face to face with might just be illusions of disturbed brain chemistry, as Western scientists claim, but they certainly hadn't seemed that way to me. On the contrary, everything that these two plant-based hallucinogens had put me through had felt *very strongly and convincingly* like the opening of doors on to other and entirely different levels of reality. The experiences had been profound, deeply moving, thought-provoking in a lasting way and also, in one case, weirdly menacing and terrifying.

I found it hard to believe that all this complexity and detail, together with amazing images that seemed to have no connection whatsoever to my previous life or interests, could simply have been generated out of nowhere by my poor drug-fried brain. My intuition was that I had been afforded glimpses, however brief and however distorted by my own cultural preconditioning, of beings that are absolutely real in some modality not yet understood by science, that exist around us and with us, *that even seem to be aware of us and to take an active interest in us*, but that vibrate at a frequency beyond the range of our senses and instruments and thus generally remain completely invisible to us.

This intuition is by no means new, or original to me. In 1901, after inhaling a psychoactive dose of nitrous oxide and passing into a trance in which he experienced intense hallucinations, the renowned psychologist and philosopher William James (brother of the novelist Henry James) was startled by a metaphysical revelation about the way that human consciousness interacts with reality:

> One conclusion was forced upon my mind at that time, and my impression of its truth has ever since remained unshaken. It is that our normal waking consciousness, rational consciousness as we call it, is but one special type of consciousness, whilst all about it, parted from it by the filmiest of screens, there lie potential forms of consciousness very different. We may go through life without suspecting their existence; but apply the requisite stimulus and, at a touch, they are there in all their completeness . . . No account of the universe in its totality can be final which leaves these other forms of consciousness quite disregarded . . . At any rate, they forbid a premature closing of our accounts with reality.[1]

Half a century later, in 1953, the author Aldous Huxley began to feel exactly the same way after consuming four-tenths of a gram of mescaline, the psychoactive alkaloid derived from the peyote cactus. Having reflected upon that first and other subsequent experiences with mescaline – and also with psilocybin and LSD – Huxley's mature and thought-out suggestion was that 'the function of the brain and nervous system and sense organs is in the main *eliminative* and not productive' – i.e. that these organs operate primarily as a 'reducing valve' that protects us from being overwhelmed and confused by [a] mass of useless and irrelevant knowledge, by shutting out most of what we should otherwise perceive or remember at any moment, and leaving only that very small and special selection which is likely to be practically useful . . . What comes out at the other end is a measly trickle of the kind of consciousness which will help us to stay alive on the surface of this particular planet . . . Most people, most of the time, know only what comes through the reducing valve and is consecrated as genuinely real by local language. Certain persons, however, seem to be born with a kind of by-pass that circumvents the reducing valve. In others, temporary by-passes may be acquired either spontaneously, or as the result of deliberate 'spiritual exercises', or through hypnosis, or by means of drugs. Through these permanent or temporary by-passes there flows . . . something more than, and above all something different from, the carefully selected utilitarian material which our narrowed, individual minds regard as a complete, or at least sufficient, picture of reality.[2]

In 1983, the Swiss scientist Albert Hoffman, who first synthesised LSD (and frequently self-experimented with this powerful hallucinogen), noted that

reality is inconceivable without an experiencing subject. It is the product of the exterior world, of the sender, and of a receiver, an ego, in whose deepest self the emanations of the exterior world, registered by the antennae of the sense organs, become conscious . . . The entry of another reality under the influence of LSD may be explained by the fact that the brain, the seat of the receiver, becomes biochemically altered. The receiver is then tuned into another wavelength than that corresponding to normal, everyday reality. Since the endless variety and diversity of the universe correspond to infinitely many different wavelengths, depending on the adjustment of the receiver, many different realities . . . can become conscious . . . The true importance of LSD and related hallucinogens lies in their capacity to shift the wavelength setting of the receiving 'self', and thereby to evoke alterations in reality consciousness. This ability to allow different, new pictures of reality to arise, this truly cosmogenic power, makes the cultish worship of hallucinogenic plants as sacred drugs understandable.[3]

Especially so, we might add, if such changes of receiver wavelength were to give us veridical access to 'higher spiritual agencies'. William James again:

> Just as our primary wide-awake consciousness throws open our senses to the touch of things material, so it is logically conceivable that *if there be* higher spiritual agencies that can directly touch us, the psychological condition of their doing so *might be* our possession of a subconscious region which alone should yield access to them. The hubbub of the waking life might close a door which in the dreamy Subliminal might remain ajar or open . . . If there be higher powers able to impress us, they may get access to us only through the subliminal door.[4]

In 2001 a leading American psychiatrist, Rick Strassman MD, of the University of New Mexico, published the results of the first federally approved and funded human hallucinogen research in the US in over two decades.[5] Dr Strassman's project had involved 11 years of closely monitored studies in which dimethyltryptamine (DMT), the principal psychoactive alkaloid in the ayahuasca brew, was given by injection in a purified form to human volunteers who then reported their experiences. Precisely *what* they reported was so extraordinary, so unexpected, and so difficult to explain, as we'll see in Chapter Eighteen that it caused Strassman to re-examine his view of reality. Like Huxley and Hoffman, he was forced to consider the possibility that hallucinogens might change the receiver wavelength of the brain, allowing it to make contact with 'unseen worlds and their residents',[6] opaque to us in normal states of consciousness but nonetheless completely real. Drawing an analogy between the brain and a TV set, he observed that what DMT seems to do is not merely to adjust brightness, contrast and colour (as might be said of alcohol and other non-hallucinogenic drugs); instead it switches our attention to a new channel altogether:

No longer is the show we are watching everyday reality, Channel Normal. DMT provides regular, repeated, and reliable access to 'other' channels. The other planes of existence are always there. In fact, they are right here, transmitting all the time! But we cannot perceive them because we are not designed to do so; our hard-wiring keeps us tuned in to Channel Normal. It takes only a second or two – the few heart-beats that the 'spirit molecule' [DMT] requires to make its way to the brain – to change the channel, to open our mind to these other planes of existence. How might this happen? I claim little understanding of the physics underlying theories of parallel universes and dark matter. What I do know, however, causes me to consider them as possible places where DMT might lead us . . .[7]

Two main lines of research

So it seemed that I was in good company in keeping my mind open to the possibility that the 'spirit worlds' and 'supernatural entities' of which the shamans spoke, and that I myself had experienced, might after all have some kind of objective existence that the hallucinating brain was capable of interacting with – rather than being simply fantastic subjective concoctions of the selfsame hallucinating brain. I felt encouraged that thinkers of the stature of William James, Aldous Huxley and Albert Hoffman had self-experimented with hallucin-ogens in order to test the boundaries of socially constructed reality and try to discover what might lie beyond. Their insights reinforced my sense that this was a valid and potentially fruitful research method and helped give me courage to extend my own explorations with shamanic drugs.

I decided to experiment with psilocybin because of its suspected role as the catalyst for the visionary cave art of Upper Palaeolithic Europe.

Pure DMT also held great interest for me because of the aston-ishing and disturbing results of Rick Strassman's work. The detailed reports of his lab volunteers left no room for doubt that when the alkaloid was isolated and injected in concentrated purified form its effects differed in intriguing ways from those of the ayahuasca brew.

The reader will recall that other ingredients in ayahuasca inhibit certain enzymes in the stomach that normally render DMT inactive orally (see Chapter Three). Though much less psychoactive than DMT, these other ingredients (principally harmaline) also have their own distinct effects in the brain and thus contribute further to setting a 'receiver wavelength' that is specific to ayahuasca.[8]

The obvious implication of Strassman's research is that pure DMT, separated from the other ingredients, sets a receiver wavelength all of its own. This is confirmed by a number of tribes of Amazonian Indians who make regular of use of psychoactive snuffs, extracted from plants of the virola family, containing extremely high concentrations of pure DMT.[9] The Tukano, for example, consume ayahuasca frequently and have the greatest possible respect for it (see Chapter Seven). Nevertheless, the anthropologist Gerardo Reichel-Dolmatoff found that Tukano shamans nominate a virola snuff that they call *viho* as 'the most important means by which one can establish contact with the supernatural sphere in order to consult the spirit beings above'. Amongst these spirits, *Viho-mahse*, 'Snuff Person' (the owner and master of snuff), is considered paramount. He is said to dwell in the Milky Way, from where he continuously watches the doings of mankind.[10]

I knew that I was most unlikely to be able to locate synthetic injectable DMT of the sort that Strassman had used in his federally approved research project, but learned that it could sometimes be bought in smokeable form on the black market. Another alternative, if it could be obtained, was virola resin, which I could prepare as a snuff, or a resinous extract of pure DMT from the bark of an Australian acacia tree which could be smoked in a pipe.

There were many other hallucinogens that I might try if I so wished, but I had no plans to do so. Nor, after my intense experiences with ayahuasca and ibogaine, did I feel in any great or pressing hurry to begin my experiments with psilocybin and DMT. Far from it! The truth is that I have very mixed, ambiguous feelings about hallucinogens and about their effects on my consciousness. I welcome their ability to jolt me – even temporarily – into a spiritually receptive state of mind that I am normally too neurotic and preoccupied to permit myself to enter. I welcome the unexpected riches that this state of mind reveals. But like most people who have had acquaintance with powerful hallucinogens and taken them seriously, I'm also permanently afraid of their (or my own?) dark side, afraid in all sorts of nameless ways of the otherworldly vistas that they uncover and of the strange and sometimes terrifying entities they bring us into contact with, afraid that they could lure me to some spiritual hell-world from which I might not emerge sane. Such fear, I think, is appropriate. In investigating the supernatural, as the Peruvian shaman Don Emilio Andrade Gomez told the anthropologist Eduardo Luna, one should impose limits on the knowledge one seeks to acquire, and above all, 'one should not be too eager'.[11]

Far from eager, I was downright scared! But I also knew that I had to overcome my fear if I wanted to complete this side of my research. I therefore began looking for ways, preferably legal, to get my hands on the requisite substances, and to prepare myself psychologically for whatever surprises or tribulations they had in store for me.

Meanwhile, I was also well advanced on a second line of enquiry.

This took me back to the mystery of the wounded men in Upper Palaeolithic cave art and David Lewis-Williams' suggestion, reported in Chapter Ten, that these tortured figures 'represent a form of shamanistic suffering, "death" and initiation that was closely associated with hallucinations'. The reader will recall the gory and graphic details of some of the agonies and ordeals that shamans from as far afield as Australia and Greenland say they have endured in the spirit world at the hands of supernatural beings. Although they are bizarre, and although ethnographic and anthropological studies of hunter-gatherer societies make frequent mention of them, such reports of 'magical surgery', implantation of 'crystals' into the bodies or heads of initiates, 'dismemberments', 'piercings', extraction of brains and eyes, and so on and so forth, have never tempted scholars to ask whether something very odd *but real* could possibly lie behind them. So although they are studied for the light they supposedly shed on the tensions and dynamics of hunter-gatherer societies, and other sociological concerns, the reports in themselves are believed to have no truth value and are loftily dismissed as the brutal, ritualistic and superstitious fantasies of pre-scientific cultures and their mentally deranged shamans. Imagine my surprise, therefore, when I discovered that virtually identical experiences are routinely reported today by very large numbers of sane, sophisticated, respectable, well-educated individuals in technologically advanced countries such as the United States, Britain and Japan that long ago distanced themselves from the shamanic view of reality.

Abductions and other unusual personal experiences

In an exhaustive series of three national polls conducted by the Roper Organisation in 1991 it was established that approximately one out of every five adult Americans has, at one time or another in their lives, woken up paralysed with the sense of a strange figure or presence in the room. In addition:

- nearly one adult in eight has experienced a period of one hour or more in which he or she was apparently lost but could not remember why;
- one adult in ten has felt the experience of actually flying through the air without knowing why or how;
- one adult in twelve has seen unusual lights or balls of light in a room without understanding what was causing them;
- one adult in twelve has discovered puzzling scars on his or her body without remembering how or where they were acquired.[12]

The Roper polls, which had been nominally directed at gathering data about 'unusual personal experiences', were commissioned, and their results analysed, by Dr John Mack, Professor of Psychiatry at Harvard Medical School, Dr David Jacobs, Associate Professor of History at Temple University, John Carpenter, a psychiatric therapist from Springfield, Missouri, Dr Ron Westrum, Professor of Sociology at Eastern Michigan University, and Budd Hopkins, a New York based author, researcher and counsellor with specialist knowledge of the so-called 'alien abduction' or 'UFO abduction' phenomenon.[13] Indeed, the specific but hidden agenda of the surveys, behind the more innocuous declared interest in 'unusual personal experiences', was to get some sort of statistical measure of the prevalence in the general population of individuals who had been afflicted by the constellation of extremely unusual personal experiences associated with classic UFO abductions.

The belief that one might have been abducted by alien entities in an unidentified flying object is generally taken as a sign of an unbalanced mind in our society, and provokes ridicule. The pollsters' strategy was therefore to avoid direct questions on this subject and to focus, more obliquely, on 'experiences known to be associated with UFO abductions'.[14] Such experiences, in their turn, had been extracted from thousands of hours of interviews with deeply troubled and perplexed people conducted – often under hypnosis – by John Mack, John Carpenter, David Jacobs and Budd Hopkins. The interviewees had all undergone distressing episodes in their lives, often beginning in childhood and continuing into adulthood, that felt real to them but that seemed objectively impossible. In many cases they shamefacedly attributed these episodes to abduction by 'extraterrestrial beings' who took them up to 'spaceships in the sky' (or sometimes underwater or underground) and did painful, humiliating and unpleasant things to them there, before returning them to their home environments. More frequently, however, they did not remember exactly what had happened – only that *something* had happened – but under hypnosis had full recall of repeated 'abductions by aliens' at intervals throughout their lives.

Because so many interviewees were unable to remember being abducted until the details were extracted using hypnosis, the questions in the Roper surveys concentrated on the kinds of odd experiences that these individuals *had* been able to recall prior to hypnosis – often the very experiences that had led them to seek therapy in the first place. The five 'strong indicators' listed above (i.e. waking up paralysed in the night with a strange figure in the room, inexplicably flying, puzzling scars on the body, an hour or more of missing time, seeing balls of light) were reported particularly frequently by UFO abductees. The poll designers therefore decided that if any respondents answered yes to at least four out of the five indicators then they would count these individuals as probable abductees. Altogether 2 per cent of the total survey sample fell into this category:

This suggests that two per cent of the adults in the American population have had a constellation of experiences consistent with an abduction history. Therefore, based on our sample of nearly 6,000 respondents, we believe that one out of every fifty adult Americans may have had UFO abduction experiences.[15]

In 1991, when the Roper polls were conducted, 'one out of every fifty adult Americans' was equivalent to almost four million people.[16]

My own position on 'UFOs' and 'aliens'

Before going further, I wish to state, very clearly and for the record, that when I started to explore the avenue of investigation set out in this and the next five chapters I did not believe that UFOs were 'nuts-and-bolts' spaceships from other planets. Likewise I did not believe that the 'aliens' frequently associated with UFO sightings were physical beings from extraterrestrial civilisations who for some reason visited the earth, abducted certain specially selected humans, inflicted all manner of strange and intimate procedures on them, and then returned them to their homes, only to abduct the same individuals again and again – often over periods of many years – in order to carry out more strange procedures.

In Chapter Three I described my own direct observations of entities resembling the popular conception of aliens – entities who appeared to me in hallucinations seen under the influence of ayahuasca. The absolutely convincing and indeed terrifying nature of these hallucinations (which included objects like flying saucers) raised the possibility in my mind that the UFO sightings and alien abductions so widely and sensationally reported all around the world in recent years are likely to be best understood as experiences stemming from altered states of consciousness rather than nuts-and-bolts physical encounters of any kind.

Now, as I write these words after completing my research, my lack of belief in physical, extraterrestrial explanations for UFOs and aliens, and my intuition that they must be visionary phenomena, has hardened into something close to a certainty. I give readers fair warning, therefore, that nothing will be found in the pages that follow to support the idea that aliens are visitors from outer space. No one can rule out such a possibility entirely, but the evidence I have gathered suggests they are something far more interesting and far more mysterious than that.

Needles, surgery and pain

There is one particularly unusual, distressing and distinctive personal experience that people who believe they have been abducted by UFOs report more often and more consistently than almost any other. This is the humiliating and traumatising experience of being subjected by the abducting entities to forced medical examinations and to painful and incomprehensible surgical procedures that often leave behind permanent visible scars and sometimes even mysterious implants in abductees' bodies.[17] For full details, the reader is referred to the published work of John Mack, David Jacobs and Thomas Bullard, where hundreds of pages of such reports can be found.[18] Here a few examples will have to suffice to convey the peculiar character of the overall phenomenon.

In 1961 Betty and Barney Hill claimed that they were followed in their car by a UFO and abducted by small humanoid beings with

rather odd-shaped heads, with a large cranium, diminishing in size as it got toward the chin. And the eyes continued around to the sides of their heads . . . The texture of the skin was greyish, almost metallic looking . . . I didn't notice any hair . . . I didn't notice any proboscis, there just seemed to be two slits that represented the nostrils.[19]

Once on board the UFO the couple were separated and Betty was subjected to a medical examination during which a long needle was inserted into her navel, causing her agonising pain.[20]

The high point of Sandy Larson's 1975 UFO abduction was a view 'of the earth in space through the end of a luminous tunnel'.[21] The low point was an extremely unpleasant experience of bizarre and radical surgery in which 'beings' removed her brain and set it down beside her.[22]

In the autumn of 1950, Betty Aho was abducted by humanoids that she described as about three feet tall with 'pear-shaped' heads and large unblinking eyes. Dramatic events followed. The UFO 'plunged into the sea and came out again, then entered huge crystalline caverns which broadened into a vast underworld'.[23] Later, Aho was 'floated' on to a table:

> She felt stuck to it while the beings removed her right eye and implanted a tiny device deep within her head using a luminous needle. A being's hand on her forehead relieved her pain. They . . . implanted objects in her spine and heels. The beings passed hand-held instruments over her spine and pointed needle-like devices at her head, causing her to feel the implants inside her.[24]

Some 40 years later, at the beginning of the 1990s, John Mack's patient 'Scott' recalled that during one of his numerous abduction experiences he found himself in what he took to be a spaceship, stretched out on a table flanked by two 'doctor-like' figures. His head lay on a block and four 'prongs' were being pressed into his neck, 'high up, just below the scalp'. Scott believed these were electrodes, Mack reports, 'that were used to manipulate and control his movements and feelings'.[25]

'Jerry', another of Mack's patients, remembered an abduction in which she was brought into a large spaceship with a domed roof and then into 'a circular room' within it which was 'shiny and metallic-looking and contained what looked like equipment'.[26] Here small, dark human-like beings performed incomprehensible tests on her body under the guidance of a taller, lighter entity who she thought of as male and as 'the leader'. At one point he asked her telepathically (but confusingly) if 'the medication has been okay up till now?' Immediately afterwards, she reported, 'something sharp, like a needle', was driven from a high angle down into the side of her neck: 'They're turning it! Ohhhh! It's inside of me . . . They stuck that thing inside me.'[27]

Like many other abductees, 'Catherine's' experience – having been brought against her will on board what she believed was a UFO – involved first being taken into a metallic room, 'like burnished aluminium but darker', and made to lie on a table there. She noted that the room had muted lighting and that present in it with her were a number of small beings. The leader, or 'examiner', though taller than the others, was nonetheless shorter than Catherine. His skin appeared to be 'very smooth – whitish grey' and his manner was intimidating: 'He's looking at me like you look at a frog before you dissect it.'[28]

Next Catherine remembered being subjected to a series of painful gynaecological procedures and was convinced that samples had been taken from her ovaries.[29] We will return in Chapter Thirteen to the possible significance of these (also very common) 'reproductive' aspects of the UFO abduction experience. Meanwhile, Catherine's ordeal was far from over. She described a metal instrument 'maybe a foot long' that was inserted 'perhaps six inches' into one of her nostrils – i.e. into her brain:

> I could feel something breaking in my head. When he pushed it through, he broke whatever it was and pushed it all the way through, up even further . . . I'm wondering what they broke . . . I don't know the anatomy, and he broke something to get it through, to get it into my brain . . . I don't know what it was. I want to know if it's going to heal.[30]

'Joe' recalled being abducted by a humanoid 'with a triangular face and a large forehead, narrow chin, and large, black, elliptical eyes' that first 'floated' him up to a spaceship that was 'much bigger inside than outside' and then used mind control to make him lie on a table.[31] Here he was suddenly surrounded by eight to ten small beings. One standing to his left fell upon him with 'a large needle about a foot long, with a kind of hilt'. The needle entered the left side of Joe's neck below the ear, 'against the skull', causing severe pain: 'They're putting a picture in my mind of a small, silver, pill-shaped thing that they're leaving there which has four tiny, tiny wires coming off it.'[32] After the needle was removed, Joe reported that he received this telepathic message from the beings: 'We are close. We are with you. We're here to help you. We're here to guide you, to make it through your difficult times.'[33]

On another occasion, Joe was abducted together with his baby son

Mark and witnessed the beings holding 'crystals' against the child's head and 'shining a light on his eyes and on his hand'.[34]

John Mack's patient 'Eva' saw a grey spaceship, panicked, blacked out, then found herself on a table in a room with two beings inspecting her:

> I was in a foetal position, my back to them. They were doing something to my spine. My entire spine was stinging and cold. It was awful! It felt as though they were going inside my body with some very sharp instrument and inserting it between my flesh and my skin.[35]

'Karin' also found herself in a room on a spaceship: 'They opened up my chest and took out my heart.'[36] Similarly, 'Carlos' told Mack of how he had been 'floated' up through the sky 'on a beam of light' to what he took to be a spacecraft. He found himself in the 'rotunda' of this circular vessel in a spacious instrument-filled room where many small humanoid creatures went about their business seemingly with no expectations of him. However, one of them eventually led him to another part of the ship, where he was placed on a table that he described as 'a block of crystal'.[37] Here a female being with huge oblique eyes, but 'hardly a nose and hardly a mouth',[38] instructed 'reptilian-faced, insectile-bodied, or robotlike entities' to perform an operation on him.[39] The operation was excruciatingly painful and involved the use of crystals:

> Whatever these crystals are, metal-like more than glasslike, there is light. I can see it . . . It is like a squared tube of crystal with the sides lopped off so that at the ends each tube appears eight-sided . . . And then the end of it is shaped like a step-pyramid. It shoots laser light into the body, but it feels like a needle because it hurts, and it resembles a needle.[40]

Same phenomenon, different cultural setting?

I was already familiar with the sorts of initiatory ordeals that hallucinating shamans the world over believe they suffer at the hands of spirits. The limited extracts from the vast ethnographic literature on this subject that are given in Chapter Ten are sufficient to make it clear that these ordeals frequently and graphically involve procedures that Westerners would very likely construe as 'medical' or 'surgical' in nature. I was satisfied that close and persuasive parallels exist between these often baffling and painful episodes of shamanic surgery on the one hand, and the piercing and spearing of the wounded men figures in Upper Palaeolithic cave art on the other. But it was unsettling to discover equally strong parallels in the supposed surgical procedures on board spaceships described under hypnosis by people of the late twentieth century who believed that they had been abducted by UFOs:

Jerry reported 'something sharp, like a needle' being driven from a high angle down into the side of her neck . . . A small being plunged 'a large needle about a foot long, with a kind of hilt' into Joe's neck below the ear, 'against the skull', causing severe pain . . . A metal instrument 'maybe a foot long' was inserted deeply into Catherine's brain through one of her nostrils: 'he broke something to get it through, to get it into my brain . . .'

Compare the above with these ethnographic accounts of shamans' hallucinatory experiences cited in Chapter Ten:

'Three black devils thrust a lance through his head . . .' (Yakut) 'A spirit throws an invisible lance at him, which pierces his neck from behind, passes through his tongue, making therein a large hole, and then comes out through his mouth . . .' (Arunta, Australia) 'A snake is put in their heads and their noses are pierced by a magical object . . .' (Warramunga, Australia)

Returning to the UFO abductees:

Betty Aho's right eye was removed and a tiny device was implanted deep within her head – with additional devices implanted in her spine and heels . . . Joe believed that a 'small, silver, pill-shaped thing' with wires coming off it had been implanted in his brain, and witnessed beings holding 'crystals' against his son's head and 'shining a light on his eyes and on his hand'

. . . Crystals were used as surgical instruments in the excruciatingly painful operation that Carlos experienced as part of his UFO abduction.

From the shamanic ethnographies:

'They cut his head open, take out his brains, wash and restore them to give him a clear mind to penetrate the mysteries . . . They insert gold dust into his eyes . . .'[1] (Dyak, Borneo) 'Then comes a man with a stick; he thrusts the stick into the neophyte's head and puts a magical stone the size of a lemon into the wound. Then the spirits appear . . . to teach him the art of healing . . .'[2] (Wotojobaluk, Australia) 'The Cobeno shaman introduces rock crystals into the novice's head; these eat out his brain and eyes, then take the place of those organs and become his strength . . .' (South America) 'Once they are in the sky, the master inserts into the candidate's body small rainbow-serpents and quartz crystals. After this operation the candidate is brought back to earth . . .'[3] (Forrest River, Australia)

UFO abductees:

Two beings operated on Eva's spine: 'It felt as though they were going inside my body with some very sharp instrument and inserting it between my flesh and my skin.' A long needle was inserted into Betty Hill's navel, causing her agonising pain.

The shamanic ethnographies:

'I saw the form of a man . . . whose head was surrounded by a bright glow . . . He spoke: "Wait without fear until I have said and done everything that I intend." Then I felt various instruments, first like sharp knives, then like needles, penetrate my flesh . . .'[4] (Ojibwa, North America) 'The aspirant to the Kuksu Society is believed to have his navel pierced with a lance and an arrow by Kuksu himself . . .' (River Patwin, North America)

After Sandra Larson had been taken on board a UFO she had a memorable and most unusual experience:

But even here hallucinatory initiations offer striking parallels. For example, in the case of a Yakut shaman cited by Eliade:

'The spirits cut off his head, which they set aside.'[45]

Mystery of the bones

I found other remarkable parallels, not all of which there is space to list here, between these medical aspects of the abduction phenomenon and the descriptions of spiritual surgery that feature so frequently and prominently in ethnographies. One that is particularly striking – because so odd – concerns the ritual of the 'counting of the bones' which is reported from many different shamanic cultures. A typical case is that of a Tungus shaman who entered a deep trance during which he experienced a ritual of initiation at the hands of spiritual beings:

> They pierced him with arrows until he lost consciousness and fell to the ground; they cut off his flesh, tore out his bones and counted them; if one had been missing he could not have become a shaman.[46]

In another Siberian account, the shaman Kyzlasov told how he had been 'cut into pieces on a black table' by 'two black and two fair' beings who counted his bones on the orders of their chieftain:

> They found a bone around the ribs, which had a hole in the middle. This was the excess bone. This brought about my becoming a shaman. Because, only those men can become shamans in whose body such a bone can be found.[47]

It seemed most unlikely that there would be anything like this in the UFO abduction literature, but I soon discovered that there was. David Jacobs of Temple University, who has conducted extensive interviews with hundreds of abductees, and himself completely rejects any connection between their experiences and those of shamans,[48] nevertheless notes that they frequently make reference to the prodding and palpation' of their bones and joints:

> The Small Beings look closely at the subject's ribs and rib cage. Sometimes [they] make a small incision on the abductee's left side . . . They methodically touch and press each individual vertebra from the neck to the coccyx . . . They take a long time with the vertebrae as their fingers manipulate each bone structure.[49]

Likewise John Mack's patient Catherine, whom we met earlier, described an experience in which small beings with 'huge black almond eyes'[50] floated her up to an enormous silver-metallic UFO and then into one of its cavernous rooms 'the size of an airplane hangar'. As her captors led her through the room she noticed rows of tables on either side. Some of these were empty but on others she saw procedures being done on what she estimated were 'between one hundred and two hundred humans'. Catherine was forced to sit on one of the tables and then the following explicitly 'bone-counting' experience unfolded:

> They're running their little fingers down my spine like they're counting the vertebrae in my spinal column. 'What the hell's that for?' 'To make sure everything's okay,' he says.[51]

Troublesome things

My curiosity had been aroused but my initial reaction to what looked like a series of remarkable unexplained cross-cultural commonalities was one of scepticism. I simply could see no reason why hunter-gatherer shamans, who deal with 'spirits' and make rain, should have anything in common with sophisticated American city-dwellers who happen to believe that they've been abducted by aliens. So I worked hard to downplay the similarities I was seeing and to persuade myself that they must all result from coincidence.

As other such coincidences began to pile up, however, I became increasingly perplexed at the level of detail. Why should spirits in one part of the world and at one period of history, and aliens in another part of the world at another period of history, both abduct men and women, insert mysterious objects into their heads, stick lances or massive needles into their necks and skulls, implant crystals into their bodies, count their bones, take out their eyes and brains, etc., etc.? On reflection, I could see how ludicrous it was to imagine that people from such different cultural backgrounds as shamans and UFO abductees could have independently invented what were essentially the same utterly bizarre entities and the same utterly inexplicable medical/surgical procedures.

But if that wasn't what was going on here, then what was?

I had the sense that I had stumbled on the outline of an underlying pattern, deeply buried, and of troublesome things waiting to come to light.

CHAPTER TWELVE

Shamans in the Sky

Most readers of this book will have heard something about UFO abductions. Some will know a great deal about them; others will know very little. Many will believe (wrongly) that the phenomenon has been successfully debunked as a mixture of hoaxes and crazed delusions. Many others will feel that the reports they have heard are too numerous, and the people making them too decent and reliable, for them to be completely without foundation. Amongst the latter group there will be some who have no theory at all about who or what is responsible for abductions, but most will probably take the view, popularised in the famous 1990s television series *The X-Files*, that they are the work of 'ETs' – in other words extraterrestrials, in other words technologically advanced aliens from other planets who have travelled across interstellar space in order to abduct us for arcane reasons of their own.

Needless to say, there is no hard evidence for this or any other theory. There is a phenomenon. It is massively documented. It appears to have involved millions of people. But there is not a scintilla of proof that the abducting agencies – if they exist in any useful sense at all – are extraterrestrials. Nor, though we almost automatically assume it to be so, is there the slightest reason for us to believe that the saucer-like UFOs to which abductees frequently say they have been taken are in fact spaceships. All such ideas are just assumptions built upon speculations that have been conjured out of conjecture and rest ultimately on the public mindset of the twentieth century.

Remember what happened in the twentieth century. We invented space travel. We went to the moon. We put landers on Mars. And we were the first generation who had to contemplate seriously the possibility, since we ourselves are a technologically advanced species living on a planet, that there might be other species living on other planets who were perhaps even more technologically advanced than we are. So when metallic-looking UFOs began to be noticed flying at impossible speeds and performing manoeuvres that defied the laws of physics in the skies over America, Europe and Japan from the late 1940s onwards, and with increasing frequency during the 1950s and 1960s, it's hardly surprising that 'aliens in spaceships from other planets' was the explanation that leapt most readily to our minds.

The first abductions – and with them the first bizarre surgical procedures – began to attract attention in the 1960s. The earliest publicised case was that of Barney and Betty Hill in 1961. During it Betty underwent an ordeal, described in Chapter Eleven, that she experienced as a long needle being thrust into her abdomen through her navel. Over the following three decades thousands of others reported similar experiences, the grotesque character of which was summed up for many in Whitley Strieber's bestselling book about his own abductions (*Communion*, published in 1987, and subsequently made into a Hollywood film starring Christopher Walken). In 1989 Dr John Mack at Harvard University began to offer therapy as part of his psychiatric practice to people who believed they had been abducted by aliens. His extensive interviews, often conducted under hypnosis, revealed that many of his subjects remembered multiple abductions going back to their childhoods. In some cases it became clear that their first abduction experiences had occurred in the late 1940s and early 1950s, more than ten years before the Betty and Barney Hill case drew attention to this unusual syndrome.

Not the lunatic fringe

From the outset, showing unusual humility for a mainstream academic, Mack resolved to take the abductees seriously. He attracted heavy criticism and much ridicule for this from his peers. However, he was able to defend his position on excellent clinical grounds since none of the scientific surveys and psychometric tests that have been conducted on self-styled UFO abductees have provided any evidence that connects the syndrome with mental illness. For example Parnell, who administered the Minnesota Multiphasic Inventory and the Sixteen Personality Factor Questionnaire to 223 UFO abductees in 1988 – just before Mack began to see UFO abductees in his own practice – found 'no evidence of serious psychopathology'.[1] Similarly, in another study, abductees were put through nine psychological test batteries by Elizabeth Slater PhD, a trained psychologist. She herself was not informed, until after she had completed her assessments of the test results, that the subjects had all reported experiencing UFO abductions. Her conclusion was as follows:

> The first and most critical question is whether our subjects' reported experiences could be accounted for strictly on the basis of psychopathology, i.e. mental disorder. *The answer is a firm no.* In broad terms, if the reported abductions were *confabulated fantasy productions*, based on what we know about psychological disorders, they could only have come from *pathological liars, paranoid schizophrenics, and severely disturbed and extraordinarily rare hysteroid characters subject to fugue states and/or multiple personality shifts* . . . It is important to note that not one of the subjects, based on the test data, falls into any one of these categories. Therefore while the testing can do nothing to prove the veracity of the UFO abduction reports, one can conclude that the test findings are not inconsistent with the possibility that reported abductions have, in fact, occurred.[2]

Further exhaustive tests carried out by Mack's colleage Catherine McLeod at Harvard in the 1990s compared 40 abduction experiencers with 40 matched controls using a broad range of psychopathology and personality measures. Again the results were unambiguous: 'No findings of personality disorder or other psychopathology that might explain the abduction phenomenon distinguished the experiences from the control group.'[3]

On the basis of many such surveys, and of his own direct assessments of the mental health of abductees, Mack felt that the verdict was obvious:

> Efforts to establish a pattern of psychopathology other than distur-
> bances associated with a traumatic event have been unsuccessful.
> Psychological testing of abductees has not revealed evidence of mental
> or emotional disturbance that could account for their reported experi-
> ences. My own sample demonstrates a broad range of mental health
> and emotional adaptation. Some experiences are highly functioning
> individuals who seem mainly to need support in integrating their abduc-
> tion experiences with the rest of their lives. Others verge on being
> overwhelmed by the traumatic impact and philosophical implications
> of their experiences and need a great deal of counselling and emotional
> support.[4]

Crossover phenomena

In other words, people who believed they had been abducted by UFOs
were not fantasists, not mad, and not delusional, but all of them
appeared to have suffered the same constellation of unexplained traumatic experiences (indeed many showed the measurable symptoms of
post-traumatic stress disorder usually more familiar in soldiers
returning from the battlefield).[5] If they believed that they had been
abducted, therefore, Mack's decision was that he would believe them
too. But during the 15 years that he tirelessly sought a solution to this
mystery, he was careful never to extend his respectful belief in the
truth of abductees' statements to a wholesale acceptance of the
unproven popular theory that the abductions were the work of aliens
in spaceships from other planets. Something radical and extraordinary
was happening, he was certain of that, but his instinct was that it had
to do with collisions of different levels or states of reality, rather than
'nuts-and-bolts' encounters between physical human beings and
equally physical aliens from an extraterrestrial planetary culture:[6]

> What kind of matter is the alien abduction phenomenon? . . . It seems
> to belong to that class of phenomena, not even generally accepted as

existing by mainstream Western science, that seem not to be *of* this visible, known material universe and yet appear to manifest *in* it. These are phenomena . . . that seem to 'cross over' or to violate the radical separation of the spirit and unseen realms from the material world.[7]

This sense of Mack's that alien abductions are spiritual rather than material problems – but that they are nevertheless *real* and able to manifest in this world – got him into even more trouble with his scientific peers at Harvard University, who subscribe to the materialist paradigm and do not believe in spirits. During the 1990s, venomous efforts were made to have Mack fired, but he resisted with the help of a good lawyer, fought the case as an issue of academic freedom and managed to keep his job.[8] In revenge the university marginalised him, and in an exchange of emails with me during April and May 2004, he admitted that his work had forced him 'into the ontological and epistemological wilderness'.[9] (Ontology is the branch of metaphysics that deals with the nature of being; epistemology is the critical study of the validity of knowledge.) As we tried to set up a meeting for later in the year, he told me that after August there were 'no bad months'.[10] In September 2004 he was run over and killed by a drunk driver.[11]

Aliens and spirits

Could 'aliens' and 'spirits' be the same thing – or the same class of thing? And if so, what might this mean for our understanding of the human condition and of the nature of reality? Could the realm from which UFOs appear – and then seem to disappear back into again 'between one blink of the eye and the next' – be the 'spirit world', as John Mack came increasingly to believe? More intriguingly, what are the chances of this being the same spirit world, with its well-charted supernatural geography and inhabitants, that shamans have entered and negotiated with by means of hallucinatory out-of-body journeys since times immemorial?

The idea seems absurd by the tenets of Western science, which holds *all* spirit worlds to be illusory projections of the contents of our own minds. Still, I couldn't help being intrigued by the close parallels I'd found between the piercings and inexplicable surgical procedures supposedly carried out on shamans by spirits, and the same sorts of procedures experienced by UFO abductees at the hands of aliens. I began to re-examine ethnographic studies of shamanism side by side with casebooks of UFO abductee reports to see if there were other such similarities. Gradually I became fascinated and immersed – for there seemed not just to be similarities here but a whole network of closely interwoven and interdependent connections so intricate and extensive that they could not possibly have arisen by chance.

An example is the way most abductees report that at the beginning of the experience they are 'floated' out of their houses or cars and up to the sky to where the UFO awaits. Similarly, most accounts of shamanic initiations also begin with a sky journey (because the realm of the gods and spirits is located in the sky – for example *Viho-mahse*, the Tukano god of hallucinogenic snuff, lurking in the Milky Way). Now the sky itself is universal to all cultures and periods, always over our heads, always beckoning, glittering with stars, so the fantasy of sky journeys might occur spontaneously to anyone and could easily have been invented independently by many different cultures. That was why I didn't pay much attention to this obvious and elementary parallel until I began to look in detail at the *methods* used by abductees and shamans to reach the sky.

The gentle art of floating (1)

Abductees speak of three principal means by which they are floated through the sky to and from the waiting UFOs. The first is just that – floating. A few examples of how it is described:

> I've got this impression of floating above my bed, like being kind of levitated out the doorway to the hall.[12] (Catherine)

> We kind of walked, kind of floated into the bottom of the ship.[13] (Joe)

They then support me somehow off the table and down out of the ship . . . They levitate me or something.[14] (Dave)

I sort of feel like I'm on an elevator except there's no walls or anything around it, it's just up, fast . . .[15] (Barbara Archer)

I can remember floating down. I came from very far away. We were very high up in the sky, it seemed to me. And when I was put down they put me down gently.[16] (Karen Morgan)

They glided me into that thing . . . I couldn't resist them, I just floated . . .[17] (Charles Hickson)

In the second type of experience of floating, abductees associate their sudden levitation and flight through the air with a beam of light which often encloses them completely:

I'm inside the beam of light. I'm going up, and there's a hole above me, and it's dark, but there's light all around it. It's like a blue light . . . a blue beam of light come down to the ground, and then it was almost like going through a tunnel . . .[18] (Nona)

He's taking me up, up the diagonal. We just kind of fly off. We're not going straight up. We're going across too. 'This is too fast! Why are you going so fast? I'm going to fall off the beam! I'm going to fall down there!' And he just kind of says: 'No, you won't.'[19] (Catherine)

The third type of experience is more unusual but is nonetheless reported in a good number of cases. It involves ropes, wires, strings or threads of light which the abductees must float along, or climb, in order to reach a UFO hovering far above them.[20] For example, John Mack's patient Andrea was wakened in her bedroom by a flash of blue light 'like a big headlight on a car' and the presence of two small, thin beings with bulging heads and huge eyes. 'They're very skinny,' she remembered, and 'they look like they're made of light. But then underneath there's some physicalness to them.' One of the beings was 'holding a stick or a rod' which he now pressed to the back of Andrea's ear. Her next recollection was of being 'floated' feet first 'right through' the glass of her bedroom window and high over trees. She reported that a 'line' or 'thread' of light extended from her navel to the beings and that 'streamers' of light were coming out from one of the beings to her body. These 'threads of light' seemed to be used to pull her up to the ship.[21]

Similarly, as his abduction began, Arthur saw a 'light like a thread, a spider's thread that's lit' extending down from the night sky. At the same moment he saw a group of 'little lighted beings clustered all together' who told him: 'Don't be afraid or it will break the thread.' Next Arthur found himself in the air, in some way supported by the thread, which he estimated to be no more than one-eighth of an inch in diameter: 'like a kite string, maybe'.[22]

> The thread or string seemed to be bathed in a light that was everywhere and as the beings were telling him 'not to be afraid' Arthur was 'just going along it, standing erect', pulled as if by an unseen force. The string seemed to go into the craft, 'like a phone line or something'.[23]

The gentle art of floating (2)

Shamans, too, float, or are wafted aloft in various ways, as they begin their journeys in the spirit world:

> He saw the roof of his hut open above his head and felt himself carried off to the sky, where he met a multitude of spirits . . .[24] (Basuto shaman, South Africa)

> I was carried up to the spirit-village of those who live in the sky, a doctor's village, and there I was instructed . . .[25] (Winnebago shaman, North America)

What is particularly puzzling, however, is that the striking motif of a rope, or string, or spider's web, or thread of light that occurs as a means of ascent in some UFO abductions is also commonly found in accounts of shamans' sky journeys. In north-western Australia, for instance, shamans say that they reach the sky on 'ropes of air',[26] while the shamans of the Kulin and Kurnai tribes hallucinate a fine thread emerging from their bodies: 'It comes out of their mouths like a spider's web and they climb to heaven on it.'[27]

Likewise, the bushmen of southern Africa almost always make use of threads, strings and ropes in their hallucinatory sky journeys. As was the case with the now extinct San rock artists, the reader will recall from earlier chapters that for the *!Kung* shamans of the Kalahari, the trance dance remains the principal means of entering a deeply altered state of consciousness and summoning up sufficient *n/um* (supernatural power) to ascend to the spirit world. The *!Kung* shaman Bo explains that when the power is strong he sees

> lines or strings of light that go up into the sky. These lines may be the thickness of a blade of grass or as big as a rope or chain. They are white in colour or shiny like silver metal . . . When I see a rope of light I walk towards it. As soon as I get to it or near to it, I start floating up to the sky . . . You don't have to grab it or touch it. You just float away with that rope. That line just takes you. You become so light that you simply fly away.[28]

According to another shaman, Mabolele Shikwe:

> The rope can take away anyone who comes to the dance. If you are very strong and you don't fall to the ground, the rope can take you away while are dancing.[29]

A Kalahari shaman named *Cgunta !elae*:

> When I go to the rope, it makes me float up to the sky. Sometimes I travel to another place the instant I go toward it. At other times you simply walk along it.[30]

The same informant:

> When we go up the rope we sometimes see other doctors from our

San rock art depiction of shamans
climbing ropes to the sky (RARI).

community who are also going up the same rope. The ropes will be
there forever. They point down to us from the sky. The place in the
sky is where the Big God lives . . .[31]

Here's old *K"xau*, a famous *!Kung* shaman whom we have already met
briefly in Chapter Ten:

My friend, that's the way of this *n/um* . . . I dance . . . When I emerge
I am already climbing. I'm climbing threads, the threads that lie over
there in the South . . . I take them and climb them. I climb one and
leave it, then I go climb another one. I come to another one and climb,
then I come to another one. Then I leave it and climb on another.
Then I follow the thread of the wells, the one I am going to go enter!
The thread of the wells of metal. When you get to the wells you duck
beneath the pieces of metal . . . It hurts . . . When you lift up a little,
the metal pieces grab your back.[32]

San rock art depiction of shaman
climbing to the sky: 'I follow
the thread of the wells . . . the
thread of the wells of metal. When
you get to the wells you duck
beneath the pieces of metal . . .'
(RARI)

What seems to be envisaged is some sort of contraption in the sky – 'wells of metal'. It all sounds very strange, but in fact contraptions in the sky are common elements of shamanic visions. A Yurak-Samoyed shaman of Siberia, for example, relates how

> he mounts to the sky by the help of a rope especially let down for him and how he shoulders aside the stars that block his way. In the sky he rides in a boat and then descends to earth at such a speed that the wind passes through him . . .[33]

The core image of a sky-vehicle letting down a rope also occurs in North America:

> One summer day [the shaman Bull Lodge] lay in the grass on his back with his arms out flat on the ground, elbows bent . . . As he gazed up at the sky, an object appeared . . . It was a shield, with a string or fine cord attached to it leading up to the sky . . . Then Bull Lodge heard a voice. The sound came from behind the shield . . . 'My child, look at this thing. I am giving it to you from above.'[34]

In Australia, the flying shield in the sky is replaced by a supernatural bird, but is still approached by a string:

> They took hold of the doctor's string, on the other end of which Wombu, [the god] Baimi's bird, was waiting. They travelled up through the clouds to heaven.[35]

Mircea Eliade reports that amongst the powers claimed by the shamans of the Mara Aborigines of Australia is that of 'climbing at night-time by means of a rope, invisible to ordinary mortals, into the sky, where he can hold congress with the star people'.[36]

The comparison with UFO abductees, who also say they climb to the sky by means of threads or ropes, and who also believe they hold congress with 'star people', is very clear. Meanwhile, in the depths of the Amazon, a group of shamans of the Cubeo tribe gather in a jungle shelter to drink ayahuasca so that their souls too may hold congress with the spirit world:

> And then the Star-People descend, with their shining eyes, with their brilliant eyes, and surround those sitting on their benches. The scintillating lights come and try to carry them back to the Milky Way . . .[37]

The reader will recall that many UFO abductees do not see threads or ropes but lights, or beams of light, that appear in their rooms and float them out of their beds. Some sort of 'abduction by lights' certainly seems to be implied in the case of the Cubeo and was also reported explicitly by the bushman shaman Twele, who told anthropologists: 'I don't see a string hanging from the sky, but I see a light that makes me float.'[38]

Underground, underwater

There were moments as I researched this material when I wasn't sure whether I was reading a UFO abduction report or the account of a shaman's psychedelic pilgrimage to the sky world. Despite surface differences appropriate to the very different cultural settings and periods in which the abductees and shamans had undergone their experiences, the clues kept mounting up that the two phenomena must, in some as yet unexplained way, be closely related at a deep structural level.

For example, not all shamanic journeys lead to the sky. This is the most common scenario, but the reader will recall from Chapter Ten that shamans in their trances also quite frequently report the experience of being transported into a cave – sometimes lined with crystals or calcite formations and often illuminated by a strange diffuse light with no obvious source. In other cases we've seen that they travel to an underwater location that lies at the bottom of a sea, lake, or river pool.

These are not the sorts of destinations that one automatically associates with UFOs, which are, after all, unidentified *flying* objects. Nevertheless we saw in Chapter Eleven that the UFO which abducted

Betty Aho in 1950 'plunged into the sea and came out again, then entered huge crystalline caverns which broadened into a vast underworld'.[39]

In 1979, in Florida, Filiberto Cardenas was abducted by humanoids dressed in what he described as tight white clothing. They took him to a beach, opened 'a lock' in the side of a huge boulder, then transported him through a 'tunnel beneath the sea'.[40]

In 1981, Mexican photographer Carlos Diaz saw a UFO floating over his head. 'It was made of millions of small dots of light. I tried to touch the object, but my hand went through the yellow light . . .' He felt disoriented and suddenly noticed that the craft now appeared to be standing 'inside a cave that was lined with stalactites and stalagmites . . . There was something strange about the illumination . . . It was everywhere but I couldn't find a source.'[41]

Even more to the point is the case of Lucy, abducted in October 1992 by beings who she construed as aliens, although UFOs did not feature in her experience at all. Waking up in the middle of the night, she felt a compulsion to drive her car into the Blue Ridge Mountains west of Washington DC. Finally she stopped on a deserted road to the right of which there was a steep drop 'to a field full of people in their pyjamas and nightgowns'.[42] She found herself floating in their direction and was then swept with the crowd into an opening in the side of the hill. 'It led steeply down through the limestone under the hill to a large room with a high ceiling where the abductees congregated and the aliens inscrutably watched them . . .'[43]

Similarly, Scott recalled hurtling down into 'a huge underground rock-walled place' in a fast-moving elevator[44] and Joe found himself 'in a subterranean room hewn from rock' lying on a table 'surrounded by little people with big heads, and they're putting a needle in my neck':[45] Many further examples could be cited, but the point has been sufficiently made that as well as going to technological venues in the sky – which themselves are matched in pre-scientific cultures by appropriate construals such as flying shields and boats and aerial 'wells' made of metal – UFO abductions frequently unfold in classic shamanic settings such as caverns or underwater.

The power of transformation

Aliens, shamans and the supernatural beings of the spirit realm have another completely unexpected and rather mysterious characteristic in common.

Before I began this research I had no idea that therianthropes were the subject matter of the most ancient religious art of mankind. Nor had it ever occurred to me (as seems perfectly obvious now in the light of Lewis-Williams' work) that many of the animals depicted in painted caves and rock shelters all around the world might be best understood as representations of transformed shamans or spirits in animal form seen during hallucinatory trances.

On the other side of the equation I had, at the outset, no personal interest in, and possessed only rudimentary information about, the UFO abduction phenomenon, which I did not imagine would prove relevant to my investigation of the origins of religion. I began to change my mind after my own encounters, facilitated by ayahuasca, with friendly 'light-beings' and a much less friendly large-headed 'Grey' with a heart-shaped head and huge black eyes who I had genuinely feared might abduct me in one of the flying saucers that also featured in the same vision (see Chapter Three). I was given further pause for thought when I realised that very similar figures of small humanoid beings with heart-shaped (or pear-shaped, or teardrop-shaped) heads had been depicted in the cave art of Upper Palaeolithic Europe and also in the rock art of the San hunter-gatherers of southern Africa. It was with my curiosity thus aroused that I then began to delve into the modern UFO-abduction literature of the West, alongside the extensive shamanic sources I already had to hand, and stumbled across the weird parallels and commonalities between spirits and aliens explored in the last two chapters.

My mental picture of the aliens had been heavily conditioned by what I had seen in my ayahuasca visions, which in turn accorded very well with the physical descriptions given of aliens in hundreds of UFO-abduction reports and endlessly regurgitated in the tabloid media. I was therefore completely unprepared for what I discovered next – which is that, just like spirits, these entities that Western abductees generally construe as aliens *very frequently first present themselves in the form of animals, or with hybrid animal and alien characteristics*, before appearing in their more familiar tabloid identity as small humanoid beings with heart-shaped heads, large eyes, etc., etc.

Aliens as animal spirits

Let's deal with the aliens' side of this peculiar story first. Again the most useful way to proceed is simply to allow the abductees to speak for themselves about what they saw and experienced.

In Arthur's case, the small 'luminescent and semi-transparent' humanoids (with large dark eyes),[46] who encouraged him to climb a thread of light in an episode cited earlier, for some reason strongly reminded him of rabbits: 'so close to each other they're touching each other . . . It's like a bunch of rabbits. They huddle like rabbits.'[47] This had the effect of endearing them to him.[48] Similarly, Peter's abduction began when a group of small beings appeared in his room and a beam of light lifted him off his bed. As he was floated out of his house and into the air, he got a close look at one of the beings. Its eyes, he said, were very dark and deeply set in its face: 'like an animal's eyes, like a racoon's eyes'.[49]

While he was hunting in Medicine Bow National Park, Wyoming, in 1974, Carl Higdon saw five elk together in a clearing. Instinctively he took aim and fired his rifle but, as he did so, a zone of strangeness surrounded him, the sound of the shot seemed to come from far away and time slowed down so that Higdon was able to watch the bullet as it left the gun, travelled slowly through the air and fell to the ground, 'crushed and folded like a glove', about 60 feet away. As he walked to pick up the bullet an odd-looking humanoid figure dressed in black appeared and gave him a 'pill', telling him that it would alleviate his hunger for four days. Higdon was then taken on a journey in what he presumed to be a spaceship and later returned to the National Park, bewildered and disoriented, with his body covered in scratches.[50]

Moments before her abduction by small humanoids, Virginia Horton remembered talking with an 'intelligent grey deer'[51] and added:

'there was a person inside this deer'.[52] Another woman also reported seeing a deer looking at her through a window just before she was abducted.[53] Indeed, John Mack, David Jacobs and other researchers who interviewed large numbers of abductees found such accounts of encounters with therianthropic aliens – strange humanoids that either had certain animal characteristics or were fully transformed into animals – to be extremely common. 'The aliens appear to be consummate shape-shifters,' wrote Mack, 'often appearing initially to the abductees as animals – owls, eagles, racoons and deer are among the creatures the abductees have seen initially.'[54]

Therianthropic aliens seen by six schoolchildren at Bukit Mertajam, Malaysia, on 19 August 1970. In these drawings by the children the UFO in which the aliens arrived is depicted bottom right (Ahmad Jamaludin/Fortean Picture Library)

An abductee interviewed by David Jacobs saw a wolf in her bedroom one night:

The wolf was standing squarely on her bed, looking her in the eyes. She clearly remembered its fur, fangs and eyes. Other abductees have claimed to have seen monkeys, owls, deer and other animals.[55]

Indeed, owls feature particularly often in abductee reports. For example Colin, aged two and a half, the youngest of Mack's patients, frequently complained of being taken by 'scary owls with big eyes' to a 'space-ship', which he also sometimes described as a 'big boat in the sky'.[56] The owls, he said, 'floated down' from the sky to fetch him. On one occasion he confided that 'monster owls' had 'attacked' him on the spaceship, hurting his toe.[57] The author Whitley Strieber was confronted by the large, hypnotic eyes of 'a barn owl' staring at him 'through the window' of his home at the start of an abduction in which the aliens made an incision in his right forefinger.[58] The abduction experience of a woman on the west coast of the USA began when an entity that she construed as a 'five-foot-tall owl' strode down the highway towards her parked Jeep and stared at her over the hood.[59] One of Carol's early abduction experiences began with a large owl that swooped down from the skies and hovered close to her face. Its wings did not seem to flap, and its 'big dark eyes' filled 'three quar-ters' of its head.[60]

A registered nurse from the north-eastern United States,[61] Carol's abductions were of special interest to me because another of her encounters with strange, compelling owls included further levels of transformation, as well as unexpected symbolism that she herself recog-nised as shamanic. John Mack, whose patient she was, takes up the story:

> She was lying on a grassy mound or hillside, unable to move as she watched a small speck in the sky that seemed to be spiralling down toward her. She felt a wind, heard a high-pitched buzzing sound, and saw bright light around her. As the object seemed to come closer, it appeared to be an owl, and she felt a mixture of fear and awe. She turned her head and saw what looked to be a typical shaman, with a heavy fur robe and an antlered headpiece. Carol took this to be Cerunnos, an ancient Celtic deity, half animal and half person, that presides over animals of the forest. As the owl from the sky came closer, Carol realised that it seemed much too large for an owl – its black eyes were at least four inches across, and it had no other owl-like features, such as feathers or a beak . . . Then the experience seemed to 'escalate'

quickly into a negative one . . . The owl was not an animal at all, and she was no longer outside on a hill. Instead she felt panic in the presence of a familiar small being who stood over her 'watching and controlling' . . . Mainly she remembered the eyes [of the being] which seemed like black 'bulbous eggs – maybe that's what's giving me the image of an owl'.[62]

Bernardo Peixoto, a shaman of the Brazilian Ipixuma tribe, gained a PhD, qualified as an anthropologist and held a teaching post during the 1990s at the Smithsonian Institution in Washington DC.[63] He is in addition a UFO abductee and identifies the sinister small-bodied, large-eyed beings usually known in the West as 'Greys' with spirits that the Ipixuma call the *ikuyas*. Remembering his childhood in the Amazon, he told John Mack about an occasion during a tribal ceremony when the figure of an owl was seen perching at the top of a tree. The elders chanted, '*Ikuya! Ikuya! Ikuya!*' Bernardo asked them why they thought the creature was an *ikuya* and not simply an owl:

They said that, because they were in a trance, they could see light and force around the owl, which told them it was a humanoid in disguise. Also when they shoot arrows at the *ikuyas* disguised as owls, the arrows seem to pass through them without killing them.[64]

Shamans and their spirit helpers

Lacking the benefits of Peixoto's worldwide travel and contacts, most shamans from remote tribes have never heard of aliens or of UFO abductions but, as we have seen, they know a great deal about spirits that behave in many of the same strange ways that aliens do. The reader is already familiar from previous chapters with the transformations of spirits and shamans into animals and therianthropes that are experienced in deeply altered states of consciousness. Emerging from this, an important universal theme has been identified: shamans acquire supernatural helpers or guides – spirits who teach them how to become great healers. These spirit guides almost always appear *in the form of animals or therianthropes* and frequently begin to play a role in the future shaman's life while he is still a child, long before his initiation. In this respect, too, there is a parallel with UFO abductions, which also often begin in childhood and continue into adulthood.

Mircea Eliade reports that the 'helping spirits' of future Eskimo shamans are usually

> animals appearing in human form; they come of their own volition if the apprentice shows talent. The fox, the owl, the bear, the dog, the shark, and all kinds of mountain spirits, are powerful and effective helpers.[65]

Among the Cahuilla of southern California, the shaman's powers are believed to be transmitted to him by Mukat, the Creator, through the intermediary of guardian spirits in the form of owls, foxes, coyotes and bears.[66] The Paviotso, another southern Californian tribe, say that it is the 'spirit of the night' that gives shamans 'power for doctoring', which is transmitted with the help of 'water-babies [i.e. water fairies or sprites], eagle, owl, deer, antelope, bear or some other bird or animal'.[67]

Mun-yir-yir, an Australian Aborigine of the Murngin tribe, reported the following experience at the onset of his shamanic calling:

> I leaned over and drank out of the water-hole. When I did that a doctor soul caught my nose and made me sink down into the water. The doctors, they were two boys and a girl . . . They looked like opossums . . . They opened my nose and eyes and mouth and made me well.[68]

At the end of the nineteenth century the anthropologist Franz Boas recorded the experiences of a Kwakiutl Indian who received his shamanic calling and became a healer after the intervention of an animal spirit – a wolf – that had at first made itself useful to him as a hunting companion:

> One day, however, his wolf friend pressed its muzzle against his chest

bone and vomited all its magical force into him. He fell into a deep sleep and dreamt that the wolf changed into a human being and told him he would now be able to heal the sick. When he awoke he was trembling all over. Now he was a shaman.[69]

The Gitksan shaman Isaac Tens, whom we have met in previous chapters, received his calling at the age of 30 when he began falling spontaneously – sometimes in the midst of other activities – into deep and disturbing trances. When he awoke he was often injured and bleeding and reported stressful experiences involving owls, very similar to those undergone in modern times by UFO abductees. This was what happened to Tens around the year 1890 at the end of an afternoon spent cutting wood in a forest:

Before I had finished my last stack of wood, a loud noise broke out over me . . . and a large owl appeared to me. The owl took hold of me, caught my face, and tried to lift me up. I lost consciousness. As soon as I came back to my senses I realised that I had fallen into the snow.[70]

On another occasion, while out hunting, Tens said he 'glanced upwards' and 'saw an owl' at the top of a high cedar:

I shot it, and it fell down in the bushes close to me. When I went to pick it up it had disappeared. Not a feather was left; this seemed very strange . . . A trance came over me once more and I fell down unconscious . . .[71]

When a shaman-to-be amongst the Aborigines of eastern Arnhem Land, Australia, received his calling he construed the frightening beings that initiated him during his trance as other shamans (*marrnggijt*) transformed into huge birds. This is his account, recorded by ethnographers in 1935:

He heard the *marrnggijt* slapping their sides with their wings. One was close behind his head, and the second was up in the tree above him.

Opening his eyes he saw the one in the tree, in appearance like a *jabiru* [a large bird of the region, a species of stork] *but with eyes like an owl*. Almost immediately the one behind him hit him on the head with a stick and half stunned him, while the one in the tree jumped on his chest and stood there . . . The *marrnggijt* then proceeded to thrust all manner of pointed objects into his body . . . saying, 'We are doing this to let you know that from now on you will be a *marrnggijt*.'[72]

That the onset of some shamanic initiations and of some UFO abductions should be marked by the sudden materialisation of owls – or of other birds and animals with huge owl-like eyes – is mysterious enough in itself. But what I thought made the coincidence even stranger was the way this sort of imagery seems to pick up a reflection from the caves of Upper Palaeolithic Europe. A prehistoric engraving on the wall of Trois Frères in south-west France, described in Chapter Four, features two large owls, which archaeologists judge

Humanoid owls of Trois Frères

to have distinctly humanoid characteristics.[73] In the same cave the famous therianthrope known as the Sorcerer is also found. Thought to be more than 15,000 years old, it has the legs and upper body of a human being, its face is dominated by large owl-like eyes and a beak, and antlers jut from the top of its head. It could serve as an alternative model for the antlered shaman figure seen by Carol in the abduction described earlier that also featured 'an owl with black eyes at least four inches across'.

The 'Sorcerer' of Trois Frères (Breuil, 1952)

Knowledge

Whatever animal or hybrid form they appear in, and whether terrifying or friendly at first, the purpose of a shaman's spirit guides is to
bestow upon him the power and teach him the requisite skills to
shamanise: to travel freely and at will in the spirit world, to negotiate
with its inhabitants, and to return to earth equipped to heal the sick,
influence the weather, control the movements of animals, and find out
the truth of hidden things – not for his own benefit but for the benefit
of the tribe. Very frequently, as noted above, such supernatural helpers
first make their presence felt when the shaman is still a child – particularly during episodes of stress related to his unusual abilities and
personality, or during a severe illness or emotional crisis.[74] I'm reminded
of John Mack's patient Joe, quoted in Chapter Eleven, whose alien
abductors told him: 'We are close. We are with you. We're here to
help you. We're here to guide you, to make it through your difficult
times.'[75] This pleasant expression of solidarity, as the reader may recall,
immediately followed a much less pleasant experience in which 'a large
needle, about a foot long, with a kind of hilt' had been thrust into
Joe's neck at the base of his skull.[76] But such apparent paradoxes are
as rife in the accounts of abductees as they are in accounts of shamanic
initiations.

Together with all the piercing, cutting, insertion of implants, counting of bones, removal and replacement of organs, etc., etc. with which we are already familiar from the reports of UFO abductees, it is also clear – despite their frequent feelings of confusion and trauma – that they regard their encounters with the aliens as important *learning experiences*. For example Jean, a social scientist and lecturer living in the western US, is convinced that her frequent abductions have greatly strengthened her creative powers and insights. She believes that her encounters with the aliens have in some way 'neurologically reprogrammed' her to 'take in knowledge and put it out for others'.[77] Similarly Jim Sparks, a real-estate contractor in his mid-forties, told John Mack that immediately before each abduction the aliens project a hologram-like symbol, 'most often an owl', into his visual field. When the owl appears, Sparks understands that it is time to 'prepare for school or to learn'.[78]

Is it a coincidence that shamans likewise regard their initiatory trances as *learning experiences* by which their own inner resources are bolstered and specific information is conveyed to them? Amongst the Auracanian Indians of Chile, the future shamaness (*machi*) ascends in trance to the sky. There not only does she 'meet God', as Mircea Eliade reports it, but also 'supernatural beings show her the remedies necessary for cures'.[79] Similarly, in the Kalahari, the bushman shaman Bo told anthropologist Bradford Keeney that he climbed the ropes to the sky in order to learn from 'the Big God' and his retinue of spirits:

> That's one of the ways we learn new songs, dances, and more knowledge about how to heal others. They show us what plants to use for a certain sickness or how to treat a specific person.[80]

Kgao Temi, another shaman of the *!Kung*, had the same experience:

> They teach you things and give you more power. They actually talk to you. They tell you about the dance [the trance dance that the bushmen use to attain altered states of consciousness]. They also teach you about the plants.[81]

In the Peruvian Amazon, Mestizo shamans are adamant that the ayahuasca beverage takes them to a realm where spirits, sometimes in the form of animals and sometimes in the form of 'small people of a beautiful and strong constitution', teach them everything they must know in order to shamanise.[82] Referred to as *doctorcitos* ('little doctors'), these beings equip them with *icaros*, the magic songs used during ayahuasca sessions, show how illnesses may be diagnosed, and instruct them in detail on what plants to use, and how they are to be mixed with other plants, extracted, cooked, etc., in order to effect cures.[83]

Very occasionally when shamans receive their stern lessons of pain and knowledge at the hands of the spirits, one of them may be given something more than oral teachings and demonstrations. There are cases on record in the ethnographies where a shaman claims to have been given a book. Maria Sabina, a Mazatec Indian shaman who practised in the village of Huatla de Jimenez in Mexico in the 1950s, attained her visionary state by consuming a species of psilocybin mushrooms known since time immemorial in Mexico as *teonanactl* (literally 'flesh of the gods').[84] This she did, like all true shamans everywhere, in order to heal. In one particularly strong vision, during which she penetrated further than ever before into 'the world where everything is known':

A *duende*, a spirit, came toward me. He asked me a strange question: 'But what do you wish to become, you, Maria Sabina?' I answered him, without knowing, that I wished to become a saint. Then the spirit smiled, and immediately he had in his hands something that he did not have before, and it was a big Book with many written pages. 'Here,' he said, 'I am giving you this Book so that you can do your work better and help people who need help and know the secrets of the world where everything is known.' I thumbed through the leaves of the Book, many written pages, and I thought that unfortunately I did not know how to read. I had never learned and therefore that would not have been any use to me. Suddenly I realised I was reading and understood all that was written in the Book and that I became as though richer, wiser, and that in one moment I learned millions of things. I learned and learned.[85]

331

The spirit would not allow Maria to keep the book, which, she said, 'remains in the sky'.[86] How likely is it to be a coincidence that almost exactly the same story, transferred to a UFO setting, was told by Betty Hill? During her abduction in 1961 the being that she identified as the leader of the aliens gave her a large book but reclaimed it before allowing her to leave the ship.[87] Another abductee, Betty Andreasson, was given 'a small blue book with 40 luminous pages' but it too soon afterwards disappeared.[88]

The materialised psychism and the bottomless void

Even if spirits are real – which is basically what shamans the world over have claimed for millennia and scientists have denied for about a hundred years – we still have to ask ourselves what business they have with us. The scientific faction of course says that spirits have no business with us at all, on the grounds that the spirit world does not exist and supernatural beings are just empty projections of the human mind that may naively be believed in at rudimentary stages of culture but must inevitably be abandoned in the light of modern thought and technology. Anthropologist Weston La Barre tells us, as though these things have been proven in a laboratory, that 'the notion of an ec-static or body-separable soul (brainless mind or organismless life) that can wander in space and time has long since been banished . . . and all the suposed attributes of the soul can be better explained in terms of the sciences'.[89] Babbling triumphantly about the progress of the West in the nineteenth and twentieth centuries, the influential journalist and critic H.L. Mencken praised the scientists who had pioneered this now unstoppable revolution in knowledge:

> One by one the basic mysteries yielded to a long line of extraordinarily brilliant and venturesome men . . . The universe ceased to be Yahweh's plaything and became a mechanism like any other, responding to the same immutable laws . . . Heaven and Hell sank to the level of old wives' tales, and there was a vast collapse of Trinities, Virgin Births, Atonements and other such pious phantasms.[90]

If shamanic experiences of spirits and modern experiences of aliens are essentially a single phenomenon, however, then it becomes harder to maintain certainty that all such apparitions are 'phantasms', and that the universe is just 'a mechanism like any other, responding to the same immutable laws'. This is because it is very difficult to understand how the human mind, *without any real, objective and consistent external stimulus*, could consistently generate the same bizarre sequences of unexpected procedures and experiences in two groups of people as far apart culturally as shamans in hunter-gatherer societies and UFO abductees in the United States.

We are, of course, talking about *hallucinations* here – which are conventionally defined as perceptions that are thought to be real but that lack any objective stimulus:

> 'Hallucination' derives from the Latin deponent or half-passive verb *alucinari*, 'to wander in the mind' . . . In careful, present-day usage, hallucination indicates a false appearance, in sensory form, hence seemingly external, but occasioned by an internal condition of the mind, the central suggestion of the term being its subjectivity and groundlessness . . .[91]

Entoptic phenomena in the early stages of trance are recognised by science as universal human experiences in altered states of consciousness (and ascribed to the structure of the nervous system, as we've seen). But established opinion holds that full-blown iconic and representative hallucinations – Stage 3 hallucinations in Lewis-Williams' model – are not only *not real* in any sense but also that their contents are 'derived from memory' and life experiences, and 'are all culture specific: at least in some measure, people hallucinate what they expect to hallucinate'.[92] If this established model is correct, then we need to explain what common cultural factors and common memories have led people all around the world at all periods of history to hallucinate being abducted to the sky (or underground or underwater) by small humanoids with large heads and eyes who are capable of shape-shifting into the form of animals, who perform agonising and extraordinary surgical procedures on them and who teach them transformative knowledge.

It is at this point that I begin to feel baffled. I just don't see the common memories, common life experiences, and common cultural influences that could explain, for example, Isaac Tens' 1890 hallucination of a large owl hovering directly in front of him (which he said caught him by the face and tried to lift him up) and Carol's 1990 hallucination in which a large owl swooped down from the skies and hovered close to her face. I just don't see the common memories, common life experiences and common cultural influences that could explain why both Arthur in the US and Mabolele Shikwe in the Kalahari should hallucinate floating up 'threads of light' in order to encounter beings in the sky. I just don't see the common memories, common life experiences and common cultural influences that could have led both the illiterate Maria Sabina in her remote Mexican village in the 1950s and the highly literate Betty Hill in the US in the 1960s to hallucinate being given a book (which later disappears) by a powerful otherworldly being. I just don't see the common memories, common life experiences and common cultural influences that could lead UFO abductees in the West and shamans in Australia and South America to experience the implantation of foreign objects in their bodies or piercings by long needles or spears, etc., etc.

All in all I just don't get it, and what it says to me is that yes, the experiences that shamans and UFO abductees have are indeed hallucinations, but no, hallucinations may not always be specific to the individuals who have them and may sometimes not be conditioned very much by the cultures that they come from at all. I refer here not to superficial differences that undoubtedly *are* influenced by culture – as Lewis-Williams puts it, 'a San shaman may see an eland antelope; an Inuit will see a polar bear or a seal'[93] – but to the underlying perception that both share of the presence of some kind of spirit animal. Similarly I can understand the cultural conditioning behind construals of flying objects seen in the sky as spaceships on the one hand, and as aerial 'boats', 'shields', 'wells of metal', etc. on the other, but what interests me is that there is an underlying perception in both cases that *something* strange is present in the sky *and that it is real.*

I repeat that for people all over the world to have massively recurrent shared cross-cultural experiences involving massively recurrent

334

shared external real-world events is one thing. It is quite another thing, however, when people all over the world have massively recurrent shared cross-cultural experiences in situations where science can see no evidence for any external real-world stimulus at all. I suppose one possibility that would not entirely contradict the scientific-materialist paradigm would be that some hitherto undiscovered 'library' of extra-ordinarily detailed mental images, sensations and information is hard-wired into our brains, that it is the same library for all of us, and that it can be accessed only in altered states of consciousness. In that case we would need to discover not only how such an eerie and otherworldly mental archive was compiled in the first place, but also why it is so important – presumably to our survival – that evolution has gone to the trouble of programming the entire collection into all our brains *at the genetic level*. These are interesting questions and we will pursue them further.

Even more edgy and challenging, because they collide head-on with the fundamental beliefs of Western science concerning the nature of reality, are the arguments of William James, Aldous Huxley, Albert Hoffman and Rick Strassman cited in Chapter Eleven. According to these thinkers, it is quite possible that hallucinations *do* arise from valid external stimuli that are outside what Hoffman calls the 'receiver wave-length' of our brains when they are in normal states of consciousness.

We have seen that hallucinogenic drugs, rhythmic dancing, 'audio-driving' (with loud, repetitive drumming, etc.), sensory deprivation, self-torture (e.g. the agonising body piercings of the North American Indian sun dance), starvation and other extreme austerities are all amongst the techniques that shamans have used since prehistoric times to alter their consciousness and enter the spirit world.[94] But it is well known amongst anthropologists – Eliade discusses the matter exten-sively – that there have always also been shamans who have no need of any of these tried and tested 'techniques of ecstasy' because they have acquired the gift of falling spontaneously into trance (often following a period of illness or an inner crisis marked by disturbed dreams). These specially gifted shamans, the spontaneous trancers, obvi-ously provide the closest parallel to UFO abductees, whose experiences are also spontaneous and not deliberately induced.

The limited amount of scientific research done on the abduction phenomenon – notably the Roper Organisation survey in 1991 (see Chapter Eleven) – suggests that around 2 per cent of the US population has had the constellation of shamanic experiences that we label UFO abductions. Precisely because human neurology has remained unchanged for at least the last 50,000 years, but remembering always that our brains may be receivers as well as generators of consciousness, it is therefore very likely that around 2 per cent of *every* human population possesses this same spontaneous ability. For the remaining 98 per cent of us, who lack the genetic gift but who yet feel a calling to gain knowledge of the otherworld, it is a gratuitous grace of nature that chemicals closely related to key brain hormones are found in commonly available plants and fungi distributed all over the world. Whether by ingesting these plants, or by stressing our body chemistry sufficiently through extended periods of rhythmic dancing like the *!Kung* bushmen of southern Africa, or by means of some of the other mental and physical techniques outlined above, we all have the ability to alter our brain chemistry and temporarily 'retune' our consciousness to the same remarkable experiences as the spontaneous trancer.

Either way, since 2 per cent of the population seem to be born to trance, and since the rest of us can be made to trance through judicious use of the (maybe not so gratuitous?) graces of nature, the implication is that sooner or later every culture is going to encounter the characteristic experiences, landscapes and intelligent otherworldly beings that these trance states unvaryingly reveal. That such experiences have indeed been recorded by every culture at every period of history does not – of course – prove that the experiences are real. But the remarkable mutual corroboration and cross-tallying descriptions provided by such different and completely independent witnesses as UFO abductees and shamans increases my confidence that their experiences *might* be real in some way that science – with its exclusive 'this world' focus – has so far been unable to contemplate.

In 1958 the great psychologist Carl Gustav Jung, as ever far ahead of his time, committed scientific heresy when he considered the possibility that 'UFOs are something psychic that is equipped with certain physical properties'.[95] But he also asked, 'Where would such a thing come from?' and commented that 'the notion of a materialised psychism opens a bottomless void beneath our feet'.[96] Elsewhere in his treatment of UFOs, however, Jung tantalisingly suggests exactly where he thinks 'materialised psychisms' might come from when he proposes that 'all reality' could be 'grounded on an as-yet-unknown substrate possessing material and at the same time psychic qualities'.[97] What he has in mind here, he makes clear, are the parallel universes envisaged by quantum physics.[98]

This brings me back to the point I raised a few paragraphs ago. Let's say for the sake of argument that spirits *are* real, that they have found ways, and a variety of quasi-physical forms (of which 'aliens' are only the most recent), in which to manifest in our material universe, and that they have been doing so for thousands of years. Even so, what business do they have with us? Why are they here? What do they want? What's in it for them?

In my hunt through the ethnographic sources and UFO abduction reports I found one thing – most surprising and unexpected – that spirits and aliens do seem to want very much indeed from their human counterparts. This is the subject of the next chapter.

CHAPTER THIRTEEN

Spirit Love

The Urubu Indians, who live along Brazil's Gurupi River in the Amazon rain forest, have preserved a very strange story of two shamans who were 'born at the beginning of the world' but later 'escaped into the sky' to avoid a planetary cataclysm. Their desire had been to mate with mortal women in order to breed successors who could stay behind on the physical plane and preserve their special knowledge. Intercourse was attempted but was not successful because the shamans' penises were too tiny.[1]

These first shamans of Urubu myth are so insubstantial as to be rightly classed as spirits themselves and, indeed, there are widespread traditions that the true parents of all shamans are spirits – even if the intercourse that brings about their conception takes place between spirit bodies in the spirit world.

From Siberia, for example, comes the story of Bo-Khan, a mortal who had sex with a spirit woman. The child of their union became the progenitor of 'the race of shamans'.[2] Similarly Tavgytsy, a great shaman of the Avam Samoyed in Siberia in the early twentieth century, had a vision that he himself was the child of a spirit. His first trance, in which he received his initiation, occurred sponta-neously during three days of unconsciousness due to smallpox. He was thought to have died, like many others in his village, and was about to be buried when he suddenly came back to life. He told of how he had left his body and made a journey in the company of two spirit guides (in the form of an ermine and a mouse) who led him to the underworld. There his heart was torn out and thrown into a pot (compare Karin, a UFO abductee cited in Chapter Eleven: 'They opened up my chest and took out my heart'). Then, to complete the familiar sequence of shamanic surgery, his head was cut off, his body dismembered and his bones counted. Tavgytsy was carried 'into the middle of a sea'. There a voice told him: 'From the Lords of the Water you will receive the gift of shamanising.' Finally he climbed a mountain where he met a naked woman and began to suckle at her breast. She said to him: 'You are my child; that is why I let you suckle at my breast.'[3]

Across Siberia many tribes say that such mother spirits appear in animal or therianthropic form to abduct the souls of future shamans when they are born and bring them to a huge tree in the spirit world that stands at the foot of a mountain called Jokuo.[4] Andreas Lommel, Director of the National Museum of Ethnology in Munich, has observed that the tree described in these accounts has an odd shape with its top 'broken or chopped off, and that

> Every branch and twig of this tree, from the lowest to the topmost, bears birds' nests. The shamans of the whole world are brought up on this one tree . . . The shamans themselves usually say that a raven appears as teacher, which sits on the branches of this tree and educates the souls. The shamans whose souls are brought up in the nests on the upper branches become stronger and more important than those brought up in the lower nests. The nests are attached in regular rows and rise step by step with the space of one branch between one row and the next . . .[5]

This quasi-technological vision of the souls of future shamans in neatly stacked incubators is matched amongst the Cuna, the indigenous inhabitants of islands off Panama in the Caribbean, by legends that link the birth of shamanism to the arrival 'from heaven' of a humanlike spirit named Ipeorkum on some sort of flying machine – 'a golden disk called an *olopatté*. Landing on earth, he taught the people 'heavenly knowledge' and then departed again amidst strange atmospheric effects: 'white, yellow, blue and red mists came floating down'. When the air had cleared, 'the Cuna found a child in a treetop lying on an *olopatte* like the one on which Ipeorkum had descended from heaven. Later ten more children came to earth in this fashion.' Raised by virgins, Cuna legends say that these children became the first shamans.[6]

The Paez Indians of Colombia have an altogether darker tradition about a supernatural jaguar who raped a woman of their tribe at the beginning of time. The offspring of this union, Thunder-Jaguar, became a great shaman who himself fathered many therianthropic children, part human, part jaguar.[7] These hybrids, writes the anthropologist Gerardo Reichel-Dolmatoff, 'are imagined as most voracious little creatures . . . who, upon their appearance or birth, need several human wetnurses, young girls whom they kill, in the process of growing up, by drinking their milk and blood'.[8]

Congress with spirits

In hunter-gatherer societies, it is the shaman's relationships with spirits, his great personal experience and knowledge of the spirit realm, and his mastery of techniques that allow him to enter and leave it at will that mark him out from the crowd and equip him to make his special contribution. His abilities to find game animals, to protect the community from psychic attack, and most importantly to heal the sick are gifts that the spirits bestow. But what the myths cited above suggest is that the shaman is also believed to be *reproductively integrated* with the spirit world so that he can be, at one and the same time, the child of spirits, the lover of spirits, the father of spirits and, in an altered state of consciousness, a spirit himself.

Is this all just hallucination and fantasy, or could there be something more to it?

Some years before his initiation, the neophyte shaman amongst the Buryat, a Siberian tribe, experiences a celestial journey during which he has sex with large numbers of female spirits, one of whom becomes his 'wife in the sky'.[9] Likewise, every Teleut shaman has a celestial wife whom he holds in very high regard: 'My wife on earth is not fit to pour water on thy hands.'[10]

During the trance in which he received his initiation, a shaman of the Siberian Goldi tribe reported an encounter with a spirit woman. Although very slender and only about two feet tall, she had a commanding presence and was beautiful. She announced that she was going to make him a shaman and to this end would give him assistant spirits: 'You are to heal with their aid, and I shall teach and help you myself.' She also informed him: 'I love you, I have no husband now, you will be my husband and I shall be a wife unto you.' Thereafter, the shaman claimed, they had regular sexual relations.[11]

Amongst the Warao of eastern Venezeula the initiatory trance of the shaman is induced by the consumption of immense doses of South American wild tobacco (*Nicotiana rustica*, a different and much more powerful species than the *Nicotiana tabacum* presently smoked recreationally in cigarettes all over the world).[12] In the hallucinations that follow he finds himself on what he construes as 'a bridge made of thick white ropes of tobacco smoke' leading to 'a round white house' in the sky – the 'House of Smoke' – inhabited by spirits in the form of insects. There is an obvious parallel with UFO abductions where the 'round white house' in the sky is replaced by a flying saucer and where, in addition to appearing as animals, birds and small humanoids with large black eyes, the abductors do also, quite frequently, manifest either as insects or as humanoids with insectile characteristics.[13] Similarly in my ayahuasca visions, the being who most frightened me, and who indeed had seemed about to abduct me to the sky, had the look of 'some sort of huge insect with humanoid features'. Another had eyes that I described in my notebook at the time as 'multisegmented, like those of a fly' (see Chapter Three). Curiously, the insect form of alien that is most frequently seen by UFO abductees is the praying mantis, with its long body, upright posture, triangular face and large black eyes.[14] The reader will recall from earlier chapters that Kaggen, the shaman god of the San in southern Africa, also most frequently takes the form of the mantis. Meanwhile, the 'insect-people' encountered in the House of Smoke in the sky by the Warao shaman have the form of black bees, honey bees, wasps and termites. One of these is a 'beautiful bee girl' with whom the shaman has repeated sexual intercourse and fathers four hybrid children: Elder

341

Brother Black Bee, Younger Brother Wasp, Elder Brother Termite, and Younger Brother Honey Bee.[15]

In North America the Algonquin reverse the usual direction of the shamanic abduction narrative with a story of a hunter who saw 12 ravishing young spirit maidens descending from the sky in a basket. The hunter succeeded in capturing one of these female spirits, kept her his prisoner here on earth, married her and had sexual intercourse with her. She became pregnant and bore a baby son but longed to return to the sky. Accordingly she made a small basket of her own, and 'Having entered it with her child she sang the charm she and her sisters had formerly used, and ascended once more to the star from whence she had come.'[16] For two more years she remained with her son in the heavens, but the Algonquin tradition adds an important detail. It seems that all was not well with the hybrid child in the spirit world because he needed contact with his human father. To this end a voice instructed her: 'They son wants to see his father; go down therefore to the earth and fetch thy husband.'[17]

Amongst the Saora, an aboriginal tribe of Orissa in north-west India, the future shamaness receives her calling and supernatural conse-cration during 'visits from a suitor from the Underworld who proposes marriage'. Being a spirit, he naturally has the capacity to transform himself into any bodily shape he wishes. Usually he adopts the form of a 'well dressed and handsome' man, who appears 'in the depth of the night'.[18] As with UFO abductees, who frequently experience being taken from their homes in the small hours while the other members of their family have been plunged into an unnaturally deep sleep, the Saora say that when this suitor from the spirit world enters the maiden's bedroom, 'the whole household is laid under a spell and sleeps like the dead'.[19] And also as with abductees, it is futile to resist. One shamaness named Champa told of how she refused the advances of the being who had appeared by her bed, at which 'he took me up in a whirlwind and carried me away to a very high tree where he made me sit on a fragile branch'. There, terrified, she accepted his proposal of marriage.[20] Another Saora shamaness was already a married woman when her spirit lover appeared to her. When she resisted he threat-ened to drive her mad unless she agreed. 'Finally she was obliged to

Adventures in the spirit world: Ayahuasca visions of Peruvian shaman Pablo Amaringo.

Human figures with reedbuck heads. Main Caves, the Drakensberg. Note twin serpents, also with reedbuck heads, coiled around the upper body of the figure to the right. Photo: Santha Faiia.

Chimera with two heads – feline to the left, antelope to the right – from Heaven Cave in the Karoo. Photo: Santha Faiia.

Humans transforming into antelopes perched on an entoptic zig-zag, Western Cape. Photo: Santha Faiia.

Dancing women
with entoptic patterns.
Photo: Santha Faiia.

Elephant and human
figures with entoptic dots.
Photo: Santha Faiia.

The mysterious 'bridge' scene at Junction Shelter in the Drakensberg (see Chapter Nine).
Photo: Santha Faiia.

Left, Snake Rock overview. Below, detail from Snake Rock: a serpent. bleeding from the nose, coiled around an elongated human figure. Photos: Santha Faiia.

Close up of face of one of the Junction Shelter figures. What sort of being is represented here? Photo: Santha Faiia.

Rock art panel depicting a shaman partially transformed into a hoofed animal. Note upside-down antelope-headed snake and figures of fish and eels. Photo: Santha Faiia.

Examples of entoptic patterns in San rock art. Such grids, dots and zig-zags, frequently combined with more complex figures, belong to the universal imagery of altered states of consciousness. Photos: Santha Faiia.

accept,' reports Eliade, and learned in dreams the art of shamanising. She had two children in the underworld.'[21]

In an observation reminiscent of the Algonquin tradition cited above, the Saora state that the offspring of such unions generally remain in the underworld with their spirit father, but cannot thrive there without the love and attention of their human mother. In one case a young woman was seduced by a spirit, enjoyed intercourse with him, and they married:

> Soon the young woman gave birth to a child by him in the spirit world, and he would bring it to her at night for her to breastfeed it. He came when everyone was asleep. The people in the village heard the child cry, but her own family slept as if they were dead. Later she married a man in this world, but because she had a child in the other world she did not think that she could have more children here.[22]

In Mexico, Don Soltero Perez was the shaman of a small village who received his calling when he was struck by lightning and nearly killed. He recovered but continued to lose consciousness regularly, once or twice a week, for about six months. On awakening from each of these episodes he reported that his spirit had been abducted by the *enanitos*, dwarf-sized supernatural beings well known in Mexico since Aztec times, whose purpose was to transform him into a shaman. When he attempted to refuse his calling, as he did for a long while, they tortured him and beat him from head to toe, making him 'sore all over'. Eventually, knowing that they would kill him if this punishment continued, he gave way and agreed to their demands. They then equipped him with a staff and three magical stones through which in future he would be able to focus his healing power. Last but not least they married him to an *enanita* wife who would remain in the spirit world, 'in a cave with others of her kind', where Don Soltero would be able to visit her in a state of trance. 'Since he became a healer,' reports the anthropologist Holger Kalweit, who studied this case:

> Don Soltero has not been allowed to have sexual relations with his human wife. He tried once but immediately had an attack and fell to

the floor as though he were dead. During this attack his spirit was forced to go to a cave where it was beaten by the *enanitos*. Since then Don Soltero concentrates all his sexual activity on his spirit wife . . . She and Don Soltero have children who live with their mother in the cave.[23]

In South America, throughout the Amazon region, the belief is widespread that some river dolphins (*botos*) are not what they seem but are spirits from another realm, materialised in this world. Such beings have the power to come out of the water and appear on land in the form of handsome young men and beautiful young women. Thus disguised, they seduce mortals and lure them down to Encante, the enchanted city which every boatman knows lurks far beneath the surface of that deep and turbid river:[24] 'When you are alone in the water and the *boto* comes, you are afraid . . . They make a hole under the water . . . and they really attract you. They seduce you. You must be careful.'[25]

The general view is that 'women become pregnant by botos'; however, the offspring of these unions are said to be deficient, sometimes 'monstrous' creatures that 'die very quickly'.[26] In one interesting case a woman believed that a *boto* came to her in the night, disguised as her husband, and that they 'made love as if in a dream'. She claimed that she conceived, but nine months later, when she gave birth: 'It was as if the baby was made of water. The baby just melted away.'[27]

Another spirit animal of the Amazon that likes to seduce mortals takes the form of a nutria – a large otter. Local people say that it is 'driven by an insatiable longing to seek sexual intercourse with human beings in their dreams'. As with the *botos*, when the spirit lover is male and the mother is mortal the offspring of such unions are born here on earth but sickly – in this case with 'white skin and white hair'.[28] On the other hand, when the hybrid infant is born in Encante of a mermaid mother and a human father the outcome is different. Then the child remains in the underwater realm and becomes a great shaman of that dimension.[29]

Details from two paintings of ayahuasca visions by Peruvian shaman Pablo Amaringo. Left, mermaids lure a boatman down to the enchanted city deep beneath the surface of the Amazon; right, mermaids and serpents.

Alien lovers

One of the most surprising but consistent 'subroutines' of UFO abductions, reported independently in the vast majority of cases, has been put into a concise and useful summary by John Mack:

> Abductees experience being impregnated by the alien beings and later having an alien-human . . . pregnancy removed. They see the little foetuses being put into containers on the ships, and during subsequent abductions may see incubators where the hybrid babies are being raised . . . Sometimes the aliens will try to have the human mothers hold and nurture these creatures, who may be quite listless . . .[30]

Where male abductees are concerned, sperm samples are repeatedly taken and hybrid babies are displayed to them with the strong mental suggestion that these are their offspring. Like female abductees, who are sometimes artificially inseminated and sometimes impregnated directly in acts of sexual intercourse with 'the alien beings', male abductees also have sex with alien females. Before psychologists rush in with obvious suggestions like fantasy-projection, it is worth making the point that these sex acts are rarely experienced as being pleasurable and are reported redundantly, in almost exactly the same language, over and over again, by hundreds of abductees. Based on close investigation of his own patients, Harvard psychiatrist John Mack confirmed:

> I am convinced that the reproductive narrative is powerfully real for the experiencers. To the best of my knowledge, after thousands of hours of investigation with scores of abductees, no Freudian or other individual psychodynamic explanation seems to account for its basic elements.[31]

How then are we to explain this very specific, widespread and easily identified pattern of bizarre 'non-real' experiences?

The short answer is that only in the Western context, from which spirits have been temporarily expelled by science, do such experiences seem bizarre, extraordinary, inexplicable and threatening. In the shamanic context they occur routinely and require no explanation at all.

For example, John Mack's patient Sara reported frequently being forced into intercourse with an alien male who had 'a light contour of a penis, but not like a physical penis'.[32] Similarly, based on analysis of the testimony of 60 abductees,[33] David Jacobs of Temple University provided this summary of intercourse when the male partner is alien: 'The insertion of the "penis" is quick, and the penis does not feel normal; it is usually very thin and very short.'[34] Jacobs' own view is that there is no connection between modern UFO abductions and 'myth, folklore, legend and so forth'. He believes that his evidence 'inexorably leads to the abduction phenomenon beginning in the late nineteenth century . . . and not to any time before that' (personal correspondence, May 2005). Nevertheless, his summary of alien intercourse is strongly reminiscent of the Urubu Indian descriptions, cited at the beginning of this chapter, of the mythical first shamans whose penises were so tiny that they were unable to mate successfully with human women.[35]

When we consider the number of occasions on which shamans are abducted and engage in intercourse with spirits, the 1957 abduction and subsequent rape by an 'alien' woman of a rich young Brazilian named Antonio Villas-Boas seems unmistakably to be part of the same genre. While working on his father's farm at night, Villas-Boas saw a UFO land nearby and was forced inside it by four small beings with large heads. They stripped him naked and took a blood sample from his chin. Then a small, nude female with the ethereal looks of a fairy – thin blonde hair, large slanted eyes, high cheekbones – entered the room and began to embrace him: 'Her body looked human, her feet were small, and her hands were long and pointed. She was about four and a half feet tall.'[36] Two vigorous bouts of sexual intercourse followed, leaving the young man feeling that he had been used like 'a good stallion to improve their . . . stock'.[37] He recalled later that despite her transparent and delicate looks, the alien female had emitted harsh grunts during sex, 'giving the disagreeable impression that I was with an animal'.[38]

Peter, one of John Mack's patients, remembered repeated episodes of lovemaking with an alien female but did not feel raped and abused. On the contrary, he said of his alien lover: 'It feels like she's my real wife – I want to say on a soul level.'[39]

Similar emotions of deep love and loyalty to an alien of the opposite sex, creating what Mack calls 'a moral dilemma for marriages on this Earth plane', are reported by large numbers of abductees.[40] Such triangles are highly reminiscent of the case of the Buryat shaman cited earlier who felt that his wife on earth was not even 'fit to pour water' on the hands of his celestial wife. Likewise Don Soltero Perez broke off all sexual contact with his human wife so that he could concentrate his attentions on his spirit wife.

Interestingly, however, many abductees also report that when sexual intercourse is first initiated by the aliens they are lulled into a false sense of security by a flood of imagery in their minds in which 'the abductee is made to believe that either her husband or loved one is with her. Abductees sometimes say that the face of the husband, for instance, tends to "phase" in and out of the face of the alien.'[41] The obvious parallel here, and it is a close one, is of the woman in a village along the Amazon, cited earlier, who made love 'as if in a dream' with a dolphin spirit that had taken on the appearance of her husband.

Hybrid offspring (1): tanks and nests

In some cases of UFO abductees who experience themselves to be in intense long-term 'marriages' with aliens, hybrid children are deliberately created and parented.[42] Here too there is an exact parallel to the deliberate creating and parenting of the hybrid offspring of spirits and shamans reported earlier. In addition, however, the study of large numbers of UFO abduction reports reveals consistent repeated testimony to the effect that the aliens are creating and rearing hybrid children, born of human mothers or fathers, outside anything even remotely resembling a human family unit – indeed in what sound like extremely impersonal 'battery' conditions.

Almost always what happens is that the abductee is taken by the aliens to an area set against the curving inner wall of the ship where he or she – more often she – is shown large numbers of hybrid babies stacked up in 'drawers' or 'tanks' in some sort of symmetrical grid or rack.

Here is Julie Knapp's observation of such a scene during one of her abductions in 1977:

God! It's like they've got . . . babies there. They're like in drawers in the walls; it's like little drawers that pull out and there's babies, like little, little somethings in these drawers that pull out like in a lab or something.[43]

John Mack's patient Jerry had almost exactly the same experience in a room lined with 'lots and lots and lots and lots of rectangular-shaped containers, like drawers in a cabinet, with hardly any space between them'. Inside the drawers she was shown hundreds of 'I don't know if you can call them babies or not, but I guess just little foetuses.'[44]

During one of her abductions, Catherine saw 'cases' stacked in floor-to-ceiling rows – four or five rows from top to bottom, eight or ten from left to right. The cases, she said, were 'lit from the back' and contained 'baby versions' of the aliens 'all in a liquid' and 'all facing out'.[45] Similarly in an abduction in 1980 James Austino saw what he construed as rows of fish tanks, stacked up on one another, each containing a hybrid baby: 'The whole wall's lined up . . . Sixty, maybe seventy.'[46] Another abductee, Karen Morgan, compared the room with the rack of hybrid babies to 'a big womb. There seem to be a lot of new babies in it. Fifty or maybe a hundred . . .'[47]

Allowing of course for the very different metaphor, isn't what is envisaged here rather familiar in some way? Aren't these geometrical stacks of incubation tanks, in which half-alien, half-human babies are lined up in neat symmetrical rows, in essence the same thing as the great tree of Siberian legend, described earlier, that incubates the souls of shamans in nests attached in geometric rows rising step by step with the space of one branch between each row and the next?

What makes the comparison particularly tempting is the report of Karin, one of John Mack's patients, that she had emerged during an abduction on board a UFO 'into a black space that contained a huge tree with a great canopy of leaves. On the different branches of the tree there were large nests with thick twigs and an eagle sitting quietly and peacefully in each one'.[48]

It is almost as though the symbolic array by which the spirit world represents itself to humans in shamanic cultures has here broken through and momentarily overwritten the symbolic array by which 'aliens' represent themselves to humans in modern America.

Hybrid offspring (2): parents, wetnurses and playfriends

As well as being incubated in nests on a tree, a number of other definite characteristics of the offspring of shamans and spirits are indicated in the cross-section of myths and initiation experiences cited at the beginning of this chapter. The strong themes that I take from these accounts are the association of hybrid human-spirit babies with flying discs (Cuna, Panama), their failure to thrive in the spirit world unless breastfed either by a wetnurse (Paez, Colombia), or preferably their own mother (Saora, India), their need for contact with their human father as well (Algonquin, North America), and their pale and sickly, sometimes 'monstrous' appearance (Mestizo, Amazon).

Turning now to the offspring of aliens and humans, what do we find?

The reader will recall from Chapter Twelve that the troubled toddler Colin, John Mack's youngest patient, repeatedly experienced being abducted to a flying saucer in the sky by 'scary owls with big eyes'. After one such abduction Colin announced that he did not like the flying saucer and did not want to go back, but nevertheless insisted: 'I was born there and fell from the stars . . . I was born on the space-ship . . .'[49] The comparison with the Cuna tradition of a baby left behind in a treetop by a flying disc from the sky is obvious, and indeed many UFO abductees report feeling that they too were in some way born amongst the aliens, that they are not 'from here', and that their human mother and father are not their true parents.[50]

What about the spirit child's failure to thrive unless breastfed either by his own mother or by a wetnurse, and his need for other human contact including with his father? Surprisingly these themes are richly represented in the reports of UFO abductees and shed completely new light on the sorts of experiences with spirits that must have inspired the shamanic narratives.

Many UFOs supposedly have specific recognisable rooms on board in which hybrid babies (and also older children) are presented to their human parents of both sexes. Several reluctant abductees report being told specifically by the aliens that they are involved with the hybrids whether they like it or not and that the babies 'need their mothers. They have to have their mothers. It doesn't matter if you care or not, it doesn't matter. They need their mothers.'[51] In other cases, however, such feelings seem to be reciprocated. For example, John Mack found a number of his patients who believed passionately that they had living hybrid offspring 'out there'. They suffered terrible feelings of loss at being separated from them and completely unable to gain access to them except on those occasions when

periodically the abductee mothers and fathers are brought to see the hybrid offspring and encouraged to hold and love them, which is one of the most disturbing aspects of the whole process. For the abductees are naturally filled with conflict at the prospect of forming a deep bond with an odd offspring that they can only rarely see at the pleasure of the alien beings.[52]

Hybrid babies are not only encountered by their own human mothers and fathers but also, quite frequently, by unrelated humans who are required by the aliens to serve as wetnurses and playmates to them.

Summarising the reports of 60 abductees, David Jacobs gives a helpful, moment-by-moment account of a typical 'baby presentation' and nursing sequence where the human involved is not the hybrid's mother:

The aliens bring the abductee into the child presentation room . . . The abductee stands or sits down on a bench or chair. The beings who brought her in are behind her. Then a 'female' being approaches her. She is holding a baby. The woman senses the communication 'Isn't this a nice baby? Wouldn't you like to hold the baby? Hold the baby!' The female being extends her arms with the baby in it toward the woman, and the abductee takes it. She holds the baby to her chest with the baby's head resting on her arm or shoulder. If the abductee resists she may be given a 'reason' to force her to hold the baby. One woman was told that the baby would get sick if she did not hold it, and that it would develop a rash or some other sickness if she held the baby away from her body. Therefore she had to hold the baby against her skin for as long as possible. The baby may be naked, or it may be wrapped in a 'blanket'. It is usually very small, but it can be an older and larger baby as well. Women describe the small baby as being very light in weight but with a heavy head. The woman sits with the baby, or she may get up and walk around with it. The aliens stare intently at her and the baby. The woman hears another directive: 'Nurse the baby.' 'Put the baby to your breast and feed the baby.' The woman says, 'But I do not have any milk.' The response is, 'Put the baby to your breast and nurse the baby!' Saying 'no' is futile. If she resists the aliens will put the baby to her breast anyway. It cups its mouth to her nipple. It has a very weak sucking reflex. In many instances the woman may be surprised to find that she is lactating and that her breasts are engorged. When that happens the baby will partially drain the breast. Often, however, nursing the baby is futile but seems to satisfy the watchful aliens nonetheless.[53]

After going through such an experience Jill Pinzarro commented:

I feel it's very important to the baby that it has this contact and I'm very happy to do it for it. I feel that it really needs that . . . It's like soaking up the experience of being held. That's what I think.[54]

During several of her abductions, Karen Morgan has found herself in a room with other human women, playing with naked babies:

The women hold the babies up in the air, tickle them, and make baby sounds to amuse them. The babies do not respond. They do not laugh or smile, and they do not make sounds in return. Sometimes Karen and the other women might be told to 'wash' the baby . . . Frequently the offspring the aliens tell the woman to hold in this setting is between two and ten years old, or even older . . .[55]

In one abduction Karen was required to embrace a hybrid teenage female. At first she refused, but the aliens made her wrap her arms around the girl, who returned the embrace, clinging on to her for a long while. At the end the child seemed energised. She turned to Karen and telepathically projected into her mind the words 'thank you'.[56]

John Mack's patient Peter recalled being recruited by the aliens as a playmate for hybrid children: 'Since I was a young child I had agreed to do this, and I chose to play with the babies, the other beings, the aliens.'[57]

Hybrid children (3): pale and sickly and monstrous

We've seen that the hybrid offspring of spirits and humans are frequently described as pale and sickly with white skin and white hair and also as being in some way deficient, perhaps even monstrous.[58] Although often given in more detail (as one would expect since they are recent and were recorded by trained psychotherapists) the accounts of UFO abductees ascribe exactly the same characteristics to the hybrid offspring of humans and aliens.

Monstrous hybrids are described – for example one with one arm 'almost human' while the other arm appeared 'alien', and another whose face was alien on one side and human on the other.[59] Likewise an abductee named Melissa furiously resisted contact with what she described as the 'gross baby' that the aliens presented her with – to which she reacted as though it were indeed a monster:

> It's . . . an ugly one like the little creatures. I don't want anything to do with this species, nothing at all. I'll kill it . . . It's so fucking unnatural. Fucking stupid. Disgusting thing . . .[60]

But others have more tender feelings. Debbie Tomey reported an episode in which the aliens presented her with a young adult female hybrid:

> a few feet tall, with a slim body and ivory skin and a big head and high cheekbones and no eyelashes or brows, and unnervingly sparse blonde hair, the colour of cotton, which in certain places didn't quite cover her scalp.[61]

Debbie said that she could not help feeling a pang of maternal affection for the girl.[62]

Another abductee, Barbara Archer, had this to report:

> They scared me when I first looked at them because they looked odd. They looked kind of old. They don't have much hair. They have some hair, but not much . . . They strike me as being very fragile. I feel like maybe they're what I would think of as premature babies . . . They're fragile . . . I feel like they're not real strong . . . They don't look healthy to me. They're kind of scrawny or something.[63]

Nona:

Their bodies were short for their heads. Their heads seemed oversized. They had very blue eyes. They had very thin, wispy hair . . . I would say they were probably three and a half feet tall, but they all looked the same age. 'You're our mother and we need you,' they said.[64]

Isabel:

She had long limbs, and she wrapped her arms around me, and I held her . . . on my hip and her leg was in front. The other one was dangling. Her skin looked dry and scaly and flaky, like she needed lotion. She looked so lonely. I felt she was mine in a biological sense.[65]

Peter:

They had big heads, and, like, wisps of hair, and they have bigger heads than their bodies. They have skin that's kind of like our skin. It's a little rougher – more fleshy. It's not like baby fat. It's like old-age fat, and the arms are really fragile, but they have big bellies.[66]

'Abductees universally state that the baby does not have the normal human reactions of a human infant,' adds David Jacobs. Furthermore, such a baby

is almost always listless. It does not respond to touch as a normal baby would. It does not squirm; it does not have a grasping reflex with its hands. It is lifeless, yet it is not dead. Most women think that there is something terribly wrong with the baby. They feel that they must hold the baby to help it survive.[67]

Catalyst

Although spirits frequently abduct shamans and make babies with them, they rarely bother to explain why.[68] Likewise, in all the extensive UFO abduction literature, I have found few references to attempts made by aliens to explain the very great amount of effort that they appear to put into the creation and nurture of hybrid offspring. But in answer to the question posed at the end of Chapter Twelve – what do spirits and aliens want from us? – it seems clear, even from this necessarily brief survey of the evidence, that what they want, more than anything else, is to mate with us and create hybrids. This simply begs further questions, of course – notably why do they want that, and how long have they wanted it for?

The argument has been made in Part II that entoptic phenomena and complex visions of spirit worlds and spirit beings were the inspiration for the transcendental art of the painted caves of Upper Palaeolithic Europe. We also saw how the impaled and suffering images of wounded men make complete sense in terms of what we know about the symbolism, imagery and experiences of shamanic initiations the world over. What comes as a complete surprise, however, is how much sense they also make in terms of the symbolism, imagery and experiences of UFO abductions. Since we have no ethnography from the Upper Palaeolithic, it is obvious that we cannot prove that all the other experiences reported to ethnographers by shamans, and to psychiatrists by UFO abductees, were shared by their Upper Palaeolithic predecessors, nor can we be certain what their construal of such experiences would have been. Nevertheless it would be unwise to exclude the possibility that the cave artists were as capable as we are of attaining the full range of trance perceptions. They are therefore also just as likely to have experienced abductions at the hands of supernatural beings encountered in their visions, to have received teachings of vital knowledge and the gift of healing powers, and to have paid for these in return with marriages to spirit spouses and the creation of hybrid children.

Who knows, perhaps experiences such as these might even have provided the catalyst that – virtually overnight in evolutionary terms – transformed anatomically modern but dull, uninspired and spiritually void humans into behaviourally modern, innovative, spiritually aware and interesting humans?

It seemed to me that if this were so, if interactions with mysterious supernatural beings had played such a pivotal role at such a critical moment in the story of human evolution, then the phenomenon was much too important to have confined itself to shamans in hunter-gatherer societies and UFO abductees in technologically advanced countries. No matter how well hidden by local and finite construals, it was almost certain to have been present at other moments in human history as well.

Not even sure exactly what I was looking for, but only that I would know it if I found it, I began to investigate further.

CHAPTER FOURTEEN

The Secret Commonwealth

The great Swiss psychologist and psychiatrist Carl Gustav Jung, writing in 1958, was the first to point out that the UFO phenomenon has a history, and perhaps a prehistory. Large numbers of people would later report having experienced abductions during the 1950s and even the 1940s, but in 1958 the matter had not yet received any publicity and Jung knew nothing of it. His interest was therefore limited exclusively to UFOs themselves which, since the Second World War, had generated huge numbers of eyewitness reports of 'flying saucers' and ever-rising public interest and concern. Jung described the sightings as a new form of global rumour that 'differs from an ordinary rumour in that it is expressed in the form of visions'.[1] His inclination was to treat UFOs as 'a 99 per cent psychic product' yet he admitted he was baffled by their 'apparently physical nature'[2] which, he lamented, created 'insoluble puzzles for even the best brains':[3]

> The only thing we can say with tolerable certainty about UFOs is that they possess a surface which can be seen by the eye and at the same time throws back a radar echo.[4]

In addition one other thing was clear, and this was that UFOs were nothing new:

> Though UFOs were first publicised only towards the end of the Second World War, the phenomenon itself was known long before. It was

357

observed in the first half of this century [the twentieth century], and was described in earlier centuries and perhaps even in antiquity.[5]

In August 1566, for example, 'many large black globes were seen in the air' above the city of Basel in Switzerland, 'moving before the sun with great speed, and turning against each other as if fighting. Some of them became red and fiery and afterwards faded and went out.'[6] Jung reproduced an illustration of the scene from a Basel broadsheet of 1566, noting that the 'speed and irregular motion' attributed by eyewitnesses to the black discs 'are typical UFO features'.[7]

Basel broadsheet, 1566

In April 1561 there was a spectacular UFO display over Nuremberg, Germany. Plates and globes were sighted in large numbers whirling in the sky near the sun, and also 'great tubes in which three, four and more globes were seen'.[8]

Nuremberg broadsheet, 1561

An engraving from the seventeenth century shows a pilgrim breaking through the star-strewn rim of this universe and beholding what Jung describes as

another, supernatural universe filled with . . . layers of cloud or mountain ranges. In it appear the wheels of Ezekiel and rings or rainbow-like figures, obviously representing the 'heavenly spheres'. In these symbols we have a prototype of the UFO empirical vision . . .[9]

The spiritual pilgrim
discovering another world

A fourth scene considered by Jung, called 'The Quickening of the Child in the Womb', is from the Rupertsberg Codex (twelfth century, written by Hildegard of Bingen) and shows a pregnant woman,

'The Quickening of the Child in
the Womb' (twelfth century)

reclining, approached by two groups of people bearing baskets of gifts.[10] I note in passing that a mushroom, in the hands of a small goblin-like figure, can be seen in one of the baskets.[11] Meanwhile a large quadrangular object containing a curious mixture of eyes and discs floats overhead, set against the background of a starry sky. The object is connected by a long tube to a foetus in the woman's womb.[12]

Although he knew nothing of the UFO abduction phenomenon, Jung was characteristically prescient in picking out this scene from the twelfth-century codex. Not only was something very much like the basic form of the flying quadrangular object sketched by eyewitnesses of a modern UFO sighting (the Cash/Landrum case), but also

Drawing of the Cash/Landrum UFO sighting (after Stillings, Ed., 1989).

the scene neatly symbolises one of the fundamental themes of UFO abductions – namely the impregnation of human women by aliens and the creation of hybrid offspring. In addition it may or may not be relevant that following some sightings of UFO-type lights in the sky in the US in the late 1960s, people reported experiencing strange dreams in which groups of giant eyes floated above them.[13]

Jacques Vallee and the flying saucer connection

Jung's insights were penetrating, but as he himself admitted, his research – for what was never intended to be more than a short monograph – was strictly limited. Beyond recognising that a historical background to the UFO phenomenon does exist (and examples could be multiplied from every folklore and mythology of the world), he had neither the time nor the inclination to find out more before his death in 1961.

A few years later, in 1969, the mystery of the historical background to the UFO sightings of the mid-twentieth century was explored again. This time the task was taken up with great vigour by mathematician and NASA consultant Jacques Vallee in his underground cult classic *Passport to Magonia*, unfortunately now long out of print.[14]

Vallee's contributions were manifold. Of great value is his catalogue of UFO sightings documented in relatively recent news sources. The catalogue, which stretches back long before the first modern wave of publicity for the phenomenon following World War II, begins in July 1868 when a strange 'aerial construction' bearing lights and making engine noises flew low over the Chilean town of Copiago.[15] In January 1878 a farmer in Texas was startled by a sighting of a dark flying object that he described as a 'large saucer'.[16] In 1880 a 14-year-old boy saw a luminous ball descend from the sky and hover near him. He reported feeling drawn to it but overcame his fear and escaped.[17] The examples go on and on; without needing to reproduce Vallee's entire catalogue here, the gist is that many apparently motorised and piloted UFOs, and even identifiable 'flying saucers', were in fact seen all over the world during the second half of the nineteenth century.[18]

Moreover, Vallee was able to trace the phenomenon much further back than this, and much further even than Jung had followed it. Indeed Vallee's title, *Passport to Magonia*, is taken from an account written by Agobard, Archbishop of the French city of Lyons, around the year 820. Like a modern UFO sceptic, the good archbishop's testament to posterity was a lament at the ignorance of the masses for believing in the existence

of a certain region, which they call Magonia, whence ships sail in the clouds . . . Out of the number of those whose blind folly was deep enough to allow them to believe these things possible, I saw several exhibiting in a certain concourse of people, four persons in bonds –

three men and a woman who they said had fallen from these same ships; after keeping them for some days in captivity they had brought them before the assembled multitude, as we have said, in our presence to be stoned. But truth prevailed.[19]

Doesn't it seem likely that these four unfortunates, who Agobard saved, would describe themselves as UFO abductees if their experience were to occur today? It may be relevant that a small number of modern abductees have stated that they were *not* conveniently floated directly back to their homes and beds after the experience, but dropped less gently elsewhere – sometimes miles away. It is not difficult to imagine how such a return, observed or merely reported, might have attracted the attentions of a lynch mob in the superstitious climate of the ninth century.

Another early UFO report that Vallee found comes from Japan, where Imperial records inform us of the erratic flight over Kii Province, beyond the north-east mountain of Fukuhara, of an unusual brightly lit object described as an 'earthenware vessel'. Soon 'the object changed its course and was lost to sight at the southern horizon leaving a luminous trail'.[20] Likewise, on 12 September 1271, the famous priest Nichiren was about to be beheaded at Tatsunokuchi, Kamakura, when there appeared in the sky an object like the full moon, shiny and bright . . .' Officials panicked and cancelled the execution.[21] Vallee also cites a number of other UFOs and UFO-linked phenomena that were seen and documented in Japan between the tenth and eighteenth centuries. In August 989, for example, three round, exceptionally bright objects that later joined together were observed. In September 1702 cotton-like threads fell from the heavens, apparently emanating from the sun itself, and in 1749 three more large round objects, 'like the moon', were observed continuously in the sky over a period of four days, sparking riots.[22]

In addition to such neglected and overlooked UFO reports in secular sources, Vallee argues that 'it is in the literature of religion that flying objects from celestial countries are most commonly encountered . . .'[23] Again it is not necessary here to recapitulate in any detail the evidence already published on this point, but we can easily grasp what Vallee is getting at by calling to mind the winged discs of Sumer and ancient Egypt, the Vimana 'aircraft' referenced in Hindu texts, the flying carpets of Arabia, and the 'sky-rafts' used by the 'star spirits' of ancient China.[24] Let's also not forget biblical UFO spectacles such as Elijah's ascent to heaven in 'a whirlwind' associated with a 'chariot of fire'[25] and the prophet Ezekiel's vision, again involving a whirlwind and fire, as well as mysterious creatures on board great 'wheels' (cited earlier by Jung) that 'lifted them up from the earth'.[26] In the same general vein we quite often read accounts in the Old Testament of such aerial vehicles as 'the Chariots of God'[27] and descriptions of what sound like a superior race of beings whom humans must have dealings with and 'who come from a far country, from the end of heaven'.[28] Last but not least, in keeping with two of the fundamental themes of modern UFO abductions – sex with aliens and the creation of hybrid offspring – it is surely significant that the Bible depicts women having intercourse, and making monstrous hybrid babies, with heavenly supernaturals. In a famous passage from Chapter Six of the Book of Genesis we read that the 'Sons of God', immortal beings whom scholars usually identify with angels:

> saw the daughters of men that they were fair; and they took them wives, all of which they chose . . . There were giants in the earth in those days; and also after that, when the sons of God came unto the daughters of men and they bare children to them.[29]

Whatever else might be made of these strange verses, it is clear that the 'sons of God' are not human – a matter on which every authority is agreed. Yet these non-human or superhuman spiritual powers seduce and impregnate mortal women, who in turn give birth to hybrid children. As the reader will agree, this is precisely the scenario explored in Chapter Thirteen whereby immortal spirits engage in intercourse with mortal shamans with a view to producing hybrid offspring, and whereby aliens engage in intercourse with abductees to exactly the same end.

Jacques Vallee and the fairy connection

Passport to Magonia does not consider any of the connections between UFO abduction experiences and shamanic initiation experiences, or between aliens and spirits, that I had turned up in my research. But what it does consider is another, apparently completely different but equally extraordinary, set of connections that I had been unaware of.

'The modern, global belief in flying saucers and their occupants,' wrote Vallee

> is identical to the earlier belief in the fairy faith. The entities described as the pilots of the craft are indistinguishable from the elves, sylphs and lutins of the Middle Ages. Through the observations of uniden-tified flying objects, we are concerned with an agency our ancestors knew well and regarded with terror: we are prying into the affairs of the Secret Commonwealth.[30]

I was naturally intrigued by Vallee's forthright comparison of the fairy phenomenon on the one hand and the UFO phenomenon on the other – a comparison that he documents at length and backs up with solid evidence.[31] Furthermore, the insights that he offers take us far beyond Jung on these matters because a few of the specifically abduction-related aspects of UFOs that we are familiar with today had begun to be reported during the 1960s when Vallee was doing his research. In making his case, he was therefore able to take two of the early reports very closely into account – the abductions of Antonio Villas-Boas and of Betty and Barney Hill – and to provide us with a masterful analysis of these and of their precedents in fairy folklore.

On the other hand, there was also a great deal in 1969 that Vallee did *not* know about UFO abductions – and could not have known then. Full details of the experience as we now understand it would only filter into the public domain in the 1980s and 1990s when Budd Hopkins, David Jacobs, John Mack and other psychiatric counsellors began to record extensive interviews with people who believed they had been abducted by UFOs (at the same time revealing the astonish-ing commonalities that unite all such accounts). Lacking access to the mass of data that these researchers have uncovered, Vallee obviously had very little to work with in his attempt to compare fairy and alien phenomena. Nonetheless, he found more than enough to convince me that the resemblance is strong, and intriguing.

Fairy knolls and skyships

Vallee's dark hint about 'prying into the affairs of the Secret Commonwealth' is derived from the title of a book – *The Secret Commonwealth of the Elves, Fauns and Fairies* – published in 1691 by the Reverend Robert Kirk, a church minister of Aberfoyle in Scotland.[32] Like a powerful shaman, Kirk was rumoured to possess 'the second sight'[33] – i.e. clairvoyance and other psychic abilities. By means of this gift, he claimed that he regularly encountered the small, unpredictable, often dangerous supernaturals – given many different names by many different cultures in many different epochs – that have been classed for about a thousand years throughout the Celtic fringe of western Europe under the broad rubric of 'fairies' (*feie, fata, faerie*, etc., etc.).[34] Based on his direct and powerfully felt experiences, Kirk described these fairy tribes as 'a distinct order of created beings possessing human-like intelligence and supernormal powers, who live and move about in this world invisible to all save men and women of the second sight'.[35]

What adds special poignancy to Kirk's story is that in 1692, a year after the publication of *Secret Commonwealth*, he vanished and was believed locally to have been 'taken' by the fairies. This tradition was confirmed by Walter Scott in 1830[36] and was still in circulation in 1909 when the renowned scholar of religions, W.Y. Evans-Wentz, was preparing his own careful and extensively documented study, *The Fairy Faith in Celtic Countries*.[37] Wentz visited Aberfoyle, the site of Kirk's supposed disappearance. There Mrs J. MacGregor, the caretaker of the old churchyard, where there is a tomb to Kirk, reported that 'many say there is nothing except a coffin filled with stones'. Mrs MacGregor further informed Evans-Wentz that 'Kirk was taken into the Fairy Knoll', a low hill that she pointed out on the other side of the valley, 'and is there yet, for the hill is full of caverns and in them the "good people" have their homes.'[38]

The reader will recall the frequency with which shamans experience abduction to caves by spirits during their initiatory trances and how some modern UFO abductees have also reported cave and underground settings for their experiences. In addition, as Vallee points out, fairies themselves are not confined to a troglodyte existence in any folklore, but also always have strong connections with the air, the sky and flight: 'There was the sudden vision of brilliant "houses" at night, houses that could often fly, that contained peculiar lamps, radiant lights that needed no fuel.'[39]

Numerous other sources that I have consulted – both ancient and modern – confirm this aerial – and even 'extraterrestrial' – affinity of fairies. In Ireland, for example, it was said that the fairy host travelled through the air and caused 'fairy winds',[40] while formations of 'fairy lights' were often seen moving at high speed across the sky long before the age of aeroplanes.[41] In Wales it was well known that fairies – the *Tylwyth Teg* – were only 'visitors to earth' and that as a special order of creation they had the ability to 'fly about at will'.[42] Sometimes they did this by just taking to the air in bodily form and swimming through it, but in many traditions fairies traverse the skies more grandly in cloud-like aerial vessels called 'fairy boats' or 'spectre ships'.[43] A UFO sighted in France in the 1850s was described as a 'chariot with whining wheels'. It rushed at high speed up the side of a hill and then disappeared in the air. It was driven, eyewitnesses said, by a species of small dark fairies known locally as *farfadets*.[44]

Rape, reproduction and wetnurses

Vallee did not content himself with making a prima facie case based on the broad similarities of aliens and fairies both flying around the sky in unidentified objects and having connections with caves. Much more significantly, he also picked up very early on the sexual element in the abduction of Antonio Villas-Boas (reported in Chapter Thirteen) and compared the case to traditions of fairies raping and/or marrying humans, abducting their lovers to Fairyland and producing offspring to 'strengthen their race' – often requiring the services of a human midwife or wetnurse.[45] Although unaware of the shamanic side of the story (which we have seen is also dominated by themes of rape, spirit marriage and reproduction), Vallee was certain it was no accident that the rape/reproduction sequence seemed to be common to fairy and alien phenomena. Other than the Villas-Boas case, however, which contained several highly relevant details, there were really no parallels to these reproductive narratives about fairies in the UFO abduction reports available to Vallee in the 1960s – and therefore, apparently, no comparisons to be drawn.

For example, no tales of female abductees being required to wetnurse hybrid babies had yet surfaced when *Magonia* was published. So although Vallee noticeably pricked up his ears when he found the theme of human wetnurses in the ethnographic sources on fairy abductions ('obtaining the milk and fostering care of human mothers for their own offspring', as he put it)[46] he was unable to cite a comparison in UFO abduction literature. He therefore overlooked the following passage in *The Secret Commonwealth* in which the Reverend Robert Kirk writes of 'Women . . . yet alive who tell they were taken away when in childbed to nurse Faire Children . . .'[47]

Vallee could not have known in 1969 that the predicament of these seventeenth-century women is exactly duplicated by the predicament of women in the twentieth and twenty-first centuries who have described being brought on board a UFO and into one of its many rooms – a room that they may have been in before and that is consecrated exclusively to the nursing of hybrid babies. As we saw in Chapter Thirteen:

> The aliens stare intently at her and the baby. The woman hears another directive: 'Nurse the baby.' 'Put the baby to your breast and feed the baby.' The woman says, 'But I do not have any milk.' The response is, 'Put the baby to your breast and nurse the baby!' . . . In many instances the woman may be surprised to find that she is lactating and that her breasts are engorged. When that happens the baby will partially drain the breast.[48]

Returning to the seventeenth century, Kirk's informants said that they had been brought to a grand 'lodging' where they found themselves in an anonymous room with no apparent exit:

The Child, and Fire, with Food and other Necessaries, are set before the Nurse how soon she enters; but she nather perceives any passage out, nor sees what the people does in other rooms of the lodging. When the child is wained, the Nurse dies, or is conveyed back, or gets it to her choice to stay there.[49]

If there really is a link between UFOs and fairies, then we should be grateful today that practically all UFO abductees seem to be conveyed back to this world – rather than dying, or remaining in UFO-land for ever. By contrast, it was believed and understood in olden times that those who were abducted to Fairyland very frequently failed to return – like the Reverend Robert Kirk himself. A survey of traditional accounts and of more recent fairy abduction narratives suggests a rather random process in which some of those who had been taken by the fairies did return to their normal lives and routines, sometimes mysteriously enriched. Others did not return at all and were assumed to have become permanent residents of Fairyland. Others still came back but, horrifyingly, their homecomings sometimes took place hundreds of years after all their relatives had died and after the houses they had lived in had crumbled to dust – suggesting that time runs differently in the otherworld than it does here. We will see later that UFO abductees report strange time-effects too, particularly episodes of missing time – usually periods of hours, but sometimes days, that they cannot account for, that are simply gone from their lives leaving behind only vague memories of a vast and inexplicable experience.

Widening the mystery

Almost four decades have passed since the publication of *Passport to Magonia* in 1969. Subsequently, while Vallee's thesis of a fairy–alien connection has slipped into relative obscurity, a mass of new evidence has been steadily building on the 'alien' side of the equation. I refer to the thousands of hours of tape-recorded interviews that trained counsellors such as David Jacobs and John Mack have been able to conduct with people who believe they have been abducted by UFOs.

As a result of their work, we now possess, as we did not in 1969, a solid database on the phenomena currently labelled as 'UFO abductions', and on the entities currently labelled as 'aliens', that have been experienced by millions of people, but that most scientists dismiss as purely imaginary.

Most of the post-1969 arguments about these phenomena and entities have centred around precisely this very difficult and emotive issue – i.e. is science right, or is experience right? Are UFOs and aliens brain fiction, or could they be in some way *real*? If they are brain fiction, then why and how do the brains of a minority of every population, running into tens of millions of individuals around the world, make this stuff up? And if they are real, then where do they come from – another planet, or another dimension, the future, or the earth itself? I was surprised to discover that in their often heated pursuit of interesting and important questions like these, none of the key protagonists seem to have realised the potential of Vallee's original insight connecting fairies and aliens. But if fairies and aliens are the same thing, then suddenly we have at our disposal an entire additional database on a very strange and mysterious category of human experiences apparently involving encounters with and abductions by intelligent non-human entities. Because of the strong new evidence now to hand, and because of my own parallel research into the alien/spirit/shaman connection – itself constituting a third independent database of such experiences – I therefore decided that the time had come to reopen Vallee's superb 1969 investigation.

I was soon to stumble into a labyrinth of conduits linking 'Fairyland' and its supernatural inhabitants to the otherworlds of shamans, linking fairies themselves to the spirits with whom shamans must deal, and linking all of these – fairies, shamans and spirits – to the weird traumas, adventures and experiences surrounding the supposedly modern phenomenon of UFO abductions.

CHAPTER FIFTEEN

Here is a Thing that Will
Carry Me Away

On the tiny island of Rathlin off the coast of Northern Ireland folk-lorist Linda-May Ballard found that belief in fairies was still widespread amongst the population as late as 1982. Amongst the many accounts of fairy encounters that she recorded for the archives of the Ulster Folk and Transport Museum is the story of what had happened one stormy night many years before to 'a nurse-cum-midwife' who 'lived at the far end of the island'. She had retired for the night when loud knocking awakened her. Half asleep, she went to the door and was confronted by the shadowy figure of a man and, behind him, an impressive four-wheeled coach drawn by a team of four horses. At first the midwife thought she was dreaming but then 'realised there was something strange about it':

> and the man, she couldn't see him in the darkness. He said that she was needed, there was a woman in labour and they needed her very urgently, and so she knew, and decided that no harm would come to her, that she'd get into the coach.[1]

No sooner was she aboard than the coach took off at great speed, confirming the initial strange impression it had made by floating unnaturally across impassable bogs and around obstacles where there was no road. Eventually:

> They arrived at this hill at the back of Brockley. And as they came to

the hill, the side of the hill opened up and the horse and carriage went into the hill. And inside it, you know, it was the most beautiful place, it was like a palace inside it . . . And anyway, she attended to the woman that was giving birth and everything was sorted out. But I forgot to add here that there was a lot of fairies running around, the wee folk, there was a lot of them in this hill, you see.[2]

And not only fairies. During her mission of mercy the midwife reported seeing the familiar faces inside the fairy knoll of a number of young men and women who had mysteriously vanished from Rathlin over the past few years. Until that moment 'nobody ever knew what was happening' but now it was clear they had been abducted by the fairies. There was also an obvious indication *why* they had been abducted: the midwife had been called to attend to the birth of a baby and according to her testimony, at least one of the young female abductees she saw was 'sitting nursing a small baby' and singing to it in Gaelic.[3] The midwife herself was invited to stay on in Fairyland but declined. True to the telepathic reassurance she had received at the beginning of the adventure that 'no harm would come to her', she was allowed to get into the carriage again 'and they left her back to her own door'.[4]

UFOs in disguise (1)

When I found this rather eerie account I was already well aware of the examples from modern research of people who believed they had been abducted by aliens to a cave or some other underground setting rather than to the usual flying saucer (see Chapters Twelve and Thirteen). I was also familiar with the examples of female abductees obliged to act as wetnurses for alien–human babies (see Chapter Thirteen), and even of some cases where abductees claimed that they had been 'bred' with other humans to produce presumably entirely human babies which the aliens also kept.[5] What I couldn't immediately call to mind was any case in the modern literature in which a UFO had appeared in the form of anything quite so 'this world' as four horses and a four-wheeled carriage.

Further enquiry, and a second look at some of the material I'd already explored, showed that there were precedents for this too. For example, a Long Island radio journalist named Jaye Paro underwent a typical UFO abduction in what she perceived as a black Cadillac that carried her off to a secluded area.[6] And in Chapter Twelve I told the story of Lucy, who experienced abduction by aliens into a cavernous underground chamber reached – as in the tale of the midwife – through an opening in the side of a hill. I stated there that UFOs 'did not feature in her experience at all', which is correct. However, when I took a second look at the case I noticed Lucy spoke of something else that did behave exactly like a UFO. This was a fire engine that drove noisily along her street immediately before her experience began, parked outside her house, shone a beam of light through her window and then disappeared.[7]

Noting that 'the aliens themselves seem to be able to change or disguise their form, and . . . may appear initially to the abductees as various kinds of animals, or even as ordinary human beings', John Mack also confirms that 'their shape-shifting abilities extend to their vehicles'.[8] His patients reported experiencing UFOs in disguises as varied as 'a string of motorcycles' and 'a soaring cathedral-like structure with stained glass windows'.[9] One young woman recalled 'seeing a fifteen-foot kangaroo in a park, which turned out to be a small spacecraft'.[10] A number of children claimed 'to have been transported into the sky in a small craft that appeared to them initially as a booth at a carnival in which aliens disguised as humans asked if they wanted to go on a journey'.[11]

All in all, therefore, I concluded that the story from Rathlin of a human female taken away to Fairyland in a magical flying coach to help out with an obstetric problem was well within the norm of modern UFO abduction experiences – with the only difference being that today the vehicle might take a form more appropriate to modern perceptions, such as an ambulance or stretch limousine. As John Mack suggests, it may be the case that 'the aliens assume a form or forms that are familiar or comprehensible within the individual's own perceptual background or framework . . .'[12]

UFOs in disguise (2)

Mack's insight about the apparently deliberate generation of culturally appropriate displays looks even more plausible when we realise that there sometimes seem to be errors and glitches in the process. Particularly notable, and curious, are apparent overlaps when whatever perceptual force that is exerted to give us culturally appropriate Cadillacs and flying saucers in modern America, and aerial ships and floating coaches in other less technological contexts, somehow starts broadcasting mixed signals and anachronisms. Thus for example Fortean researcher Janet Bord reports a story that was a brief local sensation in the English city of Nottingham in September 1979 when a small group of children of between eight and ten years old were in Woolaton Park at dusk and saw 'around sixty little men, about half as tall as themselves'. The children, who were deeply impressed, stuck by the details of their collective vision. It seems the men, who wore 'blue tops and yellow tights' as well as jester-style caps with a bobble on the end, had wrinkled faces and long white beards with red tips. In the drawings the children did of them, as in the verbal descriptions, they greatly resemble fairies, imps, elves, dwarves, or clowns as

A drawing of one of the 'Woolaton fairies' made by a child witness
(Fortean Picture Library)

they might have been portrayed in the Middle Ages,[13] but with one jarring, anachronistic detail. This is that they are driving around in small motorcars. The children were adamant that there were around 30 of these cars, most of them with two of the little men on board.

The cars didn't have conventional steering wheels 'but a round thing with a handle to turn'. Although there was no engine noise the cars moved fast and could jump over obstructions.[14]

Bord adds that six years before the Woolaton fairies hit the media, she had heard from a Cornishwoman, Marina Fry, who wrote giving details of her own fairy sighting when she was a child in the 1940s:

> One night she and her older sisters, all sleeping in one bedroom, awoke to hear a buzzing noise (one sister said 'music and bells'). Looking out of the window they saw a 'little man in a tiny red car driving around in circles'. He was about eighteen inches tall, and had a white beard and a 'red droopy pointed hat' . . . He just disappeared after a while.[15]

A third such case documented by Bord is a report of a fairy aeroplane seen in 1929 by a five-year-old boy and his eight-year-old sister. The tiny plane was piloted by a tiny humanoid wearing a tiny leather flying helmet. As he zoomed by, nearly colliding with a dustbin, he waved to the children in a friendly manner.

There has even been a sighting of a fairy flying saucer, all the more persuasive because it took place long before the most recent phase of UFO sightings made flying saucers a common idea. In August 1914 eight men saw a 'large, flat-topped spherical object' on the surface of Lake Huron in Canada. Next to it were small humanoids just over a metre tall. Though they had the characteristic appearance and 'violet-green' clothes of 'fairies',[16] they were doing something technical with a hose immersed in the water. Finally they inserted it into a hatch, 'and the object suddenly took off'.[17]

In 1957, after flying saucers had been widely sighted for about a decade, John Trasco of Tennessee encountered an out-of-the ordinary 'egg-shaped' UFO hovering in front of his barn. Standing between him and it, glaring at him with its 'large frog-like eyes' was a three-foot-tall humanoid dressed in 'a green suit with shiny buttons, a green tam-o-shanter cap, and gloves with a shiny object at the tip of each'. In other words, a fairy. The creature said something faintly ludicrous to Trasco: 'We are peaceful people, we only want your dog.' When he refused and expressed anger, it ran away and moments later the UFO was seen to take off straight up.[18]

Mrs Sheridan meets 'the mistress'

To return to the mystery with which this chapter opened, the figure that folklorists call 'midwife to the fairies' is widespread in global mythology, particularly in the Old World, where she is found throughout most of western and eastern Europe and in many different parts of Asia all the way to Japan.[19] Such universal themes attest to universal experiences involving reproductive contact of one kind or another with non-human intelligences – much as UFO abductees report today.

From Chapter Fourteen, the reader will recall the Reverend Robert Kirk's seventeenth-century account of Scottish mothers abducted 'when in childbed' to wetnurse fairy babies, and how the anonymous sealed rooms in 'grand lodgings' in which these nursing episodes took place are virtually interchangeable with modern descriptions of rooms on board UFOs where women are taken to wetnurse hybrid children. The degree of overlap is even more obvious in a statement given in Ireland in the early twentieth century to the folklorist Lady Gregory by a certain Mrs Sheridan, who admitted to being frequently 'away among the fairies' when she was a younger woman:

> Where they brought me to I don't know, or how I got there, but I'd be in a very big house, and it was round, the walls far away that you'd hardly see them, and a great many people all about . . . but they wouldn't speak to me nor I to them.[20]

Like the Reverend Kirk's Scottish mothers, Mrs Sheridan's function in this strange flying-saucer-like house was to breastfeed children for the fairies – a number of whom were always present, 'moving about' busily amongst the abducted humans. She said that they had 'long faces' and wore 'striped clothes of all colours'[21] – in other words typically gaudy, pre-industrial fairy attire from almost any epoch between the tenth and the early twentieth centuries. Significantly Mrs Sheridan added that they – and more directly she herself – were under the command of an important female fairy with 'a tall stick in her hand' who was 'the mistress'. When Mrs Sheridan cried and begged to be returned to her home, the fairy quietened her by touching her on the breast with the stick.[22]

Is it a coincidence that John Mack's patient Andrea, whose abduction was reported in Chapter Twelve, was controlled by an alien 'holding a stick or a rod' which he pressed against the back of her ear?[23] Indeed in virtually every procedure to which abductees are subject, notably when they are brought to the dedicated nursing rooms and 'baby presentation' rooms on board the UFOs, they will encounter an authority figure like Mrs Sheridan's fairy mistress. This figure will sometimes be identified as male, sometimes as female – although generally speaking female aliens are more frequently reported to be present when the abduction focuses around the care of hybrid babies, and male aliens are more frequently reported to be present when other procedures take precedence.[24] Mrs Sheridan referred to her fairy authority figure as 'the mistress'. Modern UFO abductees refer to their alien authority figure as 'the leader' or 'the doctor'.[25] Typically he/she will be up to a metre taller than the other 'Greys' but will otherwise be identical – with the same familiar grey skin, elf-like appearance, pear-shaped head, huge black eyes, etc., etc.[26] In the unlikely event of an abductee getting out of control, it is always 'the doctor' who restores order, sometimes with an implement or wand of some kind, sometimes with a form of hypnosis or mental compulsion exercised through the eyes.[27]

Amorous fairies

We have seen that shamans all over the world have experienced what they believe to have been sex with spirits, and that UFO abductees all over the world have experienced what they believe to have been sex with aliens. Because I could already feel that I was following a strong and reliable pattern that could be counted upon to repeat its basic features regardless of cultural or historical context, it came as little surprise to me to learn that there are numerous accounts in the ethnographic sources of humans falling for, having sex with and even marrying fairies.

In Ireland the fairies are known as the *Sidhe* and the story is told of two *Sidhe* women who loved a young prince 'and suddenly took him away into a fairy palace and kept him there three years'.[28] In England, chivalric romances of the Middle Ages describe the plight of a young man seduced and abducted by the Queen of the Fairies to spend seven years serving her in Fairyland.[29] In Wales, fairies are known as the *Tylwyth Teg*, and W.Y. Evans-Wentz was told in 1909 of 'a special sort of *Tylwyth Teg*' that lived beneath the waters of deep lakes from which they sometimes emerged to dance on the shore: 'Their fine looks enticed young men to follow them back into the lakes and marry one of them. If the husband wished to leave the lake he had to go without his fairy wife.'[30]

This latter is, of course, essentially the same story that is told in the Amazon, where female spirits in the form of dolphins lure young men down beneath the water to the otherworld city of *Encante*. Moreover, just like spirits – and of course aliens (see Chapter Twelve) – fairies frequently appear to humans in animal and therianthropic forms. For example, traditions of sea fairies abound around the islands and coasts of Britain. They are mermaids and mermen who are sometimes part fish, part human in appearance or sometimes part seal, part human. It was believed that these fairy therianthropes seduced men and women and created hybrid offspring distinguished by possessing 'webbed fingers and toes' or 'a seal's face'.[31] In northern France, Evans-Wentz recorded an old belief in a class of fairies known as lutins, related to elves, whose natural appearance was that of 'a little man dressed in green' but who could also 'assume any animal form'.[32] They were known to transform themselves particularly into black horses or goats.[33] Just as 'aliens' and 'spirits' frequently assume the form of owls and other birds, it was believed in Ireland that 'fairies assume the form of crows'.[34] Romanian fairies are said to have cat's paws or donkey's feet, while in other parts of eastern Europe fairies are associated with forest animals.[35] A pair of French woodcuts of 1500 show the medieval fairy Melusine, abductor of human babies, with the upper body of a woman and the lower body of a serpent.[36] A Flemish woodcut from

377

The medieval fairy Melusine, abductor of babies. She is a therianthrope
with a human upper body and the lower body of a serpent.

1558 shows fairies as partially transformed therianthropes with human
bodies and heads, furred cloven hoofs instead of feet, and in some
cases emerging horns.[37] The same perception of fairies as horned,

Fairies as therianthropes in a Flemish woodcut of 1558
(Fortean Picture Library)

cloven-hoofed therianthropes was also very strong in England, where
it affected popular perceptions of the Devil – who was also frequently
portrayed with cloven hoofs, a shaggy hide, and horns.[38]

We can therefore understand why the Inquisitors in the Scottish
witch trials of the sixteenth and seventeenth centuries repeatedly interpreted witches' references to fairies as though they had intended to

speak of the Devil.[39] Nonetheless, the transcripts are self-explanatory, and 'the predominance of fairy stories' in them, as Diane Purkiss, lecturer in English at Oxford University, observes, 'is proof that the accused women thought such stories believable'.[40] I take it as another sign of a well-established pattern running true to form that many of these unfortunate women, who could have made up anything they liked to mollify their interrogators, spoke primarily of sex with fairies, and of reproductive unions with fairies – in just the same ways that shamans speak of sex and reproduction with spirits and UFO abductees speak of sex and reproduction with aliens. 'In all these confessions,' reports Purkiss:

> a woman meets a man, who may be wearing black or green, or may have a specific name. He asks her to be his servant, or he offers her something. She may refuse at first, but eventually agrees. He then has sex with her . . . The being involved . . . is always otherworldly.[41]

In one summary given by the Inquisitors, 'the Devil' had appeared before a certain witch:

> in the likeness of a man in green clothes . . . [She] cannot presently remember whether he had carnal dealings with her at that time or not, but remembers perfectly that afterward he did lie with her.[42]

Another Scottish witch, Katherine Jonesdochter, told of a fairy lover she called 'the bowman' who first had intercourse with her when she was an adolescent girl and continued to visit her for sex for 40 years, gifting her with supernatural knowledge and healing skills in return.[43] There is some hint that the two had produced offspring – for 'the bowman's bairn', described as 'a little creature, a small child-sized man',[44] once mysteriously appeared and was seen playing amongst a group of children.[45]

An English witch, Susan Swapper, was put on trial in Rye in the year 1611 and told of being visited while sleeping in bed with her husband by 'four spirits in the likeness of two men and two women'. One of the women, she said, the leader of the group, wore a 'green petticoat' – standard fairy garb.[46] The description of these night visitors as 'spirits' in the court records of the time is significant, since it further confirms the increasingly obvious interchangeability of the fairy and spirit worlds. On the other hand, the sudden rather ominous appearance of the visitors in Susan's room, and their desire, soon revealed, to 'take her away' have much in common with the first stages of typical UFO abduction sequences.

It was well known in Susan's time that fairies had a constant demand and fearsome need for human children of all ages, but especially, and puzzlingly, for the newborn.[47] Since Susan was heavily pregnant and close to term when the visitors appeared, she was therefore terrified of being abducted,[48] and resisted with all her will when 'the woman in the green petticoat said to her: "Sue, come and go with me, or else I will carry thee."' Susan's response was to shake her slumbering husband and beg him to hold on to her:

And he awakening turned unto her and answered her: 'Wherefore should I hold thee?', and she replied unto him again and said, 'Here is a thing that will carry me away', and he said again unto her, 'I see nothing' and so turned about from her . . .[49]

It is quite commonly the case with modern UFO abductions that a group of aliens (and often four of them) will enter a bedroom where a couple are asleep and take one, leaving the other unaware of what has happened – and apparently incapacitated – until the abductee is returned.[50] Typically, notes David Jacobs, spouses 'sleep through the abduction. If they are awakened at the beginning of it they are made to go back to sleep immediately.'[51]

The mystery of the changelings (1)

Why should the fairies have wanted Susan Swapper's as yet unborn baby? Why did the medieval fairy Melusine steal babies? Why did women so frequently experience being brought inside Fairyland to wetnurse babies there and to assist in the delivery of yet more babies? These are all difficult mysteries of the fairy tradition, but I was beginning to hope that modern data on the alien abduction phenomenon might shed some light on them.

We all know where babies come from and how they are made. But if fairies were thought to have sexual intercourse with each other, then I have found no mention of this in the ethnographic sources, and if 'fairy babes' were born to fairy mothers and fathers, then I have found no mention of this either. On the contrary, human midwives who had multiple experiences of visits to Fairyland to deliver so-called 'fairy babes' confided that the mothers they assisted there were sometimes not fairies but humans who had 'previously been abducted into the Fairy realm'.[52]

So what we know from the examples cited above – and many others – is that fairies were believed to have sex with humans (whom they had often abducted permanently, or for very long periods, into Fairyland) and that a number of brief but unambiguous references do exist to offspring born of such unions. However, other than half sea-fairy, half human hybrids with their webbed fingers and toes and their bestial seal-like faces, detailed descriptions are never given of the appearance of these hybrid offspring or of their ultimate fate. This being the case, it is legitimate to ask what they looked like, and what happened to them. More pointedly, in the absence of any strong and clear tradition of 'pure-bred' fairy children, was it perhaps *always* hybrids who had to be delivered and nursed by human women – if, for example, the mother was a fairy and the father human, or if the father was a fairy and the human mother had been killed after delivery, as several traditions darkly hint? Since the women specially abducted as feeders and carers were invariably wetnurses who had not actually given birth to the hybrids, then they might easily have persuaded themselves that they had 'fairy babes' at their breasts.

Let's remember that we're speculating freely here about entities that scientists say are only imaginary and have never existed in any shape or form. Nonetheless, this general scenario – a requirement by the fairies for surrogate mothers to feed and cuddle hybrid offspring – would explain why so many of the women who reported this kind of abduction were mothers themselves who had recently given birth to normal babies in the human plane or, like Susan Swapper, were about to give birth, and thus were already prepared physiologically for lactation. By contrast, even when they are not pregnant or recently delivered, modern women abducted to wetnurse human-alien hybrids say that they experience induced lactation at the hands of the aliens (see Chapter Thirteen) – a technology that does not seem to have been available to the fairies.

Today, although they rarely enjoy their experiences, human wetnurses – so far as we know – are never killed, nor are they detained for more than a few hours by the aliens. A century or a thousand years ago when our aliens, or something very like them, were called fairies, we have seen that there was no such assurance. Indeed, fairies were deeply and abjectly feared as merciless killers[53] and 'for their tendencies to assault, torture, and abduct humans'.[54]

There's another big difference. Although there are cases on record of children as young as two reporting detailed UFO abduction experiences (e.g. John Mack's patient Colin; see Chapter Twelve), there are no cases of children being permanently abducted; they are always reunited with their parents. Things were not so civilised with the fairies, of course. As noted earlier, these serial abductors had a particular reputation for taking children away from their parents for ever. Quite often, too, there was a further twist. Not only did they steal healthy, happy babies but also they left not-quite-human 'changelings' in their place. The copious accounts of these creatures that have come down to us in folklore and in the ethnographies (thin and restless, ugly and malformed, physically weak but voraciously hungry, mewling and never satisfied) are the only detailed descriptions we have of 'fairy babes' – which is what changelings were always assumed to be, an interpretation that the fairies themselves seem to have encouraged. This is brought out clearly in an ancient Gaelic song in which a fairy who desires to steal a mortal woman's 'ruddy, plump and praiseworthy' child first speaks with dismay of her own child's frailty and bad looks:

> He is my ungraceful child,
> Withered, bald and light-headed,
> Weak-shouldered and weak in his equipments . . .[55]

'Withered, bald and light-headed' are all definitive characteristics of changelings, as we'll see below – and indeed the bad fairy in the song does want to exchange her weak child for the mortal woman's strong one. No matter how they were presented, however, or what assumptions were made about their identity, a close examination of the evidence undermines the view that these unhappy babies are best understood as the pure-bred offspring of fairies.

The mystery of the changelings (2)

A couple of accounts will have to suffice to give the flavour of this ancient and extremely widespread and widely reported 'changeling' phenomenon.[56]

In Norway, folklorists collected the story of Anne, a dairymaid who gave birth to a fine young boy. One night she was sitting with the child when 'a woman in black' entered the room carrying another child. Anne felt paralysed as the woman approached, touched her baby son, and left. Afterwards she discovered that a substitution had occurred: her own child was gone and a lean, difficult, ugly, hunched brat had been substituted. He grew up a fool who lowed like an ox and the mother's birth-son was never restored to her.[57]

In Ireland as late as 1981, folklorist Patricia Lysaght recorded another typical changeling tradition:

A child was about a year old and it was taken and there was a changeling put in its place, a terrible cross child left in its place. It was getting no bigger and at night they used to hear music in the room. And the mother and father were out walking the rooms with the child, crying, crying, crying.[58]

On the Isle of Skye off the west coast of Scotland around 1908, W.Y. Evans-Wentz collected a very peculiar story of a baby abduction apparently abandoned on a whim, when no child was taken and no changeling substituted:

An aged nurse who had fallen fast asleep as she sat by the fire, was holding on her knees a newly-born babe. The mother, who lay in bed gazing dreamily, was astonished to see three strange little women enter the dwelling. They approached the unconscious child, and she who seemed to be their leader was on the point of lifting it off the nurse's lap when the third exclaimed: 'Oh, let us leave this one with her as we have already taken so many!' 'So be it,' replied the senior of the party . . .[59]

Bearing in mind the 2 per cent or so of the modern population who appear to have undergone UFO abduction experiences – and the fairy's own statistical hint – one wonders indeed how *many* human babies were 'taken' by fairies over the centuries, why changelings were so often substituted and, once again, what exactly changelings are or were.

The mystery of the changelings (3)

What we have to go on are the descriptions in the folklore and ethnographies. These paint a completely clear and consistent picture of changelings:

. . . ugly . . . with an abnormally big head and with a pale, wrinkled skin as that of an old person. The changeling cries frequently and is always hungry. It is slow to learn to speak and walk and to keep itself clean, if it ever reaches such normal stages of development . . .[60]

. . . strangely and almost impossibly thin, very long feet, very long, thin legs, as though he weighed nothing at all. And he had a very strange appearance of being enormously ancient, despite the fact that he wasn't.[61]

. . . unusual features – misshapen limbs, an oversize head, slowness in learning to walk . . .[62]

. . . shrivelled up with withered face and wasted body . . . ill-favoured and deformed . . . ugly and loathsome . . . evermore craving food and yet it never grew nor throve . . .'[63]

Of particular interest are those ethnographic sources in which not only is the changeling described but also the reactions of the parents on first noticing the substitution:

There was my own fine child whipped off me out of his cradle . . . and an ugly bit of shrivelled up fairy put in his place . . . You are not my child . . . A little wizened face as ugly as a walnut . . . An ugly, wizened, crying brat . . .[64]

Now compare these to the reactions of UFO abductees to hybrid human–alien children reported in Chapter Thirteen: 'Gross baby,' exclaimed Melissa, 'it's an ugly one . . . I'll kill it . . . It's so fucking unnatural . . . Disgusting thing . . .'[65] Another abductee, not cited in Chapter Thirteen, told her counsellor David Jacobs that she found her enforced contact with a hybrid baby 'creepy . . . I can't stand to touch it . . . Their skin is like paper.'[66] In addition, as with the parents of changelings, it is normal for abductees presented with a hybrid child to suspect that in some way it might be theirs but yet to reject it on the grounds that 'It's not mine.'[67]

All in all, don't the descriptions of changelings given in the ethnographic sources make them sound much less like fairies and more like human–alien hybrid children (or for that matter like the hybrid children of shamans and spirits also described in Chapter Thirteen)? David Jacobs, who himself rejects any connection with fairy lore and is convinced that the alien abduction phenomenon began only in the late nineteenth century, provides this summary of the alien side of the story based on his case studies:

It [the alien-human hybrid] has a very large head . . . Its body is long and thin. Its hands and fingers are long and thin. Its pale-white or greyish skin is almost translucent . . . It is almost always listless . . .[68]

Likewise, the reader will recall how Barbara Archer described human–alien hybrids as looking 'kind of old' and being 'very fragile'.[69] Nona said: 'Their bodies were short for their heads. Their heads seemed oversized.'[70] Isabel spoke of the dry, scaly and flaky skin of a hybrid child.[71] Debbie Tomey mentioned 'ivory skin and a big head . . .'[72] Peter said: 'They have big heads . . . bigger heads than their bodies . . . The arms are really fragile but they have big bellies.'[73]

Needless to say, all these peculiar and distinctive physical details are the same for changelings – who, long before the nineteenth century, were also routinely described as old-looking with disproportionately large heads, elongated and misshapen limbs, pale, wrinkled papery skin, etc., etc. We will defer until later the question of whether or not we are dealing with anything *real* here (as opposed to fantasies, 'brain fiction', delusions or other dismissive scientific labels). But the close similarities between the strange, weak, large-headed hybrid children reported by modern UFO abductees and the strange, weak, large-headed changeling children of the fairies should grab our attention. These similarities, and these amazing continuities over long periods of time in unconnected cultures are most unexpected. Moreover, they go much deeper than mere surface appearances.

More permanent, more powerful

Whether we speak of a changeling fostered and nursed by a human mother in her own home, or whether we speak of a human midwife invited to a fairy knoll to deliver a 'fairy babe', or whether we speak of a human wetnurse abducted to a 'grand lodging' to breastfeed a 'fairy babe', or whether we speak of a modern woman abducted to a UFO to wetnurse a hybrid alien–human baby, there remains at the heart of the whole matter a clear, unwavering underlying concern with reproduction.

In the case of the aliens, we have seen that the very strong perception amongst abductees is that they are being used for breeding and child-nursing purposes. John Mack's summary based on large numbers of abductee reports is that a 'complex, reproductive-like process or "project" appears to be a central feature of the UFO abduction phenomenon,[74] and that its 'purely physical or biological aspect . . .

seems to have to do with some sort of genetic or quasi-genetic engineering for the purpose of creating human/alien hybrid offspring'.[75]

Most abductees who claim to have asked the aliens about this say they have received evasive answers. Nevertheless, a number of hints as to the purpose of the project do exist in the literature. The case of Kathie Davis is particularly interesting. During an extended series of abductions over the course of many years, she had multiple experiences of being impregnated by aliens. She also had subsequent encounters with two of her own hybrid offspring. One of these, a male, was introduced to her when he was still a baby. 'He looked,' she said, 'like an old man, and he looked so wise. I looked into his eyes . . . he was so . . . smart . . . more wise than anybody in the world.' She also met a 'tiny' girl aged about four years who she knew immediately was her daughter. The child's eyes were disproportionately large, her skin pale and translucent, 'her hair white and wispy'. Kathie described her as 'real pretty . . . like an elf, or an . . . angel' and felt deep attachment towards her but was told by the aliens that the girl could not survive in the physical world because 'you wouldn't be able to feed her' there.[76]

The physical description of this hybrid child (Kathie also said she had a 'really old' look) greatly resembles the traditional picture of a changeling from fairy lore. Yet as Patrick Harpur points out, there are important differences. Unlike the changelings, who are 'stunted, ugly, voraciously hungry' rejects, this little girl is 'angelic, beautiful, and unable to be fed in this world'.[77] So although she is still physically insubstantial by comparison with a fully human child, it seems that the aliens have made some sort of progress with their 'complex reproductive project'. If they are indeed the same beings that we used to call 'fairies' then perhaps they have learned a thing or two.

But what have they learned, and why? The abduction of Lori Biggs from Redondo Beach, California, in 1970 adds more to the limited information we have at our disposal. She was told by the aliens that they were able to turn themselves into light (by means of which they could also levitate objects), but that they were unable to hold their own physical form for very long: 'They wanted to learn how to combine human solid form and their luminous form into a more permanent, more powerful being.'[78] It is far from being proof, but such a scenario would certainly explain the great interest that aliens show in breeding with humans and creating hybrid babies. They want to become more material, more permanent, more powerful. They want, in other words, to stiffen their own stock with an infusion of human solidity. As Patrick Harpur puts it, their aim appears to be to 'strengthen their race'.[79]

Is it coincidence that the very same scenario of 'race strengthening' is the one most often put forward to explain why fairies were interested in breeding with humans, and why they stole vigorous, healthy human babies and replaced them with their rejected changelings? According to folklorist Peter Rojcewicz, 'Clearly the most significant form of fairy dependence upon mortals involves their genetic evolution. Humans are essential to fairies for a healthy bloodline.'[80] The Irish poet W.B. Yeats likewise believed that 'the *Sidhe* [fairies] need human robustness'.[81] Professor A.C. Haddon states of the changeling tradition in Ireland that 'dwarf or misshapen children are held to be given to a mother by the fairies in place of a healthy child they had stolen from her to renew the stock of fairies'.[82] Katherine Biggs likewise confirms a popular belief that the reason fairies abducted young men and women, and swapped changelings for healthy babies, was their need to 'inject the dwindling stock with fresh blood and a human vigour'.[83] Diane Purkiss reports a tradition that 'fairies . . . need blood. They need new blood.'[84] Edwin Sydney Hartland states: 'The motive assigned to fairies in northern stories is that of preserving and improving their race.'[85]

So it seems that not only do fairies and aliens have a shared need for sexual and reproductive contacts with humanity, but also, in both cases, they seek these contacts in order to bring about some desired transformation in their own condition.

Some conclusions on an evolving experience

A book could be written on the complex connections and continuities that bind fairy lore and alien lore together at the hip like Siamese twins. But once those links are established, what I find even more interesting are the subtle (and sometimes not so subtle) differences between the two phenomena. Thus although changelings look and behave like hybrids, we have seen that no changelings are deposited in the homes of modern UFO abductees and that no human babies are abducted for ever to UFO–land as they once were to Fairyland. Similarly, although wetnurses are used in both contexts – itself quite a remarkable correspondence in my view – we have seen that they were often killed by fairies, or stayed in Fairyland. Today the whole process, though still entirely outside abductees' control, seems much more reasonable and less final: they are taken, they lactate, they breast-feed and then they are floated back safely to their beds. So although the same sort of extremely weird experience with many identical or near-identical ingredients is clearly involved in both cases, *the experience itself seems to be evolving.*

Standing back from the data and viewing it dispassionately, we can say that the focus of this evolving experience in all the forms in which it is documented – whether spirits, fairies or aliens – has been on sexual and reproductive contact between supernatural races and humans, and on the creation of hybrid offspring to 'strengthen the stock' of the supernaturals. Beyond this, however, differences make themselves felt. To summarise what we have established thus far: (1) offspring are described in all the traditions; (2) in the case both of spirits and of aliens such offspring are clearly understood to be hybrids of monstrous or ugly appearance with pale, flaky skin, oversized heads, an old, wizened look, and an unhappy demeanour; (3) hybrids are mentioned in fairy traditions but are nowhere extensively described; (4) on the other hand we do hear a great deal about changelings – who, despite the absence of any strong and clear evidence in favour of the hypothesis, are generally presumed to be pure-bred 'fairy babes'.

I asked earlier if it is possible that changelings too were really hybrids, passed off as 'fairy babes', and also if perhaps it was *always* hybrids, and *never* pure-bred fairies who had to be delivered and nursed by human women. There can be no certainty, but my reading of fairy lore, and of hundreds of people's accounts of being abducted by fairies, as well as the similar accounts of hundreds of people abducted by aliens, convinces me that the whole phenomenon, in all times and places, has always been about creating hybrids. I see no reason why changelings should have been any exception. I therefore conclude that changelings were indeed hybrids too. More than this – although of course we tread in realms of pure speculation – could it be that they were perhaps failed hybrids who for one reason or another did not strengthen fairy stock and were therefore rejected? Keeping in mind the constant reproductive tampering that aliens do with modern abductees – many of whom forget everything until their buried memories are extracted by hypnosis – I even wonder if the families to whom changelings were returned were genetically related to the changelings without ever realising it themselves. This would explain why they were often puzzled to note that the 'ugly bit of shrivelled-up fairy' substituted for their own healthy baby always, in some odd way, resembled the missing mortal child.[86]

As to the ultimate fate in Fairyland of the abducted human babies of past centuries, who knows? Dark hints and confusing whispers are found in the ethnographies that 'in olden times' the fairies 'used to take young folks, and keep them and draw all the life out of their bodies'.[87] But what is clear in the latest alien incarnation of the experience is that while the long-term interest in reproduction remains the same, human babies are no longer permanently detained and creatures like changelings no longer appear at all. Instead, all contact with babies takes place in the dimension of the supernaturals, on board their UFOs, or in their crystal caverns, or in some enchanted, paradoxical space deep beneath the sea. The babies look almost exactly like changelings but they clearly benefit and gain vitality – in a way that changelings never did – from being breastfed, held, cuddled, caressed and generally loved by abductees who may or may not sense some sort of genetic bond with them.

So these do not seem to me to be anything like failed hybrids of the changeling type but, on the contrary, successful or potentially successful hybrids who the aliens understand need love and human warmth in order to thrive. Between fairies and aliens I therefore conclude that there has indeed been a distinct change, a distinct *evolution*, in the way the 'hybrid programme' – John Mack's phrase[88] – is handled. Any attempt to understand the phenomenon must take account of this curious ability it has to evolve and develop but must also be able to reckon with the steady and remorseless attention it seems to have paid, at all times and in all places, to the creation of a 'more permanent, more powerful' hybrid race.

It is a great mystery that people from many different cultures in many different epochs all report encountering supernaturals who are unwilling to be confined to supernatural realms and who – even while they initiate our shamans and bestow the 'second sight' and healing powers upon them – seem to want to take something of our materiality and incorporate it into their own non-physical lineage. As the first manifestations of these ancient supernatural forces in the technological age, UFO abductions and encounters with aliens have been subjected to an unrelenting campaign of ridicule and abuse by scientists who are strongly wedded to the materialist paradigm. It has been said, however, that 'the greatest trick the Devil ever played was to convince the world he doesn't exist'. Living in societies elevated by technology to almost godlike heights, we have convinced ourselves, against the wise advice of our ancestors, that there are no supernatural intelligences – that spirits do not exist, that fairies are crazed delusions and that aliens are just figments.

We may be wrong.

CHAPTER SIXTEEN

Dancers between Worlds

Andrea, one of John Mack's patients whose abduction experience was reported in Chapter Twelve, said that the aliens 'look like they're made of light. But then underneath there's some physicalness to them.'[1] The reader will recall that Sara, another of Mack's patients, reported frequently being forced into intercourse with an alien male who had 'a light contour of a penis, but not like a physical penis'.[2]

It is precisely this paradoxical 'non-physical physicality' that characterises spirits in all their interactions and sex acts with humans described in Chapters Eleven through to Thirteen, and – not surprisingly – the same turns out to hold true for fairies. Writing in the seventeenth century, the Reverend Robert Kirk described fairy bodies as 'so pliable through the subtlety of the spirits that agitate them that they can make them appear or disappear at pleasure'.[3] Folklorist Peter Rojcewicz points out that this description is strongly reminiscent of supernatural beings known as the *Siddhas*, said in ancient Indian scriptures to be capable of 'becoming very heavy at will or as light as a feather, and which travel through space and disappear from sight'.[4] In the same way the fairies of Brittany were said in the nineteenth century to have bodies that are 'aerial and transparent',[5] a group of fairies seen in Suffolk, England, in 1842 were 'light and shadowy, not like solid bodies'[6] and fairies in the west of Ireland were described as 'pale beings, almost grey in colour'.[7] Summing up many traditions, Rojcewicz concludes that 'fairies have light, changeable bodies ... capable of altering their form at will. Fairies have something of the nature of a mist or condensed cloud.'[8]

In the legends of Scandinavia, elves, a tribe of the worldwide fairy race, are depicted as 'beings with oversized heads, tiny legs and long arms'.[9] (The very word *aelf*, by the way, from which we derive the English name of these creatures, means 'supernatural'.)[10] Known as corrigans, the 'aerial and transparent' fairies of Brittany were said to be 'little beings not more than two feet high'.[11] The biggest of the Suffolk fairies cited above was 'about three feet high'.[12] In the Isle of Man, fairies were described as generally 'about two and a half feet high'.[13] In Wales, numerous accounts state that the *Tylwyth Teg* (the local name for fairies) were usually no more than three to four feet tall.[14] In County Sligo in Ireland, an elderly informant told Evans-Wentz of an occasion on the slopes of Ben Bulbin when he encountered a fairy who 'seemed only four feet high' but who informed him: 'I am bigger than I appear to you now. We can make the old young, the big small, the small big.'[15] In a similar vein, the Irish poet W.B. Yeats, who was deeply learned in these matters, warned: 'Do not think the fairies are always little. Everything is capricious about them, even their size.'[16] Indeed in all fairy traditions, amongst the mass of smaller beings in the range of two to four feet in height, individuals are occasionally mentioned who reach five feet or more and who in some cases seem 'as big as we are'.[17]

We've seen that one strong point of appearance shared by aliens and fairies is that they both frequently present themselves to abductees in animal and therianthropic forms. The above descriptions, which are representative of countless others in the ethnographies, show that the humanoid forms of both are also to all extents and purposes identical. For like fairies and elves, aliens typically have large heads and thin limbs and are, in the main, of small stature with the exception of a few individuals. Researcher David Jacobs explicitly rejects any connection with fairy lore and does not believe that his findings support such a connection (personal correspondence, May 2005). Nevertheless, from his intensive work with abductees in the US he notes that:

By far the most common types of aliens reported are the Small and Taller Beings. The Small Beings are from two to four-and-one-half feet tall, thin, slight, and even 'delicate' in appearance. They have a head, a body, two arms, two hands, fingers, two legs, two feet. They stand and walk like humans. The Small Beings are light in weight. Taller Beings stand from two to six inches above the Small Beings and have most of the same gross physical characteristics . . . By and large, most witnesses report the Small Beings' skin as just 'grey' . . . The heads of the aliens are, in human terms, disproportionately large for their bodies.[18]

Ambiguous sexuality and a hive-like social order

When W.Y. Evans-Wentz was in Ireland at the start of the twentieth century collecting reports of encounters with the *Sidhe* (fairies), he was told by informants that they had seen 'forms both male and female, and forms which did not suggest sex at all'.[19] When he asked whether any 'definite social organisation' had been witnessed 'among the various *Sidhe* orders and races', the reply came:

> I cannot say about a definite social organisation. I have seen beings who seemed to command others, and who were held in reverence. This implies an organisation, but whether it is instinctive like that of a hive of bees, or consciously organised like human society, I cannot say.[20]

These observations are interesting – and especially so bearing in mind they were made 50 years before anyone anywhere ever claimed to have encountered an alien. For here again, in tandem with all the other continuities and commonalities, we seem to have interchangeable descriptions. Aliens, too, are perceived in both male and female forms and in forms of ambiguous sexuality. Indeed, aside from the peculiar accounts of intercourse with humans (where we might hear of a 'non-physical' penis, etc., etc.), there seem to be no externally obvious anatomical features that in themselves proclaim the sex of the aliens[21] – and abductees report being completely unable to tell 'one Small Being from another'.[22] Where the Taller Beings are concerned, things are different; abductees always say they know whether they are dealing with a male or a female. Jacobs again:

The female is often the same size as the [male] Taller Being. She has no mammary glands and no hair, cranial, facial or pubic. When asked to describe the differences between the male and the female, the abductees say that the female is thinner, more 'graceful', more 'sensitive', and 'kinder'. Even with these vague descriptions, the abductees are quite clear about whether they are being tended by a male or female.[23]

Last but not least, what little is known about the social organisation of the aliens coincides with the informant's remarks, quoted above, on the social organisation of the *Sidhe*. For we saw in Chapter Fifteen that, amongst the aliens, the Taller Beings are indeed in command of, and deferred to absolutely by, the Small Beings, and that abductees do very often experience something impersonal, inhuman or hive-like in the highly programmed way that the latter in particular go about their tasks.[24]

Doors and windows no obstacle to fairies and aliens

Another quite different characteristic shared by fairies of all periods and aliens today is that they both seem to be masters of spectacularly advanced forms of camouflage and stealth technology:

Not only do fairies render themselves invisible, but they also render people, animate and inanimate things invisible.[25]

They [the aliens] cause themselves, humans and other matter to be invisible when they are outside the confines of the UFO.[26]

We have seen that both fairies and aliens can shape-shift into multiple forms and both can appear and disappear at will. Countless examples also testify to the uncanny ability of both to pass effortlessly through solid walls and closed windows.[27] More alarmingly, there are strong indications from fairy lore and definite claims on the part of alien abductees that this ability can also be harnessed in the other direction for the transport of humans; at any rate there are many cases on record of abductees who claim to have been passed bodily through solid walls and closed windows.[28]

Understandably, the experience is a strange one. John Mack reports that:

> when they are taken or floated through the wall, ceiling or window of their homes or through the door of a car, the abductees feel as if an intense energy is separating every cell, or even every molecule, of their bodies. So powerful is this feeling that experiencers often find it remarkable that they 'come back together' whole on the other side of the wall . . . The abductees speak of powerful vibratory sensations in their arms, legs and other parts of their bodies . . .[29]

An oddly convincing detail, evident over large numbers of abductions, is that the aliens seem to prefer closed windows to walls if they must pass an abductee through one or the other. According to David Jacobs: 'The beings appear to seek out a window. Sometimes the aliens will take the abductees out of their bedrooms and into another room and then out through a window there.'[30] In one typical case a mother and her son sleeping in two different rooms in a basement were abducted together. Both were walked out of their bedrooms and into the bathroom:

> She wondered why they were crowding into the bathroom and then she realised that the bathroom was the only room in the basement with a window. Soon a bright light entered and they flew out of the window.[31]

Karin, one of John Mack's patients, perhaps shed some light on this mysterious technology – and its limitations – when she described her own experience:

> It's racking just to go through the window because they have to alter your vibration in order to get a solid object to pass through another solid object, literally. And that happens. You go through a window or wall – they prefer the window.[32]

The blast

Another hint of shared fairy–alien technology comes in the spectacular ability of both to 'zap' people, strike them down, paralyse them with unseen rays, and penetrate their bodies with supernatural projectiles.[33] Once again considerations of space oblige me to cut a long story short. In a paper comparing fairy and alien lore, Peter Rojcewicz points to the mysterious force known as the 'fairy blast', widely referred to in traditional accounts, whereby fairies attacked humans and farm animals, knocking them off their feet and putting them 'immediately into a state of unconsciousness'.[34] Another weapon was 'elf-shot', often used 'by angry fairies in contexts where individuals intrude on fairy territory or cross fairy paths',[35] and which felt like an arrow or other projectile entering the body – although the skin was not broken – and left a festering *internal* wound from which foreign elements were often later surgically removed.[36] In the seventeenth century, the Reverend Robert Kirk described a similar fairy device 'flying as a dart with great force . . . mortally wounding the vital parts without breaking the skin, some of which wounds, I have observed in beasts, and felt them with my hands'.[37]

Looking for parallels in alien lore, we might mention the phenomenon of cattle mutilations, often associated with UFO sightings,[38] while assaults on humans are equally common. Rojcewicz gives details of a number of cases including those of

> Maurice Masse and Herb Schrime [who] both experienced a paralysis after being 'hit' by something from a circular object. Like those who receive the 'fairy blast', Travis Walton was 'gunned down' by a brilliant beam of bluish white light that lifted him a foot into the air before laying him out on the ground, his head thrown back, his arms and legs wide apart. A beam of green light rendered Inacio de Souza unconscious. Police sergeant Charles Moody felt 'numb' after he saw a UFO.[39]

Patrick Harpur reports a case of great interest from 1970 that overlaps characteristic elements of fairies and UFOs. Two skiers in Finland entered a wood, where they were soon 'stopped in their tracks by a round craft that hovered above them'. It sent 'an intense beam of light downwards on to the forest floor' in the midst of which a humanoid about a metre tall was seen. He held a black box that itself emitted a pulsating beam of yellow light which he aimed at the skiers. Other than this piece of technology, however, he was a typical medieval fairy, 'with thin arms and legs, a pale waxy face, small ears that narrowed towards the head and he was dressed in green with a conical hat'. One of the skiers felt a powerful force exerted on his body, which he associated with the pulsating beam of light. It was as though he had been 'seized by the waist and pulled backwards'. Moments later the UFO emitted a cloud of red-grey mist which enveloped the whole scene. When it cleared, both the UFO and the being had disappeared. The skier who had taken the force of the beam was numb on his right side, with no strength in his right leg. His friend had to drag him home.[40]

Don't interrupt fairies when they're dancing

On the basis of the evidence I have put before the reader in the last five chapters, it seems to me beyond serious dispute that fairies, spirits and aliens are all locally customised adaptations of the same extremely puzzling and mysterious core phenomena. What has been demonstrated, in contexts as different as medieval Europe, seventeenth-century Siberia and modern America is a constantly repeated pattern involving sightings and encounters, abductions by otherworldly beings, specific types of procedures carried out during abductions, settings in which abductions unfold, etc., etc. – a pattern that appears to hold true at all levels down to the minutest details. Such repetition and cross-cultural consistency should in themselves increase our confidence that we may be dealing with something real here, and at least give us reason to take these phenomena seriously – as those who have experienced them *always* do.

If we are prepared to set aside the automatic scepticism and reductionism of our age, and if we spell out the problem in plain language, then we find that we are contemplating the existence – and powerful intervention in our lives – of highly intelligent *discarnate* entities belonging to an order of creation fundamentally different from our own. Paradoxically, however, these non-physical entities seem to have mastered a 'technology', and I use the word advisedly, that enables them to enter our material world and to manifest in it in a quasi-physical, 'shape-shifting', sometimes therianthropic, sometimes large-headed and small-bodied humanoid form – but always evanescent, ephemeral, somehow luminous, almost but not quite transparent.

With that in mind, let's take a closer look at the group of fairies, mentioned earlier, seen in Suffolk in 1842:

> They were moving round hand in hand in a ring, no noise came from them. They seemed light and shadowy, not like solid bodies . . . I ran home and called three women to come back with me and see them. But when we got to the place they were all gone.[41]

It is remarkable how frequently the activity that fairies were engaged in when they were sighted was described as some sort of circular dance, 'moving round hand in hand in a ring'. It is surprising too, as we will see, how frequently those humans who stumbled upon the dance say that it culminated in the disappearance of the fairies, and how dangerous they could sometimes become if they were interrupted in the midst of it. The witness from Suffolk probably did well to run away as fast as his legs could carry him. Around the year 1908, W.Y. Evans-Wentz interviewed a certain Neil Colton of Lough Derg in County Donegal, Ireland. Then 73 years old, Colton told of a time when he was a boy out gathering bilberries with his brother and cousin and came suddenly across a group of six or eight fairies, 'and they dancing'.[42] When the fairies saw the children, things went wrong very quickly:

> a little woman dressed all in red came running out from them towards us, and she struck my cousin across the face with what seemed to be a green rush. We ran for home as hard as we could, and when my cousin reached the house she fell dead.[43]

Following the intervention of the local Catholic priest, Colton added, the girl was later revived.[44] Her condition had been one not of death but of narcolepsy.

A rather similar story comes down to us from the Reverend Edward Williams, born in Denbighshire in north Wales around 1750, and concerns events that took place there when he was about seven years old. Together with several older children, Williams was playing at the edge of a field when he observed near the middle of it:

> a company of – what shall I call them? – *Beings*, neither men, women, nor children, dancing with great briskness . . . They appeared of a size somewhat like our own, but more like dwarves than children . . .[45]

At this moment the children observed one of the company:

> starting from the rest and making towards us with a running pace. I being the youngest was the last at the stile, and, though struck with an inexpressible panic, saw the *grim elf* just at my heels, having a full and clear, though terrific view of him, with his ancient, swarthy and grim complexion . . . This warlike Lilliputian leaned over and stretched himself after me, but came not over . . .[46]

Fairies were often quick to anger and ready to do harm, ornery, unpredictable and habitually violent. In that respect the stories of Colton and Williams are not very different from many others. Still, my attention had been grabbed by the clear line of cause and effect that runs through both these reports. Remember that we are suspending disbelief here, considering accounts of fairies, spirits and aliens on their own terms, without a priori judgements about their reality status, so that we may compare them and expose any common patterns. If we stay with that method, take this story on its own terms, and do not simply insist that these Irish and Welsh children were suffering from foolish collective delusions, then it is clear in each case that their arrival on the scene must have been perceived as a *threat* to what the fairies were doing at that very moment – in other words dancing – and that in each case the attack was a direct reaction to that threat. I was reminded of my own recent encounter with the cave bees in South Africa. I had threatened them by getting too close to their hive. In response they sent out one little warrior to scare me away . . .

Why should the fairies have wanted to protect the dance? My curiosity led me to examine other accounts of this phenomenon.

Dancing and disappearing

The tribe of fairies known amongst the Breton people of northern France as *kornigan* or corrigans could, at will, assume 'any animal form' and were able, moreover, 'to travel from one end of the world to another in the twinkling of an eye'.[47] They were said to 'dance in a circle holding hands, but at the least noise disappear'.[48]

The fairy dance. Note hallucinogenic mushroom (with the characteristic spotted cap of Amanita muscaria) in the foreground, doorway into a 'hollow hill' – the entrance of Fairyland – far left, and tree spirit to the right (Fortean Picture Library)

In a field in the Isle of Man around the year 1730 fairies were seen 'playing and leaping over some stones'. Perhaps with more risk to himself than he realised, the witness managed to get close to them. 'But when he approached, as near as he could guess, within twenty paces, they all immediately disappeared.'[49]

One afternoon in 1945, J. Foot White and a companion were walking through the Dorsetshire countryside when they saw a group of about 20 small beings:

> Their hands were joined, and all held up, as they merrily danced round in a perfect circle. We stood watching them, when in an instant they all vanished from our sight. My companion told me they were fairies, and they often came to that particular part to hold their revels. It may be our presence disturbed them.[50]

As recently as 10 August 1977, well into the UFO age, fairy 'overlaps' were still occurring. On that day a police constable on early-morning patrol first saw a bank of fog – which cleared to reveal three figures dancing in a field. 'As he got nearer, however, they disappeared into thin air.' The constable described one of the figures as 'a man dressed in a sleeveless jerkin, with tight-fitting trousers; the other two figures were women, wearing bonnets, shawls and white dresses'. All had an arm raised as if dancing around an invisible maypole.[51]

Janet Bord asks rhetorically, 'Why are the fairies so often seen dancing?' but feels that this is an 'unanswerable question'.[52] Later, commenting on the huge numbers of accounts that exist of the dance, many collected together for the first time in her excellent book *Fairies: Real Encounters with Little People*, she adds that in her view these consistent descriptions

> have the ring of truth . . . though I am at a loss to explain why the fairies should so much enjoy dancing . . . Perhaps it is simply that they enjoy it and will take every opportunuity to relax in this way; perhaps they are performing rituals of some kind . . .[53]

Test-driving the dance

But perhaps something altogether different is involved. When I compare the very typical and representative accounts cited above of dances underway followed by the abrupt disappearance of the dancers, with the parallel typical and representative accounts of dances underway followed by attacks on witnesses, the hypothesis that suggests itself to me is that the fairy dance is not about revels or enjoyment at all, or even very much about rituals. What I propose instead is that its vigorous, brisk, energetic movements and generally circular pattern may be some kind of technique – or technology, just as the San trance dance is a technology – to transmit the dancers from this world to the other-world, and back again as well. I once more remind the reader that we are suspending disbelief here and speculating freely. I therefore feel at liberty to suggest that attacks on witnesses may be triggered if the dance is interrupted *before the required momentum to jump the gap between worlds has been built up*, but may become unnecessary once that momentum has been attained and disappearance is just seconds away. This would explain the evidence which shows some witnesses receiving the fairy blast and some not, apparently arbitrarily, when in reality the decisive factor may be at what point in the progression of the dance the witness appears, or whether the witness is far enough away from the dance to avoid detection or to be judged no threat.

Another of Bord's collection of fairy dance traditions illustrates this last point. It is from Carmarthenshire in Wales and dates back to 1862, when David Evans and Evan Lewis paused on the road near a place called Cwmdwr and saw a group of about 50 'small people' walking fast one after another up a hillside path some 400 yards away. A rather extraordinary scene then unfolded on the distant hilltop that is strongly suggestive of deliberately induced transit between this world and the otherworld:

> The first of those who were climbing up along the winding footpath had reached a small level spot on the top of the hill. The others quickly followed him, and each one in coming to the top gave a jump to dance, and they formed a circle. After dancing for a short time, one of the dancers turned into the middle of the circle, followed by the others, one by one till they appeared like a gimblet screw. Then they disappeared into the ground. After a while one of them reappeared again, and looked about him in every direction as a rat, and the others followed him one by one and did the same. Then they danced for some time as before, and vanished into the ground as they had done the first time.[54]

What on earth – and apparently somewhere other as well – was going on here? What was this backwards and forwards movement between realms, between the everyday world and the underworld of Fairyland – which is a dimension that we know may at one moment be found in deep caverns, at another beneath seas or lakes, and at another in the sky? What were these 50 small beings really doing when they danced themselves into the form of a corkscrew and descended beneath the hills of Carmarthenshire, then reappeared, and danced some more only for the ground to open beneath their feet and swallow them up once again? It almost seems to me as though they were trying the system out – in a sense 'test-driving' the dance. We don't know where it transported them too – other than loosely 'underground'. But if we take the story at face value, as a sighting, as an eyewitness report, then what we do know is that this particular dance does definitely seem to have been entered into and deployed with the explicit purpose of making this particular group of fairies disappear, that the dance itself was highly disciplined and structured, and that it involved the entire team working in almost hive-like co-ordination to form first a circle then a spiral that corkscrewed into the earth and vanished.

Ring portals (1)

What is unusual about this report is not only that the trick of disappearance was pulled off twice on the same spot by the same group of dancers within a few moments, but also that the performance of the dance was witnessed from beginning to end – an extremely rare state of affairs. Janet Bord's collection of relevant traditions does, however, contain one other example where the entire sequence of the dance was observed. This report dates back more than 100 years to a time when people still believed in fairies, long before the beginning of the modern UFO age. Yet, as Bord points out, it contains a number of ingredients that are more reminiscent of UFO than fairy phenomena. The eyewitness was David Williams, a manservant who lived at Penrhyndeudraeth, Gwynedd, North Wales, and he and his wife were walking home on the night in question with David lagging behind.

He was distracted, but she not, by 'a brilliant meteor passing through the air', followed

> by a ring or hoop of fire, and within this hoop stood a man and woman of small size, handsomely dressed. With one arm they embraced each other, and with the other they took hold of the hoop, and their feet rested on the concave surface of the ring. When the hoop reached the earth, these two beings jumped out of it, and immediately proceeded to make a circle on the ground. As soon as this was done, a large number of men and women instantly appeared, and to the sweetest music that ear ever heard commenced dancing round and round the circle.[55]

Williams paused to observe the scene for what he thought was about three minutes until the 'meteor' was suddenly present again, hovering above, and 'the fiery hoop' returned – at which point the lady and gentleman jumped on board their transport and disappeared into the sky. At the same moment 'the fairies vanished from sight'.[56]

Was the circle that the lady and gentleman inscribed on the ground at the beginning of the scene some kind of portal to bring the group of dancers through into this world from Fairyland, and to send them back again? I have racked my brains to try to figure out what might have been going on, what sort of procedure or process it was that David Williams observed and tried to describe in his report, and I see no easy answer. But there is one more detail that may provide a clue. Williams thought he had observed the dance for three minutes, but when he arrived home after his wife she informed him in no uncertain terms that he was a full three hours behind her. 'Does this mean,' asks Bord, 'that he unwittingly strayed into another world – fairyland – where time runs at a different speed?'[57]

The dance and time

The way that time behaves around the fairy dance is distinctly odd, and the accounts that are given of it, even when they go back centuries, seem to take for granted one of the very sophisticated notions of physics that has only been adopted by science in the past 100 years –

405

namely that the passage of time is not absolute or universal but is instead relative to the place and motion of the observer.[58] Were there to exist other dimensions, or multiple other dimensions as quantum physicists maintain, then we would expect the flow of time to be different in each one of them and to adhere strictly to local rules, regularities, circumstances and conditions in each case. It follows that any hypothetical interdimensional travellers would have to contend with the relativity of time – where, for example, three minutes in one realm might indeed prove to be equivalent to three hours in another. Remember, this is all hypothetical, so we can add, just for fun, that if the dance was a vehicle for interdimensional travel then perhaps the forces unleashed in jumping between realms might have generated a vortex powerful enough to suck in unwary humans who came too close. Could this even be why the dancers felt threatened when humans approached and rushed to frighten them off, and why they were less concerned when witnesses were a safe distance away or when they were seen too late for anything useful to be done about them?

Many different traditions attest that humans *did* get trapped in the dance, stuck fast like flies in amber. A nineteenth-century woodcut shows fairies moving in a ring around the perimeter of a circular depression. One man is being drawn in – and he looks as though he

'Twm pulling his friend Iago out of the Fairy Circle'.
Nineteenth-century woodcut.

very much wants to go. But his friend is pulling him back to safety.[59] Sometimes, when no friend was nearby to lend a hand, people trapped in this way would be invited to enter Fairyland, often with bewildering and tragic consequences. In the 1960s, folklorist Robin Glyndaff was told the following story by an elderly Welsh tradition-bearer:

Two men . . . went for a stroll and one of them lost the other . . . And what one of them saw was fairies dancing and he stopped to look at them and to listen to them. And that's where he was for a bit, for about two or three hours, he thought. Then he went home and on the way he met this man who greeted him: 'Good evening.' 'Good evening,' he replied. 'Hello,' he said, 'aren't you Jack, my cousin?' 'God yes,' said he. 'How long is it since we lost each other?' said the other man. 'Well, let me think. I've been married ten years and it was five years after losing you that I married. That makes fifteen years.' And he thought he'd only been in the company of the fairies for a couple of hours.[60]

Here's another variant of the story – or another consequence of the same phenomenon – also from Wales, in which the time penalty paid by the human victim was much more severe. It alerts us to the significance that was once accorded to the bright green circles (known colloquially as 'fairy rings' or 'fairy circles') that often appear in meadows, marshlands and floodplains. Thanks to science, we know today that these distinctive patterns are the result of soil enrichment due to subsurface fungal growth. But because extensive traditions and folklore have survived, together with numerous witness accounts collected by ethnographers, we also know that they were repeatedly identified as favoured spots for the fairy dance. Another of Glyndaff's elderly informants recalled one such 'very strange round circle', greener than the surrounding marshland in which it stood, and the fear in which it was held:

I heard about a boy who entered the circle . . . And the fairies came to dance and the boy stood in the centre looking at them. He wasn't realising that time was passing, but one of the fairies came to him. 'Would you like to come with us to our country?' 'Dear me, yes,' the boy replied. 'Well, come down these steps here this way.' And he hadn't noticed before that there were any steps there. But he goes down these steps, down and down. And after walking for a while he came to a certain country, the most beautiful he had ever seen . . .'[61]

In this land the lad was feasted and entertained, allowed to sleep overnight, and then the next day escorted to the top of the steps again:

And after he returned to the circle he makes his way for home. And he goes to the house. Dear me! There were strangers in the house. No one knew him. 'Where are my father and mother?' he asks. 'Your father and mother?' they said. 'Goodness me! We don't know who you are, tell us your name.' 'Robin Jones is my name,' he replied . . . And they said, 'We heard some talk once about a Robin who had gone into the fairy circle, but this happened over a hundred years ago.' And the boy had been in Fairyland for one hundred years and had returned. Then he didn't know anybody.[62]

The idea of a circle in the grass as some kind of portal to another world, another dimension, another frame of time, is also found in a third Welsh story where we hear of a young girl on her way home from the shops to buy a loaf of bread who takes a short cut across a field and makes the mistake of trying to jump across a fairy ring: 'But, oh dear! Before she completes her jump she has disappeared.' Eventually she does return home, with the loaf still fresh: 'Here it is, mam,' she says, 'here's the loaf for you to have tea.' 'My dear little girl, where have you been?' 'In the shop to get a loaf of bread for you.' 'Oh! No my girl. Seven years have passed since you went to the shop for a loaf.'[63]

Ring portals (2)

From Cornwall come parallel traditions that affirm the important connection between circles in the grass and all members of the fairy tribe:

Up on Sea-View Green there are two rings where the piskies [pixies] used to dance and play music on a moonlit night. I've heard they would come there from the moors. *Little people* they are called. If you keep quiet when they are dancing you'll see them, but if you make any noise they'll disappear.[64]

Also in Cornwall there were cases in the nineteenth century – long before the modern phenomenon of crop circles began – of 'piskies' coming 'at night to thrash the farmer's corn'.[65] In the sixteenth century Bishop Olaf Magnus investigated similar rings in crops and grass in Sweden which he attributed to the dance of the elves: 'They [the elves] make so deep an impression on the earth that no grass grows there, being burned with extreme heat.'[66]

When accounts like these are thrown into the melting pot, I realise we may not even have begun to understand what is going on with the phenomenon known as the fairy dance. Still, I repeat my suggestion that it feels like some sort of technology for jumping between worlds, and in particular for entering and leaving this one. I think the evidence suggests that this technology could not be used at any time and place but would only work in the context of portals that were circular in form and that were generally, but not always, to be found at certain fixed locations. Fairies dancing – presumably in the otherworld – could be brought through one of these portals into this world (as in the strange story, cited earlier, of a circle inscribed on the ground and dancers suddenly materialising around its circumference only to vanish again soon afterwards).

But generally, if a group of fairies wished to leave our world and enter another by means of the dance, then a case could be made that they were obliged to do so through a pre-established portal. That would explain why the Dorsetshire fairies cited earlier were said to hold their dances again and again at the same particular spot in the countryside – from which they would then mysteriously disappear – and why Cornish piskies travelled all the way from the moors to dance in the two rings on Sea-View Green, from which they then likewise vanished. A similar example comes from Wales in the mid-nineteenth century when John Jones, then aged about 18, was walking home late at night 'along a lonely path'. He had the sense that he was being followed and when he turned around, sure enough, he saw 'two young men or boys coming after him'. They pursued him further, moving quickly, in a way that he found threatening, then suddenly

> turned out from the path, and began to jump and to dance, going round and round *as if they followed a ring or a circle* just as we hear of the fairies. They were perfectly white, and very nimble, and . . . there was something supernatural both in their appearance and movements.[67]

Again I get the sense of a fixed mechanism at work in the dance – a mechanism that may indeed be supernatural, generating uncanny forces at the intersection of worlds. Moreover, with its circular form and its ability to materialise and dematerialise itself and its occupants instantly, it reminds me distinctly of many of the things we know, or think we know, about UFOs. Is it possible that whatever objective was achieved by the 'spiritual technology' called the fairy dance from the Middle Ages through Victorian times is more often achieved today with the mysterious apparitions that we call UFOs? After all, just as there appear to be definite signs of evolution between fairies and aliens on the matter of changelings, so too there may have been evolution in the means used to travel between this world and Fairyland/UFO-land.

Such a hypothesis does not rule out the possibility of overlaps – of both means being used together – and we've seen examples of true UFOs in the fairy period, and of the fairy dance in the UFO period.

Evolution

There are many hints in fairy lore that the dance was never exclusive technology and that there were always other means of interdimensional travel. Throughout the Celtic fringe of western Europe springs, wells, and notably caves were also widely believed to serve as portals to the otherworld, and in these cases the dance does not seem to have been used as the energising agency.[68] In Catholic Ireland of the early twentieth century, for example, caves were still popularly supposed 'to lead to Hades or an underworld of fairies, demons and spirits . . .'[69] A sixteenth-century woodcut shows a crowd of fairies inside a hollow hill. To the fore are several beautiful females who are attempting to lure a handsome young human male to join them. I draw the reader's attention in passing to the fact that a clump of mushrooms can be seen growing between the young man and the fairies.[70]

In this sixteenth-century woodcut, fairies attempt to entice a handsome young prince to join them inside a hollow hill (Fortean Picture Library)

Nor are such ideas confined to Europe. The hints and clues that certain caves, like the fairy rings, mark the spot of fixed portals to the otherworld are found everywhere. Whether we speak of the *Iruntarinia* fairies of Aboriginal Australia in their perpetually lit caverns, or the spirits who emerge through cracks in the rock to Paviotso shamans in North America, or the Inuit shaman who must enter a cave that closes behind him, we have seen many examples of this idea in previous chapters. Like the fairy dance and the fairy ring, it is an idea that is often caught up with the strange, sophisticated concept of the relativity of time.

A peculiarly evocative example from China tells of the Taoist holy man Wang Chi. Gathering firewood in the mountains one day, he came to a cave and saw inside it a group of elders playing chess. Laying down his axe, Wang Chi entered the cave to watch the game and soon afterwards one of the old men gave him a capsule about the size of a date stone and instructed him to put it in his mouth. 'No sooner had he done so than hunger and thirst passed away.' A few more hours passed, then another of the elders told him: 'It is a long time since you came here, you should go home now.' Wang Chi took his leave, but when he stepped outside the cave to pick up his axe the handle had turned to dust. When he reached his home valley he discovered that 'not hours but centuries had passed, and nothing remained of the world as he had known it'.[71]

So whatever route humans took on their temporary journeys into the otherworld, whether by the fairy dance or by some other enchantment as in this Chinese example, such stories tell us that they often became badly misplaced in time – a very heavy personal price to pay. It therefore seems to me potentially significant, despite all the other continuities and commonalities linking fairies and aliens, that this most unfortunate 'Rip van Winkle' syndrome does not seem to have been encountered even once in the 50 years since UFO abductions first began to attract publicity. There *are* time distortions and, most frequently, abductees are unable to account for short periods of their lives – usually no more than an hour.[72] But this well-known problem of 'missing time' is quite a different matter from spending what feels subjectively like a few hours in Fairyland and getting home decades or centuries later.

Once again an evolutionary process seems to have been at work, ironing out the glitches, turning the fairy dance into more efficient UFOs, relinquishing baby theft, and rigorously avoiding the late return of abductees. By whatever name we know them – spirits, fairies, aliens – it really is almost as though the beings we are dealing with have been changing and developing alongside us for thousands of years, and that they therefore cannot simply be mass delusions, as scientists would like us to believe, but must have a definite, independent reality outside the human brain.

It is to serious consideration of this possibility that we shall now turn.

PART IV
The Codes

CHAPTER SEVENTEEN

Tuning in to Channel DMT

We saw in Part I that human evolution looks very much like the evolution of every other animal species (even tool-using is not unique to man) from five million years ago down to about 40,000 years ago; then, suddenly, we seem to take an astonishing and unprecedented new tack. By 35,000 years ago in Europe and 27,000 years ago in Africa, rock and cave art have appeared, apparently already sophisticated and fully formed.[1] It is as though an inspired artistic genius in the full flow of his powers has miraculously awakened from an extremely long vegetative coma and begun to paint. His work from the outset is technically adept, magisterial and numinous, but a much bigger mystery is that it gives special importance to the depiction of therianthropic entities, part human, part beast, for which no model exists, or has ever existed, in the natural world. These, therefore, are depictions of *supernatural* beings – spirits – and we are obliged to ask from where it was that such fantastic images were conjured up. 'Imagination' alone will not suffice as an explanation, since our ancestors had managed to pass the previous five million years without ever showing even the faintest sign that they possessed any symbolic imagination at all. Clearly, therefore, something fundamental must have changed in the way that they perceived their lives, related to the world they lived in, and assessed the boundaries of their reality.

We have addressed the mystery of this great change at length in Part II and pursued David Lewis-Williams' suggestion that the catalyst was the cultivation of altered states of consciousness, most probably first experienced by our ancestors through the accidental consumption of plant or fungal hallucinogens and subsequently deliberately and systematically sought out. It seems reasonable to suppose that the overwhelmingly potent visions and experiences that we now know can be reliably elicited by psilocybin and other naturally available psychoactive substances would have exploded like incendiary bombs in the dull, somnolent, utilitarian minds of the anatomically modern but behaviourally archaic humans of 40,000 years ago. It may even be the case that *only* such a paroxysm of consciousness, capable of affecting every member of society, would have had sufficient power to demolish the barren and rigid mental structures that had hitherto masked the potential of the human brain and held back the intellectual and cultural evolution of our species.

This is *not* to say that no humans before 40,000 years ago had visionary experiences. Full anatomical modernity was achieved around 200,000 years ago,[2] or perhaps earlier according to some authorities, and much evidence supports the view that there has subsequently been no further change in the size, anatomy or complexity of the human brain. For at least 200,000 years, therefore, during which our ancestors had the same neurological equipment as we do, it follows that they must also have had our capacity to experience the visions and hallucinatory encounters of altered states of consciousness.

We know from surveys that around 2 per cent of modern adults (and this is a cautious estimate) do in fact seem to be born with the ability to fall spontaneously into very deep states of hallucination. We know that what happens to them in these states is frequently experienced as convincingly *real* and sometimes terrifying abductions by supernatural entities that often first appear to them in therianthropic or animal forms. We know, too, that this apparent genetic capacity to trance has been attested to statistically in the United States where such visions and experiences are today most frequently construed as contact with aliens – although, as I have tried to demonstrate, they are nothing new and have been construed differently by other cultures in the past.

Though it cannot be proved, I think it is highly probable that around 2 per cent of *every human population* has always been born with brain chemistry in just the right state of flux to permit them visions, prophetic knowledge and encounters with spirits without recourse either to psychoactive plants or to physical methods of trance induction such as rhythmic dancing or drumming. My guess is that such people existed and were experiencing visions and encounters long before the earliest rock art was ever painted. Perhaps it was precisely they – the first shamans, spontaneously 'shamanising' – who were responsible for the odd, isolated breakthroughs of behaviourally modern symbolism *before* 35,000 years ago (for example the shell necklace and ochre slab decorated with entoptic patterns found at Blombos Cave in South Africa and dated to approximately 77,000 years ago). I don't rule this out at all, but the archaeological record says that the influence of such visionaries on their fellows in the Stone Age was for a long while no greater then than the influence of UFO abductees is in modern society – i.e. pretty much zero.

I suggest that not only art but the entire switch to behavioural modernity came when those in any Stone Age society who lacked the genetic capacity to trance spontaneously were enabled to do so by the discovery and subsequent systematic exploitation of plant hallucinogens or one of the physical methods of trance induction. The hypothesis is that it was this 'democratisation' of altered states of consciousness, the possibility for the entire community to share in the life-changing visions and encounters that had previously been limited to a very few, that brought new, more open, more creative, more innovative, more flexible, more intuitive and frankly more intelligent ways of thinking to a point of 'critical mass' in society after society and ushered in the single most decisive shift ever to have occurred in human evolution. We need not be surprised that the archaeological record shows this moment being reached at different times in different places, sometimes with intervals of thousands of years between the awakening of one group and another. If the trigger factor in every case was the discovery of reliable means for all to enter altered states of consciousness, and if this first discovery was often accidental, then we would not expect to find modern human behaviour emerging everywhere all at once, but rather in stages and somewhat randomly – which is in fact what we see in the archaeological record. Once the process had started, however, it could not be stopped, as people who did not know how to use altered states of consciousness would sooner or later have encountered people who did and would have learned from them.

Concealed matrix and the receiving mind

The fundamental experiences of the shamanic trance in all times and places have been the otherworld journey and the shaman's initiation by, encounters with and reception of powers from supernatural entities. For reasons we have explored in Part II, we can say with a high degree of confidence that the art of the painted caves of Upper Palaeolithic Europe and the rock art of the San of southern Africa were both inspired by exactly such otherworld journeys and encounters experienced in deeply altered states of consciousness. We have seen that the outward forms in which experiences of this kind clothe themselves – in other words the ways in which they are construed and the ways in which they are portrayed – can change dramatically from culture to culture. However, we should not forget that 'normal' perceptions and experiences do so as well.

For example, if five different people witness a crime, the police are used to being given five quite different descriptions of the perpetrator. This is because interpretation is built into our perceptual processes from the outset and we each bring our own preconditioning, individual experiences and cultural preferences to bear on what we see and on how we experience reality. The fact that our hallucinations are also hugely influenced by our own preconditioning, individual experiences and cultural preferences therefore tells us more about standard mechanisms underlying *all* forms of perception than it does about the objective reality – or not – of the scenes and beings encountered in hallucinations.

Stated simply, the great variety of imagery seen in trance states by different cultures and peoples (or even by the same person in different moods and settings) does not prove that 'there is nothing there' at the source of the images, or that they are all cooked up 'within the brain' – any more than the variety of witness descriptions proves that there was no crime. The corollary, however, is that any underlying *similarities* between the hallucinated experiences of different peoples and cultures at different periods of history and prehistory should be of the greatest interest and taken fully into account in weighing up the reality status of the supernatural realms and beings that feature in such experiences.

We encounter the supernatural, or what we think of as the supernatural, in many different guises and there are as many different ways to approach and explore it. In a book there are strict limitations of space, so out of a desire for parsimony and to maintain focus, my strategy has been to concentrate on three specific manifestations of the supernatural in unconnected settings and epochs where similarities ought, legitimately, to be least expected.

The first manifestation we have explored has been the spirit world, so evident in prehistoric rock art and still actively experienced to this day in surviving shamanic cultures as far afield as central and southern Africa, Australia and the Amazon rain forest. The second manifestation has been the fascination with the supernatural beings known as fairies that captivated the imagination of Europe from medieval through to Victorian times. The third manifestation has been the modern experience, particularly strong in North America, of encounters with UFOs and aliens.

Beneath the obvious superficial and culturally determined differences, our close examination of all three cases in the previous chapters reveals the existence of a concealed matrix of deep structural similarities and connections. It is also particularly notable how certain common themes, such as therianthropic transformations, the presence of dwarf-like humanoids with large oblique eyes and oversized teardrop-shaped heads, the presence of owls, the ordeal of the 'wounded man', and the breeding of hybrid infants, seem to be expressed over and over again. Extending from the Upper Palaeolithic to the Space Age, such close and distinctive continuities and commonalities would seem extraordinary enough if they had arisen in response to easily identifiable, objective and long-lasting external stimuli that all had shared. But for them to show so much consistency over so long a period in the absence of any objective 'real world' stimulus at all is a much more mysterious matter.

It raises again the question of the mind as a receiver rather than simply as a generator of consciousness, and the possibility that everyone

419

who has ever experienced abduction by aliens or fairies, or initiation with painful piercings and tortures by spirits, automatically takes for granted – namely that the otherworlds we explore and the supernatural entities we encounter in trance states do have an objective reality all of their own and do have an independent existence outside our brains.

A common molecule with uncommon effects

It was this possibility that Dr Rick Strassman, a psychiatrist working at the University of New Mexico, was forced to contemplate when he began human trials in the 1990s with dimethyltryptamine (DMT). In Chapter Three we saw that this potent hallucinogen, which shamans in the Amazon extract from the leaves and resins of a number of jungle plants, forms the principal active ingredient of ayahuasca. But DMT is also very closely related, at the molecular level, to the fungal hallucinogen psilocybin,[3] and to serotonin (5-hydroxytryptamine), the most important neurotransmitter in the human brain.[4]

Widely distributed throughout the plant and animal kingdoms, 'DMT is, most simply, almost everywhere you choose to look,' says biochemist Alexander Shulgin. 'It is in this flower here, in that tree over there, and in yonder animal.'[5] Rick Strassman adds that it is 'part of the normal makeup of humans and other mammals; marine animals; grasses and peas; toads and frogs; mushrooms and molds; and barks, flowers and roots'.[6] In addition, our brains themselves synthesise and produce DMT, which has been found to be naturally present in human blood, in human brain tissue and in the cerebrospinal fluid bathing the brain. By any standards, therefore, we are talking about a relatively common molecule. What is most *uncommon*, however, is the storm of hallucinations unleashed in human subjects when naturally occurring levels of DMT in the brain are raised above a certain threshold.

The nominal purpose of Strassman's research was to discover whether psychoactive doses of DMT given over sustained periods of time might have any medical or therapeutic applications. To cut a long story short, no such applications were identified,[7] but instead something else, quite unexpected, came to light. Many of the subjects experienced intense encounters with supernatural, non-physical beings during their DMT trips, encounters that they often received – like the shamans of old – as profound and disturbing revelations. Several different volunteers gave accounts of virtually identical experiences and even seemed to be entering the *same* realms and communicating with the *same* beings. In a large number of instances, Strassman was stunned to realise, these experiences, realms and beings were identical to those reported to John Mack and other psychiatric counsellors by people who believed they had been abducted by aliens.[8]

Clearly there had been no physical abduction here. In each case, the subjects had remained throughout on a hospital bed in the University of New Mexico and directly under Rick Strassman's watchful eye. Yet, with intramuscular injections of DMT in doses as low as 0.2 milligrams per kilogram of body weight (only tiny quantities of this substance are required to induce hallucinations), their consciousness had been effortlessly projected to the same sorts of places that UFO abductees say they are taken, where they underwent the same sorts of ordeals at the hands of the same sorts of enigmatic beings.

In Chapter Eighteen we will look in detail at what the volunteers had to say. Their experiences were not identical to mine, but overall there were many striking similarities. The main difference, I think, was that I was obliged to use a much less efficient method of delivery and was much more frightened and unsure of my ground.

Smoking DMT

I applied the naked flame of a butane lighter to the ruby-red blob of crystalline resin, about one third the size of a pea, that I had just crumbled into the bowl of a glass pipe. There was some crackling and hissing as I inhaled deeply and filled my lungs with smoke. The taste was much less noxious than I had expected and the substance had an odd smell, not at all unpleasant, that reminded me of plasticine. I held my breath, retaining the smoke, giving the DMT a chance to work its way through the lining of my lungs and into my bloodstream. Even before I exhaled I had begun to feel very dizzy – the sort of instant buzz and disorientation that I used to get years ago from a big hit of marijuana.

I flicked the lighter on again and moved it towards the bowl. But hold on! Where was the DMT? The resin had melted into a thick clear liquid that now lay pooled in the pipe's mesh foil and was presumably already dripping through it into the bottom of the bowl. I put the flame to the liquid and inhaled again, this time getting much less smoke, which I retained in my lungs for about ten seconds before I exhaled. There was now just a smear left on the foil.

I sat back. What was I experiencing, if anything?

Well, I was definitely experiencing something. For a start I was in the midst of a serious light-headed buzz. I felt pretty good, but also scared. I wanted to lie down under a blanket and at the same time get up and pace around. I closed my eyes. If there were to be visions, that would be where I would first see them, behind my closed eyes. But I saw nothing, or perhaps not quite nothing – perhaps just the faintest hint of random lines and flashes of light, the slightest disturbance and rippling on the edge of consciousness. This too rapidly faded, and within ten minutes the buzz and disorientation had cleared completely, leaving me in full possession of all my senses and faculties.

If we lived in a free society and had made an adult choice to use hallucinogens to explore our own consciousness, then we would be able to acquire good-quality injectable DMT from our local pharmacy along with a safe system of delivery and excellent advice on how to use the drug, and on its risks, benefits and contraindications. Unfortunately, however, the powers of this world have determined that we in the wealthy industrialised countries are not under any circumstances to be permitted to use hallucinogens for consciousness exploration, or any other purpose, and that if we do we may be sent to prison for up to 30 years. Naturally this brazen and inexplicable breach of our basic human right of sovereignty over our own minds does make it quite difficult to acquire DMT – and particularly to acquire pure high-quality DMT.

So this was my problem. Given the choice, given the liberty to act rationally and wisely in the best interests of my health, I would have preferred to be like Rick Strassman's very fortunate volunteers and to receive my DMT in the form of injections. But because my society denies me that choice, and would imprison me for making it, and because government-sanctioned projects like Strassman's are as rare as hen's teeth, I had been forced to acquire the drug 'on the street'. It came to me through contacts I trust, so I had no doubt that what I was getting would be of tried-and-tested quality, not some dangerous rip-off cocktail of bogus chemicals – always a possibility with street drugs. But I had to take what was available, and what was available was this ruby-red resinous tree-bark extract, loaded up by nature with very high concentrations of DMT. Smoking it was a hit-and-miss method of delivery, far less efficient than Rick Strassman's wonderfully precise intramuscular injections, and potentially very wasteful of the substance into the bargain – as I had now discovered.

I took stock of what remained of my stash. There was one solid lump of resin about twice as large as the piece I had already burned. And in a separate plastic bag I had what looked like the same amount again but broken up into powder and flakes.

Dose was absolutely crucial with this drug, and in my first session I had smoked too little. This was obviously because I had not used enough of the resin and because the little that I had used melted down and became unsmokeable almost immediately. I removed the foil with its smear of salmon-coloured residue from my pipe and replaced it with a fresh one. I had strong feelings of apprehension, and indeed fear, about using DMT, and had it not been essential for my work to get acquainted with this molecule I do not think I would ever have got this far with it. Now I could not bear the thought of my low-level dread of the DMT experience carrying on for even another hour. I had to get this done! I therefore decided to smoke all of the rest of the main lump in one session – which would give me at least double the dose I'd had already. Presumably the trick would be to apply the flame in such a way that not all of the resin burned at once, thus allowing at least four or five good hits on it before it disappeared.

The resin broke up easily between my fingers into crystalline crumbs, which I sprinkled on to the new, clean foil. It made quite a formidable little pile. And I was going to smoke all this? At once? I

423

must be crazy. Santha was sitting beside me now and handed me a glass of spring water from the shrine of the Blessed Virgin Mary at Lourdes which we'd visited together eight months previously. I'm not a Christian, but the grotto at Lourdes was a fairy cave before Catholicism adopted it, and when little Bernadette Soubirous experienced visions in front of it in the mid-nineteenth century, she initially described the female figure she saw not as the Virgin Mary but as *un petito damizela*, 'a little lady' – a term redolent of the fairy lore of the Pyrenees.[9] Another thing that is not widely known about Lourdes is that a large quantity of portable Upper Palaeolithic art was found there,[10] but this is a matter that we will return to.

Whirlwind

I clicked on the lighter, held it over the edge of the bowl and tried to avoid igniting all the resin at once. There was crackling and hissing as before, and I inhaled deeply, this time drawing down what felt like a large amount of smoke into my lungs. I held it there for some seconds, then slowly breathed out and reinhaled about half the smoke. The immediate rapid buzz was back, multiplied in strength. I exhaled again, peered into the bowl. Hmm, quite a lot left this time! I flicked the lighter back on and applied the flame to the other side of the diminished melting pile. Crackle. Hiss. Another big inhalation . . . hold it, breathe out, reinhale, breathe out. Fire up the lighter again. This time the target is that solid little chunk of resin standing out of a sea of meltdown. Click. Crackle. Hiss. Inhale. Breathe out . . .

By now I was feeling way beyond buzz, way beyond disoriented. I needed to lie down fast. But there was still something that could be smoked left in that bowl. Having come this far, I knew it was my duty to smoke it all and make certain I got a good dose. Click. Crackle. Hiss. Inhale. I handed the pipe and lighter to Santha, and stretched out full-length on the couch with my eyes closed.

Although my rational observing consciousness never left me for a moment, I now found myself fully immersed in an extremely potent psychedelic episode. I felt as though I were being drawn up out of my body by some utterly irresistible impersonal force like a flood or a whirlwind and carried off to a far-off, high-up place. Then, while I was still in the midst of that vertiginous upwards rush, a seething mass of incredibly rich, deeply saturated colours presented themselves across my entire field of vision, coiled into serpentine internested wave patterns decorated with bright dots like the bodies of a thousand snakes – the whole glowing, luminous mass pulsating and writhing and filled with an extraordinary and indescribable sense of menace. I felt real fear now. My heart was beating faster. I was sweating. Santha had her cool hand on me but after a while I started to be afraid that somehow she would get drawn into this vortex and asked her to sit back. I groaned and moaned. And all the while, eyes open or closed, the mass of seething colours invaded my consciousness and called insistently for my attention.

Then suddenly . . . WHOOSH!! It happened unbelievably fast. One second I was outside the wall of colours, mesmerised and menaced by it. The next second . . . BAM! I was projected through it into some strange, pristine geometrical space on the other side of the wall.

High-speed machine beings

What was this place? Where was I? How had I got here? I hardly had time to ask any of the basic questions when things started happening and information started flowing.

The first thing was that I felt the presence of other intelligences with me in this weird geometrical room with transparent planes and impossible angles. What I could see were hints and suggestions of very rapid, purposive activity around the edges of the room, as though beings were there but moving so fast that they were a blur.

At this point I said out loud: 'I'm scared. This is a scary place. I want to get out of here.' I was shaking and trembling, partly with genuine fear, partly because I was suddenly feeling very cold. But I knew that I couldn't escape from any of this until the DMT let me go.

I paid attention to the fast-moving little entities zipping around the margins of the geometrical room as though they were running on rails around the circuit boards of a giant computer, and gradually the scene opened up to me. Still I could not see the beings, exactly, could

425

not make out definite form, but I felt a strong sense of communication with them. It dawned on me that this place I was in had something to do with teaching. I was here to learn and these high-speed little machine-like beings were my instruments of instruction.

At that moment, and for perhaps the next one or two minutes of real time, I was introduced – to the limited extent I was able to grasp it – to a true otherworld, organised completely differently from our own, where our laws of physics do not apply, where there are more than three dimensions, and where vast amounts of information have been stored. I had the strong sense that I was being shown around very, very quickly – 'this is how we do things here; this is how we are' – and that the purpose of the lesson was as a kind of induction to enable me to use their world properly. To that extent I was a bit like an immigrant, not knowing the language, being given a lecture by earnest local officals. They meant well and definitely had useful things to tell me. I meant well and definitely wanted to hear what they had to say. But we couldn't understand one another.

Towards the end of the experience I was shown a lozenge-shaped screen filled up with the same internested serpentine wave patterns in the same seething colours that I had seen on the way in. I felt drawn towards the patterns. Then . . . WHUUMPH! As suddenly as it had started, I was back on Channel Normal.

The first and most powerful emotion I felt was relief.

Script

I was now reduced to the powdery substance in the plastic bag. It wasn't identical to the resin I had finished. Perhaps it was older. Or perhaps it had been derived from a different species of DMT-producing plant. I started off with a third of it, but this was a mistake since – quite predictably – it got me only as far as the buzz.

I immediately filled up the pipe bowl with everything I had left, and by working round the edges of the pile of powder with the flame managed to get what felt like four good hits out of it.

I lay back, did some shivering and shuddering, groaned and moaned some more, felt mightily afraid again. This time I didn't get the colours, and I didn't find my way into any geometrical otherworldly rooms. Instead a different but equally purposive and meaningful communication aimed directly at me started to come my way.

The first thing I noticed was that there was a thick, ivory-coloured, organic-looking tube running horizontally across approximately the lower third of my visual field. Then black lines faded into view on the surface of the tube and began to move and rearrange themselves in ordered vertical and horizontal registers and in chaotic spirals and zig-zags. Very often strings of almost recognisable numbers and letters would appear, but just as frequently I would see sections of script from languages that were completely unknown to me – sometimes expressed in what looked like hieroglyphs, picture writing, or signs. Constantly shifting, sorting and juggling like a computer programme running through a thousand different alphabets in an instant, the lines themselves seemed to come alive at certain moments and to behave in a way that reminded me of small, diligent mechanical ants and spiders.

Then the display changed in the blink of an eye and it wasn't simple monochrome lines any more but pairs of colourful writhing snakes wrapped around one another, drawn down to a minute, submicroscopic scale, as though I were being allowed to peer deep into the nucleus of a cell and to witness the dance of DNA – the ultimate 'Master of Transformations'.

What did it all mean? What was I being told here? Why was I being shown this? Behind the interwined helices I just had time to notice that the display of numbers and letters had started rolling again before . . . WHOOMPH! ZAP!

I had smoked DMT and survived.

CHAPTER EIGHTEEN

Amongst the Machine Elves

My experience with DMT was qualitatively different from the realms and beings ayahuasca introduced me to. For whereas the ayahuasca worlds seemed rich, luxurious, and abundant in the transformations of organic and supernatural life, DMT brought me to a world – or to some aspect of a world – that appeared from the outset to be *highly artificial, constructed, inorganic, and in essence technological.*

Perhaps this was not so very far apart from the technological props that spirits, fairies and aliens have always been linked to – the circular dance, flying saucers, flying shields, etc., etc. Moreover, as we'll see, a number of the volunteers in Rick Strassman's DMT project at the University of New Mexico did report experiences that closely paralleled some elements of my ayahuasca visions. Still, nothing that I personally encountered under ayahuasca was anything like the transparent geometrical space into which DMT projected me on the first of my two trips. With its sense of intelligent little entities scurrying around on printed circuit boards stuffing vast quantities of incomprehensible data into my brain, it had the impact of a technological array that had been created explicitly to give very rapid courses of instruction in complex information.

To be more specific, the technology of the room seemed to be about displaying some sort of *recording* that had been set in playback mode by the arrival of my consciousness. It seemed to me to be a very powerful and special kind of recording, one that was *interactive* beyond the wildest dreams of today's computer programmers. It would adjust its output according to the psychology, habitual perceptions and culture of each individual plugging into it, and could be played slow or fast, again dependent on interactive feedback.

I was a panicked subject, inexperienced in the use of mental technology and tuned in to Channel DMT only for a few moments. Recalling the scene now, I feel that when my consciousness was in that room – wherever or whatever it was – I behaved like a terrified animal that had inadvertently blundered into a machine shop. My disrupted hold on reality, my utter vertigo at being in so alien and unexpected a space, and my deep-seated fear at the presence of non-human intelligences caused me to thrash about in panic in a full-scale fight-or-flight reaction and prevented me from observing and trying to assess the set-up that confronted me.

Nevertheless, I came out of the experience with the weird feeling that enormous amounts of data had been transferred to me. It's a strange thing to say but I remained thoroughly aware for a long while afterwards of all this new data – just as one might be aware of the presence of a massive new file suddenly downloaded on to the hard disk of a computer. And just as it is possible to download a file but impossible to open it unless we have the right software, I found that what I had received during my DMT sessions was a great deal of information that I simply could not 'read'. Whether I would in due course learn to read it was another matter, but for now I had what felt like a million gigabytes of raw binary code awaiting my attention and could understand none of it.

So part of the experience was this continual vast flow of information. But the other part – though I have only the haziest recall of their appearance – concerned the entities that presented or channelled this information to me during my first trip. What I remember most of all about them, anyway, was not their appearance but their *intelligence* – which struck me immediately as utterly different in its emotional temperature from contact with human intelligence. It felt more like being in the presence of big-brained robots than people – robots who probed and tested me for my reactions and adjusted the volume and tone of the data-flow accordingly. Moreover, their exclusive function seemed to be to show stuff to me – *indeed, to put on a show for me* – often in a rather entertaining or amusing way, leaping about through six dimensions, and uncovering panels of moving patterns before my eyes with a certain flourish as though they had pulled off a very clever trick that they were pleased with. I was sure that they had been in the room before I entered it, that they remained in it after I left it and that they were, in short, part of its basic equipment. Indeed, I imagined the entire interactive ensemble falling instantly into 'sleep' mode the moment the DMT ran out and I was hauled back to Channel Normal.

Machine realms

My experience of being brought into an otherworldly space that was distinctly technological in character was widely shared by the volunteers in Rick Strassman's project. This is what Jeremiah had to say after receiving an injection of DMT at the intensely psychoactive dose (for this extremely potent substance) of 0.4 milligrams per kilogram of bodyweight – the highest dose available under Strassman's study:

> It's a different world. Amazing instruments. Machine-type things . . . I was in a big room . . . There was one big machine in the centre, with round conduits, almost writhing – not like a snake, more in a technical manner. The conduits were not open at the end, They were solid blue-grey tubes, made of plastic? The machine felt as if it was rewiring me, reprogramming me . . . I observed some of the results on that machine, maybe from my brain. It was a little frightening, almost unbearably intense.[1]

Other volunteers reported seeing the 'inner workings' of machines on their DMT trips and 'inside a computer's boards',[2] and on the final dose of a four-dose tolerance study, Sara suddenly announced:

> I always knew we weren't alone in the universe. I thought that the only way to encounter them is with bright lights and flying saucers in outer space. It never occurred to me to actually encounter them in our own inner space. I thought the only things we could encounter were things in our personal sphere of archetypes and mythology. I expected spirit

guides and angels, not alien life forms . . . I saw some equipment or something . . . It looked like machinery.[3]

Carnivals and clowns

The peculiar impression I'd come away with of a 'show' being put on for me by machinelike mannequins – who I might easily have construed as 'clowns', or 'elves' – and of information or data being transferred, was also reported quite frequently by Rick Strassman's DMT volunteers. Marsha had this to say when she returned to normal consciousness after a DMT session at the high dose of 0.4 mg per kg:

> You know what happened? I was on a merry-go-round! There were all these dolls in 1890s outfits, life-sized, men and women . . . They were all whirling around me on tiptoes . . . And there were some clowns, flitting in and out, not really the main characters, but busier, somehow more aware of me than the mannequins.[4]

At the same dose Cassandra reported:

> Something took my hand and yanked me. It seemed to say, 'Let's go!' Then I started flying through an intense circus-like environment. I've never been that out of body before. First there was an itchy feeling where the drug went in. We went through a maze at an incredibly fast pace. I say 'we' because it seemed like I was accompanied. It was cool. There was a crazy circus sideshow – just extravagant. It's hard to describe. They looked like Jokers. They were almost performing for me. They were funny looking, bells on their hats, big noses. However, I had the feeling they could turn on me, a little less than completely friendly.[5]

Chris:

> They were trying to show me as much as possible. They were communicating in words. They were like clowns, or jokers or jesters or imps. There were just so many of them doing their funny little thing.[6]

Sara:

> I was scared, but I kept telling myself, 'Relax, surrender, embrace.' Then
> I saw what I can only describe as a Las Vegas casino type of scene, all
> flashing and whirling lights . . . Then . . . I 'flew' on and saw clowns
> performing . . . animated clowns . . .'[7]

Given DMT's crucial role in the psychoactivity of ayahuasca, it is
perhaps predictable that the South American brew also sometimes
seems to tune the brain to the strange 'receiver wavelength' of pure
DMT – very far from Channel Normal – in which the entities encountered quite frequently appear in the guise of clowns against a
background of carnivals or circuses. This is not to say that the ayahuasca
and DMT experiences are identical; on the contrary, I have been
careful to emphasise that they are not. The reader will recall that
ayahuasca contains other psychoactive alkaloids as well, notably harmaline, that extend the 'trip' to several hours in duration (rather than the
20 minutes that is typical for pure DMT). Nevertheless, Benny
Shanon, Professor of Psychology at the Hebrew University in
Jerusalem, reports that across a sample of several hundred individuals
whose ayahuasca experiences he has documented, 'The frequency of
facilities pertaining to amusement parks in the visions is, it seems to
me, disproportionately high. Especially noted are carousels and Ferris
Wheels.'[8]

As an example of this, Michael Harner, an American anthropologist who did his fieldwork in the Amazon in the early 1960s, saw what
he described as 'a supernatural carnival of demons' on the night that
he first drank ayahuasca.[9]

In Chapter Sixteen I reported the case of a group of children in
the United States who had certainly *not* been drinking ayahuasca but
who claimed to have been transported to the sky by a UFO that had
appeared to them initially in the guise of 'a booth at a carnival in
which aliens disguised as humans asked if they wanted to go on a
journey'.[10] In the same chapter the reader will also find the story of
another sighting by schoolchildren. Aged between eight and ten years,
these were English kids who saw a group of about sixty small beings

dressed in blue tops, yellow tights and jester-style caps with a bobble on the end. Although reportedly driving around in little cars that travelled at high speed and could jump soundlessly over obstacles, the overall style and appearance of the beings was not at all modern or technological. Drawings were done of them by the children at the time, and in these they very closely resemble fairies, imps, elves, dwarves or clowns as they might have been portrayed in the Middle Ages.[11]

In Chapter Twelve we met Maria Sabina, a Mazatec Indian shaman who practised in the village of Huatla de Jimenez in Mexico in the 1950s. I reported the story of the 'big Book with many written pages' that she claimed to have been shown by a spirit during one of her psilocybin-induced trances, and I drew the comparison with similar books that have been shown to UFO abductees by beings they presume to be aliens. Thanks to ethnographers who were sometimes allowed to be present, and who made recordings and transcriptions, a large number of the sacred chants that Maria Sabina used in her 'mushroom *veladas*' (all-night shamanic healing vigils) have survived. It is of interest that these include frequent mention of clowns and that Maria often referred to the hallucinogenic mushrooms themselves as 'little clowns'.

On one night when she consumed 13 pairs of *Psilocybe mexicana*, she described them as 'Thirteen superior whirlwinds. Thirteen whirlwinds of the atmosphere. Thirteen clowns. Thirteen personalities.'[12] Later during the same *velada*, the transcript tells us that Maria cried out: 'Woman lord of clowns am I, Woman lord of the holy clown am I.'[13] And towards morning: 'Woman chief of clowns am I . . . Woman of the holy clown am I.'[14]

On another occasion, while giving her life story to the American anthropologist Joan Halifax, Maria recalled the time when she first consumed the hallucinogenic mushrooms and began her career as a shaman:

My soul was coming out of my body and was going toward the world that I did not know but of which I had only heard talk. It was a world like this one, full of sierras, of forests, of rivers. But there were also other things – beautiful homes, temples, golden palaces. And there was my sister, who had come with me, and the mushrooms, who were waiting for me – mushrooms that were children and dwarfs dressed like clowns . . .[15]

For Maria Sabina these hallucinated experiences under the influence of psilocybin were unquestionably real even if they took place in a world that she had never encountered before and that was not accessible to her in her normal state of consciousness. For most Western scientists, on the other hand, the otherworld Maria believed she had entered and the 'dwarfs dressed as clowns' that she saw there cannot possibly have been real because it is known that she did not go anywhere during her *veladas* but remained very much physically present throughout. Like Rick Strassman's volunteers 40 years later, who never left their hospital beds, it seems that the receiver wavelength of the Mazatec shaman's brain had been temporarily returned to pick up broadcasts from Channel DMT – and since psilocybin is closely related to DMT, as we've seen, this need not surprise us.

But what exactly is this 'channel' and why should millions of years of physical evolution have equipped us to experience encounters with beings who look like clowns when the level of a hormone that is already naturally present in our brains is boosted above a certain threshold? Also, and this is not a small point, where did the idea for clowns come from in the first place? Were the visions of carnival-type figures seen by Strassman's subjects, Maria Sabina, Michael Harner and others influenced by strictly modern and culturally contingent television and circus spectaculars? Or is it possible that the direction of influence really flows the other way and that the inspiration for the earliest clowns came from visions and hallucinations seen in altered states of consciousness – whether entered spontaneously or under the influence of DMT-linked hallucinogens? We know that at least as far back as ancient Greece, a land rich in psychoactive plants, stage plays, farces and mimes frequently featured performances by dwarves and children dressed up in ways quite similar to modern circus buffoons.[16] Before that the history of such theatrical figures is obscure – as well it might be if they had emerged from occult realms that were originally accessible only in visions.

Paradigm wars

It is impossible for Western science as it is presently structured to give serious consideration to the shamanic explanation of experiences like those of Maria Sabina and Rick Strassman's volunteers, and indeed of the experiences that I myself have had under the influence of hallucinogens. This is not because the way that shamans explain reality has ever been falsified. Nor is it because there is anything inherently weak, faulty or illogical about their world view. The reason is simply that the opposing materialist paradigm, upon which all the progress and achievements of Western technology have been built, would face catastrophic implosion if the shamans were ever proved right.

According to the shamanic explanation, when Maria Sabina, Rick Strassman's volunteers and I consumed hallucinogens, our bodies remained in the material world while the 'plant spirits' temporarily liberated some aspect of our consciousness to travel in other, non-physical realms and to interact with intelligences there. It is perhaps a sign of how profoundly Strassman's research has changed his own world view as a scientist that he refers to DMT as 'the spirit molecule' and is prepared to contemplate the possibility that humans have evolved a relationship with it precisely because it 'leads us to spiritual realms':[17]

> These worlds are usually invisible to us and our instruments, and are not accessible using our normal state of consciousness. However, just as likely as the theory that these worlds exist 'only in our minds' is that they are, in reality, 'outside us' and freestanding. If we simply change our brain's receiving abilities, we can comprehend and interact with them.[18]

Strassman is to be commended for exploring such ideas. But he himself would be the first to point out that it was partly because of his subjects' interactions with what they took to be the inhabitants of other realms – and because it was difficult to describe the therapeutic benefit of such experiences according to the norms and expectations of Western healthcare – that he eventually decided to give up his potentially explosive research project.[19] He was, he explained frankly, 'unprepared for the overwhelmingly frequent reports of contact with beings. They challenged my view of the brain and reality.'[20]

Looking back on the project in 2001, he elaborated on this point:

When reviewing my bedside notes I continually feel surprise in seeing how many of our volunteers 'made contact' with 'them' or other beings. At least half did in one form or another. Research subjects used expressions like 'entities', 'beings', 'aliens', 'guides', and 'helpers' to describe them. The 'life-forms' looked like clowns, reptiles, mantises, bees, spiders, cacti, and stick figures. It is still startling to see my written records of comments like 'There were these beings', 'I was being led', 'They were on me fast'. It's as if my mind refuses to accept what's there in black and white. It may be that I have such a hard time with these stories because they challenge the prevailing world view, and my own.[21]

Return of the fairies and elves

Quite a number of the encounters reported by Strassman's volunteers after their DMT trips were with fairy-like or elf-like beings – sometimes explicitly named as such in the reports. For example Cassandra spoke of meeting 'the DMT elves . . . They were jovial and they had a great time giving me the experience of being loved.'[22] Eight minutes into a high-dose 0.4 mg-per-kg session, however, Karl had a slightly less friendly (and certainly more perplexing) encounter with the same type of beings:

That was real strange. There were a lot of elves. They were prankish, ornery, maybe four of them appeared at the side of a stretch of interstate highway I travel regularly . . . They held up placards, showing me these incredibly beautiful, complex, swirling geometric scenes in them. One of them made it impossible for me to move. There was no issue of control; they were totally in control. They wanted me to look![23]

After her second dose on the day when she took part in the four-dose tolerance study of DMT, Sara reported:

> This time the aggressive spinning colours were almost familiar. Suddenly, a pulsating 'entity' appeared in the patterns. It sounds weird to describe it as 'Tinkerbell-like' [i.e. fairy-like]. It was trying to coax me to go with it. At first I was reluctant, because I didn't know about finding my way back. By the time I made up my mind I did want to go with it, I could tell the drug was starting to wear off, and I wasn't 'high' enough to follow it. I told it, 'I can't go with you now. See, they want me back.' It didn't seem to be offended and, in fact, 'followed' me back until I sensed it had reached its boundary. I felt like it was saying goodbye . . .[24]

Sean also participated in the tolerance study, receiving four 0.3 mg/kg doses of DMT at hourly intervals. During the first session the following extraordinary interactive vision unfolded:

> I watched a low-lying city . . . on the far horizon mutate through a variety of colours and hues, with many ill-defined 'things' floating in the air above the city. Then I noticed a middle-aged female, with a pointed nose and light greenish skin, sitting off to my right, watching this changing city with me. She had her right hand on a dial that seemed to control the panorama we were watching. She turned slightly toward me and asked, 'What else would you like?' I answered telepathically, 'Well, what else have you got? I have no idea what you can do.' Then she stood up, walked up to my forehead, touched it and warmed it up, and then used a sharp object to open up a panel in my right temple, releasing a tremendous amount of pressure. This made me feel much better than I'd felt before, even though I realised that I'd felt fine in the first place.[25]

As well as the presence of the green-skinned, witch-like fairy, there is more than a hint in this strange account of other themes the reader is already familiar with from earlier chapters – 'shamanic surgery', for example (during which initiates frequently believe their heads have

437

been penetrated or opened), and the painful but often beneficial operations that aliens supposedly carry out on abductees.[26]

Playrooms

In Chapter Thirteen we saw that UFO abductees are frequently brought to so-called 'child-presentation rooms', to rooms where they are required to play with hybrid babies, and to rooms where they are required to nurse hybrid babies. Under the influence of DMT Strassman's subjects did not report seeing babies but did report finding themselves in spaces that seemed like playrooms or nurseries.

'There were some scenes or forms like in a nursery,' said Gabe after receiving a high dose of 0.4mg/kg:

> There were cribs and different animals, vibrant. I went to a childhood scene, or feeling. It was like I was in a stroller, kid images. It was sort of scary. I can't describe it. I could draw it maybe. It was like being in a room, as a child, with a stroller. There were cartoonlike people in the room, but they weren't what I wanted to see.[27]

Soon after he had received his 0.4 mg/kg dose Aaron found himself – or at any rate his consciousness – in a sealed room. Just like so many of the featureless rooms to which UFO abductees say they are taken, and like the transparent geometrical room that my first dose of DMT projected me into, it lacked any obvious entrance or exit:

> There are no doors, there's nothing to go through. It's either over here – it's dark; or over there – there are images. You just can't do anything with them. It was Mayan hieroglyphics. It was interesting. The hieroglyphics turned into a room, like I was a child. There were toys there, like I was a kid. It was like that. It was cute.[28]

Also on the high dose, 50-year-old Jeremiah discovered that his consciousness had vaulted into a similar room:

> It was a nursery. A high-tech nursery with a single Gumby, three feet

tall, attending me. I felt like an infant. Not a human infant, but an infant relative to the intelligences represented by the Gumby. It was aware of me, but not particularly concerned. Sort of detached concern, like a parent would feel looking into a playpen at his one-year-old lying there. As I went into it I heard a sound: *hmmm*. Then I heard two to three male voices talking. I heard one of them say, 'He's arrived.'[29]

Tales of the alien laboratory

The playrooms are the first of many strong and obvious similarities between the experiences of UFO abductees and the hallucinations of injected DMT. In the accounts given above, for example, it is already clear that the subjects frequently felt they had no control at all over the places their consciousness was being taken to. That was exactly how I felt too, and we've seen in earlier chapters that this is a common feeling and experience amongst UFO abductees – and, of course, amongst those abducted by fairies as well. Moreover, further study of the hundreds of pages of statements made by Strassman's volunteers reveals an overall atmosphere, setting, cast of characters, *and sequence of procedures* at the heart of their DMT experiences that overlaps to a remarkable degree with the typical progression of UFO abductions.

After a high-dose session of 0.4 mg/kg Lucas reported:

There is nothing that can prepare you for this. There is a sound, a *bzzzz*. It started off getting louder and louder and faster and faster. I was coming on and coming on and then POW! There was a space station below me and to my right. There were at least two presences, one on either side of me, guiding me to a platform. I was also aware of many entities inside the space station – automatons, androidlike creatures . . . They were doing some kind of routine technological work and paid no attention to me. In a state of overwhelmed confusion, I opened my eyes.[30]

It is exactly the same overwhelmed confusion that many UFO abductees feel when they are floated up threads or beams of light to flying saucers in which they first see ranks of robotic little creatures busily working on incomprehensible tasks, and are then frequently taken to or simply find themselves in an examination room where medical procedures are performed on them.

'I was in a white room experiencing certain emotions and feelings that gave me a feeling of co-reality,' reported Eli, one of Strassman's volunteers, after receiving a dose of 0.4 mg/kg of DMT. 'The white room consisted of light and space. There were cubes stacked with icons on the surfaces . . . It was light but there was a lot of other information coming in.'[31]

Aaron:

There was no turning back. After a moment or two I became aware of something happening to my left. I saw a psychedelic, Day-Glo-coloured space that approximated a room whose walls and floor had no clear separations or edges. It was throbbing and pulsing electrically. Rising in front of 'me' was a podium-like table. It seemed that some presence was dealing/serving something to me. I wanted to know what it was and 'sensed' the reply that I had no business there. The presence was not hostile, just somewhat annoyed and brusque.[32]

Such non-hostile but annoyed and brusque alien presences are of course frequently encountered by UFO abductees – who generally describe them as somewhat taller than the drone-like Greys. These beings are usually also in charge of the bizarre surgical procedures to which abductees are subject during which they believe that their bodies have been cut open, pierced and probed and that implants have been placed in their eyes, brains, arms, spinal columns, or other parts of their anatomy. We cannot always be 100 per cent certain that abductees' bodies did *not* in fact go to the places where their consciousness went – because there are rarely witnesses to report one way or another. But we do know for sure that the bodies of the volunteers in Rick Strassman's project stayed in the hospital room when he injected them with DMT. Nonetheless, they too experienced probes, implants and surgery.

'There were clinical researchers probing into my mind,' reported Jim during one of his DMT experiences. 'There were sort of long fibre-optic things that they were putting into my pupils.' Jim knew that his body could not actually be experiencing this invasive eye procedure because it was lying safely in a hospital bed in the University of New Mexico. His mind was experiencing it, however, and – paradoxically – seemed to have acquired some sort of bodily form of its own in whatever dimension the procedure was taking place. Jim was matter-of-fact about all this in a way that those who believe they have been abducted by aliens rarely are. 'It was pretty weird,' he said, 'but I figured it was just the drug.'[33]

Ben stayed silent for 36 minutes during his high-dose DMT session, then reported how he had arrived in another reality and been received by the beings who inhabited it:

> There were four or five of them. They were on me fast . . . They weren't benevolent but they weren't non-benevolent. They probed, they really probed. They seemed to know time was limited. They wanted to know what I, this being who had shown up, was doing. I didn't answer. They knew. Once they decided I was okay, they went about their business . . .[34]

A few moments later he added:

> I felt like something was inserted into my left forearm, right here, about three inches below this chain-link tattoo on my wrist. It was long. There were no reassurances with the probe. Simply business.[35]

Dimitri was well aware that his DMT experience resembled the publicly reported experiences of UFO-abductees. The instant the injection took effect:

> WHAM! I felt like I was in an alien laboratory . . . A sort of landing bay or recovery area. There were beings . . . They had a space ready for me. They weren't as surprised as I was . . . There was one main creature, and he seemed to be behind it all, overseeing everything. The others were orderlies, or dis-orderlies. They activated a sexual circuit, and I was flushed with an amazing orgasmic energy . . . When I was coming out, I couldn't help but think 'aliens'.[36]

441

Sexual bonding

The reader will recall that there is very frequently a sexual element to the contacts that take place between aliens and humans during UFO abductions, and Dimitri was by no means unique amongst Strassman's DMT subjects in reporting similar experiences. Of particular interest is the well-established pattern, noted in previous chapters, of the UFO abductee who establishes close, loving and often sexual bonds with a particular alien figure sometimes explicitly identified as belonging to the opposite sex. Dimitri again:

> These beings were friendly. I had a bond with one of them. It was about to say something to me or me to it, but we couldn't quite connect. It was almost a sexual bond . . . I was filled with feelings of love for them. Their work definitely had something to do with my presence. Exactly what remains a mystery.[37]

A very similar story was told by Rex after a low dose of DMT (0.2 mg/kg):

> The beings were there and they were doing something to me, experimenting on me . . . There was a female. I felt like I was dying, then she reappeared and reassured me . . . When I was with her I had a deep feeling of relaxation and tranquillity . . . She had an elongated head.[38]

Rex also reported other interesting details:

> There were rays of psychedelic yellow light coming out of the face of the reassuring entity. She was trying to communicate with me. She seemed very concerned for me, and the effects I was experiencing due to her attempts at communicating. There was something outlined in green, right in front of me and above me here. It was rotating and doing things. She was showing it to me, it seemed like, how to use this thing. It resembled a computer terminal. I believe she wanted me to try to communicate with her through that device. But I couldn't figure it out.[39]

It is almost as though we are the aliens to the inhabitants of the DMT world. But when we make unscheduled visits to their dimension – not as abductees but as psychedelic voyagers – do they have some way of knowing we are coming? We will return to the disturbing implications of this question in due course.

Insects with an agenda

One of Rex's other DMT sessions included a terrifying, 'demonic' encounter with 'insect creatures'. Elements of his description, and a similar description given separately by Aaron, remind me of nothing I saw in my two DMT sessions – but who knows what I would have seen next if I'd had more resin to burn? What Rex's and Aaron's descriptions do remind me very strongly of, however, is the being who most frightened me in my ayahuasaca visions (see Chapter Three) and who I described in my notebook at the time as having the look of 'some sort of huge insect with humanoid features'. This is what Rex told Strassman:

> When I was first going under there were these insect creatures all around me. They were clearly trying to break through. I was fighting letting go of who I am or was. The more I fought, the more demonic they became, probing into my psyche and being. I finally started letting go of all parts of myself, as I could no longer keep so much of me together . . . They were interested in emotion. As I was holding on to my last thought, that God equals love, they said, 'Even here? Even here?' I said, 'Yes, of course.'[40]

UFO abductees frequently report encountering aliens in the form of insects or of insect-humanoids. We've seen examples of this in previous chapters and parallel examples of the insect-like spirit beings encountered by shamans – such as the 'bee-people' of the Warao of eastern Venezuela,[41] or Kaggen, the mantis god of the San of southern Africa.[42] The reader will recall that part of the hallucinogenic mission of the Warao shaman is to find a 'beautiful bee-girl' and have sex with her repeatedly in the 'round white house' in the sky where these insect spirits dwell.[43] Interestingly, Rex's negative alien-insect DMT experience also developed in a sexual direction:

> They were still there but I was making love to them at the same time. They feasted as they made love to me. I don't know if they were male or female or something else, but it was extremely alien, though not necessarily unpleasant. The thought came to me with certainty that they were manipulating my DNA, changing its structure. And then it started fading. They didn't want me to go.[44]

In a later DMT session Rex (like the Warao shamans) experienced his new insect friends as part of a bee-like social structure:

> I was in a huge infinite hive. There were insect-like intelligences everywhere. They were in a hypertechnological space . . . They wanted me to join them, to stay with them. I was tempted . . . There was another one helping me . . . It was very intelligent. It wasn't at all humanoid. It wasn't a bee but it seemed like one.[45]

During his first high dose of DMT Aaron reported seeing:

> a mandala-like series of visuals, fleur-de-lis type visions. Then an insect-like thing got right into my face, hovering over me as the drug was going in. The thing sucked me out of my head into outer space. It was clearly outer space, a black sky with millions of stars. I was in a very large waiting room, or something. It was very long. I felt observed by the insectlike-thing and others like it. Then they lost interest.[46]

Aaron concluded that the experience was 'like being possessed' by an 'alien-type, insectoid, not-quite-pleasant' entity:

> There is sense of someone, or something else, there taking control. It's like you have to defend yourself against them, whoever they are, but they certainly are there. I'm aware of them and they're aware of me. It's like they have an agenda.[47]

Same beings, same experiences, same worlds

When ayahuasca brought me face to face in the Amazon with what I construed as an insect-humanoid alien who wanted to abduct me, I know that I felt exactly the same sense of demonic attack and psychic intrusion that both Rex and Aaron described, the same sense of an agenda aimed at me, and the same need to defend myself.

Rex, Aaron and I therefore represent a nice little micro-mystery all of our own – three people who do not know each other but who both experienced very similar 'non-real' encounters with very similar 'non-real' beings. At first glance it looks as though the mystery should be easily solved, since all three of us had received psychoactive doses of DMT immediately prior to these encounters: in my case together with a cocktail of other alkaloids delivered by the ayahuasca brew; in the case of Aaron and Rex in pure form and delivered by injection. But even with DMT as an important common factor, current theories of the way the human brain supposedly concocts hallucinations cannot even begin to explain the shared details and characters in the peculiar visions that confronted us. We are, after all, completely separate individuals who have never been in contact with one another, who come from different cultures and backgrounds, and who received DMT a decade apart in starkly contrasting settings (the jungle in my case; the University of New Mexico for Aaron and Rex). It follows that if what David Lewis-Williams calls Stage 3 hallucinations are 'culturally controlled' and 'derived from memory', as orthodox scientists teach,[48] then there is simply no way that Rex, Aaron and I, with so little in common, could have experienced such similar encounters with unpleasant and intrusive 'alien-type insectoids'.

The problem is compounded when we remember that several of Rick Strassman's other volunteers also encountered these alien-type insectoids on their DMT trips, and that encounters with insectoids are also very commonly reported by UFO abductees who have never taken DMT in their lives. I stress again that present theories about hallucinations cannot explain the recurrence of such complex common themes amongst such disparate groups of people – and doubly so when some of them are drugged and some are not.

As well as the insectoids, we've seen that Strassman's volunteers reported meeting more obviously humanoid beings during their DMT trips, who they often described as small-statured with epithets such as 'the little presences',[49] 'the small gremlins'[50] and, in one memorable case, as a three-foot-tall 'Gumby'.[51] Frequently set in an operating-theatre-type environment, and featuring surgical procedures, implants, etc., it must be obvious to any reader of this book that the volunteers' DMT-occasioned encounters with those little humanoids follow very much the same general pattern as UFO-abductees' encounters with aliens. There are differences, but the overall similarity of tone is striking.

'They were hurting me, they were not human'

Confronted by this data, the sceptic might very reasonably respond that once again there is no mystery. By the 1990s when Strassman was doing his research, so-called alien abductions had received more than three decades of massive publicity. All of his volunteers there-fore must have been familiar with alien and UFO imagery from popular culture and simply dredged up some of these stored images and notions during their hallucinating state. The same would go for my own alien visions under ayahuasca, and the machine intelligences that commun-icated with me under DMT – not real perceptions of usually invisible entities, not even tremendous feats of the imagination, just a spewing-out of internalised tabloid clichés.

But Strassman has a complete answer to all such arguments.

In the 1950s, a decade before any UFO abductions had ever been publicly reported anywhere in the world, a Hungarian medical doctor named Stephen Szara gave DMT to large numbers of human subjects in trials to assess its possible utility as a psychiatric drug. Similar research was also done in the United States during the distinctly pre-abduction 1950s by William Turner MD and Sidney Merlis MD. All these investigators asked their subjects to report their experiences during their DMT trips and, as Strassman points out, their replies were 'remarkable in their foreshadowing of the stories we were going to hear almost forty years later'.[52]

On 30 April 1956, for example, Szara's patient KV was injected intramuscularly with a massive 1 mg/kg dose of DMT. After 32 minutes she reported the characteristically shamanic experience, also shared by some UFO abductees as the reader will recall, of feeling that her heart had been removed. At 38 minutes she proclaimed: 'I saw strange creatures, dwarfs or something, they were black and moved about.' She also announced that she was flying, 'as if I were floating between earth and sky'.[53]

Similarly, on 21 June 1957, one of the American DMT subjects reported a characteristic experience of both UFO and fairy abductions when she found herself 'In a big place, and they were hurting me. They were not human. They were horrible.'[54]

In 1966, a few years after UFO abductions had begun to be publicised, but long before an 'insectoid' image of the aliens had become established, the famous psychedelic guru Timothy Leary took DMT. Two minutes into the experience he described what he saw: 'There squatting next to me are two magnificent insects . . . skin burnished, glowing metallic, with hammered jewels inlaid.' A few moments later he found himself exploring 'A huge, grey-white mountain cliff, moving, pocked by little caves and in each cave a band of radar-antennae, elf-like insects merrily working away.'[55]

That 'alien-like' and 'insectoid alien-type' entities should have popped up in scientific papers in the 1950s and 1960s doing exactly the same kinds of things to hallucinating DMT subjects as aliens would much later become famous for doing to abductees is extremely significant. It certainly rules out any simplistic attempt to derive the alien imagery in the reports of Strassman's volunteers from the mass culture of the 1990s and makes it more likely that the popular imagery itself is in some way derived from visionary experiences.

Living with an endogenous psychedelic

On the basis of all this, therefore – and compressed into a nutshell – Rick Strassman's theory is that people who believe they have been abducted by aliens are those whose brains from time to time spontaneously overproduce DMT.[56] We are dealing here with what has rightly been described as an 'endogenous human psychedelic',[57] so naturally when its overproduction exceeds a certain threshold we can understand why its effects might be virtually indistinguishable from those experienced by normal subjects like Strassman's volunteers who had been injected with the drug – or for that matter by shamans who had consumed it in plant form.

Indeed, in my view Strassman's simple, elegant theory does most parsimoniously and satisfactorily explain many aspects of the alien abduction phenomenon and of the closely interlinked phenomena of fairies and spirits that we have explored in Part III. But it is important to assert, and for the reader to be very clear, that Strassman is not a reductionist. Nowhere does he insist that these extraordinary experiences are simply *caused* by an increased level of DMT in the brain, only that the experiences are 'made possible' by the DMT.[58] And although he professes embarrassment and consternation at volunteers' numerous reports of contact with what they took to be other 'freestanding realities', we have seen already that Strassman is with Huxley, Hoffman and James in strongly advocating the 'receiver' model of the brain. He therefore makes a point of remaining open to the possibility that the beings encountered on these trips – and by UFO abductees – are absolutely real but normally opaque to us until our 'receiver wavelength' is reset by DMT or other similar hallucinogenic molecules.

Entoptic phenomena

In a few of the accounts of their DMT experiences cited above, the reader may have noted that Strassman's volunteers refer to visual effects such as 'complex, swirling geometric scenes' and 'aggressive spinning colours'. These are entoptic phenomena of the kind that appear in all three of the stages of trance envisaged in David Lewis-Williams' neuropsychological explanation of cave art. Moreover, further study of the volunteers' reports turns up many more references to imagery that is clearly and unmissably entoptic, sometimes standing alone as in Stage 1 and sometimes combined with complex 'iconic' Stage 3 hallucinations.

On a relatively low dose of DMT, Vladan reported: 'There were visuals at the peak, soft and geometric. There were 3-D circles and cones with shading. They moved a lot.'[59] Also on a low dose Rex described finding himself in the midst of 'creatures and machinery', and noted that 'there were brilliant psychedelic colours outlining the creatures and machinery' – a characteristic entoptic effect.[60] Similarly Saul experienced striking entoptic phenomena merging with fully iconic figures. He reported that 'complicated and beautiful geometric patterns' had overlaid his visual field. Out of these patterns the forms of beings emerged: 'I "stared" with my inner eyes, and we appraised each other. As they disappeared back into the torrent of colour, now beginning to fade, I could hear some sounds in the room. I knew I was coming down.'[61]

Other entoptic phenomena reported by Strassman's subjects are too numerous to list here but included, in no particular order, 'kaleido-scopic geometric patterns', 'beautiful, colourful pink cobwebs', 'tremendously intricate, tiny geometric colours, like being one inch from a colour television', 'tunnels', 'stairways', 'ducts', and 'a spinning golden disc'.[62] Flecks and dots of light 'shooting off in all directions'[63] were mentioned by many of the volunteers.

It provides further broad support for Strassman's theory that UFO abductees also report noticing identical entoptic phenomena at various points during their experiences. To cite just a few examples here, Patti Layne told researcher David Jacobs of seeing 'stars and lines, images, geometric things' during one of her abductions. 'Geometric images?' asked Jacobs. 'I guess,' Patti replied, 'they're like lines and dots, things like that.'[64] In other words, entoptic phenomena.

John Mack's patient Shiela saw something that looked like 'a huge, red stained-glass window with brown and fold lattice work separating the panes'.[65] This sounds like a construal of a classic entoptic lattice form. Anne, another of Mack's patients, sketched a specific entoptic pattern – very like the patterns known as 'meanders' drawn on cave walls and ceilings in the Upper Palaeolithic – that she had seen repeat-edly projected on to her visual field following her abduction experiences.[66]

Top, drawing by modern UFO abductee: 'When I turn the lights out at night, this has been the show for the past week. I can see it with my eyes closed as well as open.' (Mack, 1995, 308). Centre left and right, prehistoric 'meanders' – finger tracings on clay in the caves of Hornos de la Pena (Spain) and Gargas (France). Bottom, prehistoric 'meanders' on the ceiling of the cave of Altamira in Spain (Breuil, 1952).

And let's not forget the case of Carlos Diaz (see Chapter Twelve), who saw a UFO 'made of millions of small dots of light' floating over his head. He was baffled to find, when he tried to touch the object, that his 'hand went through the yellow light . . .'[67] In the next moments, the reader will recall, Carlos found that both he and the craft had been transported 'inside a cave that was lined with stalactites' and decorated with 'works of art'.[68]

Back to the caves

Hallucinating an entoptic UFO inside a painted cave, Carlos brings us back, quite appropriately, to the riddle with which we began this book, described by David Lewis-Williams as 'the greatest riddle of archaeology – how we became human and in the process began to make art and to practise what we call a religion'.[69] Indeed, the combination of entoptic phenomena with fully iconic figures was an important clue leading Lewis-Williams to formulate his neuropsychological theory in the first place, and to propose hallucinations seen in altered states of consciousness as the most likely inspiration for the extraordinary hidden art of the deep, dark caves of Upper Palaeolithic Europe.

'Owl-Man', the 'Sorcerer', 'Lion-Man', 'Bison-Man', 'Aurochs-Man' – the supreme images of the caves are unmistakably those of *supernatural* beings, of 'spirits'. Our ancestors depicted them as therianthropes and fully transformed animals because this is exactly how they encountered them in their visions, and how they continue to be construed and depicted to this day by the shamans of surviving hunter-gatherer cultures all around the world. In more complex and sophisticated societies the same entities are sometimes no longer thought of as spirits. Even in the guise of fairies and aliens, however, two of their most recent manifestations in the West, we've seen in earlier chapters that they are still shape-shifters and that they frequently appear in therianthropic and animal form.

I've made the case that what we are dealing with here are not multiple, different, very strange phenomena, but *a single very strange phenomenon*, truly Protean in its character, that has been construed in different ways by different cultures at different times, that cannot be pinned down anywhere in the material world, but that nevertheless behaves exactly as though it possesses an independent freestanding reality of its own. It is remarkable that this phenomenon has been so long-lived and that it has maintained its integrity and hidden consistency across the transformation that we have documented from spirits through fairies into aliens. It would be truly extraordinary, however, if it were found to have been at work not only in bizarre abductions and initiations, operations and implants, hybridisation programmes and interspecies love affairs, but in the dawn of art and religion – perhaps the very innovations that made us fully human and set us on our present evolutionary path.

Today such possibilities need no longer be left unexplored for lack of data. The close family resemblances that we have documented interlinking spirits, fairies, aliens, and the beings encountered on DMT trips suggest a completely new approach to the fundamental mystery of our past. By their very existence these family resemblances build bridges across the ages and invite us to make use of the unsettling data that modern scientists have gathered on aliens and the DMT beings as a means to assess the true significance, agenda and impact of the therianthropic spirits that so impressed our ancestors in the Upper Palaeolithic.

We have seen already that the modern research reveals remarkable consistencies across a range of supposedly 'non-real' experiences – consistencies that cannot be explained within the present scientific model of hallucinations. Moreover, when huge numbers of people over enormous periods of history from entirely unrelated cultures keep on experiencing the same 'unreal' things – as we know has consistently and continuously been the case – then perhaps the time has come for us to stop dismissing and discounting such visions and to seek out a proper explanation for them instead.

Dark matter, quantum worlds

One very plausible, and for me very persuasive, explanation, in the school of thought of Huxley, James and Hoffman, is that there do indeed exist 'separate, freestanding realities' – or 'parallel dimensions' of the kind quantum physics predicts – that vibrate at a different frequency to our own and thus are invisible to us *except when we approach them in altered states of consciousness*. These other realities seem to be inhabited by intelligent beings who are non-physical in our dimension – although they would apparently like to acquire permanent physical forms – and who have had a long-term interest in us, interfering in and manipulating human affairs in the guise of spirit guides, supernatural teachers, fairies and recently aliens. Perhaps it was even they, in the therianthropic forms they have continued to show to shamans ever since, who launched us on the path of modern behaviour just 40,000 or 50,000 years ago? After all, one of the key functions performed by such beings, in all their manifestations, has traditionally been initiation and the bestowal of wisdom on the human seeker during a hallucinated ordeal represented by the wounded man figure in one epoch, stories of shamanic surgery in another, and reports by abductees of alien operations today.

We've seen that Rick Strassman, for all his empirical caution, was ultimately obliged by his research to accept the possibility that DMT does provide our consciousness with access to real parallel dimensions. He speculates freely about this in his major work on the subject – *DMT: The Spirit Molecule*, published in 2001. 'It may be,' he writes, 'that DMT alters the characteristics of our brains' so that we are able to perceive what the physicists call 'dark matter' – the 95 per cent of the universe's mass that is known to exist but that at present remains invisible to all our senses and instruments.[70] Strassman devotes a good deal of attention to the concept of 'different levels of reality permeating and suffusing our own' and reminds us of the 'surprisingly common' reports by his volunteers that they were *expected* by the beings they encountered on their trips, and even 'welcomed back' when they returned again and again. But how could this be possible? 'How might these beings be even dimly aware of our presence if we normally don't have an inkling of theirs?' Warning that 'we're treading on extraordinarily thin ice', Strassman suggests:

Perhaps we are not dark for the denizens of dark matter, or parallel to those intelligent beings who have mastered quantum computing? We are limited to inferring these alternative realities exist by employing powerful mathematical treatment of massive amounts of experimental data. It may be that those who have evolved in different universes, or according to their own unique laws of physics, actually can observe us directly with their own senses or by using particular types of technology.[71]

So following this line of reasoning, I have no objection in principle to the possible free-standing other-dimensional existence of 'spirit worlds' and 'spirit beings' – at least as a working hypothesis. I'm also with Strassman on the notion that hallucinogens like DMT might allow us to undertake rational, targeted and repeated explorations of an infinity of such worlds that might hypothetically surround us in every direction though normally unseen. Indeed, it sometimes seems to me that the actual existence of parallel non-physical realms and beings is a far more plausible explanation than anything that orthodox scientists have so far offered us for the consistent story told in alien lore, fairy lore and spirit lore for as far back as anyone can remember.

Seeing DNA on DMT

On my second good dose of DMT, as well as a scrolling palimpsest of scripts, signs and numbers displayed on an ivory-coloured tube in the lower third of my visual field, I had seen the forms of serpents arranged in pairs each coiled into double helices – 'as though I were being allowed to peer deep into the nucleus of a cell and to witness the dance of DNA'.

When I looked back on the notes of my ayahuasca experiences in the Amazon (reported in Chapter Three), I found that I had experienced an almost identical vision there:

> snakes arrange themselves into patterns of interlaced wheels and spirals. Then they merge into one large mass and finally break apart into pairs of individuals that wind around each other like the DNA double helix.[72]

Double helix of serpents. Detail from a painting of an
ayahuasca vision by Peruvian shaman Pablo Amaringo

I reread the reports that Rick Strassman's volunteers had given of their
DMT experiences and found that many of them had also spoken of
DNA. In one case, already cited above, the reader will recall Rex's
insistence that the insect-beings he encountered had 'manipulated' his
DNA and 'changed its structure'.[73] Likewise Karl saw 'spirals of what
looked like DNA, red and green',[74] Cleo saw a 'spiral DNA-type thing
made out of incredibly bright cubes',[75] and Sara said:

> I felt the DMT release my soul's energy and push it through the DNA
> . . . There were spirals that reminded me of things I've seen in Chaco
> Canyon [an ancient rock-art site in Arizona]. Maybe that was DNA.
> Maybe the ancients knew that. The DNA is backed into the universe
> like space travel. One needs to travel without one's body. It's ridicu-
> lous to think about space travel in little ships.[76]

455

For Eli, the experience was eerily similar to my first DMT trip:

> like threads of words or DNA or something. They're all around here. They're everywhere . . . When I looked around it seemed like meaning or symbols were there. Some kind of core of reality where all meaning is stored. I burst into its main chamber.[77]

Likewise, Vladan was presented with symbols filled with meaning in an experience that was again close to mine:

> It was almost like looking at an alphabet, but it wasn't English. It was like a fantasy alphabet, a cross between runes and Russian or Arabic writing. It felt like there was some information in it, like it was data. It wasn't just random.[78]

Something supernatural about DNA?

If, hypothetically, one was the master of an astonishingly advanced biotechnology, and wished to record a vast amount of information in an indelible and as near as possible immortal form, then it would be difficult to think of a more suitable recording medium than DNA. For only DNA would stay the same through all the vicissitudes and transformations that evolution might bring about in the course of life on a planet, and if enough DNA were given over to this task then the genome of all living creatures would still be carrying copies of the original recording billions of years later. Moreover, although a certain amount is known about the 3 per cent of our DNA gathered up in our genes, nothing at all is known about the function of the other 97 per cent – so-called 'junk DNA'.[79]

What an ideal place to store data – in a bio-genetic system of truly 'supernatural' construction that already encodes the secret of life itself.

CHAPTER NINETEEN

Ancient Teachers in Our DNA?

Eyewitness reports of human encounters with 'supernatural beings' have been documented as far back as the painted caves of Upper Palaeolithic Europe 35,000 years ago and brought right up to date with bizarre accounts of abductions by aliens in the twenty-first century. Such reports include powerful common themes that we have explored in detail in Part III and that science is unable to explain. In particular we've seen the massive universality of the experience that spirits, fairies and aliens (though themselves taken to be non-physical or only quasi-physical in nature) are interested in interbreeding with men and women – an interest that *in every case* is said to have led to the production of hybrid offspring. Equally universal is the belief that supernaturals can and frequently do present themselves in the form of therianthropes – part human, part animal. The same widespread distribution applies to the 'wounded man' experience – whether construed as 'shamanic surgery' in hunter-gatherer societies, 'torture by fairies' in the European Middle Ages, or 'alien operations' today. Finally, let us not forget the astonishing range of unusual motifs that are shared by all three domains – for example dwarfish humanoids with large oblique eyes and oversized heads, the experience of climbing or floating up 'threads of light', and the experience of abductions to sky, cave and underwater settings.

It is striking that many of these same experiences can be reproduced in the minds of people who have consumed certain types of hallucinogens (or used non-drug trance techniques such as rhythmic

457

dancing, austerities and sensory deprivation) which temporarily reset the electrochemical balance of the brain. This can be made to happen quite reliably, even under laboratory conditions as we saw in Chapter Eighteen. We may therefore conclude that altered states of consciousness, which are themselves universals of human neurology, are fundamental to 'supernatural' encounters.

What remains to be discovered is the true status of the visions that we all see in such altered states. Are they simply quaint 'brain fiction'? Most mainstream scientists would say so – although they cannot explain why evolution should have installed identical, highly imaginative Gothic novelists in all our brains. Or could it be that these strange, complex, universal experiences with evolving storylines are in some way as *real* as those we take for granted in normal states of consciousness?

The reader knows already that I am not with mainstream science on this. I do not regard it as an a priori impossibility that spirit worlds and beings may in some significant sense be real. Nonetheless, just as my research seemed to be luring me inevitably towards that deeply anti-scientific conclusion, another theory that seemed to account equally well for all the anomalous evidence began to force itself upon me. This is the theory that DNA, the fundamental mechanism for the reproduction of all forms of life on earth, contains, or is driven by, intelligence – and that information originating with this intelligence can, under special circumstances, become accessible to our consciousness. If the information were in some way 'written' or recorded on DNA that we all share, and if nature has designed us to access this information in trance states by means of our shared human neurology, then all the otherwise inexplicable commonalities, and all the universal motifs, imagery and phenomena that are experienced by different hallucinating individuals would make perfect sense.

Clever entities

It's good to be clear. By 'information', I am not referring to the ordered and highly specific chemical instructions that DNA gives to our cells to assemble long chains of amino acids into proteins. This is, itself, a miraculous process that goes on every minute of every day and that unites our life processes at the submicroscopic level with those of daisies, flatworms, blue whales, elephants, monkeys, mice, sharks, sprats, plankton, cabbages, coral and all the rest of the biosphere. But it is not what I have in mind here. I mean actual messages, intelligent, structured communications, a system of symbols conveying meaning, as in any other language.

It does not surprise me at all that the late great Terence McKenna was the first to suggest this extraordinarily fertile idea – or that he conceived it in the Amazon after a month spent drinking ayahuasaca supplemented by 'heroic' doses of psilocybin mushrooms.[1] McKenna, who died on 3 April 2000, was a radical and original thinker, an advocate of hallucinogen use for consciousness exploration, and a specialist in the ethnomedicine of the Amazon basin. His intensive ayahuasca/psilocybin experiments were done at La Chorrea in Colombia in 1971. He never gave detailed written treatment to his intuitions about DNA, However, in his classic study *The Invisible Landscape*, co-authored in 1975 with his brother, the neurobiologist Dennis McKenna, he speculated that:

> information stored in the neural-genetic material might be made available to consciousness . . . by intercalation of tryptamines [e.g. DMT] and beta-carbolines [e.g. harmaline, the second essential ingredient of ayahuasca] into the genetic material. We reasoned that both neural DNA and neural RNA were involved in this process.[2]

Ten years later, Bruce Lamb put forward a somewhat similar suggestion, also following research in the Amazon and also in the context of ayahuasca:

> Perhaps on some unknown, unconscious level the genetic encoder DNA provides a bridge to biological memories of all living things, an aura of unbounded awareness manifesting itself in the activated mind.[3]

Ten years later again, the Swiss anthropologist Jeremy Narby developed the concept much further and took it in several exciting new

459

directions in his important book *The Cosmic Serpent: DNA and the Origins of Knowledge*, first published in 1995.[4] When I met Narby at his home in Switzerland almost a decade after that, on 27 May 2004, I asked him to clarify his position and whether he still stood by it. 'Correct me if I'm wrong,' I said, 'but when I read *Cosmic Serpent*, if I were to take your idea as far as it would go, it's almost that there's a message, encoded in our DNA, which we can read, or see, or interact with through ayahuasca. Is that right?'

'Or a bunch of messages. I think that we haven't even found all that goes with it.'

'Who put the message there?' I asked

'I don't have the faintest,' Narby replied, 'but I think it was some entity, or several entities, that were rather clever.'

The cosmic serpent: DNA and the origins of knowledge

Part of Narby's argument involves reminding us of some easily forgotten facts of the submicroscopic kingdom. A double strand of DNA ten atoms wide and nearly two metres long is coiled up inside every human cell[5] and DNA is found in every cell of every living creature – the one unifying factor that runs unchanged through the whole story of the evolution of life on earth from the advent of the first bacteria to the emergence of modern humans. 'DNA is a master of transformation, just like mythical serpents,' says Narby:

> The cell-based life DNA informs made the air we breathe, the landscape we see, and the mind-boggling diversity of living beings of which we are a part. In four billion years, it has multiplied itself into an incalculable number of species, while remaining exactly the same.[6]

Drawing on his years of field research amongst tribal peoples in the Amazon basin, and several direct experiences of his own with ayahuasca, Narby's *Cosmic Serpent* forcefully advances the seemingly extraordinary and unbelievable hypothesis that DNA is in some mysterious way 'minded' and that ayahuasca opens a door to non-material levels of reality where that mind can be contacted. In Narby's view, the famous double-helix structure discovered in 1953 by Nobel Prize-winners Francis Crick and James Watson has been rightly described by some biologists as nothing less than

an ancient, high biotechnology containing over a hundred trillion times as much information by volume as our most sophisticated information-storage devices. Could one still speak of a technology in these circumstances? Yes, because there is no other word to qualify this duplicable, information-storing module. DNA is only ten atoms wide and as such constitutes a sort of ultimate technology. It is organic and so miniaturised that it approaches the limits of material existence.[7]

Most orthodox evolutionary scientists might accept the *metaphor* of DNA as a technology but would certainly not agree that it is *in fact* a technology, or that it could be in any way 'minded' or 'intelligently designed'. In their framework, blind Darwinian forces of natural selection alone are quite sufficient to explain the structure and workings of DNA and its involvement with life; no other explanation need be sought for its miraculous miniaturisation and perfection. But Narby means something much more guided:

DNA and the cell-based life it codes for are an extremely sophisticated technology that far surpasses our present understanding and that was initially developed elsewhere than on earth – which it radically transformed on its arrival some four billion years ago.[8]

Of course, this is an outrageous thought from the perspective of mainstream science. But it is no more outrageous than the hypothesis to which Narby reconfirmed his commitment when I met him at his home in Switzerland in 2004 – namely that as well as its more routine functions, which are in themselves miraculous and unexplained, the DNA code may conceal purposeful, intelligent messages for us emanating from whichever 'clever entities' invented the technology in the first place. Narby nowhere commits as to the exact status or provenance of these entities, but it is their messages, he hints, that have been accessed by shamans from all parts of the world for millennia. All any of them needed to do was to find a way to tune their consciousness to the right frequency – efficiently achieved with hallucinogens like ayahuasca, as McKenna long ago suggested – and then they could decode their own DNA and learn from it everything they needed to know.

A new slant on spirit teachers

Narby reminds us that the 'coded' nature of DNA is not in dispute amongst scientists, most of whom would also agree with the linguist Roman Jakobson that until the discovery of the genetic code, such encryption systems were considered to be 'exclusively human phenomena – that is phenomena that require the presence of an intelligence to exist'.[9] Moreover, there is certainly room for intelligent hidden messages in the astonishing total of 125 billion miles of submicroscopic strands of DNA, 10 atoms wide, estimated to be folded up within the cells of each and every adult human body.[10] Indeed, despite rapid advances in genetics, scientists admit that 'the vast majority of DNA in our bodies does things that we do not presently understand'.[11]

As we saw at the end of Chapter Eighteen, the truth is that genes, of which we now do have some knowledge, make up only about 3 per cent of our DNA, while the function of the other 97 per cent remains entirely unknown. Does it make sense to suppose, as most scientists do, that this 'junk DNA' has no function at all? Or is it possible, as Narby contrarily suggests, that hidden messages, teachings and revelations were long ago coded into it by 'clever entities' – messages that Amazonian shamans have accessed for thousands of years through the use of ayahuasca?

I began to realise that if Narby's questions led anywhere, then here, potentially, was another radical way to explain the mysterious revolution in human consciousness that took place around 40,000 years ago, producing the first art and religions, and initiating the whole suite of recognisably modern behaviour. Alongside the possibility of 'spirit worlds' and 'spirit beings' coexisting and interacting with our own three-dimensional reality, accessible to us in trance states, and intervening at crucial moments to catalyse our development, there was now a rather different question to consider – one that my own recent DMT experiences had primed me for.

Perhaps our ancestors' discovery of trance techniques and widespread use of hallucinogens not only shattered five million years of mental rigidity with extraordinary and life-changing experiences, but also gave them access to *specific information*, recorded billions of years previously in their DNA, deposited there by Narby's 'clever entities', to await the evolution of creatures that could make use of it. Perhaps this information was packaged by its makers in such a way as to be responsive to, and highly interactive with, the cultural preconceptions of just about any creatures above a certain level of intelligence that evolution might eventually produce. And perhaps the interactive display in the case of modern humans most frequently takes form as therianthropic 'spirit teachers' – just like those man-beasts that first began to be painted on cave walls around 35,000 years ago, right at the dawn of modern human behaviour.

In this case we would be dealing not with visions of 'real' spirits seen by Upper Palaeolithic shamans, but with the teaching devices of some sort of guidance and control system for intelligent beings, installed like a time-bomb in DNA at the moment that life began on earth, to await activation billions of years later by a combination of the right sort of brain with the right sort of electrochemical trigger. Such messages from a higher intelligence would presumably provide immense adaptive advantages, as they perhaps did during the Upper Palaeolithic 'revolution'. They would also be democratic. Those who found the trigger, used it properly and paid attention would receive tangible benefits.

Plant teachers of the Amazon and the Kalahari

It is widely recognised that the Indians of the Amazon have unparalleled knowledge of the properties of jungle plants, and of their uses as medicines and poisons. One of the most remarkable aspects of this knowledge is that many of the individual plants required for the recipes are entirely inert on their own and can only be brought into activity through long preparation and mixture with other plants. This is the case with ayahuasca, as we saw in Chapter Three, and at the other end of the spectrum, it is the case also with the neurotoxin curare, used for thousands of years by hunters in the Amazon and now extensively adopted by Western medicine for its life-saving properties during radical surgery and anaesthesia. Jeremy Narby's view is that the secrets of such substances are most *unlikely* to have been revealed by chance experimentation, no matter how long we might hypothetically allow for that to occur:

> There are forty types of curares in the Amazon, made from seventy plant species . . . To produce it, it is necessary to combine several plants and boil them for seventy-two hours, while avoiding the fragrant but mortal vapours emitted by the broth. The final product is a paste that is inactive unless injected under the skin [on the tip of an arrow or spear, for example]. If swallowed it has no effect. It is difficult to see how anybody could have stumbled on this recipe by chance experimentation.[12]

Amazonian shamans do not claim that they stumbled upon their tribal archives of biochemical secrets by chance experimentation, or by any other such rational and quasi-scientific device. What they claim, very simply – but unanimously – is that a variety of 'plant spirits', amongst which ayahuasca is paramount, have taught them everything important they need to know about the properties of other plants in the jungle, thus allowing them to make powerful medicines, to heal the sick, and, in general, to be good doctors and *vegetalistas*.[13] Ayahuasca itself is said to be a 'doctor', possessing a strong spirit, and is considered to be 'an intelligent being with which it is possible to establish rapport, and from which it is possible to acquire knowledge and power'.[14]

The anthropologist Angelica Gebhart-Sayer, who studied the Shipibo-Conibo Indians of the Amazon, notes that under the influence of ayahuasca 'the shaman perceives, from the spirit world, incomprehensible, often chaotic *information* in the form of luminous designs . . .'[15] As Gebhart-Sayer sees it, it is the shaman's function to decode and 'domesticate' this raw, unprocessed data beamed at him by the plant spirits by 'converting it' into therapy for the tribe as a whole. Similarly among the Campa, another Amazonian tribe, herbal recipes alone are not effective in bringing about improvements in health unless they are specified by a plant spirit encountered by a shaman in an ayahuasca trance.[16]

When the anthropologist Eduardo Luna interviewed mestizo shamans around the Amazonian town of Iquitos in the early 1980s, one of them, Don Celso, remarked that he himself had never had a shaman as a teacher and did not require one, because ayahuasca was an infallible source of true knowledge:

> That is why some doctors believe that the *vegetalismo* [or science of the plants] is stronger than *la medicina de studio* [Western medicine], because they learn by reading books. But we just take this liquid [ayahuasca], keep the diet, and then we learn.

Another of Luna's subjects, Don Jose, also claims that the spirits of the plants taught him everything he knows. Likewise Don Alejandro said that what he learnt directly from ayahuasca very quickly surpassed his lessons from his human teacher, an old Indian shaman, because the spirits of the plants taught him so much.[17] 'The spirits . . . present themselves during the visions and during the dreams,' Luna concludes:

> They show how to diagnose the illness, what plants to use and how, the proper use of tobacco smoke, how to suck out the illness or restore the spirit to a patient, how the shamans defend themselves, what to eat, and, most important, they teach them *icaros*, magic songs or shamanic melodies which are the main tools of shamanic practices.[18]

It is notable that in the Amazonian traditions, the 'plant teachers' are said to assume not only plant forms, but also to appear as animals (the boa constrictor is a particularly common manifestation of the spirit of ayahuasca) or as human beings. Quite often they adopt the guise of 'small people of beautiful and strong constitution',[19] a description strongly reminiscent of European fairies. Picking up on another ancient theme found across the domains of spirits, fairies and aliens that we have explored throughout this book, Amazonian shamans also routinely report plant teachers appearing to them in the shape of hybrids and therianthropes – 'the product of the mating of human fathers with mermaids', in the words of Luna's informant Don Jose.[20]

Notable too, in every case, is the role of ayahuasca as a vehicle or a portal that allows the shaman to gain access to the hidden realms of information in which the plant teachers reside. This belief is prevalent throughout the indigenous cultures of the Amazon, notes Benny Shanon, Professor of Psychology at the Hebrew University in Jerusalem and one of the world's leading academic experts on ayahuasca:

> In these [Amazonian] cultures, knowledge of the ultimate realities as well as all major cultural achievements are attributed to this brew . . . Ayahuasca – along with other psychotropic agents – is considered to be 'the only path to knowledge'. The world revealed through the consumption of these agents is taken to be real whereas the ordinary 'real' world is often regarded as illusory.[21]

Significantly, though they attain their deeply altered states of consciousness without using any drugs, the bushmen shamans of southern Africa speak of their trance dance in much the same way that their counterparts in the Amazon speak of ayahuasca – as a vehicle for encountering spirits who deliver practical teachings to them. The reader will recall the imagery of 'threads of light' and 'ropes to the sky' that is so common in the bushmen accounts. According to the Kalahari shaman Bo:

> Only the strongest doctors go up the rope and learn from their ancestors and the Big God. That's one of the ways we learn new songs, dances, and more knowledge about how to heal others. *They show us what plants to use for a certain sickness* or how to treat a specific person.[22]

Another bushman shaman, Kgao Temi, describes similar experiences:

When we dance we sometimes travel underneath the ground. There's a line that goes to the sky and a line that goes under the earth. One line takes you to the Big God and the other line brings you back. When you're up in the sky, you can see the line below you . . . The people who sit around the fire can touch your body, but you're not there. You disappear, while your body remains behind. It feels like you float up to the sky . . . The people from the past may come and take you. They teach you things and give you more power. They actually talk to you. They tell you about the dance. They also *teach you about the plants.*[23]

Whether construed as the apparitions of ancestors in southern Africa, or as 'plant teachers' in the Amazon, it is clear that these entities, 'hallucinations', 'interactive recordings', 'spirit beings' – whatever they may be – are everywhere experienced in much the same way. By some mechanism or other they do actually talk to people, and many of those who listen believe that the communications thus received are from intelligent beings.

Westerners come to the school

Benny Shanon has drunk ayahuasca more than 130 times and strongly affirms the widespread Amazonian perception of it as a powerful source of knowledge. As his experience with the brew increased, he says, he realised that he was 'entering a school':

There were no teachers, no textbooks, no instructions, yet there was definitely structure and order to it. The teacher was the brew, the instruction was conducted during the period of intoxication without the assistance of any other person.[24]

During one ayahuasca session, Shanon reports experiencing a series of different visions that all pertained to one common theme – the life of nocturnal animals:

In each vision a different species appeared: jaguars, jackals, several kinds of birds, insects and organisms smaller than insects. In each case I was shown how the animals in question behave. My eyes accommodated and I could see what the animals themselves saw. In effect, the entire set of visions was a very instructive course on animal behaviour.[25]

Such structuring of experiences in an ordered flow, like a lesson, is quite common in Shanon's view:

As one gains more experience with the brew, one discovers that what happens to one under the intoxication is not haphazard – it seems to have an internal logic and order. It is as if there is, within the brew itself, a wise teacher who decides what one should experience and learn in each session.[26]

In addition to his own direct experiences of ayahuasca, which he describes extensively in his important book, *The Antipodes of the Mind*, Shanon has interviewed a large sample of ayahuasca users in South America and collated their accounts with those of a separate group of outsiders who have come to the hallucinogenic brew from many different countries.[27] He reports the case of a European informant, participating in a private ayahuasca session held in Europe

who was struck by the feeling that a plant-being was in his body and that he had a strong, intimate relationship with it. This man felt that the plant was a being in its own right and that it was passing knowledge to him. This is in line with the indigenous conception of plants as teachers, a topic with which this subject was not familiar.[28]

In 1999, three Western molecular biologists travelled to the Amazon to participate in ayahuasca sessions with a Peruvian shaman. Two subsequently reported that they had experienced contact with 'plant teachers' in the form of 'independent entities' that had permanently altered the way they thought about reality. One, an American biologist whose specialist subject is the human genome, said she saw 'a chromosome from the perspective of a protein flying above a long strand of DNA'. She claimed to have received a specific technical teaching from the vision concerning the hitherto-unknown function of certain DNA sequences called 'CpG islands', found upstream of about 60 per cent of all human genes.[29]

Francis Crick, LSD and the double helix

Those from rational, technological societies who have not drunk ayahuasca must naturally rebel at the notion of any plant teaching us about anything in the sense that is meant here – let alone teaching us about something so specific, and frankly so technical, as CpG islands and the mysteries of our own DNA. Yet it is not very hard to find evidence that something like this does in fact take place. As it happens, one very clear example concerns the discovery of the structure of DNA itself.

As the reader is already well aware, DMT, the active ingredient of ayahuasca, is a prominent member of a family of hallucinogenic and non-hallucinogenic molecules known collectively as the tryptamines. These are the very molecules highlighted by Terence McKenna earlier in this chapter for their possible role in making 'information stored in the neural-genetic material . . . available to consciousness'.

We saw in Chapter Seventeen that one of the best known tryptamines is the neurotransmitter serotonin, 5-hydroxytryptamine, which is itself entirely non-psychedelic. Another well-known – and definitely psychedelic! – tryptamine is psilocybin. Ibogaine, the African psychedelic that put me on my back for 48 hours, has a tryptamine core, and so too does the most famous psychedelic in the world, lysergic acid diethylamide (LSD),[30] discovered by Albert Hoffman in Switzerland in 1943 and elevated to cult status by the hippie movement in the 1960s. Peculiarly appropriately, one of the key amino acids with which DNA does its mysterious work of constructing and replicating life is tryptophan,[31] the parent molecule from which all the tryptamines, including DMT, are derived.[32]

In late July 2004, the Nobel Prize-winning biologist Francis Crick, co-discoverer of the structure of DNA, died at the age of 88, and soon afterwards a little-known fact of his life hit the tabloid press. This was

Serotonin

Tryptamine

Dimethyltryptamine (DMT)

Psilocybin

Ibogaine

LSD

Serotonin, DMT, psilocybin, ibogaine and LSD all contain a nucleus, or basic building block, of tryptamine, derived from the amino acid tryptophan. (after Strassman, 2001, pp. 34–36)

that when he was working at the Cavendish Laboratory in Cambridge in the early 1950s, he frequently used LSD (which remained legal until the mid-1960s) as a 'thinking tool' to boost his mental powers. According to a report published in London on 8 August 2004 in *The Mail on Sunday*, Crick had privately admitted to colleagues that he was under the influence of LSD in 1953 at the moment when he 'perceived the double helix shape' and unravelled the structure of DNA.[33]

Nobel Prize genius Crick was high on LSD when he discovered the secret of life

FRANCIS CRICK, the Nobel Prize-winning father of modern genetics, was under the influence of LSD when he first deduced the double-helix structure of DNA nearly 50 years ago.

The abrasive and unorthodox Crick and his brilliant American co-researcher James Watson famously celebrated their eureka moment in March 1953 by running from the now legendary Cavendish Laboratory in Cambridge to the nearby Eagle pub, where they announced over pints of bitter that they had discovered the secret of life.

Crick, who died ten days ago, aged 88, later told a fellow scientist that he often used small doses of LSD – then an experimental drug used in psychotherapy – to boost his powers of thought. He said it was LSD, not the Eagle's warm beer, that helped him to unravel the structure of DNA, the discovery that won him the Nobel Prize.

Despite his Establishment image, Crick was a devotee of novelist Aldous Huxley, whose accounts of his experiments with LSD and another hallucinogen, mescaline, in the short stories The Doors Of Perception and Heaven And Hell became cult texts for the hippies of the Sixties and Seventies. In the late

SPACED OUT: LSD is popular with hippies

Sixties, Crick was a founder member of Soma, a legalise-cannabis group named after the drug in Huxley's novel Brave New World. He even put his name to a famous letter to The Times in 1967 calling for a reform in the drugs laws.

It was through his membership of Soma that Crick inadvertently became the inspiration for the biggest LSD manufacturing conspir-

acy the world has ever seen – the multi-million-pound drug factory in a remote farmhouse in Wales that was smashed by the Operation Julie raids of the late Seventies.

Crick's involvement with the gang was fleeting but crucial. The revered scientist had been invited to the Cambridge home of freewheeling American writer David Solomon – a friend of *hi min* LSD guru Timothy

Leary – who had come to Britain in 1967 on a quest to discover a method for manufacturing pure THC, the active ingredient of cannabis.

It was Crick's presence in Solomon's social circle that attracted a brilliant young biochemist, Richard Kemp, who soon became a convert to the attractions of both cannabis and LSD. Kemp was recruited to the THC project in 1968, but soon afterwards

devised the world's first foolproof method of producing cheap, pure LSD. Solomon and Kemp went into business, manufacturing 'acid' in a succession of rented houses before setting up their laboratory in a cottage on a hillside near Tregaron, Carmarthenshire, in 1973. It is estimated that Kemp manufactured drugs worth £2.5 million – an astonishing amount in the Seventies – before police stormed

The headline in *The Mail on Sunday*, 8 August 2004

While he was using LSD, as he supposed, to free himself from rigid preconceptions, is it possible that the drug's tryptamine core brought Crick inadvertently into that hypothetical hall of records in our DNA to which ayahuasca gives us access, where 'clever entities' long ago hid away the secrets of the universe? Since his mind was already well prepared in that direction, and his consciousness temporarily returned to the right wavelength, could he have picked up high-quality information encoded in his own DNA . . . about the structure of DNA itself?

Francis Crick and the mysterious origins of DNA

In the Amazon, a fellow ayahuasca drinker gave Benny Shanon this eloquent thought about the kind of knowledge that might possibly be unlocked by the tryptamine-rich brew:

> God wanted to hide his secrets in a secure place. 'Would I put them on the moon?' He reflected. 'But then, one day human beings could get there, and it could be that those who would arrive there would not be worthy of the secret knowledge. Or perhaps I should hide them in

the depths of the ocean,' God entertained another possibility. But again, for the same reasons, He dismissed it. Then the solution occurred to Him – 'I shall put my secrets in the inner sanctum of man's own mind. Then only those who really deserve it will be able to get to it.'[34]

The moral of the story is that drinking ayahuasca, or ingesting some other similar hallucinogen, may for most of us be *necessary* if we wish to open secret chambers in our own minds – but it is certainly not *sufficient*. For just as a horse may be brought to water but not made to drink, so a man or woman may consume ayahuasca without gaining any revelation – unless he or she 'really deserves' it. All the shamans in the Amazon would agree, however, that revelations are there to be had if ayahuasca is used properly, and that what is needed is a prepared mind and a cool head to grasp the import of the information received and make the most of it.

Few men's minds could have been better prepared, or heads cooler, than Francis Crick's when he came to his LSD experiences. Along with James Watson and Maurice Wilkins, he broke the genetic code of DNA and won the Nobel Prize. It's hard to be more orthodox or more mainstream than that. Indeed, in a sense Crick was one of those who defined the mainstream. Where he led, generations of less inventive and less original scientists have been happy to follow. When he spoke, no matter what the subject, he was listened to. Indeed, one of his favourite topics was a matter on which it is difficult to see that he had any special qualification to pronounce judgement – namely the supposed impossibility of the soul's existence.[35] But when Crick spoke on DNA, there can be no doubt, as the co-discoverer of its molecular structure, that he did so with special authority.

He always recognised that the big problem was not how life perpetuated itself through natural selection *after* DNA had come on the scene, but how DNA came on the scene in the first place. 'At first it seems highly unlikely that this complicated mechanism could have arisen by chance,' he wrote in 1966, 'but it really is quite possible that some primitive version of it started in that way and although not perfect was sufficiently accurate to enable the system to get along.'[36]

Over the next 15 years Crick changed his tune entirely and in 1981 he published a remarkable book entitled *Life Itself: Its Origin and Nature*, in which he set out his view that DNA could not, in fact, have arisen on earth 'by chance', but rather that the seeds of life and of all future evolution, most likely in the form of simple, resilient bacteria, must have been sent here in spaceships by an alien civilisation. The aliens' motive, he speculated, might have been to overcome the certain doom of a supernova explosion (or some such cataclysm) by preserving at least their DNA in stripped-down bacterial form and sending it out into the universe in crewless, automated ships programmed to seek and crash into certain sorts of planets at certain stages of development – there to release their cargo of bacteria to begin all over again the long process involved in the evolution of fully conscious beings.[37]

Perhaps the early earth was one such planet? Perhaps it was seeded with bacteria containing the DNA of intelligent beings from the other side of the galaxy who had evolved their civilisation billions of years before the earth was even formed and whose technology was astonishingly, almost magically advanced?

These are Francis Crick's speculations, not mine. But if our DNA is not 'of this earth' and originated with an alien civilisation in command of advanced genetic engineering technologies, as he proposes, then we cannot rule out the possibility that its scientists might have been able to record meaningful information, 'messages' or 'wake-up calls' in the language of DNA. If they were clever enough, they might even have transcribed the entire accumulated knowledge of their culture into DNA to await the evolution and attention of intelligent species on whichever planets anywhere in the universe the original cargoes of bacteria had happened to land . . .

CHAPTER TWENTY

The Hurricane in the Junkyard

Francis Crick's hypothesis that life on earth was 'seeded' with the DNA of an alien civilisation from a far-off planet is oddly similar in its essence to the cosmology of the ayahuasca-drinking Yagua Indians of the Peruvian Amazon, who told the French anthropologist Jean-Pierre Chaumeil: At the very beginning, before the birth of the earth, this earth here, our most distant ancestors lived on another earth . . .'[1]

Crick called his version of the Yagua belief 'directed panspermia', and although it sounds a little crazy coming from a Nobel Prize-winner, he got away with it – well, because he was Crick, and because he made it clear that he was just punting a hypothesis. Besides, another scientist of almost equal eminence, though from a different field – the astrophysicist Sir Fred Hoyle – was also promoting a panspermia theory at around the same time, and also succeeded in keeping his career intact despite it.[2] Hoyle envisaged the spores of life being carried randomly through space on great interstellar comets – rather than the intentional, intelligent dissemination favoured by Crick – but what both men had in common was the strong conviction that life was already too complex when it first appeared on earth to have evolved here. Accordingly, they both believed that the first and most difficult steps – the steps from non-life to life that no scientist has ever been able to replicate – must have been taken somewhere else.

The story begins around 4.5 billion years ago when the earth's mass had formed as a planet orbiting the sun. For the next 600 million years it remained a molten lava fireball, but by 3.9 billion years ago cooling was sufficiently advanced to produce a thin outer crust of solid rock.[3] It is supposed that around the same time pools of water enriched with minerals began to take shape beneath an atmosphere of simple gases. In these pools of primeval, prebiotic 'soup', many scientists believe that the first very primitive life-forms appeared suddenly and almost instantaneously as a result of the accidental collision of molecules.[4] Others, Crick amongst them, argue that 'the odds against such instant life are beyond the astronomical – more unlikely than the assembly of a Boeing 707 by a hurricane in a junkyard'.[5]

Whatever one's view, the fact of the matter – on which scientists are generally agreed – is that life appears to have spread across the earth almost as soon as a prebiotic soup could be supported. The crust had not formed fully until about 3.9 billion years ago, yet by 3.8 billion years ago – a window of just 100 million years – there is abundant though secondary evidence that the planet had already been colonised by bacterial life.[6] This evidence becomes firm at 3.4 billion years ago, the date of the oldest fossilised bacteria so far discovered[7] – still barely half a billion years after the earth's first rocks had formed.

Source code

Crick was a biophysicist, and no mean mathematician, and he had statistical objections to the notion that life got its start on 'this earth here' in a period of half a billion years or less. He had no problems with the notion of a prebiotic soup but he did not see how the 'formation from the soup of a primitive, chemical, self-reproducing system' – i.e. the beginnings of the DNA/RNA system that he played so large a part in decoding – could have occurred spontaneously, or even at all, in the relatively short time available.[8] The argument here is not an anti-evolutionary one. Once such a system was in place, as it appears to have been from the very beginning of life on earth, once individual organisms could inherit 'adaptive' characteristics which improved their survival chances, it is easy to see how Darwinian natural selection would begin to interact with DNA, favouring different traits in different circumstances and thus providing the fundamental mechanism for the evolution of all the myriad forms of life that presently girdle the planet. But Crick's difficulty had to do with how the system got up and running in the first place – even if it was granted much more than half a billion years to do so. No matter how long he allowed in his models, the odds against this kind of organised complexity taking shape *on its own* remained vanishingly immense.

To understand why, we need to understand a little bit about the family of molecules known as the proteins on which much of the structure and metabolic machinery of all living cells are based, and we need to know more about DNA.

'A protein molecule is a macromolecule, running to thousands of atoms,' explains Crick:

> Each protein is precisely made, with every atom in its correct place. Each type of protein forms an intricate three-dimensional structure, peculiar to itself, which allows it to carry out its catalytic or structural function. This three-dimensional structure is . . . based on one or more 'polypeptide chains', as they are called . . . [which the cell constructs] by joining together, end to end, a particular set of small molecules, the amino acids . . . Surprisingly just twenty kinds of them [amino acids] are used to make proteins, and this set of twenty is exactly the same throughout nature . . . A protein is like a paragraph written in a twenty-letter language, the exact nature of the protein being determined by the exact order of the letters . . . Animals, plants, microorganisms and viruses all use the same set of twenty letters . . . The set of twenty is so universal that its choice would appear to date back to very near the beginning of all living things.[9]

A second chemical language of equal antiquity can be seen in the nucleic acids, DNA and RNA.[10] Classified amongst that broad category of naturally occurring and synthetic compounds known as the polymers, they are giant chain molecules, each of which is characterised by repeating patterns – 'bases' – of only four chemical elements. For RNA these are adenine, cytosine, guanine and uracil (represented by their initial letters A, C, G and U). For DNA, the first three bases are the same – namely adenine, cytosine and guanine, while the fourth base is thymine (T), such a close relative of uracil that it creates no incompatibility in the constant interactions that take place at the cellular level between strands of DNA and strands of RNA.[11]

These two polymers (with DNA usually 'in command' and RNA playing subordinate, 'messenger' functions) carry all the genetic information required to construct living organisms, and are the fundamental templates of inheritance.[12] Moreover, DNA and RNA, with their four bases, remain *exactly the same* and fulfil *exactly the same functions* in all living things, whether bacterium or elephant, flea or dog, jellyfish or acacia tree, cabbage or butterfly, minnow or whale, worm or man, four billion years ago or today. All that changes is the order of the letters A, C, G and T in the genetic code written into the DNA of each organism, and of course the amount of DNA that each organism has. Thus the intestinal bacterium *E. coli* consists of only a single cell within which is coiled a half-millimetre-long ribbon of the DNA polymer;[13] by contrast, as we have seen, every one of the thousands of billions of cells making up the human body contains *two metres* of the same DNA – obviously loaded with many more paragraphs of genetic code than poor little *E. coli* has room or need for. Still, a great deal of information is required to code for even the simplest forms of life. *Mycoplasma genitalium* is the smallest bacterium known to science, but nevertheless requires enough DNA to carry its genetic code of 580,000 letters. The much more extensive genetic code that specifies a human being consists of approximately *three billion* letters, strung out along every one of those two-metre-long ribbons of DNA coiled inside every one of our cells.[14]

The great biological breakthrough of the 1960s, again in large part thanks to Crick's work, was the unravelling of this genetic code – the small dictionary 'similar in principle to the Morse Code', as Crick put it, 'which relates the four-letter language of the genetic material to the twenty-letter language of protein, the executive language'.[15]

Without going into this submicroscopic alchemy in any depth, let's just state briefly that meaningful combinations of any three of DNA's four chemical letters mobilise cells to join amino acids together in a particular order so as to synthesise specific proteins – thus determining the final shape, form and functioning of every organism according to its own inherited code. Given the vast apparent diversity of life on earth, I find myself newly amazed every time I am reminded that exactly the same breathtakingly simple cipher can be reshuffled in a sufficient number of ways to specify us all, with only the order of the letters making the difference between geranium and giraffe, ant and elephant, ape and man (exactly as they do in written words, of course). But it all comes down to maths, as Crick explains:

> Since the nucleic acid language has just four distinct letters, there are sixty-four possible triplets (4 x 4 x 4). Sixty-one of these 'codons', as they are called, stand for one amino acid or another. The other three triplets stand for 'end chain'.[16]

As we have already seen, only 20 amino acids are actually used by living cells in the construction of proteins. Inevitably, therefore, there is quite a lot of 'ambiguity' – with most triplets coding for more than one amino acid and different triplets coding for the same amino acid. It is not known how cells decide on the right amino acid when several

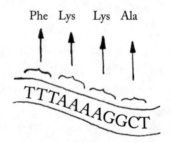

Codons specifying amino acids: TTT = phenylalanine; AAA = lysine; AAG = lysine; GCT = alanine (After Calladine et al., 2004, page 13).

alternatives seem to be equally specified. Indeed, and I mention it without drawing any inference, there are only two amino acids that DNA treats as too important for any ambiguity to be tolerated, since it specifies them unequivocally with a single codon in each case. One is methionine. The other is tryptophan, the source molecule of all the tryptamine hallucinogens.[17]

Miracle

It should be obvious from the above that both nucleic acids and proteins, which in all cases are very large, complex macromolecules, are required for anything that we might call life, at least on this planet. Crudely, the nucleic acids are needed because they carry the genetic code and they can replicate themselves – two things that proteins cannot do. Proteins on the other hand are needed for all the dynamic body-building tasks of cells, including the construction and replication of DNA itself. Without the inherited instructions already contained in DNA – 'pick this amino acid', 'put it together with that one', 'stop', etc., etc. – no protein chains would be synthesised and cells could not do their work. But since DNA could not be made and could not replicate itself in the absence of proteins, we are faced with a chicken-and-egg situation.

What bothered the statistician in Crick was the absolute improbability of even a single fully assembled protein made up of a long chain of amino acids emerging as a result of chance – no matter how nutritious the prebiotic soup or how many billions of years the ingredients were allowed to stew. Based on an average protein about 200 amino acids in length (others are much bigger), he calculated the odds of this happening as just one chance in a 1 followed by 260 zeros. To provide some sort of benchmark, all the atoms in the entire visible universe (not just our own galaxy) amount to a 1 followed by 80 zeros – quite a paltry number by comparison with the odds against the chance assembly of a single protein.[18] How much less likely would it be, therefore, that life itself – which even at the bacterial level calls for complex cellular mechanisms and makes use of many proteins – could have got started through the chance collisions of molecules?

This sense of an amazing ordered complexity, right down to the atomic scale, is reinforced by a closer look at DNA's double-helix structure. Remember that in every human cell, each cell being one millionth the size of a pinhead, there is a double 'ribbon' of DNA two metres long and ten atoms wide.[19] Indeed the reduction factor is even greater than that required to stuff two metres into a pinhead since the entwined strands of DNA are entirely housed in the cell nucleus which

Because of the 'upside-down' symmetry of its coiled strands, the DNA molecule is frequently compared to two identical serpents wound around each other and facing head to tail

is much smaller than the cell itself with a diameter of just ten micrometres. The result is a feat of compaction that has been compared to folding fifty miles of kite string into a shoe box. The two identical polymer ribbons are generally wound around each other like two serpents facing head to tail, each an 'upside-down' duplicate of the other and joining at their bases in a specific order (A always with T, C always with G).[20] Scientists correctly speak of them as the 'master copy' and the 'back-up copy' because if any errors are introduced on one ribbon the cell has a mechanism for repairing them with reference to the other.

Strung out along the DNA polymer ribbons, as we have seen, the genetic information in each cell is recorded chemically in detailed base sequences that code for the synthesis of proteins. The beauty and complexity of the system is that these instructions are not implemented directly from the cell's DNA archive but are first copied (the technical term is 'transcription') on to single-stranded RNA molecules ('messenger RNA') which then initiate the synthesis without the need for further reference to the master and back-up copies safely stored inside the double helix.

RNA

DNA   DNA

Transcription of information from DNA onto single-stranded 'messenger' RNA. (After Calladine et al., 2004, page 65)

'It is quite remarkable,' notes Crick, 'that such a mechanism exists at all, and even more remarkable that every living cell, whether animal, plant or microbial, contains a version of it.'[21] As with the 20-letter protein code, to which it is intimately linked by its amazing 'translation' mechanism, this universality tells us that the genetic code is extremely ancient. Indeed it, and the DNA/RNA system which embodies it, must have been present in the first living organisms from which we are all descended. Yet the system itself is built of component parts and, in Crick's view, 'is far too complex to have arisen at one blow. It must have evolved from something simpler.'[22]

The problem is that there is no evidence for that simpler thing – no evidence that any such evolution took place anywhere on earth before the spread of the first DNA-based bacteria between about 3.9 billion and 3.4 billion years ago. The implications are obvious, but as an arch-rationalist and committed atheist it clearly pained Crick to admit that 'the origin of life appears at the moment to be almost a miracle, so many are the conditions which would have needed to be satisfied to get it going'.[23]

Perhaps it was in subconscious rebellion against any sort of spiritual explanation of this 'miracle' that Crick came up with his panspermia theory. He did not believe in the supernatural, but the evidence convinced him that the four-letter DNA 'language', together with the 20-letter protein 'language', and the translation mechanism that links the two, were most unlikely to have arisen naturally on earth through chance collisions of matter. In some sense the system appeared to have been engineered, even 'created', *before* it ever went into action here. But by whom? Crick would have been going against his own character to consider the possibility that it might have been a supernatural entity of the kind that most people call God. He much preferred the scenario of intelligent aliens on a distant planet sending rocket-loads of bacterial DNA out into space targeted at promising solar systems.

Recording the music of life

It is rather odd to think that our bodies are built and our parts function according to a complex set of coded chemical instructions half of which we have inherited from our mothers and half from our fathers. Then, as we delve deeper, we realise that they too inherited half their DNA from their mothers, half from their fathers – and so on, counting along the chain of generations all the way back to the beginning of life on earth. The one constant factor, from the first bacterium more than three and a half billion years ago to the most exalted members of the modern human race, are these little polymer ribbons of self-reproducing 'recording tape' that make up the DNA system.

We have already noted that inside every human cell a two-metre length of this 'tape' is coiled up containing the complete genetic information for the construction of a human being. As a polymer, the tape itself is chemically related to the vinyl records on which the hit songs of the 1960s were played, but the information recorded on it is the endlessly duplicable, endlessly renewable music of life:

> Growth occurs by the process of cell division: each cell divides into two new cells, and these cells in turn divide, and so on. Just before any cell divides, it duplicates all of its DNA, so that every new cell contains a complete set of DNA, which again contains all the genes of the organism. Only a small fraction of the genes present on this DNA are activated in any given type of cell . . . A little thought indicates that this scheme for providing every cell with a complete set of DNA is, in fact, an extremely simple way of providing the necessary information, in all places where it is required – even though, of course, the

Just before any cell divides it duplicates all of its DNA, so that every new cell contains a complete set of DNA which again contains all the genes of the organism (after Calladine et al., 2004, p. 10 and 65)

scheme requires a vast amount of repetitive copying and duplicating of DNA.[24]

The theme of apparently redundant copying and duplicating is one that comes up again and again. First there is the double helix itself – an original and a copy. Then there is the role of RNA, busily copying specific segments of code from DNA in order to initiate protein synthesis. In any one cell at any one moment the end result is that most of those highly meaningful clusters of code on the DNA ribbons that we call genes have no function whatsoever. They are 'off-line':

Thus cells which develop into an eye use only the genes which programme for the growth of eye cells. How cells 'know' which kind of organ they belong to is a large and only partly understood area of research.[25]

What is clear is that it seems to be part of the normal functioning of DNA for most of it to be off-line most of the time with only specific segments being activated for protein synthesis. Moreover, it would be wrong to think that DNA's only function is to make proteins according to the inherited instructions of the genetic code. On the contrary, even within genes, less than 1 per cent of the bases contain programs to synthesise specific proteins.[26] The issue looms larger when we remember that genes themselves make up only around 3 per cent of the DNA in each cell. Figures vary, and some authorities assign 5 per cent, others as much as 10 per cent of DNA to genes – but even on the highest estimate it still means that 'the vast majority of DNA in our bodies does things that we do not presently understand'.[27] All that we know for sure about these huge libraries of DNA – remember, we are speaking of between 90 and 97 per cent of the total – is that they contain immense amounts of information written in exactly the same language as the genetic code, but in this case not coding for the construction of proteins or any other recognised function. Some areas of such 'non-coding' text consist of long sequences of bases repeated over and over again, sometimes thousands of times, apparently uselessly. Understandably, therefore, scientists for a long while had the idea that this must be 'junk DNA', superfluous, meaningless code, with no function, that survived simply because it was automatically replicated whenever cells divided.

But why would natural selection preserve such a huge volume of useless gibberish and go to all the trouble of reproducing it in every living cell?

Coming at the problem from many different directions, scientists today are finding that the answer is quite straightforward. The old throwaway theory is wrong. So-called junk DNA does in fact play a vital role in regulating cellular processes and is every bit as important to the overall health and functioning of the organism as the better-known coding sections. But this is not the place to describe the medical implications of the expanding scientific exploration of non-coding DNA. What I'm interested in is something else, discovered by scientists as a chance by-product of other enquiries, about the information recorded on these long and so far still mainly mysterious segments of polymer.

It has to do with the patterns in which that information is organised.

The message of Zipf

All human languages have a very strange and most unexpected secret in common. It is called Zipf's Law, after the linguist George Zipf, who discovered it in 1939. He studied texts in many different languages and ranked the words in order of frequency. What he found, which has since proved to be true whether the language is English or Inuit, Japanese or Xhosa, Arabic or Urdu, is that a direct, exact, unvarying and utterly counter-intuitive mathematical relationship exists between the rank of a word and the actual frequency of occurrence of that word. No matter which text he selected, when Zipf created a histogram that plotted word frequency against word rank, the surprising result was a straight line 'with a slope of -1 for every human language'.[28]

In order to grasp the general principle here, imagine a book of any given number of words, 60,000, or 114,000, or any number, it doesn't matter. If the most common word in the book – i.e. the word with the rank of one – appears 10,000 times, then you can be certain that the tenth most common word (i.e. ranked ten) will appear 1,000 times and the one hundredth most common word will appear just 100 times. The numbers will vary, obviously, from text to text dependent on overall length, but the exact mathematical proportions between rank and frequency will always turn out to be the same in any human language at any time. This, in a nutshell, is Zipf's Law.[29]

Now here is the even stranger thing. In the mid-1990s, researchers from Boston University and Harvard Medical School examined 37 DNA sequences containing at least 50,000 base pairs each, as well as two shorter sequences and one with 2.2 million base pairs. Where possible, they evaluated both coding and non-coding regions.[30] They noticed that distinct patterns of three, four, five, six, seven and eight base pairs – comparable to individual 'words' – existed in all the sequences. This led them to apply two standard linguistic tests to the material. One of these was Zipf's test, and following Zipf's own method, the DNA 'words' were ranked in order of frequency and a histogram plotting the rank of each word against the actual number of times that it appeared in each 'text' was drawn up.

In every case where coding regions were evaluated, they turned out *not* to obey Zipf's Law. This is precisely as one would expect, since the coding regions are just codes, not languages – and are better thought of as templates for the construction of particular proteins.[31] 'The coding part has no grammar,' explains lead researcher Eugene

Stanley. 'Each triplet [of bases] corresponds to an amino acid [in a protein]. There's no higher structure to it.'[32]

So far so predictable, and so reassuring. Of course our DNA doesn't contain intelligent messages and isn't trying to communicate them to us in a language! If it did, all the basic principles of modern evolutionary science would be turned head over heels! Still, what happened next was most unexpected – 'really remarkable', in Eugene Stanley's appraisal: 'There's no rhyme or reason why that should be true.'[33] This really remarkable and totally unexpected discovery was that *in every case where non-coding regions of DNA had been evaluated, they turned out to demonstrate a perfect Zipf Law linear plot.*[34] If these DNA sequences had been books filled with pages of indecipherable printed

Plotting frequency against rank for arbitrary 'words' in non-coding DNA yields the linear plot found in human languages. By contrast coding DNA does not conform to this law (After Eugene Stanley, *Science*, 25 November 1994).

letters, then this result would oblige us to conclude that the letters were not random alphabet soup but words in an organised language. Stanley didn't shy away from the implications of this. In his opinion, the non-coding DNA sequences do contain 'a structured language fundamentally unlike the coding in genes'.[35] Even though it doesn't code for proteins, we therefore need to consider the possibility that '"the junk" DNA may carry some kind of message'.[36]

Such a daring proposition receives further support from the second linguistic test that the team also applied to the DNA sequences. Developed in the 1950s by information theorist Claude Shannon, this test distinguishes texts written in true languages from texts written in alphabet soup by quantifying the 'redundancy' of any string of characters. The test works, and is universal, because 'languages are redundant sequences . . . You can fill in a typographical error by noting nearby characters. A random sequence, in contrast, has no redundancy.'[37]

Again, when the test was applied to coding regions of the DNA, these were shown *not* to have the properties of a human language – as we would predict. The genetic code is not, and cannot be, a redundant sequence in which errors can be corrected with reference to the general context; on the contrary, geneticists are well aware that even a single mistake involving a single base pair on a single gene can scramble the code and produce catastrophic abnormalities. By contrast, the researchers found that the *non-coding* sections of DNA 'revealed a surprising amount of redundancy – another sign that something was written in these mysterious stretches'.[38]

In short, these completely unexpected discoveries allow us to contemplate something astonishing. The chemical 'writing' on so-called junk DNA may not only possess 'all the features of a language'[39] but may in fact *be* a language like any human language. When I contacted Professor Eugene Stanley at Boston University in June 2005 to ask if he still stood by his electrifying 1994 findings, or if they had subsequently been refuted, he told me: 'You bet I stand by them! Nothing has been refuted.'

The ancient anonymous author

As a general rule of thumb, the more complex an organism is, the more non-coding DNA it will have. There are, however, a great many simple organisms that possess a great deal of non-coding DNA, and even the simplest organisms have some. Indeed, these long sequences of apparently meaningless code are found so widely distributed amongst all categories of living things that they may even descend from the DNA of our remotest common ancestors – those first single-celled replicating bacteria that colonised the earth almost four billion years ago.[40]

We have much more in common with primitive organisms and lower animals than we imagine. An Australian National University study of 1,300 DNA sequences from the coral *Acropora millepora*, published in December 2003, found more than 500 coding and non-coding areas that were also present in humans.[41] Similarly, in 2004 researchers at the University of California showed that long sections of the non-coding DNA of mice and humans are identical despite 50 million years of divergent evolution from their last common ancestor.[42] 'It absolutely knocked me off my chair,' comments Professor Haussler, the leader of the University of California team. 'It's extraordinarily exciting to think there are these ultra-conserved elements that weren't noticed by the scientific community before.'[43]

What I find much more exciting, however, is the possibility envisaged by Eugene Stanley and his colleagues at Boston and Harvard that 'some kind of message' might be written on these ultra-conserved sequences of code that occupy up to 97 per cent of our DNA but have no known function. It is difficult to see how the accidental processes of chemistry alone could have produced the intense language-like organisation embedded in the so-called junk sequences. But if it really is some kind of message, rather than a freak of chance and nature that just looks like a message, then who, or what, might have written it? For those who feel uncomfortable with the intervention of gods or spirits in our affairs – and most of all in our creation – Francis Crick's theory of directed panspermia provides what looks like a thoroughly reasonable, 'nuts-and-bolts' alternative. Yet let's recall, despite being one of the great rational atheists of the twentieth century, that Crick received his vision of the structure of DNA while he was in an LSD trance, and ultimately felt obliged to conclude that the double helix must have been introduced to this planet on board the spaceships of an advanced alien civilisation.

The teachers within

It is bizarre not only that Crick's hypothesis reflects the ayahuasca-inspired mythology of the Yagua of the Amazon, as we saw at the beginning of this chapter, but also that a number of Westerners who did not know one another or compare notes, and who experimented with ayahuasca or with pure DMT at different times, nevertheless arrived separately at what were essentially very similar visions involving DNA. In Chapter Eighteen we saw that several of the volunteers in Rick Strassman's DMT project at the University of New Mexico experienced intense visions featuring 'threads of DNA'[44] and 'spirals of DNA'.[45] In Chapter Nineteen the reader will find the case of the American biologist who received detailed images of specific DNA sequences under the influence of ayahuasca, and in Chapter Three I reported my own ayahuasca visions of 'snakes that wind around each other like the DNA double helix'.

Indeed, this theme seems to be everywhere abundant amongst people who have encountered hallucinogens, like DMT, LSD, psilocybin and ayahuasca, which have a tryptamine core. In 1961 the American anthropologist Michael Harner was one of the first Westerners to participate fully in an indigenous ayahuasca ceremony in the Amazon – in his case in a Conibo Indian village beside a remote lake off a tributary of the Rio Ucayali. After drinking a large dose of the bitter hallucinogenic brew he received a spectacular vision in which he saw dragon-like creatures that came to earth fleeing something, perhaps an enemy, 'out in space' after a journey that had lasted for 'aeons':

> The creatures showed me how they had created life on the planet in order to hide within the multitudinous forms and thus disguise their presence. Before me, the magnificence of plant and animal creation and speciation – hundreds of millions of years of activity – took place on a scale and with a vividness impossible to imagine. I learned that the dragon-like creatures were thus inside all forms of life, including man. They were the true masters of humanity and the entire planet, they told me. We humans were but the receptacles and servants of

these creatures. For this reason they could speak to me from within myself. In retrospect one could say they were almost like DNA, although at that time, in 1961, I knew nothing of DNA.[46]

Much later, in the 1990s Jeremy Narby's experiences of ayahuasca evoked a similar chain of thought. During his first session with the brew he reports that he suddenly found himself

> surrounded by two gigantic boa-constrictors that seemed fifty feet long. I was terrified. These enormous snakes are there, my eyes are closed and I see a spectacular world of brilliant lights, and in the middle of these hazy thoughts, the snakes start talking to me without words. They explain that I am just a human being.[47]

Despite superficial differences, it seems to me that Narby and Harner's ayahuasca experiences have much in common with Crick's LSD experience, and his subsequent elaboration of the directed panspermia theory. In essence, what all three seem to envisage is a control system for the human race that is not of this earth, that is serpent-like in form, that now dwells inside us, and that is superior to all of us. Crick calls it the double helix, coils it up inside bacteria and has it sent here from across the galaxy on alien spaceships. For Harner it is creatures that he sees as dragons that have likewise come to earth from space after a journey of 'aeons', that have found a way to perpetuate themselves here inside all life, and that are the 'true masters of humanity'. Narby is put in his place by twin serpents, notes that the double helix of DNA resembles 'two entwined serpents',[48] calls it 'an extremely sophisticated technology . . . that was initially developed elsewhere than on earth',[49] and goes on to write a book called *The Cosmic Serpent*, in which the notion that DNA may be minded, and may encode intelligent messages that we can access in altered states of consciousness, receives its fullest elaboration.[50]

I feel that the possibility cannot be discounted that these insights into the mysteries of DNA that have been given to scientists and anthropologists, just like the insights into the properties and combinations of plants that ayahuasca gives to shamans in the Amazon, may not be accidental. If our DNA is at root an artifice of technology, as Crick suggests, then there is every reason to suppose that its makers would expect such a technology to result in the evolution of beings of high intelligence – sooner or later. In that case, the one certain way to send those future beings a message, no matter what unpredictable paths their mental and physical development might follow, would be to encode it in their DNA – indeed in the most basic elements of DNA that everyone and everything would have to possess some of but that might accumulate preferentially in higher organisms.

Making up 97 per cent of the total DNA library in the cells of modern human beings, this is why the 'junk' non-coding sequences with their mysterious language-like properties are so interesting. It may be the case that hallucinations of the sort that convey veridical knowledge about DNA or about plants, or about how to cure a certain sickness, or about the nature of reality, are as effective a technology as bio-engineering and genetic manipulation for exploring the true potential of the legacy stored inside all our cells. It may be, in other words, that the ancient teachers of mankind have been inside us all along but that we must enter altered states of consciousness in order to hear what they have to say.

PART V

The Religions

The Hidden Shamans

Since it first began to leave definite traces in the archaeological record in the painted caves around 35,000 years ago, religion has undoubtedly been one of the two or three great influences on human behaviour – as universal and as far-reaching in its effects as the struggle to meet basic physical needs.

Its importance in our affairs is not a thing of the past.

Despite the advance of science, which has no space and no patience for the supernatural, roughly two out of every three human beings alive today continue to hold strong beliefs in supernatural entities and in the existence of spirit worlds. Hindus and Buddhists recognise the veridical existence of limitless non-physical realms, entities, intelligences and states of existence. Traditional Jews believe that Moses talked to God face to face, as the Torah states, and received from him 'heavenly writings' in the form of the Ten Commandments. Muslims are taught that Muhammad had encounters with a majestic supernatural being, later identified with the Angel Gabriel, whose apparitions were preceded by 'a peculiar sound like the tinkling of bells', and who subsequently revealed to the Prophet the entire text of the Koran.[1] Interestingly, with a mind to the UFO abductees and shamans we have met in previous chapters who believe they were shown a book that is kept in the otherworld, and gained some revelation from it, Muslims believe that the Koran is 'a perfect transcription of an eternal tablet preserved in heaven'.[2] Another parallel is found in the Mormon belief that Joseph Smith received his revelation from an angel named Moroni, who gave him the text of the Book of Mormon on golden plates that later vanished into thin air.[3]

Mani, eponymous founder of the Manichean religion in the third century AD, claimed to have received all his teachings from an angel who first visited him when he was 12 years old and told him he had a mission to educate mankind. This being, who inspired Mani throughout his life, frequently appeared to him like a dazzling 'flash of lightning'.[4] Likewise St Paul, the great apostle of Christianity, began his mission with a supernatural encounter on the road to Damascus when suddenly he heard a voice accompanied by 'a light from heaven' so bright that it knocked him to the ground and blinded him for three days.[5] The shamanic theme of Paul's initiation fits comfortably into the framework of the Christian religion as a whole – founded as it is on a belief in the life, death and resurrection of a supernatural being whose father was a god, whose mother was a mortal woman and who was thus, himself, a particularly special, important and effective kind of spirit-human hybrid. Christians generally also believe in angels, the Devil, demons of various sorts, and other supernaturals such as the Blessed Virgin Mary and the Holy Ghost. The heaven and hell of Christianity are of course spirit worlds.

We cannot escape it. Belief in the supernatural – whether manifested through spiritual beings thought to have been born in human form, or through revelations to particular humans – has been responsible for social, political, economic and cultural developments 'of monumental significance in the history of mankind'.[6] Moreover, we need only watch a few minutes of international television news daily to realise what a huge force religion *still* is, how deeply and effectively it controls the minds of billions of people all around the globe, and the extent to which it underlies the hot political issues of our times. Few scientists would agree with the suicide bomber's firm belief that when he blows himself up his soul will go straight to paradise, but none would argue with the power of such beliefs to shape events in the 'real world'.

The bureaucratisation of shamanism

Since religious beliefs are so important, it should not be controversial to state clearly what the evidence shows about their ultimate source and inspiration. And what the evidence shows, if we probe deeply enough into the foundations of all the world's great religions, is that they rest upon a bedrock of supernatural encounters and experiences involving powerful and charismatic individuals with the gift to communicate what they *knew* to others. Although such beliefs quickly crystallise into dogmas passed on from generation to generation, it is clear, even from the few examples given above, that they were not originally conjured out of thin air, or arrived at through scholarly study, or deliberately devised to assuage supposed human needs, but that they arose in every case solely out of attempts to describe, depict and explain the supernatural *experiences* of their founders – who were, by any standards, shamans of the highest order. The evidence we have explored in these pages suggests that experiences of this sort have been inextricably tangled up with altered states of consciousness since the dawn of human culture and indeed that they derive from, and in fact are only attainable in, such profoundly altered states – more often than not induced by the consumption of psychoactive plants. Anthropologist Weston La Barre goes so far as to assert that:

> All our knowledge of the supernatural derives *de facto* from the statements made by religious visionaries and ecstatics, i.e. prophets and shamans . . . Priests only administrate the ecclesia established on this supernatural basis . . .[7]

I find La Barre to be entirely correct and highly perceptive in this observation. In the case of all the great religions of the modern world, the original supernatural experiences and revelations of their founders are now so far in the past that salaried priests, ministers, rabbis, mullahs and bishops have taken over entirely – presenting themselves not just as administrators but as true and exclusive intermediaries between humanity and the otherworldly powers. The reader is well aware by now that this role of intermediary is the shaman's role. Unfortunately for us, however, the imposing bureaucrats and managers whose modern monopoly over our relationships with the otherworld has often been brutally built up by centuries of repression are not shamans. On the contrary, they are no more likely than most members of their congregations to encounter spirits in their daily experience. They teach, and adhere, often rigidly, to what they themselves have been *taught* about the supernatural, but they have no special abilities and have practised none of the special skills needed to penetrate supernatural realms and return with hard-won knowledge of real value to their communities. Unless they happen to belong to the 2 per cent of our species who are capable of spontaneously entering trance states, or consume psychoactive drugs, or use arduous physical techniques such as long sessions of rhythmic dancing (like the San of southern Africa) in order to induce such states, we can therefore be quite certain that these functionaries will *never* present us with any new supernatural experiences of their own to refresh the original inspirations, revelations and insights of the religions they now direct and control. Perhaps this is part of the tragedy of the modern world – that the blind have for so long been allowed to mislead the blind about the very experiences and revelations that may have made us human in the first place.

What hope do we have of rediscovering the truth? In a sense it is always there waiting for us. Indeed, it is our birthright. Shamanic ecstasy lies at the root of all religions and, as Weston La Barre admits, 'the nature of the shamanic ecstasy may be illuminated by attention to ancient hallucinogens . . .'[8] That has been the path pursued throughout this book. By paying close attention to ancient hallucinogens, we have attempted to illuminate the contribution of shamanic ecstasy to the emergence of modern human behaviour. In the process we have also been drawn inevitably to explore the full spectrum of human consciousness and the multiple realities it is capable of recognising – rather than confining ourselves to 'the carefully selected utilitarian material', wrongly perceived as 'a complete or at least sufficient, picture of reality', that is normally admitted into consciousness by the 'reducing valve' of the brain.[9]

The reducing valve is plainly necessary, as Aldous Huxley observed (see Chapter Eleven), to prevent us from being overwhelmed and confused by a mass of useless and irrelevant knowledge, by shutting out most of what we should otherwise perceive or remember at any moment, and leaving only that very small and special selection which is likely to be practically useful . . .[10]

At the same time as equipping us with such an obviously adaptive device, however, and presumably for some equally important reason, evolution has also given us access to a variety of shamanic techniques by which almost anyone can bypass the reducing valve in his or her own brain. It is a sad irony that these 'gratuitous graces', which our ancestors originally used with caution and reverence to explore and learn from non-ordinary reality, have, with the passage of much time, been diverted by bureaucrats into the spiritual dead end of the 'ecclesia', where everything is dogma, endlessly repeated, where almost no one has first-hand experiences of the supernatural any more, and where nothing new may be discovered or learnt.

Primitive Christians

Arguably the rot sets in from the moment that any culture begins to devalue its shamans as madmen and visionaries, to deny the legitimacy of direct revelation amongst 'ordinary people', and to place its spiritual trust in a sacerdotal class who can only teach what they have been taught by others rather than what they themselves have experienced.

Let's take a closer look at Christianity by way of example. After its foundation around 2,000 years ago it was, at first, an overtly shamanistic religion. This is hardly surprising since Christ was so obviously and so profoundly a shaman. It is not only his pedigree as a half-human, half-divine hybrid that makes him so, or his heaven-sent gifts as a healer. His ordeal of crucifixion and piercing followed by death and subsequent resurrection as a spiritualised being equipped with the power to save souls is essentially the story of the wounded man – the story that is told by all shamans everywhere of their own initiatory agonies, death and resurrection.

The primitive Christians who called themselves Gnostics believed that salvation was to be attained through a special sort of 'knowledge of the true nature of things' that could not be taught but only revealed directly to the initiate. They also believed, like the Jivaro of Ecuador, that this material world in which we live is essentially an illusion in which the soul is trapped and that the only way for us to see reality is to enter the visionary state. We do not know how the Gnostics did it (although some certainly practised severe austerities and there is inferential evidence of a mushroom cult).[11] In the case of the Jivaro, however, there is absolutely no doubt that hallucinogens – principally ayahuasca – are used. As anthropologist Michael Ripinsky-Naxon explains:

> The spiritual and metaphysical contingencies of the energies of life may be tapped, the Jivaro believe, by means of hallucinogens. The spiritual realm, this antipodal World, thus entered, is where knowledge of the great cosmic causality can be apprehended. All the events that occur inside the Otherworld are manifestations of the 'true' reality and exert an impact on the daily, physical aspect of existence. Consequently, the everyday non-visionary life is considered 'fake' and 'false'.[12]

During approximately the first to sixth centuries AD, this was precisely how the Gnostics, and their 'pagan' cousins the Hermeticists, described the human predicament in a world of material illusions:

> All things on earth then, my son, are unreal; but some of them – not all, but some few only – are copies of reality. The rest are illusion and deceit, my son, for they consist of mere appearance. When the appearance flows in from above, it becomes an imitation of reality. But apart from the working of power from above it remains an illusion.[13]

> All things which the eye can see are mere phantoms, and unsubstantial outlines; but things which the eye cannot see are the realities.[14]

> You must understand that that which ever is, and that alone, is real. But man is not a thing that ever is; and therefore man is not real, but is only an appearance.[15]

One can find many similarly subversive statements about the sham nature of daily reality, and the contrasting truth of the visionary realm, in the Hermetic texts and in the library of original Gnostic texts rediscovered at Nag Hammadi in Upper Egypt in 1945.[16] Such views, however, were ferociously repressed from the fourth century AD onwards by the emerging Catholic Church, whose priests preached blind faith in an extremely crude, 'down-to-earth' and literal interpretation of the tightly censored range of Christian scriptures that became the canonical New Testament. Far from encouraging the personal search for revelation (and thus escape from illusion) amongst their 'flock', these Catholic 'men of God' presented themselves and their Church as the exclusive channel by which divine wishes reached the masses and by which the masses could communicate with the divine. Indeed, so determined were they to maintain and enforce their spiritual monopoly that by the thirteenth century the Pope had made it illegal across large parts of Europe for lay persons to possess any of the books of the Old and New Testament 'with the exception of the Psalter, the Breviary and the Book of Hours of the Blessed Virgin'. Even these could only be owned if they were in Latin. To attempt to translate them into any vernacular tongue that might be understood by the masses, and worse still to circulate vernacular copies, was considered heresy and called for the attentions of the Inquisition.[17]

Shamanic survivals from Santa Claus to St Sebastian

Against such a background of censorship and persecution, including the execution of tens of thousands of Gnostic 'heretics' during the Albigensian Crusades in the twelfth and thirteenth centuries,[18] I'm not surprised that Christians today are mostly unaware of the shamanic roots of their religion.

Yet by no means all of those roots have been amputated.

An example is the way that Christmas Day, arguably the most important annual Christian festival, has been thoroughly overtaken in the public imagination by strange non-Christian ceremonials and symbolism involving the figure of 'Santa Claus'. American ethnobotanist

Jonathan Ott proposes that what all this goes back to are ancient shamanistic cults amongst the reindeer-herding tribes of Siberia in which the hallucinogenic red and white fly agaric mushroom was consumed to induce visions – particularly around the time of midwinter:

> The winter dwelling, or yurt, had a smokehole in the roof, supported by a birch pole. At the midwinter festivals, the shaman would enter the yurt through the smokehole, perform his ceremonies, ascend the birch pole and leave. Santa Claus is robed in red and white, the colours of the fly agaric. He enters and leaves by the chimney, and he has reindeer. Santa Claus also flies, an accomplishment that he shares with the shaman.[19]

Numerous shamanic vestiges are also to be found in the cults of saints that are so popular amongst both the Catholic and Orthodox branches of Christianity. For instance, the Greek St Christophoros is often portrayed in Orthodox Christian art in therianthropic form with

The Greek St Christophoros (after Ripinsky-Naxon, 1993, p. 3)

the body of a man and the head of a dog.[20] Moreover, it is common for individuals to relate themselves especially to a particular saint who they believe intercedes on their behalf with the supernatural powers.

All of this of course would be intensely shamanic even if it were not for the additional fact that most saints are saints in the first place by virtue of having performed feats of healing or other miracles that would clearly mark them out as shamans in hunter-gatherer societies. Very often, too, if we examine the life story of a saint, we will find that he or she has been through a recognisably shamanic initiatory ordeal.

There are hundreds, if not thousands, of such cases of which the most famous and most obvious is St Sebastian, who was supposedly made a target by Roman archers and then beaten to death with clubs. Always depicted in Church art as a naked youth pierced by multiple

Left, wounded man of Pech Merle; centre, St Sebastian; right, wounded man of Eastern Free State, South Africa

arrows, Sebastian should be instantly recognisable to readers of this book as another form of the ubiquitous image of the wounded man that has been with us since the Upper Palaeolithic.[21]

St Ursula underwent the same ordeal of piercing by arrows.[22] Similarly St Justina is depicted as a damsel with both breasts pierced by one sword[23] while St Stanislaus is always shown as a bishop being 'hacked to pieces' at the foot of an altar[24] (a direct echo of the traditions of shamanic dismemberment from all around the world that we have examined in previous chapters). Though never physically martyred, the sixteenth-century Spanish nun St Theresa of Avila also underwent a classic shamanic ecstasy of piercing and agonising pain:

To my left I saw an angel in bodily form . . . its face so fiery that it seemed to belong to the highest of angels, who appear to be all flame . . . In its hand I beheld a long golden spear at the point of which a small flame seemed to flicker. I felt as if the angel pierced that spear several times through my heart, that it penetrated to my bowels, which were extracted when the spear was withdrawn, leaving me all aflame with an immense love of God.[25]

Sisters in vision and prophecy

Very often the Church reacts badly at first to potential saints, seemingly dumbfounded as to what to do with them, but ultimately finds ways to capture and channel their energies within the dominant orthodoxy. Jeanne d'Arc, who communed directly with the spirit world and its supernatural inhabitants, 'and thereby miraculously saved her king and her country',[26] was ultimately executed for her shamanic powers when the ecclesiastical authorities determined that her 'voices' (modern psychiatrists would call them auditory hallucinations) were those of demons not of angels. In an act of infamy that has rung down the ages, Jeanne was burnt at the stake at Rouen, France, on 30 April 1431. In April 1909, almost five centuries later, the Catholic Church belatedly decided that her spirit guides had after all been angels, not demons, and this great shaman of the late Middle Ages was at last canonised as a saint.[27]

What is less well known about Jeanne d'Arc is that when she stood before the Inquisition accused of witchcraft, the first questions her interrogators asked were if she had 'any knowledge of those who went to Sabbath with the fairies' or if she had not assisted 'at the assemblies held at the fountain of the fairies, near Domremy, around which dance malignant spirits'.[28]

Another matter the inquisitors were eager to learn about was a certain 'fairy tree' that Jeanne was accused of frequenting. She did not deny knowledge of it and said that it was called the Tree of the Mistress, or sometimes the Tree of the Fairies, because long ago in the past fairies had been at the tree. She reported that girls used to hang bunches of flowers on the tree and admitted that she herself had 'made wreaths there for the picture of our Lady of Domremy'. Near the tree was a spring, Jeanne added, 'where sick people would scoop up water to drink; the water healed them'.[29]

Dianne Purkiss, who teaches English at Oxford University, has taken a special interest in these fairy connections and points out that Jeanne d'Arc's testimony before the Inquisition often seems to mix up standard vernacular terms for the fairies – 'white ladies', 'good ladies' – with those for the Virgin ('Our Lady').[30] Nor is this confusion confined to Jeanne d'Arc or to the fifteenth century. Exactly the same thing happened hundreds of years later on another occasion when recognisably shamanistic experiences and supernatural encounters erupted in the face of an initially reluctant Catholic Church. This is the case from the mid-nineteenth century, briefly cited in Chapter Seventeen, of Bernadette Soubirous. Her visions of a supernatural entity later identified with the Virgin Mary were much more quickly co-opted and accommodated by the Vatican than those of Jeanne d'Arc, and led to the foundation of the world-famous shrine at Lourdes in the French Pyrenees, which is today visited by more than two million Christian pilgrims every year and where miracles of healing through contact with the waters of a sacred spring are still regularly reported. Although the copious publicity about Lourdes that the Church now churns out attributes these miracles to the powers of the Blessed Virgin Mary, the truth is that the place had a miraculous reputation long before any such association was made. As Diane Purkiss explains, this reputation derived from a much more ancient connection with the supernatural beings that we know as fairies:

> Jeanne did not have much luck conflating the Virgin Mary with 'the good ladies', but her much later sister in vision and prophecy, Bernadette Soubirous, was to be more fortunate. Like Jeanne, Bernadette frequented a site linked with the fairies, and like Jeanne, she saw visions of a beautiful lady there. Like Jeanne, Bernadette associated the sight with a healing spring, a spring in which the sick could shed their illness. Like Jeanne, Bernadette chose a term redolent of fairy lore to describe what she saw, saying that her lady was *uo petito damizela*, a little lady; Pyrenean fairies were often dwarfish . . . Unlike Jeanne, her visions

were accepted and her healing spring became the fountain at Lourdes. Of course, nothing was said about the fairies by the Church, but the influence of Pyrenean fairy stories is evident at Lourdes.[31]

The influence of Pyrenean fairy *stories*? I think Purkiss makes the wrong emphasis here, since she does not address the question of where the stories themselves originally came from. I hope I have conclusively demonstrated in Part III that such traditions are for the most part not made up but reflect genuine personal experiences, widely reported down the ages, of supernatural beings seen in altered states of consciousness and construed sometimes as spirits, sometimes as aliens and sometimes as fairies, depending on the epoch and the local cultural context. It is not a big jump from the Fairy Queen to the Blessed Virgin Mary, and the really interesting issue here is that Bernadette Soubirous clearly saw *something* that shook her to the core, as powerful hallucinations often do, and that quickly led to real effects in the real world touching the lives and beliefs of huge numbers of people and delivering to many the characteristically shamanic gift of healing.

'I beheld a lady dressed in white . . .'

When she had her first vision, on 11 February 1858, Bernadette was a half-starved, asthmatic 14-year-old from a very poor family, out that cold day with her friends Toinette and Baloume to collect firewood and any animal bones that they might find on richer people's rubbish tips. Following advice on where to look given to them by an old woman who crossed their path, they eventually found their way to the banks of a stream running alongside the Hill of Espeluges, where a cave was long ago cut by water into the imposing rocky outcrop known as Massabielle.[32]

The cave and the massif had a mysterious glamour and, as Diane Purkiss points out, were 'linked with the fairies'. Now, as everyone knows, fairies sometimes unpredictably present those they favour with gifts. Perhaps this was why the children were not too surprised to see that a great 'mass of wood and bones' – exactly what they were out looking for – lay stacked up in the mouth of the cave. All they had to do was cross the icy waters of the stream and the prize they sought would be theirs.[33]

Toinette and Baloume did not hesitate. They pulled off their shoes and stepped at once into the stream. As Bernadette later told the story:

> My two companions began crossing the water in front of the Grotto. They began crying. I asked them why they were crying. They replied that the water was bitterly cold. I remained alone on the other side.[34]

Desperately wanting to cross the stream herself, and yet afraid of catching a chill that might set off her breathing difficulties, Bernadette's rising sense of urgency and distress becomes palpable in her account at the moment that Toinette and Baloume reach the other side and unkindly decline to make special arrangements to get her across with dry feet:

> I asked them to help me by throwing stones in the water so that I could cross without taking off my shoes. They told me to do as they had. Then I went a little further down to see if I could get across with my shoes on. I could not. I came back towards the Grotto and I started taking off my shoes . . .[35]

At this point, physically weak, hungry, anxious, agitated and contemplating the impending shock of cold water, it is obvious that Bernadette Soubirous was a prime candidate for an instant altered state of consciousness even if she had not been (as she almost certainly was) one of the 2 per cent of all human populations who are able to enter trance spontaneously. 'Hardly had I taken off my first stocking,' she tells us:

> when I heard a sound as though there had been a rush of wind. I looked around towards the meadow. I saw the trees quite still. So I continued to take off my shoes. Again I heard the same noise. I looked up towards the Grotto. I beheld a Lady dressed in white. She wore a white dress, a blue sash and a yellow rose on each foot . . .[36]

In another, more detailed account of that vision, Bernadette said that she 'lost all power of speech and thought' after hearing the rushing wind noise the second time. Turning her head towards the Grotto, she saw

> at one of the openings of the rock a rosebush, one only, moving as if it were very windy. Almost at the same moment there came out of the interior of the Grotto a golden-coloured cloud, and soon after a Lady, young and beautiful . . . the like of which I had never seen, came and placed herself at the entrance of the opening above the rosebush . . .[37]

The 'Lady', who appeared to Bernadette at the same spot 17 more times over the next five months, wore the typical garb of a fairy (though coupled in this case with a politically expedient rosary). It was only much later that she became identified with the Virgin Mary. On her way home with Toinette and Baloume after the first vision, Bernadette reports quite explicity: 'I told them I had seen a Lady in white, but that I did not know who it was . . .'[38] Even the term 'Lady in white' is a giveaway in a land where, as we saw above, fairy women were commonly referred to as 'white ladies'.

Just as spirit-helpers in the Amazon today teach hallucinating shamans the properties of plants, so on 25 February 1858 'Our Lady of Lourdes' instructed Bernadette concerning a certain 'herb': 'Go and drink from the fountain and wash yourself and eat of the herb which is at the side . . . ["*Vous mangerez de l'herbe qui est à côté . . .*"]'[39] I can't help wondering what sort of 'herb' was growing that day by the side of the Grotto of Massabielle at Lourdes, and whether what was meant might not have been some crop of psychoactive mushrooms such as *Psilocybe semilanceata* that might help explain Bernadette's repeated sessions of pure shamanic ecstasy.

There is another curiosity too that I don't want to make too much of but will simply mention in passing. Lourdes stands near the geographical centre of that large area of south-west France and northern Spain where the greatest number of painted caves dating from the Upper Palaeolithic have been found. The hill of Espeluges at Lourdes, at the foot of which the Grotto is located, also contains another much larger cave, situated about 65 metres higher up, that was used by our ancestors during the Upper Palaeolithic.[40] In 1889 Church authorities decided to build a chapel inside this cave and in the process removed over 2,000 cubic metres of deposits from its floor, which were then scattered over nearby land. Archaeologists note that 'many items of Palaeolithic portable art [were] subsequently discovered in these discarded sediments'.[41]

It seems at least permissible to guess, therefore, that the Grotto of Lourdes that Christians today describe as 'an open door to another world',[42] and that we know was linked with fairies in medieval times, could possibly have been part of some shamanic pilgrimage tradition as far back as the Upper Palaeolithic. Perhaps the place itself has special qualities that science doesn't understand but that have been discovered empirically, and forgotten, and rediscovered again and again by successive societies and cultures down through the ages.

Michael Persinger and electromagnetism

The last point is pure speculation, nothing else. Nonetheless it rests on almost 30 years of solid research by Dr Michael Persinger, head of the Neuroscience Laboratory at Laurentian University in Ontario. His work has shown that certain almost imperceptible electromagnetic fields, often associated with earthquakes and other seismic events, seem to interact with the human brain in such a way as to trigger temporarily altered states of consciousness every bit as deep and every bit as 'hallucinatory' as those induced by drugs like DMT, psilocybin and LSD. These effects are especially pronounced in the case of individuals with unusually excitable temporal lobes.[43]

Persinger's theory provides a neat, one-stop explanation for why large numbers of people gathered together in the same location sometimes all start to hallucinate at once and often say that they have seen broadly the same things, though some more intensely than others. Indeed Persinger's volunteers, subjected to strong electromagnetic fields under laboratory conditions, routinely report hallucinations of small beings standing near them.[44] As with my approach to drugs, my use of the word 'hallucination' here implies no judgement concerning the actual reality status of what is seen. Just as DMT may conceivably retune the receiver wavelength of our brains to 'pick up' veridical alternative realities, so too it is conceivable that electromagnetic fields might have the same effect. Even Persinger, who is himself not much in favour of spirit worlds, has to admit the possibility that:

> The experience [occasioned by an electromagnetic field] actually represents what was perceived. From this perspective, the experiences reported by the thousands of normal people who have reported visitation phenomena – from the Virgin Mary to the most repugnant alien – are primarily veridical. The similarity of experiences would be due to the similarity of actual stimuli that produce them rather than to a mundane stimulus that simply activates an intrinsic pattern of complex neuronal activity.[45]

Persinger does not seem to be aware of the pitfalls that confront this preferred notion of his – i.e. supposedly 'intrinsic' patterns of complex neuronal activity, somehow installed in the human brain, that when suitably stimulated yield experiences like abductions by aliens or encounters with the Blessed Virgin Mary. If such intrinsic patterns exist, which no scientist has yet demonstrated, then we have to be able to explain how they evolved, and that, as we will see in Chapter Twenty-Three, is no easy matter and leads us into a mystery every bit as deep as any spirit world. It is to Persinger's credit, however, despite his reductionist instincts, that he does not entirely rule out the shamanic alternative that spiritual beings seen in altered states of consciousness may in some way be real, noting that 'in the pursuit of the Unknown, all possibilities must be considered'.[46]

The shaman and the Fairy Queen

Probably we will never know how Bernadette Soubirous induced her altered states of consciousness, but we have the reports of eyewitnesses that she frequently fell into a deep trancelike condition during her encounters with 'the Lady' (whatever the true identity of this supernatural being). These trances, or raptures, were very much like those of a shaman communing with spirits. For example, on 4 March 1858, in the presence of a crowd estimated at 10,000 (none of whom saw the Lady). 'Bernadette went into a rapturous ecstasy that lasted well over an hour in an atmosphere of fervour and peace . . .'[47] Earlier, on 24 February, she had put on an even more classically shamanic display to a smaller audience of around 200 (who again did not see the Lady themselves):

> After a few minutes, Bernadette's face saddened, her eyes filled with tears; then she was seen to advance on her knees into the hollow of the Grotto which opens out on the outside recess. The child conversed with the Lady who was now quite near her. She smiled. Thus, for some minutes Bernadette came and went from the outside into the interior of the Grotto; on her face tears changed into smiles and smiles into tears. Now and again she would kiss the ground.[48]

Just as the shaman intercedes with spirits to bring the gift of supernatural healing to his people, so we can see that Bernadette's encounters at Lourdes with the mysterious 'Lady in the cave' led ultimately to the bestowal of a potent healing grace upon mankind. Indeed, the miracles that happen every day to ordinary human beings as they bathe themselves in the spring waters that flow forth from the Grotto seem to me to be prime examples of a very powerful and ancient kind of 'shamanic healing' in action.

I visited Lourdes on an ordinary midweek in June 2004, yet I found myself amongst more than 8,000 hopeful, damaged people, many in wheelchairs, or on crutches, or supported by friends and relatives, as they made their way painfully down the long processional avenue that leads to the great Basilica, to the Crypt where the relics of St Bernadette are now kept, and to the sanctum sanctorum of the Grotto itself. Night was falling and we all held candles as we spilled into the large square in front of the Basilica. There volunteers marshalled us into a winding, sinuous procession that gradually and majestically coiled forward to form the glowing body of a gigantic serpent of light with its tail towards the secular world of the town and its head already penetrating the otherworld of the ancient cave where Bernadette received her visions.

A tiny point of illumination amongst so many flickering sparks, I drank the waters of the healing spring, bathed my face and hands and, entering at last within the mouth of the Grotto, felt drawn to touch its craggy stone walls worn smooth as any marble by the generations of pilgrims before me who had responded to the same instinct. I was powerfully reminded that sections of wall in many of the Upper Palaeolithic painted caves, and in the rock shelters of southern Africa, are worn smooth in exactly the same way – and perhaps for exactly the same reason.

Some who have been healed at Lourdes have left written messages of gratitude inside the Crypt close to Bernadette's relics. Their simple statements and affirmations bear witness to a form of direct experiential contact with supernatural powers that long pre-dates Christianity:

Grateful. Cured of deadly cancer 1974, John B. Flachs, Hamilton, Canada.

Merci NDL [*Notre Dame de Lourdes*] *pour avoir sauvée notre maman, mai 1980.*

Deep gratitude for favours obtained through our lady. M. Argier.

Thank you. Anne, Angela and Joseph Chang-Hoi Phin, 18 June 1979.

One need not remain very long at Lourdes to realise that the quest for direct intervention, help and healing from the realm of the spirits that anthropologists most commonly associate with shamanism in hunter-gatherer societies is still a strong force in the modern world. Bernadette's role was fundamentally that of a shaman, and – far from being supplanted by Christianity – it is the Fairy Queen who still rules in the enchanted realm of the Grotto.

The Virgin in the flying saucer

During the course of the twentieth century, shamanic visions and encounters like those of Jeanne d'Arc and Bernadette Soubirous with entities described as 'ladies in white' who were later officially co-opted by the Church as true apparitions of the Virgin Mary seem to have occurred at a steady rate of around three per year; however, there are no figures on the number of sightings that have not been reported to the Church or that the Church rejects.[49] The overlap between such direct experiences of supernaturals and the entities formerly known as fairies is obvious and, as we have seen, is often made explicit by the visionaries themselves. It is therefore of interest that the Virgin Mary phenomenon also has strong overlaps with UFOs and the sorts of supernatural entities who might just as easily be described as 'aliens'.

Limitations of space forbid a lengthy treatment here, and two brief examples will have to suffice.

The village of Knock in County Mayo, Ireland, became a world centre of Christian pilgrimage after a group of 'shining' beings, one of whom the Church later accepted as the Virgin Mary, appeared there on the evening of 21 August 1879. The apparition was witnessed from different sides of the field in which it occurred by three men, six women, two children and three teenagers. What they reported would be taken as a UFO sighting today since it began with the arrival of 'a large globe of golden light' which settled somewhat above the grass of the field. Within the light could be seen three glowing and radiant human-like beings – two men and a woman. One of the men, construed as St John, was said to have had the manner of a teacher and held an open book in which the lines and letters could be seen – a common enough theme of UFO abductions and shamanic encounters with spirits. Another figure, construed by all the witnesses as the Virgin Mary, was a classic 'lady in white'; her robe was described as 'strikingly white' and she wore in addition 'a large white cloak'. Bridget Trench, one of those who was there that night, rushed to embrace her feet but found her to be non-physical:

I felt nothing in the embrace . . . yet the figures appeared so full and so lifelike and so lifesize that I could not understand it and wondered why my hands could not feel what was so plain and distinct to my sight.[50]

Almost immediately afterwards, as at Lourdes, healing miracles began to occur at Knock and have continued to this day.[51]

The second example of 'UFO crossover' is the so-called Miracle of Fatima in 1917. In this famous case Lucia, Francisco and Jacinta, three Catholic children of the small town of Fatima in Portugal, had repeated encounters over a period of six months with a mysterious supernatural being who said she was 'from Heaven' and who they naturally construed as the Virgin Mary.[52] Their fame quickly grew and on a number of occasions the encounters occurred in the presence of crowds of tens of thousands of people – many of whom saw visions and reported effects identical to those associated with modern UFO sightings.

It is worth nothing that before the Fatima apparitions began on 13 May 1917, Lucia, Francisco and Jacinta had each reported other supernatural encounters. On several occasions during 1915, when she was eight, Lucia had been visited by 'a transparent white cloud and a human form'. Likewise in 1916 when they took shelter from a rainstorm in the mouth of a cave near Fatima, all three of the children had a close encounter with a being who they construed as an 'angel'.[53] He appeared to them initially as a bright light, 'whiter than the driven snow', amidst a strong wind that shook the trees above their heads – a description that could apply to many modern UFO sightings. Coming closer, he then revealed himself in the form of 'a young man, transparent and resplendent with light'.[54]

All the subsequent Virgin Mary apparitions that the children experienced between 13 May 1917 and the miraculous climax of these events on 13 October 1917 took place in a wide, amphitheatre-like meadow near an ancient sacred spot called *Cova da Iria* (the Cave of St Irene). On the first occasion the children were tending their sheep in an adjoining pasture when they saw a blinding flash of light over *Cova da Iria*. They ran towards the light, which hovered above a tree, and in its midst they saw the figure of 'a little woman' who instructed them to return every month to the same place.[55]

On 13 June 1917 a crowd of 50 spectators gathered in the hope that the Virgin Mary would appear again as promised. Though none were rewarded with visions of the Virgin themselves, they did see the children transported in shamanic ecstasy while Lucia, the eldest of the three, appeared to address an unseen entity. Only Lucia could hear the Virgin's replies, although one member of the crowd reported being aware of a very faint voice like the buzzing of a bee[56] (such buzzing sounds are often associated with shamanic altered states of consciousness and are frequently construed as bees). At the end of the dialogue all witness heard a loud bang and reported the presence of a small cloud surrounding the tree above which the children had seen the Virgin.[57]

On 13 July 1917, more than 4,000 witnesses were present for the third apparition and reported phenomena that Jacques Vallee regards as 'specific enough to be compared to UFO data'.[58] As on the second occasion, these phenomena included 'a buzzing or humming sound, a decrease in the Sun's glow and heat, a small whitish cloud about the tree of apparitions, and a loud noise at the Lady's departure'.[59]

On 13 August 1917 the children were not present to witness the scheduled appearance of the Virgin as they had been imprisoned by a local official who believed the whole thing to be a hoax. They were released by a mob later the same day but in the meantime the 18,000 people who had gathered in the meadow at *Cova da Iria* heard a loud explosion followed by a bright flash and saw a small white cloud gather about the tree before dissipating a few moments later. Nature took on psychedelic tones. Clouds in the sky changed colour in weird ways, rapidly alternating from crimson, to pink, to yellow, to blue. Witnesses spoke of 'coloured light, like a rainbow on the ground', of 'clouds around the sun reflecting different colours on the people', and of 'flowers' falling from the sky. Manuel Pedro, one of the eyewitnesses, reported *una especie de globo luminoso girando nas nuevas* – 'a luminous globe spinning through the clouds'.[60]

Alongside a crowd of 30,000, two Jesuits who had come to debunk the apparitions witnessed the events of 13 September 1917. By the end of the day they were sceptics no longer, convinced of everything the children claimed. In their report they describe how 'a globe of light was seen by all, advancing slowly down the valley, from east to west, toward the children', how it came to rest on the tree where the Virgin always appeared, how a white cloud formed, and how 'petals' began to fall from the sky:

> As the people stare at this strange sight they soon notice that the falling, glistening globules, contrary to the laws of perspective, grow smaller and smaller as they near them. And when they reach out their hands and hats to catch them they find they have somehow melted away.[61]

It would be hard to think of a better description of a hallucinatory fog of entoptic dots and dashes raining down from the sky. Meanwhile the three children were in touch with the figure of the little woman inside the globe of light and received a communication from her – on 13 October a miracle would occur. The globe then ascended and vanished into the sun.[62] Afterwards, one of the priests described it as 'a heavenly vehicle that carried the Mother of God from her throne above'.[63]

The final apparition, on 13 October 1917, was attended by a crowd of 70,000, none of whom saw the Virgin or heard a word she said to the children. What all the spectators did see was 'the miracle': 'a revolving, multicoloured disk in the sky which plunged downwards and then, again, upwards into the sun'.[64] This large flying disc, which many believed would crash into their midst, was described at the time as having pursued a zig-zag course – the characteristic 'falling-leaf trajectory' of UFO sightings, as Jacques Vallee points out.[65] Another intriguing parallel is that a witness who studied the disc with binoculars reported seeing 'a ladder and two entities' emerging from it.[66]

As had been the case at Lourdes, and as at Knock, there was a shamanic aftermath to the apparitions at Fatima: hundreds of people with previously life-threatening illness reported miraculous, spontaneous cures.[67]

Ezekiel on ayahuasca?

Much more evidence could be given of the shamanic vestiges, active shamanic practices, and unmistakably shamanic experiences wrapped up in modern Christianity, but this is not intended to be a comprehensive survey of these ancient influences on any one religion. My purpose is rather to convey to the reader the broader truth, suggested earlier, that if we scratch the surface of *any* religion deeply enough we will sooner or later come to shamanism and to the distinctive supernatural realms, beings and phenomena that shamans everywhere encounter in their visions.

Before Christianity there was Judaism, and before the New Testament there was the Old Testament. In these more ancient sources, too, shamanic allusions, supernatural beings and visionary flying discs abound.

We have already seen in Chapter Fourteen the direct comparison made in 1958 by the psychologist Carl Gustav Jung between the so-called 'wheels of Ezekiel' and modern UFOs. The Old Testament description (Ezek I: 4–19) involves a whirlwind and fire, as well as mysterious creatures on board great wheels that 'lifted them up from the earth'. In 2003 Benny Shanon, Professor of Psychology at the Hebrew University in Jerusalem, drew attention to these same verses in the Book of Ezekiel, but from a different – though by no means contradictory – perspective. In his view they describe hallucinations very similar to those seen under the influence of ayahuasca. The reader will recall from the last chapter that Shanon has himself consumed ayahuasca more than 130 times and is well qualified on this subject, having, in addition, interviewed hundreds of other users and collated their reports. He points out that

> Ezekiel opens his text with noting that the heavens opened. Many powerful ayahuasca visions present the same pattern. Like Ezekiel who recounts that 'the heavens opened, and I saw visions of God' [Ezek I:1], drinkers of the brew report that the heavens opened and celestial and heavenly scenes were revealed to them.[68]

Shanon argues that the descriptions of light and fire in Ezekiel parallel ayahuasca visions.[69] Additionally:

The materials prevalent in ayahuasca visions are gold, brass, gilded wood, crystal (especially palaces of crystal), precious stones and fine textiles. In the Ezekiel vision gold and textiles are not mentioned. Apart from these, all the materials common in ayahuasca visions are encountered in Ezekiel. Furthermore, all the materials mentioned in the Ezekiel vision pertain to the set of materials commonly seen in ayahuasca visions.[70]

Large revolving wheels and disembodied eyes are other features common to Ezekiel and to ayahuasca visions,[71] as are therianthropes:

The creatures described in Ezekiel have four faces – those of a human being, a lion, a bull and an eagle. Furthermore, while having 'the likeness of a man', these creatures were winged and their soles of feet were those of a calf. *Chimeras* (in the extended sense of the term) or *hybrid* creatures – that is, creatures which are half-human, half-animal – are very common in ayahuasca visions. Such creatures encountered in the corpus I have collected include hybrids of, on the one hand, humans and, on the other hand, fish, felines, reptiles, birds and canines. Also frequent are creatures who ordinarily do not have wings but in the visions do – e.g. winged horses and winged elephants. In my corpus there are also several instances of creatures with multiple faces. Usually, these creatures are encountered in heavenly scenes in which the ayahuasca drinker [as was the case with Ezekiel] feels that some ultimate secrets are being revealed to him or her . . .[72]

To cut a long story short, Shanon puts forward a tentative hypothesis that the origins of the Hebrew religion are rooted in experiences of this sort (Moses' 'burning bush' vision is another archetypal example) made possible – as they still are today in the Amazon – by the consumption of psychoactive plants. He points out that combinations of acacia (*Mimosa tortilis* and *Mimosa raddina*) with *Peganum harmala* (the plant known as Syrian rue) 'produce a biochemical configuration identical to that produced by the Amazonian plants of which ayahuasca is made'.[73]

Since the relevant acacia and Syrian rue species grow widely in several arid areas of the Middle East, including the Land of Israel, the Sinai Peninsula and Mesopotamia, Shanon argues that hallucinatory experiences arising from the use of these plants cannot be ruled out and are, on the contrary, strongly indicated by the character of many of the visions reported in the Old Testament.[74]

Drugs and genuine religious experiences

It is Benny Shanon's controversial view that 'all the paradigmatic characteristics of the mystical experience are encountered with ayahuasca ...'[75] He also asks if the 'meaning and value of religious and spiritual experience induced by the ingestion of psychoactive agents' are 'comparable to the experiences of mystics attained without external agents', and replies: 'My empirical study of ayahuasca leads me to answer with a categorical "yes".'[76]

It may at first seem absurd that anything like a genuine religious experience could be induced by activities as simple and apparently as materialistic as eating, drinking or smoking certain species of plants. But we should feel less surprised when we remember that the plants in question contain chemicals intimately related to brain hormones and neurotransmitters such as dopamine and serotonin. Although the neurological details are difficult to grasp, the fact is that these chemicals and others like them are intrinsic to *all* the functions of our brains, while our brains in turn are involved in *everything* we experience – even if we choose to define some of those experiences as real and some as non-real. Whether we like it or not, in other words, and whether or not we augment them or tinker with their balance in any way, it is beyond serious dispute that these chemicals *already* play a fundamental role in spontaneous (i.e., non-drug-induced) religious experiences. And since such spontaneous experiences occasioned by brain chemistry are regarded as genuine, then there is no reason why the deliberate induction of the same brain chemistry with hallucinogens should result in experiences that are any less genuine.

It was for this exact reason that Aldous Huxley, who had no doubt of their mystical and religious value, often referred to hallucinogens as 'gratuitous graces'.[77] Those of us reared in puritanical moral climates might feel that we cannot possibly deserve something so wonderful and enlightening as a religious experience without working and suffering for it, but this is not a logical position. Besides, no matter how powerful the hallucinogen we may consume, the truth is that we will *not* have a religious experience with it unless we have prepared ourselves properly and have indeed made ourselves in some way deserving.

Huston Smith, the renowned American scholar of religions, agrees that many drug experiences may be entirely lacking in religious features: 'They can be sensual as readily as spiritual, trivial as readily as transforming, capricious as readily as sacramental.'[78] Nevertheless he reports recent research which demonstrates that under the right circumstances with properly prepared subjects, drugs can and do

> induce religious experiences that are indistinguishable from such exper-
> iences that occur spontaneously . . . The way the statistics are currently
> running, it looks as if from one-fourth to one-third of the general
> population will have religious experiences if they take certain drugs
> under naturalistic conditions . . . Among subjects who have strong reli-
> gious proclivities, the proportion of those who have religious experiences
> jumps to three-fourths. If such subjects take the drugs in religious
> settings, the percentage soars to nine out of ten.[79]

I feel compelled to re-emphasise at this point that my full accept-ance of the role that brain chemistry plays in consciousness does not mean that I think brain chemistry *causes* consciousness or that reli-gious experiences – whether or nor induced by hallucinogens or other means – are necessarily 'made up' in the brain. I see no evidence for such reductionism. The alternative model that I have adopted throughout this book is of the brain as a biochemical and bioelectric *receiver* that may be 'retuned' by a variety of techniques to allow atten-tion to be paid to other levels of reality not normally accessible to our consciousness. Those 'retuning' techniques include the use of hallucinogenic drugs combined with the skilful manipulation of the 'set' and 'setting' of participants to generate maximum sensitivity and openness on their part.[80]

Inspired by the progress that David Lewis-Williams has made cracking the visionary code of Upper Palaeolithic cave art, more and more scholars are coming to suspect that the answers to some of the greatest mysteries of antiquity may lie in further research into the role of hallucinogens in triggering spiritual experiences. It seems that very often those experiences were sought in theatrically staged subterranean settings, selected, like the caves themselves, to maximise visionary 'retuning' of the brain. Specific suggestions have been made on the basis of large bodies of convincing evidence that the religions of ancient Greece, ancient India, ancient Egypt, and the ancient Maya of Central America – to name but a few – were rooted and grounded in direct spiritual experiences that the devotees themselves attained through the use of psychoactive plants. If this is so, then one would expect to find many strong shamanistic traces in all of these religions.

Perhaps not surprisingly, it turns out that we do, and that in a number of cases it is even possible to identify the specific hallucinogens that were used.

The end of life and its god-sent beginning

Barely half an hour's drive outside the modern city of Athens lies the ancient shrine of Eleusis, humbled and in ruins now but once the centre of the most famous 'mystery cult' of antiquity, dedicated to the myth of Demeter and Persephone. The myth tells the story of Demeter's journey to the underworld to claim back from death the soul of her daughter Persephone – a shamanic mission that honours the forces of life, rebirth and regeneration. So vital were these forces held to be that once a year, in our month of September, thousands of pilgrims from all parts of Greece used to converge on Eleusis, where it was believed that the living Persephone had burst forth from the earth. The terminus of their journey was the great Telestrion, the darkened Hall of Initiation, with its forest of columns, focused around an inner enclosure known as the Anaktoron, from which, at the climax

521

of the ceremonies, a figure apparently materialised 'in the midst of a great light'.[81] The figure was often construed as that of Persephone 'returning from the dead with her new-born son conceived in the land of death'.[82]

It is hard work to discover anything else about the visions that the pilgrims saw at Eleusis. The shrine was astonishingly successful at guarding its mystery over a period that some authorities suggest may have been as long as 2,000 years of continuous functioning before it was finally closed by Christian diktat in the fourth century AD.[83] Hundreds of thousands passed through its gates down the ages, including some of the most famous names of Classical Greece, such as Plato, Aristotle and Sophocles, but almost everyone stayed very quiet about what they had seen – which, indeed, they were obliged to keep secret 'on pain of death or banishment'.[84] We have few specifics, therefore, but from many of the pilgrims there have survived more general reports telling us that the rituals at Eleusis and the visions seen there were transformatory and that afterwards they were never the same as before. Very commonly they claimed to have utterly lost their fear of death and to be prepared for life beyond it in the land of shadows. In the words of Sophocles after his initiation at Eleusis: 'Thrice happy are those of mortals, who having seen those rites depart for Hades; for to them alone is granted to have a true life there. For the rest, all there is evil.'[85] The poet Pindar likewise said that what he had seen validated the continuity of existence beyond the grave, and that he had learned great truths from his experience at Eleusis:[86] 'Happy is he who, having seen these rites, goes below the hollow earth; for he knows the end of life and he knows its god-sent beginning.'[87]

As archaeologist George Mylonas puts it, when we read these and many other similar statements by the great and nearly great of the ancient world:

We cannot help but believe that the Mysteries of Eleusis were not an empty, childish affair devised by shrewd priests to fool the peasant and the ignorant, but a philosophy of life that possessed substance and meaning and imparted a modicum of truth to the human soul. That belief is strengthened when we read in Cicero that Athens has given nothing to the world more excellent or divine than the Eleusinian Mysteries. Let us recall again that the rites of Eleusis were held for some two thousand years; that for two thousand years civilised humanity was sustained and ennobled by those rites. Then we shall be able to appreciate the meaning and importance of Eleusis . . .[88]

Mylonas was certain that the shrine succeeded so spectacularly for so long because it 'satisfied the most sincere yearnings and deepest longings of the human heart'[89] – but neither he nor anyone else when he wrote these words in 1961 really had the faintest idea *how* it managed to pull off a trick like that. It's all very well to hint that it must have had something to do with 'a philosophy of life', but a philosophy takes time to absorb, while it is clear that what all the pilgrims were struck and transformed by at Eleusis was a powerful and immediate *experience* that they went through during their night inside the Telestrion and that seems to have included visions seen, sounds heard and supernatural beings encountered.

The oath of secrecy and the passage of thousands of years means that the pickings are thin in the relatively limited range of primary sources on Eleusis that have come down to us. Nevertheless, scattered here and there, some clues have survived that have helped researchers build up a clearer picture of what was really going on inside the Telestrion. Aristotle confirms that it was 'an experience rather than something learned'.[90] The pilgrim Sopater tells us that he saw a *schema ti*, 'a form or appearance of some kind hovering above the ground'.[91] Plato was perhaps a little more explicit when he spoke of *phantasmata* or ghostly apparitions, while Pausanias records that the initiation hall 'became filled with spirits'.[92] Also relevant are the physical symptoms reported by many:

fear and trembling in the limbs, vertigo, nausea, and a cold sweat. Then there came the vision, a sight amidst an aura of brilliant light that suddenly flickered through the darkened chamber. Eyes had never before seen the like . . . The division between earth and sky melted into a pillar of light.[93]

Spot the hallucinogen

What are we to make of this distinctive constellation of symptoms combining spectacular visions with physical malaise? Carl A.P. Ruck, Professor of Classical Studies at Boston University, is in no doubt:

> Clearly an hallucinatory reality was induced within the initiation hall and since at times as many as three thousand initiates, a number greater than the population of an ordinary ancient town, were afforded such a vision annually on schedule, it would seem obvious that some psychotropic drug was involved.[94]

Together with the world-famous mycologist R. Gordon Wasson, and Albert Hoffman, the discoverer of LSD, Ruck was the third member of a team of eminent scholarly detectives who spent much of their spare time during the first half of the 1970s trying to solve the mystery of Eleusis. They drew attention to the well-documented fact that on entering the Telestrion every pilgrim was obliged to drink 'a special potion, the *kykeon*, that was an essential part of the Mystery'.[95]

Could the potion have been psychedelic? Fortunately its ingredients are recorded in a Homeric hymn to Demeter dating to the seventh century BC, so we ought to be able to find out. At first glance they don't look anything like hallucinogens, being listed rather innocently as barley (*alphi*), water, and mint (*glechon*).[96] However, Gordon Wasson, the mycologist on the research team, knew that barley and other wild and cultivated grasses often support a fungal parasite called ergot that does contain hallucinogenic alkaloids. Indeed, it was from precisely the same fungus that Albert Hoffman had first synthesised LSD in 1943. Hoffman tells the story as follows:

> In July 1975 I was visiting my friend Gordon Wasson in his home in Danbury when he suddenly asked me this question: whether Early Man in ancient Greece could have hit on a method to isolate an hallucinogen from ergot which would have given him an experience comparable to LSD or psilocybin. I replied that this might well have

been the case and I promised to send him, after further reflection, an exposition of our present knowledge on the subject.[97]

It took Hoffman two years and much laboratory work to complete his task, since ergot-contaminated rye was known as a dreaded poison in the Middle Ages (see Chapter Eight) and he had to satisfy himself that it would have been possible for the priests of Eleusis to isolate the hallucinogenic alkaloids from the toxic and deadly ingredients. What he discovered is that ergonovine and lysergic acid amide, the two principal hallucinogens in ergot, are both water-soluble, whereas the poisonous alkaloids such as ergotamine and ergotoxin are not. Throughout Greece ergot is a parasite of barley, which we know was one of the ingredients of the *kykeon*, and in Hoffman's opinion it would have been relatively easy for the priests to extract the visionary alkaloids: 'The separation of the hallucinogenic agents by simple water solution from the non-soluable ergotamine and ergotoxin alkaloids was well with the range of possibilities open to Early Man in Greece.'[98]

Although the priests of Eleusis were dedicated in particular to the cultivation of wheat and barley in the name of Demeter, goddess of grains, Hoffman points out that an even easier method than washing contaminated barley was available to them. *Paspalum distichum*, a wild grass that grows throughout the Mediterranean basin, supports *Claviceps paspali*, a species of ergot

> which contains only alkaloids that are hallucinogenic and which could even have been used directly in powdered form . . . In the course of time the hierophants could easily have discovered *Claviceps paspali* growing on the grass *Paspalum distichum*. Here they would be able to get their hallucinogen direct, straight and pure. But I mention this only as a possibility or a likelihood, and not because we need *P. distichum* to answer Wasson's question . . . The answer is yes. Early Man in ancient Greece could have arrived at an hallucinogen from ergot.[99]

Any remaining doubt that the sacred potion of Eleusis was indeed a psychoactive brew was dispelled when the researchers came across evidence of a notorious scandal . . . uncovered in the classical age, when it was discovered that numerous aristocratic Athenians had begun celebrating the Mystery at home with groups of drunken guests at dinner parties.[100]

The revellers included Alcibiades, the brilliant but unscrupulous politician and military commander who was convicted of profaning the Eleusinian Mysteries in 415 BC and defected to Sparta rather than face the death penalty.[101] As well as showing the seriousness with which such matters were treated by the Athenian authorities, the significance of this story lies in what it tells us about the true nature of the visionary experiences at the heart of the Mysteries. We now know that these experiences were not exclusive to the sacred precincts of Eleusis but could even be enjoyed at private dinner tables by the simple expedient of drinking the *kykeon*.[102] The conclusion that they were drug experiences is more or less inevitable, as is the obvious parallel with the modern recreational use of once sacred plant hallucinogens.

Last but not least, it is surely significant that Demeter herself, the goddess of Eleusis, was sometimes known by the name of *Erysibe*, which means, literally, 'ergot',[103] while we read three times in the Hymn to Demeter that her robes were 'purple dark', the colour of the fruiting bodies of ergot.[104]

For all these reasons, and many more, Professor Ruck concludes: 'I and my colleagues interpreted the Eleusinian mysteries as communal shamanic ceremonies involving the ingestion of drugs.'[105]

The mystery of soma

As becomes apparent under modest magnification, 'fruiting bodies' of ergot are in fact clusters of tiny purple mushrooms.[106] Another much larger species of mushroom, *Amanita muscaria* – the fly agaric – has been identified by the mycologist R. Gordon Wasson, together with Indologists Stella Kamrisch and Wendy O'Flaherty, as the most likely candidate for the mysterious soma, the famous consciousness-altering drug of ancient India's Vedic scriptures.[107]

The Rigveda, the oldest of the four Vedas that stand at the root of modern Hinduism, is thought to date back more than 3,000 years and perhaps a great deal longer. It describes soma as a god, as a plant, and as a beverage extracted or pressed from that plant.[108] The Vedas run to millions of words, and tens of thousands of them are devoted to soma, but we need only cite a few lines here to convey the sense of its hallucinogenic attributes and its unmistakably shamanic undertones:

> Like currents of wind, the drinks have lifted me up. Have I not drunk soma?

> One of my wings is in heaven, the other trails below. Have I not drunk soma?

> I am huge, huge! Flying to the clouds. Have I not drunk soma?[109]

> In the navel of the earth [is situated soma], which is also the mainstay of the sky.[110]

> The filter of the burning [soma] has been spread in heaven's home. Its dazzling mesh was spread afar . . .[111]

> We have drunk the soma, we are become Immortals, we have arrived at the Light, we have found the Gods.[112]

The identity of the original soma plant had long been forgotten by Hindus by the beginning of the historical period. The problem first came to the attention of Western scholars in 1784, when it was mentioned in a note to a translation of the Bhagavad Gita, and has been the subject of heated discussions ever since. Wasson's evidence linking soma to the hallucinogenic fly agaric has, however, proved the most convincing. Briefly:

- The Vedic descriptions of the soma plant make no mention of leaves, roots or branches;[113] a mushroom best fits this bill.
- The Vedas frequently refer to soma as *aja ekpad* (literally 'not-born, one-foot'). This strongly suggests a mushroom, 'which, springing up mysteriously and without seed could be said to be "not-born".

Likewise, if thought of anthropomorphically, its stipe (stem) could be conceived of as "one-foot".[114]

- Soma's colour is sometimes described with the word *hari* in the Rigveda, meaning bright red to tawny brown. Bright red is the colour of fresh fly agaric, while the dried mushrooms are tawny brown.[115]
- It is very likely that the mushrooms were preserved dried (in which state they anyway undergo certain chemical reactions that make them more potent) and when needed were rehydrated with water, milk or ghee before being 'pressed' out, just as described in the soma ritual.[116]
- The word most frequently used in the Rigveda to describe the effects of soma has 'a range of meanings including delight, intoxication, and inspiration. It also refers to the heavenly bliss of the gods and ancestors and is, in the context of soma, best translated and interpreted as rapture or elation.'[117]

Much other evidence too detailed to enumerate here is also cited. But even setting aside all this, there is one passage in Rigveda IX:74 which on its own appears to contain sufficient detail to vindicate Wasson's thesis that soma is *Amanita muscaria*. The passage reads as follows:

Soma, storm cloud imbued with life, is milked of ghee, milk. Navel of the Way, Immortal Principle, he sprang into life in the far distance. Acting in concert, those charged with the Office, richly gifted, do full honour to soma. The swollen men urinate the on-flowing soma.[118]

The reason that the Vedic image of priests with swollen bladders pissing out 'the on-flowing soma' is so firmly diagnostic of *Amanita muscaria* is that the fly agaric is the only psychoactive plant that retains, or even strengthens, its activity after being passed through the 'filter' of the human digestive system. It can thus be said quite accurately to flow onwards into urine. Wasson's wide research on hallucinogenic fungi throughout the world had taken him on field trips amongst the shamans of Siberia long before he became interested in India, and he was therefore very well aware that in Siberia:

He who drinks the juice of the hallucinogenic mushroom saves his urine, and others drink this urine with inebriating effect, perhaps heightened, for there is reason to think that certain nauseating ingredients in the original mushroom are filtered out in passing through the human organism. This use of the urine can be repeated over and over again, it is said, until it has passed through five human bodies, when at last it loses its virtue.[119]

Wasson further points to other passages in the Rigveda in which the god Indra is said to drink soma, 'pissing it out day by day', and in which the mythical Rudras in the shape of horses seem to have pissed soma likewise.[120] But this is all very curious unless we are prepared to accept that an ancient hallucinogenic cult exploiting the well-know shamanic virtues of the fly agaric mushroom provided the visionary spark out of which the Vedas first emerged fully formed in remote prehistory. Wasson's logic is, in my view, impeccable:

When one drinks tea, or coffee, or milk, or beer, one later urinates, not tea, coffee, milk or beer, but urine. Why does Indra, why possibly do the Rudras, urinate soma? How did the Vedic priests learn that soma-urine was also soma unless they had drunk it?[121]

A vital role

The reader will recall from Part II that David Lewis-Williams has faced stiff resistance from a faction of archaeologists who appear to object *in principle* to the notion that the first religious experiences of our ancestors were induced by hallucinogens. It is not surprising, therefore, that there has been hostility towards those scholars like Gordon Wasson, Albert Hoffman and Karl Ruck who have argued that shamanic plants and practices continued to play a vital role long after the prehistoric period was over and are directly implicated in the genesis of all the great historical religions.

I have already made it clear that my purpose here is to sketch out rather than to record in detail the shamanic and hallucinogenic themes that weave their way continuously through the entire fabric of human religion since it first manifested its presence in the painted caves and rock shelters 35,000 years ago. There is neither space nor need to trace these threads in every religion, but it will repay our effort to look a little more deeply in the next chapter at the case of ancient Central America, where the spiritual role of hallucinogens has never been in doubt, and the case of ancient Egypt, where the most elaborate steps were taken to induce altered states of consciousness and the most sublime and mysterious shamanic religion of historical antiquity was practised.

CHAPTER TWENTY-TWO

Flesh of the Gods

The high civilisations of ancient Egypt and of the ancient Maya maintain an air of occult mystery. We would like to know what made them tick, get inside their souls. We are familiar with their numinous religious art and its capacity to transport us to other realms. We have experienced the magnetism of their majestic and extraordinary sacred architecture. We have read their surviving scriptures. Even so, full understanding remains elusive. We sense that they were engaged in the exploration of some tremendous mystery, and much suggests that it had to do with the quest for life after death, but our prevailing scientific biases make it hard for us to accept that they could ever have had any realistic hope of attaining their desired goal of immortality.

The ultimate origins of these great and mysterious religions of antiquity, one in the Old World, one in the New, are lost in time, but it is certain that at some stage, and for a very long while, shamanism, the techniques of shamanism, the experiences of shamanism and the discoveries of shamanism played a central role in the evolution of both of them.

As I make this statement, I can already hear the academic critics, who have digested many books but few hallucinogens, protesting that what went on amongst the ancient Egyptians and the ancient Maya cannot be described as shamanism because their societies were urbanised, sophisticated, etc., etc., and shamanism is the religious domain of hunter-gatherers. But we have been through these arguments before. Shamanism is not confined to specific socio-economic settings or stages of development. It is fundamentally the ability that all of us share, some with and some without the help of hallucinogens, to enter altered states of consciousness and to travel out of body in non-physical realms – there to encounter supernatural entities and gain useful knowledge and healing powers from them.

The hero twins, Osiris and the journey of the dead

We have seen again and again in previous chapters how it is diagnostic of the shamanic initiatory trance that it should involve a spiritual ordeal – often construed as an otherworld journey culminating in tortures of piercing, dismemberment and skeletonisation followed finally by the 'rebirth' of the newly energised and empowered shaman.

The Popol Vuh, a book of the ancient Quiche Maya of Guatemala that survived the Conquest and the Inquisition, tells just such a story when it describes the descent of the hero twins Huhnapu and Xbalanque into the netherworld, Xibalba, sometimes depicted as a true underworld and sometimes as a 'nocturnal celestial dome over the earth'.[1] Interestingly, the twins' adventure begins when they are abducted from their home by the 'messengers' of Xibalba – supernaturals described as owls whose 'horrible faces frightened people'.[2] The reader will recall from Chapter Twelve that fearsome-looking owls play a role as spirit messengers in other shamanic cultures, that images of owl therianthropes are found in the painted caves of Upper Palaeolithic Europe, and that modern UFO abduction experiences frequently begin with the appearance of owls with huge black eyes.

As is usually the case with shamans in altered states of consciousness, Huhnapu and Xbalanque transform themselves into therianthropes in order to confront the perils of the spirit realm and are shown in Mayan art with patches of spotted jaguar skin on their faces and bodies.[3] We need not rehearse here the many trials, travails and tortures that they undergo in such places of supernatural terror as 'the Dark House', 'the Rattling House', 'the Jaguar House', 'the Bat House' and 'the Razor House'.[4] At the end of it all, finally and predictably, they allow themselves to be defeated by the evil spirits of

The hero twins
(drawing by Karl Taube)

Xibalba[5] – the shaman's classic 'submission to a higher order of knowing'.[6] They are then 'cooked in an oven and their bones ground and tossed into the river'.[7]

Needless to say, a very similar fate was experienced by many of the shamans from all around the world whose accounts we examined in earlier chapters, and, like those shamans, Huhnapu and Xbalanque were naturally reborn after an interval and returned with supernatural powers to vanquish wickedness and disease amongst their people and to heal the earth.[8] For these reasons the anthropologist Michael Ripinsky-Naxon believes that 'Xibalba actually means the Otherworld as perceived through shamanistic visions.'[9]

We may also make a direct comparison here with the well-known story of the god Osiris in ancient Egypt who was killed and hacked to pieces by his brother, the evil god Set – always depicted as a therianthrope with a human body and the head of an unknown animal with distinctive ears and a long snout. Set buried the 14 parts of the dismembered body throughout the land of Egypt but then the Goddess Isis retrieved them and with her magic brought Osiris back to life for long enough to engage him in copulation and conceive their child – the hawk-headed therianthrope Horus. Thereafter Osiris became king of the afterlife-realm known as the Duat through which the souls of the dead must journey after death.

In ancient Egyptian cosmology this realm was not located underground but in the sky – as are many shamanic netherworlds. Indeed, as Robert Bauval and I have shown in previous books, the Duat was viewed quite specifically as the sky region, divided by the Milky Way, lying between the constellations of Orion and Leo. The figure that we call 'Orion' was identified directly with Osiris.[10]

The Maya were interested in exactly the same region of the sky and connected it to similar ideas of afterlife journeys and spiritual rebirth. On a mural in the Temple of the Foliated Cross at the Mayan site of Palenque in Mexico's Chiapas province, we see the Milky Way represented by a maize tree rising from 'the place of Creation near Orion'.[11]

The Milky Way is flanked by two figures – the spirit of Lord Pacal, the deceased former ruler of Palenque, and his son and successor Chan-Bahlum, who are shown in shamanic communion with one another. As the father ascends to the heavens, the son is transformed from 'the status of heir apparent into king'.[12] At the same time it is understood that the deeds and rituals performed by the son are essential if the father's hoped-for rebirth amongst the stars is to be achieved. Indeed, this is the whole point and message of the mural – a message that has been described by David Friedel, Linda Schele and Joy Parker as 'the central mystery of Maya religion'.[13]

It is extremely curious that an identical mystery lies at the heart of the ancient Egyptian royal rebirth cult in which the deceased pharaoh is cast in the role of Osiris and the pharaoh-to-be plays the role of Horus, the son who assures his father's rebirth in the spirit world.[14] In Egypt, as amongst the Maya, the stellar context involves Orion and the Milky Way. In Egypt, as in Mexico, a journey through the netherworld must be undertaken by the deceased.[15]

A key shamanic function in virtually every culture where shamanism has been studied is that of the psychopomp, guiding the souls of the dead. In ancient Egypt this function was memorialised in permanent form by the so-called Books of the Dead, which serve as Baedekers for the soul's journey through the Duat netherworld. As we will see later, these remarkable texts, which we cannot doubt are direct records of the *experiences* of shaman priests on out-of-body journeys in deeply altered states of consciousness, instruct the deceased on how to overcome the dangers of the afterlife journey, enable him to assume the form of several mythical creatures, and equip him with the passwords necessary for admission to the various stages, or levels, of the scary parallel universe called the Duat.

Is it a coincidence, or is it because the same parallel universe could be accessed by all humans in an appropriately altered state of consciousness, that the peoples of ancient Central America preserved a similar vision of the perils of the afterlife? There the netherworld was said to consist of nine strata through which the deceased would journey for four years, overcoming dangers and obstacles on the way.[16] In both ancient Central America and ancient Egypt it was believed that certain segments of the deceased's afterlife voyage were made in a boat accompanied by 'paddler gods' who ferried him from stage to stage.[17] The tomb of Double-Comb, an eighth-century ruler of the Mayan city of Tikal, was found to contain a representation of this scene.[18] Similar

| Stingray paddler | Iguana | Spider monkey | Dead king | Parrot | Kankin dog | Jaguar paddler |

Paddler gods in the barque of Double-Comb, who ruled the Mayan city of Tikal in the eighth century (drawing by Linda Schele © David Schele, courtesy FAMSI).

images appear throughout the royal tombs in ancient Egypt's Valley of the Kings.[19] The passengers in the canoe in which Double-Comb makes his final journey include deities in the form of a dog, a bird and a monkey. The passengers in the barque of the dead pharaoh frequently include Horus, who has the head of a bird, Upuaut, the 'Opener of the Ways', who has the head of a dog, and Thoth, the god of wisdom, who sometimes appears in the form of an ape and sometimes as a bird-headed therianthrope (an ibis).[20]

Baby Jaguar

In the Americas there is firm archaeological evidence dating back almost 10,000 years for the use of hallucinogenic plants to alter consciousness, and there is no doubt whatsoever, as we will see, that the Maya were sophisticated users of hallucinogens with an extensive shamanic pharmacopoeia at their disposal. As virtually every chapter of this book has demonstrated, visions of therianthropes – half-man, half-beast hybrids – are amongst the imagery most consistently seen in altered states of consciousness. It is therefore only to be expected that Maya art should feature therianthropic transformations – as indeed it does, very frequently in specifically visionary contexts.

Thus, for example, certain painted murals from the Classic period show strange ceremonial dances which scholars believe 'combine the

Transformation into jaguars (left) and monsters (right) in shamanic pageants of the ancient Maya (drawings by Linda Schele © David Schele, courtesy FAMSI)

dynamics of pageants with the mystical transformation of human beings into supernaturals by means of visionary trance'.[21] The dancers are shown just as we know that shamans all around the world still experience themselves today – i.e. partially transformed into animals such as jaguars and birds of prey and in some cases into fantastic

Mayan lord entering hallucinatory state reaches for vision-serpent emerging from the conch shell in front of him (drawing by Linda Schele © David Schele, courtesy FAMSI)

monsters.[22] Similarly a carved conch shell shows a Maya aristocrat of the Late Classic period (around AD 600–800) smoking a thin hallucinogenic cigar. Out of the back of his elongated skull a second head appears to grow – that of a deer – and he reaches for a 'vision-serpent' emerging from the conch shell in front of him.[23]

Gigantic rearing 'vision-serpents' with the bodies of huge snakes and human heads are a repeated theme of Mayan art of all periods.[24] Again

Vision-serpent and penitent (drawing by Ian Graham)

they are frequently presented in contexts that leave little doubt that altered states of consciousness were involved, since associated human figures are often shown smoking or otherwise consuming hallucinogens, or self-torturing – another tried-and-tested shamanic technique for inducing visions. The Celestial Monster of Maya cosmology is a

The Celestial Monster, a hybrid of human, reptilian and animal parts
(drawing by Linda Schele © David Schele, courtesy FAMSI)

hybrid of many reptilian and animal parts. It has two heads, one of which is fully human.[25] J. Eric Thompson, the leading authority on Mayan religion, notes that most Mayan gods 'show a blending of human and animal forms . . . The god of number nine, for instance, borrows both snake and jaguar features' – the latter in the form of feline whiskers and spots on his otherwise human chin.[26] Similarly, the Mayan divinity known to archaeologists as God III 'walks and acts like a human' but is depicted fully transformed into a jaguar with a water-lily blossom or leaf (the hallucinogenic significance of which we will come to in a moment) placed on top of his head. Supposedly brought to life by the

God III, a jaguar who walks and acts like a human (drawings by Linda Schele © David Schele, courtesy FAMSI).

Water-Lily Jaguar
(drawing by Linda Schele ©
David Schele, courtesy FAMSI).

mating of a human mother and a spirit-jaguar father,[27] his other manifestion, particularly common in the Early Classic period, is in the very peculiar form of 'Baby Jaguar': 'His features are subject to some variation, although he is always anthropomorphic. His feet and hands may be human or feline, but he always has a jaguar tail.'[28]

God III manifesting as Baby Jaguar (drawings by Linda Schele © David Schele, courtesy FAMSI)

Baby Jaguar is a reminder of how ancient such hallucinatory notions of spirit–human hybrids are in the amazing prehistoric religions of Central America. Before the Maya, going back some 3,000 or 4,000 years, we come to an even more mysterious people who built pyramids in the jungles along the Gulf of Mexico in what are now the states of Veracruz and Tabasco. Known to archaeologists as the Olmecs, they frequently depicted themselves in sculptures as human beings

Olmec jaguar-human therianthropes

partially transformed into jaguars; very often, baby were-jaguars were shown.[29] David Gillette, a student of Central American religions, draws the following conclusions:

A being of mystery and terror, the jaguar was almost certainly the Olmecs' primary deity. He appears to have been for them what he was for the later Maya, a vision from the demon-haunted regions . . . The

Jaguar-god lived in caves, especially those with pitch-black pools of water in their lower reaches. These pools of water in the deep interior of caves were entrances to the realm of death and spiritual transformation.[30]

Pitch-black pools . . . Deep, dark caves . . . These, we know, have been seen as portals to the otherworld by shamanic cultures since before history began. Likewise, the part-animal, part-human infant, the changeling, the attempt by aliens or spirits or fairies to mingle their supernatural essence with human DNA are all very archaic and at the same time very modern themes.

The player in the maze of serpents

Ancient Egyptian art abounds in eerie and disturbing therianthropes of the kind that are only seen in profoundly altered states of consciousness and of which our ancestors have been making images since the Upper Palaeolithic. In the case of the Maya, it is not controversial to state that hallucinogens were used to induce these trance states since the role of psychoactive drugs in their society is relatively well known and documented. But with the ancient Egyptians, too, as we will see, there is strong evidence to suggest that therianthropes like dog-headed Anubis, lion-headed Sekhmet, crocodile-headed Sobek, hawk-headed Horus and ibis-headed Thoth (who could also manifest in the form

Left Anubis, dog-headed guide of human souls in the underworld; centre Horus; right Thoth

of an ape) were not concoctions of pure imagination but were seen and experienced by shaman priests in altered states of consciousness who sought to explore and map the netherworld and win useful knowledge from the supernatural beings residing there.

Nor is it simply a matter of therianthropes, the ubiquitous presence of which can be confirmed by any tourist visiting the majestic temples and tombs arranged along the banks of the sacred river Nile. Other hallucinatory themes with which we have become familiar are also found everywhere in ancient Egyptian religious art. These include extensive entoptic patterns of stars, zig-zags, dots and grids,[31] flying discs (from which rays ending in human hands are sometimes seen to project),[32] spirit beings, disembodied eyes, and an extraordinary menagerie of gigantic serpents, many of which are coiled around each other, or have multiple heads, or spit fire, or are elaborately winged and feathered.

The ancient Egyptian text known as *Per em am Duat*, the *Book of What is in the Duat*, plunges the reader into a nightmare maze of

Water-filled tunnel in the Duat

Serpent and spirits spitting fire into pits of fire in the Duat

narrow, often water-filled tunnels and secret chambers, caverns where monsters lie in wait, and pits of fire. I have viewed an almost complete version of this extensively illustrated text arranged around the ovoid walls of the tomb of Thuthmosis III in the Valley of the Kings. The scenes depicted, though 3,500 years old, have something of the feel of a computer or video game, while many of the beings shown are 'wire people' and stick figures of the kind frequently reported by modern lab volunteers during DMT sessions. Overall there is a sense of quest

Fourth Division of the Duat. The scenes depicted, though 3,500 years old, have something of the feel of a computer or video game, with a maze-like underworld of tunnels and corridors. Many of the beings shown are 'wire people' or 'stick figures' of the kind frequently reported by modern lab volunteers during DMT sessions.

as the 'player' – supposedly the soul of the deceased pharaoh – battles his way through the perils of the Duat to win immortal life in the Judgment Hall of Osiris. He knows what to expect, has the pass-words to all the gates, can subdue all the monsters because others – the great shaman priests and ultimately Osiris himself – have been there before him and mapped out the way: 'Whosoever knoweth these things shall, when he passeth by these beings, not be driven away by their roarings and he shall never fall down into their caverns.'[33]

Today people who drink ayahuasca sometimes report a similar maze-like underworld of tunnels and corridors, with or without the threatening beings. Alex Polari, a *padrinho* of the Santo Daime ayahuasca church in Brazil, describes the following Duat-like experiences under the influence of the sacred brew:

> I found myself in the salon of a castle illuminated by torches. The salon was oval, slightly oblong, with semicircular doors, placed at regular intervals. At the same time I saw an atrium situated in front of the principal wall . . . Thousands of tunnels, galleries, corridors, secret doors, staircases, inclined planes criss-crossed . . . These led to sumptuous palaces, lofty halls, sarcophagi, caverns or temples. In some of these were sentinels appearing as medieval figures.[34]

The strange, intelligent serpents whose images are found in every one of the 12 divisions of the Duat also turn up, in all their different

Vision-serpents of the Duat.

manifestations, in modern ayahuasca visions. The experienced ayahuasca drinker Benny Shanon reports:

> About a third of the serpents I have seen were mythical or non-naturalistic in one way or another. Some of the serpents were adorned with flowers or shining scales. Phantasmagoric serpents like those of

543

mythology were also reported by my informants. Amongst these were gigantic serpents, serpents characterised as 'cosmic', winged serpents, and ones made of or emitting fire. At times, serpents appear entwined in pairs, with one serpent coiled around another.[35]

Before ayahuasca enabled me to make my own first explorations of visionary realms, I used to study ancient Egyptian art for its beauty, for the secrets I hoped it might reveal about the origins of Egyptian civilisation, and for what I believed was simply its extraordinary imaginative power. Now, having encountered my own vision-serpents, having witnessed miraculous transformations of animal and human forms that spoke to me of the unity of all being, having met and interacted with spirit entities, and having peered in my own limited way into the abyss of the supernatural, I look at the tomb paintings and temple reliefs with new eyes. By all means there is a system here, set rules, a canon. There are even definite schools and styles, long-lasting conventions, automatic habits in the art. Nevertheless it seems obvious to me that *the original inspiration* behind every depiction of supernatural realms and beings that the ancient Egyptians left us can ultimately be traced back to the visions received by shaman priests in deeply altered states of consciousness.

Shaman priests

Let me be clear again about what I mean by shaman priests, since I know that the term is an anthropological contradiction in terms. My focus is on the role of altered states of consciousness in the origins of religion, in the cultivation of authentic religious experiences, and in the inspiration of religious imagery. My own opinion is that once 'religions' abandon, forget, or even outlaw the deliberate induction and use of altered states of consciousness, then they lose contact with their roots and wellsprings, and great ugliness and materialism can be expected to ensue. In hunter-gatherer cultures, in close touch with the powerful rhythms and energies of nature, this is least likely to happen and the shamanic adventure thrives. But as societies grow more complex, it is easy to see how techniques of ecstasy could fall into disuse and even disrepute, and how secrets of knowledge acquired through millennia of shamanic exploration of visionary realms and contact with 'supernatural' beings might thus be lost.

If we want examples of the sort of societies where that has already happened, or is happening now, then the highly technological and industrialised nations of the northern hemisphere come immediately to mind. On the other hand, if we seek an example of a society which achieved an advanced level of civilisation, sophistication, urbanisation and economic development (built on a secure agricultural base), but which at the same time did *not* sever its shamanic roots – and on the contrary celebrated them from first to last – then we need look no further than ancient Egypt.

It is in this context, therefore, that I speak of shaman priests. I am referring to functionaries, associated with the great temples and cult centres of Egypt, who might properly be called priests in the modern sense of the term, who lived with the economic and social realities of an advanced urban civilisation, but who were also masters of ancient techniques of ecstasy through which they entered trance and systematically explored the experiences that became accessible to them as a result. When they did this, they were doing the same things that shamans all over the world have always done, projecting their consciousness into the same non-physical dimensions, and meeting the same non-physical beings there – the animal spirits, the therianthropes, the vision-serpents and the monsters that have been with us since the dawn of art and religion in the Upper Palaeolithic.

A graphic representation of this sort of direct tie with the Upper Palaeolithic has been provided by anthropologist Felicitas Goodman. She has made a special study of the use by shamans from surviving hunter-gatherer cultures of ecstatic body postures in trance, meditation, dance, etc., often having her students try the postures out to the rhythmic beat of a rattle. We have already seen in Chapter Four the strong reasons to suppose that the striking bird-man therianthrope in the Upper Palaeolithic cave of Lascaux in south-west France represents a shaman undergoing hallucinatory transformation into his spirit form as a capercaillie grouse. But to this Goodman adds that we should also pay attention to his posture, leaning back at an angle of 37 degrees:

This very precise angle was a hallmark of spirit-journey postures performed by hunters, especially for journeying to the sky world . . . This same posture turned up twelve thousand years later in Egypt in a drawing of Osiris [who] underwent a typical shamanic initiation in which his body was dismembered and then reassembled by his sister before he made his spirit journey to the Upper World.[36]

Please note that although they are shown in contexts which suggest that they are 'dead' (charged down by a bison in the case of Lascaux, mummified in the ancient Egyptian example), the figures depicted in

Left, detail from the shaft scene at Lascaux; right, ithyphallic figure of Osiris

both these works of art are both equipped with prominent erections.[37] Such an 'ithyphallic' condition is frequently experienced by shamans entering trance who associate it, as we saw in Chapter Nine, with the 'boiling' excitation of 'supernatural potency' in the abdomen. 'Osiris,' Goodman concludes, 'was a shaman' and:

the figure . . . seems to point to the fact that shamanism in this form once predominated around the Mediterranean, from southern France all the way to Egypt. What is remarkable is that these elements were preserved in northern Africa over such an enormous time span, especially in light of the fact that we are dealing with two different cultural types. The shaman of Lascaux was without doubt a hunter, like everyone during that period. Osiris, on the other hand, changed into a god of the much more recent agriculturalists on the Nile without, however, losing his original character. Nor indeed did the Egyptians lose the knowledge about the correct posture, especially about the proper angle of ascending to the sky world.[38]

But it is not necessary to suggest some kind of long-term dissemination and transmission of 'shamanic knowledge'. Such knowledge can be rediscovered anywhere, at any time, whenever and wherever people are able to acquire reliable means to enter altered states of consciousness, and begin to learn the lessons that seem to be available to our species there. Very often, for mysterious reasons, whether

Serpent teachers of ancient Egypt: a scene from the
Book of What is in the Duat

in modern drug experiments or in traditional shamanic settings, the ancient teachers of these lessons present themselves in the form of serpents.

The water lily, the mandrake and the poppy

Ayahuasca is the 'serpent drug' par excellence, and we saw in the last chapter that the availability of an 'ayahuasca analogue' in the Middle East and north Africa cannot be ruled out, since plant species containing suitable ingredients do grow in the region. At present, however, it is not proven that the ancient Egyptians understood anything about how to potentiate the hallucinogenic effects of these plants – by no means an easy or an obvious process. Still, a hint that their pharmacological knowledge – and contacts – might have been wider than most historians are prepared to allow is provided by the widely reported presence in ancient Egyptian mummies of cocaine and nicotine, psychoactive drugs derived from supposedly indigenous South American plants that the Egyptians of 3,000 years ago should have had no access to.[39] A bitter academic dispute still rages around these findings, which are far from being universally accepted, but of course if they do turn out to be correct then there could be no objection in principle to the notion that other psychoactive plant alkaloids from the Americas might also have found their way to Egypt in antiquity. Any hypothetical use of DMT, whether from an Old World or a New World source, would leave no trace in mummies since excess levels of DMT are eliminated from the human body within two hours of ingestion.

Though fun to conjure with, the possibility of a prehistoric trans-Atlantic drug trade is deeply improbable and cannot be used to bolster the hypothesis that ancient Egyptian religious imagery could have been derived from altered states of consciousness induced by hallucinogens. As it turns out, however, the hypothesis has no need to rely on such exotic sources, since a perfectly suitable visionary drug was available locally and its properties were well known to the ancient Egyptians. William Emboden, Professor of Biology at California State University, has established that the blue water lily, *Nymphaea caerulea*, a plant that is indigenous to the Nile and prominent in ancient Egyptian art, has pronounced narcotic, hypnotic and hallucinogenic effects.[40] In a series of thoroughly argued scientific papers and books, he has also presented convincing evidence that it was used, along with opium, and with the mandrake (*Mandragora officinarum*, already known in Europe for its visionary qualities), to produce 'a form of shamanistic trance':[41]

Analysis of the ritual and sacred iconography of dynastic Egypt, as seen on stelae, in magical papyri, and on vessels, indicates that these people possessed a profound knowledge of plant lore and altered states of consciousness. The abundant data indicate that the shamanistic priest, who was highly placed in the stratified society, guided the souls of the living and the dead, provided for the transmutation of souls into other bodies and the personification of plants as possessed by human spirits, as well as performing other shamanistic activities.[42]

There is not space here even to hint at the wealth of evidence that Emboden adduces to support his case. Briefly, he draws attention to many scenes in ancient Egyptian art in which mandrake roots and

After Emboden, 1989, p. 62: 'Meriton, consort to Semenhkara, offers him two mandrake fruits and a bud of narcotic blue water lily. More of these flowers are held in her left hand.'

buds of the narcotic blue water lily are offered in a context of ritual healing, very frequently in association with 'emblems of opium poppy capsules'.[43] He also points out that opiate residues have been found in an unguent vessel from an Eighteenth Dynasty tomb:

To this end, it must be noted that when the Tomb of Tutankhamen was looted [in antiquity], an estimated 400 litres of fluid in sealed vessels had been taken, in preference to the gold, the decorative arts, and the vessels themselves. It was believed by the looters that these vessels contained *didi*, the elixir of life. Certainly the combined narcotic properties of water lilies, mandrakes, and the opium poppy would provide the most potent vehicle (*didi*) to a profound hypnotic state terminating in an extended period of somnolence. The symbolic death so necessary to shamanic tradition would be provided by any one of these plants. Sleep is the symbolic death that permits miraculous resurrection.[44]

A similar association is made in the tomb of Nebamun at Thebes (modern Luxor), where we see a widow with bared breasts squatting before the figure of her deceased husband. Springing from the base of the figure, Emoden draws our attention to

> a vegetal column of narcotic blue water lilies and poppy capsules (incised to release their narcotic latex) bound together and crowned with three palm fronds. It is difficult to imagine a simply fortuitous combination of narcotic water lilies and poppies. As for the palm, it was the source of palm wine and could have provided a solvent for the poppy and *Nymphaea* derivatives.[45]

After Emboden, 1989, p. 71: 'A scene of ritual mourning in which
dust is thrown upon the head of a grieving widow as she squats before a
totem of narcotic blue water lilies and incised capsules of opium poppies.
Both facilitate a trance state appropriate to mourning.'

Emboden highlights the fact that in the foundation myth of the Heliopolitan cult responsible for the rituals at the Pyramids of Giza, a central notion is that of

the creation of order out of chaos (*Nun*) in which the dark pool of nothingness gave rise to a blue water lily from which the first being arose. This legend explains the relationship between the order of the entire civilisation and the sacred quality of the narcotic blue water lily.[46]

Also of importance is a chapter in the ancient Egyptian *Book of the Dead* entitled 'Transformation into a Water Lily':

Horus is seen being petitioned by an offering of two vessels with pouring spouts. Above them are gigantic *N. caerulea* flowers . . . The water lilies indicate that these are the *didi* or elixir in the jars under them. The indication is clear that the holy water lily or narcotic water lily belongs to Horus . . . As master of the sky, Horus becomes the perfect emblem of soul flight in shamanistic ecstasy. He is portrayed in his alter ego as half falcon and half man.[47]

After Emboden, 1980: 'Horus is propitiated by an offering of two vessels whose contents are made known by overlying *Nymphaea caerulea* flowers.'

Emboden's conclusion from his study of this and many other works of art, and his own direct experiences of the psychotropic effects of the plants themselves,[48] is that:

> In the Egyptian dynasties, the essence of shamanistic trance provided by the hypnotic constituents of the mandrake and the narcotic blue water lily are clearly in evidence. They continue to be portrayed and appear in magical writings from the Fourth Dynasty until the fourth century BC. The constituents of these plants are able to provide the requisites for shamanistic trance . . . that separates the sacred from the profane and the soul from the body. The spiritual death, journey, revelation and resurrection are implicit in both writings and murals.[49]

Water Lily Jaguar and the Mayan mushroom stones

Emboden's interest in the hallucinogenic effects of the Egyptian water lily had been stimulated by his own previous studies of the use by the ancient Maya of a closely related species of water lily (*Nymphaea ampla*) for exactly the same visionary purposes. He draws attention in particular to the famous Mayan murals at Bonampak in Mexico where water lilies are shown associated with the noses and foreheads of dancers. These images, he says, 'are so like some of the Egyptian murals that the similarity is startling'.[50]

Many other Mayan artworks also depict identical themes. For example, a representation of one of the hero twins on their journey through the netherworld of Xibalba shows him wearing a water lily headdress.[51] Likewise, as we saw earlier, God III in his therianthropic manifestation as Water Lily Jaguar, wears water lily pads on his head.[52] A Late Classic vessel from Yucatán carries a polychrome depiction of a lake filled with gigantic water lilies and water lily pads intimately connected with a great serpent that inhabits the lake.[53] A polychrome pottery vase has a principal hallucinatory motif of 'a giant undersea serpent with the tail of a fish, the body of a snake and a fantastic head . . . The figure to the right . . . is a shaman with two musical horns, below which is a giant *Nymphaea ampla* bud.'[54] Recalling the universal shamanic metaphor of 'undersea' or 'underwater' in

Water Lily Jaguar as he is depicted in the Dresden Codex, one of the very
few Mayan hieroglyphic works to have survived the orgy of book burnings
ordered by Spanish missionaries following the Conquest

alluding to deep states of trance, it is interesting that the Bonampak
murals have a similar hallucinatory theme that is similarly linked to
N. ampla:

> Grotesque personages are involved in a sort of undersea dance ritual.
> Water lilies are on their foreheads and are associated with fish. One
> of the figures holds his hands aloft which are the giant claws of a
> lobster . . . As Dobkin de Rios has suggested, plant and sea familiars
> are common New World drug-linked motifs.[55]

We need not dwell further on the hallucinogenic iconograpy of the
water lily amongst the ancient Maya – who also used many other
vision-inducing drugs, some of which they likewise depicted in their
art. It is certain that *ololiuqui* (Morning Glory) seeds, which have
powerful LSD-like effects, were amongst the diverse pharmacopoeia they
resorted to.[56] Psychoactive mushrooms, more than 20 species of which
grow in the region,[57] were likewise of great importance for shamanic
journeying, which perhaps explains why the Quiche Maya of
Guatemala, the authors of the Popol Vuh, had a specific phrase, *xibal-
baokx*, meaning 'mushroom of the underworld'.[58] Mushrooms appear

Stones carved in the form of hallucinogenic mushrooms by the
ancient Maya of Guatemala

in the Popol Vuh in direct association with religious activity,[59] and
archaeologists have found hundreds of stone sculptures and ceramic
models of mushrooms in ancient Mayan tombs and religious sites in
Guatemala, El Salvador, Honduras and Mexico dating back to the
first millennium BC.[60] 'It is now clear,' writes Richard Evans Schultes,
Director of the Harvard Botanical Museum, 'that whatever the use of
these "mushroom stones", they indicate the great antiquity of a sophisticated sacred use of hallucinogenic mushrooms.'[61]

'They would see a thousand visions, especially serpents . . .'

Looking beyond the areas of Maya habitation, archaeologists and
botanists agree that hallucinogens have in fact played a formative
role in the religious beliefs, rituals and imagery of almost all the
indigenous peoples and civilisations of Central America, Mexico and
neighbouring parts of the United States. Indeed, despite the odds
against the survival of physical evidence of hallucinogen use, substantial caches of the intensely psychoactive red bean-like seeds of a
shrub known as *Sophora secundiflora*, dating back more than 9,000
years in some cases, have been found in painted caves across much
of north-central Mexico and Texas. Along the Lower Pecos River
in Texas they are associated with a remarkable complex of 8,000-
year-old rock paintings of spirit beings, therianthropes and entoptic
patterns. Even before Lewis-Williams, archaeologists were largely

agreed on a shamanistic interpretation of these paintings, relating their content to 'hallucinogenic and divinatory red bean rites'.[62] It is significant that in some sites *Sophora secundiflora* seeds (more commonly known as 'mescal beans') have been excavated from successive occupation layers dating from 7000 BC to the eleventh century AD.[63] Moreover, there are ethnographic reports from the nineteenth and early twentieth centuries of American Indians still using the seeds to pursue 'delirious exhilaration' in a religious context.[64]

8,000-year-old rock paintings of spirit beings, therianthropes and entoptic patterns, Lower Pecos River, Texas.

If we study the murals and reliefs at the pyramids and temples of Teotihuacan, 30 kilometres north of modern Mexico City, we see depictions of hallucinogenic plant species and psychoactive mushrooms everywhere coupled with fantastic and monstrous imagery. The internationally renowned mycologist R. Gordon Wasson has concluded that 'for centuries Teotihuacan was a vast sanctuary dedicated to the two or three hallucinogens that enjoyed superlative prestige'.[65]

Teotihuacan flourished around the time of Christ and reached its zenith by AD 700, afterwards rapidly falling into decline. By the early sixteenth century, when Europeans engaged in the bloody business of conquest first encountered the fierce Mexican people known as the Aztecs, the Pyramids of the Sun and the Moon at Teotihuacan were in ruins and the painted temples were overgrown and ghostly. The cults of sacred plants and mushrooms celebrated in the Teotihuacan murals were, however, not forgotten but continued to provide the principal means by which the peoples of the region established and maintained their contacts with the spirit world.

The Aztecs made particular use of *ololiuqui*, the LSD-like Morning Glory seeds mentioned earlier, and also of several different species of psilocybin mushrooms which they knew by the name of *teonanactl*, 'flesh of the gods'.[66] From the writings of the friars and other commentators who came alongside the Conquistadors and who witnessed Aztec use of these and other drugs, scholars agree it is clear that

> sacred hallucinogens played an important part not only in divinatory or curing practices on the 'folk level' of religion and ceremonial, but also in the far more complex beliefs and rituals of the priestly hierarchies that served the demanding gods of Aztec Tenochtitlan and its allies and tributaries.[67]

The descriptions of the sixteenth-century chroniclers speak for themselves:

> *Ololiuqui* . . . deprives all who use it of their reason . . . The natives communicate in this way with the devil . . . and they are deceived by various hallucinations which they attribute to the deity which they say resides in the seeds.[68]

> They all went to eat raw mushrooms, on which food they all went out of their minds . . . With the force of those mushrooms they would see visions and have revelations of the future, the Devil speaking to them in that drunken state.[69]

> At the very first, mushrooms had been served . . . When the mushrooms took effect on them, then they danced, then they wept. But some, while still in command of their senses, entered and sat there by the house on their seats; they danced no more but only sat there nodding . . . And when the effects of the mushrooms had left them, they

consulted among themselves and told one another what they had seen in vision . . .[70]

When the priests wanted to communicate with their gods, and to receive messages from them, they ate this plant [*ololiuqui*] to induce a delirium. A thousand visions and satanic hallucinations appeared to them . . .[71]

It was their custom to dance and get drunk on some mushrooms in such a manner that they would see many visions and fearful figures.[72]

A particularly detailed account was left by Fray Toribo de Benavente:

They had another way of drunkenness . . . and it was with some fungi or mushrooms . . . Eaten raw and being bitter, they drink after them or eat with them a little bees' honey; and a while later they would see a thousand visions, especially serpents . . . These mushrooms they called in their language *teunanacatlth* [*teonanactl*], which means 'flesh of god', or the devil whom they worshipped.[73]

One can see from their reactions that the friars instinctively disliked the direct communication with the spirit world that the sacred plants seemed to give the Mexican shamans. Naturally the Church and the Inquisition launched a systematic campaign after the Conquest to

Left, from the Magliabechiano Codex, illustration depicting a man eating hallucinogenic mushrooms. A terrifying supernatural figure stands behind him. Right, from the Florentine Codex, illustration of 'Satanic' mushrooms.

stamp out the religious use of hallucinogens entirely and to blacken the name and distort the memory of those who had venerated them. Historians thought that the campaign had been a complete success until 1955, when R. Gordon Wasson and his colleagues discovered a psilocybin mushroom cult still active amongst the Mazatec Indians of the mountainous country around Oaxaca. Far from being cruel and diabolic, this shamanistic cult was gentle, wise and dedicated to healing.[74]

Teaching man that which he knoweth not

We have already met Maria Sabina, the shaman of the little village of Huatla de Jimenez near Oaxaca who Wasson made famous with an article about her that he published in *Life* magazine in 1957. We saw in Chapter Twelve that on one occasion, following the consumption of a large dose of psilocybin mushrooms, she travelled more deeply than ever before into the otherworld. There she met a spirit being who had guided her on previous visits, but this time he 'had in his hands something that he did not have before, and it was a big Book with many written pages'. He told her: 'I am giving you this Book so that you can do your work better and help people who need help and know the secrets of the world where everything is known.' This seemed most inappropriate to Maria as she thumbed through the 'many written pages' of the book: 'Unfortunately I did not know how to read. I had never learned and therefore that would not have been any use to me.' At the very moment this thought crossed her mind, however, 'I realised I was reading and understood all that was written in the Book and that I became as though richer, wiser, and that in one moment I learned millions of things. I learned and learned.'[75]

I am reminded of the way, in another time and place, that the illiterate Prophet Muhammad was ordered to read by the spirit being who he identified with the Angel Gabriel. 'I am not a reader,' the prophet protested:

Then he took hold of me a third time and squeezed me as much as I could bear, and said: 'Read! In the name of the Lord who created;

created man from a clot of blood. Read! For the Lord is most beneficent, He hath taught the use of the pen; He hath taught man that which he knoweth not.[76]

Amongst the ancient Egyptians it was the god Thoth, a bird therianthrope with the body of a man and the head of an ibis, who was said to have taught the skills of reading and writing, while the shaman god Osiris was remembered as a great civiliser and the inventor of agriculture. In the same way the Mayan god Kukulkan, whose name means 'Feathered Serpent', was regarded as the supreme organiser, 'the former of laws and the teacher of the calendar'.[77]

These are not isolated examples, and once again the question arises – who are these ancient teachers, who some call 'gods', and some call 'aliens' or 'spirits', who come to us in altered states of consciousness with strange messages that have shaped the course of human history?

PART VI

The Mysteries

Doors Leading to Another World

I began this enquiry with a question about religion. When and where did our ancestors first start to believe that they could encounter supernatural realms and beings?

Although I predict that older evidence will ultimately be found in Africa, there is presently little dispute that the painted caves of Europe contain the oldest clear *surviving* evidence of the beliefs in 'spirit worlds' and 'non-real beings' that lie at the heart of all religions – no matter how far they may subsequently have evolved away from their shamanic roots. If I wanted to know about mankind's first supernatural encounters, therefore, I realised that I was going to have to learn about the caves, and their extraordinary, transcendental art, and about other ancient rock-art systems around the world.

I quite soon discovered that real knowledge about prehistoric cave art could be divided into two periods. Before Professor David Lewis-Williams began to publish widely in the 1980s, there was no good explanation of the art at all. By 1988, thanks to his work, there was an excellent explanation that made perfect sense. Precisely because it makes such good sense, though it has been opposed by a strident minority, his 'neuropsychological theory' quickly won the support of the majority of archaeologists and anthropologists specialising in this field.

For reasons that I have set out at length in Parts I and II of this book, I myself am convinced that Lewis-Williams is broadly correct: the visions and experiences of altered states of consciousness, brought on by classic shamanic techniques such as rhythmic dancing or the use of plant hallucinogens, were indeed, as he proposes, the source of inspiration for the first religious ideas of mankind. Beyond this basic but extremely important point I disagree with just about everything else Lewis-Williams has to say. In particular I disagree vehemently with the certainty he professes that the spirit worlds and beings encountered while hallucinating are not in any sense real. Likewise, he is just plain wrong to argue that only entoptic phenomena – which he attributes to the structure of the nervous system – are universally experienced in altered states, while what he calls 'fully iconic' Stage 3 hallucinations are entirely artefacts of the individual's memory and cultural background and thus differ enormously from person to person, from epoch to epoch, and from location to location.

On the contrary, even when Lewis-Williams first published on this subject, there existed a number of puzzling cases in the neuropsychological literature attesting to the universality of Stage 3 hallucinations as well. These cases were and remain puzzling precisely because they are so similar to one another despite the different cultural backgrounds and different personal memories of the individuals experiencing them. As early as 1977, for example, Dr R.K. Siegel, one of the leading US psychiatric researchers in this field, published an important study in the journal *Scientific American* reviewing some 500 hallucinations induced by LSD. Although Lewis-Williams generally relies on Siegel, he seems to have overlooked this study in which no less than 79 per cent of the subjects reported very similar complex imagery, including religious images and symbols, images of small animals, and humans.[1] As critics point out: 'This finding strongly suggests that some of the complex imagery ("iconic" hallucinations per Lewis-Williams) seen upon electrical or chemical stimulation of the visual associational cortices and temporal lobes is hard wired.'[2]

Lewis-Williams was also well aware, and indeed makes much of it in his writings, that therianthropic, part-man, part-beast figures are a universal feature of rock art in many different lands because they are universally experienced in deeply altered states of consciousness. However, he does not seem to recognise that what he is effectively admitting here is that at least some 'iconic' Stage 3 hallucinations are

apparently *not* strongly culturally constrained. Everyone sees therianthropes even if the therianthropes they see are part man, part bison
in Upper Palaeolithic Europe, part man, part eland in southern Africa,
or part man, part jaguar in the Amazon jungle.

In 1990, Robert Bednarik of the Australian Rock Art Association
took Lewis-Williams to task for overlooking evidence of this sort. In
a critique published in the journal *Current Anthropology* he drew attention to research which has demonstrated that certain universal themes
appear in the ayahuasca visions of people from quite different cultures,
and suggested that further investigation of such shared 'non-real'
experiences might demonstrate the existence of 'a collective unconscious of "iconic form constants"'.[3]

On the basis of everything I've learnt, I'm certain Bednarik is right
to draw attention to the mysterious universality of Stage 3 hallucinations. But to say that they derive from a 'collective unconscious of
"iconic form constants"' is to say that we all unknowingly share
immense quantities of bizarre otherworldly images of utterly unfamiliar places and beings that have somehow been 'hard-wired' into
our brains. This of course is not an explanation of the problem but
merely a description or reformulation of it. What we really want to
know is *why* so many people all around the world see the same 'non-
real' things once they enter altered states of consciousness.
Furthermore, though Bednarik would undoubtedly be aghast at the
comparison, his idea that we each possess a hard-wired neural archive
filled with 'iconic form constants' depicting supernatural realms and
beings comes remarkably close to Jeremy Narby's off-beat notion that
intelligent interactive video messages have been recorded on DNA by
some higher intelligence and that we all see the same things because
we are all one at the level of DNA.

Eyewitnesses to the non-real

I began to understand that this problem of human experiences of the
supernatural – judged to be non-real but nonetheless universal and
apparently very ancient – lay at the heart of the matter I was investigating. It was precisely such experiences, documented in the painted

caves, and duplicable by drugs such as ayahuasca, psilocybin, ibogaine and DMT, that seemed to have accompanied mankind's leap into fully modern symbolism.

The next step was to look elsewhere – in folklore, in mythology, in the annals of ancient and contemporary religions and in modern news sources – for other examples, not necessarily connected with drugs, of complex, detailed but supposedly non-real experiences reported in very similar terms by large numbers of people with nothing in common.

For practical reasons it was necessary to impose constraints on the scope of my enquiry and in particular to make some difficult decisions about which aspects of it to write about and which to keep to myself. But because of the direction from which I had approached the problem, my primary research focus was inevitably on the 'spirit world' that our ancestors depicted for the first time in prehistoric rock art, that continued as the great obsession of the high religions of antiquity, and that is still actively experienced to this day in surviving shamanic cultures as far afield as central and southern Africa, Australia and the Amazon rain forest. Then there was the modern supernatural phenomenon of encounters with and abductions by UFOs and aliens, and in between the two there were the fairies and elves, the imps and goblins, the nymphs and sprites that were so commonly encountered in Europe from medieval through to Victorian times.

Once I started digging, I found clues leading in all directions and multiple interconnections linking areas of enquiry that I had previously thought to be entirely separate. Most important of all, in a field of study that has been neglected by modern researchers, I found that the ethnographies and folklore collections were stuffed with statements by earnest and sincere eyewitnesses describing supernatural beings and events.

Many scientists dismiss such accounts as hoaxes, or delusions, or 'mere hallucinations', and don't consider the possibility that the eyewitnesses might have seen something real. However, this is a knee-jerk response driven by deeply embedded materialist prejudices about the nature of reality rather than by any solid research or evidence. I therefore decided to undertake a thorough examination of some of these bodies of eyewitness testimony – not a patronising sociological or psychological study of mass delusions (just about the only approach that scholars have made to this material up to now) but an attempt at a deliberately open-minded appraisal, ruling out nothing in advance. I hoped if I treated the evidence with respect, and allowed it to speak for itself, that it might have something useful to teach me about the supposed supernatural realms and beings to which it refers – which I myself had experienced and which I was willing to accept might *not* be real, or might, on the other hand, be real in some way that scientists did not presently understand.

What I found, set out in Chapters Eleven to Sixteen, is that essentially the same pattern of bizarre non-real experiences has been consistently reported over and over again by people from all parts of the earth and all periods of history. Furthermore, despite the glaring underlying similarities, there is clear evidence of evolution in these experiences – notably in the way that the issue of hybrid infants is handled and in the way that the technology for navigating between worlds, and even the clothing worn by the 'beings', seems to change and develop. It seems to me completely obvious that when people from all times and places consistently and reliably report the same non-real experiences – especially experiences as extraordinary and distinctive as those typically associated with spirits, fairies and aliens – then it is not good enough to say that all the eyewitness are 'mad' or deluded. Nor will it do to dismiss their testimony on the grounds that they must be hallucinating, since that does not explain but merely restates the problem – which is, of course, that they are all hallucinating the same things! The real issue that science keeps dodging is *why* they are all hallucinating the same things. Why do the same otherworlds and spirit beings keep appearing, and what does this all mean?

Hard-wired program

I was already aware of how closely 'supernatural' experiences are linked to altered states of consciousness, very often brought on by the use of plant hallucinogens. This is, after all, the entire basis of shamanism in the Amazon. But it was only when I began to study Rick Strassman's work that I realised how such experiences could be occasioned virtually instantaneously by DMT – which turns out to be a substance that the human brain produces naturally in minute quantities. Even in laboratory and hospital settings, as we saw in Chapters Seventeen and Eighteen, a dose of DMT above a certain minimum threshold is guaranteed to send just about anyone on a very rapid, intense and convincing otherworld journey. Moreover, despite some notable differences, which we will return to in a moment, it is, once again, essentially *the same* otherworld to which shamans and alien abductees and those taken by the fairies have always been transported.

Rick Strassman and others working in this field repeatedly warn that the ease with which DMT can *facilitate* such experiences does not mean it has *caused* them. On the contrary, we have seen that there is considerable support at top scientific levels for the notion of the brain as a receiver that may be temporarily retuned by hallucinogens to pick up frequencies that normally fall below the threshold of our senses. Theoretically if it were possible for beings to exist at those frequencies, we would be unable to see them without the assistance of a substance like DMT – though they might be 'round us thick as flies' (as used to be said of fairies).

Yet my own experiences with DMT also suggested another possibility. Despite their general similarities to other alternative realities I had encountered in trance states, I was haunted by the mechanical, artificial and even technological overtones of the DMT 'world'. Unlike the rich, abundant supernatural life revealed by ayahuasca, the effect of pure, concentrated dimethyltryptamine had felt less like an encounter with spirits and more like a personal session with an interactive computer program designed to tailor its output to my individual psychology, habitual perceptions and cultural background.

Now the weird thing, as we saw in Chapter Eighteen, is that everyone else who takes DMT seems to engage with the same computer program – as though it is somehow hard-wired into all of us. Such an interactive system, just conceivable somewhere far beyond the limits of twenty-first-century biotechnology, would require vast amounts of information, stored within our bodies on

Top, the 'twisted cord' of DNA, a physical medium within our bodies for the storage of vast amounts of information. Above, 'Those who carry the twisted cord', from the ancient Egyptian *Book of Gates* (tomb of Rameses VI).

some physiological medium that would allow it to be accessible to consciousness. We saw in Chapters Nineteen and Twenty that this is not impossible, that there are good reasons to believe our DNA did not evolve on this planet, and that neural DNA with its billions upon billions of supposedly 'junk' letters is an obvious candidate to carry an interactive message written by 'clever entities', as Jeremy Narby suggests.

Video-game people

If we continue for the moment to speculate – with Narby – that alongside all its other miraculous properties, our DNA contains interactive recordings of intelligent messages that we can activate in altered states of consciousness, then the hybrid and therianthropic imagery documented in visionary experiences from the painted caves of Europe 35,000 years ago to the Amazon jungle today make deep symbolic sense. How better could an intelligent, interactive system express the essence of DNA as a fundamental animating principle uniting the attributes of all living things than to summon up virtual teachers that merge the characteristics of different species into composite beings? It is perhaps no accident, while about half the group saw aliens and flying saucers in one form or another, that many of Rick Strassman's volunteers also reported encounters with therianthropes during their

569

DMT sessions, mostly in the form of insect-like or reptilian hybrids who seemed to be driven by a bizarre urge to *teach* them. Chris, for example:

> It was wild. There were no colours. There was the usual sound: pleasant, a roar, a sort of an internal hum. Then there were three beings, three physical forms. There were rays coming out of their bodies and then back to their bodies. They were reptilian and humanoid, trying to make me understand, not with words, but with gestures. They wanted me to look into their bodies. I saw inside them and understood reproduction, what it's like before birth, the passage into the body.[4]

Note the theme of reproduction – with the added twist that what is being envisaged is the passage *into* the body, 'before birth', presumably of some non-physical entity. Was the lesson Chris says he was given about this 'mechanism' just brain fiction with no broad significance at all? Was it a revelation, vouchsafed to him by 'spirits', of some fundamental truth about the nature of physical existence? Or could it have been an encounter with high-tech virtual teachers in his own DNA?

Gabe, another of Strassman's volunteers, reported 'an initial sense of panic' on receiving an intravenous dose of 0.4mg/kg of DMT:

> Then the most beautiful colours coalesced into beings. There were lots of beings. They were talking to me but they weren't making a sound. It was more as if they were blessing me, the spirits of life were blessing me . . . At first it felt like I was going through a cave or tunnel or into space, at a fast rate, definitely. I felt like a ball hurtling down to wherever it was.[5]

If modern lab volunteers conclude that the beings they encounter in altered states of consciousness are 'spirits' (and meet them in caves and tunnels!), then it is easy to understand how our ancestors in similar trance states – whether induced by drugs or other techniques – would have come to similar conclusions. But by no means all the volunteers in Rick Strassman's study believed they were dealing with spirits, and the descriptions that many gave of their experiences accord equally well with the 'virtual teacher' hypothesis.

Sean:

I couldn't watch it all, it was so busy. Something asked me, 'What do you want? How much do you want?' I answered that I wanted to see fewer things, but more of it. That reduced the intensity of the busy, crackling, colourful Chinese-like panels. It became more manageable and focused. I'm feeling freer about going out there. I'm not lost. I'm asking questions and getting answers.[6]

On another day, after receiving the third of four consecutive doses of DMT, the same subject reported:

The trip started with an electric tingling in my body, and quickly the visual hallucinations arrived. Then I noticed five or six figures walking

Scene from the ancient Egyptian *Book of Night*, Tomb of Rameses VI (circa 1150 BC). The existence of such archaic depictions suggests that 'wire people' and 'stick people' of the kind repeatedly seen by subjects under the influence of DMT do not result from the influence of modern 'cartoons' and video games but are part of a mystery buried deeply in the structure of the human mind.

rapidly alongside me. They felt like helpers, fellow travellers. A humanoid male figure turned toward me, threw his right arm up toward the patchwork of bright colours, and asked, 'How about this?'[7]

On his fourth dose Sean found himself in a place with

wire people everywhere riding bicycles, like programmed people, like video-game people . . . I watched them. They were blue-green, running all around me . . .[8]

Another participant in the same four-dose tolerance study was Sara. 'This time, I quickly blasted through to the "other side",' she said soon after receiving her third injection:

I was in a void of darkness. Suddenly, beings appeared. They were cloaked, like silhouettes. They were glad to see me. They indicated that they had had contact with me as an individual before. They seemed pleased that we had discovered this technology . . . They wanted to learn more about our physical bodies. They told me humans exist on many levels . . .[9]

Sara's experience after her fourth dose seemed to continue the scenario from the third:

I went directly into deep space. They knew I was coming back and they were ready for me. They told me there were many things they could share with us when we learn how to make more extended contact. I wish you [Strassman] didn't control who gets DMT![10]

In a later interview she added:

I have the feeling of remembering those entities. My experience of them was so real it doesn't fade with time like other things do. They want us to come back and teach us and play with us. I want to go back and learn.[11]

Dimitri said that he was 'confused and in awe' about the beings he encountered during his DMT trips:

I knew that they were preparing me for something . . . They had things to show me. But they were waiting for me to acquaint myself with the environment and movement and language of this space . . .[12]

Jeremiah felt that DMT was 'not like some kind of drug':

It's more like an experience of a new technology than a drug. You can choose to attend to this or not. It will continue to progress without you paying attention. You return not to where you left off, but to where things have gone since you left. It's not a hallucination, but an observation.[13]

But an observation of what? Neural pulp-fiction? Or real spirits from parallel otherworlds? Or virtual teachers broadcasting interactive lectures at us from our DNA?

Or none of the above?

The baffling of Strassman and Shanon

Implausible, mind-boggling, universal experiences of the kind described repeatedly in this book do not often attract serious academic attention. Those few scientists who have studied them in depth, however, have concluded that there is something deeply mysterious about their universality and that it in fact raises profound questions about what is real and what is not. Rick Strassman, for one, admits to being 'baffled and nonplussed' during his DMT research by the

surprising and remarkable consistencies among volunteers' reports of contact with nonmaterial beings . . . [in an] 'alien' realm . . . or high-technology room. The highly intelligent beings of this 'other' world are interested in the subject, seemingly ready for his or her arrival and wasting no time in 'getting to work' . . . They . . . communicated with the volunteers, attempting to convey information by gestures, telepathy, or visual images. The purpose of contact was uncertain, but several subjects felt a benevolent attempt on the beings' part to improve us individually or as a race.[14]

As a clinical research psychiatrist, Strassman says, it was natural for him to presume that the regularity and consistency of these reports, as well as their strong sense of reality, must arise from some biological cause. He speculated that the DMT was 'activating certain hard-wired sites in the brain that elicit a display of visions and feelings in the mind. How else could so many people report similar experiences: insect-like, reptilian creatures?'[15] However, the volunteers were not satisfied with such reductionism: '"Yes," they would reply, "but what about what I just saw and felt? Are there brain centres for clowns, elves and aliens? Where did this really come from?"'[16]

In due course Strassman found himself agreeing that there was a problem. 'Why do we all have DMT in our brains?' he asked:

> Why is there a compound . . . that generates experience of 'alien-contact', death, space-travel, and other extraordinary effects?[17] How could anyone believe there were chunks of brain tissue that, when activated, flashed encounters with beings, experimentation and reprogramming?[18]

Benny Shanon, Professor of Psychology at the Hebrew University in Jerusalem, has arrived at very similar conclusions about ayahuasca. After interviewing a sample of several hundred ayahuasca users from many different cultures and backgrounds, he found that no less than 75 per cent reported visions of death, birds, reptiles, divine beings, creatures and beings, palaces and temples, and forests and gardens.[19] Serpents and felines were the most common visionary creatures,[20] and significantly, there was much content that had nothing whatsoever to do with drinkers' life histories, including 'all sorts of animals, phantasmagoric creatures and beings, royalty and religious figures, objects of art and magic, and divine beings . . .'[21] Like many ayahuasca users, Shanon himself reported seeing spaceships twice during his ayahuasca visions[22] and notes that amongst his interviewees, 'beings referred to as extraterrestrials' were often 'seen along with spaceships'.[23]

What are we to make of such unexpected universal themes? 'A reductionist would argue that the commonalities in the ayahuasca experience are directly due to neuroanatomical structures and brain processes,' says Shanon, 'and hence should be explained in biological terms':[24]

> While at first glance such an explanation may seem most natural, further reflection reveals that it is far from being obvious. Would we say, for instance, that the recurrence of visual elements such as serpents and jaguars, palaces and works of art are due to there being specific brain centres in which such information is stored? . . . It seems to me that, at least in the present state of our understanding of the brain and nervous system, the postulation of such specific centres simply does not make sense.[25]

What most directly affronts common sense is the notion that natural selection could ever have allowed the evolution of such a potent and spectacular hallucinatory mechanism, requiring those equipped with it to become helpless in the real world and to devote close attention to non-real things instead. If the materialist view of the universe is correct, then it is hard to see how attending to *anything* 'non-real' could have been at all adaptive or could have contributed usefully to our ancestors' chances of survival – especially in the early days when such an adaptation would have had to provide spectacular immediate payoffs in evolutionary terms if it was to become established in the genome.

On the other hand, if the shamanic view of the universe is correct, then attending closely to spirit realms and beings makes complete sense, as does their universality, even if Western scientists persist in their delusion that such realms and beings are not real. Moreover, as Rick Strassman reminds us:

> By conceiving of the brain as a receiver of information . . . one can accommodate the biological model of changing brain function with a chemical. At the same time, it allows for the possibility that what is

being received, while not usually perceptible, is consistently and verifiably existent for a large number of individuals. It may, indeed, reflect stable, free-standing, and parallel planes of reality.[26]

Benny Shanon is also open to this possibility, with all its implications, and admits that often the things he saw under the influence of ayahuasca impressed him as being so real that

> the conclusion seemed to be unavoidable: truly existing other realities had been revealed. Believing that this is the case is very common with the drinkers of ayahuasca. Both during the course of the intoxication and afterwards the question repeatedly forces itself: Does this really exist?[27]

Shanon states that ayahuasca brought him, for the first time in his life, 'to doubt the validity of the Western world view'.[28] At the same time he is clearly uncomfortable, as a scientist, with any accommodation with the supernatural, and informs us that 'recourse to the paranormal is foreign to my thinking'.[29] Acknowledging what he calls 'the enchanted nature of the ayahuasca experience', he says, as 'a Western university professor, a psychologist, and a philosopher', that he prefers to try to account for it in a way that respects 'frames of thought and canons of judgement that define my own cultural and professional heritage'.[30] But he acknowledges this may be impossible and that:

> If the commonalities in the ayahuasca experience cannot be accounted for in ordinary psychological terms, then perhaps we have no choice but to shift from the internal domain to the external one and consider the possibility that these commonalities reflect patterns exhibited on another, extra-human realm.[31]

Internal domain?

For our purposes, the upshot is that Strassman and Shanon, despite their acknowledged expertise as the top scientists in this field, are unable to offer any definitive explanation for the mysterious universal hallucinations of spirit beings that our ancestors first depicted in rock art 35,000 years ago, that took the form of gods and goddesses for the high civilisations of antiquity, that were known as fairies, elves, demons and goblins in the European Middle Ages, and that continue to manifest in the twenty-first century as spaceships and aliens while still retaining much of their ancient 'enchantment' and many of their traditional disguises. Nothing that Strassman and Shanon have discovered rules out the possibility that these complex hallucinations, and the distinctive themes such as therianthropy, hybridism, abduction and the wounded man that run through them from the earliest times until today, might represent veridical encounters with alternative realities. But despite the complexity of such hallucinations, both authorities also acknowledge that they might in some way have been generated inwardly – although they can offer no suggestion as to what process, evolutionary or otherwise, could have brought this about.

Let's first address this problem of the universal inward generation of non-real perceptions.

The one thing that is clear is that 'coincidence' – that much overused longstop of materialist arguments – cannot explain the massive universality of the many supposedly 'non-real' human experiences described in this book. If we are to think of them all as inwardly generated hallucinations, therefore, then we are more or less obliged to conclude, as some academics do, that evolution has hard-wired the bizarre images, sensations and information that they contain into the modern human nervous system. The moment that we try to take this proposition seriously, however, we collide with the evolutionary paradoxes outlined earlier – namely the difficulty of seeing *why* natural selection should have favoured the survival of such a large amount of useless information (along with ingenious means for its admission into consciousness), and *how* it could possibly manifest itself in the form of universal images, ranging from therianthropes to aliens and angels to demons, in settings as diverse as caves and UFOs.

The problem looms larger if we ask *when* the alleged hallucinatory database was downloaded on to the human genome (from where, thereafter, it would be duplicated in every newly made human being).

Those who want us to believe that blind evolutionary forces acting on their own could have compiled such a database and impressed it permanently on all our brains ought to have an instant answer to this question, but, as it turns out, they do not.

We have seen that there are no grounds for attributing the human ability to hallucinate to any kind of neurological change. Although the earliest surviving evidence that our ancestors were experiencing hallucinations comes in the cave paintings of 35,000 years ago, it is the scientific consensus that our species had undergone no neurological evolution whatsoever for at least 160,000 years before that. The brains of the great shaman artists of the Upper Palaeolithic did not differ in terms of size, complexity or structure from the brains of the most ancient anatomically modern humans so far discovered, who lived in Ethiopia around 196,000 years ago.[32] The difference was all in behaviour, with the symbolic abilities that are expressed so fluently in the cave paintings being found to lie at the root of all the significant innovations – then and since – that have elevated human beings above animals and allowed us to take our destiny into our own hands.

From this we may deduce that any evolution required to install the ability to hallucinate on our mental hard-drives must have occurred much further back in the human story than just 35,000 years ago, or even 196,000 years ago, *but that this ability was for a long while inconsequential in its effects*. I have argued that a small percentage of every human population has always been able to hallucinate spontaneously without the need for drugs or other shamanic techniques, but that most of our ancestors probably didn't know how to 'switch on' this ability in any sort of systematic way until such a time as they encountered and began to make deliberate use of psychoactive plants and fungi. I am certain that the ability was already present amongst our pre-sapient hominid ancestors all the way back to the Australopithecines, and I do not doubt that they would from time to time have encountered and enjoyed psychoactive plants without being transformed by them in the way that later humans would be.

Indeed, scientists have established that the ability to hallucinate is not confined to humans but is shared by other mammals and also by birds, bees, butterflies, ants and spiders, many of which are known actively to seek out psychoactive substances.[33] Of course we cannot know what mental events they experience – or even if they experience any mental events at all – under the influence of a drug. What we can be sure of is that their behaviour changes. Spiders on LSD, for example, weave fantastic, convoluted, 'arabesque' webs. There are ants that become addicted to the abdominal secretions of a certain beetle, specimens of which they collect, nurture and breed so as to ensure a permanent supply on hand in their colonies. Once under the influence of the secretions the ants stagger around, and abandon their normal work. Similarly moths in Arizona favour the nectar of hallucinogenic datura flowers over all other sources available. After visiting just a few flowers they become clumsy, researchers report, and often 'miss the target and fall onto the leaves or the soil. They right themselves slowly and awkwardly. When they take to flight again, their movements seem erratic, as if they were confused. But the moths seem to like this effect and return to suck more nectar from those flowers.'[34]

That such different categories of creature as insects and humans should both turn out to have an evolved ability to alter their state of consciousness with hallucinogens is highly significant. It means that the actual process by which the ability to hallucinate was 'naturally selected' and imprinted on DNA (so that it could thereafter be replicated from generation to generation) must have taken place before the last common ancestor of them all. This is so because the Arthropoda (the line to which insects and spiders both belong) and the Chordata (the line to which humans and other vertebrates belong) have been separate from the very first records of multicellular life and their last common ancestor is thought to have lived around a billion years ago. It is a hypothetical creature, for no physical remains have survived, and the general view amongst biologists is that it would have been little more than a ball of cells without eyes, a face or a brain.[35] Nevertheless we can be certain that some such creature did exist, and that its descendants separated and formed the Arthropod and Chordate lines because of the astonishing similarities that still connect insects and humans at the genetic level. Thus, for example, although the compound eyes of a fly and the camera-like eyes of a human being are completely different in structure their development turns out to be controlled by exactly the same group of genes – i.e. segments of DNA that are identical in both flies and humans. Likewise the same gene clusters that regulate the differentiation of the paired and segmented antennae of the head region in fruit flies are also involved in the differentiation of the head region in mice and humans. The implication is that these genes were 'retained in invertebrates and vertebrates from a common ancestor that lived aeons upon aeons ago'.[36]

By the same logic the genes that control the response of insects and humans to hallucinogens must also have been present in the common ancestor of both. That hypothetical faceless, eyeless and brainless ball of cells bobbing mindlessly in the waters of the primeval ocean a billion or more years ago must, in other words, have already been equipped with the same genetic coding that makes it possible for modern humans to experience complex universal hallucinations.

One cannot say that nature gave the common ancestor this equipment which it could not use itself so that it would much later be available for more evolved species – since every step of evolution has to pay its way *at the time*. So if we want natural selection to explain our ability to hallucinate and to account for the specific types of content that are seen universally in altered states of consciousness – including flying discs, 'wheels', therianthropes, beings with multiple faces, clowns, 'white ladies', small humanoids with large heads, and serpents coiled around each other like the double helix – we must first explain why it was useful for the last common ancestor of insects and humans to have the necessary instructions on its DNA to enable it to hallucinate even though it did not yet have any brain cells to hallucinate with! If it is not immediately obvious how possessing the ability to see 'non-real' things could confer survival advantages on an advanced mammal like a human being, it is a thousand times more difficult to explain how or why such an ability could have evolved in the first place in much earlier and simpler forms of life.

But perhaps it did not evolve. Or anyway not here. Perhaps Narby and Crick are right and our DNA really is an 'ancient high biotechnology . . . that far surpasses our present understanding and that was initially developed elsewhere than on earth'.[37]

Far better than vain attempts to bend natural selection to explain why the DNA of creatures ancestral to insects and humans should have been equipped with blueprints to enable their descendants to observe the unreal is to suppose that the blueprints were always present in some vital area of DNA right from the moment that life first began replicating on this planet, and that they were put there by 'clever entities' in the expectation that the processes of evolution would one day result in a creature that could understand and make use of them.

If there is any truth to this scenario, then it could be that the next stage in our evolution depends on our willingness to give full attention to the ancient interactive teachers in our DNA. Perhaps Rick Strassman's volunteer Jeremiah came as close to the truth as anyone when he announced in the middle of a high-dose DMT session: 'I felt evolution occurring. These intelligences are looking over us.'[38]

Extra-human realm?

The alternative to experiences like these being inwardly generated, as Benny Shanon admits, is that they genuinely do 'reflect patterns exhibited on another, extra-human realm'. Much of the evidence we have explored in these pages is at least suggestive of this possibility.

For example, what final reckoning are we to reach with the parallels between flying saucers (circular, rotating fast, instrumental in the abduction of humans, linked to the appearance and disappearance of aliens) and the fairy dance (circular, rotating fast, instrumental in the abduction of humans, linked to the appearance and disappearance of fairies)? They often seem like two different technologies for doing the same thing, with the fairy dance the equivalent of the analogue version and the UFO showing off its tricks as the latest digital model. But if they are technologies of any kind, rather than abstract mental images, then we can only be dealing with perceptions of extra-human realms and beings.

The alternative, 'inward' notion that we are interacting with intelligent virtual agents in our DNA does not seem to provide a good explanation for data of this sort. It is also unable to account for the many physical elements of abductions by spirits, fairies and aliens that have been reported down the ages – ranging from the complete disappearance of individuals in medieval times, to radar echoes of UFOs today, and to the small but distinct traces, such as scars and implants, that are often left on the bodies of abductees. Far from being 'virtual' and inwardly generated, such phenomena seem to meet most of the standard tests that we apply to exterior reality.

What I find most persuasive, however, is the consistent tradition of interbreeding between humans and spirits/fairies/aliens, together with the parallel themes of wetnursing, hybrid children, etc., etc., and clear indications of change and development taking place within these peculiar phenomena over the course of relatively recent human history. Such experiences do not seem to accord at all well with Narby's scenario, since it is difficult to guess why even the most creative and interactive virtual teachers should have been designed to convince us that we are having intercourse and making babies with them, let alone whey they should further require us to return repeatedly to the classroom to cuddle and nurse our poor, sickly, hybrid (and of course *virtual*) offspring.

Also, although the 'lessons' envisaged by the virtual-teacher hypothesis would have been designed to draw on and tailor themselves sensitively to the existing mental imagery of the pupil (thus accounting for bison therianthropes in Upper Palaeolithic Europe, eland therianthropes in southern Africa, and jaguar therianthropes in the Amazon), it is much harder to understand how the actual content and structure of the lessons could change if they had indeed been pre-loaded on to DNA at the start of life on earth. We have seen, for example, that the 'hybrid project' has maintained a consistent focus on producing offspring that are half human and half spirit (or fairy, or alien), and that this seems to have been going on for thousands of years. The reader will recall that many intricate details of this supposed mental figment have remained exactly the same as far back as records go, but that there also appears to have been significant streamlining of standard operating procedures (e.g. no more changelings and no more permanent abductions of adults and children into the otherworld – see Chapter Fifteen).

Such evidence can only add weight to the scary but intriguing possibility that the reason why human experiences of the 'non-real' demonstrate so many astonishing commonalities is that they do in fact 'reflect patterns exhibited on another, extra-human realm'. The bottom line would be that non-human, apparently non-physical intelligences, whose first interactions with us are documented in rock paintings of therianthropes dating back 35,000 years, and who inspired all the world's religious traditions, are still present amongst us today following their own agenda according to their own timetable and purposes.

We know that about 2 per cent of humans have the spontaneous ability to enter the altered states of consciousness that are required for seeing and hearing such beings. The rest of us – including many of the most accomplished shamans – require the help of a range of techniques in order to induce the requisite state of consciousness. Amongst these, by far the simplest, the most certain and the most immediate is the consumption of large doses of one or other of the many plant and fungal hallucinogens that have evolved alongside us. Indeed, when we look at the pattern globally we can see that psychoactive flora are so widely available in nature that evolution seems to have taken almost a 'belts and braces' approach to ensuring that they would sooner or later be encountered by any intelligent species that might evolve on this planet.

It so happened that the first species on earth with the brain power to do more than just enjoy these plant catalysts – as even ants and spiders seem to do – was our own, *Homo sapiens sapiens*. Other species seek out hallucinogens, and demonstrate behavioural changes while intoxicated, but soon revert to rigid instinctive patterns when the drug effects have worn off. Earlier hominids no doubt did so too. Modern humans, on the other hand, are frequently transformed by the same substances. As we saw in Chapter Twenty-One, studies where subjects have been questioned on such matters emphasise that their drug experiences had profound effects on their views of reality and often left them with long-lasting spiritual leanings and metaphysical interests.[39]

We have no reason to suppose that it would have been any different for our ancestors in the Upper Palaeolithic. On the contrary, the evidence is overwhelming that their great leap forward 35,000 years ago was causally linked with the experiences that they went through in altered states of consciousness and documented so fluently in the dark depths of the painted caves. They believed that they were encountering supernatural beings from non-human realms. After all we know now, who are we to say that they were wrong?

Psilocybin at Avebury

Under the influence of five dried grams of psilocybin mushrooms, the acerbic American comedian and social commentator Bill Hicks had experiences that changed his outlook on life completely:

> I have seen UFOs split the sky like a sheet . . . I have seen seven balls of light come off a UFO, lead me onto their ship, explain to me telepathically that we are all one and there is no such thing as death . . . I laid in a field of green grass for four hours going, 'My God . . . I love everything.' The heavens parted, God looked down and rained gifts of forgiveness onto my being, healing me at every level, psychically, physically, emotionally. And I realised our true nature is spirit, not body, that we are eternal beings.[40]

I too had seen UFOs under the influence of a drug – in my case ayahuasca – and come to similar realisations. But then the DMT in ayahuasca and the psilocybin in the mushrooms that Hicks ate are closely related. Indeed Rick Strassman defines psilocybin as orally active DMT.[41] Psilocybin is also a plausible candidate for the hallucinogen used to induce trances by the shamans of the Upper Palaeolithic, since *Psilocybe semilanceata* and a number of other highly psychoactive mushroom species grew in Europe during the Ice Age.[42] In addition, scholars have implicated the consumption of *Psemilanceata* as most likely to have inspired the later Neolithic art of Europe's great megalithic monuments at sites such as Carnac in Brittany, and Newgrange and Dowth in Ireland.[43] Though fully iconic figures are lacking, many of the same entoptic phenomena abound and there is a sense of continuity – as though the great project of the painted caves never quite died out but somehow re-emerged amongst the megaliths thousands of years later.

There is another strange connection too. In European folklore the Neolithic monuments have always been strongly associated with fairies. The tumuli – or ancient burial mounds – were often taken to be 'fairy hills' and the stone circles and megalithic passage-graves such as Gavrinis, New Grange and West Kennett Longbarrow were feared and avoided as entrances to Fairyland.[44]

A megalithic setting therefore seemed appropriate to attempt what I was determined would be one final experiment with psilocybin – a final experiment because I had already taken hefty doses of *Psilocybe cubensis*, *Psilocybe mexicana* and *Psilocybe semilanceata* and was frankly scared of further encounters.

I'm not sure why I felt as afraid as I did, because nothing particularly terrifying had happened to me under the influence of the drug. Far from it! Mushrooms are very hit-and-miss, and on two of the three previous occasions I didn't have a psychedelic experience at all. The third occasion was different, but perhaps that was because I took 13 dried grams of *P. semilanceata* (far too much, apparently – almost three times as much as the dose that put Bill Hicks on to a UFO). I tipped the little mushrooms into a pot of water and cooked them at well below boiling point for half an hour until I had about a litre of dark brown stock. Then I hauled out the tangled, soggy mushroom mass from the bottom of the pot, put it in a sieve, squeezed most of the liquor in it into the pot, ate a handful of the mushrooms out of the sieve and then drank all the soup (which didn't taste at all bad).

Within half an hour I was immersed in a heavy visual storm of entoptic patterns and ever-changing colours, and as I let these develop, the room around me and even members of my family who were in it with me underwent a slightly sinister metamorphosis. Walls bent and breathed, the floor expanded, facial features were distorted, skin took on strange tones and pallor. It was as though everything in my familiar reality had surreptitiously shifted half a step to one side and now was somehow different. At the same time I knew clearly who I was, where I was, who I was amongst, and that these were just the characteristic perceptual effects of the drug I had taken which would wear off in six hours or less.

I listened to our daughter Shanti playing beautiful music on our old piano. The notes seemed to take shape in the air – sometimes as huge curtains of light rippling across my visual field like the aurora borealis, sometimes as fireworks and starbursts, sometimes almost as winged beings. I found that there was a curious way my consciousness could follow and be guided by these notes in flight, or sometimes be lulled by them as though into a gentle rocking motion like a soft swell out at sea.

When Shanti stopped playing I stood up and walked around. At some point I looked down at my feet and found that they were ridiculously far away – at least two floors beneath me. Later I noticed that my left hand seemed to be surrounded by a fuzzy glowing aura. I held it up to study it, splaying my fingers out, and realised that the effect was almost exactly like the negative handprints, each surrounded by a penumbra of spray-paint, that I had seen in so many of the painted caves of Europe.

I started to feel cold and lay down on the couch, wrapping myself in a blanket. Santha sat with me. After a while our daughter Leila came into the room and recounted a harrowing story about hunters in Africa slaughtering a pregnant chimpanzee for 'bush meat'. The story filled me with an unutterable and inconsolable sense of sorrow and desolation and I spent the next hour in tears. By the time I pulled myself together the psychedelic side of the trip was well and truly over.

So . . . emotional, yes, a bit disturbing, yes, a lesson, yes (both my daughters taught me different important lessons about the beauty and sadness of life), but scary – no. There was nothing out-and-out scary about where psilocybin had taken me because it hadn't really taken me anywhere at all. Unlike ayahuasca and DMT, which had propelled me into convincing otherworlds, and ibogaine which had introduced me to the spirits of the dead, the large dose of mushrooms I had consumed had not plunged me into anything like a full-scale visionary state. What the drug had done, however, was play around enough with my sense of reality to hint at the limitless powers that it still held in reserve and what it could do to me if it let rip. Everyone has their own threshold and clearly mine for psilocybin was high, but if I wanted to get into as deep a trance as Hicks had done, and as perhaps the cave artists had done, then I was going to have to test my threshold and break through it. In practice that would mean what? Twenty dried grams? Thirty?

The otherworld can be a very scary place and I began asking myself how much I wanted to see it again. Psilocybin was clearly a vehicle that would get me there if I was willing to brave a truly heroic dose, but how much did I really want or need to do that? And what more did I hope to find out? Was there any real chance, even if I 'asked the mushrooms' (as the Mazatec shaman Maria Sabina used to do in Mexico back in the 1950s) that any kind of definitive insight, or any answers at all, would come out of a big psilocybin trip? Well, honestly, yes there was. Was there any hope that I might meet the spirit of my father and be reconciled to his loss? Again, honestly, yes there was – I have heard regular users of hallucinogens report stranger things. But did I have the stomach for a trip like that now, after two years of research and writing, with my energy at a low ebb and my fear of the spirit world high? I wasn't at all sure that I did.

Nonetheless, a couple of weeks before the spring equinox in 2005, I made my way to the 5,000-year-old megalithic stone circle at Avebury in Wiltshire with three friends who are all experienced users of psyche-delics. Santha and our son Luke came along to lend reassurance and help out in case of any problems. Again the mushroom of the day was the Liberty Cap, *Psilocybe semilanceata*, which has grown in profu-sion across huge swathes of Ireland, the British Isles and mainland Europe since times immemorial. One of us had brought the little fungi in a rucksack and we chewed them up pretty much as they came out of the earth, just as our ancestors might have done.

I lost count after a while but I know that I ate at least 50 caps and stalks. I have no idea what that would amount to in dry grams, but certainly it was many fewer mushrooms than had gone into the soup I'd made before. Since I hadn't broken through into the visionary state then, it followed that I was most unlikely to break through to it now on what felt like less than half the dose, yet at the same time I found myself strongly resisting the idea of eating more.

We were perched up amongst the exposed roots of an ancient tree on the ridge of the immense ditch and embankment in the form of a fairy circle that surrounds the principal henge at Avebury. I looked around at the colossal earthworks and at the weathered, imposing megaliths, standing stark, in silhouette, like doors leading to another world. It was early afternoon, cold and grey, with a chill wind blowing, the trees were bare, and there were very few people around.

Then I ate five more mushrooms and closed the rucksack . . .

Appendices

APPENDIX I

Critics and Criticisms of David Lewis-Williams' 'Neuropsychological Theory' of Rock and Cave Art

(NB This Appendix amplifies points originally raised in Chapters Seven and Eight and some short sections of text are repeated from those chapters.)

Since obtaining his doctorate from the University of Cambridge in 1979, the British archaeologist Paul Bahn has risen to become one of the most powerful figures in the production, management and control of public knowledge about cave art. A prolific academic essayist, he has authored and co-authored literally hundreds of highly regarded papers in learned journals. Meanwhile his television documentaries, and the series of popular books that he has written and edited, have established him as the one of the main channels by which information about the ideas and discoveries of cave-art researchers filter down to the man in the street.[1] In 1986 he delivered the first public lecture on Palaeolithic art by a foreigner in China since the Abbé Breuil 54 years earlier. In 1988, his authoritative study *Images of the Ice Age*, hailed as 'an outstanding critical synthesis and review of current research on Palaeolithic art' and as 'a major scholarly contribution',[2] also enjoyed great popular success. Revised and republished in 1997 as *Journey through the Ice Age*, it remains the single most influential overview of Upper Palaeolithic art available to the general public.[3]

In 2003 Bahn added new lustre to his reputation when he led the team of archaeologists who made the first ever discovery of cave wall and ceiling art in Britain (previously only small portable pieces had been known). The find, provisionally dated to around 12,500 years ago, was made at Cresswell Craggs in Derbyshire on 14 April 2003, and consists of two separate groups of engraved figures, including a male ibex or other caprid, and two birds.[4] Subsequent investigations throughout 2004 have uncovered a much wider array of figures, with 'up to 80 carvings of animals, dancing women and geometric patterns'.[5]

The vicissitudes of Bahn

At the mention of cave art in which geometric patterns are juxtaposed with human and animal figures, anyone persuaded by David Lewis-Williams' neuropsychological theory of prehistoric shamanism is bound to start thinking in terms of trances, entoptic phenomena, full-scale hallucinations, and spirit journeys to the otherworld as the inspiration of the artists. And indeed, when the neuropsychological model first became widely known in 1988, Paul Bahn was amongst its early supporters, declaring: 'It may well provide some long-needed insight into what lies behind some of the "signs" of the Upper Palae-olithic.'[6] At times he even seemed prepared to make imaginative leaps of inference and to take the line of argument that cave art could be based on hallucinations into speculative territory that David Lewis-Williams himself was not prepared to enter. In *Images of the Ice Age*, for example, Bahn suggested that the model had the potential to

> account for some of the more disturbing cross-cultural parallels in images that are far more complex than meanders or simple geometric shapes. For example, in southern African [San] rock art, there are images of a medicine man in trance next to a dying eland (an analogy between the animal's state and the shaman who 'died' in trance) which resemble the Shaft scene at Lascaux with its bird-headed man and wounded bison; similarly the Lascaux man, with his erection and his 'bird on a stick', is remarkably like an Arizona rock-engraving depicting an ithyphallic man with a bird on a stick ... Are these simply remark-able coincidences? Or are they indicative of some widespread phenomenon such as 'universal myths' of very remote antiquity, or

perhaps something akin to phosphenes – images seen under trance conditions?[7]

Bahn never seems to have followed up on these interesting questions. On the contrary, as the 1990s passed, he became ever more antagonistic towards the neuropsychological model. It remained closely associated with the personality and achievements of David Lewis-Williams, who continued to attract glowing international plaudits as a result. By the time *Journey through the Ice Age* was published in 1997, Bahn had undergone a notable transformation and was ready to insist that Lewis-Williams' ideas were no more than 'wishful thinking' based on flawed research that should be dropped entirely from archaeological curricula.[8] And in 2001, noting that public interest in the theory remained strong, despite his warnings, and that even mass-circulation newspapers were now giving it favourable coverage, he protested:

> Such reckless dissemination of misinformation in the popular media is particularly reprehensible and will have untold repercussions for the public's view of the past. That is why this situation has become intolerable, and it is time for this dogma to be exposed for what it is: Piffle, or indeed Piffle-Lite.[9]

Other attacks that Bahn has made on Lewis-Williams have appeared in the scientific literature under such witty titles as: 'Membrane and Numb Brain,'[10] 'Desperately Seeking Trance Plants'[11] and 'Save the Last Trance for Me'.[12] Bahn is also by no means alone in delivering these often deeply discourteous and highly personalised broadsides but has marshalled a substantial lobby of allies and supporters – Patricia Helvenston, Henri-Paul Francfort, Roberte Hamayon, Cyril Hromnik and Anne Solomon to name but a few.[13] Some members of this group have recently begun to work together in a co-ordinated and public manner.[14] Their published statements make it clear that they regard the popular acclaim that the neuropsychological theory has received, and its growing uptake by rock-art researchers around the world, as a serious threat to proper public understanding of the past – a threat that indeed has become 'intolerable' and must be countered at every step. To this end, as we will see, they have sought to raise a cloud of question marks over Lewis-Williams' scholarly reputation and to surround the theory in a fog of abuse and opprobrium that is sufficiently foul and off-putting to dissuade any more researchers from trying to make use of it.

'Some dangerous spirit of dogmatism'

In 2002, Paul Bahn and his colleague Patricia Helvenston, a retired American clinical psychologist, felt sure they had the information that would finally bring Lewis-Williams to his knees. They hastily submitted their material to the *Cambridge Archaeological Journal* 'in the hope of rapid publication by October 2002'.[15] Following normal procedures, *CAJ* sent Bahn and Helvenston's paper out for peer review. Unexpectedly, however, some of the academic referees advised that there were serious problems with it, and that these should be remedied before it could appear in print. When *CAJ*'s editor suggested that the article be reworked and published in the next issue, Bahn and Helvenston were incensed:

> We felt very strongly that our paper should appear as rapidly as possible so that the rock art community, and the archaeological world at large, could be made aware of the fallacies underlying the shamanic model . . . Since the length and format of the paper preclude rapid publication in any other journal, we have therefore resorted to the methods of some earlier scholars in deciding to publish the paper ourselves, in order to disseminate the facts as swiftly as possible.[16]

The result, *Desperately Seeking Trance Plants*, which runs to 62 pages, appeared in 2002.[17] A much shorter version was also eventually printed in the *Cambridge Archaeological Journal* in 2003 under the title 'Testing the "Three Stages of Trance" Model'.[18] It is not clear to me whether cutting more than 50 pages of the argument to produce this four-page 'summary' did in fact deal with all the problems that the original referees had objected to – because, as we'll see, a great many serious errors still remain in the abridged version. In the 'Comments' from peers that are published alongside it, moreover, it is troubling to note that a contribution from the Cambridge University archaeologist and rock-art expert Christopher Chippendale was heavily edited by *CAJ*. In the remnant, Chippendale reports that any research issues raised by Helvenston and Bahn's attacks on Lewis-Williams' work are unfortunately overshadowed by a 'social context' within the archaeological world that he describes as 'unusual, peculiar and deeply unsatisfactory'.[19] His unedited comment, he states, had provided 'specific facts' to show that his concerns were well founded, but it was these that had been refused publication:

> *CAJ*'s readers, unable in this way to have access to the pertinent facts of the social context, are still entitled to know the consequences: my inclination is to discount Helvenston and Bahn's arguments entirely, as likely to be too much based on partisan presuppositions rather than on open-minded consideration of the material information. I regret I cannot publish here the good reasons that gradually have brought me unhappily to that dismaying and dismal view.[20]

It sounds like an impasse, but that's nothing new in the temperamental world of rock- and cave-art research. It is, however, most unfortunate that academic opinion should have become so polarised around the first theory in 100 years of research that makes sense, that explains not only the broad range but also the specific details of the evidence, and that resolves what are otherwise extremely perplexing cross-cultural commonalities. By all means we can allow that the shamanic-neuropsychological approach has faults, that there might be many ways of improving and refining it, and that it should not be retained if it fails a battery of fair and reasonable tests. Nevertheless, the history of cave-art research warns us to stay open to the possibility that 'some dangerous spirit of dogmatism' may have blinded those who seek to trash this line of approach completely, without even a second thought – just as partisan presuppositions blinded Cartailhac and his colleagues to the truth of Altamira for more than 20 years.[21]

Accusations of distortion and misrepresentation

One of Paul Bahn's earliest attacks on David Lewis-Williams and the shamanic-neuropsychological model was made in *Journey through the Ice Age*:

> The African research on which the new approach is founded is itself based on massive assumptions, wishful thinking, and extreme selectivity of image and interpretation. In fact there is no hard ethnographic evidence to link any prehistoric southern African rock art with shamans, let alone with trance phenomena. For example the written ethnographic records contain no mention of trance whatsoever, nor of any practices, dreams or beliefs involving it. Yet it has been claimed that there is impeccable ethnographic evidence here for linking 'medicine men' and rainmakers with shamanism, and in turn linking the shamans with the rock art.[22]

Earlier, in 1991, in the *Rock Art Research* journal, the South African scholar Cyril Hromnik had similarly accused Lewis-Williams of subjecting the nineteenth-century ethnographic data, such as the Bleek and Lloyd documents, 'to a process of readjustment and reinterpretation' to make them provide 'a semblance of support for the theory'.[23] In reality, Hromnik revealed:

> None of Bleek's writings cited by Lewis-Williams expressly states that any of the described practices, dreams or beliefs involved trance, and Bleek's *A Bushman's Dictionary* has no entry for trance.[24]

Both as expressed by Bahn, and in its earlier Hromnik incarnation, this is tantamount to accusing Lewis-Williams of intellectual fraud. Effectively what is being alleged is that he distorted and misrepresented the record to fool us into thinking that the nineteenth-century ethnography from southern Africa provides 'support for the theory' when in fact it does no such thing.

Hromnik even goes a stage further and charges Lewis-Williams with misrepresenting the modern ethnographic record of the *Ju'/hoansi*

(*!Kung*) bushmen in the Kalahari as well. The reader will recall from Chapter Seven that the survival of the trance dance and shamanistic healing practices amongst the *Ju/'hoansi* provide important strands in Lewis-Williams' argument about similar practices amongst the nineteenth-century San. Yet Hromnik asserts that

> Katz [the American anthropologist Richard Katz, one of Lewis-Williams' key sources on the *Ju/'hoansi*], who made a detailed study of the magico-medicinal practices of the Kalahari *!Kung* bushmen with whom he stayed for several months, did not find a single medicine man who could rightfully be called a shaman. Their healing practices were devoid of trance.[25]

Interrogating the ethnographic records

If either or both of these allegations about Lewis-Williams' use of his sources turns out to be true, then it would rightly deliver a damaging blow to his credibility. Very surprisingly, however, given their gravity, and the supposed seriousness of the publications in which they appear, neither allegation is true. Worse, six years before Bahn repeated the slur that he had misused the nineteenth-century ethnography, Lewis-Williams had publicly refuted Hromnik on this exact same point, yet Bahn makes no mention of this.

The refutation is simple. It is strictly true that Bleek's dictionary (itself by no means a complete lexicon of the lost San language),[26] 'has no entry for trance', but it is *not* true, as Bahn alleges, that the 'ethnographic records contain no mention of trance whatsoever, nor of any practices, dreams or beliefs involving it'. On the contrary, unless one works with a unique, idiosyncratic and highly unusual definition of what trance is, one could hardly fail to note the frequent occurrence in the ethnographic records of the San word /xau, which connotes a sense of disassociation from one's body[27] – one of the defining characteristics of trance. The Bleek family documents translate this word /xau as 'to go on a magical expedition'.[28] An appropriate modern rendering might be the hippie word 'tripping'.

Moreover, again contradicting Bahn, the ethnographic records describe very specific practices, involving dance and supernatural healing, for which it was absolutely essential that some people enter the state of /xau. The records also document intriguing beliefs in a mysterious power called !gi (see Chapter Seven), said to have been required to launch an individual from his ordinary, everyday state into the state of /xau. This word !gi is translated by Lucy Lloyd and other members of the Bleek family as 'magic power', or 'sorcery', and we learn that people in San society who were believed to possess a lot of !gi were given a special name.[29] Lewis-Williams, who in all cases provides detailed references to his original sources, puts it this way:

> The 'magic power', or 'sorcery', as the Bleek family had it, employed on these occasions was . . . called !gi . . . A person who possessed this power was called a !gi:xa (pl.!gi:ten). The suffix xa means '-ful' as in the English word 'powerful'. W.H.I. Bleek and Lloyd translated !gi:xa as 'sorcerer', and D.F. Bleek devoted three instalments of extracts from the manuscript collection to the activities of these people. A !gi:xa was thus a person who was 'full' of supernatural power that he or she could use to heal, go on extracorporeal journeys, put sickness into people, turn into a lion or other creature, make rain, protect people from thunderstorms, and so forth . . .[30]

Bahn's second charge is that the ethnographic records contain no evidence linking San 'medicine men' and 'rainmakers' with shamanism. The word !gi:xa is indeed sometimes translated today as 'medicine man'.[31] As noted above, however, and more extensively described in Chapter Seven, the rainmaking, supernatural healing, animal transformations, out-of-body journeys, etc., etc. of the !gi:ten are amongst the classic feats of shamans in many different parts of the world and are in fact extensively described in the San ethnographic records. What else but shamanism are we to call the bizarre behaviour of the !gi:ten in a state of /xau?

> The San !gi:ten are said to have entered a frenzy in which they bit people, trembled so violently that they had sometimes to be held down, sniffed sickness out of people, bled from the nose, and in which their

veins stood up and became rigid. During this dangerous time other people danced and sang.[32]

As David Lewis-Williams concludes:

> The behaviour of, and beliefs about the *!gi:ten* show that they were . . . what I and other writers believe can be called 'shamans' who enter 'trance'. Trance was indeed a central and pervasive component of San belief, and the connection between it (together with its corollaries of supernatural power, shamans, transformation and out-of-body travel) and rock art should come as no surprise.

The third allegation that Bahn makes against Lewis-Williams in the passage cited earlier is that there is in fact 'no hard ethnographic evidence to link any prehistoric southern African rock art with shamans'. Bearing in mind the constant cross-translation and confabulation of the words 'shamanism' and 'sorcery', Bahn's position finds little obvious support from what is – so far as I know – the only surviving statement in the ethnographic records that seems to comment specifically not only on who the painters were but also on what the paintings were used for. Given to the geologist George William Stow by a San informant in the nineteenth century, this enigmatic remark informs us that that the paintings are 'sorcery's things'.[33] Or, as Lewis-Williams might put it, 'shaman's things'.

Besides, once we take note of the quintessentially shamanic experiences, behaviour and social role of the San *!gi:ten* as described in the ethnographic records, and the rare but nevertheless clear references that also exist which link *!gi:ten* to the rock art, Bahn's position becomes even less tenable.

Dia!kwain, one of the most important of Bleek and Lloyd's nineteenth-century San informants, was shown a high-quality copy by G.W. Stow of an ancient San rock painting. The painting featured a large hybrid animal, part buffalo, part hippo, that Dia!kwain called *!khwa-ka xorro*. It was being led by men who Dia!kwain called *!khwa-ka !gi:ten*. We've already discussed the meaning of *!gi:ten* at some length, and *!khwa* means 'rain'. A fair translation of the whole phrase would therefore be 'shamans of the rain'.[34] The San word *xorro* means 'large animal', so we can translate *!khwa-ka xorro* as 'large animal of the rain'.[35] These hallucinatory 'rain animals' and the shamans who were believed to lead them through the rock face from the spirit world on the other side are described in Chapter Seven. Dia!kwain's reference to the presence of *!khwa-ka xorro* and *!khwa-ka !gi:ten* in the painting does therefore provide the sort of 'hard ethnographic evidence linking prehistoric southern African rock art with shamans' that Bahn wants to persuade us does not exist.

Nor is this an isolated example. Qing, another of the nineteenth-century San informants whose testimony has become part of the ethnographic record, also explained the same painting. Speaking in rather cryptic and metaphorical terms, he said that the men leading the animal were 'people spoilt by the dance, because their noses bleed'.[36]

As the reader already knows from Chapter Seven, the ethnographic record tells us that the San *!gi:ten* frequently bled from the nose during the trance dance. What is particularly interesting about Qing's observation, however, is that in Stow's copy of the painting the figures of the *!gi:ten* are *not* in fact shown to be bleeding from the nose.[37] It is as though Qing knew these figures were shamans, knew nose-bleeds were a common feature of the shamanic trance dance, and therefore attributed nose-bleeds to the figures. The sense that this is what happened is reinforced by Qing's account of the trance dance itself, which he claimed had been given to the San by the god Kaggen – 'the Mantis' – and which would serve to describe the *!Kung* trance dance today:

> It is a circular dance of men and women, following each other, and it
> is danced all night. Some fall down; some become as if mad and sick;
> blood runs from the noses of others . . . and they eat charm medicine
> . . . When a man is sick, this dance is danced around him, and the
> dancers put both hands under their arm-pits and press their hands on
> him . . .'[38]

Even more telling, although equally cryptic and metaphorical, was Qing's interpretation of another painting – this time not a copy that

600

had been brought to him, but on-site in front of an original panel. It is in a rock shelter that still exists named Melikane in a remote part of the Moloti mountains (just inland of the Drakensberg), and it features a group of three therianthropic figures with human bodies and the heads of antelopes. All three are in the bending-forward posture that we saw in Chapter Seven was frequently adopted by San shamans in a state of trance. Qing had this to say about the figures: 'They are men who had died and now lived in rivers, and were spoilt at the same time as the elands and by the dances of which you have seen paintings.'[39]

Decoding this, on the face of things, rather odd remark, is reasonably straightforward, as David Lewis-Williams has shown. 'Death', the state of being 'spoilt' and the state of being 'underwater' – including the specific notion of 'living in rivers' (or sometimes of descending underground through a 'waterhole') – are all well established from the ethnography as San metaphors for the shamanic trance state.[40] The majestic eland, largest of the antelopes, was also another common metaphor for the shaman. Moreover, as Bahn himself had observed in 1987 in a comment quoted earlier, many of the rock paintings exploit an observed similarity between the behaviour of a shaman in trance and the behaviour of a dying eland.[41] This analogy is especially appropriate, Lewis-Williams adds, when we consider

an eland that is succumbing to the effect of a poisoned arrow. Both shaman and animal tremble violently, sweat profusely, stagger, lower their heads, bleed from the nose, froth at the mouth, and finally crash to the ground. In addition, a dying eland's hair stands on end and San people told Bleek and Lloyd that lion's hair sometimes grows on a shaman's back.[42]

Last but not least, it cannot be an accident that the surviving *!Kung* bushmen in the Kalahari, whose culture shares so much with the lost culture of the southern San, use the single word *kxwia* to mean both 'to spoil' and 'to enter deep trance'.[43] Lewis-Williams cites the evidence of American anthropologist Megan Biesele that when a shaman lies completely unconscious and possibly cataleptic, people say that he has been 'spoilt'. That Qing meant this and not 'spoil' in the daily sense is confirmed by his statement that the men with rhebuck [antelope] heads were 'spoilt . . . by the dances of which you have seen paintings'.[44]

It is not such a strange idea. In England today we say someone is 'smashed' when we mean he is in a drunken stupor. By the same token, San or *!Kung* shamans who fell into a deep hallucinatory state after dancing for hours were said to be 'spoilt'. So when Qing used the word for the figures in the rock paintings, it was his idiom to tell us that they depicted trancing shamans.

It seems, therefore, that Bahn is incorrect to accuse Lewis-Williams of misapplying the ethnography and that there is after all impeccable evidence linking shamans with the rock art. Indeed, not only on this point, but at every stage of the argument, the bottom line is that the ethnography does in fact provide the support that Lewis-Williams claims for his theory, which for some reason Bahn and Hromnik want to convince their readers it does not.

The truth about Katz

The same goes for Hromnik's accusations about misuse of modern anthropological material concerning the *!Kung*, and particularly his suggestion that Lewis-Williams misrepresented Richard Katz, one of the key anthropological sources on the Kalahari bushmen. In the extract quoted earlier, Hromnik says plainly that Katz judged *!Kung* healing practices to be 'devoid of trance' and failed to find even 'a single medicine man who could rightfully be called a shaman'.[45]

Again, if these statements are correct, then the consequences are devastating for Lewis-Williams' credibility – since he makes much of trance and shamanism amongst the *!Kung*. Once again, however, the accusations turn out to have no solid basis. As we saw in Chapter Seven, a profoundly altered state of consciousness called *!kia* is at the heart of the traditional 'healing' or 'trance' dance of the *!Kung*. Richard Katz is extensively on record on this matter and repeatedly makes clear that

that the *!Kung* word *!kia*, which he defines shamanistically as 'that altered state of the consciousness which is the key to healing',[46] is routinely translated by the English word 'trance' (e.g. '*!kia*, usually translated as "trance"',[47] and '*!kia* has been translated by other fieldworkers as "trance"').[48] Katz does have reservations about the word 'trance' itself – in any context, *!Kung* or otherwise – simply because there is no standard scholarly definition of what 'trance' is and 'its referents remain ambiguous, its use inconsistent'.[49] When writing about these matters, he therefore generally prefers to 'keep the *!Kung* word *!kia* and to build an understanding of the phenomenon through examining the *!Kung's* discussion of it'.[50] It is quite wrong, and indeed 'intolerable', on the basis of this semantic point, for Hromnik to persuade his readers that Katz finds *!Kung* healing practices to be 'devoid of trance' when he knows perfectly well that Katz finds *!Kung* healing practices to be filled to the brim with the state of *!kia*. Katz's very insistence that *!kia* is usually translated into English as 'trance' leaves us in no doubt that this is exactly what he is talking about, as does his repeated description of *!kia* as an 'altered state of consciousness':

> *!Kia* can be viewed as an altered state of consciousness, altered to the degree and quantity where it becomes transcendence . . . During *!kia* a !Kung experiences himself as existing beyond his ordinary level of existence . . . Also, a !Kung practices extraordinary activities during *!kia*. He performs cures, handles and walks on fire, claims X-ray vision, and at times says he sees over great distances . . . Transcending himself, he is able to contact the supernatural, a realm where the ghosts of dead ancestors live . . .[51]

If this is not the phenomenon that – in its many different manifestations around the world – is rightly labelled as 'shamanic trance healing', then what is? Even the most cursory reading of the literature leaves Hromnik without a leg to stand on in this regard, since virtually every scholar who has ever commented on the *!Kung* has recognised the trance dance as a form of exactly what Hromnik says it is not, i.e. shamanistic trance healing. 'Specially trained healers are able to enter trance and heal the sick,' notes R.B. Lee. 'The central ritual event in traditional !Kung life is the medicinal trance dance,' writes M. Shostack. L. Marshall comments: 'After an hour or two the medicine men begin to go into trance and perform their healing rite.' According to M. Guenther: 'The explicit purpose of the shamanistic trance dance . . . is to heal.'[52] Megan Biesele's observations are particularly pertinent:

> The central religious experiences of Ju'/hoan [*!Kung*] life are consciously, and as a matter of course, approached through the avenue of trance. The trance dance involves everyone in society, those who enter trance and experience the power of the other world directly, and those to whom the benefits of the other world – healing and insight – are brought by the trancers.[53]

It is extremely hard to understand why Hromnik did not acknowledge these and so many other scholarly voices that so resoundingly confirm the existence of shamanic trance healing amongst the *!Kung*.

Shamans full of supernatural power

Interestingly, Katz even reports (though again we hear none of this from Hromnik) that student shamans who have difficulty entering *!kia* through the normal strenuous methods (see Chapter Seven) are sometimes given 'an indigenous drug' at the beginning of the trance dance:

The drug is offered as a training device, which may vault [the student] over his intense fears as well as bringing him to the *!kia* state. The drug experience itself also becomes a preparation for *!kia* since both experiences are forms of altered states of consciousness. As with other techniques used during the dance, the dosage and time of ingestion of the drug are carefully regulated by the teacher. The drug is supposed to help the student over the barrier of fear and into *!kia*.[54]

Hromnik also misleads us when he says that the *!Kung* have no shamans. On the contrary, if we define shamans in the most widely used sense as those individuals in society who enter altered states of consciousness in order to contact supernatural realms and beings on behalf of their tribe, clan, band, etc., then on Katz's estimates:

Many !Kung, approximately half the older adult males and one-third of the adult women, learn to !kia. During the !kia state, they heal and fulfil many religious functions . . .[55] The healer who is in !kia goes to each person at the dance whether he shows symptoms of illness or not. All receive the protection of healing. The healer pleads and argues with the gods to save the person from illness. He lays his hands on each one, and pulls out the sickness with eerie, earth-shattering screams and howls that show the pain and difficulty of his healing.[56]

As we saw in Chapter Seven, the name the !Kung give to these trance healers is n/om k"xausi, 'owners of supernatural power', i.e. the same concept exactly as the San !gi:ten, who were also 'full of' supernatural power. Since there is absolutely no doubt that the most accurate and direct way to translate what such people are and what they do into the English language is to refer to them as 'shamans', it seems that Hromnik's entire argument to suggest otherwise consists of nothing more than semantic hairsplitting. The truth is that the !Kung do have a phenomenon that is rightly referred to as 'trance' – the altered state of consciousness they call !kia – and they do have shamans, their n/om k"xausi, who volunteer on behalf of the rest of their people to enter !kia and travel out-of-body in the hallucinatory otherworld, sometimes in the form of lions, to intercede there with gods and spirits on behalf of the sick.[57] As one !Kung n/om k"xau described it to Katz:

In !kia your heart stops, you're dead, your thoughts are nothing, you breathe with difficulty. You see ghosts killing people, you smell burning, rotten flesh. Then you heal and you pull sickness out.[58]

A fair test?

In their privately published tract *Desperately Seeking Trance Plants* (2002), and in the much shorter 'summary' of it ('Testing the "Three

Stages of Trance" Model') that eventually appeared in *CAJ* in 2003, Paul Bahn and the clinical psychologist Patricia Helvenston emphasise and extensively document what they call a fair test of the neuropsychological model, while at the same time presenting evidence that they believe refutes the model completely. This is supposedly hard scientific evidence that the three-stage trance process described by Lewis-Williams and Dowson in their landmark 1988 paper[59] does *not* have the wide general applicability to all human beings in all places and times that its proponents claim for it. It is, of course, this very quality – i.e. wide general relevance because of shared human neurology – that allows Lewis-Williams and Dowson to apply their model to arts as diverse as those of the San in southern Africa, the Coso in North America and, most controversially of all, to the remotely ancient cave art of Upper Palaeolithic Europe. If they can be proved to have made false claims for such wide relevance then the model would – to say the least – be severely compromised.

The gist of Helvenston and Bahn's argument is as follows. Having undertaken what they describe as a 'systematic consideration of the most common trance states', they inform us loftily, as though citing divine writ – or at least empirically established and widely agreed facts – that:

The only trance states that are consistent with those described in the TST ['three stages of trance'] model are drug-induced trances caused by plants containing mescaline, lysergic acid diethylamide (LSD), or psilocybin. The TST model does not describe naturally induced trance states nor trance states induced by other hallucinogens contained in plant materials.[60]

Towards the end of their longer paper, *Desperately Seeking Trance Plants*, the two critics make the same point, perhaps a little more clearly:

No naturally induced altered states of consciousness are consistent with Lewis-Williams' and Dowson's 'neuropsychological model' . . . The only drug-induced trance states that are consistent with the model are those produced by LSD, mescaline and psilocybin.[61]

And just so there are no misunderstandings, the assertion is repeated in the *CAJ*: 'No altered states of consciousness are consistent with the TST model except those elicited by mescaline, LSD or psilocybin.'[62]

Bahn and Helvenston's second main point flows directly out of this supposed 'fact' – on the basis of which they assert that the neuropsychological model must be regarded as *refuted*, at least with reference to the painted caves of Upper Palaeolithic Europe, unless Lewis-Williams and Dowson are able to prove (a) that plants containing mescaline, psilocybin or LSD 'were readily available in Western Europe in the late Ice Age'[63] and (b) that the remains of such plants have in fact been found by archaeological excavation of 'the sediments of the site where the proponents of the model claim the art has been inspired by LSD, mescaline or psilocybin-induced trance'.[64] They add that by 'examining the TST model from this perspective' their approach provides 'the first direct method for empirically testing its validity'.[65]

Out-of-date sources, or no new research?

Hidden between the two prongs of Bahn and Helvenston's attack are a range of other lesser stabs and gouges – for example that Lewis-Williams and Dowson extensively misuse neuropsychological terminology[66] and (we've heard this one before!) that what they claim is shamanism is not shamanism,[67] that few of their sources are more recent than the 1970s and therefore that their conclusions have been bypassed by later research,[68] and that there are so many different kinds of trance that it is impossible to talk about 'trance' in the general manner in which the word is used in the neuropsychological model.[69]

I will not try the patience of my readers by going over the semantic games about shamanism again (see Chapter Seven). These simply seem to be part of the standard equipment used by the debunking industry that feeds parasitically off Lewis-Williams' initiatives, original thinking and hard work. For the same reason, let's not get mired in the pettifogging debate about terminology.

The accusation of reliance on out-of-date sources is that Lewis-Williams and Dowson's so-called 'neuropsychological model' is in fact based on very old neuropsychological literature, most of it dating back to the 1970s or earlier, that has been superseded by more recent and modern research.[70]

It is hypocritical of Bahn and Helvenston to take such a position, since they themselves rely extensively on neuropsychological research done during and before the 1970s (Ludwig's work, for example, to which they devote one sixth of their treatise, as we'll see below, was published in 1968).[71] Besides, they fail to make clear that most of the best science on altered states of consciousness produced by psychotropic drugs was done prior to the mid-1970s – at which time the so-called 'War on Drugs' put a halt to almost all properly funded research in this field. Against this backdrop it is plainly absurd for Bahn and Halvenston to suggest that a great deal of significant new science has been done since the mid-1970s into the three drugs they themselves nominate – namely LSD, psilocybin and mescaline. This is completely untrue; worldwide, *almost no scientific research at all* has been done into the effects of these hallucinogens on humans since the end of the 1960s, for the simple reason that such research is highly illegal in all the major science-funding nations! To complain of out-of-date sources on a subject that has seen so little new research for more than 30 years is nothing short of deeply misleading.

When is a trance not a trance?

On the issue of trance, Bahn and Helvenston devote 10 pages to a verbatim reproduction and lengthy discussion of 75 different ways of getting into an altered state of consciousness listed by a certain Arnold M. Ludwig in a book published in 1968. At the time, Arnold Ludwig was Director of Education and Research at the Mendota State Hospital in Madison, Wisconsin, and no doubt his work is of the highest quality. For some reason, however, Bahn and Halvenston want to persuade us that this estimable body of research undermines Lewis-Williams' and Dowson's basic thesis:

> Given this huge variety of some seventy-five different trance states, only one of which refers to shamanistic trance, how could anyone who

is informed about the complexities of neuropsychological research suggest that all trance states have the same characteristic three stages?[72]

In fact, if we consult Ludwig himself, we find that he does not talk about 75 'different' trance states, but rather about 75 different ways to *produce* trance states[73] – a very different matter. It is quite true that only one of these refers to what Ludwig calls 'shamanistic, divination, and prophetic trance states', which he lists as being 'produced' by 'increase of exteroceptive stimulation and/or motor activity and/or emotion'.[74] Of course Ludwig is not an infallible resource on such matters and is mistaken not to mention shamanic trances a second time when he deals later with altered states of consciousness induced by 'the administration of pharmacological agents . . . narcotics, etc.'[75] The reader will recall from Chapter Seven that amongst the Tungus nomads of Siberia (from whom the very word 'shamanism' derives), 'Some shamans eat narcotic mushrooms and in their hallucinations visit the world of spirits, where they get the answers to questions posed to them.'[76] Indeed not just the Tungus, but shamans the world over, more frequently make use of hallucinogenic drugs than of any other technique to enter altered states of consciousness.

The real problem with all this, however, is not what Ludwig does or doesn't say about shamanism, but the very strong impression given to readers that by identifying all sorts of other trance states that are not overtly 'shamanic', Bahn and Halvenston have dealt a mortal blow to Lewis-Williams' and Dowson's neuropsychological model. This is far from the truth. When you go back to the original source, the evidence that fills up this 10-page diversion in the middle of *Desperately Seeking Trance Plants* (one sixth of the overall length of the text) turns out to be completely irrelevant to the neuropsychological model. Yes, let it be true, as Ludwig tells us, that there is such a thing as a 'reading trance, especially with poetry';[77] yes, no doubt free association during psychoanalysis may sometimes produce a trance state;[78] yes, by all means let us accept that even 'prolonged masturbation' may bring about 'trance-like states'[79] – etc., etc. In the final analysis, however, none of this has any bearing on the phenomenon at hand. Whatever name different factions wish to give to it, this is the phenomenon described in Chapter

Seven, based on the universal capacity of all humans to enter altered states of consciousness, to experience hallucinations in those altered states that are interpreted as supernatural contacts with a 'spirit world' or 'otherworld' (usually said to be located above us in the sky or beneath us underground), and to use these contacts to bring back to this world what are believed to be healing powers, control over the weather, control over the movements of animals, and other useful benefits.

We already know very well that Lewis-Williams and Dowson are concerned exclusively with this phenomenon, which they call 'shamanistic trance', but that others may prefer to find a different name for. They are not at all concerned with 'reading trances', 'masturbation trances', 'free-association trances', or any other such states of mind, and nowhere do they claim that these sorts of trance 'have the same characteristic three stages'. It is therefore misleading for Bahn and Helvenston to cite Ludwig's evidence as though it undermines their theory. On the contrary, if there are 75 ways to enter trance, and if by chance *any* of these trance states produce the same sort of hallucinatory imagery and experiences that are common with psychotropic drugs, then the theory is strengthened, not weakened. All it calls for is that people be capable – by a variety of means – of getting into such deeply altered states of consciousness that they hallucinate. We already know, it is a truism, that people are capable of doing this – and, indeed, that there are extant cultures in which people not only hallucinate in a socially structured way but also make paintings of their visions afterwards. If Ludwig's list cited by Bahn and Halvenston contains information about a few more means of getting into such deeply altered states, then so much the better. But it certainly does nothing to refute the neuropsychological model of rock and cave art, and should not be claimed so to do.

It is a debating trick to imply that Ludwig had listed 75 different types of trance when in fact he had listed 75 different ways to get into trance. The purpose of the trick seems to be to suggest that Lewis-Williams and Dowson are falsely creating a special niche, that 'their' kind of trance, involving drugs or rhythmic dancing, is just a small part of a much bigger picture and not worth drawing any general conclusions about. Thus Bahn and Helvenston also devote several pages of *Desperately Seeking Trance Plants* to the subject of hypnotic trance, a specialist interest of Helvenston's, apparently.[80] This is all very well, but since hypnosis is not implicated in Lewis-Williams' and Dowson's model, what people do and don't experience under hypnosis is again irrelevant to the discussion. It feels like just a thick fog of facts and observations thrown together to suggest some semblance of an argument where really there is none. Partially obscured but unchanged by it is the universal phenomenon of people entering deep trance and experiencing hallucinations as real contacts with supernatural beings from a 'spirit world'. There may be 75 or 75,000 different ways of getting into trance, and there may even be 750,000 different kinds of trance, but to reiterate a point that I have already made several times, none of this has any bearing whatsoever on the verified existence in many different cultures of the phenomenon itself.

Besides, quite contrary to the impression given in *Desperately Seeking Trance Plants*, Ludwig's list of 75 different ways of getting into a trance is *not* followed by any assertion that this means 75 or more different kinds of trance. On the contrary, one of the most intriguing conclusions of Ludwig's research for some reason goes unreported by Bahn and Helvenston. This is that altered states of consciousness (ASCs) 'share many common features' and that, moreover, 'certain general molding influences . . . appear to account for many of the apparent differences in the outward manifestation of ASCs'.[81] A little later Ludwig speaks of the 'common denominators' linking a wide range of supposedly different ASCs.[82] Indeed, in this paper which Bahn and Halvenston rely on so extensively to demonstrate the *differences* amongst trance states, I was surprised to discover that Ludwig in fact devotes only five pages to his list of 75 different ways to get into a trance (which, to reiterate, was never claimed to be a list of 75 different kinds of trance and should not have been spun that way). By contrast, though we get no hint of this from the two critics, he devotes 10 pages to exploring the common denominators and amazing similarities that seem to link almost all states of trance, for example 'alterations in thinking', 'disturbed time-sense', 'loss of control', 'change in emotional expression', 'body-image change', 'perceptual distortions', 'change in meaning or significance', 'sense of the ineffable', 'feelings of rejuvenation', and 'hypersuggestibility'.[83]

Accordingly, despite the spin put on it by Bahn and Halvenston, I find nothing in Ludwig's paper that undermines Lewis-Williams' case by even a hair's breadth. Quite the opposite: there is much in it that supports him but which, in a most unsatisfactory manner, the two critics simply don't tell their readers about.

To give a closing example of this sort of behaviour, we have seen that a central element of Bahn and Helvenston's argument rests on the supposed uniqueness of three plant-based drugs. These are mescaline, LSD and psilocybin, which – they repeatedly and firmly assert in statements cited earlier – are *the only agents* capable of inducing the mixture of abstract and geometrical patterns with full-scale iconic figures that is essential for the success of Lewis-Williams' neuropsychological model. We have also seen that they make a particular point of emphasising that hypnotic trances and indeed *all* other kinds of trances are totally *different* from trances induced by these three specific named drugs. Despite their tendency to quote extensively from Ludwig's paper when it can be made to serve their argument, it is therefore easy to understand why they fail to inform their readers about the views that he expresses on the supposed 'uniqueness' of LSD, mescaline and psilocybin in the same paper:

> The psychedelic experiences attained through peyote, LSD, psilocybin or mescaline tend to resemble the subjective experiences attained through marihuana, certain anaesthetics, or opium, all of which may closely resemble the subjective experiences gained in the hypnotic trance, mystical states, creative states, or during acute psychotic or toxic episodes.[84]

Last but not least . . .

The claim that no altered states of consciousness 'except those elicited by mescaline, LSD or psilocybin'[85] are consistent with the types of hallucinations and experiences described in the neuropsychological model, and the parallel claim that none of these substances were available in Europe in the Upper Palaeolithic, stand at the very heart of Bahn and Helvenston's critique. As demonstrated in Chapter Eight, however (and more extensively in Appendix II, below), DNA and other evidence, together with expert testimony, confirms that the hallucinogenic mushroom *Psilocybe semilanceata* is a native Old World species that would have been present in Europe in the Upper Palaeolithic. Contrary to Bahn and Helvenston's argument, it therefore cannot be ruled out as the hallucinogenic agent that inspired the cave art – and indeed suggests itself as a very plausible candidate. We have seen in addition that approximately 30 other species of psilocybin-containing mushrooms are also native to Europe and are equally likely to have served as trance agents for the shamans of the painted caves. The fact that these species have only relatively recently been taken up again for hallucinogenic purposes tells us nothing about their use or potential use by hunter-gatherers in the Upper Palaeolithic who – like hunter-gatherers of all epochs and places – are likely to have possessed knowledge far superior to our own of the medicinal and other properties of local plants and fungi.

APPENDIX II

Psilocybe semilanceata – a hallucinogenic mushroom native to Europe

by Professor Roy Watling, OBE, winner of the Royal Society of Edinburgh's Patrick Neill Medal for research in mycology

Although the hallucinogenic mushroom Psilocybe semilanceata *is widespread in Europe today, the claim has been made that it is not an ancient native species but was introduced from the New World after trans-Atlantic contact began in the late fifteenth century. Professor Watling investigates this claim and gives his opinion on the provenance of the species.*

Psilocybe semilanceata, or 'Liberty Caps', a colloquial name pertaining to the cap resembling the helmet of the First World War French infantry (before the general term 'magic mushroom' was introduced), is well known to naturalists and forayers – and more recently those collecting wild recreational drugs. Scientifically it is classified amongst the *basidiomycetes*, a group which includes the bracket fungi, puffballs and the like, in addition to the mushrooms and toadstools, the last two together called agarics. Within this group the Liberty Cap is placed in the *Cortinariales* along with the cultivated mushroom, and it resides in the family *Strophariaceae*.

As a species, *Psilocybe semilanceata* is well defined and belongs to a relatively small genus, as presently understood, even after the recent expansion by Noordeloos (1995), but despite being well known, *P. semilanceata* is not particularly characteristic of the genus when all the world species are taken into account. The majority of non-European species have been described as new to science in the last half-century by those actively involved in the documentation of hallucinogenic taxa.

Guzman (1983) has monographed the world species and examined material of *P. semilanceata* from nearly all European countries, in addition to Australia, Chile and North America. It has been recorded many times by European authors since its formal description by the Swedish botanist Elias Fries in 1838. Indeed, it has been the subject of ecological studies in more recent years and molecular analyses have been undertaken which demonstrate a uniformity within the taxon. It is, however, rather significant that Stamets (1996), who monographed the hallucinogenic fungi, records it only from west of the Cascades in the United States, from northern California to British Columbia during the autumn and early winter, and sometimes in Oregon and Washington during the spring months. This distribution when linked with its European distribution fits in with many other known organisms; in contrast the eastern United States ties up with the temperate and subtropical areas of Asia. Charles Peck, the influential pioneer American mycologist, recorded *P. semilanceata* and indicated it was common in grasslands but failed to keep any material, something unusual for him. Material was sent to him from all over North America during his career, so he could have thought it was common in America if the specimens sent to him by his contacts included those from the west. Examination of specimens in his herbarium in Albany, however, has ascertained that he had confused the Liberty Cap with what was then known as *Psilocybe foenisecii*. This latter species we now know as *Panaeolus* or *Panaeolina foenisecii*, depending on the authority. Regardless of the generic placement, this fungus agrees with those placed in a totally different family of fungi to the *Strophariaceae*. Thus old records of *P. semilanceata* from eastern North America are at most extremely limited or totally confused. Strange for a fungus considered to be common! No?

In Britain, *P. semilanceata* extends from the northernmost islands of Orkney and Shetland, including even some of the smaller non-inhabited islets in the archipelagos, and the Hebrides, including the far-flung St Kilda, to the eastern and western extremities of southern England. It is considered native to these islands. It is found in semi-natural grassland communities often unimproved in even historic times, and even perhaps since they were originally formed after woodland clearance.

Equally it is a widespread species in Europe, its distribution reaching northernmost parts of the continent, in addition to the Faeroes, as attested by published records, the author's own collecting and that of his colleagues from Norway, Sweden, Denmark and the Netherlands, including some who have monographed *Psilocybe* for their respective countries. All agree that there is no evidence to suggest that the Liberty Cap is not native to Europe. The uniformity of *P. semilanceata* throughout its range is supported by little or no morphological differences between collections from different areas and by molecular studies. The latter indicate that there are no differences in the portions of DNA studied between specimens from Scotland and Spain (Watling and Martin, 2003).

P. semilanceata is also uniform over other large parts of the world. It possibly has been introduced to Australia but the finding of it in high-altitude grasslands in New Zealand needs careful interpretation. In Europe as in New Zealand *P. semilanceata* is a grassland species with a propensity for areas where there is nitrogenous input; it is not, however, coprophilous (the closely related annulate *P. fimetaria* fills this habitat niche). Although often associated with hill and lowland pastures supporting domesticated animals (cows, sheep and even horses), *P. semilanceata* is also found in grassy glades in woodlands and in copses frequented by deer. It has obviously spread from such sites to lawns and playing fields and therefore closer to habitation, and evidence has been accumulated on the movement of populations of man and *Psilocybe* in Shetland connected with the oil industry.

Nowhere in its range has *P. semilanceata* demonstrated the explosive expansion generally associated with an incomer, such as the false truffle *Paulocotylis* in Britain, or an expansion of distribution as a result of the availability of a new substrate as seen in the spread northwards in the last 40 years of the native and southern *Schizophyllum*. We are all by now familiar with the devastating and rapid spread of the causal organism of Dutch Elm disease, *Ceratocystis ulmi*, after its recent entry into the country from imported timbers. Certainly there have been historic connections between Spain and Britain, but any uniformity shown between the Liberty Caps of these countries should be reflected also in the DNA of North American specimens if the hypothesis is correct that North America is the origin of *P. semilanceata*. Instead the North American information available to us shows several differences to the European material. Unfortunately dried voucher specimens, although available to support the European sequences, are apparently not available for the New World collections which have been flagged up on the international GenBank. Cross-checking cannot therefore be conducted, for as shown above there has been some confusion in the identity of *Psilocybe* spp. abroad. The differences exhibited, however, indicate that there has been much longer separation between New and Old World populations, differences which would hardly have occurred in the period of a few centuries.

In South America, *P. semilanceata* is rather infrequent and few records are known; indeed, collectors have been particular in noting its absence except in Chile. Surely if this fungus moves so easily between continents, South America would be a very good site as the Spanish colonists were prominent there. As this is not the case, evidence for *Psilocybe semilanceata* being native to Europe is supported.

References
Guzman, G., 1983, 'The Genus Psilocybe', *Beih. Nova Hedw.*, 74: 1–439.
Noordeloos, M., 1995, Notulae ad Floram Agaricinum Neerlandicum XXII, 'Psilocybe & Pholiota', *Persoonia*, 16: 127–9.
Sowerby, J., 1815, *Coloured figures of English Fungi or Mushrooms*, R. Wilks, Chancery-Lane, London.
Stamets, P., 1996, *Psilocybe mushrooms of the world*, Ten Speed Press, Berkeley, California, 245pp.
Watling, R., and Martin, M., 2003, 'A sequestrate Psilocybe from Scotland', *Bot. J. Scotland*, 55: 245–8.

APPENDIX III

Interview with Rick Strassman MD

Rick Strassman lives and practises psychiatry in western New Mexico, and is Clinical Associate Professor of Psychiatry at the University of New Mexico School of Medicine. He has published nearly 30 peer-reviewed scientific papers, and has served as a reviewer for several psychiatric research journals. He has been a consultant to the US Food and Drug Administration, National Institute on Drug Abuse, Veterans' Administration Hospitals, Social Security Administration, and other state and local agencies. Dr Strassman's clinical research at the University of New Mexico included an investigation of the function of the pineal hormone melatonin in which his team documented the first known role of melatonin in humans. As we saw in Chapters Eleven and Eighteen, he also began the first new US government-approved and funded human hallucinogen research in North America in over two decades, the results of which were published in his important and thought-provoking book, DMT: The Spirit Molecule (Park Street Press, Rochester, Vermont, 2001). This interview was conducted in May 2005.

Graham Hancock: For me the most intriguing aspect of your extraordinarily interesting DMT research has to do with your volunteers' detailed reports of encounters with 'entities', 'beings', etc., and the implications that these reports might have for an open-minded enquiry into the nature of reality. You point out the striking similarities between the reports that were given to you after DMT sessions and reports of encounters with 'aliens' given to John Mack (and others) by people who believe they have been abducted by UFOs. In addition, you are probably aware of the numerous almost identical reports from folklore and ethnography of encounters with 'fairies', 'elves', etc., and of shamanic encounters with 'spirits' of various sorts. Since we know that your volunteers' experiences were 'hallucinations' as conventionally defined, it is therefore not a very big jump to infer – as you yourself propose vis-à-vis 'aliens' – that these other categories of very similar experiences might also have been hallucinations. If this is so, however, then are established scientific theories about how the brain 'concocts' complex hallucinations (from memories, personal history, etc.) able to explain such a huge range of commonalities in apparently 'non-real' experiences reported by so many different people from such different cultural backgrounds and periods of history?

Rick Strassman: The crux of this concern hinges on whether one believes that all of these phenomena are internally generated, or externally perceived, or some combination thereof. Clearly, the brain is affected by one's experiences. It's as though the brain learns a particular language through experience – it obtains a vocabulary, perceptual, emotional and cognitive – based on that with which we come into contact, and the constraints of our brain's hardware and software.

With that in mind, it's possible to take a larger view of the visionary experiences people may have on psychedelics. While certainly there are just 'releases' of previously, or normally, repressed or suppressed images, thoughts, feelings, and the like – particularly at lower doses of these drugs, or in those with reduced sensitivity to them (for either biological or psychological reasons) – in the more nether regions where these drugs may lead our consciousness, something else may happen. That is, we are forced to clothe, or engarb, the *external* forces, or beings, or influences that otherwise might be invisible to us, in a manner that we are able to recognise. This follows what many others have suggested – that angels, demons, imps, elves, dwarves, etc. are similar 'creatures' but ones that appear in a guise that is culturally or personally flavoured or determined. Like Captain Cook's ships, which the indigenous people of the South Pacific saw either as large ocean waves, or as nothing at all – not until they actually came up to the ships and touched them could they see them in their true form.

So, beneficent beings may be seen as 'angels', malevolent forces as 'demons', strange forces taking on strange appearances and emotional colouration – assuming personally and socially specific shapes and valences that convey the nature of the forces or information they are representing or conveying.

Drugs like DMT would provide access to these forces or beings, and then our own personalities and cultures would act as the prisms through which we see them. This is also where religious, ethical, moral training may be important. It's necessary to have as unsullied a personality and psychology as possible. No matter how powerful a drug might be, if it's working on a polluted, avaricious, sadistic level of consciousness, we're not going to be able to perceive things that someone who's been working on themselves for decades might be able to perceive. And, once we come 'down' from the expanded level of consciousness, what we can remember, and then put into practice, is certainly dependent upon our pre-existing personality organisation and structure.

Actually I don't come out in favour of explaining my volunteers' experiences as 'hallucinations'. I sort through a variety of possible, relatively plausible, models to explain their experiences.

However, there were problems which I encountered with explaining away, as it were, their experiences as something other than they seemed to be. First, most of the volunteers described their experiences as more real than real. More intensely visually constructed, more emotionally powerful, more cognitively and spiritually profound than anything they'd ever undergone before. In addition, they nearly unanimously stated that they never could have imagined, made up, or otherwise invented or hallucinated these experiences.

I *do* first begin with the 'hallucination' model; that is, 'this is your brain on DMT'. However, volunteers rejected this theory as unrealistic – 'How could there be brain centres for such complexly constructed story lines, visions, messages?' I then tried the Freudian unconscious model: that what they were undergoing was of the nature of symbolic representation of unexpressed drives, impulses, feelings, or the like. This, too, was laughed at by the volunteers. I offered a Jungian model, along the lines of their visions representing archetypal constructs. Again, a lead balloon. In some cases, the visions did seem to meet many of the criteria of dreams, and in those cases, there was little problem coaxing volunteers through those pathways – investigating what the 'dreams' might be representing in their lives – but these types of experiences were rather rare.

Finally, I decided to treat the experiences 'as is'. That is, if they were envisioning and interacting with beings from what seemed to be other dimensions of reality, I accepted this as such. In other words, I stopped making their experiences into something other than they seemed to be. By doing so, volunteers began confiding more and more about the utter strangeness of their experiences under DMT. Also, I could rest a bit easier and work more readily with the volunteers' experiences, because there seemed to be such commonalities among them.

If they were really what they seemed to be, then where could such realities reside? It was then I began allowing myself to consider that DMT provides a portal into alternative dimensions of reality – perhaps parallel universes, or dark matter, about which I speculate rather freely in the book.

Graham Hancock: Are you still open to this hypothesis, and would you be prepared to elaborate further on the problems that it raises for scientific understanding of the nature of reality and consciousness?

Rick Strassman: I remain more wedded to this idea than ever. The primary problem right now in validating and extending my theories is the lack of technical equipment, other than our mind/brains, that is, to verify such phenomena as existing outside of this time-space continuum. If we could photograph things like this, we'd all be able to come to an agreement that they exist. However, I am quite impressed with the commonalities existing in the reports of our volunteers; and in the subsequent large number of reports I've received from those who have had such experiences on psychedelic drugs, or spontaneously without drugs – perhaps through elevated levels of endogenous DMT generated by various means such as meditation, stress, sleep disorders, etc.

The scientific method generates scientific understanding. Charles Tart wrote a neat little paper about 'state specific sciences' in the 1970s for the journal *Science*, in which he describes the requirements for 'state specific scientists' who would explore different states of consciousness using the fundamental tools of the scientific method: field data based on 'anecdotal' reports, hypothesis generating, experiments, gathering more data, revising theories based on new data, and so on. Training a cadre of scientists to be experts in negotiating through these 'laboratories'. However, in this case, Tart recommended studying states of consciousness with this permutation of the scientific method, rather than objective external reality. If you replace 'state of consciousness' with 'states of reality', I think we'd be in a similar situation.

Graham Hancock: You oppose the biological reductionism of many scientists with an important idea that has also been entertained by William James, Aldous Huxley, and Albert Hoffman amongst others. This is the idea of the brain as a receiver that can be retuned by certain hallucinogens (and other techniques) to pick up different wavelengths of a much wider 'reality' than is normally available to our senses. Are you aware of any evidence within the prevailing materialist/empiricist scientific paradigm that is capable of refuting the 'receiver' model? If not, then on what basis do you think so many mainstream scientists are so dismissive of hallucinations and so adamant that the information they contain can in no way be veridical?

Rick Strassman: This almost would fall into the 'philosophy of science' field. About which I know little. I'm sure someone could 'disprove' the receiver model using a materialistic argument. Because such a theory falls outside of what we 'know', or what is 'real', it cannot happen. This seems a rather immature way of looking at things, and one which science itself has disproven countless times in its history. This is where science becomes another agent of evil's use of fundamentalism.

The receiver model is just that. The brain receives information at the level for which it happens to be tuned at that particular time. Clearly, there are examples of objective technical equipment changing what we're able to see: the microscope, or night-vision goggles, or radar, the telescope. Meditation is a 'subjective' technique or tool that seems relatively well established as a method by which we can experience things not normally accessible. So is 'biofeedback', in which case we are trained, by the aid of a machine, to 'feel' various physiological functions previously believed to be outside our realm of perception.

Theories about psychedelics providing even greater ranges of what is perceivable are little more than extensions, albeit somewhat radical extensions, of what we already have incorporated into our scientific biomedical world view.

The remarkable thing about DMT is that it is endogenous, the brain's own psychedelic. And the fact that it is capable of eliciting such amazing and earth-shattering effects makes theorising about what its role might be in human consciousness so compelling.

Graham Hancock: Another model that you contemplate is that 'We were activating certain hard-wired sites in the brain that elicit a display of visions and feelings in the mind. How else could so many people report similar experiences: insect-like reptilian creatures?' (*DMT: The Spirit Molecule*, p. 200) But you clearly also see many problems with this 'hard-wired' model and ask on the same page: 'How could anyone believe that there were chunks of brain tissue that, when activated, flashed encounters with beings, experimentation and reprogramming?' Where do you come down on this today? After all, it is widely argued, pretty much without contest, that so-called entoptic phenomena are seen universally in certain altered states of consciousness because they are 'hard-wired' into the structure of our nervous systems. Why shouldn't much more complex experiences like those reported by your volunteers also in some way be 'hard-wired'?

Rick Strassman: The entoptic phenomena are the bytes of information from which more complex constructs are made. It may be a bit of turning the whole issue upside down. Rather than the brain constructing the mind, perhaps the mind constructs the brain. That is, the entoptic bits of brain structure are just what the mind needs in order to display the phenomenon which it accesses.

The television analogy is always handy, and one for which in this incarnation I owe a debt of gratitude to my friend and mentor, Rupert

Sheldrake. We can take apart a television set and investigate the ways in which each transistor and switch work. However, we cannot explain the programmes which come in through the TV by understanding the mechanisms of action of each component part.

We all have DNA, mitochondria, tissues and cells. However, they are put together in a very special way to make organs, limbs, and these are then themselves organised in a particular manner, to make a human body. Even then, it is just a body, lifeless, a hunk of flesh. Without the overriding principle that enlivens and directs all this matter, there really is not much to speak of. In a similar vein, the entotpic bits and pieces that people believe are hard-wired into the brain would exist in an absolute vacuum unless they were organised and directed in the particular manner coming through as visionary experience.

Graham Hancock: To expand on the above a bit, are you able to envisage any sort of evolutionary process (over the five- or seven-million-year story of human evolution since our last common ancestor with the chimps) that might have the capacity to hard-wire 'flashed encounters with beings, experimentation and reprogramming' into all human nervous systems? This for me is one of the real problems with the 'hard-wired' theory that is so often deployed as if it explains all commonalities. If such information is hard-wired into us, then how, when and why did this hard-wiring occur?

Rick Strassman: This mechanism, say through the aegis of DMT, seems to be hard-wired into every mammal that has been investigated. DMT exists in the brain and blood and spinal fluid of humans, mice, rats, other primates. In addition, DMT has been found in an enormous number of plants. Fish, too. Invertebrates.

No religion of any merit discounts the spiritual nature of all existence, including that of plants, animals, minerals, space, time, light/energy, and what have you. At least on the material biological realm, DMT seems to be the link, the mechanism of action by which this spiritual nature is manifest, and through which a divine connection seems, at least in certain circumstances, possible.

God wants us to be godly. So, by being close to God, we can learn to emulate God. Perhaps DMT is one of the ways in which we are able to communicate with God that much more intensely – for better or worse.

Graham Hancock: Can you see any way in which the experiences that DMT occasions could be described as 'adaptive' in conventional evolutionary terms?

Rick Strassman: This touches upon what I have spent the last several years pondering, which is, what is the evolutionary/adaptive role of endogenous DMT? A few years back, I was asked to write a response to Kari Jansen's paper in *Journal of Near Death Studies* regarding his theory of an endogenous ketamine-like compound being involved in the near-death experience. Karl is a good friend and colleague, and we had batted around these ideas at some length.

Karl, I believe, proposes that such compounds as putative endogenous ketamine-like substances function like ketamine, which has a neuroprotective effect on the brain when it suffers oxygen deprivation in near-death circumstances. Ketamine also is quite psychedelic in and of itself. Karl proposed that ketamine-like endogenous substances produce NDEs as a side effect of its primary role – which is to protect the brain from damage when it is being traumatised.

It is worth mentioning that the initial reports of such ketamine-like endogenous compounds have not been replicated.

Nevertheless, I come down on the side of believing the other way around. That is, DMT and its ilk produce such psychedelic experiences during the NDE, because that is what our consciousness is experiencing at that time – it is what we see, feel, hear, think, as we are dying, and DMT is the aegis through which this happens. And, rather than DMT just producing a blank, dark, empty nothing state, which some people think is what happens at death, it produces quite the opposite. And that may be, I believe, because what happens *is* quite the opposite. It is on DMT's wings, so to speak, that consciousness takes flight from the body on its way towards death. That is what's happening, and this is the mechanism by which it occurs.

I hope I'm being clear. The NDE is not a hallucination – it is what happens as we die. It is what our consciousness experiences. How else could there be such an astonishingly consistent reporting of such experiences throughout time and cultures? How could it be an artefact? How much more proof do we need? Why in the world would nature or God have set things up in such a way? It would have been much more kind to just let us drift into oblivion, if such was the function of compounds easing our transition to death. On the contrary, death does not seem to be that way, and DMT shuttles us along as we make that transition.

Graham Hancock: Apropos of this you write (in *Entheogens and the Future of Religion*, pp. 158–9): 'Why do we all have DMT in our brains? Why is there a compound, when given (or produced), that generates experience of "alien-contact", death, space-travel, and other extraordinary effects? However, the comparable question is not asked of silicon in computer chips. Rather silicon is in computer chips because it works; it's the best molecule for the function needed. In the same way, we have DMT in our brains because it works. It's the best molecule for the function needed, to retune the perceiving abilities of the brain to different levels.' In which case, the evolutionary question then becomes, 'Why would we need such abilities if the conventional scientific model of reality is correct?'

Rick Strassman: Our conventional scientific model of reality is correct, for this level of reality. And, taking into account the endogenicity and nature of DMT's effects, we can expand that conventional model into what are now believed to be the unconventional realms, those that have previously been under the purview of religious, spiritual, and shamanic disciplines.

One of the problems, I believe, with the DMT work, and the conclusions I come to, is that they don't fit into anyone's world view very well – that is, at least the scientific and spiritual ones. And the 'new age' one ignores the real dangers inherent at both the spiritual and physical levels.

The scientific model is generally limited to objective reality, although some of the developments in physics and astronomy are pretty psychedelic in themselves – but they haven't quite trickled down into everyday parlance and thinking very well, especially not in psychiatry. And, the fact that these ideas partake of non-corporeal, non-physical levels of existence, which are usually referred to as 'spiritual', cause my colleagues to bristle (at the worst), or quickly lose attention (which is most common).

And the fact that DMT allows a relatively reliable entry into states of consciousness or levels of reality that had heretofore been the primary turf of religious organisations and doctrines raises the hackles of members of those institutions. No need to study, pray, take vows, wear unique clothes and hairstyles, exchange special bows and handshakes.

I wish there were some way of bridging those gaps. Why not take the best of both worlds? That is, the scientific methodology with its mastery of the physical/natural world (read: access to DMT), and the ethical/moral advances that exist within religion?

Graham Hancock: Subsequent to the publication of *DMT: The Spirit Molecule*, have you had any opportunity to follow up your hypothesis that 'the alien abduction experience is made possible by excessive brain levels of DMT'? Did you ever have the chance to compare notes directly with John Mack before his tragic death in a car accident last year?

Rick Strassman: John thought there were striking similarities, and I think, if time had permitted, might have agreed to collaborate on a study giving DMT to some of his subjects, to determine how close the two phenomena were.

I haven't followed up with such a study. Many of the notes I've gotten from people since the book came out confirm what I believe – that is, many of those who have their spontaneous 'being contact' experiences appear to be having what otherwise would be indistinguishable from a big dose of DMT on our clinical research unit.

Some people have argued against my theory by pointing to the lack of physical 'stigmata' of abduction, and the relatively sparse (nearly zero) reports of the typical 'greys' of the literature.

Regarding the stigmata issue, I have come to believe there is probably a spectrum of 'encounters', from the purely consciousness-to-consciousness variety, to the purely physical-to-physical variety – the latter might be the ones in which the stigmata occur, but are the ones about which I have the least knowledge and opinions. The consciousness-to-consciousness encounters, however, could very likely be mediated via DMT.

Regarding the relative absence of 'greys', there is nothing that precludes these beings donning other garb!

Graham Hancock: In *DMT: The Spirit Molecule* you ask: 'What would happen to the study of spirit realms if we could access them reliably using molecules like DMT?' As a matter of interest, what do you think would happen?

Rick Strassman: I'm not sure what would happen. I think it would be a bit too much for fundamentalistic members of any religion, and they would suppress or ignore it. It also would be too much for fundamentalistic scientists – that is, those scientists who mistake what is known so far for all that is possible and to-be-determined-as-true.

For those who were interested, it could revolutionise our understanding of the spirit realms, and therefore might have a positive effect on our evolution as a species. However, the forces of evil seem to be gathering a lot of strength right now, and that is primarily through using a black-and-white fundamentalist approach to reality. Shades, nuances, and even shockingly obvious contradictions to the fundamentalistic world view don't have much of a chance when they are so outnumbered and feared.

Not that we would learn anything we weren't already ready to learn – if it's just too much out of our sphere, we won't see/hear/understand it. That's why spiritual/religious/shamanic training is so important – we must be ready to entertain the strangest and most unexpected phenomena and information. And there's nothing about realms of the spirit that is inherently good. There certainly are dark spiritual forces. We don't want to be seduced by something that solely by its non-physical nature promises to be helpful.

By revolutionising our understanding of spirit realms, hopefully our understanding of the physical/material realms would evolve – into more ethical, co-operative and beneficent practices. It will take a lot of optimism and fearlessness.

NOTES AND REFERENCES

Chapter One: The Plant that enables Men to See the Dead

[1] James W. Fernandez, *Tabernanthe Iboga: Narcotic Ecstasis and the Work of the Ancestors*, in Peter T. Furst (Ed.), *Flesh of the Gods: The Ritual Use of Hallucinogens*, Praeger Publishers, New York, 1972, p. 245.

[2] ibid., pp. 245–6.

[3] Richard Evans Schultes, *Plants of the Gods: Their Sacred, Healing and Hallucinogenic Powers*, Healing Arts Press, Rochester, Vermont, 2001, p. 58.

[4] My dose was 14 mg per kg, a total of 1.2 grams.

[5] *Plants of the Gods*, p. 112.

Chapter Two: The Greatest Riddle of Archaeology

[1] *Guide de Visite de la Grotte du Pech-Merle, Cabrerets-Lot*, Editions du Castelet, Boulogne, March 1999, p. 8

[2] Paul Bahn, *Journey through the Ice Age*, Weidenfeld and Nicolson, London, 1997, p. 197.

[3] At the French cave of Chauvet and the Italian cave of Fumane – see detailed discussion in Chapter Four.

[4] See, for example, discussion in Robert Bednarik, 'The Earliest Evidence of Palaeoart', *Rock Art Research*, 2003, Vol. 20, No. 2, pp. 89–135. See also Daniel Kaufman, 'Redating the Social Revolution: The Case for the Middle Palaeolithic', *Journal of Anthropological Research*, Vol. 58, 2002, pp. 477–92.

[5] The consensus is most clearly summarised in Richard G. Klein and Blake Edgar, *The Dawn of Human Culture*, John Wiley and Sons Inc, New York, 2002.

[6] *The Times*, London, 17 February 2005, citing *Nature* of the same date, reports

the discovery in Ethiopia of anatomically modern skeletal remains dated to 196,000 years ago – approximately 35,000 years older than any previously discovered anatomically modern human remains. The discovery was made by a team of scientists from the University of Utah led by veteran fossil hunter Dr Frank Brown.

[7] For example the renowned palaeo-anatomist Philip Tobias, in an interview with Graham Hancock at the University of Witwatersrand, South Africa, on 13 April 2004, expressed the view that humans may have achieved full anatomical modernity as early as 300,000 years ago.

[8] William H. Calvin, *A Brain for all Seasons: Human Evolution and Abrupt Climate Change*, University of Chicago Press, 2002, p. 39: 'Homo erectus persisted until about 50,000 years ago in China. *Erectus* was the longest-running species in hominid history.'

[9] See Henry Gee (Senior Editor, *Nature*), 'Flores, God and Cryptozoology', published online 27 October 2004, http://www.nature.com/news/2004/041025/full/041025-2.html: 'Probably descended from full-sized *Homo erectus* that made landfall on Flores as much as 900,000 years ago, the islanders dodged the [Komodo] dragons and hunted the elephants. Killers and quarry became smaller with each generation, instances of the well-known phenomenon of endemic dwarfing in small, inbred island populations, until they were transformed into new species. *Homo erectus* became *Homo floresiensis*.'

[10] *The Times*, London, 14 March 2005.

[11] *The Independent*, London, 28 October 2004, pp. 1–2, 12–13; Richard Dawkins in *The Sunday Times*, 31 October 2004 (News Review) p. 6; *The Guardian*, 28 October 2004, pp. 1–2; Henry Gee, Senior Editor, *Nature*, writing in *The Guardian*, 28 October 2004, (Life section), pp. 4–6.

[12] The dates given for the earliest Neanderthals vary widely from scholar to scholar between the range of 300,000 years ago down to about 150,000 years ago or less. For example Professor Dr Joao Zilhao, *Anatomically Archaic: Behaviourally Modern: The Last Neanderthals and their Destiny*, Drieentwintigste Kroon-Voordracht, p. 9, refers to 'the view that the classical Neanderthals are the last of a variety of humans that inhabited Europe from at least 300,000 BP onwards.' Matthias Krings, et al., 'Neanderthal DNA Sequences and the Origin of Modern Humans', *Cell* Vol. 90, 11 July 1997, p. 19, assert that 'Neanderthals are a group of extinct hominids that inhabited Europe and western Asia from about 300,000 to 30,000 years ago.' Ian Tattershall and Jeffrey Schwartz, *Extinct Humans*, Westview Press, 2001, p. 176, write: 'The Neanderthals were a distinctive group of hominids who occupied Europe and Western Asia in the period between about 200,000 years ago and 30,000 years ago.' James Shreeve, *The Neanderthal Enigma*, Viking, New York, 1995,

p. 5, states that the Neanderthals appeared first in Europe 'about 120,000 years ago.' Ian Tattershall, *The Last Neanderthal: The Rise, Success, and Mysterious Extinction of our Closest Human Relatives*, Westview Press, 1999, p. 120: 'The Neanderthalers lived between 200,000 and 30,000 years ago.' Christopher Stringer and Clive Gamble, *In Search of the Neanderthals*, Thames and Hudson, London, 1994, p. 69: 'We currently believe the "early" Neanderthals had evolved in Europe by 230,000 years ago.'

[13] See discussion in David Lewis-Williams, *The Mind in the Cave*, Thames and Hudson, London, 2002, pp. 67–96. See also Robert H. Gargett, 'Grave Short-comings: The Evidence for Neanderthal Burial', *Current Anthropology*, Vol. 30, No. 2, April 1989, pp. 157–90; and Robert H. Gargett, 'Middle Palaeolithic Burial is not a Dead Issue', *Journal of Human Evolution* (1999), 37, pp. 27–90; Philip G. Chase and Harold L. Dibble, 'Middle Palaeolithic Symbolism: A Review of Current Evidence and Interpretations', *Journal of Anthropological Archaeology* (1987), 6, pp. 263–96. Although it is the consensus amongst scholars that 'the available evidence fails to indicate the presence of symbolic thought or symbolic behaviour before the Middle/Upper Palaeolithic transition' (Chase and Dibble), there are some strongly held dissenting views according to which the Neanderthals were capable of symbolic activity and did engage in symbolism. Robert Bednarik is the champion of this minority point of view. See, for example, his 'Palaeoart and Archaeological Myths', *Cambridge Archaeological Journal* 2 (1) (1992), pp. 27–57. Most scholars agree that the Neanderthals began copying the designs and symbolically crafted tools of anatomically and behaviourally modern humans after their arrival in Europe, and that this copying activity is reflected in the so-called 'Chatelperronian' archaeological assemblage. See Frederick L. Coolidge and Thomas Wynn, 'A Cognitive and Neuropsychological Perspective on the Chatelperronian', *Journal of Archaeological Research*, Vol. 60, 2004, pp. 55–73. See also discussion in Lewis-Williams, *The Mind in the Cave*, pp. 86–7 and 94–5.

[14] E.g. the so-called Howieson's Poort technology, and finds at Klassies River Mouth caves. See H.J. Deacon and Janette Deacon, *Human Beginnings in South Africa: Uncovering the Secrets of the Stone Age*, Altamira Press, London, 1999, pp. 93–106.

[15] Chris Henshilwood in an interview with Graham Hancock at Blombos Cave, 15 April 2004. See also Christopher Henshilwood, et al., 'Middle Stone Age Shell Beds from South Africa', *Science*, April 2004; *The Times*, London, 12 August 2004, T4, p.14; Christopher Henshilwood et al., 'Emergence of Modern Human Behaviour: Middle Stone Age Engravings from South Africa,' *Science*, Vol. 295, 15 February 2002, pp. 1278ff.

[16] For dates for the anatomically modern human presence in Australia see

Spencer Wells, *The Journey of Man: A Genetic Odyssey*, Penguin, London, 2002, pp. 60, 66. For the cited (controversial) 75,000-year date see Robert Bednarik, 'The Earliest Evidence of Palaeoart', *Rock Art Research*, 2003, Vol. 20, No. 2, p. 94.

[17] Wells, *Journey of Man*, p. 66.

[18] ibid. For the controversial date of 75,000 years ago for the earliest Australian art, and discussion of the controversy surrounding this date, see Bednarik, 'The Earliest Evidence of Palaeoart', p. 94.

[19] Klein and Edgar, *The Dawn of Human Culture*, p. 8.

[20] There is an extreme view (associated with Richard G. Klein – Professor of Anthropology at Stanford University – and others) that modern human behaviour was a package deal that appeared everywhere about 50,000 to 60,000 years ago. This view frequently assigns the introduction of the 'package' to some hypothetical neurological change but seems to have been too much formed by scholars who looked at the western European data alone. The more gradual trends in evidence elsewhere do not support the notion of a species-wide neurological adaptation. See Lewis-Williams, *The Mind in the Cave*, p. 96.

[21] *The Times*, London, 17 February 2005.

[22] ibid.

[23] Tattershall and Schwartz, *Extinct Humans*, p. 224.

[24] Lewis-Williams, *The Mind in the Cave*, p. 7; 'Three-Dimensional Puzzles: South African and Upper Palaeolithic Rock Art', *Ethos*, Vol. 66, 2, 2002, p. 260.

[25] Lewis-Williams, *The Mind in the Cave*, p. 7.

Chapter Three: Vine of Souls

[1] Pascal Boyer, *The Naturalness of Religious Ideas*, cited in Steven Mithven, *The Prehistory of the Mind: A Search for the Origins of Art, Religion and Science*, Thames and Hudson, London, 1996, pp. 174–5: 'Boyer explains that a belief in non-physical beings is the most common feature of religions; it may indeed be universal. In fact, ever since the classic work of E.B. Tylor in 1871 on *Primitive Cultures*, the idea of non-physical beings has been taken for the very definition of religion itself.'

[2] See discussion by Chris Knight in *Cambridge Archaeological Journal*, 12:1, 2002, p. 89.

[3] Dozens of titles could be cited but for a quick overview see Peter Furst (Ed.), *Flesh of the Gods: The Ritual Use of Hallucinogens*, Praeger Publishers, New York, 1972, in particular in this volume, Weston La Barre, 'Hallucinogens and

the Shamanic Origins of Religion', pp. 261–78. See also Peter T. Furst, *Hallucinogens and Culture*, Chandler and Sharp Publishers, 1988.

4 See for example Arnold M. Ludwig, 'Altered States of Consciousness,' in Charles T. Tart (Ed.), *Altered States of Consciousness*, Harper, San Francisco, 1990, pp. 19–22.

5 Discussed more fully in Chapter Seven.

6 See, for example, David Lewis-Williams, *The Mind in the Cave*, Thames and Hudson, London, 2002; Jean Clottes and David Lewis-Williams, *The Shamans of Prehistory: Trance and Magic in the Painted Caves*, Harry N. Abrams, 1998; David Lewis-Williams, *A Cosmos in Stone*, Altamira Press, Walnut Creek, 2002.

7 J.D. Lewis-Williams and T.A Dowson, 'The Signs of All Times', *Current Anthropology*, Vol. 29, No. 2, April 1988, pp. 201–45.

8 See for example discussion in G. Reichel-Dolmatoff, *The Shaman and the Jaguar: A Study of Narcotic Drugs Among the Indians of Colombia*, Temple University Press, Philadelphia, 1975, pp. 167–81.

9 Luis Eduardo Luna and Pablo Amaringo, *Ayahuasca Visions: The Religious Iconography of a Peruvian Shaman*, North Atlantic Books, Berkeley, California, 1999.

10 Richard Evans Schultes, Albert Hoffman and Christian Ratsch, *Plants of the Gods: Their Sacred, Healing and Hallucinogenic Powers*, Healing Arts Press, Rochester, Vermont, 2001, pp. 124–35.

11 Jeremy Narby, *The Cosmic Serpent: DNA and the Origins of Knowledge*, Victor Gollancz, London, 1995, p. 11.

12 Richard Evans Schultes, 'An Overview of Hallucinogens in the Western Hemisphere', in Furst (Ed.), *Flesh of the Gods*, pp. 38–9, cited in Narby, *Cosmic Serpent*, pp. 10–11.

13 See discussion in Chapter Eight.

14 David Lewis-Williams and Thomas Dowson, *Images of Power: Understanding Bushman Rock Art*, Southern Book Publishers, Johannesburg, 1989, p. 60, discuss the ability of southern African San bushmen to enter trance without hallucinogens but by means of intense, prolonged dancing, and refer to the neuropsychological experiments, conducted largely with LSD, on which their model is based: 'The state of consciousness induced by this drug does not differ materially from the effects of a wide range of drugs or from the states induced by sensory deprivation, pain, rhythmic movement or sound, intense concentration, hyperventilation, and even, in some respects, migraine headaches. This means that although Bushmen shamans may not have depended on hallucinogens as heavily as shamans in other parts of the world, their experiences would have been similar to those of other shamans and

also to those of Western subjects who take part in neuropsychological experiments.'

Chapter Four: Therianthropy

[1] For a general overview see David S. Whitley (Ed.), *Handbook of Rock Art Research*, Altamira Press, Walnut Creek, CA, 2001.

[2] It may simply be a matter that much more prehistoric archaeology needs to be done in these regions. Whitley (Ed.), *Handbook of Rock Art Research*, pp. 760–823.

[3] Where ethnographic records are available it is clear that much of the art is motivated by spiritual purposes. In some cultures its use is entirely secular and practical, however. See Whitley, *Handbook of Rock Art Research*, p. 312.

[4] J.D. Lewis-William and T. A. Dowson, 'The Signs of all Times', *Current Anthropology*, Vol. 29, No. 2, April 1988, pp. 201ff.

[5] For example, both Poussin and Leonardo encoded secret messages in their paintings.

[6] *Science*, Vol. 290, 20 October 2000, p. 419.

[7] Jean Clottes, *Return to Chauvet Cave Excavating the Birthplace of Art: The First Full Report*, Thames and Hudson, London, 2003, pp. 32–3.

[8] *The Guardian*, 19 October 2000; *Science*, Vol. 290, 20 October 2000, p. 419.

[9] See Chapter Three

[10] Clottes, *Return to Chauvet Cave*, p. 170

[11] Jean Clottes and David Lewis-Williams, *The Shamans of Prehistory*: Trance and Magic in the Painted Caves, Harry N. Abrams, New York, 1998, p. 45; Clottes, *Return to Chauvet Cave*, p. 170

[12] Clottes, *Return to Chauvet Cave*, p. 170. It is arguable that the effect is achieved by a superimposition of feline over human form at this point.

[13] Excavations at Geissenkosterle have yielded a slab fallen from the ceiling buried in sediments more than 30,000 years old; the slab bears traces of black, red and yellow paint but no recognisable image.

[14] 16 identifiable pieces of sculpture from Hohlenstein-Stadel, Geissenkosterle and Vogelherd: see Thomas A. Dowson and Martin Porr, 'Special Objects – Special Creatures: Shamanistic imagery and the Aurignacian art of south-west Germany', in Neil Price (Ed.), *The Archaeology of Shamanism*, Routledge, London, 2001, p. 165; three identifiable pieces of sculpture from Hohle-Fels: see Nicholas J. Conrad, 'Palaeolithic Ivory Sculptures from southwestern Germany and the origins of figurative art', *Nature*, Vol. 426, 18/25 December 2003, p. 830.

[15] Dowson and Porr, 'Special Objects – Special Creatures', p. 168: 'Datable

material from the upper Aurignacian level, containing the statuettes, at Geissenkosterle has produced a large number of AMS dates which fall between 32,300 plus or minus 700 and 36,800, with a mean value of 33,500 plus or minus 350.'

[16] Conrad, 'Palaeolithic Ivory Sculptures', p. 831.

[17] Dowson and Porr, 'Special Objects – Special Creatures', p. 174; Conrad, 'Palaeolithic Ivory Sculptures', p. 831.

[18] Dowson and Porr, 'Special Objects – Special Creatures', p. 170

[19] For example, J. Hahn cited by Dowson and Porr 'Special Objects – Special Creatures', p. 170, is quite explicit in claiming that 'nothing supports the assertion that this statuette might represent a human wearing a mask.'

[20] Conrad, 'Palaeolithic Ivory Sculptures', p. 831.

[21] *Science* Vol. 290, 20 October 2000, pp. 419–21.

[22] The rock the plaquettes are composed of is not the same type as the rock of the cave. See Randall White, *Prehistoric Art: The Symbolic Journey of Mankind*, Harry N. Abrams Inc., New York, p. 158.

[23] National Museum of Namibia internet page: http://www.natmus.cul.na/events/rockart/apollo11.htm.

[24] W.E. Wendt, '"Art Mobilier" from the Apollo 11 Cave, South West Africa: Africa's Oldest-Dated Works of Art', *South African Archaeological Bulletin*, 1976, 31, p. 8: 'The conclusion is reached that this "art mobilier" was created between 30,000 and 25,000 years BP and that with a probability close to certainty even an age between 27,500 and 25,500 years BP can be assumed, thus making it by far the oldest dated art known on the African continent.' See also White, *Prehistoric Art*, p. 158; Paul Bahn, *Journey through the Ice Age*, Weidenfeld and Nicolson, London, 1997, pp. 30–1; Conrad, 'Palaeolithic Ivory Sculptures', p. 831 in *Nature*, Vol 426, op. cit., 831; National Museum of Namibia internet page (http://www.natmus.cul.na/events/rockart/apollo11.htm); Peter Garlake in Whitley (Ed.), *Handbook of Rock Art Research*, p. 640: 'The earliest painted fragments so far found are seven painted slabs, some with recognisable images, from the inappropriately named Apollo 11 Cave in southern Namibia. They were in the topmost levels of a Middle Stone Age deposit dated to between 28,500 (plus or minus 450) and 26,300 (plus or minus 450) YBP [years before the present]. There has been much discussion about whether the spalls were intrusive from the immediately overlying Later Stone Age deposit, dated to approximately 18,500 to 19,750 YBP. The consensus now appears to be that the association with the earlier deposit is valid.'

[25] Bahn, *Journey through the Ice Age*, p. 30.

[26] David Lewis-Williams and Thomas Dowson, *Images of Power: Understanding Bushman Rock Art*, Southern Book Publishers, Johannesburg, 1989, p. 22;

Conrad, 'Palaeolithic Ivory Sculptures', p. 831; White, *Prehistoric Art*, p. 159; National Museum of Namibia internet page.

27 However, Wendt himself believed it had 'bovine traits', with vestigial horns possibly apparent. In that case it is a similar sort of hybrid to the human-bovid of Fumane cave. See Wendt, "Art Mobilier"', p. 10.

28 On the bison-man identity of the El Castillo stalagmite figure see Bahn, *Journey through the Ice Age*, pp. 107, 166; L.G. Freeman, et al., *Altamira Revisited and other Essays on Early Art*, Institute for Prehistoric Investigations (Chicago/Santander), Centro de Investigacion y Museo de Altamira, 1987, pp. 242–3.

29 Bahn, *Journey through the Ice Age*, p. 107.

30 John E. Pfeiffer, *The Creative Explosion: An Inquiry into the Origins of Art and Religion*, Harper and Row, New York, 1982, p. 107; White, *Prehistoric Art*, p. 119.

31 David Lewis-Williams, *The Mind in the Cave*, pp. 235–6.

32 Miguel Angel García Guinea, *Altamira and other Cantabrian Caves*, Silex, Madrid, 1979, pp. 114–16; Pedro A. Saura Ramos, *The Cave of Altamira*, Harry N. Abrams, New York, 1999, pp. 70–1.

33 See Chapter Two, above; and Clottes and Lewis-Williams, *The Shamans of Prehistory*, p. 74; see also M. Lorblanchet and A. Sieveking, 'The Monsters of Pergouset', *Cambridge Archaeological Journal*, 7:1 (1997), pp. 52–3.

34 Bahn, *Journey through the Ice Age*, pp. 154–6; Anne Sieveking, *The Cave Artists*, Thames and Hudson, London, 1979, p. 149.

35 Count Begouen, 'The Magic Origin of Prehistoric Art', *Antiquity*, 3 (1929?), p. 17.

36 Though the latter organ, comments John F. Pfeiffer delicately, 'is drawn in a position more appropriate for a feline than a man', Pfeiffer, *The Creative Explosion*, p. 107; Begouen, 'Magic Origin', p. 17.

37 Mario Ruspoli, *The Cave of Lascaux: The Final Photographs*, Harry N. Abrams, New York, 1987, pp. 100 and 176; Lewis-Williams, *The Mind in the Cave*, p. 240.

38 Lewis-Williams, *The Mind in the Cave*, p. 240.

39 So much so that the figure is 'sometimes interpreted as men in a skin', Bahn, *Journey through the Ice Age*, p. 181.

40 Lewis-Williams, *The Mind in the Cave*, p. 262; Ruspoli, *The Cave of Lascaux*, p. 201.

41 Pfeiffer, *The Creative Explosion*, pp. 30–1. Fragments of three-ply rope have been excavated elsewhere in the cave.

42 The only rhinoceros figure reported from Lascaux: French scholar Annette Laming-Emperaire cited in D. Bruce Dickson, *The Dawn of Belief: Religion*

in the Upper Palaeolithic of Southwestern Europe, The University of Arizona Press, Tucson, 1996, p. 133.

43 Demorest Davenport and Michael A. Jochim, *Antiquity*, 62, 1988, pp. 558–62.

44 ibid p. 561.

45 L.G. Freeman and J. Gonzalez Echegaray, 'El Juyo: A 14,000-year-old Sanctuary from Northern Spain', *History of Religions*, 1981, 21 (1), pp. 12–13.

46 ibid., p. 13.

47 ibid., p. 16.

48 For example, at Wonderwerk Cave, Northern Cape, a slab bearing a fine line engraving of part of an animal has been dated to 10,200 BP. Later deposits in the same cave, dated to between 5200 and 4000 BP, contained slabs engraved with geometric patterns by the same technique. Peter Garlake, in Whitley (Ed.), *Handbook of Rock Art Research*, p. 641. The earliest identifiably 'bushman' skeletal remains so far discovered in southern Africa date to around 10,000 years ago. 'These very early proto-Bushman people were descended from much earlier African populations represented by such skulls as those found at Hopefield in the Cape, Florisbad in the Orange Free State, and Kabwe in Zambia,' Lewis-Williams and Dowson, *Images of Power*, p. 9.

49 Professor John Parkington interviewed by Graham Hancock at the University of Cape Town, April 2004.

50 ibid.

51 Peter Garlake, in Whitley (Ed.), *Handbook of Rock Art Research*, p. 657.

52 ibid.

53 Bahn, *Journey through the Ice Age*, p. 30.

54 Cited in Dickson, *The Dawn of Belief*, p. 105; Noel W. Smith, *An Analysis of Ice Age Art: Its Psychology and Belief System*, Peter Lang Publishers, New York, 1992, p. 29; Bahn, *Journey through the Ice Age*, p. 214, note 19 to Chapter Three: David Coulson and Alec Campbell, *African Rock Art: Paintings and Engravings on Stone*, Harry N. Abrams, New York, 2001, p. 77.

55 Bahn, *Journey through the Ice Age*, p. 214, note 19 to Chapter 3.

56 F.T. Masao in his Introduction to Tanzanian rock art (http://www.brandshawfoundation.com/tanzania/) makes the common mistake of assuming that these figures are meant to portray humans wearing animal head masks. General arguments against this frequent misinterpretation of rock art therianthropes are given in J.D. Lewis-Williams, *A Cosmos in Stone*, Altamira Press, 2002, pp. 127ff.

57 E.g. Coulson and Campbell, *African Rock Art*, pp. 136–7; White, *Prehistoric Art*, pp. 166–7.

58 See for example Coulson and Campbell, *African Rock Art*, p. 136; White, *Prehistoric Art*, p. 167.

[59] Peter Slingsby, *Bushman's Kloof: A Comprehensive Guide to the Rock Art of Bushman's Kloof, Rock Art of the Western Cape*, Book 2, The Fontmaker, South Africa, 1997, p. 45, points out that the cleverness of the figure is that from a different perspective it can look like a woman facing forward with a large hairstyle.

[60] David Lewis-Williams in Price (Ed.), *The Archaeology of Shamanism*, op. cit., page 19.

[61] ibid.

[62] For example, in Heaven Cave, La Cachette Farm, Baviance (Karoo).

[63] Lewis-Williams in Price (Ed.), *The Archaeology of Shamanism*, p. 19.

[64] Lewis-Williams and Dowson, *Images of Power*, p. 68.

[65] H.C. Woodhouse, *Bushman Art of Southern Africa*, Art Publishers, Johannesburg, p. 26.

[66] See discussion in David Lewis-Williams and Geoffrey Blundell, *Fragile Heritage: A Rock Art Fieldguide*, Witwatersrand University Press, 1998, p. 43; Slingsby, *Bushman's Kloof*, p. 48.

[67] R. Townley Johnson, *Major Rock Paintings of Southern Africa*, David Philip Publishers, Cape Town, 1979, p. 57; Clottes and Lewis-Williams, *The Shamans of Prehistory*, p. 34.

[68] Woodhouse, *Bushman Art of Southern Africa*, p. 4.

[69] David Lewis-Williams, *Images of Mystery: Rock Art of the Drakensberg*, Double Storey, Cape Town, 2003, pp. 36–7.

[70] Coulson and Campbell, *African Rock Art*, p. 117

[71] E.g. Lewis-Williams and Blundell, *Fragile Heritage*, p. 191; Townley Johnson, *Major Rock Paintings of Southern Africa*, p. 85.

[72] Lewis-Williams and Dowson, *Images of Power*, p. 134.

[73] E.g. Peter Garlake, *The Hunter's Vision: The Prehistoric Art of Zimbabwe*, British Museum Press, 1995, pp. 80–4.

[74] Slingsby, *Bushman's Kloof*, p. 47.

[75] E.g. Garlake, *Hunter's Vision*, pp. 68 and 134; Lewis-Williams in Price (Ed.), *The Archaeology of Shamanism*, p. 23.

[76] E.g. see Bradford Keeney, *Ropes to God: Experiencing the Bushman Spiritual Universe*, Ringing Rocks Press, Philadelphia, 2003, p. 55; Lewis-Williams and Dowson, *Images of Power*, pp. 132–3; Townley Johnson, *Major Rock Paintings of Southern Africa*, p. 27.

[77] Reported in *The Observer*, London, 25 November 2001.

[78] Jean Clottes, 'Thematic Changes in Upper Palaeolithic Art,' *Antiquity*, 70, 1996, p. 287.

[79] ibid.

Chapter Five: Riddles of the Caves

[1] Jean Clottes and Jean Courtin, *The Cave Beneath the Sea: Palaeolithic Images at Cosquer*, Harry N. Abrams, New York, 1996, p. 13.

[2] The excavators have concluded that there were only two periods of decoration, one at approximately 27,000 years ago and the second around 18,500 years ago. During the 8,500-year interval between these two periods it was not visited: Clottes and Courtin, *The Cave Beneath the Sea*, p. 7.

[3] ibid., p. 155.

[4] ibid., pp. 127–39 for general discussion of sea animals in Cosquer Cave, and p. 131 for reproductions of the eight images of impaled seals.

[5] ibid., p. 155.

[6] ibid., p. 156.

[7] ibid., pp. 155–6.

[8] ibid., p. 156 (emphasis in the original).

[9] ibid., p. 155.

[10] ibid., p. 157.

[11] E.g. ibid., p. 157.

[12] E.g. David Lewis-Williams, *The Mind in the Cave*, Thanes and Hudson, London, 2002, p. 278.

[13] Clottes and Courtin, *The Cave Beneath the Sea*, p. 156.

[14] Several sources refer to the figure of a third wounded man at Cougnac so faded as to be no longer visible. If it is there I was unable to make it out.

[15] Clottes and Courtin, *The Cave Beneath the Sea*, p. 158.

[16] ibid., pp. 158–9.

[17] ibid., pp. 159–61.

[18] In the South African example the figure, otherwise human, has the ears of an antelope or is wearing a cap with antelope ears stitched to it. See David Lewis-Williams, *A Cosmos in Stone*, Altamira Press, Walnut Creek, CA, 2002, p. 235; *The Mind in the Cave*, p. 276.

[19] Lewis-Williams, *Cosmos in Stone*, p. 235; *Mind in the Cave*, p. 276.

[20] Peter Garlake, *The Hunter's Vision: The Prehistoric Art of Zimbabwe*, British Museum Press, 1995, p. 130.

[21] ibid., p. 166.

[22] ibid., p. 159.

[23] Lewis-Williams and Dowson, 'The Signs of All Times', *Current Anthropology*, Vol. 29, No. 2, April 1988, pp. 201 ff.

[24] ibid., p. 201.

[25] Joelle Robert-Lambling writing in Jean Clottes, *Return to Chauvet Cave Excavating the Birthplace of Art: The First Full Report*, Thames and Hudson,

London, 2003, p. 201.

26 Clottes, *Return to Chauvet Cave*, pp. 65–8.

27 ibid., p. 82.

28 See ibid., p. 81.

29 ibid., pp. 81–2.

30 Anne Sieveking, *The Cave Artists*, Thames and Hudson, London, 1979, p. 209.

31 Thomas A. Dowson and Martin Porr, 'Special Objects – Special Creatures: Shamanistic Imagery and the Aurignacian Art of south-west Germany', in Neil Price (Ed.), *The Archaeology of Shamanism*, Routledge, London, 2001, p. 169.

32 ibid., p. 170.

33 ibid., p. 171.

34 Sieveking, *The Cave Artists*, op. cit., p. 110.

35 Paul Bahn, *Journey Through The Ice Age*, Weidenfeld and Nicolson, London, 1997, p. 197; Jean Clottes, 'Thematic Changes in Upper Palaeolithic Art: a view from the Grotte Chauvet', *Antiquity*, 70 (1996), p. 285.

36 Clottes and Courtin, *The Cave Beneath the Sea*, p. 165.

37 ibid., p. 137.

38 ibid., p. 150.

39 Randall White, *Prehistoric Art: The Symbolic Journey of Mankind*, Harry N. Abrams, New York, p. 97.

40 Mario Ruspoli, *The Cave of Lascaux: The Final Photographs*, Harry N. Abrams, New York, pp. 109–25; 200–1.

41 ibid., p. 156.

42 ibid., pp. 158–9.

43 ibid., p. 158.

44 Pedro A. Saura Ramos, *The Cave of Altamira*, Harry N. Abrams Inc., New York, 1999, p. 53.

45 Personal observations in Altamira II. See also Saura Ramos, *The Cave of Altamira*, p. 37; L.G. Freeman et al., *Altamira Revisited and Other Essays on Early Art*, Institute for Prehistoric Investigations, Chicago/Santander, 1987, p. 221.

46 Saura Ramos, *The Cave of Altamira*, p. 144; Miguel Angel García Guinea, *Altamira and other Cantabrian Caves*, Silex, Madrid, 1979, p. 151.

47 Saura Ramos, *The Cave of Altamira*, p. 155; Guinea, *Altamira and other Cantabrian Caves*, p. 86.

48 John E. Pfeiffer, *The Creative Explosion: An Inquiry into the Origin of Art and Religion*, Harper and Row, New York, 1982, pp. 136–137; Sieveking, *The Cave Artists*, p. 66; Denis Vialou, *Our Prehistoric Past*, Thames and Hudson, London,

1998, pp. 90–1.

49   Sieveking, *The Cave Artists*, p. 9.

50   Vialou, *Our Prehistoric Past*, p. 51; Sieveking, *The Cave Artists*, p. 9; Jean Clottes and David Lewis-Williams, *The Shamans of Prehistory*: Trance and Magic in the Painted Caves, Harry N. Abrams, New York, 1998, pp. 76–7, 93.

51   Personal observation, and see Sieveking, *The Cave Artists*, p. 47.

52   Personal observation.

53   Sieveking, *The Cave Artists*, p. 209.

54   Lewis-Williams and Dowson, 'The Signs of All Times', p. 201.

55   See, for example, Bradford Keeney, *Ropes to God: Experiencing the Bushman Spiritual Universe*, Ringing Rocks Press, Philadelphia, 2003, pp. 61–5.

56   David Lewis-Williams, *Images of Mystery: Rock Art of the Drakensberg*, Double Storey, Cape Town, 2003, p. 78.

57   David Lewis-Williams and Geoffrey Blundell, *Fragile Heritage: A Rock Art Fieldguide*, Witwatersrand University Press, 1998, pp. 66–8.

58   Personal observation. See also Lewis-Williams and Blundell, *Fragile Heritage*, p. 44.

59   ibid., pp. 76–7.

60   Garlake, *The Hunter's Vision*, pp. 91–2.

61   ibid., p. 93.

62   Personal observation.

63   Personal observation, and see Lewis-Williams and Blundell, *Fragile Heritage*, p. 48.

64   Personal observation, and see ibid.

65   Lewis-Williams, *Cosmos in Stone*, p. 153.

66   This is the argument of David Lewis-Williams in *Cosmos in Stone*, p. 174.

67   ibid.

68   In France: Arcy-sur-Cure, Rouffignac, Villars, Bara Bahau, Cougnac, Merveilles (Rocamadour), Cap Blanc, St Cirque (Grotte du Sourcier), Font de Gaume, Combarelles, Niaux, Bedeilhac, and Gargas. In Spain: Las Monedas, El Castillo, Covalanas, and El Pendo. In addition two replica caves (where the originals are closed to the public) were also visited: Lascaux II in France and Altamira II in Spain.

69   For the number and predominance of mammoths in Pech Merle: Jean Clottes, 'Thematic Changes in Upper Palaeolithic Art: a view from the Grotte Chauvet,' *Antiquity*, 70 (1996), p. 285.

70   Cited in Sieveking, *The Cave Artists*, pp. 49–51.

71   For example Pech Merle – see Chapter Two.

72   Personal observation.

73   Lewis-Williams, *The Mind in the Cave*, p. 240.

74 Cited in ibid., p. 249.
75 ibid., p. 251.
76 Clottes, *Return to Chauvet Cave*, p. 88.
77 Lewis-Williams, *The Mind in Cave*, p. 213, and personal observation.
78 Personal observation.
79 Personal observation.
80 Personal observation.
81 Clottes and Lewis-Williams, *The Shamans of Prehistory*, p. 86.
82 See for example Bahn, *Journey through the Ice Age*, p. 106.
83 See Clottes and Lewis-Williams, *The Shamans of Prehistory*, p. 87.
84 Personal observation and information from local guides.
85 See for example Clottes and Lewis-Williams, *The Shamans of Prehistory*, p. 82.
86 Lewis-Williams, *Cosmos in Stone*, pp. 104–6.
87 ibid., pp. 104–105.
88 Peter Slingsby, *Bushman's Kloof: A Comprehensive Guide to the Rock Art of Bushman's Kloof, Rock Art of the Western Cape*, Book 2, The Fontmaker, South Africa, 1997, p. 25.
89 Anne Solomon, 'Southern African Rock Art Research', in Christopher Chippendale and Paul S. Tacon (Eds), *The Archaeology of Rock Art*, Cambridge University Press, 1998, p. 282. The figure seems to be male. For a second example, with what is probably a female figure, see Gavin Anderson, *Bushman Rock Art*, Art Publishers, Johannesburg, p. 31.
90 R. Townley Johnson, *Major Rock Paintings of Southern Africa*, David Philip Publishers, Cape Town, 1979, p. 52.
91 Thomas A. Dowson in Chippendale and Tacon, *The Archaeology of Rock Art*, p. 79.
92 Personal observation.
93 M. Lorblanchet and A. Sieveking, 'The Monsters Of Pergousset', *Cambridge Archaeological Journal*, 7:1 (1997) p. 52.
94 Clottes and Courtin, *The Cave Beneath the Sea*, p. 122.
95 Jean Marie Chauvet et al, *Dawn of Art: The Chauvet Cave*, Harry N. Abrams, New York, 1996, p. 83.
96 Personal observation.
97 D. Bruce Dickson, *The Dawn of Belief: Religion in the Upper Palaeolithic of Southwestern Europe*, the University of Arizona Press, Tucson, 1996, pp. 114–15.
98 Ruspoli, *Lascaux*, p. 55.
99 Lewis-Williams and Blundell, *Fragile Heritage*, pp. 95–6.
100 David Lewis-Williams and Thomas Dowson, *Images of Power: Understanding Bushman Rock Art*, Southern Book Publishers, Johannesburg, 1989, pp. 58–9.
101 Clottes, *Return to Chauvet Cave*, pp. 84–5.

[102] Chauvet et al., *Dawn of Art*, p. 58.

[103] See discussion of Fumane Cave in Chapter Four.

[104] Personal observation.

[105] Lorblanchet and Sieveking, 'The Monsters of Pergousset', pp. 37–56.

[106] Slingsby, *Bushman's Kloof*, p. 28.

[107] Garlake, *The Hunter's Vision*, p. 82.

[108] Clottes and Lewis-Williams, *The Shamans of Prehistory*, p. 58.

[109] Clottes, *Return to Chauvet Cave*, p. 172.

[110] Lewis-Williams, *The Mind in the Cave*, p. 240; Ruspoli, *The Cave of Lascaux*, p. 104.

[111] Pfeiffer, *The Creative Explosion*, p. 219.

[112] All positive handprints in southern Africa, with the paint applied directly to the palm of the hand and then pressed against the rock face. In Europe the handprints are mainly negative – i.e. the paint was sprayed directly over the hand pressed against the cave wall; however there are also some positive handprints – as at Arcy-sur-Cure for example.

[113] See Lewis-Williams, *Images of Mystery*, p. 51; Clottes and Lewis-Williams, *The Shamans of Prehistory*, pp. 70–1.

[114] White, *Prehistoric Art*, pp. 162–5.

[115] Clottes and Lewis-Williams, *The Shamans of Prehistory*, p. 44.

[116] Lewis-Williams, *Cosmos in Stone*, p. 247.

Chapter Six: The Shabby Academy

[1] David Lewis-Williams, 'Harnessing the Brain: Vision and Shamanism in Upper Palaeolithic Western Europe', in Conkey et al. (Eds.), *Beyond Art: Pleistocene Image and Symbol*, Memoirs of the California Academy of Sciences No. 23, San Francisco, 3 October 1997, p. 321.

[2] Paul G. Bahn, 'New Developments in Pleistocene Art', *Evolutionary Anthropology*, 1995/96, Vol. 4, No. 6, pp. 213–14. Bahn remains 'sceptical about whether it is either possible or necessary for any single theory to encompass so many millennia and so many different types and contexts of art.'

[3] Benite Madariaga de la Campa, *Sanz de Sautuola and the Discovery of the Caves of Altamira*, Fundacion Marcelino Botin, Santander, 2001, pp. 21–2. See also p. 46.

[4] ibid., p. 24. The figure of 14,000 years is given in Paul Bahn, *Journey through the Ice Age*, Weidenfeld and Nicolson, London, 1997, p. 17.

[5] Bahn, *Journey Through The Ice Age*, pp. 14–16. The first pieces had been discovered as early as 1827.

[6] ibid., p. 17.

[7] Madariaga de la Campa, *Sanz de Sautuola*, p. 44.

[8] Miguel Angel García Guinea, *Altamira and Other Cantabrian Caves*, Silex, Madrid, 1979, pp. 12, 23.

[9] Bahn, *Journey Through The Ice Age*, p. 17.

[10] Madariaga de la Campa, *Sanz de Sautuola*, p. 36; P. Bahn, *Journey through the Ice Age*, p. 18.

[11] Madariaga de la Campa, *Sanz de Sautuola*, p. 44.

[12] García Guinea, *Altamira And Other Cantabrian Caves*, op.cit., pp. 44–5.

[13] ibid.

[14] Bahn, *Journey through the Ice Age*, p. 22.

[15] ibid., pp. 18–19.

[16] Madariaga de la Campa, *Sanz de Sautuola* p. 43: '*Il semble probable qu'elles ont été faites dans l'intervalle des deux premières visite de M. de Sautuola, de 1875 à 1879.*'

[17] Madariaga de la Campa, *Sanz de Sautuola*, pp. 40–41; Garcia Guinea, *Altamira and Other Cantabrian Caves*, p. 37.

[18] Cited in Madariaga de la Campa, *Sanz de Sautuola*, pp. 40–1.

[19] Cited in ibid.

[20] Cited in García Guinea, *Altamira and other Cantabrian Caves*, p. 44.

[21] Bahn, *Journey Through The Ice Age*, p. 20.

[22] Cited in García Guinea, *Altamira And Other Cantabrian Caves*, p. 46.

[23] Madariaga de la Campa, *Sanz de Sautuola.*, p. 43–4.

[24] García Guinea, *Altamira and other Cantabrian Caves*, p. VIII, Prologue by Emilio Botin Sanz De Sautuola.

[25] In ibid., page VII, Prologue.

[26] H. Kuhn, *El arte de la epoca glacial*, cited in Garcia Guinea, *Altamira and Other Cantabrian Caves*, p. 32.

[27] Garcia Guinea, *Altamira And Other Cantabrian Caves*, p. 28.

[28] ibid., p. 37.

[29] Madariaga de la Campa, *Sanz de Sautuola*, p. 62.

[30] Bahn, *Journey through the Ice Age*, p. 22.

[31] ibid.

[32] ibid., p. 21.

[33] ibid.

[34] ibid., p. 22.

[35] Madariaga de la Campa, *Sanz de Sautuola*, pp. 62–3.

[36] Bahn, *Journey through the Ice Age*, p. 22.

[37] García Guinea, *Altamira and Other Cantabrian Caves*, p. 51.

[38] Cited in Pedro A. Saura Ramos, *The Cave of Altamira*, Harry N. Abrams,

New York, 1999, p. 24.

39 Jean Clottes and David Lewis-Williams, *The Shamans of Prehistory: Trance and Magic in the Painted Caves*, Harry N. Abrams, New York, 1998, p. 38.

40 Bahn, *Journey through the Ice Age*, p. 22.

41 Cited in Madariaga de la Campa, *Sanz de Sautuola*, op. cit., p. 65.

42 Cited in García Guinea, *Altamira and Other Cantabrian Caves*, p. 65.

43 André Rosenfeld and Paul Bahn (Eds.), *Rock Art and Prehistory*, Oxbow Monograph 10, Oxford, 1991, p. v.

44 ibid.

45 Clottes and Lewis-Williams, *The Shamans of Prehistory*, p. 66.

46 ibid., p. 65.

47 ibid.

48 Count Begouen, 'The Magic Origin of Prehistoric Art', *Antiquity*, 3 (1929?), p. 5.

49 Clottes and Lewis-Williams, *The Shamans of Prehistory*, p. 68; Randall White, *Prehistoric Art: The Symbolic Journey of Mankind*, Harry N. Abrams, New York, pp. 55–6.

50 Begouen, 'Magic Origin', p. 5.

51 David Lewis-Williams *The Mind in the Cave*, Thames and Hudson, London, 2002, p. 33.

52 Begouen, 'Magic Origin', p. 8.

53 ibid., p. 10.

54 Lewis-Williams, *The Mind in the Cave*, p. 47.

55 Paul Bahn, Foreword in Jean Marie Chauvet et al., *Dawn of Art: Chauvet Cave*, Harry N. Abrams, New York, 1996, p. 9.

56 Bahn, *Journey through the Ice Age*, p. 60.

57 See Chapter Five. See also Lewis-Williams, *The Mind in the Cave*, p. 258; Evan Hadingham, *Secrets of the Ice Age*, Walker, New York, 1979, p. 108: only 19 painted caves in western Europe contain pictures of reindeer – the main food species – comprising well under 150 beasts in all. Reindeer occupies 7th or 8th position as a subject for cave artists – far behind horse and bison.

58 Bahn, *Journey through the Ice Age*, p. 177.

59 Lewis-Williams, *The Mind in the Cave*, p. 47.

60 Bahn, *Journey through The Ice Age*, p. 173. Cosquer is another cave with many such images – 28 figures out of 142.

61 ibid.

62 ibid.

63 ibid.

64 Clottes and Lewis-Williams *The Shamans of Prehistory*, p. 70.

65 Lewis-Williams *The Mind in the Cave*, p. 57.

66 ibid.

67 ibid.

68 Cited in ibid.

69 Cited in ibid.

70 White, *Prehistoric Art*, p. 56.

71 Bahn, *Journey through the Ice Age*, p. 190.

72 White, *Prehistoric Art*, p. 56.

73 Bahn, *Journey through the Ice Age*, p. 190; Lewis-Williams, *The Mind in the Cave*, pp. 60–1.

74 Lewis-Williams, *The Mind in the Cave*, p. 61.

75 Rosenfeld and Bahn (Eds.), *Rock Art and Prehistory*, page v.

76 Bahn, *Journey through the Ice Age*, p. 190.

77 ibid.

78 ibid., p. 191.

79 Bahn in Chauvet et. al., *Dawn of Art*, p. 8.

80 ibid., p. 10.

81 Robert G. Bednarik, 'A Major Change in Archaeological Paradigm', *Anthropos* 98, 2003, p. 514.

82 Bahn in Chauvet et al., *Dawn of Art*, p. 10.

83 Bahn, *Journey through the Ice Age*, p. 197.

84 Jean Clottes, in Christopher Chippendale and Paul S. Tacon (Eds), *The Archaeology of Rock Art*, Cambridge University Press, 1998, p. 122. See also Chauvet et al., *Dawn of Art: Chauvet Cave*, p. 127.

85 Jean Clottes, in Chippendale and Tacon, *The Archaeology of Rock Art*, pp. 121–2.

86 ibid., p. 121.

87 Robert G. Bednarik, 'A Major Change', p. 515.

88 Cited in David S. Whitley (Ed.), *Handbook of Rock Art Research*, Altamira Press, Walnut Creek, CA, 2001, p. 643.

89 David Lewis-Williams and Thomas Dowson, *Images of Power: Understanding Bushman Rock Art*, Southern Book Publishers, Johannesburg, 1989, p. 7.

90 ibid.

91 Lewis-Williams, *A Cosmos in Stone*, Altamira Press, Walnut Creek, CA, 2002, p. 166.

92 D. Bruce Dickson, *The Dawn of Belief: Religion in the Upper Palaeolithic of Southwestern Europe*, The University of Arizona Press, Tucson, 1996, p. 152.

93 Cited in ibid., p. 152.

94 Conkey et al., *Beyond Art*, p. 1.

95 Bahn, 'New Developments in Pleistocene Art', p. 213.

96 E.g. Robert Layton. See Bahn, *Journey through the Ice Age*, p. 211.

[97] García Guinea, *Altamira and Other Cantabrian Caves*, p. 67.

Chapter Seven: Searching for a Rosetta Stone

[1] See *The Times*, London, 17 Feb. 2005: 'Modern man has just got older – by 35,000 years'. The article, based on a research paper published in *Nature*, announces the discovery in Ethiopia of anatomically modern human skeletal remains dated to 196,000 years ago.

[2] See Clive Gamble, *The Palaeolithic Societies of Europe*, Cambridge University Press, 1999, p. 273; H. Knecht, et al., *Before Lascaux: The Complex Record of the Upper Palaeolithic*, CRC Press, Ann Arbor, 1993, pp. 48, 57, 59, 279; Ofer Bar-Yosef, 'The Upper Palaeolithic Revolution', *Annual Review of Anthropology*, 2002, 3, p. 373; Randall White, 'Beyond Art: Toward an Understanding of the Origins of Material Representation in Europe', *Annual Review of Anthropology*, 1992, 21, p. 546.

[3] Matthias Krings et al., 'Neanderthal DNA Sequences and the Origin of Modern Humans', *Cell*, Vol. 90, 11 July 1997, pp. 19–30.

[4] See discussion in David Lewis-Williams, *The Mind in the Cave*, Thames and Hudson, London, 2002, pp. 71–85; the possible latest date of 27,000 years for the survival of Neanderthals in Spain is given on p. 83.

[5] The Chatelperonnian archaeological assemblage. See Frederick L. Coolidge and Thomas Wynn, 'A Cognitive and Neuropsychological Perspective on the Chatelperonnian', *Journal of Anthropological Research*, Vol. 60, 2004, pp. 55–73.

[6] See discussion in Lewis-Williams, *The Mind in the Cave*, pp. 67–96. See also Robert H. Gargett, 'Grave Shortcomings: The Evidence for Neanderthal Burial', *Current Anthropology* Vol. 30, No. 2, April 1989, pp. 157–90; and Robert H. Gargett, 'Middle Palaeolithic Burial is not a Dead Issue', *Journal of Human Evolution* (1999), 37, pp. 27–90; Philip G. Chase and Harold L. Dibble, 'Middle Palaeolithic Symbolism: A Review of Current Evidence and Interpretations', *Journal of Anthropological Archaeology* (1987), 6, pp. 263–96. Although it is the consensus amongst scholars that 'the available evidence fails to indicate the presence of symbolic thought or symbolic behaviour before the Middle/Upper Palaeolithic transition' (Chase and Dibble), there are some strongly held dissenting views according to which the Neanderthals were capable of symbolic activity and did engage in symbolism. Robert Bednarik is the champion of this minority point of view. See for example, Robert Bednarik, 'Palaeoart and Archaeological Myths', *Cambridge Archaeological Journal* 2 (1), (1992), pp. 27–57. Most scholars agree that the Neanderthals began copying the designs and symbolically crafted tools of anatomically and behaviourally modern humans after their arrival in Europe, and that this

copying activity is reflected in the so-called 'Chatelperonnian' archaeological assemblage. See Coolidge and Wynn, 'A Cognitive and Neuropsychological Perspective on the Chatelperonnian'.

7   Randall White, *Prehistoric Art: The Symbolic Journey of Mankind*, Harry N. Abrams, New York, 2003, pp. 132–3.

8   Robert G. Bednarik, 'The Earliest Evidence of Palaeoart', *Rock Art Research*, 2003, Vol. 20, No. 2, p. 94.

9   J.D. Lewis-Williams and T.A. Dowson, 'The Signs of All Times', *Current Anthropology*, Vol. 29, No. 2, pp. 201–45.

10 Charles Tart (Ed.), *Altered States of Consciousness*, Harper, San Francisco, 1990; Raymond Price (Ed.), *Trance and Possession States*, R.M. Bucke Memorial Society, 1968 – see in particular paper by Arnold M. Ludwig, 'Altered States of Consciousness', who writes as follows (pp. 69–70): 'I shall regard "altered states of consciousness," hereafter referred to as ASCs, as those mental states induced by various psychological or pharmacological manoeuvres or agents, which can be recognised subjectively by the individual himself (or by an objective observer of the individual) as representing a sufficient deviation, in terms of subjective experience or psychological functioning, from certain general norms as determined by the subjective experience and psychological functioning of that individual during alert, waking consciousness.'

11 Michael Ripinsky-Naxon, 'Shamanistic Knowledge and Cosmology', in Helmut Wautischer (Ed.), *Tribal Epistemologies: Essays in the Philosophy of Anthropology*, Ashgate Publishing, Aldershot, 1998. The quote continues as follows: 'The critical importance of the shaman's worldview in the development of cosmo-religious metaphors and symbolic syntax cannot be fully understood without giving serious consideration to the role played in the process by hallucinogenic substances . . . Such perceptions more often than not reflect the recognisable imagery derived from psychotropic experiences.'

12 See extended discussion in Chapter Twenty-Two.

13 For further discussion of peyote religions in the United States see Weston La Barre, *The Peyote Cult*, University of Oklahoma Press, 1989; Stacy B. Schaeffer and Peter T. Furst (Eds.), *People of the Peyote*, University of New Mexico Press, 1996; Barbara G. Meyerhoff, *Peyote Hunt*, Cornell University Press, 1974; Edward F. Anderson, *Peyote: The Divine Cactus*, University of Arizona Press, 1996.

14 Ludwig, 'Altered States of Consciousness', pp. 19–22.

15 ibid., p. 22.

16 Joan Halifax, *Shaman: The Wounded Healer*, Thames and Hudson, London, 1982, p. 41.

17 Piers Vitebsky, *The Shaman*, Duncan Baird Publishers, London, 1995, p. 79.

[18] ibid., p. 70.

[19] ibid., p. 52.

[20] ibid., p. 79.

[21] See, for example, Louis Cholden MD (Ed.), *Lysergic Acid Diethylamide and Mescaline in Experimental Psychiatry*, Grune and Stratton, New York, 1956; Louis J. West, *Hallucinations*, Grune and Stratton, New York, 1962; R.K. Siegel and L.J. West, *Hallucinations: Behaviour, Experience and Theory*, John Wiley and Sons, New York, 1975.

[22] David Lewis-Williams, *A Cosmos in Stone*, Altamira Press, Walnut Creek, CA, 2002, pp. 20.

[23] ibid., p. 17–18.

[24] ibid., p. 20.

[25] David Lewis-Williams (1972), cited in ibid., page 27.

[26] ibid., p. 51.

[27] ibid., p. 28.

[28] ibid., p. 22.

[29] ibid., p. 49.

[30] ibid.

[31] ibid., p. 193: 'We have to guard against what Richard Bradley has called Mr Micawber archaeology: Keep at it long enough and something is bound to turn up. When we have enough "facts" their meaning will become evident. In other words, data precede and lead to theory. Empiricism, the philosophical name for Micawberism, is, however, not an infallible program for the production of explanations . . . We need some other methodological routes to the uncovering of "meaning".'

[32] ibid., p. 51.

[33] Jean Clottes and David Lewis-Williams, *The Shamans of Prehistory: Trance and Magic in the Painted Caves*, Harry N. Abrams, New York, 1998, p. 9.

[34] Lewis-Williams, *A Cosmos in Stone*, p. 169.

[35] ibid., p. 51.

[36] ibid; Lewis-Williams, *The Mind in the Cave*, p. 137.

[37] Lewis-Williams, *The Mind in the Cave*, p. 137.

[38] Lewis-Williams in Neil Price (Ed.), *The Archaeology of Shamanism*, Routledge, London, 2001, p. 19.

[39] Clottes and Lewis-Williams, *The Shamans of Prehistory*, pp. 11–12.

[40] David Lewis-Williams and Thomas Dowson, *Images of Power: Understanding Bushman Rock Art*, Southern Book Publishers, Johannesburg, 1989, p. 28.

[41] Cited in Lewis-Williams, *The Mind in the Cave*, p. 138.

[42] ibid.

[43] Lewis-Williams, *A Cosmos in Stone*, p. 169.

44 Michael Ripinsky-Naxon, *The Nature of Shamanism: Substance and Function of a Religious Metaphor*, State University of New York Press, 1993, p. 69.

45 ibid., p. 74.

46 Weston La Barre, *The Ghost Dance: The Origins of Religion*, George Allen and Unwin, London, 1970, p. 178.

47 But see the following: Marlene Dobkin de Rios, 'Enigma of Drug-Induced Altered States of Consciousness among the !Kung Bushmen of the Kalahari Desert', *Journal of Ethnopharmacology*, 15 (1986), pp. 297–304; Michael Winkelman and Marlene Dobkin de Rios, 'Psychoactive Properties of !Kung Bushmen Medicine Plants', *Journal of Psychoactive Drugs*, Vol. 21 (1), Jan.-Mar. 1989, pp. 51–9; P.A.G.M. De Smeet, 'Some ethnopharmacological notes on African Hallucinogens', *Journal of Ethnopharmacology*, 50 (1996), pp. 141–6.

48 See, for example, Lewis-Williams, *A Cosmos in Stone*, p. 122. The southern San spoke of 'shamans turning themselves into creatures such as jackals (Bleek 1935, 15–17), birds (1935, 18–19) and lions (Bleek 1936, 131–3). One informant gave a long account of a female shaman becoming a lioness and visiting his camp.'

49 Lewis-Williams, *The Mind in the Cave*, pp. 147, 168; *Images of Mystery: Rock Art of the Drakensberg*, Double Storey, Cape Town, 2003, pp. 38, 40–1.

50 Lewis-Williams, *The Mind in the Cave*, p. 141: 'Transformation into a lion or some other animal is a key part of San spiritual experience.'

51 ibid., pp. 149, 160.

52 Lewis-Williams, *Images of Mystery*, p. 35.

53 Cited in Lewis-Williams, *A Cosmos in Stone*, p. 58.

54 Lewis-Williams, *Images of Mystery*, pp. 34–5.

55 Cited in ibid., p. 26.

56 Lewis-Williams, *The Mind in the Cave*, pp. 147, 168; *Images of Mystery*, pp. 38, 40–1.

57 Paul Bahn and Jean Vertut, *Images of the Ice Age*, Windward, 1988, p. 190.

58 Lewis-Williams, *Images of Mystery*, p. 35.

59 Lewis-Williams, *A Cosmos in Stone*, p. 62.

60 Lewis-Williams, *Images of Mystery*, p. 35.

61 E.g. see Lewis-Williams and Dowson, *Images of Power*, pp. 92–5; Lewis-Williams, *Images of Mystery*, p. 72.

62 Lewis-Williams, *Images of Mystery*, p. 72.

63 Lewis-Williams, in *Antiquity*, 2003, Vol. 77, No. 295, p. 167.

64 Lewis-Williams sets out his definition of shamanism in *Antiquity*, 2003, Vol. 77, No. 295, p. 166: 'Hunter-gatherer shamanism is fundamentally posited on a range of institutionalised altered states of consciousness. The visual, aural and somatic experiences of those states give rise to perceptions of an altern-

ative reality that is frequently tiered (hunter-gatherers believe in spiritual realms above and below the world of daily life). People with special powers and skills, the shamans, are believed to have access to this alternative reality. The behaviour of the human nervous system in certain altered states creates the illusion of dissociation from one's body . . . Shamans use dissociation experiences of altered states of consciousness to achieve at least four ends: contact spirits and supernatural entities; heal the sick; control the movements and lives of animals; change the weather. These four functions of shamans, as well as their entrance into an altered state of consciousness, are believed to be facilitated by supernatural powers and entities that include: variously conceived supernatural potency, or power; animal-helpers and other categories of spirits that assist shamans and are associated with potency.'

[65] Paul Bahn, *Journey through the Ice Age*, Weidenfeld and Nicolson, London, 1997, p. 183.

[66] Lewis-Williams, *A Cosmos in Stone*, p. 122: 'Out-of-body travel is so closely associated with lions that the !Kung [Ju/'hoansi] use the word for "pawed creature" (*jum*) to mean "to go on out-of-body travel".'

[67] Lewis-Williams, *The Mind in the Cave*, p. 139.

[68] ibid.

[69] ibid., p. 140.

[70] See for example Richard Katz, 'Education for Transcendance: !Kia-Healing with the Kalahari !Kung,' in Richard B. Lee and Irven Devore (Eds) *Kalahari Hunter-Gatherers: Studies of the !Kung and their Neighbours*, Harvard University Press, 1976, pp. 284ff.

[71] Cited in Bradford Keeney, *Ropes to God: Experiencing the Bushman Spiritual Universe*, Rolling Rocks Press, 2003, p. 31.

[72] E.g. see ibid.

[73] Lewis-Williams, *Images of Mystery*, pp. 32–3.

[74] ibid., p. 33.

[75] G. Reichel-Dolmatoff, *The Shaman and the Jaguar: A Study of Narcotic Drugs amongst the Tukano Indians of Colombia*, Temple University Press, Philadelphia, 1975.

[76] See Chapter Three.

[77] See Benny Shanon, *The Antipodes of the Mind: Charting the Phenomenology of the Ayahuasca Experience*, Oxford University Press, 2002, p. 13; Jeremy Narby and Francis Huxley, *Shamans through Time*, Thames and Hudson, London, 2001, pp. 196, 267.

[78] Reichel-Dolmatoff, *The Shaman and the Jaguar*, photographic plates between pp. 174 and 175, 178 and 179.

[79] ibid., pp. 167–173.

[80] In this context the different patterns are accorded particular meaning by the Tukano. Animals painted in red are those they wish the 'Master of Game Animals' to release from the spirit world for them to hunt in this world: 'Geometric motifs painted adjacent to the animal figures represent fecundity. Rows of dots depict drops of semen, and zigzag lines the succession of generations. Geometric shapes inside the bodies of animal paintings denote the animals' fertility.' (Robert Layton in David S. Whitley (Ed.) *Handbook of Rock Art Research*, Altamira Press, Walnut Creek, CA, 2001, p. 314). Reichel-Dolmatoff realised that what was happening here was that standardised visual forms, generated universally by the human nervous system in trance states, were being construed and interpreted by the Tukano (naturally enough!) according to the particular views and setting of Tukano culture. In other cultures the same forms would be seen and described but would be construed differently, according to the local setting.

[81] See Chapter Five.

[82] Reichel-Dolmatoff, 1978. Drug-induced optical sensations, etc., cited in Lewis-Williams, *The Mind in the Cave*, p. 131.

[83] G. Reichel-Dolmatoff, *The Shaman and the Jaguar*, p. 172.

[84] ibid.

[85] ibid.

[86] ibid.

[87] Lewis-Williams and Dowson, 'The Signs of All Times'.

[88] G. Reichel-Dolmatoff, *The Shaman and the Jaguar*, p. 173.

[89] ibid., p. 174.

[90] ibid.

[91] ibid., p. 173.

Chapter Eight: The Code in the Mind

[1] David Lewis-Williams, *A Cosmos in Stone*, Altamira Press, Walnut Creek, CA, 2002, p. 169.

[2] J.D. Lewis-Williams and Thomas Dowson, 'The Signs of All Times', *Current Anthropology*, Vol. 29, No. 2. p. 202.

[3] ibid.

[4] ibid.

[5] ibid., p. 203; Heinrich Kluver, *Mescal and Mechanisms of Hallucinations*, Phoenix Books, The University of Chicago Press, 1966, p. 66.

[6] Lewis-Williams and Dowson, 'The Signs of All Times', p. 203.

[7] H. Kluver, 'Mescal Visions and Eidetic Vision', *American Journal of Psychology*, 37 (1926), pp. 502–15; H. Kluver, *Mescal: The Divine Plant and its Psychological*

Effects, London, Kegan Paul, Trench, Trubner and Co., 1928; H. Kluver, 'Mechanisms of Hallucinations, Studies in Personality', Q. McNemar and M.A. Merrill (Eds), McGraw Hill New York.

[8] E.g. Horowitz, 'Hallucinations: An information-processing approach', in R. Siegel and L. West (Eds.) *Hallucinations: Behaviour, Experience and Theory*, Wiley, New York, 1975, cited in Lewis-Williams and Dowson, 'The Signs of All Times', p. 202.

[9] Lewis-Williams and Dowson, 'The Signs of all Times', p. 202.

[10] ibid.

[11] ibid., p. 203.

[12] Kluver, *Mescal and Mechanisms of Hallucinations*, p. 66.

[13] Lewis-Williams and Dowson, 'The Signs of all Times', p. 203.

[14] See Chapter Seven.

[15] Lewis-Williams and Dowson, 'The Signs of all Times', p. 203.

[16] ibid., p. 204.

[17] ibid.

[18] ibid.

[19] ibid.

[20] ibid.

[21] ibid.

[22] ibid.

[23] ibid.

[24] ibid., p. 205.

[25] Cited in ibid., p. 204.

[26] Cited in ibid.

[27] Robert Layton in Whitley (Ed.), *Handbook of Rock Art Research*, Altamira Press, Walnut Creek, CA, 2001, p. 321.

[28] Cited in Lewis-Williams and Dowson, 'The Signs of all Times', p. 204.

[29] Richard Evans Schultes, Albert Hoffman and Christian Ratsch, *Plants of the Gods: Their Sacred, Healing and Hallucinogenic Powers*, Healing Arts Press, Rochester, Vermont, 2001, pp. 78, 106 ff.

[30] ibid., p. 110.

[31] See Chapter Three

[32] Lewis-Williams and Dowson, 'The Signs of all Times', p. 206.

[33] ibid., pp. 208 ff.

[34] ibid., pp. 208–10.

[35] ibid., p. 210.

[36] ibid., p. 211.

[37] ibid., p. 205.

[38] ibid., p. 208.

[39] ibid., pp. 211–12.

[40] ibid., p. 212.

[41] ibid.

[42] ibid.

[43] ibid.

[44] ibid.

[45] ibid.

[46] ibid., p. 212

[47] Cited in ibid., p. 212

[48] Cited in ibid., from Siegel and West (Eds), *Hallucinations: Behaviour, Experience and Theory*, p. 104–5.

[49] See Chapter Seven

[50] Lewis-Williams and Downson, 'The Signs of all Times', p. 212

[51] ibid.

[52] ibid.

[53] ibid.

[54] ibid.

[55] ibid., p. 215. Alexander Marshack, *The Roots of Civilisation: The Cognitive Beginnings of Man's First Art, Symbol and Notation*, McGraw-Hill, New York, 1972 (and many other works), is one of the principal advocates of this point of view.

[56] Lewis-Williams and Dowson, 'The Signs of all Times', p. 215.

[57] ibid.

[58] ibid.

[59] ibid.

[60] ibid.

[61] ibid., citing John Halverson, 'Art for Art's Sake in the Palaeolithic', *Current Anthropology*, 28, 1987, pp. 63–98.

[62] Lewis-Williams and Dowson, 'The Signs of all Times' p. 215.

[63] ibid.

[64] ibid., p. 216.

[65] ibid., p. 202.

[66] ibid., p. 213.

[67] See Chapter Six.

[68] Now Professor Emeritus since his retirement from the University in 2003.

[69] Jean Clottes and David Lewis-Williams, *Shamans of Prehistory: Trance and Magic in the Painted Caves*, Harry N. Abrams, New York, 1998.

[70] Robert Layton, *Cambridge Archaeological Journal*, 10:1 (2000), p. 169.

[71] David S. Whitley Introduction to Lewis-Williams, *A Cosmos in Stone*, p. ix.

[72] *Cambridge Archaeological Journal (CAJ)*, 13:2, 2003, p. 215.

[73] ibid., p. 213

[74] Patricia A. Helvenston and Paul G. Bahn, *Desperately Seeking Trance Plants: Testing the Three Stages of Trance Model*, RJ Communications, New York, 2002, pp. 31–9.

[75] ibid., p. 34.

[76] *CAJ*, 13:2, p. 214.

[77] Helvenston and Bahn, *Desperately Seeking Trance Plants*, p. 37.

[78] ibid., p. 39.

[79] See my own experiences with ayahuasaca recounted in Chapter Three

[80] Rick Strassman MD, *DMT: The Spirit Molecule: A Doctor's Revolutionary Research into the Biology of Near-Death and Mystical Experiences*, Park Street Press, Rochester, Vermont, 2001; Benny Shanon, *The Antipodes of the Mind: Charting the Phenomenology of the Ayahuasca Experience*, Oxford University Press, 2002.

[81] E.g. Lewis-Williams and Dowson, 'The Signs of All Times', p. 204: 'These three stages are not necessarily sequential. Some subjects appear to move directly into the third stage, while others do not progress beyond the first . . . Nor should the stages be considered discrete . . . The three stages we propose should therefore be seen as cumulative rather than sequential.'

[82] See discussion by David Pearce, '"Testing" and Altered Stages of Consciousness in Upper Palaeolithic Art Research', *Cambridge Archaeological Journal*, 14:1, 2004, pp. 82–3: 'The "three stages" were suggested as classes of experience-types that may be experienced by people in altered states of consciousness. The three levels of trance act as heuristic devices to help researchers recognise imagery that may have been generated in altered states. That individuals experience "entoptic" and iconic hallucinations for a variety of reasons is indisputable. Whether or not any given mechanism of hallucination leads to the experience of all three levels is irrelevant to Lewis-Williams' and Dowson's central argument.'

[83] Christopher Chippendale in *CAJ*, 13:2, p. 219.

[84] Helvenston and Bahn, *CAJ*, 13:2, 2003, p. 222.

[85] Helvenston and Bahn, *Desperately Seeking Trance Plants*, p. 38.

[86] ibid., p. 39.

[87] ibid., p. 37.

[88] Steven Hayden Pollock, 'The Psilocybin Mushroom Pandemic', *Journal of Psychedelic Drugs*, Vol 7:1.

[89] ibid., page 75, cited in Helvenston and Bahn, *Desperately Seeking Trance Plants*, p. 37.

[90] Paul Stamets, *Psilocybin Mushrooms of the World: An Identification Guide*, Ten Speed Press, Berkeley, California, pp. 108–9.

[91] ibid., p. 144.

[92] Schultes et al., *Plants of the Gods*, p. 72.

[93] Helvenston and Bahn, *Desperately Seeking Trance Plants*, p. 37, footnote.

[94] Stamets, *Psilocybin Mushrooms of the World*, p. 144.

[95] Schultes et al., *Plants of the Gods*.

[96] Helvenston and Bahn, *Desperately Seeking Trance Plants*, p. 37, footnote.

[97] Schultes et al., *Plants of the Gods*, p. 72.

[98] Email, subject 'Psilocybe', from Professor Roy Watling to Graham Hancock, dated 23 November 2004.

[99] Email, subject 'Psilocybe.doc', from Chris Scarrre to Graham Hancock, dated 16 December 2004.

[100] Roy Watling to Graham Hancock, 18 December 2004.

[101] Roy Watling to Graham Hancock 16 December 2004 and 6 January 2005.

[102] Email from Giorgio Samorini to Graham Hancock, 17 December 2004.

[103] Stamets, *Psilocybin Mushrooms of the World*.

[104] Email, subject 'Psilocybe semilanceata', from Paul Stamets to Graham Hancock, 1 January 2005.

[105] Email, subject 'Psilocybe', 15 April, 2005, from Roy Watling to Graham Hancock. And see Roy Watling and Maria Martin, 'A Sequestrate Psilocybe from Scotland', *Botanical Journal of Scotland*, 55 (2), pp. 245–57.

[106] Watling to Hancock, 6 January 2005.

[107] Watling to Hancock 16 January 2005.

[108] ibid.

[109] Bahn in Henri-Paul Francfort and Roberte N. Hamayon (Eds), *The Concept of Shamanism, Uses and Abuses*, Akademiai Kiado, Budapest, 2001, p. 52.

Chapter Nine: Serpents Of The Drakensberg

[1] See Chapter Six. Breuil's first visit was in 1929: David Lewis-Williams and Thomas Dowson, *Images of Power: Understanding Bushman Rock Art*, Southern Book Publishers, Johannesburg, 1989, p. 6.

[2] David S. Whitley, *Handbook of Rock Art Research*, Altamira Press, Walnut Creek, CA, 2001, p. 643.

[3] See Chapter Six; and Lewis-Williams and Dowson, *Images of Power*, pp. 6ff; Whitley, *Handbook of Rock Art Research*, p. 643.

[4] David Lewis-Williams, *Images of Mystery: Rock Art of the Drakensberg* pp. 110–11; Christopher Chippendale and Paul S. Tacon, *The Archaeology of Rock Art*, Cambridge University Press, 1998, p. 253.

[5] Lewis-Williams, *Images of Mystery*, p. 111.

[6] ibid., p. 109.

[7] ibid.

[8] ibid., p. 111.

[9] ibid., p. 112.

[10] ibid.

[11] Lewis-Williams and Dowson, *Images of Power*, p. 36; Lewis-Williams, *Images of Mystery*, pp. 113, 116.

[12] See Chapter Seven.

[13] Lewis-Williams, *Images of Mystery*, pp. 67–8; Chippendale and Tacon, *The Archaeology of Rock Art*, p. 263.

[14] Chippendale and Tacon, *The Archaeology of Rock Art*, p. 257.

[15] ibid., p. 264.

[16] ibid., pp. 76, 259.

[17] ibid., p. 75.

[18] ibid.

[19] ibid., pp. 75–6.

[20] ibid.

[21] Cited in ibid., p. 76.

[22] ibid., p. 259.

[23] ibid.

[24] See Chapter Seven.

[25] E.g. David Lewis-Williams, *The Mind in the Cave*, Thames and Hudson, London, 2002, pp. 128–9; 209; Jean Clottes and David Lewis-Williams, *The Shamans of Prehistory: Trance and Magic in the Painted Caves*, Harry N. Abrams, New York, 1998, pp. 26–7; Lewis-Williams, *Images of Mystery* p. 54; Lewis-Williams, *A Cosmos in Stone*, Altamira Press, Walnut Creek, CA, 2002, pp. 108ff., 202.

[26] Lewis-Williams, *A Cosmos in Stone*, p. 109.

[27] ibid.

[28] ibid.

[29] ibid., p. 110.

[30] Chippendale and Tacon, *The Archaeology of Rock Art*, p. 75.

[31] ibid.

[32] For this reason I am not convinced by occasional attempts that have been made by a few scholars to attribute the therianthropes featured in San rock art in southern Africa to mythological rather than visionary sources. (See, for example, Anne Solomon, 'What is an Explanation? Belief and Cosmology in Interpretations of Southern San Rock Art in Southern Africa', in Henri-Paul Francfort and Roberte N. Hamayon (Eds), *The Concept of Shamanism: Uses and Abuses*, Akedemiai Kiado, Budapest, 2001, pp. 162–4; Anne Solomon, 'On Different Approaches to San Rock Art', *South African Archaeological Bulletin*, 55, 2000, p. 78; Harald Pager, 'San Trance Performances', *Rock Art*

Research, 1994, Vol. 11, No. 2, p. 95.) It is true that there are therianthropes in San mythology, but the real question – regarding both those spoken of in myth, and those painted in the rock shelters – is *where did the idea of half-man half-animals come from in the first place?* Since we know that therianthropes are seen regularly and routinely in visions during certain altered states of consciousness, *and in no other areas of direct human experience*, the most plausible explanation is that the myths and the rock paintings both draw on the same hallucinatory sources.

33 *Cambridge Archaeological Journal* (*CAJ*), 13:2, 2003, p. 222.
34 *CAJ*, 14:1, 2004, p. 84.
35 See Chapters Four and Five.
36 See Chapter Seven.
37 Quote is from J.D. Lewis-Williams and T.A. Dowson, 'The Signs of All Times', *Current Anthropology*, Vol. 29, No. 2, p. 201. See discussion in Chapter Eight.
38 Lewis-Williams and Dowson, *Images of Power*, pp. 72ff.
39 There is an intriguing cross-cultural comparison as well. The Warao, a tribal people of Venezuela's Orinoco delta, use toxic quantities of strong indigenous tobacco (*Nicotiana rustica*) to induce trance states in which they see visions of a huge serpent with four forward-pointing horns on its head, two on each side. The serpent's body is said to look like a rainbow. See Johannes Wilbert, 'Illuminative Serpents: Tobacco Hallucinations of the Warao', *Journal of Latin American Lore*, 20:2 (1997), pp. 322–33, 325.
40 Chippendale and Tacon, *The Archaeology of Rock Art*, 259.
41 David Lewis-Williams and Geoffrey Blundell, *Fragile Heritage: A Rock Art Field Guide*, Witwatersrand University Press, 1998, p. 210.
42 Lewis-Williams and Dowson, *Images of Power*, p. 77.
43 Cited in Lewis-Williams, *Images of Mystery*, p. 87.
44 ibid.
45 Cited in ibid., p. 86.
46 Personal observation, and see ibid.
47 Felicitas Goodman, *Where Spirits Ride the Wind: Trance Journeys and Other Ecstatic Experiences*, Indiana University Press, 1990, p. 23. See also Mircea Eliade, *Shamanism: Archaic Techniques of Ecstasy*, Princeton University Press, 1974, p. 79.
48 Cited in Goodman, *Where Spirits Ride the Wind*, op cit., p. 23.
49 Cited in ibid.
50 Lewis-Williams, *The Mind in the Cave*, p. 139.
51 On the subject of Shamanic trance erections see also Andreas Lommel, *Shamanism: The Beginnings of Art*, McGraw-Hill, New York, 1967, p. 99.

[52] Demorest Davenport and Michael A. Jochim, *Antiquity*, 62, 1988, p. 561.

[53] See, for example, Clottes and Lewis-Williams, *The Shamans of Prehistory*, p. 34; Lewis-Williams and Dowson, *Images of Power*, p. 136; Peter Garlake, *The Hunter's Vision: The Prehistoric Art of Zimbabwe*, British Museum Press, 1995, pp. 78–9.

[54] See Chapter Seven. Up to one-third of all *!Kung* women are shamans.

[55] E.g. see Richard Katz, 'Education for Transcendence: *!Kia* Healing with the Kalahari !Kung,' in Richard B. Lee and Irven de Vore (Eds), *Kalahari Hunter-Gatherers: Studies of the !Kung San and their Neighbours*, Harvard University Press, 1976, p. 286: 'The primary structure for the occurrence of *!kia* [trance] is a dance which usually lasts from dusk to dawn . . . The women gather round the fire, singing *!kia* songs and rhythmically clapping their hands. The men dance in a circle around the women, some working themselves into a *!kia* state.'

[56] See Chapter Seven

[57] Lewis-Williams, *Images of Mystery*, pp. 88–9.

[58] ibid., p. 89.

[59] ibid., page 78; Lewis-Williams and Dowson, *Images of Power*, p. 87. In refutation of Bahn and Helvenston's charge that no trances other than those induced by LSD, mescalin and psilocybin, are capable of generating suitable forms of mental imagery, Lewis-Williams also cites the work of psychologist and hypnotist Etzel Cardena demonstrating that 'geometric percepts are experienced in deep hypnosis', and the work of Dominic Ffytche and Robert Howard. See J.D. Lewis-Williams, 'Neuropsychology and Upper Palaeolithic Art: Observations on the Progress of Altered States of Consciousness', *Cambridge Archaeological Journal*, 14:1, pp. 107–11.

[60] Lewis-Williams, *Images of Mystery*, p. 89.

[61] ibid., p. 90; Lewis-Williams and Dowson, *Images of Power*, p. 78.

[62] Lewis-Williams, *Images of Mystery*, p. 90.

[63] ibid.

[64] See Chapter Three.

Chapter Ten: The Wounded Healer

[1] David Lewis-Williams, *The Mind in the Cave*, Thames and Hudson, London, 2002, p. 154.

[2] David Lewis-Williams, 'Three Dimensional Puzzles', *Ethnos*, Vol. 66:2, 2002, p. 260.

[3] David Lewis-Williams, *A Cosmos in Stone*, Altamira Press, Walnut Creek, CA, 2002, p. 217.

[4] Lewis-Williams, 'Three Dimensional Puzzles', p. 260.

5 Jean Clottes and Jean Courtin, *The Cave beneath the Sea: Palaeolithic Images at Cosquer*, Harry N. Abrams, New York, 1996, p. 157.

6 Cited in Lewis-Williams, *A Cosmos in Stone*, p. 240.

7 Cited in ibid.

8 Cited in ibid.

9 Cited in ibid.

10 Lewis-Williams, *The Mind in the Cave*, pp. 270ff.

11 See ibid; Lewis-Williams, *A Cosmos in Stone*, pp. 217ff.

12 Lewis-Williams, *The Mind in the Cave*, p. 271.

13 Cited in ibid., p. 272.

14 Cited in ibid.

15 Cited in ibid.

16 Lewis-Williams, *A Cosmos in Stone*, p. 225.

17 Cited in Lewis-Williams, *The Mind in the Cave*, pp. 273–4.

18 Cited in ibid., p. 274.

19 ibid., p. 275.

20 Cited in ibid., p. 228.

21 ibid., p. 275.

22 Lewis-Williams, *A Cosmos in Stone*, p. 234.

23 ibid., p. 235.

24 Lewis-Williams, *The Mind in the Cave*, p. 276.

25 ibid., pp. 280–1.

26 Mircea Eliade, *Shamanism: Archaic Techniques of Ecstasy*, Princeton University Press, 1972; Joan Halifax, *Shaman: The Wounded Healer*, Thames and Hudson, London, 1982 (1991).

27 Eliade, *Shamanism*, p. 44.

28 ibid., pp. 37–8.

29 ibid., p. 36.

30 ibid., p. 46.

31 ibid., p. 47.

32 ibid., p. 49.

33 ibid., p. 48.

34 ibid., p. 52.

35 ibid.

36 ibid., p. 53.

37 ibid., p. 54.

38 ibid., p. 55.

39 Halifax, *Shaman*, p. 43.

40 Lewis-Williams, *The Mind in the Cave*, p. 281.

41 ibid.

[42] Eliade, *Shamanism*, pp. 51–2.
[43] *National Geographic*, November 2004, pp. 41, 47.
[44] ibid., p. 41.
[45] ibid., pp. 49–50.
[46] Eliade, *Shamanism*, p. 51.
[47] ibid., p. 52.
[48] ibid., p. 101.
[49] ibid., p. 51.
[50] Lewis-Williams, *A Cosmos in Stone*, p. 243.
[51] ibid.
[52] Professor Roy Watling, personal communication, 6 January 2005.
[53] J.D. Lewis-Williams and T.A. Dowson, 'The Signs of all Times', *Current Anthropology*, Vol. 29, No. 2, p. 204.
[54] See, for example, Francis Crick's discussion of what is known about human perception in *The Astonishing Hypothesis: The Scientific Search for the Soul*, Touchstone Books, London, 1996, Chapter 3, 'seeing', pp. 23ff.
[55] Marlene Dobkin de Rios, 'Man, Culture and Hallucinogens: An Overview,' in Vera Rubin (Ed.), *Cannabis and Culture*, Moulton Publishers, The Hague, Paris, 1975, p. 407.

Chapter Eleven: Voyage into The Supernatural

[1] William James, *The Varieties of Religious Experience*, Penguin Classics, 1902 (1985), p. 388.
[2] Aldous Huxley, *The Doors of Perception; Heaven and Hell*, Flamingo Modern Classics, 1994, pp. 11–13.
[3] Albert Hoffman, *LSD My Problem Child: Reflections on Sacred Drugs, Mysticism and Science*, J.P. Tarcher, Los Angeles, 1983, pp. 196–7.
[4] James, *The Varieties of Religious Experience*, pp. 242–3. Emphases in the original.
[5] Rick Strassman MD, *DMT: The Spirit Molecule*, Park Street Press, Rochester, Vermont, 2001. See also Robert Forte (Ed.), *Entheogens and the Future of Religion*, Council on Spiritual Practices, San Francisco, 1997, p. 180.
[6] Strassman, *DMT*, p. 322.
[7] ibid., pp. 315–16.
[8] For a highly relevant discussion of the psychotropic effects of harmaline see Claudio Naranjo, *The Healing Journey: New Approaches to Consciousness*, Ballantine Books, New York, 1975, pp. 119–69.
[9] Richard Evans Schultes, Albert Hoffman and Christian Ratsch, *Plants of the Gods: Their Sacred, Healing and Hallucinogenic Powers*, Healing Arts Press,

Rochester, Vermont, 2001, pp. 176–81.

10 G. Reichel-Dolmatoff, *The Shaman and the Jaguar: A Study of Narcotic Drugs Amongst the Tukano Indians of Colombia*, Temple University Press, Philadelphia, 1975, p. 108.

11 Luis Eduardo Luna, *Vegetalismo: Shamanism among the Mestizo Population of the Peruvian Amazon*, Acta Universitatis Stockholmiensis Stockholm Studies in Comparative Religion, Almqvist and Wiksell Publishers, Stockholm, 1986, pp. 117–18.

12 *Unusual Personal Experiences: An Analysis of the Data from Three National Surveys conducted by the Roper Organisation*, Bigelow Holding Corporation, Las Vegas, 1992, pp. 14–15.

13 ibid., pp. 5, 14–15.

14 ibid., p. 14.

15 ibid., p. 15.

16 In fact 3.7 million people, but this figure, for polling and statistical reasons, 'excludes all children, the populations of Hawaii and Alaska, and anyone living in shared, institutional quarters'. See ibid., p. 48.

17 See, for example, John Mack, *Abduction: Human Encounters with Aliens*, Simon and Schuster, London, 1995, pp. 19, 42.

18 ibid; John Mack, *Passport to the Cosmos: Human Transformation and Alien Encounters*, Thorsons, London, 2000; David M. Jacobs, *Secret Life: Firsthand Documented Accounts of UFO Abductions*, Simon and Schuster, New York, 1993; Thomas E. Bullard, *UFO Abductions: The Measure of a Mystery* (Vol. I: *Comparative Study of Abduction Reports*; Vol. II, *Catalogue of Cases*), The Fund for UFO Research, 1987.

19 Cited in Jacques Vallee, *Passport to Magonia: On UFOs, Folklore, and Parallel Worlds*, Contemporary Books, Chicago, (1969) 1993, p. 93.

20 ibid., p. 95; Jacobs, *Secret Life*, p. 40.

21 Bullard, *UFO Abductions*, Vol. I, p. 115.

22 ibid., Vol. I, p. 87.

23 ibid., Vol. I, p. 114.

24 ibid., Vol. II, p. 170.

25 Mack, *Abduction*, p. 99.

26 ibid pp. 119–20, 122–3.

27 ibid., p. 123.

28 ibid., p. 154.

29 ibid., p. 155.

30 ibid., p. 156.

31 ibid., pp. 180–1.

32 ibid., p. 182.

33 ibid.

34 ibid., p. 188.

35 ibid., p. 246.

36 Mack, *Passport to the Cosmos*, p. 142.

37 Mack, *Abduction*, pp. 354–5.

38 ibid., pp. 349–50.

39 ibid., p. 355.

40 ibid.

41 Mircea Eliade, *Shamanism: Archaic Techniques of Ecstasy*, Princeton University Press, 1972, p. 57.

42 ibid., pp. 45–6.

43 ibid., p. 132.

44 Holger Kalweit, *Shamans, Healers and Medicine Men*, Shambhala, Boston and London, 1992, p. 39.

45 Eliade, *Shamanism*, pp. 36–7.

46 ibid., p. 43.

47 Joan Halifax, *Shamanic Voices: A Survey of Visionary Narratives*, Penguin Compass, New York, 1991, p. 50.

48 Personal correspondence with David Jacobs, 31 May and 1 June 2005.

49 Jacobs, *Secret Life*, pp. 92–3.

50 Mack, *Abduction*, p. 160.

51 ibid., p. 162.

Chapter Twelve: Shamans in the Sky

1 Spanos, Cross, et al., 'Close Encounters: An Examination of UFO Experiences', *Journal of Abnormal Psychology*, 1993, Vol. 102, No. 4, p. 624.

2 Elizabeth Slater PhD, Addendum to 'Conclusions on Nine Psychologicals' (Appendices, p. 12) in Ted Bloecher, Aphrodite Clamar, and Budd Hopkins, *Final Report on the Psychological Testing of UFO Abductees*, Fund for UFO Research, 1985. Emphases in the original.

3 John Mack, *Passport to the Cosmos: Human Transformation and Alien Encounters*, Thorsons, London, 2000, p. 28.

4 John Mack, *Abduction: Human Encounters with Aliens*, Simon and Schuster, London, 1995, pp. 16–17.

5 Harvard Professor Rand McNally, in the *Journal of Psychological Science*, cited in Greg Taylor, 'Alien Abduction Stress', http://www.phenomenamagazine.com, 8 December 2003.

6 E.g. see Mack, *Abduction*, p. 3; Mack, *Passport to the Cosmos*, pp. 36–8.

7 Mack, *Passport to the Cosmos*, p. 25.

[8] Brian Appleyard in conversation with John Mack, *Sunday Times*, London, 3 October 2004, News Review, p. 7.

[9] John Mack, personal communication, 2 April 2004.

[10] John Mack, personal communication, 5 May 2004.

[11] Brian Appleyard in conversation with John Mack, *Sunday Times*, London, 3 October 2004, News Review, p. 7.

[12] Mack, *Abduction*, p. 146.

[13] ibid., p. 181.

[14] ibid., p. 277.

[15] David M. Jacobs, *Secret Life: Firsthand Documented Accounts of UFO Abductions*, Simon and Schuster, New York, 1993, p. 53.

[16] ibid., p. 214.

[17] Dennis Stillings (Ed.), 'Cyber-Biological Studies of the Imaginal Component in the UFO Contact Experience', *Archaeus*, Vol. 5, 1989, pp. 119–20.

[18] Mack, *Passport to the Cosmos*, pp. 73–4.

[19] Mack, *Abduction*, p. 161.

[20] Mack, *Passport to the Cosmos*, p. 65.

[21] ibid., p. 69.

[22] Mack, *Abduction*, pp. 378–9.

[23] ibid., p. 379.

[24] Mircea Eliade, *Shamanism: Archaic Techniques of Ecstasy*, Princeton University Press, 1972, p. 141.

[25] Holger Kalweit, *Shamans, Healers and Medicine Men*, Shambhala, Boston and London, 1992, p. 35.

[26] Holger Kalweit, *Dreamtime and Inner Space: The World of the Shaman*, Shambhala, Boston and London, 1988, p. 50.

[27] ibid.

[28] Bradford Keeney, *Ropes to God: Experiencing the Bushman Spiritual Universe*, Rolling Rocks Press, 2003, pp. 38, 42.

[29] ibid., p. 43.

[30] ibid., p. 83.

[31] ibid., p. 99.

[32] Joan Halifax, *Shamanic Voices: A Survey of Visionary Narratives*, Penguin Compass, New York, 1991, p. 61.

[33] Eliade, *Shamanism*, p. 226.

[34] Cited in Thomas A. Dowson, 'Like People in Prehistory', *World Archaeology*, Vol. 29 (3), p. 333.

[35] Holger Kalweit, *Shamans, Healers and Medicine Men*, p. 37.

[36] Eliade, *Shamanism*, p. 50.

[37] G. Reichel-Dolmatoff, *The Shaman and the Jaguar: A Study of Narcotic*

Drugs amongst the Tukano Indians of Colombia, Temple University Press, Philadelphia, 1975, p. 155.

38 Keeney, *Ropes to God*, p. 41.

39 Thomas E. Bullard, *UFO Abductions: The Measure of a Mystery*, The Fund for UFO Research, 1987, Vol. I, p. 114.

40 ibid., Vol. II, p. C-133.

41 Mack, *Passport to the Cosmos*, pp. 100–1.

42 Jim Schnabel, *Dark White: Aliens, Abductions and the UFO Obsession*, Penguin Books, London, 1994, p. 259.

43 ibid.

44 Mack, *Abduction*, p. 103.

45 ibid., p. 180.

46 ibid., p. 297.

47 ibid., p. 379.

48 He referred to the beings as 'just cute': ibid., p. 379.

49 ibid., p. 297.

50 Patrick Harpur, *Daimonic Reality: A Field Guide to the Otherworld*, Pine Winds Press, Ravensdale, WA, (1994) 2003, pp. 205–7.

51 Budd Hopkins, *The Ongoing Problem of Deception in UFO Abduction Cases*, Special Report No 1, Intruder Foundation, 1990, p. 2.

52 Cited in Harpur, *Daimonic Reality*, p. 190.

53 Schnabel, *Dark White*, p. 174.

54 Mack, *Abduction*, p. 32.

55 Jacobs, *Secret Life*, p. 50.

56 Mack, *Abduction*, pp. 115–16.

57 ibid., p. 115.

58 Cited in Keith Thompson, *Angels and Aliens*, Fawcett Columbine, New York, 1993, pp. 204–5.

59 Hopkins, *The Ongoing Problem of Deception*, p. 2.

60 Mack, *Passport to the Cosmos*, pp. 139–40.

61 ibid., p. 43.

62 ibid., pp. 146–7.

63 ibid., pp. 158–68.

64 ibid., p. 140.

65 Eliade, *Shamanism*, p. 90.

66 ibid., p. 103.

67 ibid., p. 105.

68 Halifax, *Shamanic Voices*, p. 163.

69 Kalweit, *Dreamtime and Inner Space*, pp. 78–9.

70 Halifax, *Shamanic Voices*, p. 184.

71 ibid., p. 185.

72 Webb (1935) cited in Christopher Chippendale, Benjamin Smith and Paul S.C. Tacon, 'Visions of Dynamic Power: Archaic Rock Paintings, Altered States of Consciousness and "Clever Men" in Western Arnhem Land (NT), Australia', *Cambridge Archaeological Journal*, 10:1 (2000), p. 75. Emphasis added.

73 Leroi-Gourhan believed these owls to be therianthropes. See Paul Bahn, *Journey through the Ice Age*, Weidenfeld and Nicolson, London, 1997, p. 156, who adds: 'Indeed in some cases it is not sure whether faces on cave walls belong to owl-like birds or to humanoids.'

74 E.g., see Eliade, *Shamanism*, pp. xii, 33.

75 Mack, *Abduction*, p. 182.

76 ibid.

77 Mack, *Passport to the Cosmos*, pp. 46, 68, 88.

78 ibid., pp. 46, 149.

79 Eliade, *Shamanism*, p. 141.

80 Keeney, *Ropes to God*, p. 44.

81 ibid., p. 71.

82 Luis Eduardo Luna, 'The Concept of Plants as Teachers', *Journal of Ethnopharmacology*, 11 (1984), pp. 141–2

83 ibid., p. 142.

84 See discussion in Richard Evans Schultes, 'Teonanactl, the Narcotic Mushroom of the Aztecs', *American Anthropologist*, NS, 42, 1940, pp. 429–43.

85 Halifax, *Shamanic Voices*, pp. 133–4.

86 ibid., p. 212.

87 Bullard, *UFO Abductions*, Vol. I, p. 119.

88 ibid.

89 Weston La Barre, 'Anthropological Perspectives on Hallucination and Hallucinogens', in Siegel and West (Eds), *Hallucinations: Behaviour, Experience and Theory*, Wiley, New York, 1975, p. 10.

90 Cited in David M. Jacobs, *UFOs and Abductions: Challenging the Borders of Knowledge*, University Press of Kansas, 2000, p. 149.

91 Weston La Barre, 'Anthropological Perspectives on Hallucination and Hallucinogens', pp. 9–10.

92 David Lewis-Williams, *The Mind in the Cave*, Thames and Hudson, London, 2002, p. 129; Jean Clottes and David Lewis-Williams, *The Shamans of Prehistory: Trance and Magic in the Painted Caves*, Harry N. Abrams, New York, 1998, p. 19; and for a more extensive presentation of this point of view see Louis Jolyon West MD, 'A Clinical and Theoretical Overview of Hallucinatory Phenomena', in Siegel and West, *Hallucinations*, pp. 287–311.

93 Clottes and Lewis-Williams, *The Shamans of Prehistory*, p. 19.

94 Substantial caches of the intensely psychoactive red bean-like seeds of a shrub known as *Sophora secundiflora*, dating back more than 9,000 years in some cases, have been found in painted caves across much of north-central Mexico and Texas. In the Lower Pecos River in Texas they are associated with a remarkable complex of 8,000-year-old rock paintings of spirit beings, therianthropes and entoptic patterns. See discussion in Chapter Twenty-Two.

95 Carl Gustav Jung, *Flying Saucers: A Modern Myth of Things Seen in the Sky*, Routledge, London and New York, (1958; 1959) 2002, p. 125.

96 ibid., p. 125.

97 ibid., p. 120.

98 ibid: 'In view of the trend of modern theoretical physics, this assumption [i.e. that all reality is grounded on an as-yet-unknown substrate possessing material and at the same time psychic qualities] should arouse fewer resistances than before.'

Chapter Thirteen: Spirit Love

1 Michael Ripinsky-Naxon, *The Nature of Shamanism: Substance and Function of a Religious Metaphor*, State University of New York Press, 1993, p. 79.

2 Mircea Eliade, *Shamanism: Archaic Techniques of Ecstasy*, Princeton University Press, 1972, p. 77.

3 The full story is told in ibid., pp. 39–42.

4 Andreas Lommel, *Shamanism: The Beginnings of Art*, McGraw-Hill, New York, 1967, p. 62.

5 ibid., pp. 62–3.

6 Holger Kalweit, *Shamans, Healers and Medicine Men*, Shambhala, Boston and London, 1992, p. 11.

7 G. Reichel-Dolmatoff, *The Shaman and Jaguar: A Study of Narcotic Drugs amongst The Tukano Indians of Colombia*, Temple University Press, Philadelphia, 1975, pp. 51–2.

8 ibid., p. 52.

9 Eliade, *Shamanism*, p. 75.

10 ibid., pp. 76–7.

11 ibid., p. 72. As we would expect, this spirit woman is also a therianthrope and sometimes appears as a wolf and a winged tiger.

12 Warao, see Joan Halifax, *Shamanic Voices: A Survey of Visionary Narratives*, Penguin Compass, New York, 1991, pp. 226 ff.; Tobacco, see William Emboden, *Narcotic Plants: Hallucinogens, Stimulants, Inebriants, and Hypnotics, their Origins and Uses*, Studio Vista, London, 1979, pp. 35ff.

[13] See John Mack, *Abduction: Human Encounters with Aliens*, Simon and Schuster, London, 1995, pp. 37, 207, 211, etc.; Dennis Stillings (Ed.), 'Cyber-Biological Studies of the Imaginal Component in the UFO Contact Experience', *Archaeus*, Vol. 5, 1989, pp. 153ff.; John Mack, *Passport to the Cosmos: Human Transformation and Alien Encounters*, Thorsons, London, 2000, pp. 19, 57, 139ff.

[14] John Mack, *Passport to the Cosmos*, pp. 19, 57, 230.

[15] Halifax, *Shamanic Voices*, pp. 226–32.

[16] Hartland, cited in Jacques Vallee, *Passport to Magonia: On UFOs. Folklore and Parallel Worlds*, Contemporary Books, Chicago, 1969, 1993, p. 42.

[17] ibid.

[18] Eliade, *Shamanism*, p. 423.

[19] ibid.

[20] ibid., pp. 423–4; Holger Kalweit, *Dreamtime and Inner Space: The World of the Shaman*, Shambhala, London and Boston, 1998, pp. 130–1.

[21] Eliade, *Shamanism*, p. 424.

[22] Kalweit, *Dreamtime and Inner Space*, p. 132. See also Eliade, *Shamanism*, p. 423.

[23] Kalweit, *Dreamtime and Inner Space*, pp. 141–2.

[24] Sy Montgomery, *Journey of the Pink Dolphin: An Amazon Quest*, Touchstone/Simon and Schuster, New York, 2000, pp. 18–19.

[25] ibid., p. 271.

[26] ibid., p. 270; Luis Eduardo Luna, *Vegetalismo: Shamanism among the Mestizo Population of the Peruvian Amazon*, Acta Universitatis Stockholmiensis, Stockholm Studies in Comparative Religion, Almqvist and Wicksell Publishers, Stockholm, 1986, p. 84.

[27] Sy Montgomery, *Journey of the Pink Dolphin*, p. 270.

[28] Luna, *Vegetalismo*, p. 86.

[29] ibid., p. 83: 'The offspring of a mermaid and a human being may become a powerful *vegetalista* [shaman]. Both Don Jose Coral and Don Santiago Murayari told me that when they take ayahuasca and cure, among the spirits they call are *vegetalistas* who live under the water and whose mothers are mermaids.'

[30] Mack, *Abduction*, pp. 38–9.

[31] Mack, *Passport to the Cosmos*, p. 114.

[32] Mack, *Abduction*, pp. 210–11.

[33] David M. Jacobs, *Secret Life: Firsthand Documented Accounts of UFO Abductions*, Simon and Schuster, New York, 1993, p. 15.

[34] ibid., p. 206.

[35] ibid.

[36] ibid., p. 39.

37 Villas-Boas, cited in ibid.
38 Jim Schnabel, *Dark White: Aliens, Abductions and the UFO Obsession*, Penguin Books, London, 1994, pp. 22–3.
39 Mack, *Abduction*, pp. 319–20.
40 See, for example, Mack, *Passport to the Cosmos*, p. 114, and Jacobs, *Secret Life*, p. 104.
41 Jacobs, *Secret Life*, p. 206.
42 Mack, *Passport to the Cosmos*, p. 120.
43 Jacobs, *Secret Life*, p. 122.
44 Mack, *Abduction*, p. 132.
45 ibid., p. 157.
46 Jacobs, *Secret Life*, pp. 154–5.
47 ibid., pp. 156–7.
48 Mack, *Passport to the Cosmos*, p. 140.
49 Mack, *Abduction*, p. 116.
50 ibid., p. 17.
51 Jacobs, *Secret Life*, p. 164.
52 Mack, *Cosmos*, pp. 124–5; Mack, *Abduction*, p. 414.
53 Jacobs, *Secret Life*, p. 168.
54 ibid., p. 170.
55 ibid., p. 178.
56 ibid., p. 186.
57 Mack, *Abduction*, pp. 322–3.
58 Sy Montgomery, *Journey of the Pink Dolphin*, p. 270; Luna, *Vegetalismo*, pp. 84, 86.
59 Mack, *Passport to the Cosmos*, p. 253.
60 Jacobs, *Secret Life*, p. 272.
61 Cited in Schnabel, *Dark White*, p. 61.
62 ibid.
63 Jacobs, *Secret Life*, p. 166.
64 Mack, *Passport to the Cosmos*, p. 117.
65 ibid.
66 Mack, *Abduction*, p. 323.
67 Jacobs, *Secret Life*, p. 172.
68 Compare Diane Purkiss, *Troublesome Things: A History of Fairies and Fairy Stories*, Penguin, London, 2000, p. 60: 'Why did fairies want babies? No one knows.'

Chapter Fourteen: The Secret Commonwealth

[1] Carl Gustav Jung, *Flying Saucers: A Modern Myth of Things Seen in the Sky*, Routledge, London and New York, (1958; 1959) 2002, p. 1.

[2] ibid., p. 19.

[3] ibid.

[4] ibid., p. 123.

[5] ibid., p. 105.

[6] Broadsheet of Samuel Coccius, cited in ibid.

[7] ibid., p. 106.

[8] ibid.

[9] ibid., p. 109.

[10] Supposedly representing 'the fates that preside over the awakening of the soul', ibid., p. 113.

[11] Jung assimilates the figure with the devil.

[12] ibid., pp. 110–13.

[13] Jim Schnabel, *Dark White: Aliens, Abductions and the UFO Obsession*, Penguin Books, London, 1994, p. 151.

[14] Jacques Vallee, *Passport to Magonia: On UFOs, Folklore and Parallel Worlds*, Contemporary Books, Chicago, 1969, 1993.

[15] ibid., p. 179.

[16] ibid., p. 4.

[17] ibid., p. 180.

[18] ibid., pp. 179ff.

[19] ibid., pp. 9–10.

[20] ibid., pp. 4–5.

[21] ibid., p. 5.

[22] ibid., p. 6.

[23] ibid., p. 3.

[24] Winged discs of Sumer and Egypt: see discussion in Jeremy Black and Anthony Green, *Gods, Demons and Symbols of Ancient Mesopotamia: An Illustrated Dictionary*, British Museum Press, 1992, pp. 185–6; Vimanas: See for example David Hatcher Childress, *Vimana Aircraft of Ancient India and Atlantis*, Adventures Unlimited Press, Stelle, IL., 1991; China: Edward H. Schafer, *Pacing the Void: T'ang Approaches to the Stars*, University of California Press, Berkeley, 1977, p. 146.

[25] II Kings 2:11.

[26] Ezekiel 1:4–19.

[27] Psalms 68:17.

[28] Isaiah 13:5.

29 Genesis 6:2, 4.

30 Vallee, *Passport to Magonia*, p. 57.

31 ibid. See in particular chapters 3 and 4.

32 ibid., p. 64.

33 Peter Narvez (Ed.), *The Good People: New Fairylore Essays*, The University Press of Kentucky, (1991) 1997, p. 98.

34 For Kirk see ibid., p. 100; for antiquity of usage of term 'fairy' see Purkiss, *Troublesome Things: A History of Fairies and Fairy Stories*, Penguin, London, 2000, pp. 11–12ff., 73; Narvez, *The Good People*, pp. 159, 463.

35 W.Y. Evans-Wentz, *The Fairy Faith in Celtic Countries*, New Page Books, Franklin Lakes, NJ, 2004 (fascimile reprint of original 1911 edition with a modern Introduction by Carl McColeman), p. 224, note 20.

36 Walter Scott, *Demonology and Witchcraft* (1830), cited in Narvez, *The Good People*, pp. 100–1.

37 Evans-Wentz, *The Fairy Faith in Celtic Countries*.

38 ibid., p. 110.

39 Vallee, *Passport to Magonia*, p. 50.

40 Narvez, *The Good People*, p. 201.

41 Janet Bord, *Fairies: Real Encounters with Little People*, Michael O'Mara Books, 1997, pp. 5–6.

42 Narvez, *The Good People*, p. 481; Evans-Wentz, *The Fairy Faith in Celtic Countries*, p. 159.

43 Narvez, *Good People*, p. 484.

44 Vallee, *Passport to Magonia*, pp. 58–9.

45 E.g. see ibid., pp. 101–5, 116–19.

46 ibid., p. 105.

47 Kirk, *Secret Commonwealth*, cited in Purkiss, *Troublesome Things*, p. 185.

48 David M. Jacobs, *Secret Life: Firsthand Documented Accounts of UFO Abductions*, Simon and Schuster, New York, 1993, p. 168.

49 Kirk, *Secret Commonwealth*, cited in Purkiss, *Troublesome Things*, pp. 185–6.

Chapter Fifteen: Here Is a Thing that Will Carry Me Away

1 Peter Narvez (Ed.), *The Good People: New Fairylore Essays*, The University Press of Kentucky, (1991) 1997, pp. 53–4.

2 ibid., p. 54.

3 ibid.

4 ibid.

5 See, for example, David M. Jacobs, *Secret Life: Firsthand Documented Accounts of UFO Abductions*, Simon and Schuster, New York, 1993, p. 158; John Mack,

Abduction: Human Encounters with Aliens, Simon and Schuster, London, 1995, pp. 38–39, 416.

6 Jim Schnabel, *Dark White: Aliens, Abductions and the UFO Obsession*, Penguin Books, London, 1994, p. 153.

7 ibid., p. 258.

8 Mack, *Abduction*, p. 396.

9 ibid.

10 ibid.

11 ibid.

12 John Mack, *Passport to the Cosmos: Human Transformation and Alien Encounters*, Thorsons, London, 2000, p. 144.

13 Or in more recent times. A Victorian Shetlander described fairies as having a 'yellow complexion . . . red eyes and green teeth', while in the Orkneys in the same period one informant described a fairy as 'a small man about a foot high clad in green and red'. Narvez, *Good People*, p. 134.

14 Janet Bord, *Fairies: Real Enbcounters with Little People*, Michael O'Mara Books, 1997, pp. 55–6.

15 ibid., p. 57.

16 For a discussion of fairies and the colour green see Purkiss, *Troublesome Things: A History of Fairies and Fairy Stories*, Penguin, London, 2000, pp. 63–4: 'fairies are always linked with green'.

17 Valerii I. Sarnov, 'On The Nature of Flying Saucers and Little Green Men', *Current Anthropology*, Vol. 22, No. 2, April 1981, p. 165.

18 Jacques Vallee, *Passport to Magonia: On UFOs, Folklore and Parallel Worlds*, Contemporary Books, Chicago, 1969, 1993, pp. 43–4.

19 Narvez (Ed.), *The Good People*, p. 126.

20 Cited in Bord, *Fairies*, pp. 125–6.

21 ibid., p. 126.

22 Bord, *Fairies*, p. 126.

23 Mack, *Passport to the Cosmos*, p. 69.

24 Jacobs, *Secret Life*, p. 162: 'Abductees nearly always say that the aliens attending the babies are females.' See also pp. 104, 226.

25 Mack, *Abduction*, p. 37.

26 ibid.

27 Jacobs, *Secret Life*, pp. 271–2.

28 W. Y. Evans-Wentz, *The Fairy Faith in Celtic Countries*, New Page Books, Franklin Lakes, NJ, 2004, p. 297.

29 Purkiss, *Troublesome Things*, p. 68.

30 Evans-Wentz, *The Fairy Faith*, p. 156.

31 Narvez (Ed.), *The Good People*, p. 245.

[32] Evans-Wentz, *The Fairy Faith*, pp. 204–5.

[33] ibid., p. 205.

[34] ibid., p. 267.

[35] Purkiss, *Troublesome Things*, pp. 146–7.

[36] ibid., Plates 5 and 6.

[37] ibid., Plate 9; Bord, *Fairies*, p. 10.

[38] Bord, *Fairies*, pp. 113–14.

[39] Purkiss, *Troublesome Things*, p. 89: 'When these women talked about fairies, interrogators thought they were hearing about a pact with the devil . . .'

[40] ibid., p. 88.

[41] ibid., p. 89.

[42] Cited in ibid., p. 89.

[43] ibid., p. 110: 'The fairy man gives Katherine knowledge, and knowledge is power. He gives her magical weapons which allow her to cure her cows, and do anything else she wishes.'

[44] ibid.

[45] ibid.

[46] ibid., pp. 116–17.

[47] ibid., p. 60: 'Why did fairies want babies? No one knows.'

[48] ibid., p. 116: 'She [Susan Swapper] is expecting a child, and in her mind, this makes her a target.'

[49] ibid., pp. 116–17.

[50] E.g. see Mack, *Abduction*, p. 277.

[51] Jacobs, *Secret Life*, p. 55.

[52] Patrick Harpur, *Daimonic Reality: A Field Guide to the Otherworld*, Pine Winds Press, Ravensdale, WA, (1994) 2003, p. 214.

[53] Purkiss, *Troublesome Things*, pp. 73–4.

[54] Narvez (Ed.) *The Good People*, p. 491 and see also p. 169; Evans-Wentz, *The Fairy Faith*, p. 9.

[55] Cited in Purkiss, *Troublesome Things*, p. 58.

[56] Detailed first-hand reports and descriptions of changelings are best known from Europe where ethnographers worked assiduously in the 19th and 20th centuries to preserve and record all aspects of fairy lore in the face of rapid social and economic change. But traditions and experiences involving changelings are by no means limited to Europe. The same 'bizarre tale of a supernatural race exchanging one of their own ill-thriven infants . . . for a handsome human infant' is globally distributed and detailed examples have been recorded from as far afield as Egypt, India, China and America's Pacific northwest. See Joyce Underwood Munro in Narvez, *Good People*, op. cit., p. 251.

[57] Cited in ibid., p. 221.

58 Cited in ibid., p. 34.

59 Evans-Wentz, *Fairy Faith*, p. 115.

60 Narvez, *Good People*, p. 220.

61 ibid., p. 225.

62 ibid., p. 234.

63 ibid., p. 258.

64 ibid., p. 257.

65 Jacobs, *Secret Life*, p. 272.

66 Karen, cited in ibid., pp. 277–8.

67 Melissa, cited in ibid., p. 272.

68 Jacobs, *Secret Life*, pp. 172–3.

69 ibid., p. 166.

70 Mack, *Passport to the Cosmos*, p. 117.

71 ibid.

72 Cited in Schnabel, *Dark White*, p. 61.

73 Mack, *Abduction*, p. 323.

74 John Mack in David M. Jacobs (Ed.), *UFOs and Abductions: Challenging the Borders of Knowledge*, University Press of Kansas, 2000, p. 253.

75 Mack, *Abduction*, p. 39.

76 Harpur, *Daimonic Reality*, pp. 210–13.

77 ibid., pp. 213–14.

78 Thomas E. Bullard, *UFO Abductions: The Measure of a Mystery*, The Fund for UFO Research, 1987, Vol. II, p. C 184.

79 Patrick Harpur, *The Philosopher's Secret Fire: A History of the Imagination*, Ivan R. Dee, Chicago, 2003, p. 22.

80 In Narvez, *The Good People*, p. 493.

81 Cited in Harpur, *The Philosopher's Secret Fire*, p. 22.

82 Cited in Bord, *Fairies*, p. 93.

83 Cited in ibid., pp. 93–4.

84 Purkiss, *Troublesome Things*, p. 69.

85 Cited in Vallee, *Passport to Magonia*, p. 105.

86 Narvez, *Good People*, p. 258, 'But always the changeling bears a physical resemblance to the real child . . .'

87 Evans-Wentz, *Fairy Faith*, p. 98.

88 E.g. see Mack, *Passport to the Cosmos*, p. 112.

Chapter Sixteen: Dancers between Worlds

1 John Mack, *Passport to the Cosmos: Human Transformation and Alien Encounters*, Thorsons, London, 2000, p. 69.

[2] John Mack, *Abduction: Human Encounters with Aliens*, Simon and Schuster, London, 1995, pp. 210–11.

[3] Cited in Peter Narvez (Ed.), *The Good People: New Faiylore Essays*, The University Press of Kentucky, (1991) 1997, p. 482.

[4] ibid., p. 482.

[5] W.Y. Evans-Wentz, *The Fairy Faith in Celtic Countries*, New Page Books, Franklin Lakes, NJ, 2004, p. 208.

[6] Cited in Janet Bord, *Fairies: Real Encounters with Little People*, Michael O'Mara Books, 1997, p. 27.

[7] Evans-Wentz, *Fairy Faith*, p. 90.

[8] Narvez, *Good People*, p. 482.

[9] Jacques Vallee, *Passport to Magonia: On UFOs, Folklore and Parallel Worlds*, Contemporary Books, Chicago, (1969) 1993, p. 38.

[10] Narvez (Ed.), *The Good People*, p. 465.

[11] Evans-Wentz, *The Fairy Faith*, p. 208.

[12] Cited in Bord, *Fairies*, p. 27.

[13] Evans-Wentz, *Fairy Faith*, p. 137.

[14] ibid., p. 156.

[15] ibid., p. 76.

[16] Cited in ibid., p. 248

[17] ibid., p. 137.

[18] David M. Jacobs, *Secret Life: Firsthand Documented Accounts of UFO Abductions*, Simon and Schuster, New York, 1993, p. 222.

[19] Evans-Wentz, *Fairy Faith*, p. 91.

[20] ibid.

[21] Jacobs, *Secret Life*, p. 226: 'the physical description is not unique enough to suggest anatomical differences'.

[22] ibid., p. 223.

[23] ibid., p. 226.

[24] For example, see Mack, *Abduction*, p. 37: 'The greys are mainly two kinds – smaller drone *or insect-like workers*, who move or glide robotically outside and inside the ships and perform various tasks, and a slightly taller leader or "doctor" as the abductees most often call him' (emphasis added).

[25] Narvez (Ed.), *The Good People*, p. 496. See also: Evans-Wentz, *The Fairy Faith*, p. 177: 'The land of pixy was supposed to be able to render its devotees invisible, if they only anointed their eyes with a certain green salve made of secret herbs gathered from Kerris-moor. In the invisible condition thus induced, people were able to join pixy revels, during which, according to the old tradition, time slipped away very, very rapidly . . .' ibid., p. 153: 'As a race, the Tylwyth Teg [fairies] were described as having the power of invisibility; and

it was believed they could disappear like a spirit while one happened to be observing them. The world in which they lived was a world quite unlike ours . . .'

26 Jacobs, *Secret Life*, p. 220.

27 Aliens, e.g. see Mack, *Abduction*, pp. 19, 279; Mack, *Passport to the Cosmos*, pp. 45, 71. Fairies: see Evans-Wentz, *The Fairy Faith*, p. 93: 'Fairies passing through stone walls', and p. 148: 'When I was a boy here on the Island [Anglesey, Wales], the *Tylwyth Teg* [fairies] were described as a race of little beings no larger than children six or seven years old, who visited farmhouses at night after all the family were abed. No matter how securely closed a house might be, the *Tylwyth Teg* had no trouble to get in.'

28 E.g. see Mack, *Abduction*, pp. 19, 279; Mack, *Passport to the Cosmos*, pp. 45, 71.

29 Mack in David M. Jacobs (Ed.), *UFOs and Abductions: Challenging the Borders of* Knowledge, University Press of Kansas, 2000, pp. 254–5.

30 Jacobs, *Secret Life*, p. 51.

31 ibid.

32 Mack, *Passport to the Cosmos*, p. 57.

33 Patrick Harpur, *The Philosopher's Secret Fire: A History of the Imagination*, Ivan R. Dee, Chicago, 2003, p. 179: 'Encounters with the Sidhe often include a "touch", or a "stroke" which leaves us tender, scarred, even witless. Contact with UFOs or "aliens" often includes a zap from a beam of light or a ray-gun, which leaves the contactee dizzy, sick, disoriented, "touched", numb or irradiated.'

34 Narvez, *The Good People*, p. 491.

35 ibid., pp. 10–11

36 ibid., p. 225: A man takes a short cut across marshy land. 'And halfway across he got a jab in the left leg, in the calf of the left leg, sort of like something jabbed him. Well, he went on home and it felt troublesome and so on and so forth. It felt troublesome, felt troublesome. And 'twas beginning to protrude, expand, turn black up to the knee and down to the ankle, and they got a doctor in. And the doctor cut this open and out comes little bunches of grass and little splinters of wood, out of this man's leg. There was so much damage done, they cut the man's leg off up to the knee.'

37 Cited in Patrick Harpur, *Daimonic Reality: A Field Guide to the Otherworld*, Pine Winds Press, Ravensdale, WA, (1994) 2003, p. 195.

38 See, for example, Vallee, *Passport to Magonia*, pp. 45–8.

39 Narvez, *The Good People*, pp. 491–2.

40 Harpur, *The Philosopher's Secret Fire*, pp. 11–12.

41 Cited in Bord, *Fairies*, p. 27.

[42] Evans-Wentz, *Fairy Faith*, p. 98.

[43] ibid.

[44] ibid.

[45] Cited in Bord, Fairies, p. 25.

[46] Cited in ibid.

[47] Evans-Wentz, *Fairy Faith*, p. 208.

[48] ibid.

[49] Cited in Bord, *Fairies*, p. 26.

[50] Cited in ibid., p. 39.

[51] ibid., pp. 41–2.

[52] ibid., p. 30.

[53] ibid., p. 36.

[54] Cited in ibid., p. 31

[55] Cited in ibid., pp. 81–2.

[56] ibid., p. 82.

[57] ibid.

[58] Jacques Vallee was the first to point this out. See Vallee, *Passport to Magonia*, pp. 105–6, 162.

[59] Bord, *Fairies*, p. 128.

[60] Narvez (Ed.), *The Good People*, p. 186.

[61] ibid., p. 183.

[62] ibid., pp. 183–4.

[63] ibid., p. 191.

[64] Evans-Wentz, *Fairy Faith*, p. 182.

[65] ibid., p. 175.

[66] Harpur, *Daimonic Reality*, pp. 142–3.

[67] Cited in Bord, *Fairies*, p. 29, emphasis added.

[68] Narvez, *The Good People*, p. 161: 'The various methods of getting in and out of this magical realm [Fairyland] . . . include open caves, magical rocks, and underground passages, as well as lakes, pools, river banks, marshy ground. It was also possible to enter the otherworld through fairy circles and rings.'

[69] Evans-Wentz, *The Fairy Faith*, p. 448.

[70] See Bord, *Fairies*, p. 3.

[71] Vallee, *Passport to Magonia*, p. 107.

[72] In general on this phenomenon amongst abductees see Budd Hopkins, *Missing Time: A Documented Study of UFO Abductions*, Richard Marek Publishers, New York, 1981.

Chapter Seventeen: Tuning in to Channel DMT

1 As noted in earlier chapters, it is highly probable that rock art older than the oldest in Europe will eventually be found in Africa. The problem is that huge areas of the continent have received little attention from archaeologists interested in the emergence of modern human behaviour.

2 *Nature*, 17 Feb 2005, cited in *The Times*, London, 17 Feb 2005, p. 23, reports the discovery of anatomically modern human remains in Ethiopia dated to 196,000 years ago. Such a date for the emergence of anatomically modern humans, supported by DNA studies, confirms that 'there was a great time gap between the appearance of the modern skeleton and modern behaviour'.

3 Rick Strassman MD, *DMT: The Spirit Molecule: A Doctor's Revolutionary Research into the Biology of Near-Death and Mystical Experiences*, Park Street Press, Rochester, Vermont, 2001, pp. 36–7.

4 ibid., pp. 34–5.

5 Alexander Shulgin and Anne Shulgin, *Tikhal: The Continuation*, Transform Press, Berkeley, 1997, p. 249. TIKHAL is an acronym. It stands for Tryptamines I Have Known And Loved.

6 Strassman, *DMT*, p. 42.

7 See for example ibid., pp. 276–7.

8 ibid., pp. 216–19.

9 Purkiss, *Troublesome Things: A History of Fairies and Fairy Stories*, Penguin, London, 2000, p. 66.

10 Paul Bahn, *Journey through the Ice Age*, Weidenfeld and Nicolson, London, 1997, p. 58.

Chapter Eighteen: Amongst the Machine Elves

1 Rick Strassman MD, *DMT: The Spirit Molecule: A Doctor's Revolutionary Research into the Biology of Near-Death and Mystical Experiences*, Park Street Press, Rochester, Vermont, 2001, p. 194.

2 ibid., p. 147.

3 ibid., pp. 215–16.

4 ibid., p. 164.

5 ibid., p. 169.

6 ibid., p. 192.

7 ibid., p. 213.

8 Benny Shanon, *The Antipodes of the Mind: Charting the Phenomenology of the Ayahuasca Experience*, Oxford University Press, 2002, p. 128.

9 Michael Harner, *The Way of the Shaman*, Harper, San Francisco, (1980) 1990, p. 3.

10 John Mack, *Abduction: Human Encounters with Aliens*, Simon and Schuster, London, 1995, p. 396.

11 Janet Bord, *Fairies: Real Encounters with Little People*, Michael O'Mara Books, 1997, pp. 55–6.

12 Cited in Joan Halifax, *Shamanic Voices: A Survey of Visionary Narratives*, Penguin Compass, New York, 1991, pp. 195–6.

13 Cited in ibid., p. 204.

14 Cited in ibid., p. 212.

15 Cited in ibid., p. 131.

16 *Encyclopaedia Britannica*, Micropedia, 3:402.

17 Strassman, *DMT*, pp. 53–4.

18 ibid., p. 54.

19 ibid., p. 292.

20 ibid.

21 ibid., p. 185.

22 ibid., p. 173.

23 ibid., p. 188.

24 ibid., p. 213.

25 ibid., pp. 243–4.

26 See Chapters Eleven and Twelve.

27 Strassman, *DMT*, p. 180.

28 ibid., p. 181.

29 ibid., p. 193.

30 ibid., pp. 189–90.

31 ibid., p. 180.

32 ibid., p. 182.

33 ibid., p. 193.

34 ibid., pp. 198–9.

35 ibid., p. 199.

36 ibid., pp. 196–7.

37 ibid., p. 197.

38 ibid., p. 208.

39 ibid., p. 209.

40 ibid., pp. 206–7.

41 See Chapter Thirteen.

42 See Chapter Four.

43 See Chapter Thirteen.

44 Strassman, *DMT*, p. 206.

[45] ibid., pp. 209–10.

[46] ibid., p. 189.

[47] ibid.

[48] See discussion in Lewis-Jolyon West MD, 'A Clinical and Theoretical Overview of Hallucinatory Phenomena', in R. Siegel and J. West (Eds), *Hallucinations: Behaviour, Experience and Theory*, Wiley, New York, 1975, pp. 287–311, and particularly pp. 299–301. See also J.D. Lewis-Williams and T.A. Dowson, 'The Signs of All Times', *Current Anthropology*, Vol. 29, No. 2, p. 204.

[49] Strassman, *DMT*, p. 171.

[50] ibid., pp. 224–5.

[51] ibid., p. 193.

[52] ibid., p. 187.

[53] S. Szara MD PhD and Z. Boszormenyi MD PhD, 'Dimethyltryptamine Experiments with Psychotics', *Journal of Mental Science*, 104, 1958, p. 446.

[54] William J. Turner MD and Sidney Merlis MD, 'Effect of some Indolealkylamines on Man', *AMA Archives of Neurology and Psychiatry*, 81, 1959, pp. 121–9.

[55] Timothy Leary, 'Programmed Communication during Experiences with DMT', *The Psychedelic Review*, 8, 1966, pp. 83–95.

[56] Strassman, *DMT*, p. 216: Strassman speaks of 'the striking resemblance between these naturally occurring contacts and those reported in our DMT study. This remarkable overlap may ease our acceptance of my proposition that the alien abduction experience is made possible by excessive brain levels of DMT.'

[57] ibid., p. 48.

[58] ibid., p. 216.

[59] ibid., p. 178.

[60] ibid., p. 208.

[61] ibid., pp. 344–5.

[62] ibid., p. 147.

[63] ibid., p. 344.

[64] David M. Jacobs, *Secret Life: Firsthand Documented Accounts of UFO Abductions*, Simon and Schuster, New York, 1993, p. 147.

[65] Mack, *Abduction*, p. 83.

[66] ibid., p. 388.

[67] John Mack, *Passport to the Cosmos: Human Transformation and Alien Encounters*, Thorsons, London, 2000, p. 101.

[68] ibid.

[69] See Chapter Two.

[70] Strassman, *DMT*, p. 318.

[71] ibid., pp. 320–1.

[72] See Chapter Three.

73 Strassman, *DMT*, p. 206.

74 ibid., p. 176.

75 ibid.

76 ibid., pp. 177–8.

77 ibid., p. 179.

78 ibid., p. 178.

79 Jeremy Narby, *The Cosmic Serpent: DNA and the Origins of Knowledge*, Victor Gollancz, London, 1998, p. 100.

Chapter Nineteen: Ancient Teachers in Our DNA?

1 Terence McKenna and Dennis McKenna, *The Invisible Landscape: Mind, Hallucinogens and the I Ching*, Harper, San Francisco, (1975) 1993. See Chapter 6, pp. 95 ff: 'An experiment at La Chorrea'. Sadly Terence McKenna died on 3 April 2000.

2 ibid., p. 104.

3 Bruce Lamb, *Rio Tigre and Beyond*, p. 2, cited in Jeremy Narby, *The Cosmic Serpent: DNA and the Origins of Knowledge*, Victor Gollancz, London, 1998, p. 203.

4 First published as *Le serpent cosmique, L'AND et les origins du savoir*, Georg Editeur SA, Geneva.

5 Narby, *The Cosmic Serpent*, p. 86.

6 ibid., p. 92.

7 ibid., pp. 103–4.

8 ibid., p. 104.

9 ibid., p. 135, citing Jakobson.

10 ibid., p. 88.

11 Molecular biologists Chris Calladine and Horace Drew, cited in ibid., p. 100.

12 ibid., p. 40.

13 Luis Eduardo Luna, 'The Concept of Plants as Teachers', *Journal of Ethnopharmacology*, 11, 1984, p. 135.

14 Luis Eduardo Luna, *Vegetalismo: Shamanism among the Mestizo Population of the Peruvian Amazon*, Acta Universitatis Stockholmensis, Stockholm Studies in Comparative Religion, Almqvist and Wiksell Publishers, Stockholm, 1986, p. 62. See also Glen H. Shepard Jr., 'Psychoactive Plants and Ethnopsychiatric Medicines of the Matsigenka', *Journal of Psychoactive Drugs*, Vol. 30 (4), October-December 1998, pp. 323ff: 'Matsigenka consider hallucinogenic plants to be sentient beings with superhuman souls, described as "owner", "master" or "mother" of the plant.'

15 Cited in Luna, *Vegetalismo*, p. 62. Emphasis added.

[16] ibid., p. 65.

[17] Luna, 'The Concept of Plants as Teachers', p. 142.

[18] ibid.

[19] ibid., p. 141.

[20] ibid., p. 139.

[21] Benny Shanon, *The Antipodes of the Mind: Charting the Phenomenology of the Ayahuasca Experience*, Oxford University Press, 2002, p. 251.

[22] Bradford Keeney, *Ropes to God: Experiencing the Bushman Spiritual Universe*, Rolling Rocks Press, 2003, p. 44 (emphasis added).

[23] ibid., p. 71 (emphasis added).

[24] Shanon, *The Antipodes of the Mind*, p. 8.

[25] ibid., p. 109.

[26] ibid., p. 302.

[27] ibid., p. 44. Shanon reports that a total of 178 persons were interviewed, 122 males and 56 females. Of the informants, 16 were indigenous or persons of mixed race, 106 were residents of the urban regions of South America, and 56 were foreigners, that is, persons residing outside South America. Shanon estimates that the total number of ayahuasca sessions probed in these interviews is of the order of 2,500.

[28] ibid., p. 120

[29] Jeremy Narby and Francis Huxley (Eds) *Shamans through Time*, Thames and Hudson, London, 2001, p. 302.

[30] See Rick Strassman MD, *DMT: The Spirit Molecule: A Doctor's Revolutionary Research into the Biology of Near-Death and Mystical Experiences*, Park Street Press, Rochester, Vermont, 2001, pp. 34–6.

[31] Francis Crick, *Life Itself: Its Origin and Nature*, Futura Macdonald, London, 1982, pp. 171–3.

[32] Strassman, *DMT*, p. 34.

[33] *Daily Mail*, London, 8 August 2004, pp. 44–5.

[34] Shanon, *The Antipodes of the Mind*, Epigraph.

[35] Francis Crick, *The Astonishing Hypothesis: The Scientific Search for the Soul*, Touchstone Books, London, 1995.

[36] Francis Crick, *Of Molecules and Men*, Prometheus Books, New York, (1966) 2004, pp. 69–70

[37] Crick, *Life Itself*. See in particular pp. 113–40.

Chapter Twenty: The Hurricane in the Junkyard

[1] Cited in Jeremy Narby, *The Cosmic Serpent: DNA and the Origins of Knowledge*, Victor Gollancz, London, 1998, p. 59.

[2] Fred Hoyle and Chandra Wickramsinghe, *Lifecloud: The Origin of Life in the Universe*, J.M. Dent and Sons, London and Toronto, 1978.

[3] Lyn Margulis and Dorion Sagan, *Micro-Cosmos: Four Billion Years of Microbial Evolution*, Summit Books, New York, 1986, p. 43.

[4] ibid., p. 51.

[5] ibid., p. 51.

[6] ibid., pp. 71–2. The sedimentary rocks of the Isua formation in Eastern Labrador and southwestern Greenland are 3.8 billion years old and believed to be 'the graveyards of what were flourishing films and scums of Archean bacteria'.

[7] ibid., p. 70. The discovery was made in rocks of the Kromberg Formation, Swaziland.

[8] Francis Crick, *Life Itself: Its Origin and Nature*, Futura Macdonald, London, 1982, p. 15.

[9] ibid., pp. 44–5.

[10] Deoxyribonucleic acid and ribonucleic acid.

[11] See Crick, *Life Itself*, pp. 46, 171–5.

[12] ibid., p. 46.

[13] David S. Goodsell, *The Machinery of Life*, Copernicus, New York, 1998, pp. 60–1.

[14] Narby, *The Cosmic Serpent*, pp. 99, 143, 212,; see also Crick, *Life Itself*, p. 46.

[15] Crick, *Life Itself*, p. 46.

[16] ibid.

[17] ibid., pp. 171–2.

[18] ibid., p. 51.

[19] Narby, *The Cosmic Serpent*, p. 86.

[20] Chris R. Calladine, Horace R. Drew, Ben F. Luisi, Andrew A. Travers, *Understanding DNA: The Molecule and How it Works*, Elsevier Academic Press, 2004, p. 29.

[21] Crick, *Life Itself*, p. 70.

[22] ibid., p. 71.

[23] ibid., p. 88.

[24] Calladine, et al., *Understanding DNA*, p. 10.

[25] ibid.

[26] ibid., p. 13: 'Only a small fraction of the long DNA molecule in a chromosome – about 1 per cent in humans – contains programmes to make specific proteins.'

[27] ibid.

[28] *Science*, Vol. 266, 25 November 1994, p. 1320.

[29] *Science News*, 146 (24), 10 December 1994, p. 391.

[30] ibid.

[31] ibid.

[32] *Science*, Vol. 266, p. 1320.

[33] ibid.

[34] ibid.

[35] *Science News*, 146 (24), p. 391.

[36] *Science*, Vol. 266, op. cit., p. 1320.

[37] ibid.

[38] ibid.

[39] ibid.

[40] 'A study of 191 non-coding sequences of human chromosome 21 revealed that they were more identical among 14 mammalian species than DNA that codes for proteins . . . Recent completion of genome sequencing for many diverse vertebrates has revealed long sequences (at least 200 bp) of non-coding DNA that are identical or nearly identical. Between humans and mice, 481 of these sequences are 100 per cent identical. Between humans and dogs, the sequences are 99 per cent identical. Even between humans and chickens the sequences are 95 per cent identical.' Rich Deem, 'When Junk DNA isn't Junk', http://www.godandscience.org/evolution/junkdna.htm.

[41] 'Invertebrate DNA raises questions about evolution models', *Nature*, 16 December 2003: http://www.nature.com/nsu/031215/031215-2.html.

[42] '"Junk" throws up precious secret,', BBC News Online Science Staff, 12 May 2004: http://news.bbc.co.uk/2/hi/science/nature/3703935.stm

[43] ibid.

[44] Rick Strassman MD, *DMT: The Spirit Molecule: A Doctor's Revolutionary Research into the Biology of Near-Death and Mystical Experiences*, Park Street Press, Rochester, Vermont, 2001, p. 179.

[45] ibid., pp. 177–8.

[46] Michael Harner, *The Way of the Shaman*, Harper, San Francisco, (1980) 1990, p. 4.

[47] Narby, *Cosmic Serpent*, p. 7.

[48] ibid., p. 56.

[49] ibid., p. 104.

[50] ibid.

Chapter Twenty-One: The Hidden Shamans

[1] F.A. Klein, *The Religion of Islam*, Curzon Press, London, (1906) 1971, pp. 5–9.

[2] *Encyclopaedia Britannica*, Micropedia, 9:866.

[3] ibid 8:328, and see discussion in Patrick Harpur, *Daimonic Reality: A Field*

Guide to the Otherworld, Pine Winds Press, Ravensdale, WA, (1994) 2003, p. 136–7.

4 Andrew Wellburn, *Mani, the Angel and the Column of Glory: An Anthology of Manichean Texts*, Floris Books, Edinburgh, pp. 11–13.

5 Acts 9: 3–10.

6 *Encyclopaedia Britannica* 8:396, with specific reference to the Prophet Muhammad, but the remark is applicable to all major religions.

7 Weston La Barre, 'Hallucinogens and the Shamanic Origins of Religion', in Peter Furst (Ed.), *Flesh of the Gods: The Ritual Use of Hallucinogens*, Praeger Publishers, New York, 1972, p. 261.

8 ibid.

9 Aldous Huxley, *The Doors of Perception; Heaven and Hell*, Flamingo Modern Classics, 1994, pp. 11–13, cited in Chapter Eleven.

10 ibid.

11 Founded by Mani in the third century AD, the Manichean religion began as a Christian Gnostic sect (see discussion in Graham Hancock and Robert Bauval, *Talisman: Sacred Cities, Secret Faith*, Michael Joseph, London, 2004, pp. 76–86) and was certainly in touch with other Gnostic movements of the period. It is therefore of interest that the world-renowned ethnomicologist R. Gordon Wasson detected the possible traces of a hallucinogenic mushroom cult amongst the Manicheans, noting that St Augustine's infuriated attacks on them (Augustine was himself a former Manichean) included the accusation that they gratified their appetites with mushrooms; similar accusations in a similar tone of high indignation were made against Manichean sects in China a few centuries later. R. Gordon Wasson, *Soma, Divine Mushroom of Immortality*, Harcourt Brace Jovanovich, New York, 1968 pp. 71–4.

12 Michael Ripinsky-Naxon, *The Nature of Shamanism: Substance and Function of a Religious Metaphor*, State University Press of New York Press, 1993, p. 133.

13 Walter Scott (Ed. and Trans.), *Hermetica: The Ancient Greek and Latin Writings which Contain Religious or Philosophic Teachings Ascribed to Hermes Trismegistus*, Shambhala, Boston, 1993, Excerpt II A, Hermes to Tat, p. 383.

14 ibid., Libellus VI, p. 169.

15 ibid., Excerpt II A, Hermes to Tat, p. 387.

16 James M. Robinson (Ed.), *The Nag Hammadi Library in English*, E.J. Brill, Leiden, 1988; Scott, *Hermetica*. See Hancock and Bauval, *Talisman: Sacred Cities, Secret Faith*, Penguin, London, 2005, Chapter 9, for a study of the close links between Gnosticism and Hermeticism and their overlapping texts such as the Asclepius.

[17] See discussion in Hancock and Bauval, *Talisman*, pp. 131, 149–50.

[18] The heretics were the Cathars of Occitania. See discussion in ibid., Chapters 2–7 and 9, of the truly Gnostic nature of the Cathar religion.

[19] *New Scientist*, 25 December 1987–1 January 1988, 'Father Christmas flies on toadstools', p. 45.

[20] See Ripinsky-Naxon, *The Nature of Shamanism*, op. cit., pp. 2–3.

[21] *The Book of Saints*, A & C. Black, London, (1921) 1989, pp. 500–1.

[22] ibid., p. 556.

[23] ibid., p. 329.

[24] ibid., pp. 519–20.

[25] Cited in Holger Kalweit, *Dreamtime and Inner Space: The World of the Shaman*, Shambhala, London and Boston, 1998, p. 94.

[26] W.Y. Evans-Wentz, *The Fairy Faith in Celtic Countries*, New Page Books, Franklin Lakes, NJ, 2004 (facsimile reprint of original 1911 edition with a modern Introduction by Carl McColeman), pp. 264–5.

[27] ibid., p. 265.

[28] ibid.

[29] Diane Purkiss, *Troublesome Things: A History of Fairies and Fairy Stories*, Penguin, London, 2000, p. 65.

[30] ibid.

[31] ibid., pp. 65–6.

[32] A. Ravier SJ, *Lourdes*, pp. 5–6.

[33] ibid., p. 7.

[34] ibid.

[35] ibid.

[36] ibid., pp. 7–8.

[37] Cited in Harpur, *Daimonic Reality*, pp. 97–8.

[38] A. Ravier, *Lourdes*, p. 10.

[39] Inscription inside the crypt at Lourdes. Personal observation.

[40] *Lourdes Magazine*, Grotto Special, October/November 2003, pp. 28–9.

[41] Paul Bahn, *Journey through the Ice Age*, Weidenfeld and Nicolson, London, 1997, p. 58.

[42] *Lourdes Magazine*, Grotto Special, p. 13.

[43] Jim Schnabel, *Dark White: Aliens, Abductions and the UFO Obsession*, Penguin Books, London, 1994, pp. 126–9; Michael Persinger in David M. Jacobs (Ed.), *UFOs and Abductions: Challenging the Borders of Knowledge*, University Press of Kansas, 2000, pp. 281, 286, 289; Michael Persinger in Dennis Stillings (Ed.), 'Cyber-Biological Studies of the Imaginal Component in the UFO Contact Experience', *Archaeus*, Vol. 5, 1989, pp. 157–71.

[44] Jim Schnabel, *Dark White*, p. 130; Michael Persinger in David M. Jacobs (Ed.),

UFOs and Abductions, pp. 262–302; Michael Persinger in 'Cyber-Biological Studies', pp. 157–71.

45 Michael Persinger in David M. Jacobs, *UFOs and Abductions*, p. 300.

46 ibid.

47 Father Joseph Bordes, *Lourdes: In Bernadette's Footsteps*, MSM, 1991, p. 29.

48 A. Ravier, *Lourdes*, p. 18.

49 Harpur, *Daimonic Reality*, p. 97: Researchers have established that between 1928 and 1975 a total of 230 visions of the Blessed Virgin Mary were acknowledged by the Roman Catholic Church.

50 Cited in Jacques Vallee, *Passport to Magonia: On UFOs, Folklore and Parallel Worlds*, Contemporary Books, Chicago, (1969) 1993, p. 134. I have relied largely on Vallee's account here, pp. 132–5.

51 ibid., pp. 134–5.

52 Harpur, *Daimonic Reality*, p. 100.

53 Jacques Vallee, *The Invisible College*, E.P. Dutton, New York, 1976, pp. 148–9.

54 Harpur, *Daimonic Reality*, p. 101.

55 Jacques Vallee, *The Invisible College*, p. 143.

56 ibid.

57 ibid., pp. 143–4.

58 ibid., p. 144.

59 Cited in ibid., p. 144.

60 ibid., p. 145.

61 Cited in ibid.

62 ibid., p. 146.

63 Cited in ibid., p. 147.

64 Bryan Appleyard, *Aliens: Why They Are Here*, Scribner, London, 2005, p. 138.

65 Vallee, *The Invisible College*, p. 148, Appleyard, *Aliens*, p. 138.

66 Vallee, *The Invisible College*, p. 152.

67 ibid., p. 150.

68 Benny Shanon, 'The Biblical Merkava Vision and Ayahuasca Visions', *Studies in Spirituality*, 2003, 13, p. 34.

69 ibid.

70 ibid., p. 36.

71 Indeed, as well as 'wheels' (e.g. see Benny Shanon, *The Antipodes of the Mind: Charting the Phenomenology of the Ayahuasca Experience*, Oxford University Press, 2002, p. 128) ayahuasca drinkers frequently report specific visions of flying saucers. See the paintings of the Amazonian shaman Pablo Amaringo (in Luis Eduardo Luna and Pablo Amaringo, *Ayahuasca Visions: The Religious Iconography of a Peruvian Shaman*, North Atlantic Books, Berkeley, CA, 1999, and see Shanon, *The Antipodes of the Mind*, p. 122. Disembodied eyes are also

frequently seen in ayahuasca visions. E.g. see Shanon, *The Antipodes of the Mind*, pp. 133, 140.

72 Shanon, 'The Biblical Merkava Vision', p. 35.

73 ibid., p. 40.

74 ibid.

75 Shanon, *The Antipodes of the Mind*, p. 263.

76 ibid.

77 Huxley, *The Doors of Perception*, p. 55.

78 Huston Smith, *Cleansing the Doors of Perception: The Religious Significance of Entheogenic Plants and Chemicals*, J.P. Tarcher/Puttnam, New York, 2000, p. 20.

79 ibid.

80 ibid.: set = the psychological make-up of the individual; setting = the social and physical environment in which the drug is taken.

81 R. Gordon Wasson, Carl A.P. Ruck, Albert Hoffman, *The Road To Eleusis: Unveiling the Secret of the Mysteries*, Harcourt Brace Jovanovich, New York and London, 1978, pp. 78–9.

82 ibid., p. 37.

83 ibid., p. 38 suggests a date of the 14th century BC for the first performance of the ceremony at Eleusis. See p. 76 for the 4th century AD closure of the shrine by Christianity.

84 Paul Devereux, *The Long Trip: A Prehistory of Psychedelia*, Penguin/Arkana, New York, 1997, p. 83.

85 Cited in Wasson et al., *Road to Eleusis*, p. 10.

86 ibid., p. 77.

87 Cited in George Mylonas, *Eleusis and the Eleusinian Mysteries*, Princeton University Press, 1969, p. 285.

88 ibid.

89 ibid., p. 284.

90 Wasson et al., *The Road To Eleusis*, p. 84.

91 Ruck in ibid., p. 80.

92 Cited in ibid.

93 Ruck in ibid., p. 37.

94 ibid., p. 80.

95 Ruck in ibid., p. 81.

96 Ruck in ibid.

97 Hoffman in ibid., p. 23.

98 Hoffman in ibid., p. 33.

99 Hoffman in ibid.

100 ibid., p. 37.

[101] ibid., p. 80; *Encyclopaedia Britannica*, 1:226.

[102] Wasson, Ruck, Hoffman, *The Road to Eleusis*, pp. 48; 80–1.

[103] Devereux, *Long Trip*, p. 82.

[104] Wasson et al., *The Road to Eleusis*, plate 9.

[105] Carl A.P. Ruck in R. Gordon Wasson, Stella Kamrisch, Jonathan Ott, Carl A.P. Ruck, *Persephone's Quest: Entheogens and the Origins of Religion*, Yale University Press, New Haven and London, 1986, p. 160.

[106] Wasson et al., *The Road to Eleusis*, plate 9.

[107] Wasson in Wasson et al., *Persephone's Quest*, p. 32.

[108] Frits Staal, 'How a Psychoactive Substance becomes a ritual: the case of Soma', *Social Research*, Vol. 68, No. 3 (Fall 2001), p. 745.

[109] Rigveda X:119, cited in ibid., pp. 751–2.

[110] Rigveda IX:72, cited in R. Gordon Wasson, 'The Soma of the Rig Veda', *Journal of the American Oriental Society*, 1971, 91(2), p. 175.

[111] Rigveda IX:86 cited in ibid., p. 176.

[112] Rigveda VIII:48 cited in ibid., p. 181.

[113] Mike Crowley, 'The God Who Drank Urine', *Fortean Studies*, Vol. 3, Steve Moore (Ed.), John Brown Publishing, London, 1996, p. 178.

[114] ibid.

[115] ibid.

[116] ibid.

[117] Frits Staal, 'How a Psychoactive Substance', p. 752.

[118] Cited in R. Gordon Wasson, *Soma: The Divine Mushroom of Immortality*, p. 29, and 'The Soma of the Rig Veda', p. 177.

[119] Cited in Wasson, 'The Soma of the Rig Veda', p. 178.

[120] Cited in ibid.

[121] Cited in ibid.

Chapter Twenty-Two: Flesh of the Gods

[1] Michael Ripinsky-Naxon, 'Shamanistic Knowledge and Cosmology', in Helmut Watishcher (Ed.), *Tribal Epistemologies: Essays in the Philosophy of Anthropology*, Ashgate Publishing, Aldershot, 1998, p. 147.

[2] Adrian Recinos, Delia Goetz and Sylvanus G. Morley (Trans.), *Popol Vuh: The Sacred Book of the Ancient Quiche Maya*, University of Oklahoma Press, (1950) 1991, p. 161.

[3] See, for example, Dennis Tedlock (Trans.), *Popol Vuh: The Definitive Edition of the Mayan Book of the Dawn of Life and the Glories of Gods and Kings*, Simon & Schuster, New York, 1996, p. 77.

[4] ibid., p. 97.

[5] Mary Miller and Karl Taube, *The Gods and Symbols of Ancient Mexico and the Maya: An Illustrated Dictionary of Mesoamerican Religion*, Thames and Hudson, London, 1993, p. 136.

[6] Joan Halifax, *Shaman: The Wounded Healer*, Thames and Hudson, London, (1982) 1991, p. 5.

[7] Miller and Taube, *The Gods and Symbols of Ancient Mexico and the Maya*, p. 136.

[8] ibid., p. 136.

[9] Ripinsky-Naxon, 'Shamanistic Knowledge and Cosmology', p. 147.

[10] Robert Bauval and Graham Hancock, *Keeper of Genesis: A Quest for the Hidden Legacy of Mankind*, Mandarin, London, 1997; Graham Hancock and Santha Faiia, *Heaven's Mirror: Quest for the Lost Civilisation*, Penguin, London, 1999; Graham Hancock. *Fingerprints of the Gods: A Quest for the Beginning and the End*, Heinemann, London, 1995.

[11] David Friedel, Linda Schele, Joy Parker, *Maya Cosmos: Three Thousand Years on the Shaman's Path*, William Morrow, New York, 1993, p. 283.

[12] ibid.

[13] ibid., p. 281.

[14] See Robert Bauval, Graham Hancock, *Keeper of Genesis*, Chapter 10, pp. 177ff.

[15] Graham Hancock, Santha Faiia, *Heaven's Mirror*, p. 37.

[16] Adela Fernandez, *Pre-Hispanic Gods of Mexico*, Panorama Editorial, Mexico City, 1992, p. 37.

[17] Miller and Taube, *Gods and Symbols of Ancient Mexico and the Maya*, pp. 128–9.

[18] Reproduced in *National Geographic Magazine*, Vol. 176, No. 4, Washington DC, October 1989, p. 468: 'Double-Comb is being taken to the underworld in a canoe guided by the "paddler-twins", gods who appear prominently in Maya mythology. Other figures – an iguana, a monkey, a parrot, and a dog – accompany the dead ruler.'

[19] Details are reproduced in John Romer, *Valley of the Kings*, Michael O'Mara Books, London, 1988, p. 167 and in J.A. West, *The Traveller's Key to Ancient Egypt*, Harrap Columbus, London, 1989, pp. 282–97.

[20] See West, *The Traveller's Key to Ancient Egypt*, p. 284, and the R.O. Faulkner (Ed.), *The Ancient Egyptian Book of the Dead*, British Museum Publications, 1989, pp. 116–30. For ancient Central America see note 18 above, re: the Mayan ruler Double-Comb.

[21] Friedel et.al., *Maya Cosmos*, p. 260.

[22] ibid., pp. 261, 238, 359.

[23] See Linda Schele, Mary Ellen Miller, *The Blood of Kings: Dynasty and Ritual in Maya Art*, Thames and Hudson, London, 1992, p. 155. The deer's head is often interpreted as a deer-head helmet.

24 E.g. see ibid., p. 190.

25 ibid., p. 45.

26 J. Eric Thompson, *Maya History and Religion*, University of Oklahoma Press, 1990, p. 198.

27 The 'Stirling hypothesis'. See Miller and Taube, *Gods and Symbols of Ancient Mexico*, p. 126.

28 Friedel et al., *Maya Cosmos*, p. 51.

29 Miller and Taube, *Gods and Symbols of Ancient Mexico*, pp. 126–7; Douglas Gillette, *The Shaman's Secret: The Lost Resurrection Teachings of the Ancient Maya*, Bantam Books, New York, 1998, pp. 9–11

30 Gillette, *The Shaman's Secret*, p. 9.

31 For example, an image of the goddess Isis offering the gift of eternal life to the soul of Pharaoh Seti I, in the Temple of Seti I at Abydos, features a classic entoptic grid on the wall to the left of the goddess, while her throne is also decorated with entoptic patterns. See *Heaven's Mirror*, p. 85. The examples of this kind of combination of entoptic with iconic imagery in ancient Egyptian art are too numerous to list. They are everywhere.

32 Alan Shorter, *The Egyptian Gods: A Handbook*, Routledge and Keegan Paul, London, 1981, p. 128.

33 *Book of What is in the Duat*, Third Division, in E.A. Wallis Budge (Trans.), *The Egyptian Heaven and Hell*, Hopkinson, London, 1925, p. 55.

34 Cited in Benny Shanon, *The Antipodes of the Mind: Charting the Phenomenology of the Ayahuasca Experience*, Oxford University Press, 2002, p. 124.

35 ibid., p. 118.

36 Belinda Gore (introduction by Felicitas Goodman), *Ecstatic Body Postures: An Alternate Reality Workbook*, Bear and Company, Santa Fe, 1995, pp. 173–5. A reproduction of the original ancient Egyptian 'drawing of Osiris' referred to here is to be found in Felicitas D. Goodman, *Where Spirits Ride the Wind: Trance Journeys and Other Ecstatic Experiences*, Indiana University Press, 1990, p. 59.

37 Source for Egyptian figure: Richard H. Wilkinson, *The Complete Gods and Goddesses of Ancient Egypt*, Thames and Hudson, London, 2003, p. 119; source for Lascaux figure, Mario Ruspoli, *The Cave of Lascaux: The Final Photographs*, Harry N. Abrams, New York, p. 151.

38 Felicitas Goodman, *Where Spirits Ride the Wind*, p. 59.

39 See discussion and full bibliography in Samuel A. Wells, *American Drugs in Egyptian Mummies: A Review of the Evidence*, http://www.colostate.edu/Depts/Entomology/courses/en570/papers_2000/wells.html.

40 Recent corroboration of Emboden's position on *N. caerulea* can be found in J. Andrew McDonald, 'Botanical Determination of the Middle Eastern

Tree of Life', *Economic Botany*, 56 (2), 2002, pp. 125–6.

[41] William Emboden, 'The Sacred Journey in Dynastic Egypt', *Journal of Psychoactive Drugs*, Vol. 21 (I), Jan.-Mar. 1989, p. 61.

[42] ibid.

[43] ibid., p. 63.

[44] ibid.

[45] ibid., p. 73.

[46] ibid., pp. 63–4.

[47] ibid., p. 65.

[48] He reports visual hallucinations and auditory hallucinations from decoctions of macerated water lily flowers. See William Emboden, 'The Water Lily and the Maya Scribe', *New Scholar: An Americanist Review*, 1982, 8:111.

[49] Emboden, 'The Sacred Journey in Dynastic Egypt', pp. 74–5. A full and authoritative presentation of Emboden's findings is also found in Emboden, 'Transcultural Use of Narcotic Water Lilies in Ancient Egyptian and Mayan Drug Ritual', *Journal of Ethnopharmacology*, 3 (1981), pp. 39–83.

[50] William Emboden, 'The Sacred Narcotic Lily of the Nile', *Economic Botany*, 32 (4), 1978, p. 395.

[51] Emboden, 'The Water Lily and the Maya Scribe', p. 116.

[52] ibid., p. 117.

[53] ibid., p. 107.

[54] Emboden, 'Transcultural Use of Narcotic Water Lilies', p. 65.

[55] ibid., pp. 65–6.

[56] R. Gordon Wasson, *The Wondrous Mushroom, Mycolatry in Mesoamerica*, McGraw-Hill, New York, 1980, p. 189.

[57] Marlene Dobkin de Rios, 'Influence of Psychotropic Flora and Fauna on Mayan Religion', *Current Anthropology*, Vol. 15, No. 2, June 1974, p. 148.

[58] Thomas M. Mcguire, 'Ancient Maya Mushroom Connections', *Journal of Psychoactive Drugs*, Vol. 14 (3), Jul.-Sep. 1982, p. 228. See also Richard Evans Schultes, Albert Hoffman and Christian Ratsch, *Plants of the Gods: Their Sacred, Healing and Hallucinogenic Powers*, Healing Arts Press, Rochester, Vermont, 2001, p. 161.

[59] Dobkin de Rios, 'Influence of Psychotropic Flora and Fauna on Mayan Religion', p. 148.

[60] ibid; Schultes et al., *Plants of the Gods*, p. 161.

[61] Schultes et al., *Plants of the Gods*, p. 161.

[62] Peter Furst, in Norman Hammond (Ed.), *Mesoamerican Archaeology: New Approaches*, Gerald Duckworth, London, 1974, pp 189–90; For examples of the paintings see Harry J. Shafer, Jim Zintgraff, *Ancient Texans: Rock Art*

and *Lifeways Along the Lower Pecos*, Gulf Publishing, Houston, 1986, pp. 138ff.

[63] Furst, in Hammond, *Mesoamerican Archaeology*, p. 190.

[64] Weston La Barre, *The Peyote Cult*, University of Oklahoma Press, (1939) 1989, p. 105.

[65] Wasson, *The Wondrous Mushroom*, p. 153.

[66] See discussion in Richard Evans Schultes, 'Teonanactl, the Narcotic Mushroom of the Aztecs', *American Anthropologist*, NS, 42, 1940, pp. 429–43.

[67] Furst, in Hammond, *Mesoamerican Archaeology*, p. 192.

[68] Schultes et al., *Plants of the Gods*, p. 170.

[69] Duran, cited in Wasson, *The Wondrous Mushroom*, p. 202.

[70] Sahagun, cited in ibid., p. 206.

[71] Francisco Hernandez, cited in Peter T. Furst, *Hallucinogens and Culture*, Chandler and Sharp, 1988, p. 67.

[72] Cited in Wasson, *The Wondrous Mushroom*, p. 218.

[73] Cited in ibid., p. xvii.

[74] Extensive discussion in ibid., pp. 3ff.

[75] Cited in ibid., p. 48.

[76] Koran, Sura XCVI, 1–5, cited in F.A. Klein, *The Religion of Islam*, Curzon Press, London, 1971, p. 7.

[77] Sylvanus Griswold Morley, *Introduction to The Study of Maya Hieroglyphs*, Dover, New York, 1975, pp. 16–17.

Chapter Twenty-Three: Doors Leading to Another World

[1] Siegel, 'Hallucinations', *Scientific American*, Vol. 237, 1977, cited in Paul Bahn and Patricia Helvenston, *Desperately Seeking Trance Plants: Testing the Three Stages of Trance Model*, R.J. Communications, New York, 2002, p. 43.

[2] Bahn and Helvenston, *Desperately Seeking Trance Plants*, p. 43. Elsewhere ('LSD Hallucinations', *Journal of Psychiatric Drugs*, Vol. 17 (4), Oct.-Dec. 1985, p. 254), Siegel notes that 'the remarkable constancies of drug-induced hallucinations lead to a consideration of their universal nature'.

[3] Robert G. Bednarik, 'On Neuropsychology and Shamanism in Rock Art,' *Current Anthropology*, Vol. 31, No. 1, February 1990, p. 78.

[4] Rick Strassman MD, *DMT: The Spirit Molecule: A Doctor's Revolutionary Research into the Biology of Near-Death and Mystical Experiences*, Park Street Press, Rochester, Vermont, 2001, p. 191.

[5] ibid., p. 190.

[6] ibid., p. 243.

[7] ibid., p. 244.

[8] ibid., p. 245.

[9] ibid., p. 214.

[10] ibid., p. 215.

[11] ibid., p. 271.

[12] ibid., p. 197.

[13] ibid., p. 195.

[14] ibid., pp. 200, 199.

[15] ibid., p. 200.

[16] Strassman in Robert Forte (Ed.), *Entheogens and the Future of Religion*, Council on Spiritual Practices, 1997, p. 157.

[17] ibid., p. 158.

[18] Strassman, *DMT*, p. 200.

[19] Benny Shanon, *The Antipodes of the Mind: Charting the Phenomenology of the Ayahuasca Experience*, Oxford University Press, 2002, p. 424.

[20] ibid., p. 431.

[21] ibid.

[22] ibid., p. 126.

[23] ibid., p. 122.

[24] ibid., p. 388.

[25] ibid., pp. 388–9. Shanon (p. 389) comments in particular on the shortcomings of the reductionist theory set out by Eugene d'Acquili and Andrew B. Newburg in their book, *The Mystical Mind: Probing the Biology of Religious Experience* (Fortress Press, Minneapolis, 1999). This book, as Shanon notes, 'suggests that religious and mystical sentiments are due to the activation of brain centres specifically responsible for such sentiments. The book had an immediate great impact and was even the topic of a *Newsweek* cover story . . . The empirical data on which the suggestion is based involve the new sophisticated technology of brain imaging. When a meditating person is inspected with imaging devices specific patterns of brain activation are observed. Much has been made of this finding and even the bombastic term 'neurotheology' has been coined. Brain imaging technology is indeed most impressive, yet conceptually, its impact is, I think, less radical than many believe. After all, everything a human being does involves brain activity. The finding of particular brain activation in conjunction with religious experience should thus be expected. By no means, however, does this finding imply that the brain *causes* the religious experience or that religious experiences (or religion, or God . . .) are to be accounted for in a biological reductionistic manner. When one speaks the brain is acting as well; this does not mean that language

and linguistic creations (think of Shakespeare's sonnets, for example) are reducible to brain activity and are to be explained in neurological terms. What the new findings may be indicating is that, like languaging, spirituality is ingrained in our very being, that the propensity for religiosity is a fundamental feature of what it is to be a human being. But do we need the supermodern technology of brain imaging to know that? Incidentally, I should add that I myself would never put ayahuasca drinkers into an fMRI machine. The experimental manipulation, its artificiality, and the discomfort associated with it are likely to affect the very experience it is set to examine. I doubt that any really powerful ayahuasca session can be entertained under such circumstances, let alone the supreme spiritual experiences that are the subject of discussion here.'

[26] Strassman in Forte (Ed.), *Entheogens and Future of Religion*, p. 157.

[27] Shanon, *The Antipodes of the Mind*, p. 165.

[28] ibid., p. 166.

[29] ibid., p. 393.

[30] ibid., p. 362. Shanon's attempt to do this leads him to suggest that the human imagination, which 'in principle . . . is without limits' (p. 138) is the key mechanism at work, and that ayahuasca visions are in some way connected to our imaginative faculty and to human creativity. He writes (pp. 398–9): 'Creation is of course a standard cognitive-psychological notion. Yet the creative accomplishments discussed here are far from being standard. First the creative power at hand is extraordinary, and while unbounded it is subject to constraints: there are some specific contents that are more likely to be created than others. These – such as serpents and jaguars, palaces and artistic objects, objects made of gold and of precious stones, angels and beings of light – do not reflect the life history, knowledge or concerns of the individual drinker, and they even seem not to be specific to members of any particular cultural group. Thus it appears that human beings, while not storing in their memories ideas of these specific semantic contents, are built in such as fashion as to be likely to imagine them . . .' Shanon emphasises (p. 399) that his suggestion should not be confused with the traditional notion of innate ideas or with the Jungian collective unconscious:

'What is being suggested rather are specific characteristics of human creative imagination. Unlike innate ideas, these characteristics are not stored in the mind of the individual as such, unlike the Jungian archetypes they cannot be reduced to existential aspects of human life, and unlike universals of music, grammar, and logic they pertain to content, not to form. Thus in some respects these characteristics resemble the Platonic Ideas – they involve specific contents and they do not reflect the life history of any individual. Where do these characteristics belong, then? My suggestion is that they are part and parcel of the make-up of human beings. Just as bees are made to produce honey and beavers to construct dams, human beings are made to build pyramids and compose sonatas. Surely, not all members of the human species will ever do this, but the species as a whole is designed so that some of its members will eventually achieve these accomplishments. With ayahuasaca the likelihood of individuals to be wonderfully creative is dramatically increased.'

This is all very well but seems to me not to explain the problem. If it is 'part and parcel of the make-up of human beings' to imagine 'serpents and jaguars, palaces and artistic objects, objects made of gold and of precious stones, angels and beings of light' then the real questions remain: why should this be so and at what point in the human evolutionary career did this specific propensity to envisage serpents, jaguars, beings of light, etc., etc., get so tightly grafted onto the human genome that today people who have absolutely nothing in common all 'imagine' (or 'create') the same things under the influence of ayahuasca?

[31] ibid., p. 392.

[32] 'Modern man has just got older – by 35,000 years', *The Times*, London, 17 February 2005.

[33] For a detailed survey of the evidence see Giorgio Samorini, *Animals and Psychedelics: The Natural World and the Instinct to Alter Consciousness*, Park Street Press, Vermont, 2002. See also R.K. Siegel and Murray E. Jarvik, 'Drug-Induced Hallucinations in Animals and Man', in Siegel and West (Eds), *Hallucinations: Behaviour, Experience and Theory*, Wiley, New York, 1975, pp. 81–104.

[34] Cited in Giorgio Samorini, *Animals and Psychedelics*, p. 63. For spiders on LSD see p. 13 and for moths on datura see p. 64.

[35] Stephen Jay Gould, *Wonderful Life: The Burgess Shale and the Nature of History*, Hutchinson-Radius, London, 1990, p. 43: 'The two phyla, Arthropodata and Chordata, have been separate from the very first records of multicellular life.' For the form of the last common ancestor see: Evolution of the Metazoa, http://www.palaeos.com/invertebrates/dafault.htm, p. 3. and for the epoch of approximately one billion years ago see http://encyclopedia.laborlawtalk.com/ Evolutionary timeline, p. 2.

[36] Jeffrey H. Schwartz, *Sudden Origins: Fossils, Genes and the Emergence of Species*, John Wiley and Sons, New York, 1999, p. 36. For discussion of the 'Hox' genes that control the development of insect and vertebrate eyes see http://www.palaeos.com/KingdomsAnimalia/Bilateria/htm, p. 4.

[37] See Chapter Nineteen.

[38] Strassman, *DMT*, p. 193.

[39] E.g. see Rick Doblin, 'Pahnke's "Good Friday Experiment": A Long-Term Follow-Up and Methodological Critique', *The Journal of Transpersonal Psychology*, 1991, Vol. 23, No. 1, pp. 1–28. See also Ronald K. Siegel, 'Religious Behaviour in Animals and Man: Drug-Induced Effects', *Journal of Drug Issues*, Vol. 7, No. 3, pp. 219–36.

[40] Bill Hicks, *Love all the People*: Letters, Lyrics, Routines, Constable, London, 2004, pp. 73–4, 193–4. Sadly, aged only 32, Bill Hicks died of pancreatic cancer in February 1994.

[41] Strassman, *DMT*, p. 37.

[42] See Chapter Eight and Appendix II.

[43] E.g. Jeremy Dronfield, 'Migraine, Light and Hallucinations: The Neurocognitive Basis of Irish Megalithic Art', *Oxford Journal of Archaeology* 14 (3), 1995, pp. 261–75. See in particular pp. 265, 271, 272; Peter Lamborn Wilson, *Ploughing the Clouds: The Search for Irish Soma*, City Lights, San Francisco, 1999, pp. 30–3; Richard Bradley, 'Deaths and Entrances: A Contextual Analysis of Megalithic Art', *Current Anthropology*, Vol. 30, No. 1, February 1989; Jeremy Dronfield, 'Ways of Seeing, Ways of Telling', in M. Lorblanchet and P. Bahn (Eds), *Rock Art Studies*, Oxbow Books, Oxford, 1993, pp. 179ff; Jeremy Dronfield, 'The Vision Thing', *Current Anthropology*, Vol. 37, No. 2, April 1996, pp. 373ff; Jeremy Dronfield, 'Entering Alternative Realities: Cognition, Art and Architecture in Irish Passage Tombs', *Cambridge Archaeological Journal* 6:1 (1996), pp. 37–72; J.D. Lewis-Williams and T.A. Dowson, 'On Vision and Power in the Neolithic', *Current Anthropology*, Vol. 34, No. 1, February 1993, pp. 55ff; Mark Patton, 'On Entoptic Images in Context: Art, Monuments and Society in Neolithic Brittany', *Current Anthropology*, Vol. 31, No. 5, December 1990, pp. 554ff; Jeremy Dronfield, 'Subjective Vision and the Source of Irish Megalithic Art', *Antiquity*, 69 (1995), pp. 539–49.

[44] Peter Narvez (Ed.), *The Good People: New Fairylore Essays*, The University Press of Kentucky, (1991) 1997, pp. 29–30, 119, 199, 201. W.Y. Evans-Wentz, *The Fairy Faith in Celtic Countries*, New Page Books, Franklin Lakes, NJ, 2004 (facsimile reprint of original 1911 edition with a modern Introduction by Carl McColeman), pp. 19, 36, 67, 166–7, 202–3, 205, 409, 413; Diane Purkiss, *Troublesome Things: A History of Fairies and Fairy Stories*, Penguin, London, 2000, pp. 6–7, 151, 204.

Appendix I: Critics and Criticisms of David Lewis-Williams' 'Neuropsychological Theory' Of Rock and Cave Art

[1] Bahn's Biography is on-line at the Archaeological Institute of America (http://www.archaeological.org/webinfo.php?page=10128&leader=9).

[2] Paul Bahn, *Images of the Ice Age*, Facts on File, 1988 (jacket text).

[3] Paul Bahn, *Journey Through The Ice Age*, Weidenfeld and Nicolson, London, 1997.

[4] P. Bahn, P. Pettit, S. Ripoll, 'Discovery of Palaeolithic Cave Art in Britain', *Antiquity*, 2003, 77 (296), pp. 227–31.

[5] John Pickrell, *National Geographic News*, 18 August 2004.

[6] Bahn comment on J.D. Lewis-Williams and T.A. Dowson, 'The Signs of All Times', *Current Anthropology*, Vol. 29, No. 2, April 1988, p. 217.

[7] Bahn, *Images of the Ice Age*, p. 190.

[8] Bahn, *Journey through the Ice Age*, p. 182. For example, Lewis-Williams is accused in this passage of 'extreme selectivity in image and interpretation'.

[9] Bahn, in Henri-Paul Francfort and Roberte Hamayon (Eds), *The Concept of Shamanism: Uses and Abuses*, p. 52.

[10] Paul Bahn, *Rock Art Research*, 1997, Vol. 14, No. 1, pp. 62–7.

[11] Patricia A. Helvenston and Paul Bahn, *Desperately Seeking Trance Plants: Testing the Three-Stages of Trance Model*, RJ Communications, New York, 2002.

[12] Bahn, in Francfort and Hamayon (Eds), *The Concept of Shamanism*, pp. 51ff.

[13] Patricia Helvenston, formerly a practising clinical psychologist in Denver and Chicago, now retired; Henri-Paul Francfort, Director of Research at at France's CNRS (National Centre for Scientific Research); Roberte Hamayon, Professor of Religious Studies at the Sorbonne; Cyril Hromnik, South African rock art researcher.

[14] Frankfort and Hamayon 'in collaboration with Paul Bahn', *The Concept of Shamanism*; and Helvenston and Bahn, *Desperately Seeking Trance Plants*.

[15] Helvenston and Bahn, *Desperately Seeking Trance Plants*, p. 4.

[16] ibid.

[17] ibid.

[18] *Cambridge Archaeological Journal*, 2003, 13:2, pp. 213–24.

[19] ibid., p. 219.

[20] ibid.

[21] The admission 'we were blinded by some dangerous spirit of dogmatism' was made by Cartailhac in 1902. Cited in Bahn, *Journey through the Ice Age*, p. 22.

[22] ibid., pp. 182–3.

23 Cyril Hromnik, 'A Testament to the Shamanistic Hallucinatory Trance Theory of the Southern African Rock Art', *Rock Art Research*, 1991, Vol. 8, No. 2, p. 100.

24 ibid.

25 ibid., p. 99.

26 ibid., Lewis-Williams reply, p. 103.

27 ibid.

28 D.F. Bleek, 1935: pp. 22–3, 29, 31; 1936: p. 132; 1956: pp. 363–4, cited in *Rock Art Research*, 1991, Lewis-Williams reply, p. 103.

29 D.F. Bleek, 1935: pp. 12, 29, 32, 35, 36, cited in *Rock Art Research*, 1991, Lewis-Williams reply, p. 103.

30 ibid.

31 David Lewis-Williams, *The Mind in the Cave*, Thames and Hudson, London, 2002, pp. 138–9.

32 *Rock Art Research*, 1991, Lewis-Williams reply, p. 103.

33 G.W. Stow, *Rock Paintings in South Africa*, Methuen, London, 1930, cited in Royden Yates and Anthony Manhire, 'Shamanism and Rock Paintings: Aspects of the Use of Rock Art in the South-Western Cape, South Africa', *South African Archaeological Bulletin*, 46, p. 8.

34 Lewis-Williams, *The Mind in the Cave*, p. 149.

35 ibid.

36 Cited in David Lewis-Williams, *A Cosmos in Stone*, Altamira Press, Walnut Creek, CA, 2002, p. 56.

37 Reproduced in ibid., p. 54, illus. B.

38 Cited in ibid., p. 58.

39 Cited in David Lewis-Williams, *Images of Mystery: Rock Art of the Drakensberg*, Double Storey, Cape Town, p. 26.

40 David Lewis-Williams, *The Mind in the Cave*, pp. 147, 168; *Images of Mystery*, pp. 38, 40–1.

41 Bahn, *Images of the Ice Age*, p. 190.

42 Lewis-Williams, *Images of Mystery*, p. 35.

43 Lewis-Williams, *A Cosmos in Stone*, p. 62.

44 Lewis-Williams, *Images of Mystery*, p. 35.

45 Hromnik, 'A Testament to the Shamanistic . . .', p. 99.

46 R. Katz, 1982, p. 8 cited in *Rock Art Research*, 1991, p. 102.

47 R. Katz, 'The Painful Ecstasy of Healing', *Psychology Today*, December 1975, 10 (7), p. 82.

48 R. Katz and M. Biesele, 1986, p. 221, cited in *Rock Art Research* 1991, p. 102.

49 ibid.

50 Katz and Biesele, 1986, p. 221, cited in ibid.

51 Richard Katz, 'Education for Transcendence: !Kia-Healing with the Kalahari !Kung', in Richard B. Lee and Irven Devore (Eds), *Kalahari Hunter-Gatherers: Studies of the !Kung and their Neighbours*, Harvard University Press, 1976, pp. 288, 287.

52 Cited in *Rock Art Research*, 1991, p. 102.

53 M. Biesele, 1993, p. 70, cited in Lewis-Williams, *The Mind in the Cave*, p. 142.

54 Katz, 'Education for Transcendence', p. 293.

55 ibid., p. 285.

56 Katz, 'The Painful Ecstasy of Healing', p. 85.

57 *Rock Art Research*, 1991, p. 102.

58 Katz, 'The Painful Ecstasy of Healing', p. 85.

59 See Chapters Seven and Eight above.

60 'Testing the Three Stages of Trance Model', *CAJ*, 2003, 13:2, p. 213.

61 Helvenston and Bahn, *Desperately Seeking Trance Plants*, p. 51.

62 *CAJ*, 2003, 13:2, p. 215.

63 ibid.

64 ibid., p. 213.

65 ibid.

66 Helvenston and Bahn, *Desperately Seeking Trance Plants*, pp. 8ff.

67 ibid., p. 16 ff.

68 ibid., pp. 9–10.

69 ibid., pp. 21–2 ff.

70 ibid., pp. 9–10.

71 Ludwig in R. Prince (Ed.), *Trance and Possession States*, 1968.

72 Helvenston and Bahn, *Desperately Seeking Trance Plants*, p. 25.

73 Ludwig in R. Prince (Ed.), *Trance and Possession States*, p. 70.

74 ibid., p. 72.

75 ibid., p. 75.

76 La Barre, *Ghost Dance*, p. 178.

77 Ludwig in Prince (Ed.), *Trance and Possession States*, p. 74.

78 ibid.

79 ibid., p. 73.

80 Helvenston and Bahn, *Desperately Seeking Trance Plants*, p. 26.

81 Ludwig in Prince (Ed.), *Trance and Possession States*, p. 75.

82 ibid., p. 76.

83 ibid., pp. 75–85.

84 ibid., p. 84.

85 *CAJ*, 2003, 13:2, p. 215.

INDEX

Aaaron (DMT volunteer), 440, 443, 444, 445
Aberfoyle, 365
Aborigines, 272–3, 275, 318, 326, 327–8, 411
Africa, 4–5, 27, 28–9, 30, 159, 164, 165, 230–8, 268, 315, 316, 401, 419, 443, 466
  rock art, 69, 77–8, 85–92, 100–2, 114–18, 123–32, 155–6, 161, 167, 168–70, 172–3, 180, 187, 194–5, 201–4, 208, 209, 229, 238, 240, 241, 242, 243, 244–61, 265, 266, 269, 321, 415, 418, 565
  see also Ju/'hoansi/!Kung; San; names of places
Agobard, Archbishop of Lyons, 361–2
Aho, Betty, 300, 303, 320
Alberto, Don, 52
Albigensian Crusades, 501
Alcibiades, 526
Alejandro, Don, 465
Alfonso XII, King of Spain, 138
Algonquin, 342, 343, 350
Altamira, 7, 80, 110–12, 114, 117, 122, 135–46, 158, 214, 215
Amaringo, Pablo 38, 65
  paintings, 43, 46, 49, 51, 52, 53, 55, 56, 59, 345, 455
Amazon, 163, 266–7, 281, 325, 344, 348, 377, 419, 460, 463–6, 565
  hallucinogens/hallucinogenic experiences in, 38–62, 164, 188, 191, 201, 210–11, 268, 294, 318–19, 331, 420, 432, 445, 454, 459, 464–5, 466, 467, 468–9, 472, 567–8
  see also Mestizo; Tukano; Urubu; Yagua
Anati, Emmanuel, 87
Andrea (abductee), 314–15, 376, 392
Andreasson, Betty, 332
Anne (abductee), 449
Anthropologie, L', 145
Antiquity, 83

Anubis, 76, 540–1
Apollo-II Cave, 77–8, 85, 86, 87, 89, 93, 161, 194
Arabia, 363
Araucanian Indians, 274, 276, 330
Arbousset, Thomas, 171
Archer, Barbara, 314, 353, 385–6
Arcy-sur-Cure, 120
Ardèche region, 72
Ariège region, 79
Aristotle, 522, 523
Arizona, 579
Arnhem Land, 327
Arthur (abductee), 315, 322, 334
Arunta tribe, 272, 303
Asia, 27, 29, 69, 165, 375
Atanga, 5
Austino, James, 349
Australia, 29, 69, 92, 161, 272–3, 274, 275, 303, 304, 315–16, 318, 327–8, 334, 411, 419
Australian National University, 488
Avam Samoyed, 338
Avebury, 587–8
Aztecs, 164, 555, 556–7

Baby Jaguar, 538–9
Bahn, Paul, 144, 157, 216–23, 224, 226, 227–8, 239, 257
Ballard, Linda-May, 370
Bantu-speaking tribes, 230, 231, 232
Bara Bahau, 122, 126
Barkly East, 125–6, 169
Basel, 358
Basuto, 315
Bauval, Robert, 533
Bednarik, Robert, 154, 155, 565
Begouen, Count, 148–9
Ben (DMT volunteer), 441

Ben Bulbin, 393
Bhagavad Gita, 527
Bible, 363 *see also* New Testament; Old
    Testament
Biesele, Megan, 179, 184, 187, 268
Biggs, Katherine, 388
Biggs, Lori, 387–8
Binbinga tribe, 273
Bitamu, 5
Bleek, Wilhelm, 170, 171, 172, 179
Bleek and Lloyd documents, 170–1, 172, 231,
    237
Blombos Cave, 28–9, 159, 417
Blue Ridge Mountains, 320
Bo, 316, 330, 466
Bo-Khan, 338
Boas, Franz, 326–7
Bomanpak, 552, 553
Book of Mormon, 496
Book of the Dead, 534, 551
Book of What is in the Duat, 541–2
Bord, Janet, 373, 374, 402, 403, 404, 405
Borneo, 304
Boston University, 485, 488
Botswana, 184
Brandhoek, 89
Brazil, 38, 39, 41, 44, 62, 338, 543
Breuil, Abbé Henri, 134, 135, 136, 139, 145,
    146, 147, 148, 149–50, 151, 153, 155, 156, 162,
    194, 230
Britain, 7, 38, 377 *see also* England; Scotland;
    Wales
British Mycological Society, 223
Brittany, 392, 393, 401, 584
Brown, Dr Frank, 31
Buddhists, 33, 495
Bulgaria, 160
Bull Lodge, 318
Bullard, Thomas, 299
Buryat, 340, 347
Bwiti, 5, 6, 9, 10, 11, 164

Cahuilla, 326
California, 326, 387
    Great Basin, 69, 200–1, 212
Cambridge Archaeological Journal (*CAJ*), 216,
    219, 224, 239
Cameroon, 4, 5
Campa, 465
Canada, 226–7, 274, 374
Cantabrico, El, 146
Cape of Good Hope Colony, 170
Cape Province, 237
Cardinas, Filiberto, 320
Caribbean, 339–40
Carlos (abductee), 302, 304
Carmarthenshire, 403–4
Carnac, 584

Carol (abductee), 324–5, 328, 334
Carpenter, John, 296, 297
Cartailhac, Emile de, 136, 139, 140, 142, 143,
    144, 145–6, 147, 215
Casares, Los, 264
Cash/Landrum case, 360
Cassandra (DMT volunteer), 431, 436
Castillo, El, 78–9, 112–13, 114, 123, 160
Catherine (abductee), 300–1, 306, 313, 314,
    348–9
Cedarberg, 89, 90, 115, 128, 129
Celestial Monster, 537–8
Celso, Don, 465
Central America, 164, 276, 521, 530, 535, 539,
    554 *see also* Maya; names of countries
Cgunta !elae, 316–17
Chaire à Calvin, La, 123
Chamisso shelter, 127
Champa, 342
Chan-Bahlum, 534
Charente region, 123
Charlie Brown shelter, 115
Chaumeil, Jean-Pierre, 474
Chauvet, 7, 72, 73–4, 76, 78, 93, 103–5, 121,
    126, 127, 129, 153, 154–5, 160, 209–10
Chile, 274, 276, 330, 361
China, 58, 274, 363, 411–12
Chippendale, Dr Christopher, 92–3, 219
Chris (DMT volunteer), 431, 570
Christ, 499
Christianity, 33, 496, 499–516, 517
Christmas Day, 501–2
Christophoros, St, 502
Church, 501, 504, 505, 509, 513, 557–8
Cicero, 522–3
Cleo (DMT volunteer), 455
Clottes, Jean, 35, 93, 96, 99, 155, 215
Cobeno, 274, 304
Coleridge, Samuel Taylor, 21
Colin (abductee), 324, 350, 382
Colombia, 38, 188, 340, 349, 459
Colton, Neil, 399–400
Combarelles, Les, 126, 144
Conibo Indians, 464, 489
Conkey, Margaret, 157
Copiago, 361
Cornwall, 38, 408–9
Coso, 200–4, 205, 206, 210
Cosquer, Henri, 94
Cosquer Cave, 94–6, 98, 99, 106–7, 117, 126
Cougnac, 97–9, 119–20, 270
County Donegal, 399
County Sligo, 393
Crete, 76
Crick, Francis, 461, 469–71, 472–3, 474, 475,
    476, 477, 478, 479, 481–2, 488, 489, 490,
    491, 580
Cubeo tribe, 318–19

Cubillas, Modesto, 136
Cuna, 339–40, 349, 350
Current Anthropology, 36, 162, 199, 200, 565

Daumas, Francis, 171
Dave (abductee), 314
Davenport, Demorest, 83, 255
Davis, Kathie, 387
Demeter, 521, 525, 526
Diaz, Carlos, 320, 451
Didima Gorge, 249
Dimitri (DMT volunteer), 441, 442, 573
Donegal, 399
Dordogne, 99
Dorsetshire, 402, 409
Double-Comb, 535
Doumremy, 504
Dowson, Thomas, 36, 156, 162, 199, 202, 204,
    206, 207, 208, 209, 210, 211, 212, 213, 219
Dowth, 584
Drakensberg, 91, 114–15, 124, 127, 168, 171,
    186, 187, 194, 238, 244–61
Druids, 33
Duat, 533–4, 542, 543
Dyak, 304

Eastern Cape Province, 117, 125, 127, 169
Eastern Free State, 101, 269
Echegaray, J. Gonzalez, 84
Ecuador, 38
Eden Project, 38
Egypt, ancient, 33, 76, 363, 530, 531, 533–5,
    540–4, 545, 546, 547–52, 559
El Cantabrico, 146
El Castillo, 78–9, 112–13, 114, 123, 160
El Juyo, 83–5
El Parlante (pseudonym), 141
El Salvador, 554
Elephant Hunt shelter, 124
Eleusis/Eleusinian Mysteries, 221, 521–6
Eli (DMT volunteer), 440, 456
Eliade, Mircea, 271, 272, 274, 276, 277, 279,
    305, 318, 326, 330, 335, 343
Elijah, 363
Emboden, William, 548–52
Encante, 344, 377
England, 373–4, 377, 378, 379–80, 392 see also
    names of places
Espeluges, hill of, 508–9
Ethiopia, 31, 159, 578
Europe, 27, 30, 159–60, 219, 220, 221, 222,
    223, 224, 225, 226, 227, 375, 410–11, 419,
    584
    Upper Palaeolithic cave art, 7–8, 13–26,
        29, 30, 35–6, 65, 69–76, 78–85, 92,
        94–100, 102–13, 114, 117, 118–23,
        126–32, 133–55, 156–8, 161–2, 163,
        167–8, 170, 182, 187, 188, 191, 192, 204,
        205–7, 209, 211, 212, 213, 217, 219–20,
        221, 229, 240, 241, 242, 243, 244, 265,
        266, 269, 277–80, 284, 295, 321, 355,
        415, 418, 451, 457, 545–6, 563, 565 see
        also names of caves
Eva (abductee), 302, 304
Evans, David, 403
Evans-Wentz, W.Y., 365, 377, 383, 393, 394,
    399
Ezekiel, 363, 517–18

Fallen Rock shelter, 129
Fatima, 514–16
Figuier, 144
Finland, 397–8
Fleagle, John, 31
Fleury, Antonio Francisco, 62
Flores, 27
Font de Gaume, 122, 144
Foot White, J., 401–2
Forrest River, 304
France, 32, 92, 94, 118, 138, 158, 366, 377,
    401, 508 see also names of caves and
    places
Francisco, Don, 54
Freeman, L. G., 84
Friedel, David, 534
Fry, Marina, 374
Fumane, 71–2, 72–3, 76, 78, 93, 127, 160

Gabe (DMT volunteer), 438, 570
Gabillou, 79–80, 100, 207, 265
Gabon, 4, 5
Gabriel, Angel, 495, 558
Gamble, Clive, 156–7
Game Pass, 91
Gamtoos River, 233, 238, 244
Garcia Guinea, Professor Miguel Angel,
    140, 143, 158
Gavrinis, 585
Gebhart-Sayer, Angelica, 464–5
Geissenklosterle, 74, 105
Genesis, Book of, 363
Germany, 74–6, 105, 358
'Ghost Ceremony' society, 274
Giant's Castle Nature Reserve, 91, 244
Gillette, David, 539
Gitskan, 268, 270, 327
Giza, Pyramids of, 551
Glyndaff, Robin, 407
Gnostics, 499–500, 501
Goldi tribe, 341
Gomez, Don Emilio Andrade, 295
Goodman, Felicitas, 545–7
Graziosi, Paolo, 119
Great Sphinx, 76
Greece, ancient, 221, 434, 521–6
Gregory, Lady, 375

Guatemala, 532, 553, 554
Gulf of Mexico, 539
Gurupi River, 338
Guruve, 115
Gxalingenwa, 124

Haddon, Professor A. C. 388
Halifax, Joan, 271, 274, 433
Harle, Edouard, 140, 141
Harner, Michael, 432, 434, 489–90
Harpur, Patrick, 387, 388, 397–8
Harriesmith District, 117
Hartland, Edwin Sydney, 388
Harvard Medical School, 485, 488
Haussler, Professor, 488
Heaven Cave, 127
Heliopolitan cult, 551
Helvenston, Patricia, 216–23, 224, 226, 227,
    228, 239, 257
Henshilwood, Chris, 28, 29, 159
Hermeticists, 500, 501
Hicks, Bill, 584, 585
Hickson, Charles, 314
Higdon, Carl, 322
Hildegard of Bingen, 359
Hill, Barney, 299, 309, 364
Hill, Betty, 299, 309, 332, 334, 364
Hinduism/Hindus, 33, 363, 495, 526–9
Hoffman, Albert, 223, 291–2, 335, 448, 452–3,
    469, 524–5, 529
Hohle-Fels, 74, 75–6, 80, 105
Hohlenstein-Stadel, 74, 75, 78, 80, 93, 105
Honduras, 554
Hopkins, Budd, 296, 297, 364
Horowitz, Mardi, 197
Horton, Virginia, 322–3
Horus, 533, 534, 535, 540–1, 551
Hoyle, Sir Fred, 474
Huatla de Jimenez, 331, 433, 558
Huhnapu, 532–3
Huxley, Aldous, 290–1, 293, 335, 448, 452–3,
    498–9, 520

Ilha de Guarantiba, 62
India, 165, 342–3, 349, 392, 521, 526–9
Indians/Native Americans, 163, 200–1, 216,
    276, 294, 463–6, 555 see also names of
    tribes
Indonesia, 27
International Congress of Anthropology
    and Prehistoric Archaeology, IXth, 139
Inuit, 274, 275–6, 334, 411
Ipeorkum, 339–40
Ipixuma tribe, 325
Iquitos, 42, 465
Ireland, 366, 370–1, 375–6, 377, 383, 388, 392,
    393, 394, 399–400, 410–11 513–14, 584
Isabel (abductee), 354, 386

Isis, 533
Isle of Man, 393, 401
Israel, 519
Italy see Fumane

Jacobs, Dr David, 296, 297, 299, 305–6, 323,
    346, 351–2, 354, 364, 368–9, 380, 385,
    393–4, 394–5, 396, 449
Jakobson, Roman, 462
James, William, 290, 292, 293, 335, 448,
    452–3
Japan, 362, 375
Jean (abductee), 330
Jeanne d'Arc, 504–5, 513
Jeffrey's Bay, 233
Jeremiah (DMT volunteer), 430, 438–9, 573,
    581
Jerry (abductee), 300, 303, 348
Jews, 495 see also Judaism
Jim (DMT volunteer), 440–1
Jivaro tribe, 268, 270, 500
Jochim, Michael A., 83, 255
Joe (abductee), 301–2, 303, 313, 320, 329
Jokuo, 339
Jones, John, 409–10
Jones, Robin, 408
Jonesdochter, Katherine, 379
Jose, Don, 465, 466
Journal of Psychedelic Drugs, 222
Judaism, 517–19 see also Jews
Ju/'hoansi/!Kung, 179, 183, 184–6, 187, 237,
    255, 256, 257–8, 268, 281, 316, 317, 330,
    336
Junction Shelter, 249, 250, 251–61, 262, 264
Jung, Carl Gustav, 336–7, 357–60, 360–1,
    364, 517
Jura mountains, 74
Justina, St, 503
Juyo, El, 83–5

Kaggen, 89, 237–8, 341, 443
Kalahari, 87, 179, 184, 186, 187, 194, 237, 256,
    263, 281, 316, 330, 466
Kalweit, Holger, 343–4
Kamberg Nature Reserve, 91
Kamrisch, Stella, 526
Karin (abductee), 302, 339, 349, 396
Karl (DMT volunteer), 436, 455
Karoo, 89, 127
Katz, Richard 256–7, 268
Kazak Kirgiz, 272
Keeney, Bradford, 330
Kgao Temi, 330, 466–7
Kii Province, 362
Kirk, Reverend Robert, 365, 367–8, 375, 392,
    397
Klein, Richard, 30
Kluver, Heinrich, 197, 198, 199, 208

Knapp, Julie, 348
Knock, 513–14, 516
Knoll, Max, 190–1, 199
Kondoa, 87–8
Koran, 495
Kuksu society, 274, 304
Kukulkan, 559
Kulin tribe, 316
!Kung /Ju/'hoansi, 179, 183, 184–6, 187, 237, 255, 256, 257–8, 268, 281, 316, 317, 330, 336
Kurnai tribe, 316
KV (Szara's patient), 447
Kwakiutl Indians, 326–7
K"xan, 268, 317
Kyzlasov, 305

La Barre, Weston, 174, 332, 497, 498
La Chaire à Calvin, 123
La Chorrea, 459
La Mouth, 144
La Pasiega, 112
Lake Huron, 374
Lakota tribe, 165
Lamb, Bruce, 459
Laming-Emperaire, Annette, 120, 151, 152, 168
Larson, Sandy, 299, 304–5
Lascaux, 7, 81–3, 108–10, 120–1, 126, 129, 150, 210, 255, 545–6
Layne, Patti, 449
Le Portel, 122, 129
Leakey, Mary, 87
Leary, Timothy, 447
Lee, Richard, 185
Lemus y Olmo, Don Alberton, 141–2
Leroi-Gourhan, A., 23, 80, 134, 135, 149, 150, 151–5, 156, 157, 162, 167, 168, 194
Les Combarelles, 126, 144
Lesotho, 124, 250
Levant, 29
Lewis, Evan, 403
Lewis-Williams, David, 31, 32, 35–7, 64–5, 69, 70, 71, 102, 113, 124, 131, 132, 135, 156, 158, 162–3, 166, 167–71, 172, 178–9, 180, 181, 182–4, 185, 186–7, 188–9, 191, 192–3, 194, 195–6, 227–8, 229, 231–2, 237, 239, 240, 242, 243, 248, 251, 256, 257, 258–9, 260, 261, 263, 264, 267–70, 271, 274, 275, 276–7, 284, 285, 295, 334, 415–16, 445, 448, 451, 521, 529, 563–5
    ideas attacked by Bahn and Helvenston, 216–27
Lloyd, Lucy, 170, 171, 179
Lommel, Andreas, 339
Long Island, 372
Los Casares, 264
Lourdes, 424, 505–9, 511–12, 516

Lower Pecos River, 554–5
Lucas (DMT volunteer), 439
Lucy (abductee), 320, 372
Ludwig, Arnold M., 165
Luna, Eduardo, 295, 465, 466
Lysaght, Patricia, 383

MacGregor, Mrs J., 365
Mack, Dr John, 296, 297, 299, 309–12, 323, 324–5, 345, 346, 350–1, 364, 368–9, 372, 373, 386–7, 396, 421
    patients (abuctees) see Andrea; Anne; Arthur; Carlos; Carol; Catherine; Colin; Dave; Eva; Isabel; Jean; Jerry; Joe; Karin; Nona; Peter; Sara; Scott; Shiela; Sparks, Jim
McKenna, Dennis, 459
McKenna, Terrence, 459, 469
Maclair district, 90
McLeod, Catherine, 310
Magar, 165
Magdalenian epoch, 78–9, 107–8, 112
Main Caves, 91, 244–9
Makoni, 102
Malay Peninsula, 274
Mama Magaba, 233, 234, 235
Mani, 496
Manichean religion, 496
Mara Aborigines, 318
Marsha (DMT volunteer, 431
Marshall, Lorna and Elizabeth, 184
Marsoulas, 144, 145
Martin, Maria, 226
Masse, Maurice, 397
Materiaux pour l'Histoire Primitive et Naturelle de l'Homme, 140
Maya, 33, 164, 274, 276, 521, 531, 532–3, 534, 535–9, 552–4, 559
Mazatec Indians, 331, 433, 558
Medicine Bow National Park, 322
Melikane, 178
Melissa (abductee), 353, 385
Melusine, 377, 380
Mencken, H. L., 332
Merlis, Sidney, 446
Mesopotamia, 519
Mestizo, 331, 350, 465
Mexico, 221, 331–2, 334, 343–4, 433, 534, 552, 554, 555–8
Middle East, 69, 519, 547
Milky Way, 533, 534
Minotaur, 76
Moloti mountains, 178
Moody, Charles, 397
Morgan, Karen, 314, 349, 352
Mormons, 495–6
Moroni, 496
Mortillet, Gabriel de, 136, 139–40, 141, 142,

143, 144, 147, 215
Moses, 495, 518
Muhammad, 495, 558–9
Mukat, 326
Mun-yir-yir, 326
Mundadji, 273
Munkaninji, 273
Murewa, 115–16
Murngin tribe, 326
Muslims, 33, 495
Mutoko, 101
Mylonas, George, 522–3

Nag Hammadi, 501
Namibia, 86, 87, 155, 184 *see also* Apollo-11
  Cave
Narby, Jeremy, 40, 459–62, 463, 464, 490,
  565, 569, 580, 582
Native American Church, 164
Native Americans *see* Indians/Native
  Americans
Nature, 31
Neanderthal Man, 27–8, 160
Nebamun, tomb of, 550
Neolithic monuments, 584–5
Nepal, 165
New Testament, 501
New York, 38
Newgrange, 584, 585
Ngun, 231–2, 233, 235, 236, 238, 247
Niaux, 108, 122, 124, 150, 158, 207
Nichiren, 362
Nona (abductee), 314, 354, 386
North America, 226–7, 274, 276, 304, 315,
  318, 342, 350, 411, 419 *see also* Canada;
  United States
North-Eastern Cape, 90, 124, 125
North-Eastern Free State, 117
Northern Cape, 115
Norway, 383
Nottingham, 373–4
Nuremberg, 358

Oaxaca, 558
O'Flaherty, Wendy, 526
Ojibwa, 304
Olaf Magnus, Bishop, 409
Old Testament, 363, 517, 519
Olmecs, 539–40
Orion, 534
Orissa, 165, 342
Orpen, Joseph Millard, 171–2, 178
Osiris, 533, 534, 542, 546–7, 559
Ott, Jonathan, 502

Pacal, Lord, 534
Paez Indians, 340, 349
Pager, Harald, 169, 253

Pair-non-Pair, 127, 144, 150
Palenque, 534
Panama, 339, 349
Parkington, John, 85–6
Parker, Joy, 534
Parlante, El (pseudonym), 141
Paro, Jaye, 372
Paul, St, 496
Pausanias, 523
Paviotso, 276, 326, 411
Pearce, David, 239
Pech Merle, 7, 13–25, 32, 35–6, 96–7, 98,
  99, 106, 117, 119, 129, 154, 260, 264,
  265, 270
Peixoto, Bernardo, 325
Pergouset, 128
Persephone, 521, 522
Persinger, Michael, 509–10
Peru, 38, 183
  hallucinogenic experiences in Peruvian
  Amazon, 38–62, 331
Peter (abductee), 322, 347, 352, 354, 386
Pindar, 522
Pinzarro, Jill, 353
Plato, 522, 523
Polari, Alex, 543
Pollock, Steven Hayden, 221–2, 223
Pomo Indians, 274
Pondomise, 230, 231
Popol Vuh, 532, 553, 554
Portel, Le, 122, 129
Portugal, 514–16
Puente Visego, 112
Purkiss, Diane, 379, 388, 505–6
Pygmy Bitamu, 5

Qing, 171–2, 178, 179
Quiche Maya, 532, 553

Rathlin, 370–1, 372
Ratier, Paul, 141
Redondo Beach, 387
Regnault, Felix, 144
Reichel-Dolmatoff, Gerardo, 163, 187–8,
  189–90, 192, 210, 294, 340
Reinach, Salomon, 147
Rex (DMT volunteer), 442, 443, 444, 445,
  449, 455
Riet River, 115
Rigveda, 526–7, 528, 529
Ripinsky-Naxon, Michael, 164, 500, 533
River Patwin tribe, 274, 304
Rojcewicz, Peter, 388, 392, 397
Romania, 377
Roper Organisation surveys, 296–8, 336
Rouen, 504
Rouffignac, 121–2
Ruck, Carl A. P., 524, 526, 529

Rupertsberg Codex,, 359–60
Rye, 379

Sabina, Maria, 331–2, 334, 433–4, 435, 558, 587
Sachamama, 42
Salmanslaagte, 116–17
Samorini, Giorgio, 225
San, 85, 86–7, 88, 89–92, 101, 114–18, 131–2,
    155, 163, 165, 167, 168–9, 170–3, 175–9, 181,
    182, 183, 184, 188, 191, 192, 195, 200, 201–4,
    205, 206, 208, 210, 217, 226, 230–3, 235–6,
    237–8, 240, 241, 242, 245, 246, 247, 248,
    252, 255, 256, 258–9, 263, 269, 270, 321,
    334, 341, 418, 443 see also Africa: rock art
Santa Claus, 501–2
Santo Daime, 543
Saora, 165, 342–3, 349
Sara (abductee), 346, 392
Sara (DMT volunteer), 430–1, 432, 437, 455,
    572
Saul (DMT volunteer), 449
Sautuola, Marcelino Sanz de, 136–7, 138, 139,
    141, 142, 143, 145, 146, 214, 215
Scandinavia, 393
Scarre, Chris, 224
Schele, Linda, 534
Schrime, Herb, 397
Schultes, Richard Evans, 40, 223, 554
Science magazine, 71, 72
Scientific American, 564
Scotland, 365, 375, 378–9, 383–4
Scott (abductee), 300, 320
Scott, Walter, 365
Sea-View Green, 409
Sean (DMT volunteer), 437, 571–2
Sebastian, St, 503
Sekhmet, 76, 540–1
Semang, 274
Set, 533
Sevilla Trail, 128
Shaman Cave, 115
Shannon, Claude, 487
Shanon, Dr Benny, 218, 432, 466, 467–8,
    471–2, 517–19, 543–4, 574–5, 576–7, 581
Sheridan, Mrs, 375–6
Shiela (abductee)), 449
Shikwe, Mabolele, 316, 334
Shipibo-Conibo Indians, 464
Shulgin, Alexander, 420
Shuna, Francisco Montes, 38, 41, 42, 44
Siberia, 272, 305, 318, 338–9, 340, 341, 349,
    502, 528–9
Siegel, Richard, 267
Siegel, Ronald, K., 197, 564
Sieveking, Anne, 105, 113, 156
Sinai Peninsula, 519
Skye, Isle of, 383–4
Slater, Elizabeth, 310

Sligo, 393
Smith, Huston, 520
Smith, Joseph, 495–6
Smith Sound, 275
Sobek, 62, 76, 540–1
Société Archaeologique de Midi, 144
Soffer, Olga, 157
Soga, J.H., 236
Soltero Perez, Don, 343–4, 347
Sopater, 523
Sophocles, 522
Sotho, 230, 232, 233
Soubirous, Bernadette, 424, 505–8, 510–11, 513
Sous-Grand-Lac, 99–100
South African Archaeological Bulletin, 168
South America, 221, 261, 276, 304, 334, 344,
    468 see also Amazon; names of countries
Southern Cape, 233
Souza, Inacio de, 397
Spain, 32, 92, 118, 138, 158, 508 see also names
    of caves
Sparks, Jim, 330
Stamets, Paul, 225–6
Stanislaus, St, 503
Stanley, Eugene, 485–6, 487, 488
Stow, George William, 172, 238
Strassman, Dr Rick, 218, 292–3, 294, 335,
    420–1, 423, 428, 434, 435–6, 445, 446,
    447–8, 453–4, 489, 568, 573–4, 575–6,
    576–7, 581, 584
    reports of volunteers in project of,
        430–2, 436–44, 448–9, 455–6, 569–73
Strieber, Whitley, 309, 324
Suffolk, 392, 393, 399
Sumer, 363
Swapper, Susan, 379–80
Sweden, 409
Switzerland, 358
Syfer, 90
Szara, Stephen, 446, 447

Tabasco, 539
Tacon, Dr Paul, 92–3
Tanzania, 87–8
Tatsunokuchi, 362
Tattershall, Ian, 31
Tavgytsy, 338–9
Teleut, 340
Tennessee, 374
Tens, Isaac, 268, 327, 334
Teotihuacan, 555–6
Tête du Lion cave, 106
Texas, 361, 554–5
Thebes, 550
Thembo, 231
Theresa of Avila, St, 503–4
Thompson, J. Eric, 538
Thoth, 535, 540–1, 559

Thunder-Jaguar, 340
Thuthmosis III, tomb of, 542
Tikal, 535
Toit, Bokka du, 233, 235
Tomey, Debbie, 353, 386
Toribo de Benavente, Fray, 557
Trasco, John, 374–5
Trench, Bridget, 513–14
Trois Frères, 79, 80–1, 89, 108, 126, 127, 328
Tukano, 181, 187–8, 189, 191, 192, 195,
    199–200, 210–11, 294, 313
Tungus, 173, 174, 181, 268, 272, 305
Turner, William, 446
Tutankhamen, Tomb of, 549
Twele, 319

Ulster Folk and Transport Museum, 370
Uniao de Vegetal (UdV), 39, 44, 62–3
Uniondale, 258
United States, 6–7, 38, 164, 200–1, 226, 227,
    298, 324, 333, 334, 336, 416, 432, 554
    see also names of places
University of California, 488
University of Cape Town, 171
Upper Palaeolithic period, 35, 36, 64–5,
    69–70, 219, 220, 221, 222, 223, 225, 226,
    280, 424, 578, 583–4
    see also Europe: Upper Palaeolithic cave
    art
Upuaut, 535
Ursula, St, 503
Urubu, 338, 346

Vallee, Jacques, 361–5, 366–7, 368, 369, 515,
    516
Valley of the Kings, 535, 542
Vedic scriptures, 526–9
Venezuela, 341, 443
Veracruz, 539
Vilanova y Piera, Professor, 139, 214, 215
Villars, 150
Villas-Boas, Antonio, 347, 364, 366, 367
Vinnicombe, Patricia, 168
Virgin Mary, 505, 506, 508, 5 13, 514, 515, 516
Vladan (DMT volunteer), 449, 456
Vogelherd, 74, 105

Wales, 366, 377, 393, 400, 403–4, 404–5,
    407–8, 409–10
Walton, Travis, 397
Wang Chi, 411–12
Warao, 341–2, 443
Warramunga, 303
Wasson, R. Gordon, 524, 526, 527–9, 555, 558
Water-Lily Jaguar (God III), 538, 552
Watling, Professor Roy, 223–5, 226–7
Watson, James, 461, 472
Wendt, Dr Wolfgang Erich, 77
West Kennett, Longbarrow, 585
Western Cape, 89, 90, 116, 124 see also
    Cedarberg
Westrum, Dr Ron, 296
White, Randall, 76
White Net, 115
Whitley, David, 35, 216
Wide Valley, 90
Wilkins, Maurice, 472
Williams, David, 404–5
Williams, Reverend Edward, 400
Wiltshire, 587–8
Winnebago, 315
Woodhouse, Bert, 252–3, 254, 256
Woolaton Park, 373–4
Wotojobaluk, 304

Xbalanque, 532–3
Xhosa, 230, 231, 232, 236
Xibalba, 532, 533, 552

Yagua, 474, 489
Yakut, 272, 305
Yeats, W. B., 388, 393
Yucatan, 552
Yurak-Samoyed, 318

Zaire, 4, 5
Zame ye Mebege, 5
Zimbabwe, 101–2, 115, 129
Zimmermann, M., 14, 15, 17, 18, 19, 20, 21,
    23
Zipf, George/Zipf's Law, 484–5
Zulu, 230